COURAGEOUS
LEADERSHIP

Career Success the Kelley Way

REVISED EDITION

*With grateful appreciation to the
Kelley School's many alumni and friends
who unselfishly contributed to this effort
and to the school's deans for their support.*

COURAGEOUS LEADERSHIP

Career Success the Kelley Way

REVISED EDITION

Terry Campbell, Chris Cook, John Hill, Eric Johnson,
Ray Luther, *and* Kelly Watkins

 KELLEY SCHOOL OF BUSINESS **Leadership Development**

Published by INDIANA UNIVERSITY PRESS

This book is a publication of

Indiana University Press
Office of Scholarly Publishing
Herman B Wells Library 350
1320 East 10th Street
Bloomington, Indiana 47405 USA

iupress.indiana.edu

ISBN 978-0-253-01920-2 (ebook)
ISBN 978-0-253-01922-6 (paperback)

1 2 3 4 5   20 19 18 17 16 15

Contents

About the Authors

Kelley Clinical Professor **Terry Campbell**, PhD, CPA, CGMA, CITP, CMA, is formerly Executive Vice President and Chief Operating Officer of a wood products company and has consulted with companies such as IBM Europe, Caterpillar, ING Bank, and Quaker Chimica Italiana. He has served as Professor of Business Administration at IMD in Lausanne, Research Professor at the International Academy of the Environment (Switzerland), Theseus International Management Institute (France), Graduate School of Management at University of Aix-en-Provence (France), Copenhagen Business School, Pennsylvania State University, INSEAD, and the University of Central Florida. At Penn State he directed the Center for Interdisciplinary Research in Information Systems. He has published articles in numerous scholarly journals and delivered over two hundred presentations and conference proceedings. Terry is Associate Editor for the *Journal of Information Technology* and the *Journal of Management Development.*

His research emphasis is measuring the unmeasurable, especially performance measurement and incentive systems. Terry served as a Russian interpreter with the U.S. Army Security Agency's Defense Language Institute and has been a Master Practitioner for the Myers-Briggs Type Indicator since 1995.

Chris Cook, MBA (Finance and Strategy), CPA, CGMA, teaches accounting at the Kelley School and has over 15 years of consulting experience specializing in financial and operational process redesign. Formerly Director at Alvarez and Marsal, Regional Manager at Scarborough International, Manager with PricewaterhouseCoopers Consulting, and Senior Analyst at Draper and Kramer, he is an expert in product and customer profitability analysis; planning, budgeting, and forecasting; financial and operational due diligence; transaction support; and mergers, acquisitions, and divestitures. He advised clients in SKU rationalization; measuring/evaluating planned versus actual performance; customer segmentations; statistical analysis; and performance measurement. Chris served clients in a variety of industries, including automotive, consumer and industrial products, energy, financial services, high tech, retail, and telecommunications. For several years Chris has taught Career Success Skills to graduate students and serves as Co-Director of the Kelley School MBA Consulting Academy.

John Hill, PhD, JD, MBA, is Professor Emeritus at Kelley and formerly Associate Dean and the Arthur M. Weimer Chair in Business with experience in business management, consulting, academic administration, and the military. A member of the Georgia Bar Association, he is currently President and Chief Operating Officer of Data2Discovery, Inc., and Business Advisor to Analog Computing Solutions, Inc. The author of over fifty journal articles and recipient of several research and teaching awards, prior to entering academe John spent 10 years in banking, 4 years as a chief financial officer. Coauthor of two textbooks adopted by over sixty schools, John has served on the faculties of the Center for Corporate and Financial Leadership and the U.S. Marine Corps Command and Staff College. He has also taught leadership and ethics to MBA students and law enforcement officers. John served as Major General, U.S. Marine Corps Reserve, with his last billet being Vice Commander, Marine Forces Atlantic, Europe, and South. He has taught in programs at the Borsa Italiano (Italian stock exchange); Nemetria, Foligno; Universita Cattolica del Sacro Cuore, Milano; Ryazan State Pedagogical University, Russia; State Bank of Vietnam, Hanoi; University of Ljubljana, Slovenia; and in numerous executive programs in Hungary, Italy, Russia, Slovenia, Vietnam, and the United States. For 10 years he served part-time as Senior Advisor with the CPA/consulting firms of CliftonLarsonAllen and RMA Associates. His international teaching/consulting experience includes European mutual fund and telecom companies and Vietnamese banks.

Eric Johnson is an Associate Director for Graduate Career Services at the Kelley School of Business, Indiana University. He is also Co-Founder and Co-Director of the MBA Leadership Academy and is a member of the Kelley Marketing faculty. Eric is responsible for coaching MBA students interested in careers in marketing and consulting and for teaching market research as part of Kelley's top-ten ranked undergraduate program. Through the MBA Leadership Academy he develops both the strategic visioning and coaching skills of the best of Kelley's MBA students. Eric's previous work spans executive team membership, business strategy, marketing strategy and implementation, organizational change, coaching and development, sales leadership, operations leadership, brand management, and market research. Prior to his work at the Kelley School, Eric spent 10 years with Eli Lilly and Company, where his most recent role was the Chief Marketing Officer for Lilly in the United Kingdom. While with Lilly Eric was a leader through many marketing challenges and change initiatives, such as the launch of Cymbalta in the United States and the initiation of the Customer Engagement Model (a new paradigm for pharmaceutical sales). Eric began his career with Regions Financial Corporation (formerly AmSouth Bank), where he was a branch manager for AmSouth's "Branch of the Future," an innovative retail approach to banking. A two-time winner of Lilly's "Manager of Choice," he is most proud that more than a dozen of his employees were promoted during his tenure as their coach.

Ray Luther, MBA, is the Executive Director of the full-time MBA program at the Kelley School of Business. He also serves as the Co-Director of the Consumer Marketing Academy and is Co-Founder and Co-Director of the MBA Leadership Academy. Over his 20-year career, Ray's work experience spans executive team leadership, strategy, market research, innovation management, organizational design, change management, and operations. Prior to his time at Kelley, Ray was a Director with the Procter and Gamble Company's Health Care Business Unit working across the Pharmaceutical and OTC product categories. Ray also served as a U.S. Army Officer in the 3rd Infantry Division, where he was in line roles as a Platoon Leader and Company Executive Officer. He was a lead designer and founding member of the Kelley MBA Me, Inc., career management course and has personally coached hundreds of students while at Kelley. Ray routinely teaches and coaches MBA students on the practice of leadership, strategic visioning, and coaching others for performance.

Kelly Watkins, MBA, is President of Expressive Concepts. The company, which she founded in 1992, specializes in highly customized training and consulting in Professional Development, Leadership, Communication, and Women's Leadership. Kelly has witnessed leadership from awesome to awful—all over the planet (on all seven continents and in all fifty U.S. states). She is a Thought Leader—helping global organizations to improve their effectiveness through employee development. Kelly currently serves on the Board of Directors for the Kelley School of Business Alumni Association and the Board for the District Export Council (position approved by the U.S. Secretary of Commerce). Kelly also serves as Global Ambassador for the International Alliance for Women. She is Past Chair of Global Development for the National Association of Women Business Owners and Past President of the National Speakers Association/KY. Kelly is the author of five books and hundreds of articles. In addition to serving as Adjunct Faculty, Kelly has spoken at hundreds of conferences and events around the globe.

Acknowledgments

This work is the product of many people: the Kelley School's leadership, instructors in its career success skills courses, key alumni who are experiencing exceptional careers, faculty, professional and support staff, and our students—all of whom gave their time and energy to help make this work a reality. We are also indebted to several of the over 800 organizations with ties to Kelley that assisted in the preparation of this book and provided critical feedback. Specifically, the following individuals have provided noteworthy assistance in supporting this effort:

Alumni

Beth Acton, formerly Chief Financial Officer, Comerica Bank, and VP and Treasurer, Ford Motor Company; currently Poling Chair, Kelley School of Business

Derek Bang, Partner and Chief Innovation Officer, Crowe Horwath, LLP

Cathy Bedrick, Transaction Services Partner, KPMG, LLP

Yassir Karam, Partner and Chief Specialized Service Officer, CliftonLarsonAllen, LLP

Jay Preston, Audit Partner, Ernst & Young, LLP

Mark Radzik, Managing Partner, Granite Creek Partners, LLC

Dave Roberts, Chairman, President, and Chief Executive Officer, Carlisle Companies, Inc., formerly CEO of Graco, Inc.

Faculty and Staff of the Kelley School

Matthew J Boyd, Instructional Technology Consultant

Haley Brown, Videographer

Mike Collins, Director, Learning Technologies and Support

Andrew Funkhouser, Videographer

Darren Klein, Director of Marketing

Michael B. Metzger, Professor Emeritus, formerly Foster Chair in Business Ethics, Associate Dean for Academics, and Chairperson, Business Law and Ethics

Jennifer Van Horn, Chief Information Officer

Byron Wolter, Videographer

Graduate Assistants

Jacqui Cuffe, MBA, Class of 2014

Nishad Gorhe, MBA, Class of 2014

Aaron Lewis, MBA in Accounting, Class of 2015

Justice Martin, MBA in Accounting, Class of 2015

Ankit Shah, MBA, Class of 2015

Erin Yacko, Master of Science in Accounting, Class of 2014

Indiana University Press

Sarah Brown, Copyeditor

Gary Dunham, Director

Peter Froehlich, Rights & Permissions Manager

Bob Sloan, Editor-in-Chief

Michelle Sybert, Project Manager/Editor

Carolyn Walters, Ruth Lilly Dean of University Libraries

Jennifer Witzke, Senior Artist and Book Designer

Bernadette Zoss, Editorial, Design, and Production Director

Preface: A Stake in the Ground

Most of our life awake is spent pursuing career interests. Career success has a great deal to do with our sense of well-being, intellectual actualization, and lifestyle satisfaction. Yet career success is often elusive—sometimes but not always because we failed to achieve our goals. Sometimes we fail because of flaws in our ethical framework, leadership, or other limitations. Sometimes it is because we chased the wrong goals or went about achieving them in ways that leave us with regrets.

We begin with the following statement of belief; our stake in the ground, so to speak: **What organizations really want (or should want) is courageous, ethical leaders who can identify and solve complex problems under conditions of uncertainty, motivate others to perform at high levels, and consistently achieve superior organizational outcomes on schedule within resource constraints.** It is no accident that *courageous* and *ethical* are linked in this statement. Courage is often required for leaders to remain ethical—hence the publication's title, *Courageous Leadership: Career Success the Kelley Way.*

At the Kelley School of Business we believe that courageous leadership is the cornerstone of career success. Why is this? Based on recent conversations with practitioners, one of the greatest problems business currently faces is the retirement of baby boomer leaders at a rate faster than they can be replaced. Given an increasingly competitive market for younger talent, hiring from the outside will be expensive and difficult. This means businesses need to grow their own leaders, which, in turn, means grooming high-performance-potential leaders to be ready to assume great responsibility earlier in their careers than has been the case in the past. Assuming greater

responsibilities earlier requires leaders to seek and be ready for *stretch assignments* that entail them being able to make quantum leaps. Former Ohio State football coach Woody Hayes was fond of saying, "When you throw the ball three things can happen, and two of them are bad." The same is true for stretch assignments. Leaders can de-

> ## "A cowardly leader is the most dangerous of all men."
>
> —Stephen King, notable fiction author

cline them, which means they may not be offered other such opportunities in the future. They can accept them but execute poorly, with the same likely result. Or leaders can accept stretch assignments and execute them well, which often launches them on a much faster career path to the top. These stretch assignments become pivotal moments requiring the courage to tale career risks.

Three threads reinforce courageous leadership and are woven through our approach to career success: (1) the **talent** to succeed, (2) the **humility** to grow, and (3) the **perseverance** to stay the course through difficult decisions and thrive in the rough seas of organizational storms. Following these threads, this monograph deals with what it takes to be successful in businesses. Success starts with understanding courageous leadership, so that's where we begin. It next flows to principles that make courageous leaders good leaders. Part of that involves an appreciation of a solid ethical foundation and assessing where we stand personally with regard to that foundation. From there we move to those personal attributes and skills that so often differentiate leaders who reach the upper echelons of organizations from those who end up in middle management. Finally, we deal with the organizational environment and how to be a savvy participant in it.

This work is not intended to be scholarly. Although it incorporates scholarly work, it is intended as practical guidance that relies significantly upon real-world experiences. Although somewhat holistic in terms of broad coverage of topics, it does not purport to be all inclusive. Space does not permit extensive coverage of every topic related to courageous leadership. Rather, our hope is to provide an overview of the many facets of courageous leadership, one that serves students as a starting point for a lifelong journey of self-improvement as courageous leaders and experienced leaders as a catalyst for honing their leadership skills. We hope you will appreciate this book's pragmatic approach, which combines principles with real-world organizational problems and the ways in which courageous leaders have solved those problems.

Coauthors' note

In creating this learning tool we draw from several types of sources including academic research, practitioner publications, business executives' experiences, the coauthors' own experiences, and a rich history of leadership development by the U.S. military. As Professor Michael Useem stated in "Four Lessons in Adaptive Leadership," "The armed services have been in the business of leadership development much longer than the corporate world . . . That's why my colleagues at Wharton and I incorporate military leadership principles in our MBA and executive MBA programs . . . We fight very different battles in business. But the armed forces provide exceptionally powerful schooling for engagements that are likely to make a difference. By looking far afield, we can often see what is close to home."

Profiles in Courageous Leadership—
Andre Galvao

Andre Galvao is a successful businessman from Brazil who lives in San Diego, California. He is also perhaps the foremost Brazilian jiujitsu practitioner in the world, having won several world championships. Brazilian jiujitsu is a very tough martial art used by various militaries around the world as part of their hand-to-hand combat training, so Andre's physical courage is unquestionable. On the mat he is a relentless warrior, dominating the sport. What might be surprising to many, however, is the moral courage that Andre exhibits. One of the coauthors relates the following story about Andre:

> The first time I attended one of Andre's jiujitsu seminars the room was full of really tough guys sitting on the mat in their gis waiting to hear about technical fighting skills from one of the world's true experts. In walks this incredibly fit young man exuding calm, humble confidence. He begins to speak. To everyone's astonishment his first words were not about jiujitsu. Instead he said, "Before we talk about jiujitsu today, I want to talk about the most important thing in the world." There was not a sound as this room full of warriors waited to hear the most important thing in the world. When Andre said, "The most important thing in the world is **love**" I suspect most of the guys were blown away just like me. Here was one of the toughest men in the world talking about the importance of love? At that moment I knew there was something special about Andre, something that defined him even more than being the greatest jiujitsu fighter. He wasn't just about toughness and physical courage; even more importantly, he was about moral courage. As he continued speaking, I knew then he was a courageous leader.

PART I
Courageous Leadership

Foreword

Part I introduces the concept of *courageous* and provides a foundation for leading. Chapter 1 introduces the topic and discusses the concept of the organization as a family—in the analogy of a pack—in which members should learn to play their roles in a manner that allows the pack to thrive. Chapter 2 presents a set of basic values and beliefs that together form a philosophy of courageous leadership. Chapter 3 deals with leadership theories and styles before introducing a particular framework we believe fits well with the concept of courageous leadership. Chapter 4 deals with the application of courageous leadership in four common situations leaders encounter in business.

CHAPTER 1

It's about the Pack!

> "For the strength of the pack is the wolf,
> and the strength of the wolf is the pack."
>
> —Rudyard Kipling, *The Law of the Jungle*

Are you a high-performance-potential person who aspires to become a leader at the highest levels of business? Would you like to be able to do this faster than most? If so, this means you will need to take risks. Early in your career you will need to accept leadership roles that will make you uncomfortable. These roles will likely involve a great deal of uncertainty about how to proceed. They will become **pivotal moments** in your career, *strategic inflection points* in your career trajectory involving *assignments that stretch your abilities as a leader.* These **stretch assignments** will require **courage**, the **tenacity** to surmount obstacles and to succeed in spite of them, the **humility** to admit mistakes and learn from them, and the **perseverance** to weather setbacks while not allowing your own disappointments to adversely affect the morale of your followers. A starting point for becoming a courageous leader is appreciating your role as a member and a leader in your organization.

1.1. You and Your Organization

It's hardly news that organizations need employees and employees need organizations. It is not simply this symbiotic relationship captured in the above quote, however, but rather the cooperative culture that should exist among organizations and their members. In a wolf pack, survival depends upon cooperation such that individual members behave in a manner that furthers the needs of the pack, and, concurrently, enables members to grow strong and healthy as individuals. The complexity of social order in a wolf pack has been described as one of the most fascinating ever observed. It involves a strict hierarchy, as businesses often entail, and, just as in business, there is fear that failure to comply with directives from the top will result in negative sanctions. It would be a mistake, however, to believe that this strict hierarchy is governed simply by fear and violence. In reality, the wolf-pack culture promotes unity and social order. It's all about the pack!

Wolves long for interaction with each other and spend a great deal of time communicating, verbally and nonverbally. Young wolves are frequently accorded a great deal of freedom and receive substantial benefits as pack members. This helps ensure the long-term survival of the pack as the younger wolves grow to take their places as adults. Older wolves set an example for younger wolves by adhering carefully to the pack's culture and mentoring the young. In fact, the entire pack is responsible for caring for its young. In the end, it is the courageous leadership of the wolves at the top of this very complex social order that ensures survival when the pack hunts to exist in what can be a very dangerous world. Young wolves that display the most courageous leadership often rise to the top of the pack. The few lone wolves that exist outside packs often live at the margin. Because they lack the strength of the pack, lone wolves are relegated to finding only small game such as rodents. It takes a pack to bring down large and dangerous game such as bison, elk, and moose.

"What is good for the manager is not always good for the company. Mission must come first, self-interest last."

—Michael Useem, Wharton professor, writing for the *Harvard Business Review*

The same is true in most thriving businesses as in wolf packs. Lone wolves determined to do it their own way without a pack find it difficult to survive. It would be a mistake, however, to interpret this statement as a condemnation of the entrepreneurial spirit. Entrepreneurial organizations can be exciting, fascinating places to work, and one of the coauthors is heavily involved with assisting startup companies get off the ground. But as entrepreneurial organizations begin to grow, entrepreneurs must make the transition from lone wolves to pack leaders or face limited future growth of the businesses. Ultimately, whether in large businesses or small, growing ones, it takes courageous leadership to rise to the top of the pack and maintenance of a cooperative culture to ensure long-term success.

What are your priorities as a leader? Getting your priorities straight has everything to do with being a courageous leader, which in turn promotes your own career success. First, just as with wolves your first priority is the welfare of the pack, your employer. For one thing, your survival is directly tied to the pack's survival. Doing the best you can for your employer and placing its mission first will helps ensure that you contribute the highest possible value and the pack thrives.

Your second priority should be to the other members of the pack, your superiors, subordinates, and fellow employees. Caring about other pack members means at times placing their immediate welfare above your own. You may have to work harder than other pack members, exercise frugality in the use of organizational resources, or even forego certain perquisites to set an appropriate example as a courageous leader. The third priority is you, your own organizational health and well-being.

Does placing your employer and fellow employees before your own interests harm you? In our experience the answer is, "It depends." There are times when out of necessity your own welfare must come first, but those instances should be the exception, not the rule. Although one may find examples that run counter to the general rule, in the long run, leaders who consistently place a higher priority on the organization and their fellow employees' interests than their own are far more likely to succeed than leaders who exhibit selfish behaviors. The former are far more likely to attract high-quality followers around them and develop a culture of the pack!

1.2. Three Premises about You

In order to have a meaningful discussion about courageous leadership in business organizations, it is helpful to establish three basic premises. You might think of these premises as stakes in the ground that become starting points for our discourse.

First, you are a **talented** person capable of and motivated to achieve success in a business career. We need a basic definition of career success in order to have clarity. Our definition includes four common attributes: (1) personal satisfaction with your career progress, (2) being a valued member of a team, (3) having a solid foundation of skills relevant to your job, and (4) enjoying most of the day-to-day transactions in which you engage. Success can be defined in multiple ways, but in order to establish what we mean by success it is desirable to embrace some fundamental definition or run the risk that the reader says something along the lines of, "My definition of success in business is that I make so much money that I can retire by age 40." Alternatively, one might say, "My definition is leaving a legacy behind so that I will be forever known as the person who invented the widget that saved mankind." We argue that those examples of very specific definitions might be subsumed in personal satisfaction with your career progress. A word of caution may be in order, however. Such narrow definitions of successful business careers are not necessarily wrong, but they can lead to a dysfunctional, myopic focus. Self-focus at some level is critical to success. We need to be ambitious, motivated, and self-directed. We need to develop self-learning feedback loops and recognize that skills that have helped us be successful to date will not necessarily be adequate to ensure continued success. But we must not forget it's about the pack.

Our second premise is that you are willing to make yourself susceptible to coaching. That is, you agree that, like all of us, you have flaws and can improve by learning. For those afflicted with narcissistic beliefs about their own infallibility, susceptibility to learning is difficult, if not impossible. Making ourselves susceptible to transformation therefore requires the **humility** to learn and grow. It takes humility to admit that we have not yet fully developed the proper skills, that we do not have the time to build them for a given task and that we must ask for help, or that perhaps we need to allow someone else to lead in order to achieve the best results for the pack.

Quantum leaps in ability are a function of the length of time and the intensity of the change process, and they frequently involve some discomfort. Real self-improvement is often not accomplished quickly and without some pain. If we

Why be so concerned about courageous leadership? This question presents an appropriate opportunity to recall our statement in the preface about what businesses want in the way of leaders: *What organizations really want (or should want) is courageous, ethical leaders who can identify and solve complex problems under conditions of uncertainty, motivate others to perform at high levels, and consistently achieve superior organizational outcomes on schedule within resource constraints.* If this is what businesses should want in their leaders, then it is also what aspiring leaders should seek to provide.

are to make a quantum leap, we must be humble enough to recognize and admit our weaknesses and seek to correct them. We must learn to marshal the talents we have, improve them, and build new talents. We must seek out others who can coach us, make us stronger, and help us apply their wisdom. We must learn to accept responsibility for failure, develop a clear understanding of our mistakes, know what mistakes are forgivable

"Anyone can hold the helm when the sea is calm."

—Publilius Syrus, first-century BC Latin writer

to our employer and what mistakes will not be forgiven, and view learning from our mistakes as a lifelong process of self-improvement—not believing we have reached some point in our careers at which we no longer need to improve.

The third premise underlying our discussion is that you have the **tenacity** to persevere in spite of difficulties and setbacks. No successful career is without its trials, obstacles, and bumps. As the quote by Publilius Syrus suggests, the real tests of how good you are as a leader will be how you respond in crises—including your own career crises. Someday you may hear your supervisor say, "Bill,

"You manage things; you lead people."

—Grace Murray Hopper, U.S. Navy rear admiral, developer of the first compiler for a computer programming language

you are outstanding in all categories of performance but one—your leadership style. You work very hard and expect the same from your subordinates. Unfortunately, although your hard-driving leadership style gets results, those results are coming at the expense of employee morale. This is clearly reflected in your 360-degree leadership assessment. Unfortunately, if you do not correct that deficiency you are unlikely to go much further in this organization." How will you react upon receiving such news? Will you become defensive, pout, argue that the supervisor is wrong, and blame others for this alleged deficiency? Or, will you view the criticism as an opportunity to improve, take a hard look at yourself, and develop a plan for overcoming the shortcoming? Even if you continue to believe that the supervisor is wrong about your alleged deficiency, obviously others' perceptions are different from yours. This means you will likely need to make changes in order to better manage their perceptions if you are to overcome this obstacle and be successful.

If you are saying to yourself that the foregoing three points seem obvious, good for you. If so, then you are already on the right track; but you might also ask yourself the question, "If they are so obvious, then why do we often observe so much dysfunctional leadership in business?" Part of the

answer likely rests in the fact that leaders often fail to do what they know they should do for various reasons, such as time constraints, frustration, and simple neglect. Another part, however, may be that leaders—even if they have intuited the foregoing—fail to discipline their thinking and actions in ways they should. Consequently, regardless of whether these ideas are new to you or whether they are simply not at the forefront of your daily thinking, this book will have accomplished a valuable end—and please note for a moment the word "end"—if it leads to a personal leadership discipline that guides in avoiding leadership problems.

The Duckworth Lab at the University of Pennsylvania focuses on two traits that predict success: self-control and grit. **Self-control** relates to one's ability to voluntarily regulate personal behaviors to include emotional response to criticism. **Grit** refers to a person's willingness to be diligent in pursuit of long-term goals. The Duckworth Lab's research suggests that self-control and grit may be even more important than talent and intellectual ability when it comes to predicting success. Moreover, these traits may change over a lifetime as people gain experience.[1] The implication, supported by the coauthors' own observations across various organizational domains, is that perseverance coupled with appropriate responses to feedback are critical to success.

1.3. Courageous Leadership

So, with these three premises we begin our journey toward becoming more courageous leaders. A logical point of debarkation for this journey is to gain clarity about our own goals and objectives versus those of the organization. Since the overarching theme is this book is courageous leadership, we begin by defining it. Although subsequent chapters are devoted to such topics as principles, styles, and techniques of leadership, it is important to understand at the onset of our journey what we mean by courageous leadership.

Before defining courageous leadership, it is best to define what we mean by leadership. Later on, our discussion of leadership will involve much more richness and detail, but for the moment allow a simple definition to suffice for brevity's sake. One way to define leadership is to contrast it with a related topic most often taught in business schools—management. Management in its simplest terms is getting employees to do what the business wants them to do. On the other hand, paraphrasing former U.S. President Dwight Eisenhower, **leadership** is the art of getting employees to *want* to do what the business wants them to do. Management can be thought of as a **push** mechanism in that it motivates employees by establishing controls that push employees toward objectives. In contrast, leadership can be viewed as a **pull** mechanism that encourages followership by creating feelings of belonging to an organizational movement.

Now that we have a simple, operational definition of leadership, let's address **courage**, a frequently misunderstood word. It is very important to understand that *courage is not the absence of fear but rather the capacity to overcome fear.* Consider the following example. You are about to cross a busy street intersection when you observe an elderly man fall in the middle of the street. There is a large truck bearing down upon the man that cannot stop in time to avoid crushing him. You dart into the street and drag the man to safety just as the truck roars by. Did this act require courage on your part? Think carefully before you answer. The correct answer is, "It depends." It depends upon whether you saw the truck barreling toward you and realized there was danger to your own physical well-being. If you had no idea that your act required you to risk your life, this gracious act was merely one of kindness not requiring courage. You only demonstrated courage if you had reason to fear that your life was in danger and your concern for the elderly man being harmed overcame your fear of being harmed personally.

Many automatically assume courage necessarily implies **physical courage** and interpret

> ## "Leadership is the key to 99 percent of all successful efforts."
>
> —Erskine Bowles,
> former White House chief of staff

that to mean an absence of fear of being harmed by some physical act. That flatly stated is a fallacy. Fortunately, physical courage is not the most common need in business. Instead, the type of courage needed in business most often is **career courage**. Career courage is the willingness to undertake fearful new responsibilities when they are presented despite the fact that failure may damage your career. Career courage is the courage to go against authority when you believe authority is wrong, ethically or merely from a best-practices standpoint. As you may well imagine, the latter version of courage is often not appreciated by an authority figure attempting to coerce other organization members into doing or not doing something ill advised morally and/or operationally. Consequently, the risk of career damage often attends both significant new responsibilities and righteous opposition to authority. Career courage is the courage to do what is morally right applied to your business career.

We need to also understand that *fear is a rational human response to danger,* whether it be physical danger or danger to one's career. No sane

> ## "Striking out is not failing. Not swinging is failing."
>
> —Babe Ruth, baseball legend

person wants to be run over by a truck. Similarly, most rational business leaders would prefer not to place their careers in jeopardy by going against authority. Consequently, fear is nothing unusual and nothing of which we should be inwardly ashamed. Rather, fear is a challenge to be conquered. Leaders must demonstrate courage in overcoming

"Leaders think and talk about solutions. Followers think and talk about the problems."

—Brian Tracy, author and motivational speaker

their fears and anxieties if they want to succeed in big ways. In the coauthors' experience, too often would-be business leaders shy away from assuming responsibilities because they fear the risks that attend those responsibilities. In doing so, new responsibilities are frequently viewed disproportionately from the perspective of their risks as opposed to that of the opportunities that accompany them. Learning to assess prudently responsibilities in terms of opportunity versus risk requires sound judgment and the ability to recognize the nature of risks and, to the extent possible, mitigate them. This leads us back to the issue of value focus and what we as employees can best do to make ourselves valuable to our employers.

1.4. What Creates Value in Businesses?

The world is full of people who can solve simple business problems. Business leaders' career success is achieved by identifying and solving complex problems. If we are to maintain our value focus, it is essential that we become leaders who do this routinely. This is a major reason career success requires courageous leadership. Consider the following real-world anecdote.

You are a midlevel commercial bank executive in charge of your bank's flagship facility in a major city. You were brought in as the facility manager to improve it 6 months ago and have achieved some success. Consequently, after months of hard work you are feeling somewhat satisfied with the facility's progress and beginning to think you might

have a moment to relax mentally. It is 3:30 PM one Thursday when, amid your self-satisfied ruminations, you receive a call from your boss telling you that your bank has just acquired a small, failed bank. Your boss says the small bank was closed by regulators earlier that day. All the bank's officers have been terminated, with only the nonofficer employees retained. Your bank has agreed to take it over and run it starting at 9:00 AM tomorrow. Your boss is directing you to have a team at the small bank's headquarters down the street to assume responsibility for its management for the foreseeable future. You will continue to be responsible for your own normal responsibilities as well. There are no additional personnel available to assist you immediately. Day-to-day supervision for the smaller bank and all its branch locations must be assumed by your leadership team. By the way, since the failed bank no longer exists as a legal entity, all its signage and forms must be changed overnight. Further, over the next few weeks your team must evaluate the failed bank's entire problematic commercial loan portfolio and decide what loans to keep for your own bank.

You would be absolutely correct if this sounds like an enormous task dropped on you with no notice, virtually no reaction time, and with no one offering to hold your hand. How would you react? Assume you have never taken over a failed bank and have no extra leadership resources in your own organization. Would you fear failure? Any rational person would. What would be the career implications if you do fail? Obviously, there would likely be negative consequences. Would you argue that you cannot possibly do a good job of carrying out these additional responsibilities given the incredibly short notice and lack of resources? Many might be tempted to argue these things. What are the career implications if you show fear of undertaking this new assignment? Aha, herein lies the crux of the matter.

Such moments described above can be career defining. Consider your boss's position. He also had this responsibility dropped on him with no notice and is in a jam. Just like you, he has other responsibilities, broader in scope and magnitude than your own. He has to accomplish this mission or risk damage to his own career. He is calling on you to be his point person in solving what is a complex, difficult problem because you have previously demonstrated the ability to solve other types of complex problems. This problem, however, is obviously something for which you have little experience and preparation, and your boss knows it, but his choices are very limited. Assigning it to you is a major expression of his belief that, at least among the leaders he might call upon, you are best suited for the mission. On one hand, if you fail to accomplish the mission successfully you may well preclude yourself from consideration as a solver of future complex problems. On the other hand, if you attempt to argue that you are ill equipped for the mission and it should therefore be assigned to someone else, your fears may result in the same outcome. In the end, there is only one good outcome possible in the above bank scenario. You must both seize the opportunity to carry out this new responsibility and discharge it well to avoid damage to your career. This requires career courage to view complex problems as opportunities and face them with confidence that you can find a workable solution.

So, how would you view this type of complex problem—as a huge risk with lots of unknown, potentially unpleasant tasks and additional work, or as a unique opportunity to create value for your employer? Learning to view complex problems as opportunities doesn't necessarily come naturally. You have to teach yourself to become a complex-problem solver, and this takes time. Just as a chess master does not become an expert by reading a book about how to play chess, complex-problem solving requires you to be willing to engage long before you enjoy. The more proficient you become in your problem-solving abilities, however, the more you will view complex problems as opportunities to demonstrate your capacity for adding value for your employer.

One critical key to success in any organization is determining what the organization values and providing it within certain ethical and organizational constraints. This is what we will refer to throughout our journey as the **value focus**. Your career success depends to a large extent upon your ability to discern the key factors that your employer values and stay focused on those values irrespective of the many noisy distractions and not-infrequent contrary signals in your employment environment. For example, if billable hours are the metric by which employees are valued in a CPA firm, spending an excessive amount of time as a member of the annual holiday party committee is probably ill advised. Albeit a nice-to-do activity in which your participation may earn you some modestly helpful good-citizen points, if your billings suffer because you become overly absorbed in such tangential activities, you have lost the value focus.

1.5. Ends/Ways/Means Thinking

Fortunately, when dealing with what one might call "emergent urgents," such as in the foregoing banking example, there are tools that can help us develop an approach to problem solving that is more likely to keep us on track than merely lunging into action. Throughout this book we will present various tools that can be very helpful in assisting you in adding value for your employer. Here we introduce the first of these tools, **ends/ways/means thinking**. At both the personal and organizational levels, this is an important, fundamental tool for gaining and maintaining clarity when it comes to identifying and solving complex problems. What are ends, ways, and means?

In simple terms, **ends** are goals that if attained constitute success or victory. In other words, they represent a desired end state. For example, suppose a business school wishes to enhance its prestige as an institution as measured by its rankings in various polls. The desired end state might be being ranked among the top-twenty business

> **"A real strategy must address three items: ends . . . ways . . . means. If your strategy does not include all three of these essentials, then you have produced trash."**
>
> —Jim Lacey, "The Death of Military Strategy," *National Review Online*

schools as opposed to the top thirty. **Ways** are the operational policies, processes, and procedures necessary to attain the ends. In our business school example, a way to achieve upward movement in rankings might be to attract more talented students by offering more scholarships. **Means** are the resources necessary to implement the ways successfully, often denominated in time, money, and personnel. Continuing our example, one means necessary to afford students scholarships could be obtaining contributions to endow scholarship funds.

Ends/ways/means thinking is in essence a mental discipline for increasing the likelihood of success in problem solving and is particularly useful when managing one's career. Ends/ways/ means thinking is more often than not neglected despite its effectiveness and simplicity. For example, people often set career goals based upon such questions as, "What am I good at?" "What is my degree in?" and "What are my colleagues doing?" In doing so they set limits on themselves that inhibit career success by narrowing their choices about the future to their earlier proclivities and decisions without considering the potential for self-improvement. What is your dream about your future? Have you ever said to yourself, "I could never achieve

that dream"? Contrast this self-limiting thinking with that used by Wernher von Braun.

As a 12-year-old child, von Braun became fascinated with the idea of rockets, so he began experimenting. After a near disaster with an experimental rocket and not being a particularly good student, he was sent away to boarding school. There he was able to view the stars through a small telescope and became enamored with the idea of man going into space. When he saw an ad in an astronomy magazine for a book about going into space, he sent for the book with the aspiration of becoming an engineer building rockets. When the book arrived he opened it breathlessly, but to his dismay it was filled with only mathematical symbols and formulas. He took the book to his math teacher and asked him to explain what the symbols and formulas meant, but his teacher told him he'd have to study math and physics in order to be able to understand them. Therein was the problem. Wernher von Braun was not a good student and not interested in math and physics. But he was so focused on attaining his desired *end,* that of becoming a rocketeer, that this desire overrode his disdain for math and physics. He determined to master these difficult subjects as a necessary *way* of realizing his dream. Books on math and physics became the resources or *means* by which he learned. Because he stayed focused on his ultimate end, today von Braun is credited with being the "Father of Rocket Science."

Businesses frequently encourage this predetermined-career mindset by focusing on **fit** rather than **talent** and potential when hiring and placing employees. Often, education in a particular subject matter and certain types of experience are deemed more important in filling a position than talent. In other words, corporate recruiters frequently try to fit round pegs in round holes and square pegs in square holes. A collegiate educational experience frequently becomes a *way* to get a job even when the desired *end* is not yet well known. The import of this is that employees are to some extent coerced into choosing their careers as students prior to knowing much about the nature of the transactions they will engage in and cultures in which they will work that naturally follow their chosen disciplines. The salient question becomes what they do once they get a better focus on their dreams. Like von Braun, however, you need not be relegated to forever being stovepiped into a particular career if you stay focused on your career ends and are determined to follow the ways that will achieve these ends even if their attainment requires some pain.

Organizations often fall prey to this same mindset when addressing complex problems by jumping into ways, as opposed to clearly understanding the ends that constitute victory. This has proven to be the case in every organizational domain in which the coauthors have worked. Famed management guru Peter Drucker teaches that within a few years after their creation, most organizations lose sight of their mission and become focused on efficiency rather than effectiveness. Recall the aforementioned problem of moving from a top-thirty business school to a top-twenty school. Convening a group of faculty to work on attaining that end can quickly devolve into a discussion of how to improve the curriculum. Why? Because faculty are usually well versed in revising curriculum. You may have heard the old expression, "When the only tool you have is a hammer, every problem looks like a nail." Regardless of whether the reasons for the school not being ranked in the top twenty result from deficiencies in the curriculum or other reasons, faculty tend to revert to what they know. This is an example of focusing on ways instead of ends.

In the 1990s most executives at pharmaceutical companies had a background in sales, and sales had been a very effective way of moving products. As competition increased throughout the decade and the healthcare landscape

> **"We could look at every field of human endeavor and find endless examples of people scrambling to the top of a ladder that is leaning against the wrong wall."**
>
> —Stephen Covey, cochairman, Franklin Covey Co.

changed dramatically, leaders continued to follow the extant model and failed to adapt their ways. Instead, they hired more and more sales personnel. This ultimately led to massive customer confusion and dissatisfaction such that the Federal Drug Administration began to regulate sales heavily.

Not focusing on the right ends also carries a serious risk. Consider the following real-world business anecdote in which a company drove itself to destruction by not focusing itself on the right ends. A family owned manufacturing company employing 300 workers was engaged in remanufacturing used automotive parts such as starters and alternators. The company was experiencing serious cash flow problems, so outside consultants were brought in to help diagnose the causes of the problems and recommend solutions. Inspection of the company's warehoused inventory revealed a substantial investment in specialty parts for which there was little demand, such as generators for 1958 Corvettes. When questioned about this policy, management indicated that it was common practice for the company to remanufacture at least fifty of a particular low-demand item because of the time required to set up to produce the item. Unsold parts were then warehoused in the hope of future sales. Over a period of years many of these items had accumulated to the point that some had been sitting in the warehouse for several years, thereby consuming needed working capital. When asked why the company bothered to remanufacture

Ignoring the ends/ways/means model often sidetracks projects. Studies, planning, and reorganizing are *ways*, not *ends*. Although usually necessary and often desirable, carried to excess they can result in stagnation. Consider the following quote by Petronius Arbiter in 210 BC: "We trained hard, but it seemed that every time we were beginning to learn to form into teams we would be reorganized. I was to learn later in life that we tend to meet any new situation by reorganizing, and what a wonderful method it can be for creating the illusion of progress while producing confusion, inefficiency, and demoralization." This quote captures the timelessness of the tendency to lose sight of desired ends by becoming bogged down in ways. If the ways are not leading to attainment of the desired ends, courageous leaders cut through the fog of the bog and move to get projects back on track.

such parts, management responded that its sales force argued vehemently that a full line of such products was necessary to satisfy their customers, automobile parts stores.

As the consultants delved further into the matter, analysis indicated that given the choice between high setup costs and high inventory carrying costs, the company would be far better off discontinuing remanufacturing low-demand, specialty parts all together. Consultants learned that none of the company competitors were offering these low-volume specialty parts, but the sales force liked more types of product because it was being compensated entirely upon sales volume as opposed to profitable sales. This is

an example of failure to think in terms of ends, ways, and means. Profitable sales, not just volume, should have been the *end*. Focusing on the wrong end led management to use a method of compensating its sales force that, in turn, led to a flawed strategy.

In summary, ends/ways/means thinking is a great tool for guiding our thinking about complex problems at both the individual and organizational levels. At the individual level it can enhance our chances of career success if we allow our desired *ends* to drive our career efforts instead of being limited by the *ways* in which we've already indulged. At the organizational level it facilitates keeping what constitutes victory for the pack in the forefront of our thinking instead of that becoming lost in the details of the ways we go about attempting to accomplish the ends. Ends/ways/means thinking can be an important tool in enhancing our value to the pack and building the balance in something we'll call our employment credibility account.

1.6. Your Employment Credibility Account

Reflect back upon the bank acquisition scenario introduced previously in this chapter. Placing yourself in the role of the manager being told to undertake this complex task, suppose you immediately decide your only choice is to embrace the mission. Would you ask your boss questions such as, "How much more will I get paid to take this mission?" "Does this mean I'm getting a promotion?" It is probably natural for anyone assuming significantly more responsibility to hope that rewards will come from doing so, but is this the time to raise that issue with your boss?

Consider the following real-world snippet. A retired associate dean at Kelley tells the story of a faculty member's response when asked in a team meeting to assist with a major curriculum revision. The faculty member's question was, "How much more money do I get paid if I do this?" When told there was certainly no immediate increase in compensation associated with the increased responsibility and no promise of same in the long run, the faculty member responded in essence, "Why should I do more if I'm not paid more?" To which the associate dean replied, "First the work, then, if done well, perhaps the reward."

How do you view this situation? For many years workers in textile manufacturing plants were paid piece rate, meaning they were paid for each piece of clothing they sewed. Do you expect your employer to reward you with each output or change in responsibility? Or, do you trust your employer to take care of you in the long run if you continuously maintain a value focus? Beyond your own self-concerns, how do you view the example you set for others with your expectations regarding rewards? If you are a business leader, how would you respond to your subordinates' questions along these lines? How you answer such questions says a lot about you, your priorities, your potential as a courageous leader and team player, and how far you will go in your career. The following analogy may be instructive.

One way to view your relationship with your employer is as a bank account—in essence your **employment credibility account**. Each time you add value for your employer you make a deposit. Each instance in which you consume organizational resources you make a withdrawal. If you consistently take more out of your account than you put in, your credibility balance will be negative. In simple words, you consume more value than you create for your employer. In your banking relationship, being continuously overdrawn risks having your account closed by the bank because you are undesirable as a customer. The same is true for your employment.

We maintain that savvy employees work hard to maintain a healthy positive balance in their

credibility accounts. Why should you add more value for your employer than you are paid for adding? One answer is to make yourself so valuable that when your employer is beset with the storms that often hit businesses, you won't be washed overboard along with others whose credibility account balances are low. Another is that life sometimes brings some unpleasant surprises and disruptions requiring you to draw down upon your credibility balance. Consider the following anecdotes.

Late one afternoon an associate dean with oversight responsibility for the Kelley School's finances sat in a budget meeting with university officials. Suddenly an administrative assistant burst into the room with the message that he had an emergency phone call from his wife. A few minutes later he learned that his son, a surgeon in Washington state, had been stricken with a terrible illness and was not expected to live another day. Amazingly his son did live but was in a coma for months and was left severely impaired. The ensuing family trauma required numerous trips to the West Coast for the next year and much time away from the school. Fortunately, the school's administration was understanding and compassionate. It helped that he had a positive balance in his credibility account.

Lest you believe such life-changing events have the probability of lightning striking and the odds are very small of something akin to this experience happening to you, consider Art. Art is a very successful partner with an international CPA/consulting firm. For many years Art labored very hard to add value for his employer, and his career

> **"It is easy to dodge our responsibilities, but we cannot dodge the consequences of dodging our responsibilities."**
>
> —Sir Josiah Stamp, 1880–1941, former director of the Bank of England

progressed accordingly. He ultimately became the partner-in-charge of its tax practice in a major city, but life has a way of throwing obstacles in career paths. Art's beloved wife was stricken with a debilitating illness, and he was forced to make a difficult choice he hadn't anticipated. He told his employer that he needed to reduce his commitment to his work in order to spend more time with his wife. That meant a reduction in his billable hours. Fortunately, Art had built up a substantial balance in his credibility account, and the firm enabled Art to free that time to be with his wife.

How does your credibility balance sit with your employer? Are you currently overdrawn? Even if you are currently a student and not employed, you still need to be concerned about a credibility balance. An educational institution is often more likely to accord a student with a 3.8 grade-point average (GPA) special consideration when needed than one with a 2.0 GPA when the student is *in extremis.* If your credibility account is overdrawn and that doesn't make you uneasy, we contend it is time for attitudinal assessment and change if you desire a successful career. It is time to stop thinking piece rate and start thinking about your compensation being the balance in your credibility account. It may not happen immediately, but in the coauthors' experience a healthy credibility balance eventually leads to much greater reward than a piece-rate attitude.

One of the coauthors tells the following story. He had just gone to work for a new employer and was sitting admiring his new office after an interi-

or decorator had just spent a not inconsiderable sum furbishing it rather luxuriously. Suddenly it dawned on him that he had left an employer where he had a healthy credibility balance for this promotion, and his new employer had spent organizational resources in acquiring his services, moving his family, and equipping him for his new responsibilities. He had yet to add a dime of value for his new employer. In other words, his credibility account was already overdrawn, and he had just begun his new job. It was time to stop admiring the new surroundings, stop patting himself on the back, and get to work. How does your credibility account look right now?

1.7. You Are Accountable to Your Pack

One way to sum up much of what is discussed above is to simply say you are accountable to your pack. This is true whether your pack is currently an employer, a class in an educational institution, or some other organization. Personal accountability is not always easy to accept because at times we fall short of the mark, and being accountable means we have to accept responsibility for failure. No one likes to fail. Moreover, failure often means someone will be blamed, and if we are responsible for the failure but don't accept responsibility, someone else may get the blame we deserve. That becomes an ethical issue. To allow someone to be blamed for something we did suggests a willingness to allow someone else to be harmed for something that is our fault.

One of the coauthors relates the following story. When a major pharmaceutical firm launched the first commercial for a new product, they closed with a call to action for patients to access the product's website. However, the website was not turned on when it was supposed to be, so it was not live when the commercials went public. The responsible party blamed others before finally being held accountable. The lack of accountability cost the company millions in sales.

Accountability has become of great interest lately in corporations because the lack of it is estimated to cost businesses tens of billions of dollars annually. Many organizations fail to achieve a record of personal accountability among their employees for several reasons. One major reason is that accountability can mean different things to different people, and organizations sometimes fail to reach consensus among members on what accountability means in their culture and context. A second major reason is that the complexities of business today often give rise to gray areas in which right and wrong become nebulous, and organizations do not always equip employees with appropriate cognitive frames for sorting out difficult ethical questions.

This brings us to the important issue of **mistakes**. All leaders make mistakes, and mistakes are frequently attended by negative consequences, both for the organization and the leader. What mistakes are usually tolerable and which are intolerable? You may find it helpful to place mistakes into three categories: (1) **Mistakes involving moral turpitude**—these are ethical violations to be avoided at all costs. A small ethical mistake is sometimes considered much more serious than a larger (in terms of financial impact) mistake not involving moral turpitude. For example, a bank officer may be forgiven for making a bad loan that costs the bank $100,000 but not for stealing $1,000. (2) **Catastrophic mistakes**—these mistakes have consequences so serious that negative sanctions are almost unavoidable. For example, a military officer whose clear and avoidable error of judgment costs the lives of personnel may expect to receive career-ending sanctions. (3) **Common mistakes**—these mistakes fall into neither of the first two categories and are often forgivable if not repeated. Mistakes fitting this category are learning opportunities for leaders. Be cautious, however, that such learning must be evinced by avoidance of repetition of the same or similar mistakes over and over. For example, if you find yourself frequently ending department meetings on a sour note due to acrimony, this could signal a problem with your leadership style in handling such meetings. If you find yourself making the same type of mistake repeatedly, change is strongly indicated.

In the end, we are accountable to the pack for our mistakes. The pack's leadership is accountable to make its members aware of their mistakes and assist them in understanding and correcting behaviors that cause mistakes. Courageous leaders are acutely aware they must always be accountable to their employer, their subordinates and co-workers, and their own ethical values. There are times when this personal accountability makes leaders uncomfortable, but it benefits both the pack and its leaders in the long run. When leaders maintain a keen sense of personal accountability for their actions they tend to err less often, thereby avoiding the adverse consequences of failure for themselves and their organizations. Avoidance of mistakes is obviously preferable, but mistakes do occur. It often takes courage to say, "I was wrong," but just saying we're wrong doesn't fulfill the requirements of accountability. True accountability means taking action to right wrongs when possible. To quote one commentator describing a particular politician's precipitous drop in popularity due to mistakes, "There is a tendency to speak of how a problem will look and how its appearance should be handled, as opposed to what the problem *is* and [what] should be done about it." Although admitting mistakes may result in some temporary loss of credibility, continuously "spinning" mistakes as something other than failure creates distrust and eventually results in far greater lost credibility. Words are important, but it is error to believe that words alone are sufficient to fulfill the requirements of accountability. Courageous leaders make themselves accountable to their pack by following their words with appropriate actions that demonstrate they really mean what they say.

Profiles in Courageous Leadership—Gunner

Want to be a courageous leader? Consider modeling yourself after a Great Pyrenees, the epitome of compassion and courage in the canine world. Giant Great Pyrenees dogs were bred in the mountains bearing their name to defend shepherds and their herds from bears and wolves. Pyres are excellent family dogs, loving and especially tolerant of children. Their normally gentle demeanor, however, belies incredible bravery when situations demand it. This gentle giant is always accountable to its pack. One of the coauthors relates the following:

My Great Pyrenees mix is 150 pounds of muscle. Gunner has a gentle disposition and, if possible, avoids conflict. If attacked by another dog, he attempts to deflect the other dog's aggression. Gunner is not naïve, though. He is wary of people and dogs who do not exhibit the right demeanor. His own gentle demeanor can change in an instant if he believes a member of his pack is threatened. If a stranger who appears menacing approaches, Gunner will utter a low growl of warning as if to say, "Convince me you are not a threat to my pack." If a dog attacks one of our smaller dogs he is ever quick to defend. Once he chased a large moose out of our camp.

Gunner is a courageous leader, highly intelligent, and often displaying independent thought, making his own decisions, and wanting to lead when on the trail. But he is always acutely aware he is accountable to his pack. There are leadership lessons to be gained from Gunner's behavior: Don't show off your power just because you have it. Humble, unassuming leaders are far easier to love than arrogant ones. Be kind to others, especially those who are weaker, but don't be naïve. Be slow to take offense personally and forgive others who offend you, but be ready to exhibit courage when the situation calls for it. When required to wield your power, do so judiciously and not vindictively, applying just enough force to rectify the problem—but do no unnecessary harm. As entrepreneur Jim Rohn once said, "The challenge of leadership is to be strong, but not rude; be kind, but not weak; be bold, but not bully; be thoughtful, but not lazy; be humble, but not timid; be proud, but not arrogant; have humor, but without folly."

CHAPTER 2

A Philosophy of Courageous Leadership

> **"If your actions inspire others to dream more, learn more, do more and become more, you are a leader."**
>
> —John Quincy Adams, sixth president of the United States

This chapter is about a philosophy of courageous leadership as opposed to leadership styles and models. The academic and practitioner literature is replete with discussion of various proposed leadership styles with the word "style" used rather loosely. It can all be somewhat confusing for someone seeking practical guidance about how to become a good leader, improve one's leadership skills if already a leader, and help build subordinates into leaders. Consequently, prior to presenting some major aspects of a courageous leadership philosophy, we begin by attempting to place some frame around our discussion by making some distinctions among leadership philosophy, style, and model. We then present several major tenets of a philosophy of courageous leadership before moving to leadership styles and methodologies in the next chapter.

A **philosophy** is a set of basic principles, concepts, and values, whereas **style** is a distinctive and identifiable form. A **model** is a schematic description of a system, theory, or phenomenon that accounts for its known or inferred properties and may be used for further study of its characteristics. Although leadership philosophy could and should clearly inform a leadership style, distinctions between them are blurry. It is often unclear where philosophy ends and style begins. Consequently, recalling that our goal is to provide a practical guide for leading courageously rather than an academic treatise on leadership, our distinction is more a matter of convenience for understanding and application than a rigorous academic position. Our fundamental position is that a philosophy of courageous leadership can be incorporated into various leadership styles.

What does it mean to lead people? There is something quite interesting about the quote above, something that is contradictory to the behaviors of lots of people today to whom the title "leader" is often assigned too casually. One hears comments such as John Jones must be a great leader because he is CEO of the XYZ Corporation, and XYZ is performing well. The assumption is that Jones's leadership is the cause of XYZ's current good performance, which may or may not be the case. Many people are drawn to people in powerful positions as a moth is drawn to a flame. Power often seems to give rise to sycophancy because many people derive vicarious utility from being around powerful people—perhaps because the sycophants feel they become more powerful themselves by associating with others' positional power.

If we accept President Adams's definition of what constitutes a leader, however, the emphasis is not on the attributes many associate with leadership—power and position. Rather, the emphasis is on the positive impact someone has on others.

"Leaders aren't born, they are made. And they are made just like anything else, through hard work."

—Vince Lombardi, legendary football coach of the Green Bay Packers

From the quote we can infer that, at least in Adams's mind, positional authority alone does not mean a person is a good leader. History is replete with examples of immoral despots who clawed their way to power. Rather, the implicit emphasis in Adams's quote is on servant leadership—that is, good leaders serve to help their pack and its members become better. This chapter explores several of the more important attributes of courageous leadership with the goal of differentiating what commonly passes for leadership from courageous leadership.

2.1. Courageous Leaders Are Made, Not Born

Many of us grew up knowing someone who always seemed to have the inside track when it came to being named to a leadership position. Perhaps it was someone who had outstanding natural athletic ability who was elected captain of a team—or perhaps someone whose physical attractiveness led to his or her being president of the class. It is tempting to think of these types of people as having been born leaders, people for whom leadership comes naturally. People who naturally possess characteristics such as athletic ability and physical attractiveness may also be more popular among their peers and therefore possess self-confidence. But are they born leaders?

The answer depends upon whether we define a leader as someone in a position of authority or whether it is defined as someone who possesses sound leadership skills. Certainly there is no natural birthing of an understanding of principles of leadership. Granted, assuming leadership positions early in life might lead to an earlier understanding of leadership acquired through experience. And make no mistake—good leadership skills cannot be learned by study alone. They must be practiced. Experience of leading acquired as a result of having gained early leadership opportunity because of some physical attribute is not the same as being a born leader, though. Just because someone has the opportunity to lead does not mean that he or she can translate that experience into superlative leadership. Consequently, if we adopt the position taken above that simply holding a position of authority does not make someone a leader, then leaders are made, not born.

What's more, early successes may actually become a deterrent to future progression as a leader. Consider Figure 2.1.

The vertical axis represents a measure of an individual's ability as a leader to function well at a given organizational level, and the horizontal axis represents the number of years' experience in business leadership roles. Leader A, represented by the blue line, had an earlier start as a result of having been accorded leadership opportunities before beginning a business career. Leader A began with leadership abilities equivalent to those of a first-level leader. Leader B, represented by the red line, had no prior leadership experience and began with no business leadership ability. Leader A's early advantage, however, led him to become somewhat complacent, comfortable that he was on the right track. Leader B, on the other hand, recognized that her lack of leadership ability was a detriment to her career and worked harder than Leader A to improve. The result is that after 10

Figure 2.1. Career Path Comparison

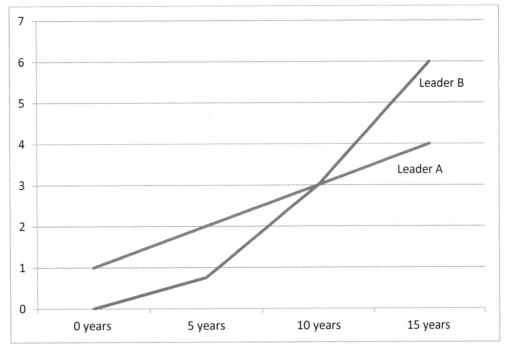

years Leader B caught up with Leader A in ability and after 15 years became capable of leading effectively at two levels above Leader A.

Note also the slopes of the two lines. Leader A improves but at a constant rate. Because she worked hard at becoming a better leader, after year 5 Leader B's ability improved at an increasing rate. Even if someone is like Leader A, for whom leadership seemed to come naturally, there is a need to be aware of the danger of assuming that the rate of improvement in leadership skills will always place you at the forefront. Modeling your leadership improvement slope after Leader B requires hard work and constant honest assessment of your performance.

Why do you suppose Leader B was so motivated to improve herself? The answer may rest with personal pain she experienced from having failed to lead well at the beginning of her business career. Stephen Covey, chairman of the Covey Leadership Center, has said that the main source of personal change is pain from disappointment and failure because pain creates the humility and motivation to learn and improve.[1] People beginning their business careers with no leadership experience should therefore not be discouraged when they experience failure if their mistakes are of the forgivable type and they learn from them. Where you find yourself in the long run in terms of leadership ability is far more important than where you start. Always keep in mind that great leaders are made, not born.

2.2. Courageous Leaders Are Trustworthy and Trusting

To be good enough to earn the right to lead we need to earn our followers' consent to follow us. Research indicates that mutual **trust** among leaders and followers is one of the most important attributes for encouraging followership. Why is trust so important? Without trust and mutual

"Leadership and learning are indispensable to each other."

—John F. Kennedy, former U.S. president

31

respect among leaders and subordinates, organizations suffer a combination of low performance and poor morale.[2] Trust is therefore an essential element in businesses' effectiveness. Research supports that, in comparison to low-trust groups,

"No man is good enough to govern another man without that man's consent."

—Abraham Lincoln, former U.S. president

members of high-trust groups experience more clarity about problems and goals, search for more alternative courses of action, and experience greater levels of mutual influence on outcomes, job satisfaction, and motivation to implement decisions.[3]

How does a leader go about earning followers' trust? Trust is earned in several ways. One is that leaders must truly care about their followers'

> Research suggests that employees who feel cared for have greater trust, loyalty, and appreciation of the work they do and perform better.

welfare and exhibit this **caring** in their behaviors. Think about the following scenario. Suppose you signed on for a guided rafting adventure on a whitewater river that has some nasty hydraulics. A hydraulic is a place where the river current is forced back upstream in such a way that a hole in the water is created. Hydraulics can be dangerous if the current is strong because they are difficult to swim out of if a rafter falls overboard into one. Prior to departure your guide is briefing you on what to do if the raft encounters rapids having bad hydraulics. Consider the following statements by two guides:

Guide A: "Don't worry much about the hydraulics. I've fallen into them before and came out fine. If it happens, you won't be able to swim out while keeping your head above water because of the force of the water pushing you down. You'll tire quickly and drown. Instead, just dive down into the hydraulic and let the current carry you out the bottom. Cowards shouldn't be doing whitewater anyway."

Guide B: "When we approach rapids having dangerous hydraulics, you need to be especially careful. If it isn't possible for us to portage the rapid, ensure that you brace yourself in the raft in the manner I discussed a few minutes ago. In the hopefully unlikely event you do fall into a bad hydraulic, I am going to explain step by step the procedure for escaping it and the assistance I'll provide."

Which of the foregoing statements inspires trust? While some might not be offended by Guide A's statements, others could be. Guide B expresses more concern for your welfare, whereas Guide A discounts the danger and makes you feel inadequate if you feel fear about something that any rational person should fear. Which guide would you trust most to take care of you? You would probably choose Guide B. If you are uncertain which, would your conclusion change if a loved one were accompanying you on the trip? The same is true in organizational settings. It is difficult for subordinates to trust leaders who do not care about them on some personal level.

Caring can be conveyed by a variety of actions such as **being concerned** about employees' concerns outside the work environment, such as family illness. Such events can be incredibly traumatic for employees and their families, and they will occur. Recall the two anecdotes in chapter 1 about an associate dean and CPA firm partner experiencing such life-changing family trauma. It is easy for leaders to get so absorbed in the exigencies of the moment that they neglect to pause and convey concern. Bosses who take no notice of such events as described in those two anecdotes act as if they are saying, "Oh well, the show must go on."

Competence is also very important. Subordinates want their leaders to be competent because leaders' competence affects subordinates' welfare. Any young officer who has led troops in combat quickly learns this lesson. When the troops' lives depend upon their officers' competence, they are much more willing to follow leaders who display competence and confidence in their own abilities to handle crises and stressful situations. Leaders who become rattled and upset cause their followers to become rattled and upset. An important point is that when leaders engage in learning activities to become more competent, they are not just furthering the organization and their own careers but also creating trust.

Other ways of conveying caring are being committed to **assisting every subordinate to improve** and **being willing to go to bat for subordinates** when the organization imposes some injustice upon them. For example, suppose a proposed new firm policy inadvertently fails to take into account an unnecessary hardship imposed upon your group. Leaders who are unwilling to raise subordinates' concerns with senior leaders for fear of offending them convey that the leaders place their own welfare above that of their followers.

Yet another way of communicating caring is to **not surprise** employees with bad news if avoidable. For example, if a subordinate is doing something incorrectly and learns about it for the first time during a formal performance review, the subordinate might well ask, "Why didn't you tell me this 6 months ago so that I could have corrected the problem then, before it became part of my employment record?" Bosses who defer dealing with unpleasant leadership tasks, such

Is trust easier to destroy than build? Decades of research assumes it is. How bad the impact of untrustworthy actions is depends, in part, upon how much trust has been created prior to the actions and how deeply ingrained trust is. One untrustworthy action is far less likely to destroy trust if the organization has worked assiduously to build trust over a long period of time.

as confronting subordinates with performance problems, are not courageous leaders and can lose followers' trust. Let your followers know where they stand.

This raises a very important point. *Trust is far more difficult to build than it is to destroy.* It can take years to build trust and only one misstep to destroy it. Although caring is the first step in engendering trust, courageous servant leaders need to be continuously aware of actions that can damage their followers' trust. A problem arises when a leader's actions do not match his or her words. Leaders who "talk the talk" but do not "walk the walk" lose the confidence of their subordinates because this conveys a lack of integrity. The old adage "actions speak louder than words"

"If you don't trust the people they will become untrustworthy."

—Lao Tzu, Chinese philosopher

applies here. Failing to deliver on promises implies an integrity problem that is one of the quickest ways to destroy trust. Never promise what you cannot deliver and be careful not to promise more than you can.

Leaders also inspire trust by **trusting their followers.** Trust is by necessity reciprocal to a large extent. It is more difficult to trust someone who doesn't trust you. Micromanaging conveys distrust by signaling a lack of confidence in subordinates' ability to handle details. One of the coauthors relates the following consulting experience: "We were working with the division of a large company. During the closing of the accounts the division CFO asked for daily updates and would become nervous with every variance instead of allowing the team to effect the close and explain any material variances. Following his poor example, the line managers acted in a similar manner. It was no surprise that the accounting department had a high turnover rate."

"There are three essentials to leadership: humility, clarity, and courage."

—Fuchan Yuan, Chan master

Employees need respect, and a pattern of not trusting conveys disrespect. By trusting followers to deliver, leaders not only convey trust but also inspire. As Lao Tzu suggests, not trusting subordinates makes them less trustworthy. In general, followers strive to live up to leaders' expectations. When leaders signal a lack of trust in followers' ability to accomplish tasks, they are implicitly signaling lower expectations, resulting in weaker performance. Courageous leaders inspire trust and have it reciprocated by setting high standards and expecting great things from their followers—but being ever ready to live to those high standards themselves and never asking anything of subordinates that the leader is unwilling to do.

2.3. Courageous Leaders Balance Power with Humility

There is something about power that fascinates humans. Why do humans like power? It is seductive. With gains in power leaders discover that many people are nicer than previously, pay them more attention, and compliment them a lot—so much so at times that these behaviors can become obsequious. It is easy for unwary leaders to begin believing that this favorable attention is coming because they are wonderful and not because of their power to reward others in some way—be the rewards financial, positional, or psychological. As a result, unless leaders are careful as they gain power, they attract followers who are drawn to them because of what they perceive the leader can do for them. Therein is an insidious danger leaders need to avoid. One characteristic of successful leaders is that they surround themselves with good subordinates. Part of what makes a follower good is having good motives. If people associate with leadership primarily for what it can do for them and not because they want to do good things, leaders can end up with organizations in which selfishness is the principal motivator. This is inconsistent with the notion of servant leadership, in which a leader's priorities should be the pack and its members first.

One way to avoid falling into this insidious trap is for leaders to balance power with **humility**. By reminding themselves constantly of the need to be humble, leaders are less likely to fall into the trap of too much self-esteem clouding their judgment. What does it mean to be humble? Humility can mean different things to different people, and in a world where many claw for power it can be interpreted to imply meekness or even weakness. That is a misinterpretation of what it means for courageous servant leaders to be humble. Humility means not resting on your laurels and recognizing, as Michael Jordan, the great basketball player, once said—that you need to earn your leadership every day. It means a willingness to admit you don't have all the answers and are willing to learn. It means being open to feedback, especially from your own subordinates. Humility means the willingness to acknowledge your own mistakes just as you ask your subordinates to acknowledge theirs. Above all, humility means recognizing that increases in power translate into increases in responsibility to both the pack and subordinates.

Any discussion of power would be remiss if it didn't address the issue of **formal versus informal power**. Often informal power can be more potent and influential than formal power. First of all, you don't need a title to be a leader. Leadership is not always top down and sometimes comes bottom up. A lower-ranking subordinate who has a leader's confidence may have more influence with the leader than a higher-ranking subordinate who lacks such confidence. The CEO's loyal administrative assistant who followed her up the organization chart over a long period may have far more actual power that a junior manager even though the assistant is below the managerial ranks. Organizationally savvy leaders recognize and appreciate how to use the informal power that exists inside their organizations. But one thing that humility helps ensure is turning people with informal power into allies instead of enemies. One of the coauthors relates the following anecdote:

> When I was a management trainee I was assigned to the CEO of another large organization as his assistant for a large charity campaign. During the campaign I became very friendly with both the CEO and his administrative assistant, Kate, in whom the CEO placed a great deal of confidence. I took care to always be friendly and kind to Kate despite the fact that my assignment was temporary, I didn't work for her company, and I was management bound and she was a clerical. At the end of the campaign the CEO attempted to hire me, but I was making excellent progress with my current employer and declined. Sometime much later I was given a new assignment under a micromanaging boss who was full of pride, hubris, and anything but humble. Then one

> "The first responsibility of a leader is to define reality. The last is to say thank you. In between, the leader is a servant."

—Max Dupree, businessman and author of *Leadership Is an Art*

day I took the initiative and dealt with a client problem because no one more senior was available. The client was pleased, but my boss who cherished his power chewed me out for exceeding my authority. Irritated because I felt I had acted in the best interests of my employer, I sat at my desk thinking about good things I'd been hearing about the CEO's company. On a whim, I picked up the phone and called Kate. She remembered me and greeted me warmly. Could she please ask the CEO to call me someday, if and when he ever had time? Two minutes later the CEO was on the line. By 6:00 PM that evening I had a new job, 50 percent pay increase, and promotion to the same level as the boss who had just chewed me out. I'd bet there was a big stack of messages on the CEO's desk and his calendar was full of appointments. Why did he call back so quickly? Kate walked into his office, handed him my message, and said, "Call him now."

Although not every act of kindness results in such good outcomes, there are several lessons about

"The best executive is the one who has sense enough to pick good men to do what he wants done, and self-restraint enough to keep from meddling with them while they do it."

—Theodore Roosevelt, former U.S. president

A Philosophy of Courageous Leadership

> **"Pride is the first step in people unraveling, companies unraveling, and relationships unraveling."**
>
> —Jeff Foxworthy, writer, actor, and comedian

power and humility in this anecdote. First, being kind because it is the right thing to do and not in anticipation of any reward paid off in an unexpected way. Second, even though Kate was a clerical employee, she had the informal power to have the CEO of a large company respond immediately to a request from a junior manager at another company. Third, the lack of humble leadership on the part of a boss full of false pride who stifled the initiative of his subordinates with micromanagement cost his company a manager rated in the top 10 percent at his level. Humility, in the end, is the opposite of false pride bred by a little power.

2.4. Courageous Leaders Delegate Authority but Retain Responsibility

The previous anecdote provides an example in which a micromanaging boss cost his company the services of a junior manager. The boss's desire to retain authority rather than delegate led to the junior manager's resignation because the latter did not feel empowered to do what was necessary to serve a client. In this case, the boss placed his own desire for power above the needs of his pack and one of its members. This raises the important issue of **decentralization** or dispersion of decision-making authority inside businesses.

Delegating authority makes subordinates feel empowered. This is not the same thing as simply off-loading tasks you'd rather not perform, but more serious delegation. When subordinates feel empowered they are more engaged and perform better. They see themselves as making greater contributions to the pack. Additionally, their professional growth is enhanced because they are given more opportunities to learn by dealing with

problems. **Self-actualization** refers to a person fulfilling his or her potential and becoming all that he or she is capable of becoming. This leads to greater job satisfaction and retention by the firm. Properly handled, delegation of authority enhances organizational performance because it speeds up responses to organizational problems, such as resolution of client dissatisfaction or requests as the junior manager did in the previous anecdote. A former military officer relates the following story:

> Many people think the U.S. military is very top down. That's a fallacy. When I left the military after 5 years' service and joined a large bank I quickly realized that I had enjoyed more responsibility as a young military officer than many who were much higher in rank than I was given at the bank. The bank had a lockstep way of training people that had been in place for many years. The assumption seemed to be that every new management trainee had to have the same experiences for the same length of time. This clearly ignored the fact that some people learn faster than others. Authority was much too centralized, and many of the more promising management trainees became bored quickly and left for other banks or careers. To make matters worse, the business climate for banking was changing rapidly at the time, but my bank's image was one of being old fashioned and a little behind the times. During my exit interview two senior officers expressed serious concern about the bank's high turnover of junior managers and asked me many questions about why I was leaving to take a better-paying job with more responsibility with another bank. They seemed to believe my reasoning was simply more money and were unable to grasp how the bank's highly centralized decision making and lockstep management development policies were affecting junior managers' self-actualization. It seemed to be a stodgy organization in which

Throughout we refer to goals and objectives, so it is important to define them. **Goals** mean end states that signify mission success as discussed later. **Objectives** are intermediate accomplishments that lead to goal attainment.

managers at the middle levels were almost afraid to make bold decisions.

One reason weak leaders are often afraid to delegate authority is that they cannot delegate the responsibility that goes with that authority. When a leader delegates authority the leader is giving up some control of outcomes in order to benefit the pack and its members. Because leaders are expected to make good decisions about when to delegate authority and which subordinates can be trusted with it, leaders retain responsibility for how the decision to delegate turns out. Consequently, delegating authority is not to be taken lightly and takes courage on the part of leaders.

A key attribute of courageous leaders is their willingness to accept responsibility for bad outcomes over which they had authority. Leaders cannot escape their responsibility by making statements such as, "I gave Jones the authority to handle that problem and he blew it. It's his fault, not mine." Courageous leaders delegate authority when appropriate, often establishing the desired outcome but allowing subordinates to figure out how to achieve it. They follow up and monitor subordinates' progress and lack of it without micromanaging their behaviors.

Directing subordinates to achieve a desired outcome but not how to do it is known in the military as **mission orders**. In other words, a leader tells a subordinate to carry out a mission but leaves the tactics of how the mission is accomplished to the subordinate. Not only does this make the subordinate feel more empowered and in control of his or her destiny, it allows for faster reaction in what is frequently a rapidly changing battlefield or business environment. In the context of the **ends/ways/means model** discussed in chapter 1, the leader gives the subordinate a *mission,* allows the subordinate to come up with the *ways* the mission will be accomplished, and then attempts to ensure the subordinate has the necessary *means* or

> "A good leader is a person who takes a little more than his share of the blame and a little less than his share of the credit."
>
> —John Maxwell, minister and author

resources to carry out the mission. One benefit of mission orders is that it allows the commander to step back from the details of a mission and retain a big-picture perspective. Why is this important? No leader can monitor all activity in any complex endeavor. Through the use of mission orders and the ends/ways/means model, leaders have the time to assess whether the ways being selected by the subordinate will accomplish the desired end and whether the means being supplied to the subordinate are adequate to support the selected ways.

One of the questions leaders continuously face is when it is appropriate to delegate. As a general rule, organizations benefit when the authority to make decisions and take actions is pushed down to the lowest level at which it can be handled well. This alleviates much of the requirement for issues, problems, and initiatives to travel up the chain of command for a decision and back

> "As we look into the next century, leaders will be those who empower others."
>
> —Bill Gates, chairman, Microsoft

down for action. The more complex the business and competitive environments become, the more the need for timely anticipation of and reaction to problems and opportunities. Today's business climate often calls for nimble decision making. Unfortunately, large organizations often become rooted in doing something in a given way simply because it has been done that way in the past, and they fail to change as their environments change.

A useful framework for thinking about delegation of authority can be borrowed from the military, which categorizes decision making into three sometimes overlapping categories: strategic, operational, and tactical. **Strategic leadership** is concerned with attaining ultimate goals or end states—in other words, victory—and the overarching plans for goal attainment. **Tactical leadership** is concerned with the details of accomplishing near-term objectives that contribute to goal attainment. In between strategic and tactical leadership is **operational leadership**, which is concerned with shaping the environment further out so that tactical-level leaders are able to accomplish their specific missions. In effect, operational authority bridges strategic and tactical authority, providing the necessary linkages between a strategy and the myriad finite tasks often required for its implementation. The following example illustrates this linkage.

Assume you are a partner in the advisory services division of a large CPA firm. After performing market studies, the firm's senior leadership has decided upon strategy for gaining a foothold in a particular niche market with the desired goal to have $50 million in annual revenues 5 years from now. You have been assigned the respon-

"He who has never learned to obey cannot be a good commander."

—Aristotle

sibility of being partner-in-charge (PIC) of this initiative and asked to develop a new unit with subunits in various locations. To accomplish the strategic goal, there will be many tactical-level tasks required, such as hiring and training junior staff and clerical personnel, developing client prospect lists, calling on prospects, obtaining clients, and servicing client needs. The PIC must establish an operational framework in which these tactical-level tasks can be accomplished. Your first responsibility is to define reality for your subordinates. This entails communicating a clear understanding of the desired ends and strategy for attaining them. It might also include such matters as creating a project team consisting of key personnel, establishing major objectives, developing a detailed operational plan for implantation including budgets, setting up the subunits, and recruiting key personnel. The PIC will need to continuously assess the mission's ends/ways/ means relationships. Are the ways adequate to attain the desired end state? Are the means sufficient to effectively implement the ways? If imbalances occur, can they be rectified by the project team or does the PIC need to request more resources from senior leadership or recommend modification to the desired end state?

Again borrowing an idea from the military, there is an old adage that a plan stays intact until the first shot is fired, after which it needs to be continuously modified because of unanticipated events and changing conditions. The PIC should continuously monitor the project's changing landscape, looking out into the future, anticipating changes before they occur whenever possible, and reacting to these future events by adjusting ways and means to fit ends so that subordinates at the tactical level can accomplish their assigned tasks. The PIC also has a responsibility to keep senior leaders at the strategic level informed, especially of any major disconnects in the project's ends/ways/means model.

2.5. Courageous Leaders Are Great Followers

Although it may be sometimes difficult to discern when observing the behaviors of some powerful and influential people society calls "leaders," courageous leaders understand that the distinction between leaders and followers is not a bright line. Leaders can become followers in a matter of minutes depending upon circumstances. One moment you may be leading a team and the next a member of another team. How well leaders transition to followers and vice versa is determined to a great extent by their pack orientation. If a leader places the welfare of the pack and its members ahead of his or her own, he or she will be far more attuned to when it is appropriate to lead and when to follow. Moreover, astute leaders can make the best followers because they understand that leaders need followers who support their leadership.

Writing for *Forbes,* August Turak notes several characteristics of great followers.[4] First among those we consider most important are loyalty and trust. Loyalty is easily misunderstood. It does not mean always agreeing with the boss. It can mean quite the opposite. Consider the following quote by a general at a promotion ceremony for a lieutenant colonel being promoted to colonel: "When John was on my staff he routinely came into my office about once a month and kicked the front of my desk in. But he was the one guy on my staff who would never let me walk off the cliff blindfolded."

What is this general saying? He is saying that his subordinate, the colonel, is not afraid to disagree when he thinks the general is making a mistake. In fact, the subordinate is so loyal that he is willing to risk offending the general in order to prevent him from making a mistake that could harm both the organization and the general's career. The colonel is placing the welfare of the unit and his commander foremost. But there is more to this than just the subordinate's loyalty. The col-

onel has earned the general's trust. If this were not the case, the general would not tolerate the colonel's occasional disagreement with him. This trust has been earned over a period of time by the colonel continuously demonstrating unselfishness in placing the welfare of the pack and its leader above

> ## "Leaders listen, take advice, lose arguments, and follow."
>
> —Irwin Federman, former CEO of Monolithic Memories

that of his own. Moreover, the colonel is also driven to the goal of betterment of his pack, demonstrating sound judgment in anticipating problems and seizing the initiative to prevent them by offering viable solutions. He has found a way to communicate with the general that apparently works well because the general listens. In a sense, the colonel has created his own job by becoming the general's trusted advisor. This trust has to be guarded carefully, however, by the colonel not advertising his special relationship to others.

Good followers must be coachable in that they are humble enough to recognize their faults and willing to receive critical feedback in pursuit of continuous improvement. In addition to being susceptible to coaching by others, they should learn to coach themselves. CNN commentator Major General Perry M. Smith notes:

> Followers can learn a great deal by observing leaders, both good and bad. By seeking and obtaining as many opportunities to exercise as the delegation, empowerment or apathy of the boss will allow, followers can prepare themselves for the great challenges that lie ahead. Followers can grow considerably if they do more than simply accomplish what their job description requires.[5]

"A leader is a dealer in hope."

—Napoleon Bonaparte

The best followers are also leaders because they understand that a leader's reaction to them as followers is influenced by their development level. Peter Northhouse notes that when development of subordinates as competent followers is low, a more directive leadership style is indicated. As development increases, a leader can move from directive to coaching. As even more development occurs, the leader is able to move into a supportive role. Finally, delegation is possible with highly developed followers. Northhouse notes:

> In brief the essence of situational leadership demands that a leader match his or her style to the competence and commitment of followers. Effective leaders are those who can recognize what followers need and then adapt their own style to meet those needs.[6]

One implication of the foregoing is that ambitious courageous leaders desiring more authority need to become highly developed followers. By doing so, they will better enable their bosses to delegate authority to them.

"People buy into the leader before they buy into the vision."

—John Maxwell, minister and author

How does one become a highly developed follower? Patrick Townsend and Joan Gebhardt provide the following suggestions.[7] Know yourself and seek improvement by becoming technically proficient. Comply with company policies and directions. Make sound, timely decisions and then take responsibility for your actions. Familiarize yourself with your leader, his or her job, and challenges, anticipating requirements and keeping him or her informed of important matters. Be a team player

but not a "yes man," and stay on the moral high ground. The best followers are actively engaged with their leaders and their organization, exhibiting critical and independent thinking. All of this suggests something that many would-be leaders overlook. Becoming a great follower takes effort, just like becoming a great leader. You have to work at it. But great followership is a prerequisite for great leadership, so become a great follower.

2.6. Courageous Leaders Paint Pictures of a Better Future, Set High Standards, and Dare to Achieve

Many people aspire to be part of something very good and meaningful, something larger than they. Elite military units attract volunteers desiring to be part of some special organization that signifies they, too, are special. Business people are often proud to work for organizations having special status as being among the best in their industry or sector. Business professors enjoy being faculty members at prestigious schools. Students often brag to their friends about having gotten internships or jobs with highly regarded firms. Savvy leaders recognize this human need to be part of something special and channel it to serve organizational goals by creating a vision of a better future attended by high standards of achievement. **Vision** is about possibilities and desired futures. The Drucker Foundation has maintained that the "capacity to paint an uplifting and ennobling picture of the future is, in fact, what differentiates leaders from other credible sources."[8]

Be careful in painting your vision, however; ensure that you can deliver and, when realized, that the vision turns out to be as advertised. There is an old joke about a man who is negotiating with the devil about going to hell. Naturally, the man has reservations. The devil says, "You'll be surprised. Hell has a bad rap. You'll like it. Come take a look and see for yourself." The devil then shows him a room full of people partying and apparently having a wonderful time. The surprised man says, "Looks great! Count me in." When he shows up the next day, yesterday's partiers are slaving away in misery. The man says, "I don't understand. Yesterday everyone seemed to be having the time of their lives. Today is horrible!" The devil replies, "Yesterday we were recruiting you. Today you start work." If you misrepresent the future to your followers, when it arrives they will feel cheated and that you cannot be trusted.

Vision is a potent tool for leaders because of referent power derived from their followers when followers feel self-actualized by their relationship to the leader and organization. The catch is that it often comes with a price. A vision that attracts followers to a leader requires leaders to set high standards for followers that are directly linked to the organization's value focus.[9] **High standards** communicate the leader's expectations of others, which in turn affects their level of aspiration. Being special, part of the best, necessarily means living up to high standards that set the organization and its members apart from the ordinary. Academic research indicates that highly successful organizations generally have high performance standards.[10] Another reason for setting high standards is that leaders' behavior toward followers is often based upon their expectations about them. When standards are high in an organization, people expect more from each other and deliver more.[11]

High standards aren't just for followers, however. Leaders have even higher standards. The old leadership adage about never asking a subordinate to do something you wouldn't do applies but doesn't go far enough.[12] The Drucker Foundation argues, "followers demand of their leaders significantly higher standards of personal conduct than they demand of themselves. Therefore, leaders have fewer degrees of behavioral freedom than those they are leading."[13] Diminished personal freedom is often the price of courageous leader-

ship because it means placing the organization and its members' interests ahead of those of the leader.

A bold vision and high standards go hand in hand with **daring to achieve**. Peter Northhouse notes, "Achievement-oriented leadership is char-

> ## "The greatest leaders mobilize others by coalescing people around a shared vision."
>
> —Ken Blanchard, author of *The One Minute Manager* and management expert

acterized by a leader who challenges subordinates to perform at the highest level possible."[14] High standards of excellence and continuous improvement are hallmarks of high-achieving leaders. One of the coauthors recalls visiting Cisco Systems years ago and being told of a work culture that got things done in "dog years." Because of a dog's lifespan being perhaps one-seventh that of a human, it is often said that one dog year equals seven human years. Cisco's culture under its high-achieving CEO John Chambers—an Indiana University MBA by the way—was to accomplish in one year what other companies would take seven years to accomplish, hence in dog years.

Developing a high-achieving organization requires developing high-achieving members. A multiyear study of Google's three major functions—engineering, global business, and administrative—called Project Oxygen examined whether management soft skills mattered in Google's culture as opposed to technical greatness. Small increases in management quality were found to have a substantial impact. Higher-achieving leaders experienced lower turnover, greater innovation, and employee satisfaction. The project identified eight skills and behaviors by high-achieving managers: (1) good coach, (2) empowers teams, (3) shows interest and concern in teams and peo-

A Philosophy of Courageous Leadership

ple, (4) productive and results oriented, (5) good listener and communicator, (6) assists subordinates with career development, (7) clear vision and strategy, and (8) uses key technical advisors. One interesting finding was that technical personnel strongly disliked being micromanaged in their work but liked having their career progression closely monitored.[15]

2.7. Courageous Leaders Make the Most of What They've Got

Courageous leaders realize that often they must use the resources they have rather than the resources they would like to have. Somehow, they find the resources necessary to achieve success; they don't just wait for someone to provide the resources. Recall the bank merger anecdote presented earlier. The manager assigned the task had very little in the way of personnel and time to meet the immediate objective of opening the bank being merged the next day, but somehow the job got done. What followed was weeks of adjustment as more issues came to light and more resources became available. This is not unusual, particularly in "emergent urgent" situations. In the bank instance, it helped that the manager had been exposed to numerous unexpected crisis situations in his military experience and was accustomed to having to deal with rapidly evolving problems using limited resources. An important lesson had been drilled into him early in his training: *When faced with a crisis, teams become demoralized*

"A good plan violently executed now is better than a perfect plan executed next week."

—General George Patton

quickly and teamwork begins to disintegrate if the leader does not take immediate action. This is not to say that thoughtful planning should not be conducted whenever possible, but rather that

Coauthor comment

"The role of the management accountant is to translate the business ideas of management into numbers— but NOT to recommend a course of action. Executives and board members don't want accountants to run the business but rather to challenge assumptions, clarify expected results, and offer insights. If assumptions are clarified and objective forecasts provided, it is management's responsibility to make the decision on a course of action. Information providers can assist by providing assessments of how supportable are alternative courses of action."

many situations call for what some have called an 80 percent solution followed by adjustment as required. Perfect solutions are elusive. Waiting for the perfect solution can mean the team and project become mired in indecision and inaction. General Electric calls this process "launch and learn."

A related trap for unwary leaders is the desire to have all relevant information. Courageous leaders realize that the perfect plan is elusive and often they need to get movement on a project and adjust as necessary. There is often one more piece of information that someone wants before making a decision to move forward. Waiting for yet another market study or focus group to report in can cause projects to bog down and the project team to lose focus. Consider how Apple's iconic leader, Steve Jobs, handled one such situation. Jobs was passionate about perfection, but he recognized when a leader has to lead rather than just listen to more reports. Once when asked whether a market study should be conducted, Jobs replied, "No, because customers don't know what they want until we've shown them." Jobs quoted the great automobile pioneer Henry Ford, who said, "If I'd asked customers what they wanted, they would have told me, 'A faster horse.'"[16]

Savvy leaders like Jobs understand that data do not always equate to useful information. When undertaking new initiatives there is often an abundance of data but a paucity of usable information. Useful information can drown in too much data, the latter obscuring the former and making it difficult to extract. Consider the following anecdote related by a military commander:

> During an operation my intelligence officer came in to brief me. He carried a stack of 3×5 cards an inch thick, each describing a datum, and proceeded to read to me about various microlevel events. After a couple minutes I stopped him and said, "I am not interested in you reading me data. I want a fused intelligence product that tells me what are the enemy's intentions and capabilities, and how confident are you in your assessment." The intelligence officer responded, "Sir, my job is to collect intelligence and present it to the commander. I don't want to prejudice the commander's point of view with my opinions." I knew immediately this was a cop-out. The intelligence officer was succumbing to his fear of making wrong predictions. I told him, "No, your job is to take intelligence data, analyze it, and fuse it in a manner that provides the commander with useful information. Leave and come back when you are able to do that." In the meantime, I had no choice but to move forward with what I believed to be the answers to my questions, making the most of what information I had, because waiting for him to do his job correctly was not an option.

This illustrates another point. For courageous leaders failure is not an option. Naturally people will sometimes fail, but courageous leaders usu-

> ## "A competent leader can get efficient service from poor troops, while on the contrary an incapable leader can demoralize the best of troops."
> —General John J. Pershing, hero of World War I

ally find a way to succeed even when success is difficult. As Debi Coleman, one of Steve Jobs's former subordinates, said of working for Jobs, "You did the impossible because you didn't realize it was impossible."[17] Courageous leaders have a low tolerance for excuses and deal with obstacles rather than allowing subordinates to whine about them. Courageous leaders sense and confront evasion of responsibility as the commander above did. Otherwise, fearful subordinates always wanting more information as a way of deferring a decision—or refusing to take responsibility for fear of being wrong—can cause projects to become moribund and leaders to be inundated with detail that obscures important issues. The case of a fearful subordinate who, lacking confidence in his own abilities, engages in these tactics has been repeated countless times in business settings. An example is captured in the following anecdote related by one of the coauthors:

> We had just instituted a new second-mortgage lending program that was growing rapidly. As I scanned the financial reports for March, I noticed that we had accrued less interest on that portfolio than in February despite having more loans, a higher average interest rate on the portfolio, there being more days in March than in February, and no interperiod adjustments having been made. I knew intuitively there had to be some discrepancy. When queried about

A Philosophy of Courageous Leadership

this, however, my controller brought me reams of data and calculations, insisting that the figures were correct, refused to accept any other possibility, and explained meticulously how carefully the accrual had been calculated. At that point I knew I needed to take control of the problem, investigated, and discovered that vendor-supplied software being used to calculate the interest accrual was not performing correctly. It was a classic case of garbage going into financial models means garbage coming out. Shortly thereafter I terminated the controller—not just because he had failed to detect this particular problem but because he did not recognize and take responsibility for his department's mistakes, becoming defensive when they were brought to his attention.

2.8. Courageous Leaders Celebrate Victories, Choose the Difficult Right Path, and Confront Problems

Courageous leaders celebrate the victories of the pack and its members. Celebrating victories in business organizations is little different that an athletic team celebrating victories. People like to be acknowledged and honored individually and be part of a winning team. Celebrating victories boosts morale and engenders pack unity. The value of psychological rewards often goes under-

"There's a rich opportunity for leaders to appeal to more than the material rewards."

—Kouzes and Posner, *The Leadership Challenge*, p. 131

appreciated in many organizations. Ways of celebrating can differ greatly, ranging from recognizing superlative performance in group meetings by awarding a special honor, to holding promotion ceremonies honoring subordinates' progression, to having an office social function following the successful completion of an especially difficult and challenging project. It is particularly important to recognize the long-term contributions of personnel leaving the organization due to retirement or promotion. Even though taking time for such celebrations may occasionally slow down work, the improvement in morale and productivity may offset the loss of time.

James Kouzes and Barry Posner list four essential keys for celebrating victories.[18] First, leaders need to cheer the key things the organization values. Value focus is critical. Members who contribute to creating real value should be celebrated. If revenue generation is what the organization desires, the extraordinary revenue generation should be applauded. Second, ceremonies should be public because such rituals bind people together and crystallize personal commitment. Third, leaders need to be personally involved in celebrations in order to underscore their importance. Fourth, including organization members in ceremonies builds a sense of team unity. People share in each other's accomplishments and joy in being recognized.

There are some caveats to celebrating victories, however. First, too-frequent celebrations and celebrations for minor accomplishments undermine their importance and credibility. Recognition given for minor task completion and routine job performance cheapens the impact of recognition of superlative performance. Second, although not every special performance recognition needs to be accompanied by a financial reward, beware of creating the impression that the organization uses psychological rewards in order to avoid giving pay increases. This creates cynicism on the part of employees and diminishes the value of psychological rewards. Third, for the same reason, avoid creating victory celebrations just as a ruse for having an excuse for social occasions.

Courageous leaders praise and reward publicly but criticize and discipline privately. Why does praising and rewarding publicly while criticizing and disciplining privately take courage? The answer is twofold. When some subordinates receive praise and reward, others may become jealous and complain to the leader, asking why their colleague deserved the recognition they did not receive. Consider the following real-but-disguised example.

Assume you are a middle-level manager and recommend a subordinate leader, Mary, for a promotion and change in title. After approval from higher authority, you make the announcement about her promotion at an organizational meeting and talk about the outstanding contributions Mary has made. Shortly thereafter you hear a rumor that two young managers who are at Mary's previous level are saying privately that it was unfair that Mary was promoted instead of them because both the young managers have MBAs, Mary doesn't, and therefore she was less qualified for her new position. Such hard feelings can arise from time to time, made worse by the leader doing the right thing—publicly acknowledging Mary's accomplishments. Mary has earned the right to have her accomplishments acknowledged, but the young managers might have been less offended without the public celebration of Mary's accomplishments. The prospect of having to deal with jealousy and selfish behaviors should not deter leaders from practicing good leadership. This is why it sometimes takes courage to do the right thing in acknowledging someone such as Mary even though it may create even more jealousy than might otherwise exist.

It is not uncommon for there to be two stories circulating about an event—in this case, the story being told by the young managers and the true story. Although it might be tempting to discredit the jealous managers' story by disclosing publicly why Mary was promoted instead of them, this is a temptation to be avoided. Although this may seem like a quick solution to the problem, not respecting your subordinates' privacy—even subordinates who are guilty of selfish behaviors—will undermine trust and your credibility as a leader in the long run even on the part of personnel not involved. By setting the example of courageous leadership in not

> ## "Outstanding leaders go out of their way to boost the self-esteem of their personnel. If people believe in themselves, it's amazing what they can accomplish."
>
> —Sam Walton, founder of Wal-Mart

succumbing to slyness, you demonstrate courage subordinates will respect. This illustrates an important principle: *Courageous leaders choose the difficult right path as opposed to the easy wrong path.* Having done the right thing as a courageous leader in acknowledging Mary, you now have to show even more courage in dealing with the injustice being wrought upon Mary, the pack, and yourself by dealing with the disaffection of the two young mangers by counseling them individually. It is your job to mute their criticism of Mary and salvage their talent for the organization if possible.

Such confrontations are frequently unpleasant, requiring careful thought, mental preparation, and patience on the leader's part. In such a confrontation you are well advised to confront the issue in a manner similar to the following. First, tell each manager that you have heard a rumor to the effect that he is upset over Mary's promotion and ask if that is true. Allow the manager to respond.

Second, if the manager acknowledges hard feelings, explain the situation compassionately but truthfully, being sure to acknowledge the manager's contributions along with those of Mary

A Philosophy of Courageous Leadership

Hiding the truth and refusing to confront unpleasant facts can often backfire on leaders. One of the coauthors tells the following story about a consulting client:

> After working with a client team for several weeks on a process evaluation and redesign, the client lead made some final edits to the presentation. When the client lead presented the findings to the project sponsor, a highly placed vice president in a key division, all of the bad news was completely eliminated from the report. What this client lead didn't know was that at the beginning of the project the VP had expressed concern that some managers reporting directly to him were "sugar coating" their reports in an effort to hide their performance problems. An unedited report was eventually presented to the VP, and the necessary steps were taken to improve the business. The client lead was subsequently moved out of the VP's division and demoted into a lesser role.

lem and seek the wisdom of senior leadership in addressing what may be a serious integrity issue.

The foregoing example is illustrative of another principle: *Addressing small problems early can often prevent them from becoming big problems later.* If Mary learns of what is being said about her by the two young managers, resentment can fester, which will undermine the morale and effectiveness of the pack. By dealing with and diffusing the problem now, you may save yourself and your pack much bigger problems later. A characteristic of courageous leaders is that they are willing to make hard decisions about people. While delegating authority early to team members, great team leaders observe how that authority is handled and decide when a team member is not a good fit for the team.[19]

Attempts to avoid blame for performance problems by covering up the truth can be found in many organizational settings, from banking businesses to military battalions. This commonly results in "escalation to commitment to a failing course of action" in which individuals make matters worse by deferring dealing with a problem now rather than later. Take, for example, loan officers whose commercial clients experience cash flow problems. Banking history is replete with examples of loan officers who, rather than acknowledge a client's inability to repay its debts, loaned even more money to the client in the vain hope that somehow the client would avoid default—or perhaps even defer default long enough to avoid becoming a blemish on the officer's record until he or she found other employment. This practice has the effect of increasing the loss when it is ultimately acknowledge and realized.

and reassure the manager by painting a positive-but-honest picture of what improvements the manager needs to make to support his own promotion. If the manager refuses to acknowledge being upset over Mary's promotion, then ask why there is a rumor circulating to that effect. If the manager still does not acknowledge the problem, then it may be wise to advise your boss of the prob-

Profiles in Courageous Leadership—
Dave Roberts

Dave Roberts is chairman, president, and CEO of Carlisle Companies, Inc., an NYSE-traded manufacturer with seventy-seven plants and warehouse facilities in the United States, Canada, Mexico, the United Kingdom, Japan, continental Europe, and China. Dave tells the following story about leadership:

> About 6 or 7 months in combat as a young Marine corporal I became the senior squad leader in Weapons Platoon. There were times that I was assigned as platoon leader of Weapons Platoon even though it was the job of an officer several ranks above me. My responsibilities as a platoon leader entailed much of the day-to-day responsibilities for running the platoon. I would attend platoon leader meetings with the company commander and inform the Weapons Platoon squad leaders of those plans. I was responsible for such leadership tasks as assigning machine gun and mortar squads to infantry platoons, selecting weapons locations when we would camp for the night, and checking my personnel. This re-

> sponsibility was a thrill for a 19-year-old high school graduate. During operations no one senior to me ever took issue with a corporal doing the job of an officer, but I also understood my place, giving the officers the respect they deserved due to their rank. Interacting with the older and higher-ranking commanders and my troops taught me how to interact with people of all ages and status.

> This experience more than any education gave me the foundation to be a leader. After returning home I went to college full-time and worked full-time, becoming the youngest supervisor in the company. Despite my peers being 25–30 years my senior with many more years of supervisory experience, my production lines were among the most productive. At first it felt odd managing people my father's age, but because of my leadership experience in combat I understood how to manage both younger and older people. I think my acceptance of those leadership responsibilities as a 19-year-old corporal was the most formative thing I've done in my career.

Dave's courage in assuming a difficult leadership role at a very young age in one of the most stressful environments imaginable provided him with the experience and confidence to become enormously successful in his business career. In carrying out those early responsibilities, Dave earned the trust of those above and below him. Today, he heads a large international corporation but continues to balance power with humility the same way he learned to do as a corporal.

CHAPTER 3

Leadership Power, Theories, and Styles

> "A leader is best when people barely know he exists, when his work is done, his aim fulfilled, they will say: 'We did it ourselves.'"
>
> —Lao Tzu, philosopher of ancient China

The previous chapter presented a philosophy, or set of values and beliefs, about what it means to be a courageous leader. This chapter deals with leadership styles. It is important to distinguish between style and stylish. The quote above suggests something quite different from popular notions of leadership. Hollywood and TV have often glorified leaders as dashing, dynamic, at-times-overwhelming, larger-than-life people others follow naturally. Sometimes leaders are portrayed as mavericks, continuously going against norms of behavior. Although these traits may be true in some circumstances, it is the exception rather than the rule in business. For every larger-than-life, movie-star leader, there are thousands of great business leaders who started as ordinary people and made themselves extraordinary by becoming courageous in taking their vision to the heights of success. Different business leaders may exhibit various styles and use different models, sometimes shifting style and model to better conform to the environment, culture, and circumstances in which they find themselves leading.

We argue that there is *no singular best leadership style* for all organizational settings and occasions, although some styles may be better suited to a particular situation, team, and mission than others. There are times when highly participative leadership is best, and other times that call for hard-driving, directive management. Development of a new organizational strategy for a division that has entered a declining phase of its life and needs a line of business to generate top-line growth and positive rate of growth in free cash flows might be best accomplished in a very participatory manner. Conversely, a crisis that calls for a quick solution or the risk of dire consequences might require strong, directive leadership that initiates immediate actions from which the organization can adjust as feedback is acquired.[1] There are times when quiet leadership works best, and times when a dynamic leader on his soapbox is needed.

Not only is there no simple formula for leadership style that guarantees success; even identifying different leadership styles can be a daunting task. Research on leadership is replete with studies proposing various typologies of style. Consequently, our approach is not about promoting a singular leadership style, a far too simplistic recipe to fit real-world business requirements. Nor is it about chronicling some set of formulaic tricks that if mastered will automatically lead to career success. Instead, we contend that astute, courageous leaders know how to modify their style to adapt to particular circumstances and choose appropriate leadership tools in order to successfully accomplish a given mission. This is not to say, however, that examples cannot be found of leaders who embrace a singular style with great success. Such leaders may use a single style that fits well with the particular circumstances in which they find themselves.

For example, General George S. Patton, commander of the U.S. Third Army in Europe during World War II, was a great operational leader and field practitioner. His relentless, hard-driving, unchanging leadership style worked well in combat when circumstances called for his army to strike hard and fast. Patton fared less well when not in combat, however, and his style sometimes clashed with organizational and societal norms.[2] Contrast Patton with General Dwight D. Eisenhower, who commanded all Allied forces in Europe during World War II. Though both were high-ranking military commanders in the same theater, Eisenhower was faced with a very different task than Patton. It was his job to help fashion an overarching strategy for winning the war in Europe and to hold together what was, at times, a fragile coalition of Allied forces dominated by egocentric personalities such as Patton and British Field Marshal Bernard Montgomery. To accomplish this, Eisenhower often had to be a consensus-seeking leader, sometimes swallowing criticism that he was too weak and not assertive enough. But in the end, Eisenhower remained steadfast to his vision of the end state, held the coalition together, made a risky and difficult decision to land Allied forces at Normandy, and secured victory when an egocentric leader such as Patton might have torn the coalition apart in personality clashes with leaders such as Montgomery, with whom Patton had a personal rivalry.[3]

So which of the two was the greatest leader? Following the war, Patton became the military governor of Bavaria but was relieved of his post because of impolitic statements. Hollywood made a movie about the colorful, dogmatic Patton that added to his folk-hero image. But Patton's wartime exploits were the zenith of his career, whereas the adaptive, team-focused Eisenhower

went on to serve 8 years as the thirty-fourth president of the United States. Eisenhower carried his adaptive-leadership, team-focused style to the presidency, helping to secure a period of peace and prosperity. Thanks to Hollywood, many people today know more about Patton than Eisenhower, but in terms of impact on a nation, the latter's influence far overshadows that of the former. We believe that the best leaders in terms of their ability to be successful in different domains, cultures, and circumstances are those who understand their particular organizational environment and the challenges they face, adapting their style to fit the circumstances.[4]

3.1. Sources of Power

From where does a leader's ability to influence others emanate? John French and Bertram Raven originally introduced five sources of power, and Patrick Montana and Bruce Charnov note these five plus two more.[5] **Legitimate power** is

> **"In matters of style, swim with the current; in matters of principle, stand like a rock."**
> —Thomas Jefferson, former U.S. president

usually the first type of power that comes to mind and refers to decision-making power resulting from holding a position in an organization. Subordinates have an obligation to follow the leader. Normally, the higher the leader's rank, the greater the legitimate power—but not always. It is not unusual to find that leaders holding the same rank (e.g., vice president) have very different legitimate power. The exercise of legitimate power is fundamental to organizational well-being and smooth functioning. Although this seems intuitively obvious, what may not be so obvious is that it is frequently important for organizational members to understand the limits of legitimate power that can be exercised at various levels, because the wrongful exercise of power under the mantle of legitimacy can be destructive. Leaders who overstep the bounds of their legitimate power can create both employee problems and legal dilemmas for their organizations.

Reward power is the power given to managers to accord positive benefits, such as pay increases, promotions, and psychological rewards like honors to organizational members. It often, but not necessarily, accompanies legitimate power. For example, a vice president not in an employee's chain of command might have the legitimate power to make decisions about programs involving the employee but have no power to provide raises or promote the employee. Often leaders holding legitimate power but not reward power can nonetheless indirectly influence rewards such as future promotions by issuing favorable performance reports. Reward power is frequently a fast way to persuade organization members to act in a certain way, but there is a danger of overuse leading to diminishing value. Awarding incremental payments for incremental tasks can devolve into a piece-rate system in which subordinates expect to get paid for each new task undertaken. As previously noted, overuse of psychological rewards reduces their impact and diminishes their value.

Coercive power is the opposite of reward power and refers to a leader's power to impose negative sanctions upon an employee. As with reward power, coercive power may accompany legitimate power but ironically may not accompany reward power. Military commanders have legitimate power over subordinates but lack the ability to provide pay increases or promotions. They do, however, usually have the power to punish subordinates up to well-defined limits. For example, a commander might punish an errant subordinate by issuing an adverse performance report or imposing nonjudicial punishments, such as restricting the subordinate to a military base for a short period of time.

Reinforcement theory explains a great deal of the impact of reward and coercive power and has three basic tenets: (1) giving rewards increases desired behaviors, (2) negative sanctions decrease undesirable behaviors, and (3) neither rewarding nor punishing behavior extinguishes the behaviors. Reinforcement theory has its limitations. A given reward or punishment may not have the same impact for different people. Punishment is sometimes difficult to mete out in ways that are completely fair to all who are being punished. For example, if several subordinates are being punished for taking part in some undesirable activity, the degree of relative guilt may differ but be indeterminate, resulting in the same punishment for all involved. Further, behavioral response to extrinsic rewards such as increased effort may be only temporary, involving no permanent change with the subordinate reverting to previous behaviors afterward.[6]

Unlike the three foregoing sources of power that derive from organizational legalism, there are other sources of power that stem from leaders' individual characteristics, traits, and abilities rather than legal directive. **Expert power** derives from a leader's talents, skills, knowledge, abilities, or previous experiences and can be informal as opposed to formal power. As a result of these attributes, a leader possessing credibility with respect to expertise is able to convince followers to trust. It should be noted that the expertise does not necessarily have to be genuine if the so-called expert is able to convey a perception that it is authentic. As a further caution, the barrier for someone to be considered an expert is sometimes a low one. Consider, for example, that the fundamental definition of an expert witness in a legal case is someone "who has knowledge beyond that of an ordinary lay person enabling him/her to give testimony regarding an issue that requires expertise to understand." Given that the majority of laypersons might have no knowledge of a technical matter, someone with any knowledge might be an "expert."[7] Although courts usually impose more stringent requirements than suggested in this basic definition, it does illustrate a point. Someone with a little knowledge of a particular subject in a group of people having none can easily portray him- or herself as an expert.

Charisma power refers to a leader who is able to persuade others to follow through the force of persona. The iconic student of organizations Max Weber defined charismatic authority as resting on devotion to a leader because of exceptional qualities such as heroism, character, and sanctity.[8] Although many people tout charisma as a positive attribute of leaders, it has its dark side. Charismatic power often endangers boundaries set by legal authority.[9] Charismatic leaders may successfully push or exceed legal boundaries to impose their wills upon organizations because of popular support. Their followers may have little understanding of the damage being done at the time. Excessive attention and devotion by followers because of charisma may cause followers to overlook major faults in leaders challenging the social orders of organizations. Charismatic leaders are often found in highly autocratic states, and, at the extreme, charisma can manifest itself in personality cults.[10]

Referent power seems to have two related but somewhat distinct meanings. It is informal power enjoyed by someone because followers have high respect, admiration, and trust for a leader with whom the person is identified.[11] For example, a White House chief of staff might have no legitimate power with respect to a member of Congress but have referent power because his or her boss, the president, is held in high esteem. It can also refer to the power a leader has because followers respect and admire him or her.

Information power derives, as its name suggests, from the possession of information that is in some way critical to organizational perfor-

mance, survival, or perception. Personnel who control the flow of important information and can determine who has access to it have the power to influence others even if they lack other forms of power. By withholding or releasing information they can influence decisions and outcomes. Once again a caution is warranted. Those who limit access to information simply for purposes of gaining power run the risk of alienating co-workers who may view such practices as selfish and disruptive of organizational efficiency.

One of the coauthors relates the following story about referent and information power:

> Once there was a colonel in a key role in a large headquarters that seemed to always hold his cards close to his vest, not sharing information. He also worked hard trying to cultivate a close relationship with the commanding general that he seemed to think gave him some sort of derived power. Later on, when he came before a brigadier general selection board, no one—including that same general who ironically happened to be president of the board—supported his promotion. His attitude of being uncooperative and playing up to the general had earned him a reputation for selfishness; the general himself seemed to recognize this, and the officer ended his career as a colonel.

How leaders use these seven sources of power says a great deal about their leadership styles. Some may rely heavily on the formal sources: legitimate, reward, and coercive power. Other leaders may attempt to develop their informal power and use power derived from authority only as needed. Followers who are attempting to become informal leaders among a peer group may wish to develop expert power as a means of rising above the flock. Whatever sources of power a leader chooses to develop and draw upon, the following is good advice: "Become the kind of leader that people follow voluntarily; even if you have no title or position."[12]

3.2. Some Theories Underlying Leadership Style

Recall that we have defined **leadership style** as a distinctive and identifiable form of leadership as opposed to a leadership philosophy (set of basic values and beliefs). This section delves into the somewhat murky topic of theories underlying leadership style, of which a number have been proposed. We do not maintain that our exploration is inclusive of all possible theories, nor do we assert that it is exhaustive of each theory discussed. Rather, it is designed to provide a flavor for the theories in which researchers have attempted to categorize styles, prior to moving on to the discussion of styles themselves, including a particular typology that we find useful for self-assessment purposes later in this book.

> **"The key to successful leadership today is influence, not authority."**
>
> —Kenneth Blanchard, author of *The One Minute Manager* and management expert

Because of the importance of leadership in organizational outcomes, from the time of the Greek philosophers leadership style has been a topic of great interest. One of the earliest theories to emerge was that of **trait theory**, which proposes that individual attributes define style. This notion of individual traits defining leadership was the topic of explorative research in the nineteenth century, such as that of Francis Galton and Thomas Carlyle, which attempted to identify the characteristics, talents, and skills of powerful people. Trait theory posited that only a few individuals are born with the right qualities for leadership and attempted to identify characteristics that

distinguish leaders from nonleaders. These characteristics include such attributes as intellect, personality, social skills, motivation, physical abilities and appearance, and education. Subsumed under the foregoing general characteristics, trait theory holds that a person's intelligence, judgment, knowledge, and decisiveness are important intellectual qualities for leaders. Aggressiveness, self-confidence, initiative, and persistence are also important, as is socioeconomic background, reflecting the theory's "leaders are born, not made" bias. Traits separating leaders from nonleaders include integrity, a desire to lead, and high energy.

Although it was to reemerge, the premise underlying trait theory of born leaders was challenged by situational and contingency theories discussed below. Studies conducted during and following World War II suggested that, although some traits are common in many leadership situations, leadership is contextual. That is, people who are leaders in some situations may not be leaders in others, implying there is no universal, extraordinary leader. Further, a particular leadership trait might not be applied in all situations in the same manner.[13] Trait theory enjoyed something of a renaissance as meta-analysis methodologies revealed a set of attributes common across many leadership situations including intelligence, self-sufficiency, being open to experiencing new ideas, social extroversion, and the ability to adjust to change. Nonetheless, trait theory continued to be criticized for a number of shortcomings, including focusing on too small a set of traits, failure to consider interactions among traits and which traits are subject to change over time, and how a set of unchanging traits could explain the behavioral diversity necessary for effective leadership.[14]

In light of these criticisms, **attribute-pattern theory** emerged, arguing that the nexus between individual traits and effective leadership is best understood by considering a leader as an integrated totality rather than a collection of individual traits.[15] Also as a result of criticisms of trait theory, **behavioral theory** posited leadership as a set of behaviors, such as a positive ego and high self-esteem, and styles, such as authoritarian, democratic, laissez-faire, and the famous Blake-Mouton Grid model with its five styles.[16] B. F. Skinner developed a model based upon the use of **positive reinforcement** by leaders to achieve behavior modification in followers.[17] **Situational contingency theory** was likewise a reaction to criticism of trait theory and posited that circumstances produce the leader, as opposed to vice versa. Some researchers then began to synthesize trait and situational theories leading to such conclusions as authoritarian leadership being effective in crises but not as effective in routine circumstances.[18]

Starting in the 1970s, more theories emerged, including functional theory, transactional theory, leader-member exchange theory, integrated-psychological theory, and neo-emergent theory. **Functional theory** maintains that the leader's role is to contribute to organizational effectiveness and cohesion by attending to group needs.[19] Central to **transactional theory** is the leader's power to perform tasks, reward performance, punish misbehavior, and develop and train subordinates. In other words, organizational member relationships are viewed as a network of transactions.[20] **Leader-member exchange theory** is similar to transaction theory in its focus on organizational-member relationships but allows for the members to vary their exchanges, leading to the emergence of in-groups (high-quality exchanges) and out-groups (low-quality exchanges).[21] **Integrated-psychological theory** attempted to combine the older theories while dealing with their limitations. James Scouller proposed a three-level leadership model categorizing leadership as public, private, and personal. Public and private leadership are outward focused and relate to how a leader behaves in influencing others. Personal leadership is internal and focuses on a leader's self-improvement.[22] **Neo-emergent theory** em-

anated from Oxford and posits leadership as a function of information available to organizational members, including the leader, as opposed to the leader's inherent behaviors. Under this theory, leaders' apparent behaviors may not reflect their actual leadership qualities but are instead a perceptual matter based upon available information. Recently, some researchers have argued that prior research is flawed in that it does not consider the physiological nature of brain patterns. These researchers argue that breakthroughs in **neuroscience** allow the observation of how people react to various stimuli and conclude that change is painful to organizational members, rewards and punishments do not work well, soft approaches to dealing with subordinates are overrated, expectation shapes reality, and repeated, purposeful, and focused attention (attention density) can lead to personal improvement.[23]

The diversity of the foregoing theories of leadership suggests that the study of leadership has yet to produce anything close to a universally agreed-upon theory of how leaders should behave to attain optimal results. As a result, the topic of preferred style is similarly fuzzy. Without a theory to guide optimal leadership behaviors, leaders are largely left to develop their own styles. Moreover, almost any experienced leader can point to instances when some behavior has worked well and another has not. This might lead some to the conclusion that no style is better than any other, but that would be fallacious in our opinion. Our own experiences and intuition tell us that some styles work better than others in a particular set of circumstances. Consequently, an understanding of leadership styles is important so that leaders can adapt to often-changing environments.

3.3. A Brief Review of Better-Known Leadership Styles

The application of the foregoing theories and others led to researchers positing various leadership styles. This section discusses some of these styles as a prelude to our selecting a particular typology for our use. This list is by no means all inclusive, but we believe it is nonetheless instructive. Nothing herein is meant to imply that one of these approaches is always preferable to another. Rather, one may be more appropriate when used in a particular culture or context.[24]

Take, for example, an **autocratic style**—also known as authoritarian leadership—which is a leadership style characterized by individual control over decisions with little input from followers.[25] In military combat, where decisions about life and

"A ruler should be slow to punish and swift to reward."

—Ovid, one of the three canonic Roman poets of Latin literature

death must sometimes be made instantly and orders carried out without debate, an autocratic approach is necessary. The same may sometimes be true in hospital operating rooms when lives hang in the balance. There are also many situations not involving life and death that call for autocracy, such as when one is training team members to do simple tasks that require all to respond in a particular manner, such as rowing a scull. For the team to win, the coxswain by necessity needs a demanding leadership style that requires each crew member to follow instructions. There is no room for debate during the race about the rowing cadence. All crew members need to row in unison. In some cases an autocratic approach may be actually desired by subordinates who realize that their own lives depend upon a leader taking charge and controlling situations. Similarly, football teams usually appreciate having a quarterback who is confident and clearly takes charge of leading the team on the field.

Carried to an extreme and applied in the wrong circumstances, however, an autocratic

approach can become highly dysfunctional. Consider, for example, the dictator Adolf Hitler, who exhibited a consistently pronounced autocratic style. Hitler's approach accompanied by his intervention in military strategy led to disastrous military defeats for the Wehrmacht, the German army, during World War II. Further, his tendency to severely punish those who disagreed with him violated Ovid's admonition in the box on the left. His dictatorial insistence on continuously having his predisposed ideas and plans followed without dissent led to subordinates fearing to disagree with him even when he was wrong. Such fear among Hitler's generals on the Wehrmacht general staff led to suppressed dissention and serious morale problems.

Extreme autocrats like Hitler often self-destruct. When it is appropriate to apply an autocratic approach, it is wise to follow some general rules. First, leaders taking an autocratic approach need to respect their subordinates. Doing so improves morale and reduces resentment. Second, when insisting that something must be done a particular way, time permitting, explain why. Third, be consistent and fair in taking hard-line positions. Inconsistency and unfairness breed mistrust. It is difficult to trust someone who applies policies differently in similar circumstances. Fourth, leaders should ensure that subordinates understand what their expectations are up front. This helps prevent miscommunication and reduces surprises. Fifth, again time permitting, listen to others' points of view even if you don't change, and provide logical explanations for why you are unable or unwilling to adopt their ideas.[26]

In contrast to autocratic leadership, leaders using a **paternalistic style** nurture subordinates in the manner of a parent, demonstrating concern, taking care of their needs, and developing a familial culture.[27] This family culture can help control behaviors in uncertain situations where other types of control are difficult to apply. Given their affinity for one another, organizational members may be more inclined to act in the best interests of the family when given the opportunity to behave in various ways. There is also the issue of self-selection by subordinates to leaders and organizations utilizing a paternalistic style. Employees who follow paternalistic leaders may have better morale and organizational skills than workers in autocratic organizations. Paternalistic leaders inspire trust and loyalty, so subordinates feel more comfortable in paternalistic organizations. The downsides of a paternalistic style are that it may not result in rapid response in crises and that, as in biological families, paternalistic leaders may devote more attention to some family members than others, giving rise to jealousy.[28]

A **democratic leadership style** is driven by the belief that every organizational member should have a voice in what goes on and is characterized by social equality and sharing of authority with subordinates. Because idea sharing is fundamental, democratic leadership can foster innovation and creativity. It works best in situations where organizational members are knowledgeable, skilled, and have ample time to contribute. It can become suboptimal in situations in which members' roles are unclear or time is of the essence.[29]

In **laissez-faire leadership** all decision-making authority is delegated to organizational members with little or no guidance unless requested by the members. There is obviously a high degree of autonomy for members, so there is risk of confusion, dissension, and lack of direction. These problems can lead to member dissatisfaction.[30]

Transactional leadership derives its name from its underlying theory discussed in the previous section and is focused on rewards and punishments. One important element of this style is rewards that are contingent on performance. Transactional leaders set goals and objectives,

agree explicitly or implicitly to provide rewards if these are attained, monitor members' performance, and manage by exception. Managing by exception means focusing on performances that are outliers; that is, too far out of an acceptable range. Typically transactional leaders are interested in measuring efficiency and effectiveness. Transactional leadership is common in many organizations, but it has the downside of not working well in situations where member emotions are high.[31]

Adaptive leadership, drawn from evolutionary biology, is an approach that seeks to influence positive change by enabling organizations and their members to thrive. In simple terms, autocratic leaders insist that followers adapt to their will, whereas adaptive leaders seek to foster a culture that honors a diversity of opinion and uses collective knowledge for the good of the organization.[32] Adaptive leaders view leadership as more of a process of enabling change than merely a set of competencies. They are concerned with preserving the key elements necessary for the organization to survive, divesting it of those that are unnecessary, and creating new arrangements that help the organization thrive. Adaptive leaders connect organizational change to stakeholders' vision and core values, foster a culture of collaboration, help members learn and improve, and resist pressure to take shortcuts.[33] Although other styles may at times embrace some of these same elements, the culture of collaboration and concern for organizational members' vision of the future embodied in the adaptive approach in achieving organizational improvement is greater.

Two of the more intriguing leadership styles to have been studied relatively recently are transformation and servant leadership. **Transformational leaders** are primarily concerned with changing organizations by changing members' beliefs and perceptions and redirecting thinking. The focus is on the leader who is concerned with progress and development. **Servant leaders** are focused on the organization and its members, as opposed to the leader who is primarily motivated by self-interest, with servant leaders being concerned instead with developing their followers. Figure 3.1 depicts models comparing the two styles.[34]

Gregory Stone, Robert Russell, and Kathleen Patterson stipulate that both styles involve vision, trust, influence, credibility, delegation, integrity, modeling, and valuing organization members by listening, mentoring, teaching, and empowering them.[35] But the models indicate differences in the

Figure 3.1. Transformational versus Servant Styles

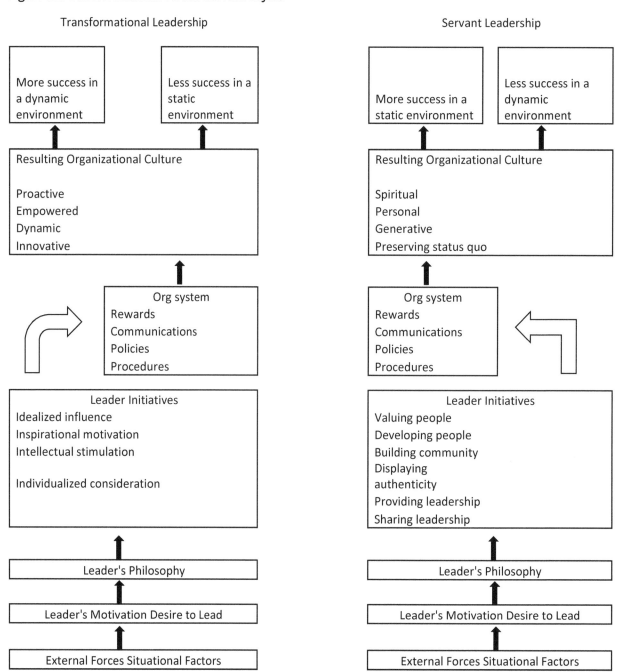

Source: Adapted from B. N. Smith, R. V. Montagno, and T. N. Kuzmenko, "Transformational and Servant Leadership: Content and Contextual Comparisons," *Journal of Leadership and Organizational Studies* 10, no. 4 (2004): 80–91.

two leadership styles. External forces and situational factors affect a leader's motivation to lead in both models. This motivation, in turn, influences the leader's philosophy, which drives the leader to take various initiatives. The initiatives, however, differ with philosophy. For example, a transformational leadership philosophy drives the leader to engage in inspirational motivation. Vision is very important because it challenges and inspires members, providing excitement and purpose. Duane Schultz and Sydney Ellen Schultz suggest that transformational leaders often promote themselves, exhibit high energy, take unorthodox approaches to problem solving, and intellectually stimulate organization members to think independently.[36] On the other hand, the servant leadership philosophy causes servant leaders to take different initiatives. Servant leadership involves a much greater emphasis on service to followers, with servant leaders gaining power by virtue of being unselfish.

The leader's initiatives then impact the organization's system of rewards, policies, procedures, and communications with the resulting organizational cultures being different for the two styles. Transformational leadership results in a culture of dynamism, proactivity, empowerment, and innovation. Servant leadership results in more of a culture of community, stewardship of organizational resources, and commitment to individual growth.[37] Transformational leadership works best in dynamic environments requiring organizational adaptation to change, whereas servant leadership tends to work better in static environments. The implication from this comparison is clearly that some styles are a better fit for some organizational contexts than others.

The foregoing styles are not all inclusive of everything that has been termed a leadership style. They do, however, provide a flavor for the many different styles that have been identified. One conclusion we draw is that deciding on a leadership style is a complex decision, and the style chosen might best be based upon the context in which it is being used. Each of the coauthors has had the benefit of having worked in different types of organizations. These include manufacturing, professional services, banking, and consumer products firms. Some have also served in the military, and all in academe. Although there are certainly many commonalities in terms of leadership issues across all of these settings, there are also substantial differences in the cultures prevalent in different types of organizations and even within firms in the same industry. For example, the culture in a large professional services firm operated as a partnership can be decidedly different than a corporation with a very vertical leadership hierarchy. Because partners have an equity stake and a vote in partnerships, a more consensual style may be called for than in a large, shareholder-owned corporation in which the majority of the ownership does not work for the company.

Consider the situation faced by the former CEO of a corporation who becomes the dean of a business school. Although both organizations share the common attribute of being about business, the cultures are markedly different. Business schools are governed to a significant extent by faculties whose members, once tenured, are accustomed to a great deal of autonomy with many issues that require faculty vote. As a result, faculty members are far less likely to respond well to authoritarian directives than corporate executives. CEOs who become academic administrators and fail to recognize cultural differences and modify their leadership styles may soon find that their goals and plans lack the necessary faculty support for implementation. The culture in business schools works because serious crises are less common than in many businesses. Business schools are not faced with such issues as volatile stock prices, shareholder lawsuits, product liability, and falling sales and earnings. Also, autonomy encourages the creation of new ideas and concepts through research, a major function for professors. A simple adaption analogy from nature explains our belief regarding leadership style. An orange lizard on a brown rock gets eaten by a bird. An orange lizard that changes its color to brown when it finds itself on a brown rock has a much better chance of surviving.

3.4. Does Style Matter?

At this juncture you may be asking the question, "With so many alternatives to consider, does style really matter?" The answer seems to be yes. Bernard Bass notes that followers of transformational leaders are more effective than those of transactional and contingent-reward leaders. Followers of transactional and contingent-reward leaders are, in turn, more effective than those of laissez-faire leaders.[38] In the comparison of transformational and servant leadership styles in the previous section we observed that which of these styles is most effective is contextually dependent.

A team of researchers led by Daniel Goleman performed a 3-year study involving over 3,000 middle-level managers. Their purpose was to provide evidence of the impact of specific leadership styles and behaviors on corporate climate and performance. Their research indicates that leadership style made as much as a *30 percent difference in the profitability* of the companies studied. Their results indicate that leaders should not rely on a single style and should adapt their styles to organizational context and circumstances to attain better results. In other words, these findings strongly call for a situational approach.[39]

Situational leadership, mentioned earlier in brief, is a term coined by Paul Hersey and Kenneth Blanchard to describe the adaptation of style to context.[40] This theory maintains that leadership has both directional and supportive dimensions, and leaders must ascertain followers' development to determine when to apply each dimension.

Depending upon the followers' developmental characteristics, the leader can assume a style based upon some appropriate combination of directing and supporting followers. For example, a very highly developed subordinate (e.g., a scientist performing a research task) might require little ongoing direction and little support, whereas an undeveloped subordinate (e.g., one performing a physical task) might require considerable ongoing direction but not much support. An inexperienced manager dealing with a complex project might require both considerable direction and considerable support.

Does the situational leadership approach work? Situational leadership training is prescriptive in nature and has been widely used in corporate training programs suggesting its practicality. It emphasizes the need for leaders to adjust their style to their followers, discover subordinates' needs, and meet the requirements of varying situations. Followers are treated as individuals who need opportunities to learn and grow. Despite these positives, there are criticisms of situational leadership. One of the major criticisms is that conceptualization of follower development is nebulous, and some studies have failed to support the basic prescriptions of the approach. Another criticism is that the approach does not consider sufficiently how some important individual characteristics of followers such as gender, education, age, and experience influence the need for a given style. This would seem to be a serious shortcoming given that research has shown that such factors as education and job experience influence followers' preferences for a particular leadership style.[41] In our belief situational leadership suggests the right path for leaders to follow but does not go far enough in explicating the leader/follower relationship. Consequently, a model is needed that extends the idea of leader adaptation more deeply into follower characteristics and preferences. This brings us to the Path-Goal Model.

3.5. The Path-Goal Model

Unlike academics, practitioners cannot be content to just describe various phenomena. Due to the demands of practice they strongly prefer prescription to description. As a current or future practitioner you need description to lead to prescription. Therefore, in this section we embrace a particular typology of leadership style that we strongly believe has practical implications, the **Path-Goal Model**. We choose this model over others and dedicate more in-depth attention to it for several reasons: (1) It fits well with our courageous leadership philosophy presented in chapter 2 and the coauthors' beliefs that the best leaders are those who understand (a) themselves, (b) the contextual environment in which they are operating, and (c) their subordinates' characteristics, and (d) who adapt their style accordingly. (2) The Path-Goal Model fits well with ends/ways/means thinking because the ultimate end goal is made explicit. (3) We find it useful in linking to assessment methodologies that we will use later to facilitate leaders' self-understanding. (4) Path-Goal Theory emphasizes the relationship between leadership style and subordinate characteristics as well as the work setting. (5) We believe that it is parsimonious enough—yet rich enough in context—for practitioners to apply successfully in everyday leadership situations.

Path-Goal Theory was first proposed by Martin Evans (1970) and Robert House (1971) and differs from situational contingency theory because it emphasizes the leader/subordinates relationship in arriving at an appropriate style to fit subordinate characteristics as well as work settings.[42] The leader is challenged to meet the needs of subordinates who are motivated by three principal beliefs: (1) they are capable of performing assigned tasks, (2) they believe their efforts will results in a desired outcome, and (3) they believe the rewards for achieving the desired outcome are worth their efforts. The leader should engage in behaviors that complement or supplement whatever is missing in the work environment that would cause followers to internalize these beliefs. The model is based upon leaders helping followers to select a path that leads to the desired goal by overcoming obstacles, as depicted in Figure 3.2.

Figure 3.2. The Path-Goal Concept

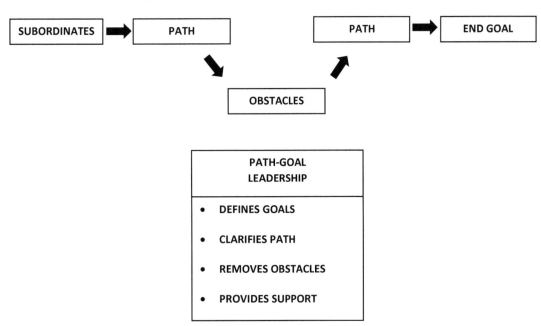

Source: Adapted from Professional Faculty Leadership Association, Ball State University, http://facultyleadership.weebly.com /uploads/9/9/3/8/9938172/how_it_work1.jpg.

The Path-Goal Model works by focusing on three things: (1) leader behaviors, (2) subordinate behaviors, and (3) task characteristics. Leaders may adopt one of four basic styles: (1) directive, (2) supportive, (3) participative, or (4) achievement oriented. As shown in Figure 3.3, leaders should use a directive style when subordinates are dogmatic and authoritarian in their own behaviors and when tasks are ambiguous and complex and rules are unclear. This involves providing subordinates with specific instructions about tasks, to include how the tasks are to be performed, in what time frame, and the desired results. A supportive style is used when subordinates need nurturing and affiliation with leadership and when tasks are repetitive, unchallenging, and mundane. This style involves being friendly and approachable, with leaders attempting to make work more enjoyable. A participative style is called for when followers are autonomous but there is a need for control and clarity because tasks are ambiguous and unstructured. Leaders using this approach invite followers to share in decision making by eliciting and integrating their ideas into the work plan. An achievement-oriented style is indicated when followers have high expectations and a need to excel and tasks are ambiguous, complex, and challenging. Achievement-oriented leaders establish high standards of excellence and challenge followers to work at the highest levels.[43]

Peter Northhouse cites House and T. R. Mitchell (1974) positing that leaders should be adaptive and might use any or all of these styles across different situations and subordinates—or even with a particular subordinate depending upon task

Figure 3.3. Three Aspects of Goal Theory

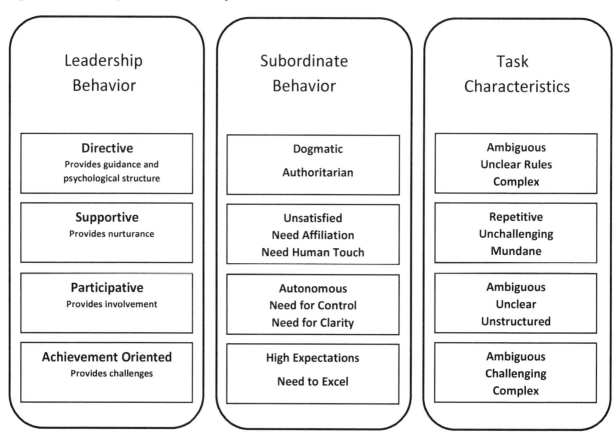

Leadership Behavior	Subordinate Behavior	Task Characteristics
Directive Provides guidance and psychological structure	**Dogmatic** **Authoritarian**	**Ambiguous** **Unclear Rules** **Complex**
Supportive Provides nurturance	**Unsatisfied** **Need Affiliation** **Need Human Touch**	**Repetitive** **Unchallenging** **Mundane**
Participative Provides involvement	**Autonomous** **Need for Control** **Need for Clarity**	**Ambiguous** **Unclear** **Unstructured**
Achievement Oriented Provides challenges	**High Expectations** **Need to Excel**	**Ambiguous** **Challenging** **Complex**

Source: Adapted from Professional Faculty Leadership Association, Ball State University, http://facultyleadership.weebly.com /uploads/9/9/3/8/9938172/how_it_work1.jpg.

Courageous Leadership

Figure 3.4. Two Principal Tools in Path-Goal Theory

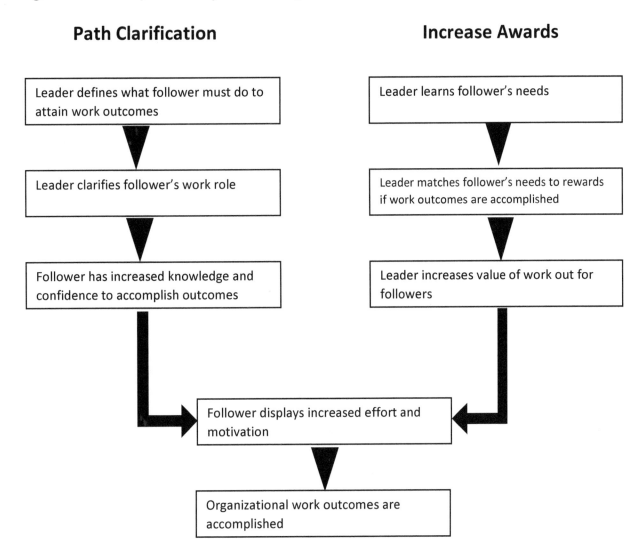

Source: Adapted from http://www.tusculum.edu/faculty/home/tmcfarland/ppt/chp16_files/slide0011_image024.jpg.

and subordinate characteristics.[44] *Two principal tools at leaders' disposal are clarifying paths and increasing rewards, as shown in Figure 3.4.*

The Path-Goal Model is pragmatic and, at the same time, rich enough in its predictions to be useful in practice. It represents a situational/contingency approach that explains the need for leader adaptation. It predicts how different styles interact with subordinate behaviors and task characteristics, thereby affecting subordinates' motivational levels. It is unique in attempting to in-

corporate expectancy theory and its principles of motivation into general recommendations about leadership behaviors. It can be used by leaders at all organizational levels and is helpful in answering questions such as the following suggested by Northhouse: How can I motivate subordinates to feel that they have the ability to do the work? How can I help them feel that, if they successfully do their work, they will be rewarded? What can I do to improve the payoffs that subordinates expect from their work?[45]

How much does leadership style matter? Here is one take by Robyn Benincasa, author and two-time Adventure Racing World Champion:

"My favorite study on the subject of kinetic leadership [turning vision into action] is Daniel Goleman's 'Leadership That Gets Results,' a landmark 2000 *Harvard Business Review* study. Goleman and his team completed a 3-year study with over 3,000 middle-level managers. Their goal was to uncover specific leadership behaviors and determine their effect on the corporate climate and each leadership style's effect on bottom-line profitability. The research discovered that a manager's leadership style was responsible for *30 percent of the company's bottom-line profitability*! That's far too much to ignore. Imagine how much money and effort a company spends on new processes, efficiencies, and cost-cutting methods in an effort to add even 1 percent to bottom-line profitability, and compare that to simply inspiring managers to be more kinetic with leadership styles. It's a no-brainer."

—Robyn Benincasa, "6 Leadership Styles, and When You Should Use Them," http://www.fastcompany.com/1838481/6-leadership-styles-and-when-you-should-use-them (accessed March 20, 2014).

The Path-Goal Model is not without its drawbacks. Its richness comes with the price of some complexity. Obviously, subordinates' behaviors and task characteristics usually exist along some continuum, but the model classifies these behaviors and characteristics as separate and distinct. The leader is left with such tasks as, for example, deciding how much directive versus supportive leadership to utilize when a task is moderately ambiguous and repetitive. Nonetheless, as a practical guide we believe the Path-Goal Model may be among the most useful tools leaders can have in deciding how to adapt to followers' characteristics and needs in order to move them to perform optimally.

CHAPTER 4

Four Common Business Leadership Situations

> "The problem is not that there are problems.
> The problem is expecting otherwise and
> thinking that having problems is a problem."
>
> —Theodore Rubin, former president of the American Institute for Psychoanalysis

Not every common leadership situation is a problem, but every leader will experience and have to deal with problems, as the quote above indicates. Recalling what was said earlier about what adds value for businesses, leaders exist because they get paid to solve problems. Many of these problems require courageous leadership for optimal solutions. This chapter deals with four of the common types of situations leaders face in business: performance reviews, counseling problem employees, hiring new employees, and terminating employees. Because of the associated complexities, we reserve client-interface problems for an entire later chapter. Before we proceed some words of caution are in order.

Our discussion of these four leadership situations is not intended to be legal advice on how to deal with delicate employee matters such as lawsuits, threats of lawsuits, wrongful discharge allegations, and so forth. In situations where there is a reasonable probability that problems could result in legal action, leaders are well advised to consult with both the organization's human resources (HR) unit and legal counsel. Further, leaders should be aware of organizational policies and have a general understanding of laws and regulations governing matters with potentially serious legal connotations. If our advice conflicts with or-

ganizational policies and rules, then leaders are advised to follow their organization's established protocol for dealing with a given problem.

Our thoughts come from expert commentators and our own experiences. There is no guarantee they will work in all instances. Human beings are complex and so are the workplace situations they create. Instead, readers should view our positions as general guidelines. Your organization's HR department is central to guidelines for dealing with employee situations. You should have a clear understanding of the role of HR. At times, HR personnel may appear to act as an advocate for either management or employees, but in the end doing what is in the best interests of the organization is HR's primary responsibility. HR representatives are not obligated to keep confidential what you say to them about personnel matters if they feel it needs to be shared with organization officials. On the other hand, HR may be aware of things they may not disclose to you. For example, HR may know that your boss has just been asked to resign by senior leadership, but senior management is not yet ready to make the announcement. So, when you suggest a meeting to HR involving your boss, HR, and you, HR may not agree. But if for some reason you are routinely not getting information you believe you should from HR, find out why.

Be in sync with your employer.

When dealing with personal or personnel matters, it is important to read and understand any policies, rules, and guidelines promulgated by your employer. If your employer's position differs in some material way from the guidance in this section, you are well advised to check with your books and/or the HR department before deviating from your employer's guidelines. Also be aware that your employer's guidance may change over time, and you should read carefully any information disseminated regarding the handling of employee situations.

Respect HR's role and responsibilities, but do not allow HR personnel to dictate how you operate in terms of hiring, promotions, and terminations. HR is a staff function that supports the organization and, by inference, line management. You are responsible for your personnel decisions, and the authority to make these decisions should accompany that responsibility as long as you conform to your firm's policies and rules. If personnel decisions go wrong, don't blame HR. Sometimes, HR assumes more authority than it should. Leaders need the courage to push back if you think HR representatives are insinuating themselves into your leadership role. Finally, there can be high variance in the quality of HR departments and how they operate. If you change firms, don't assume your new employer's HR department functions as your old one did.[1]

4.1. A General Model for Resolving Workplace Issues

Fortunately there are some general guidelines on how to go about resolving workplace issues that fit many but not all situations. The Myers-Briggs Type Indicator (MBTI) literature proposed what is termed the "Zig-Zag Method of Problem Solving," shown in Figure 4.1. The name "Zig-Zag" derives from the movement from quadrant to quadrant.

The underlying theory posits that decision makers attempting to solve problems cycle through a particular mental process. At any given time decision makers are continually and alternatively (1) **perceiving** by *sensing* or *intuiting,* or (2) **judging** by *thinking* or *feeling.* Both perceiving and judging are required for problem solving, although not necessarily in equal proportion. Sensing involves gathering facts, collecting data, and examining what is already known about the problem. From sensing decision makers move to intuition, which involves brainstorming, being imaginative, and keeping an open mind. Next comes thinking about the problem, deciding on a set of decision criteria, and applying these criteria in a reasonable, logical manner. From there, decision makers move to feeling out whether they really like the solution selected and how it affects the organization, others, and themselves. Feelings may cause the decision maker to do more sensing, seeking more data and information about the problem, and cycling through the process again.

The theory then proposes a series of seven conscious, decision-making steps. Perception is used in steps 1, 2, and 7, whereas judgment is used in steps 3, 4, 5, and 6.

> Step 1: Define the situation using perception in examining all the facts. Be realistic and avoid feelings and wishful thinking that might distort reality.

Figure 4.1. Zig-Zag Model

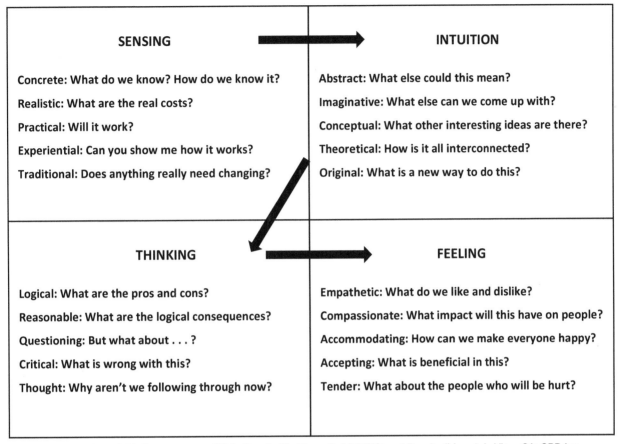

SENSING	INTUITION
Concrete: What do we know? How do we know it?	**Abstract: What else could this mean?**
Realistic: What are the real costs?	**Imaginative: What else can we come up with?**
Practical: Will it work?	**Conceptual: What other interesting ideas are there?**
Experiential: Can you show me how it works?	**Theoretical: How is it all interconnected?**
Traditional: Does anything really need changing?	**Original: What is a new way to do this?**
THINKING	**FEELING**
Logical: What are the pros and cons?	**Empathetic: What do we like and dislike?**
Reasonable: What are the logical consequences?	**Compassionate: What impact will this have on people?**
Questioning: But what about . . . ?	**Accommodating: How can we make everyone happy?**
Critical: What is wrong with this?	**Accepting: What is beneficial in this?**
Thought: Why aren't we following through now?	**Tender: What about the people who will be hurt?**

Source: Adapted from J. M. Kummerow and N. L. Quenk, *Working with MBTI® Step II Results* (Mountain View, CA: CPP, Inc., 2005). All rights reserved. Reprinted with permission.

Step 2: Consider all possibilities using intuitive perception. List the possible courses of action (COAs). Put the COAs into words in order to make conscious each possible COA. Be imaginative. Avoid eliminating a COA you like at this point because you feel it cannot be done due to organizational constraints and lack of resources.

Step 3: Determine what the result of each COA will be and assess the consequences (ends). List what steps are necessary to implement each COA (ways) and what resources are required (means). Then list the advantages and disadvantages of each COA given its ends, ways, and means. Make a tentative decision about the preferred COA.

Step 4: Weigh each COA in terms of how you *feel* about. How deeply do you care about the costs and benefits?

Step 5: Decide on a COA.

Step 6: Implement it. Do not agonize or procrastinate over implementation.

Step 7: Evaluate implementation. Is your COA working as anticipated? If not, then seek new information and cycle back through the steps and reconsider other COAs.[2]

These steps represent a controlled process for using sound perception and judgment one step at a time. Developing this as a mental discipline for decision making will help you avoid making inferior decisions. The following exercise about a real-world-but-disguised employee situation provides an example of how to implement the Zig-Zag Method.

You are a young manager who has just been promoted and sent out to take over a peripheral unit of a bank. The position of administrative assistant to the manager is currently open and you have authorization to hire. Before you can interview anyone, however, you receive a call from your new boss. He asks you if you would do him a favor and take someone asking to be transferred from headquarters as your administrative assistant. He tells you that Susan is smart and talented but had to be counseled recently about her inability to get along with her current boss, one of the bank's senior officers. This puts you on the spot, but you want to be cooperative with your new boss so you agree without disclosing your reservations. Just before your boss hangs up he says, "According to her current boss, Susan is impossible. But the good news is she's very attractive."

You have a potential problem. How should you handle it? You decide to follow the seven-step process outlined in the Zig-Zag Model. Reflecting on the problem, your facts are limited. Your new secretary is apparently smart and talented but has boss problems. You catch yourself wishing this problem had not been forced on you, but you remind yourself to avoid wishful thinking. In reality, you have little to go on. You decide to ask to review Susan's performance reports the next time you are at headquarters. Then you consider the possibilities. One is that Susan has interpersonal relations problems. Another is that her old boss was difficult to work for due to his own issues. A third is that Susan is experiencing something in her personal life that may be adversely affecting her work performance. You decide on two possible COAs: (1) act as if you have no indication of Susan's past problems and treat her as you would any new employee, or (2) confront her with the issue and indicate that you are more than willing to give her a new start but you expect none of the problems experienced by her previous boss. What are the consequences of each? If you act as if you have no knowledge of the previous problems, will she be more inclined to repeat them? Possibly, but if you mention them, Susan may feel you are already prejudiced against her. You weigh these alternative COAs, and your intuition tells you to say nothing about her previous problems.

Susan turns out to be pleasant, attentive, and neat in appearance but subdued like a dog that has been abused by her master. Over the next several days you observe her closely. She is intelligent, dedicated, and works hard, sometimes staying late. The quality of her work is excellent, and she seeks out new responsibilities. She never mentions her past issues with her old boss. One day you have a meeting at headquarters and stop by HR and look at Susan's performance reports. She has been with the bank 2 years, after graduating from a small liberal arts college with a degree in psychology. Her first two reports written by a lower-level manager were excellent, and consequently she was promoted to an executive administrative assistant to her former boss. Her former boss also wrote two reports. The first was a regular periodic report and favorable, stating that Susan is very intelligent, works hard, and has promise. The second was a special report, highly unfavorable, stating that Susan is resistant to instruction, prickly in temperament, and the quality of her work has declined recently. You wonder why she was not placed on probation.

Returning from headquarters, you reflect on your new information and consider the possibilities. Whatever the problems with Susan may have been, they arose fairly recently and you have observed no evidence of them. You consider two possibilities. One, the cause of the problems has been resolved. Two, Susan has a repetitive pattern of starting strong but worsening over time.

That doesn't fit with her first boss's reports, but you consider that sometimes weak leaders avoid having to deal with confronting employee issues by recommending that the employee be promoted out of their unit. You reconsider the possible COAs. Once again, after weighing the potential consequences and how you feel about each, you decide not to raise the issue and instead continue to observe her performance.

Susan's story will be continued in the next section when we deal with counseling for performance evaluations. So far, what we've observed is an application of the principles of the Zig-Zag Model that has worked well. Using the mental discipline the model embodies has helped the young manager deal with a potentially difficult situation and make the most of it.

> ### Do you know your own beliefs?
>
> Have you ever sat down and written out your fundamental beliefs about leadership and compared them to those of others? The young manager in Susan's story had thought out and committed his own leadership philosophy to writing. One of his beliefs—*making the most of what you've got*—was covered in chapter 2. Early in his relationship with Susan, that belief made him determined, if possible, to turn a bad situation around for the bank, Susan, and himself.
>
> Take the time to sit down and write out your leadership credo. Writing it will help clarify your thoughts, and you can refer back to your credo from time to time, adjusting it as you gain new knowledge and experience.

Employee problems are virtually continuous, not because most employees are problems but because they are human beings. Human beings are fallible and therefore prone to creating problems and subject to having things happen to them that are not of their making. Sooner or later most leaders will have to address employee shortcomings or comfort a subordinate who is experiencing personal problems of one form or another that are affecting the employee's personal life and work performance.

Not all employee issues are problems, however. Many times leaders have the pleasant task of praising their followers for doing a good job. This praise should most certainly not be limited to formal periodic performance reviews. Informal feedback is important, too. Taking time to praise subordinates when they do a good job on a major project or handle some difficult situation is good practice. Be careful not to overdo it, however, or its impact will be diminished. Give praise only when praise is truly deserved, but give it then without reservation.

4.2. Performance Reviews

At first blush, the idea of writing performance evaluations might not seem to take much courage. The coauthors' experience is just the opposite. We have seen many instances in which managers were reluctant to confront employee problems and many others in which performance reports were inflated because managers inflated them out of fear of offending good-but-not-great subordinates. Most large organizations and many others have an established process for formal, periodic reviews. These reviews are usually conducted privately with only the leader and subordinate present. There are times, however, when it may be appropriate to have a third person present. One of those situations is when the subordinate is being disciplined for poor performance, as discussed in a section below. Another is when the leader is training an inexperienced subordinate leader in the subordinate's chain of command on how to give a performance review. Even if the subordinate is receiving a mostly favorable report, because employees almost always have some area in which they could improve, sometimes managers dread performance reviews because of the need to provide some constructive criticism. This need not be the case. By properly preparing and following the guidelines below, this "problem" can become an opportunity and positive experience.

1. First, do your homework. Apply the Zig-Zag Model. Gather all the facts, information, and performance data, analyze these data, and define the employee's situation. Hopefully you have kept track of good and poor instances of performance during the reporting period. Develop alternative COAs for the review. For example, should you take an inductive approach, starting with details using illustrations of the employee's good and poor performances on various projects, and work to the conclusion? Or, do you want to take a more deductive approach, starting with your conclusions and then providing details as necessary? Knowing your subordinate is a big help in making this decision. How would you characterize the subordinate's style of interacting? For example, is he or she someone who likes to get to the point quickly and loses interest in long conversations? Or, is he or she someone who wants to know the facts before agreeing with an opinion? Having observed your subordinate over time should give you clues about such preferences, but, as we discuss in chapter 5, it is even better to test your assumptions about the employee against measurements such as the MBTI if your organization has performed such measures.

2. Once you have gathered and analyzed your facts and decided on an approach,

write the review. In writing a performance review, it is very important to first decide what message you want to communicate to the subordinate—that is, What is the overall impact you are seeking? Do you want to encourage a high-performing employee to perform even better? Do you wish to encourage a mediocre performer to pick up the pace a bit? Do you want to communicate that a marginal performer is at risk of hitting the ceiling in terms of progression or even being separated from the organization down the road if the performance isn't improved? If the report calls for numerical rankings such as where the subordinate stands among others at the same level, be honest. Too many leaders have difficulty telling a subordinate that he or she ranks six of six at his or her level. The subordinate needs to know this in order to avoid being deceived about how he or she is being perceived. Human beings often have difficulty perceiving themselves as others perceive them. In verbal parts of the report, use short, descriptive phrases that get a point across and collectively paint a picture of the performance. Consider the following example:

Ambitious, hardworking, and loyal to the company. Responsible, punctual, completes requirements on time. Gets results. Intelligent, incisive, seeks to learn. Bill holds himself to high standards in terms of work product but sometimes openly expresses disappointment in others whose standards are not as high. Sometimes struggles in dealing with deviations from plan when unexpected events arise. Works hard to improve but occasionally resists constructive feedback if not delivered in a soft manner. High promise assuming improvement in interpersonal skills, greater flexibility, and tolerance for critical feedback. I plan to meet with Bill soon to help him develop a plan for dealing with the issues noted so that he can fulfill his substantial potential while continuing to be a high producer.

Taken as a whole, what picture of the subordinate does that set of statements paint? Do you see the subordinate as someone talented who really wants to succeed, but who is somewhat dogmatic and sometimes gets upset if things don't go exactly as planned? Someone who is sensitive to criticism? Someone who is openly critical of others whose career path might be blocked unless he makes changes? Is the picture sufficiently considerate of the employee so as not to sound overly critical and disheartening but yet clear enough that the employee can get the message of the need for improvement and what improvements are needed?

There is skill and art in writing good performance reviews. Notice that the above set of statements starts by accentuating several positives before turning to the negatives. Notice that it ends on an encouraging note, saying that the employee has great promise if he makes certain improvements. The closing statement suggests you are not leaving Bill to work out his performance issues alone. You care about him and want to help him fulfill his potential.

3. Avoid placing surprises in the report unless they very recently emerged. If you have provided informal feedback to the subordinate on an ongoing basis, surprises can hopefully be avoided. For example, if you know that the subordinate has been working hard and hoping for a promotion, saying, "Sorry, your performance does not justify promotion at this time" may disappoint less if it isn't a surprise.

4. If there are negative aspects in the report that require employee actions to correct,

ensure the report contains clear statements as to what those actions are, the time frame in which correction must be accomplished, and the possible range of adverse consequences if the employee fails to correct them. If probation is involved, ensure that is clearly stated as well.

5. Note also that you are not just fulfilling a requirement by documenting a file with a performance report; you are creating an employment history. In the future others may read what you have written and form conclusions about your subordinate. You should be careful not to communicate misinformation, positive or negative. Inflating performance reports in an effort to help an employee harms the organization. If Janice is a good employee but not great, simply say she is good and explain why. Don't make her sound like a superstar she isn't. If you are uncertain about something that concerns you, attempt to resolve it before placing reference to it in the report. Recall from chapter 2 one basic attribute of courageous leaders is that they deal with small problems before they become big ones. For example, Janice may have been late for work three times within the past month. Before making reference to a problem of tardiness in a performance report, address the issue with her when you first observe what may be a pattern emerging, asking questions such as, "Janice, I've noticed that you have been late a few times recently. This is not like you. Is there some problem of which I'm unaware?" Janice may simply be experiencing a temporary problem with childcare arrangements becoming unreliable and currently seeking new arrangements. Including minor, temporary issues of that nature in a performance report many convey a wrong impression to a reader who doesn't know Janice.

69

6. Anticipate how the subordinate will respond to any negative feedback and be prepared to take responsibility for what you write and say. Have facts to support your statements whenever possible. If you have received negative feedback about the subordinate from a credible third party and have done your best to verify its accuracy, believing the third party has the best interests of the pack in mind, including this feedback in the report means you have to take responsibility for using it. If confronted by a subordinate's response such as, "That isn't correct. Who said that?" you have to be prepared to respond with something like, "I investigated this, and based upon the facts I believe it to be accurate." You should not disclose your third-party source. It isn't fair to the third party providing the feedback, who is trying to help the organization. Moreover, disclosing sources may mean losing their trust, creating reluctance to provide such information in the future. If your statements involve perceptions, ensure they are stated that way. For example, "My perception is that Bill dislikes team tasks because he never volunteers to be part of a team that is forming." However, it may be best just to note that Bill never volunteers for teams, a factual statement. There could be other reasons Bill doesn't volunteer, such as an already heavy workload. Be careful also of drawing conclusions based upon too few observations. Because Bill didn't volunteer for teams last week or the week before does not necessarily mean he doesn't enjoy teamwork.

7. Once you have written your report, apply step 7 of the Zig-Zag Model and objectively evaluate what you have written. Put your report aside for a day or so and reread it when your mind is clear. For this reason it is best not to write performance reports at the last minute prior to performance reviews. Does it communicate what you intend? Does it present a fair balance of the positive and negative performance aspects? Have you focused too much on one negative and not enough on several positives? Have you buried the negatives in the positives such that the message that improvement is needed doesn't come through very clearly? What are the evidentiary weak spots? Do you need to try to collect more evidence?

8. When you discuss the report with the employee, stay on the moral and professional high ground. Stick with issues related to the performance and workplace. Avoid meandering off on tangents. Avoid the tendency to think ahead while the subordinate is talking and listen carefully, assessing his or her feedback. Give the employee time to fully express feelings. If the employee attempts to rebut portions of the report, listen carefully to the rebuttal. Avoid arguing if at all possible. After the employee has expressed feelings, make summary statements that you understand those feelings but do not agree. Such statements should express concern for the employee. For example, "Bob, I understand the points you are making and that you disagree with my conclusions, but I'm afraid we'll just have to disagree. Even if you do not agree with me, I must do what I feel is best for the organization. Because I care about you and your future here, I hope that you will take my comments to heart and make the necessary corrections."

9. Follow your organizational procedures regarding the employee signing the report. Some organizations require the employee to sign, while others do not. If the employee disagrees with the report and is reluctant to sign, offer to let the employee write a

rebuttal statement and attach it to the report. Also, you might inform the employee that signing the report does not constitute agreement with its contents but rather that the employee was offered the opportunity to read the report. If the employee still refuses to sign the report, write a statement to that effect, stating that you presented and discussed the report with the employee but the employee refuses to sign, and attach the statement to the report.

Granted, following the procedure outlined above takes time, but performance reviews are one of a leader's most important responsibilities. Do not allow a heavy workload or other excuses to lead you to do a poor job of discharging this responsibility. You have an obligation to your organization and your followers to do this to the best of your ability.

Returning to Susan, it is now time for her periodic performance review. She has continued to seek responsibility and handle it well, so you delegated more tasks. Soon she is performing tasks well above those of an administrative assistant. You decide that she has potential to go well beyond her current level, but you are hesitant because of her previous difficulties. You follow the above steps but are still somewhat uncertain about promising too much. During her review, you cite the outstanding job she has been doing and your feelings that she has high potential. You then ask about her professional aspirations. Susan hangs her head, saying she has no hope of promotion with the bank as a result of the difficulties with her previous boss. This opens the door for you to ask about those difficulties. She tells you she would have resigned except that she is a single mother and desperately needs a paycheck. She fears if she leaves she won't be able to get another job because of a bad reference. You say you don't understand. Her performance in your unit is superb.

How important are performance reports?

The answer is "very important." One of the coauthors says the following: "Over many years I wrote hundreds of reports and read thousands. I've presided over military promotion boards and participated in countless meetings in business and academia in which employee promotions were discussed. Conversation in these meetings usually centered on the content of written reports. It was obvious whether leaders had done a good job of creating these reports, and their diligence sometimes made the difference between a worthy subordinate being promoted or not and an unworthy one being promoted because of inflated reports when the leader lacked the courage to tell it like it is."

Over time you've earned Susan's trust and loyalty. You have provided positive feedback about her excellent performance and shown her you trust her to carry out assignments. Now, because of that she opens up. Somewhat hesitantly and with tears in her eyes, she explains that her former boss, a married man, had wanted to have sexual relations with her. When she repeatedly refused, trying to deflect his advances while not offending him, he felt rejected and became enraged. Then, to cover his tracks he created a bad performance report, perhaps hoping that if she filed a grievance he could say she was just trying to get revenge for the bad report. You detect no disingenuity in Susan's story and ask why she didn't file a grievance. She says it would be her word against the senior officer's, so proof was impossible. She hadn't wanted the embarrassment and gossip that would come from the story possibly becoming known. Again, you consider the facts. It all makes sense. She wasn't placed on probation because that might have provoked her into filing a grievance. You then ask, if she could paint a picture of her future at the bank, what would it look like? She responds that she'd really like to make it to the management ranks but feels locked into being a clerical. You ask how hard she is willing to work to achieve that goal. She says, "Very hard."

How do you feel you have handled Susan's situation so far? By following the Zig-Zag Model's principles, not jumping to conclusions based upon scant information—misinformation at that—and carefully considering the alternative COAs, you refrained from prejudicing your relationship with Susan. In earning her trust and loyalty by showing that you have confidence in her abilities, you have helped turn her into a valuable employee. You have now counseled Susan regarding her annual performance, and she is appreciative of your confidence in her and the favorable review. What are your leadership responsibilities regarding Susan's future with the bank? Keep this question in mind, because we will return to Susan's story again in a later chapter dealing with mentoring by applying the Path-Goal Model.

4.3 Counseling Errant Subordinates

Although many managers might not admit it, counseling an errant subordinate can be an intimidating proposition and requires courage. All managers sooner or later face situations in which errant employees require counseling. Effective counseling is an art form, a skill often gained through experience. The most informative experiences are usually gained by failing in first attempts and learning from those failures. Despite

counseling being art, we need not have to learn by failing and trying over and over. Fortunately, guidelines exist to assist in becoming better counselors.

When faced with a need to counsel someone, whether it be a routine performance review or a specific problem, start by getting the facts. Don't rely on rumor and innuendo. If possible, observe the subordinate's behaviors and work products personally. One of the observations we can make from the preceding anecdote was that the so-called facts about Susan were completely wrong. Given the opportunity, she demonstrated that she was a fine employee.

For many years one of the coauthors used what he calls the "three-strikes rule," a baseball analogy. If the discrepancy is minor and it is a first instance, an informal, private counseling is often used. In this "first strike," the employee is made aware of the problem and asked to comment on it and suggest how it may be resolved. This session should be upbeat, not overly focused on the problem to the exclusion of positive performance attributes, but the employee needs to agree to resolve the problem. If informal counseling does not resolve the problem, a second private session ("strike two") needs to be conducted using the following steps:

1. Advise your immediate superior of the problem and the steps you propose taking. Obtain the superior's advice and input. It is almost never a good idea to allow your superior to get "ambushed" by bad news about an employee problem.

2. Apply the Zig-Zag Model to analyze the situation and decide on a course of action.

3. When you confront a subordinate about a performance problem, clearly communicate what you believe the problem to be.

4. Then ask open-ended questions and allow the employee the opportunity to explain circumstances. Once you believe you have an accurate assessment of the problem, ask the employee what solution he or she thinks would resolve it.

5. Try to reach agreement with the employee on the definition of the problem. If you and the employee have defined the problem in different ways, it is far less likely the problem will be resolved. If the employee refuses to agree with your definition of the problem, explain the consequences of it not being resolved. You may need to explain that even if the employee's perceptions differ from yours, as the leader you have no choice but to do what you believe is in the best interests of the organization. Try again to reach agreement on a problem definition.

6. Develop a plan for problem resolution and attempt to obtain a commitment from the employee to accept responsibility for carrying out the plan. Be sure the plan contains a time frame for correcting the problem as well as indicators of problem resolution. For example, if the problem is a lack of effort, you might indicate that a measure of problem resolution would be productivity equal to that of the average of the group. Make sure the employee understands that it will be your judgment as the whether to improvement goal has been met.

7. The plan together with a memo clearly stating the problem, time frame, and consequences if not resolved should be committed to writing, with copies to the employee, your superior, and the employee's file.

8. Observe the employee carefully and provide feedback privately, both positive and corrective. Do not allow the time frame to expire without having informed the employee that adequate progress is not being made.[3] It is usually a good idea to also alert your immediate superior if the employee is failing to make the required progress. Don't surprise your superior by dropping the bad news that the employee failed after it's too late.[4]

Consider the following real-world-but-disguised example of counseling an errant subordinate. Because your unit performed well you have been promoted recently to become the manager of the bank's flagship facility in the heart of a big city. The previous manager was a senior officer who had other responsibilities that distracted him from giving the unit the necessary attention. A decision was made to place you in charge with the mission of bringing the unit to excellence. After a few weeks you have made substantial progress and are feeling somewhat self-satisfied. Years later you will understand that such feelings often breed complacency, and, when complacency sets in, bad things are often about to happen.

You have heard stories about one of your direct reports in the unit, Tommy, who has a reputation for being difficult to deal with, and you have been meaning to look into the situation but hadn't gotten around to it. Tommy is a clerical employee who works alone and reports directly to you. His function is to monitor cash at each of the bank's branches and order shipments from the Federal Reserve Bank via an armored car service to maintain prescribed levels of cash. In addition, sometimes a commercial customer has special cash requirements that are also ordered through Tommy. Today, one of the bank officers who reports to you says, "Something has to be done about Tommy. I received another call from an official I know personally at the Federal Reserve Bank complaining about Tommy's rudeness. That's the third time he's called me. Tommy is continually rude to his employees." You call Tommy to your office and ask him about the report of rudeness.

73

You: Tommy, apparently we've gotten multiple complaints from the Fed about your interactions with some of their employees. Can you shed any light on this?

Tommy (fidgeting in his chair and not looking you in the eye): Those people over there have an attitude of superiority. They are always talking down to me.

You: I'm sorry you feel that way about them, Tommy, but might it be possible you are contributing in some way to the difficulties?

Tommy (testily): I haven't done anything to them. They think they're better than other people because they work for the Fed.

You: Why do you believe they feel that way?

Tommy (eyes darting): Every time I call over there to order money they act like it's a chore. Aren't we their customer?

This sort of exchange continues for a while, and you realize Tommy is not going to accept any responsibility for the problem. You end by saying that, even if Tommy feels someone at the Fed is being rude to him, he should not be rude in return. You ask if the two of you can at least agree on that. Tommy agrees and leaves.

A week later another complaint arises, this time from one of the bank's branches. The manager says the branch did not receive an adequate cash supply as it should. When her head teller called to inquire about it, Tommy became belligerent and accused the head teller of making him look bad. After you discuss the incident with the branch manager, it appears that the fault rested with Tommy. You pull Tommy's personnel jacket and learn that he has been with the bank for only a few months. He attended college for 2 years before dropping out, apparently due to declining grades. He has no criminal record: otherwise he would not have been hired and placed in his

position. His former boss tells you he had heard some rumors about Tommy being difficult, but he was so busy with his main responsibilities that he never had time to pay attention to Tommy. After some consideration, you decide that the complaints about Tommy's behavior justify placing him on probation, so you prepare a memo documenting the problem and inform HR. The following dialogue takes place at your counseling session with Tommy:

You: Tommy, we've had another complaint about your rudeness, this time from one of our own branches. Can you help me understand what this is about?

Tommy (again fidgeting, eyes darting): I haven't been rude to anybody. The head teller out there is just trying to shift the blame to me for them running low on cash. They should have called and told me they'd disbursed more cash than usual the day before.

You: Is not part of your job description to monitor the cash levels at all the branch locations online and order cash for them as necessary?

Tommy (avoiding the question): Everybody makes mistakes. She shouldn't rub my nose in it.

You: First, running out of cash presents a real problem for the branches. Second, I don't think attempting to resolve a cash shortage is rubbing your nose in your mistake. Third, we agreed that you would stop being rude to people even if you believe they are being rude to you.

Tommy (angrily): I'm not anybody's patsy! I don't have to put up with people being rude to me!

You: Tommy, this discussion is not getting us anywhere. I'd like for you to have a good memo outlines the conditions. Please sign both copies and keep one for yourself.

Tommy signs the copies, tosses the pen on your desk, and walks out of your office without saying anything else. Based on his poor attitude, you consider terminating him now; but, except in extraordinary circumstances, the bank's policy is not to terminate employees for cause without first providing a formal written warning, placing the employee on probation, and allowing sufficient time for the employee to correct the problems. Tommy's case doesn't fit moral turpitude or a catastrophic failure. With no paper trail on file, you find yourself wishing your predecessor had done a better job of overseeing Tommy and documenting his problems. You decide that it is better to ensure that you follow policy and give Tommy one more chance, hoping that being placed on probation will be a sufficient incentive to improve.

If your predecessor had done a better job of leading, you might not be faced with Tommy. The topic of the next section should help you avoid having to deal with situations like Tommy.

4.4. Hiring Decisions

Hiring decisions are critical. Not only do they have a large impact on organizational performance; taking the time to make good hiring decisions will save leaders an enormous amount of time in the future by avoiding having to deal with such issues as correcting employee mistakes, dealing with complaints, counseling employees about substandard performance, and terminating poor performers. There is plenty of advice on how to hire. Consider, for example, the following seven questions proposed by one author: (1) Competent—necessary skills, experience, and education? (2) Capable—responsible with potential for growth? (3) Compatible—interpersonal skills? (4) Commitment—willing to stay with employer? (5) Character—good values aligned with organization's and yours? (6) Culture—does the prospect

employment experience here, but that's not going to happen with your present attitude. You've got to make some major adjustments as outlined in this memo. I'm placing you on probation. You will be terminated if there are any more complaints about rudeness from any credible source in the next 90 days. This fit culture? and (7) Compensation—adequate to satisfy applicant?[5] Although such a list can be useful guidance, it is anything but a complete answer to choosing the right employee.

Consider that the above list of "seven Cs" places competence as the number one factor to be considered and character as number five. We respectfully disagree. If you suspect a job applicant lacks the requisite ethical values, no matter how otherwise qualified the applicant may be, hiring would be a huge mistake. In our experience, hiring someone who lacks the right values will come back to haunt you. One of the coauthors is fond of saying, "You can't make a pet out of a rattlesnake. No matter how many mice you feed him, sooner or later he'll bite you." In other words, if you cannot trust an employee you don't want him or her.

Another point of difference with the above list is that competence in a particular set of skills may not always be an important capability. One of the coauthors says, "I'll often take talent over fit when it comes to technical skills if talent can be made to fit." In other words, in certain situations he would rather have a highly talented employee than one with less talent who apparently has skills and experience in a job as long as the talented employee can acquire the necessary technical skills. Granted, you would probably not hire someone as CFO without a substantial financial background, but there are times when talent trumps skills. Yet another point of difference with the list above is that an employee's commitment can change because of job satisfaction and growth. An applicant may sound committed but may not remain so if the job turns out to be insufficiently fulfilling. On the other hand, someone whose commitment might be questionable based upon his or her circumstances may turn out to be very loyal. Consider the following disguised-but-real-world episode as we join a corporate CFO interviewing an applicant to be his executive assistant:

CFO: You have undergraduate and master's degrees in English with a background in secondary education, but no experience as an executive assistant. Why are you applying for this position?

Applicant: I want to be totally candid with you. My husband was just transferred here with his employer. There are no jobs in English in the school system here, and there is a long waiting list of qualified applicants. My chances of being hired as an English teacher are virtually nonexistent.

CFO: If a teaching job did become available, would you quit here, assuming equal compensation?

Applicant: Again, being completely candid, that would depend upon whether my job here is fulfilling and whether there are possibilities for growth that would not exist in teaching.

CFO: I'm impressed with your intelligence, interpersonal skills, and honest answers to my questions. I'd like to give you a little test and see how you perform. This is a letter that I received this morning from a senior officer at one of our largest customers describing a problem with our service. I'd like for you to go into my conference room, read the letter, and draft a response apologizing for the problem and outlining our basic steps to resolve it.

The CFO relates the following outcome:

The applicant returned in half an hour with her response. It was outstanding—clear, concise, respectful, and well-conceived. I hired her. She was one of the best executive assistants I ever had—the type of employee to whom you could give a mission with basic guidance and count on it be carried out with complete professionalism.

I gave her increasingly challenging assignments and eventually she rose to management.

One very useful skill in hiring is the ability to prescreen applicants, including reading between the lines on resumes. Here is some useful guidance that will help keep you from wasting time and result in better hiring decisions: (1) Before soliciting applicants, develop a job description that accurately describes the person you are seeking. The job description sitting in an old personnel binder may not fit your needs. (2) Write down the critical attributes you are seeking in applicants. Rank them in order of importance. (3) Skim resumes for obvious red flags. If an applicant is missing a key attribute, make a note of that. Look for gaps in employment. If gaps exist and you still want to interview the applicant, write down the gaps and decide during a phone interview if the applicant is capable of closing them. (4) Read the resume carefully. If you decide to interview the applicant, reread the resume and make an outline for a phone interview. (5) Prescreen the applicant on the phone, asking basic questions such as the applicant's reason for leaving the current or last position, gaps in employment, and changes in career direction.[6]

Assuming you decide to hold an in-person interview following your prescreening, make a list of questions you want to ask. During the interview there are several important points to keep in mind. First, keep it professional, legal, and relevant to the job. Ensure that you know what you can and cannot say to an applicant and your firm's policies. For example, questions about religion, national origin, age, physical characteristics, marital status, disability, or gender are off-limits unless they are genuinely essential to the job. If you are interested in such activities as volunteer work for charities as evidence of community service because that it something your firm values, then approach that in an open-ended way by asking questions such as, "We value employee service to their communities.

How do you feel about that?" rather than, "I notice you don't list any community service on your resume." Try to keep your mind reasonably open and avoid making subjective snap judgments.[7]

Ask applicants to describe past experiences and how specific skills were used and to provide examples of how problems were handled successfully and unsuccessfully. Has the applicant been a member of and led teams? Ask about teams and why the teams were successful or unsuccessful. Does the applicant take all the credit for successes and avoid accepting any responsibility for failures? Ask for examples of problems with other team members and how the applicant handled them. Attempt to get the applicant to think extemporaneously with questions such as, "Give an instance where something would not have happened if you weren't leading," "Describe how you persuaded team members to do something your way," or "Describe a situation with an irate customer and how you handled it."

Pay close attention to the applicant's verbal responses and body language. Do difficult questions make the applicant especially nervous? Does the applicant avoid eye contact when providing responses? Once the interview is over, assuming you have significant interest in the applicant, immediately take a few minutes to jot down some notes before details are lost to memory.[8]

In interviews there are some behaviors you should avoid. A 15-minute interview does not allow enough time, so plan on your interview and notes afterward taking an hour. Listen more than you talk, and don't ask leading questions that beg the answer you're seeking. Avoid telling stories about yourself. Have the courage to ask difficult questions, but don't stress the candidate. Don't rank candidates against one another until you've completed your interviews to avoid recency effect, in which someone following a weaker candidate interviews well in comparison. Always treat candidates respectfully. Never use abusive tactics designed to frustrate or irritate just to see how the applicant reacts. As the sidebar indicates, this behavior may cost you a good applicant.[9] Ask the applicant if it is acceptable to contact his or her current employer for a reference. Often current employers are unaware that employees are seeking employment elsewhere, and you must be careful not to jeopardize an applicant's current job.

Checking an applicant's references is a critical step in the hiring process that often gets less than a complete effort. Some firms outsource reference checking to third parties, but assuming you are personally involved, the following guidelines are useful. The references you really want are current and former supervisors who can attest to the applicant's work performance. Carefully plan the questions you will ask during a reference check, but go into it with open eyes with respect to the information you will receive. Many organizations are very cautious in providing reference checks—and especially reluctant to provide negative information—because of legal risks of damaging a current or former employee's chances of getting a job and subsequently being sued. Also, the applicant's current employer may be attempting to unload someone who is not a good performer without having to fire him or her. Consequently, you are unlikely to get a complete and fully honest appraisal of the employee's performance, but there are things you can learn by asking the right questions.

The following are good areas of inquiry during a reference check. What responsibilities did the applicant have when working for you, and how well were these responsibilities discharged? Explain the responsibilities of the job for which the applicant is applying and ask how well he or she is capable of performing in that capacity. Ask about the applicant's leadership style and how well others responded to it. How reliable was the candidate? What suggestions for future development

Applicants deserve respect.

One of the coauthors was once invited to interview for a position with another firm.

"I was doing very well with my firm, but an older friend, another firm's CFO, insisted that I interview with his firm's CEO, saying there were great opportunities there. The CEO had a reputation for being a real bulldog. When I sat down in his office, he began by asking, 'What makes you think you're good enough to work for me?' Over the next half hour there was a continuous barrage of similarly brash questions that I suspected were designed to rattle me. Despite him interrupting my responses, I attempted to answer each calmly to the best of my ability. At one point he asked, 'So, tell me again why you want to work for us?' My patience was finally exhausted with his boorish behavior and I replied, 'I really can't think of a reason at the moment,' stood up, thanked him for his time, and left him sitting at his desk slack-jawed. I didn't want a boss who treated his employees that way."

were made to the candidate and how did he or she respond to these suggestions? What was the candidate's reason for leaving? Would you hire this person?[10] In asking questions of references ask questions that are neutral in tone to avoid prejudicing responses. For example, "Does the candidate prefer to work in groups or does she perform better working alone?" is preferable to "Can the candidate work in a team?"

Once you select the applicant you want to hire and obtain all the requisite clearances from HR, such as background checks, be prepared with the details of your firm's offer. Know and respect the applicant's need for confidentiality, ensuring there are no administrative slipups. Do not allow yourself to be placed in the position of having gotten an applicant in difficulty with a current employer because of some administrative slipup. Never delegate the task of calling to verify some aspect of an applicant's background or credentials to a clerical employee.

When you call the candidate, ask if it is an appropriate time to speak about your recent discussions. If the candidate is currently employed, the employer may not know the candidate is seeking another position. If you leave a message for callback, just leave a name and number to avoid alerting the person taking the message that the applicant might be seeking another position. Ensure that both you and the applicant fully understand all relevant major details of the offer, such as the position and title, compensation, when the applicant will begin work, and so forth. Indicate that an offer letter will be sent containing detailed information. Be sure to indicate excitement about the candidate joining your firm. If the applicant asks for time to think over the offer, he or she may be waiting to hear from other potential employers. Ask when the applicant thinks he or she will be able to make a final decision, but don't allow yourself to be kept in suspense indefinitely. You may wish to indicate that if he or she is unable to give you a decision now that the offer is contingent on you not hiring someone else prior to the decision. Sometimes firms issue "exploding offers" expiring after a certain period.

Hiring is a critical function of leadership. Good hiring practices will minimize the amount of time you spend dealing with the topic of the next section—terminating employees.

4.5. Terminating Nonperformers

Recall that earlier we categorized mistakes into three types: (1) mistakes involving moral turpitude, (2) catastrophic mistakes, and (3) other mistakes that are forgivable if not repeated too frequently. Moral turpitude involves an act or behavior that gravely violates the moral sentiment or accepted moral standards of the organization. Examples are criminal acts, hateful acts such as deliberately spreading damaging false information about another employee, and serious violations of organizational policies, rules, and regulations, such as sexual harassment. Catastrophic mistakes are so serious that they must not be repeated. An example might be a very large financial loss brought about by the shear negligence of the employee for failing to secure the appropriate legal documents in a large transaction with complete disregard for the organization's policies and procedures. Mistakes in categories 1 and 2 often can and often should result in termination regardless of whether the employee has been given prior warning. Moral turpitude presents unacceptable ethics, and, if employees are allowed to commit such acts and get away with them, the organization will suffer harm to its reputation, lower morale, and possibly more acts because some employees will see that it is possible to commit them and get away with it. Catastrophic mistakes may not involve ethical problems, but their cost is so high that the organization can ill afford a repetition. For example, suppose through negligence and dereliction of duty an employee fails to fulfill a commitment to the firm's largest client that results in the loss of the client. It may be desirable to terminate the employee to signal other employees that these behaviors are intolerable. The third category of mistake, however, usually calls for a reasonable opportunity for the employee to take corrective action prior to termination.

Termination situations often require courageous leadership, and they are not to be delegated. It is usual and often most appropriate for the employee's direct supervisor to be the one terminating the employee. Once again, the Zig-Zag Model procedures form a sound basis for preparing to terminate someone. Gather the facts, documentation, and any other evidence of the problem to possibly include written statements by people who have observed the behaviors. Ensure that the circumstances have been thoroughly documented to include the most recent incidents that have led to the decision to terminate. Consider any alternative courses of action for conducting the termination meeting. For example, do you think an inductive or deductive approach is best and why? Should your boss be present or is an HR representative the only requirement? Do you anticipate the possibility that the employee may become unruly and even violent? If so, you should notify security and have security personnel standing by close to the meeting.

Once you have considered the alternative COAs, decide on the approach you will take. Ensure that all participants other than the employee are briefed on the circumstances prior to the termination meeting. Schedule the meeting on a morning early in the week, not on Friday afternoon. Evidence suggests that terminating employees just prior to a weekend prevents them from immediately seeking new employment and makes it more likely that they will stew over the weekend, returning Monday with intentions of disrupting the workplace and possibly committing acts of violence.

During the meeting, you as the direct supervisor should act with the utmost professionalism, demonstrating both strength of conviction and compassion. Do not hurry the meeting. Termination is a difficult emotional experience, and the employee may want to express feelings about you and the organization. It is very important to demonstrate compassion for the employee, saying such things as, "This is difficult for all of us. We care about you as we do all our employees, but circumstances leave us no choice." Allow the employee ample time to "blow off steam," and don't become embroiled in arguing. If the employee asks questions, attempt to provide clear, concise answers. Don't prattle. One common question is what will be the response if a prospective employer requests a reference. You should know this in advance of the meeting and be able to respond. Alternatively, this is a question to which the HR representative can respond. If the employee disputes evidence, don't argue, just listen, and when he or she is finished affirm your belief that the evidence speaks for itself. The employee may attempt to talk you out of termination and feel he or she has done so with the arguments, so once the employee is finished be clear in the fact that termination is still the result of the meeting and when it takes effect. Often this will be at the end of the meeting so that the employee has as little opportunity as possible to spread dissension among other employees, steal data, and commit sabotage. Ensure that all keys, computer pass cards, firm identification, and credit cards are collected, and have the employee be escorted to his or her workspace, collect any personal items, and be escorted from the building.[11]

Let's return to Tommy, our errant employee. The problem with Tommy has not been resolved. You have received yet another complaint about his rudeness, this time from yet another source. The time has come for "strike three." You advise your boss and HR that Tommy has once again misbehaved after being told that the next incident would be the last. Now you intend to take the action stipulated in the plan and memo that followed the second counseling—terminate his employment. The day and time for your termination meeting arrive, and there is a representative from HR present. The following conversation takes place with the three of you sitting in a conference room with the door closed:

You: Tommy, we're here today because we've received yet another complaint about you being rude to someone, this time from a commercial customer who called about ordering a special currency shipment. The customer's representative said you told him that his failure to get the request to you before 10:00 AM was his problem, not yours, and that you further stated that a failure on his part did not mean a crisis response on your part. You weren't going to jump through a hoop just to please him because he was too lazy to get his request in on time. Is that accurate?

Tommy (angrily): I never said that! He's lying. People lie all the time. They lie about me!

You: Tommy, what the customer rep is saying is similar to reports we've had from the people at the Fed and the recent complaint from a branch that caused you to be placed on probation.

Tommy (fidgeting nervously): I don't see why I have to jump through a hoop just because he didn't call in time. If I let customers walk all over me I'll never get my shipments ready for pickup.

You: Tommy, the customer is very upset and threatening to move their business elsewhere. You do understand, don't you, that the bank depends upon customers to generate revenue to pay our salaries, so our relations with them are critical?

Tommy (bloodshot eyes darting back and forth between you and Ms. Carroll, the HR representative): If I made your salary I'd pay more attention to that sort of thing. You get what you pay for in this world.

You (disgusted): Enough of this. Two weeks ago you were counseled and placed on probation with the provision that another oc-

currence of rudeness would result in your termination. You signed the memo saying that . . .

Tommy (interrupting): Yeah, but that just pertained to the complaints from the Fed.

You (becoming angry): That's inaccurate. The memo clearly states ANY complaints, not just complaints from the Fed. See, it says so right here that . . .

Tommy (interrupting again in an accusing tone and jumping out of his chair): You're distorting this whole thing. You've never liked me. This is nothing but a personality conflict. My previous boss never had any problems with me. We got along fine. I haven't got time to read that bunch of crap. If you keep wasting my time I won't get my shipments out, and you'll blame me for that, too. I'm going back to work!

You (angrier): Sit down, Tommy! We covered that at the counseling session. I talked with your previous boss before that session, and he told me he never pursued any complaints because he was too distracted with other responsibilities and hadn't had time to . . .

Tommy (defiantly, still walking rapidly around the room): I don't believe it! He never told me anything like that. You're making this up because you don't like me. My other boss knew how to treat me, not the way you people and that guy at the Fed do.

You (completely frustrated): Enough of this foolishness! You are terminated effective immediately! You will be escorted by security to collect your personal belongings and then escorted out of the bank. Turn in your employee ID card to Ms. Carroll now.

Tommy (screaming): You can't do this! I'm going to go talk my OLD boss. He'll stand up for me! He's got real experience! You're just an arrogant, young guy who has let power go to his head! You've got no right to treat ME this way! I'm filing a complaint about you with the government! Ms. Carroll, he's the one who should be fired for treating people this way (pointing at you)!!!

You (reaching for the phone): This meeting is over. I'm calling security now.

Tommy (highly agitated, flailing his arms): DO THAT and see what happens! If those goons touch me I have every right to resist! My rights as a human being are being violated. You'll pay for this! You can't fire me! It's not fair and it's illegal!!!

You (looking at Ms. Carroll, who appears to be in shock): Ms. Carroll, security is on the way. I suggest you leave with me.

The foregoing exchange is a recollection of an actual termination gone wrong. What should the leader have done differently? First, he didn't take the time to use the Zig-Zag Model. Even if he hadn't known about the model, he should have thought about and planned the termination more carefully. Second, if the supervisor had paid closer attention and not rushed his counseling session with Tommy, he might have recognized symptoms of possible illegal drug use and taken appropriate precautions. If he had, then he should have reported his observations to HR at that time. By not having security standing close by outside the conference room during the termination meeting, he placed both himself and Ms. Carroll in unnecessary danger had Tommy become physical. Third, he showed no compassion for Tommy. His approach and tone suggested no concern for Tommy. Fourth, he was impatient. Instead of attempting to rebut Tommy's self-serving arguments, he would have been better advised to allow Tommy to

fully vent his feelings and then calmly announced the outcome remained the same.

Did the supervisor do anything right? Although he became angry with Tommy's unreasonableness, he did not get into a shouting match with Tommy and remained somewhat under control during Tommy's outbursts. He did not allow Tommy's behavior to intimidate him into giving Tommy another chance. He also showed concern for Ms. Carroll's well-being.

Could Tommy's bizarre behaviors been prevented? This is questionable, especially if Tommy was under the influence of illegal drugs, which was never determined. Nonetheless, the termination was not handled well by the supervisor, who should have taken a more thoughtful and better-guided approach. Terminations are difficult leadership situations and require careful preparation and execution. A heavy workload and hectic schedule are insufficient justification for a leader not doing the best job possible when circumstances require an employee to be terminated. A good rule is to enter the termination meeting hoping for the best but prepared for the worst. Also, each termination is an opportunity for personal growth as a leader. Let's face it—terminations are not enjoyable. But if you enter the termination process with the attitude of making the most of a learning opportunity rather than simply dreading an unpleasant task—focusing on being as absolutely professional as possible and grading your own performance—your countenance during the meeting can be more positive and professional.

Situations such as the ones discussed in this chapter often require courageous leadership. Dealing with employees is a responsibility that requires more diligence and investment than busy managers are sometimes willing to make. Too frequently, "hip-shot" responses to employee situations do the organization and its members, includ-

Tommy's former supervisor

"That was my first termination and I clearly blew it. But I learned. Over time I improved and most of my subsequent terminations went about as well as could be expected. There was one incident much later, however, involving a very senior leader that I also blew. My problem was that I let my personal liking for the guy get in the way of my professionalism. I should have just placed the cards on the table compassionately and allowed the guy to talk as much as he liked. Instead, my feelings about him being a nice guy caused me to commiserate with him, going on about how much I admired him and liked him personally. All I succeeded in doing was weakening the message. I gave myself a failing grade on that one. I guess the moral is stick to the script and don't get complacent and careless thinking you've got the process down cold."

ing the employee, a disservice. Learning to deal appropriately with these situations takes thought and personal development. Personal development begins with knowing yourself and manifests itself in being able to lead your subordinates into growing themselves into ever-improving followers. Part II addresses these topics.

PART II
The Inner Self

Foreword

Having dealt with what courageous leadership means, some underlying principles, and some leadership situations, part II discusses the notion of self-understanding for both the leader and the organization. Chapter 5 deals with self-assessment and employs Myers-Briggs Type Indicator and emotional intelligence
to facilitate our self-understanding. Chapter 6 discusses business ethics, which
constitute the organization's inner self. Chapter 7 explores motivating others
and yourself, and chapter 8 tackles fostering growth in others and yourself.

Understanding Others and Yourself

> "If you know the enemy and know yourself, you need not fear the result of a hundred battles. If you know yourself but not the enemy, for every victory gained you will also suffer a defeat. If you know neither the enemy nor yourself, you will succumb in every battle."
>
> —Sun Tzu, *The Art of War*

Hopefully most of us will not have to experience war, but regardless of the difficult situations in which we find ourselves—Tommy's termination in chapter 4 represents just one scenario—knowing ourselves to the extent possible offers an advantage in improving our personal and professional relationships. Because behaviors are a function of personality and the environment, we examine personality defined as the complete set of ways that a person reacts to and interacts with others.[1] There is no perfect tool for knowing ourselves or others, but the **Myer-Briggs Type Indicator (MBTI)** is a useful anchor point for information processing and decision making leading to individual improvement.[2] MBTI refers to a four-letter designator for one of sixteen different and somewhat distinct personality preference profiles, each with its own characteristic behaviors that, in the aggregate, are different from other MBTIs.

As the quote above indicates, courageous leaders need to know themselves and others in order to resolve problems. Recalling what was said earlier about what adds value for businesses with an added behavioral twist, leaders are paid to identify the *right problems* to solve and the *right people* to solve the *right problems*. Many problems require courageous leadership in peo-

ple selection and problem identification processes. In one sense, the leadership task is the reconciliation of differences among subordinates. This reconciliation process involves the leader dealing with subordinates' preferences, determined in part by personality, as well as other issues.[3] The pervasive nature of human behavioral patterns makes this possible.

An important caveat is in order before proceeding, however. Although MBTI offers significant insights into human behavior in a broad domain of activities, neither personality nor MBTI explains all human behaviors. Properly utilized, however, it can help better inform leaders about individuals, teams, organizations, selling, conflict resolution, coaching, careers, change, project management, leadership, innovation, emotional intelligence, and decision making.[4]

5.1. How Does MBTI Basically Work?

MBTI uses **pattern recognition** of people's behaviors, personalities, and relationships to assist leaders in resolving human conflicts. It is a well-accepted tool that has demonstrated excellent validity, and consequently the tool we choose to perform behavioral assessments. Although personality does not fully explain all human behaviors, MBTI patterns represent a well-validated starting point that has been used effectively since the 1960s. Phrases used frequently in common discussions such as "comfortable in my own skin" and "out of my comfort zone" are related in MBTI terminology to **Best-Fit Type**. Best-Fit Type is gradually revealed as subjects move along a path of self-discovery to identify the type that best fits their behavioral patterns.[5]

As an indicator, MBTI prompts us to think seriously about patterns of behavior. Underlying patterns of behaviors begin at an early age. Individuals engage in various behaviors but over time develop preferences for certain specific behaviors. As these preferences grow more pronounced, greater competence and comfort are developed with some behaviors versus others. This leads to some behavioral options being excluded. Followers are more comfortable when preferred behaviors are supported by leaders and circumstances. When this is not the case, although followers may temporarily modify their preferences, often over time followers revert to their original preferences.[6] **Type Talk** refers to statements that expose and clarify these preferences. When one hears a statement about someone such as, "This is just not like him," more than likely his behaviors are inconsistent with Best-Fit Type. We are interested in the behaviors associated with each type.[7]

Behaviorally anchored rating scales (BARS) refers to a tool used to assess behavioral aspects of individuals, teams, and even learning organizations to ascertain whether behaviors match individuals' and others' beliefs about themselves.[8] BARS ask respondents to assess the *frequency* of their engagement in certain specific behaviors as opposed to questions involving their own perceptions about the *quality* of these behaviors.[9] This is because self-assessments of quality tend to be more biased than self-assessments of frequen-cy. Since any self-assessment, however, may not result in an objective assessment, assessments other than the subjects' self-assessments are also used to arrive at Best-Fit Type.[10]

A BARS approach is also used to assess subjects' learning to improve performance, allowing both the evaluator and subjects being evaluated to exchange feedback. When an evaluator is attempting to assist a subject in assessing current versus desired performance, BARS give greater clarity than a raw, global performance rating such as simply rating a performance as good, fair, or poor. This same conceptual framework is used to understand type. Basic behaviors are first identified and then the relative frequency, comfort, and confidence that subjects have in these behaviors are measured until eventually arriving at a Best-Fit Type. Figure 5.1 shows a BARS used to assess how well an individual learns. The middle column describes in general terms the amount of learning activity taking place. The right column describes the types of activity. The left column assigns a numeric score based upon frequency and types of behaviors.

Upon meeting someone for the first time, many thoughts enter our minds. Initially, these are about physical similarities or differences we observe, but as we go beyond these initial impressions MBTI is a useful tool for better understanding behaviors by categorizing patterns of normal preferences in normal people as follows:

1. **Extraversion–Introversion**: two different and normal ways of focusing energy.

2. **Sensing–Intuition**: two different and normal ways of processing information.

3. **Thinking–Feeling:** two different and normal ways of making decisions.

4. **Judging–Perceiving**: two different and normal ways of arranging one's life.

Figure 5.1. BARS Example of Individual Learning Performance

In a learning individual the style of learning should be open and committed to maximize the benefits from alternative opinions.

Numeric Scale	Relative Amount of Activity	Examples of Activities Related to This Factor
9 8 7	More than usual amount of typical activity on effort related to this factor	**What/how can I learn as I resist minimally?** Active exchange of ideas and information is frequently and actively sought across boundaries. People are prepared to challenge assumptions, to question, and to exchange ideas to gain the maximum learning. People accept the discomfort or comfort in the learning process in order to make progress. **What/how may I learn as I resist minimally?**
6 5 4	Usual amount of typical activity or effort related to this factor	**What/how can I learn as I slightly resist?** Less than full participation is given by oneself or sought from others. Individuals slightly resist the challenge of assumptions and resulting discomfort to themselves. Some prefer to passively involve themselves, but this leaves others without the benefit of their insights. Some search for comfort or "fun" as a sign of learning in spite of the overwhelming evidence that learning is as much about unlearning as it is about learning. **What/how may I learn as I slightly resist?**
3 2 1	Less than usual amount of typical activity or effort related to this factor	**What/how can I learn as I actively resist?** People are hostile to exchanging information or receiving ideas from others. This is seen as threatening and the style of communication is closed, sullen and suspicious. Some attempt to actively resist via offline discussions to undermine the learning activities of others without attempting to gain or share insights. **What/how may I learn as I actively resist?**

Source: Adapted from Terry Campbell, *European Consortium for the Learning Organization*.

These four preference categories combine to form a matrix producing sixteen types explored in more detail later in this chapter.

Recall the **Zig-Zag Model** whose underlying theory posits that decision makers attempting to solve problems cycle through a particular mental process. At any given time decision makers are continually and alternatively (1) **perceiving** by *sensing* or *intuiting,* or (2) **judging** by *thinking* or *feeling.* Both perceiving and judging are required for problem solving, although not necessarily

Understanding Others and Yourself

in equal proportion. Sensing involves gathering facts, collecting data, and examining what is already known about the problem. From sensing decision makers move to intuition, which involves brainstorming, being imaginative, and keeping an open mind. Next comes thinking about the problem, deciding on a set of decision criteria, and applying these criteria in a reasonable, logical manner. From there, decision makers move to feeling out whether they really like the solution selected and how it affects the organization, others, and themselves. Feelings may cause the decision maker to do more sensing, seeking more data and information about the problem and cycling through the process again. The Zig-Zag Model focuses attention on the aforementioned four behavioral patterns in judging and perceiving, exposing such behaviors as someone jumping directly from sensing to thinking in making a decision, thereby bypassing intuition, and others jumping to feeling. Alternatively, a person may go from intuition to feeling, bypassing facts sensing and consequences (thinking). The Zig-Zag Model posits, therefore, that decision making is improved when all four personality elements are engaged.

5.2. Does MBTI Deliver Good Results?

The primary purpose for which MBTI was created was to help others gain mutual understanding and avoid destructive conflicts.[11] Swiss psychologist Carl Jung and American mother-daughter team Isabel Briggs Myers and Katharine Cook Briggs were more or less in the same time period (early to mid-1900s) gaining an understanding for human behavior. For example, Jung proposed that people cannot simultaneously and completely focus on details *and* the big picture, so normally people do more of one and less of the other, usually in sequence. As time passed, improvements were made in MBTI to include finer granulation regarding preferences. For example, one may be an introvert very clearly and very comfortably

and also engage in some extraverted activities despite a preference for introversion. A particular introvert will prefer introversion but may not be as reserved as other introverts, and he or she may even appear to be an extravert at times. Initially, improvements emanated from observations and insights, but later questionnaires were developed to take advantage of statistical analyses.

Although MBTI was not initially overwhelmingly promoted in the academic psychology community, over time actual results demonstrated the value of MBTI, and it has become one of if not the most used psychological instruments. The publisher, Consulting Psychologists Press, reports on its website that millions of individuals have used the MBTI.[12] One of the coauthors has been using MBTI on a global basis since the mid-1990s.[13] Having firsthand experiences in numerous countries with several thousand managers and executives confirmed many of the observations and insights noted by Jung, Myers, and Briggs. More importantly, the efforts to find Best-Fit Type reflected actions speaking louder than words, and realization of Best-Fit Type produced positive outcomes. Best-Fit Type explained a sufficient amount of behavior such that these executives were able to improve their leadership abilities. Knowing one's preferences provides indications of one's strengths because people operate best within their preferences. Consequently, to the extent that Best-Fit Type helps identify strengths, and inasmuch as some have argued that the key to leadership success is to emphasize one's strengths first, leaders can be well served by knowing their types.[14]

5.3. Determining Best-Fit Type

Determining a Best-Fit Type begins with identification of basic preferences, and a starting point for that is identifying preferences along the four attributes of energy, perception, judgment, and orientation, as shown in Figure 5.2.

Figure 5.2. Contrast of Preference across Four Behavioral Attributes

Extraversion Prefers the external world	Energy	Introversion Prefers the internal world
Sensing Prefers to scan back for data with the five senses	Perception	Intuition Prefers to scan ahead for possibilities and new ideas
Thinking Prefers to step back from the situation and make an objective and logical decision	Judgment	Feeling Prefers to place him or herself into the situation and make a personalized subjective decision
Judging Prefers a planned approach, motivated by the deadline	Orientation	Perceiving Prefers a spontaneous approach, motivated by pulling off the task at the last minute or in the last hours

Figure 5.3. A First Attempt at Assessing Preference

Extraversion		Energy	Introversion	
			Y	X
Sensing		Perception	Intuition	
			Y	X
Thinking		Judgment	Feeling	
X	Y			
Judging		Orientation	Perceiving	
X	Y			

Source for Figures 5.2 and 5.3: Adapted from J. M. Kummerow and N. L. Quenk, *Working with MBTI® Step II Results* (Mountain View, CA: CPP, Inc., 2005). All rights reserved. Reprinted with permission.

The intensity can vary across people with the same preference. In other words, a person might be strongly introverted or weakly introverted. It is therefore helpful to use a visual indicator when assessing preferences. Consider the cases of persons X and Y as illustrated in Figure 5.3.

X and Y are both introverted, but X much more so than Y. The same is true on the other three preference categories. In other words, X's prefer-ences are much more pronounced than Y's. Recall preferences are just that. People are both capable and often required to operate outside their prefer-ences but are more comfortable when operating within their preferences. Moreover, a person can be close to the midpoint on any or all dimensions but still lean toward preferring one behavior over another. Clarifying preferences is merely a start-ing point for understanding yourself and others.

Figure 5.4. The Sixteen Types

ISTJ	ISFJ	INFJ	INTJ
ISTP	ISFP	INFP	INTP
ESTP	ESFP	ENFP	ENTP
ESTJ	ESFJ	ENFJ	ENTJ

Combining the four preferences results in the following sixteen types shown in Figure 5.4.

The initial assessment of Best-Fit Type is made by identifying which of the sixteen types a person's four preferences suggest. Once one has determined an initial assessment of Best-Fit Type, the next step is to explore the preferences with more specificity. This involves reconsidering the initial assessment by proceeding through a series of steps as follows using two hypothetical people, Sue and Bob.

The preferred focus of extraversion (E) is the external world. Extraverts are energized by people. Key words associated with extraverts are external, active, people, sociable, many, expressive, and breadth. Extraverts need sufficient introversion for balance, and lacking it may appear to be shallow to introverts. Conversely, the preferred focus of introversion (I) is the internal world. Introverts are energized by thought. Key words associated with introverts are internal, reflective, privacy, reserved, few, quiet, and depth. Introverts need sufficient extraversion for balance, and lacking it may seem withdrawn to extraverts.

Sensing (S) prefers to scan back for data with the five senses. Key words associated with sensing are details, present, practical, fact, sequential, repetition, and stability. Sensing needs sufficient intuition for balance, and lacking it may seem materialistic to intuitives. Conversely, intuition (N) prefers to scan ahead for possibilities and new

Figure 5.5. Preferred Focus of Extraverts and Introverts

The preferred focus of extraversion (E) is the external world	Energy	The preferred focus of introversion (I) is the internal world
Sue		Bob

Figure 5.6. Preferred Data Perception of Sensors and Intuitives

Sensing (S) prefers to scan back for data with the five senses	Perception	Intuition (N) prefers to scan ahead for possibilities and new ideas
Bob		Sue

Figure 5.7. Preferred Decision-Making Strategy of Thinkers and Feelers

Thinking (T) prefers to step back from the decision and make an objective and logical decision	**Judgment**	Feelings (F) prefer to place themselves into the situation and make a personalized subjective decision
Bob		**Sue**

Figure 5.8 Preferred Lifestyle of Judgers and Perceivers

Judging (J) prefers a planned approach, motivated by the deadline	**Orientation**	Perceiving (P) prefers a spontaneous approach, motivated by pulling off the task at the last minute or in the last hours
Bob		**Sue**

ideas. Intuitives gather information with a "sixth sense." Key words associated with intuitives are patterns, future, imaginative, innovation, random, variety, and change. Intuitives need sufficient sensing for balance, and lacking it may seem to be dreamers to sensing types.

Thinking (T) prefers to step back from the decision and make an objective and logical decision. Thinking decides logically and objectively. Key words associated with thinking are head, justice, cool, criticize, analyze, precise, and principles. Thinking needs sufficient feeling for balance, and lacking it may seem cold to feeling

Feelings (F) prefer to place themselves into the situation and make a personalized subjective decision. Feeling decides personally and subjectively. Key words associated with feeling are heart, harmony, caring, appreciate, empathize, persuasive, and values. Feeling types may seem emotional to thinking types. Feeling types need thinking for balance.

Judging (J) prefers a planned approach, motivated by the deadline. Judging lifestyle is decisive

and planned. Key words associated with judging are organized, structure, control, decisive, closure, plan, and deadlines. Judging needs sufficient perceiving for balance, and lacking it may seem rigid to perceiving types. Conversely, Perceiving (P) prefers a spontaneous approach, motivated by pulling off the task at the last minute or in the last hours. The perceiving lifestyle is flexible and spontaneous. Key words associated with perceiving are flexible, flow, experience, curious, openness, wait, and discoveries. Perceiving types need judging for balance, and lacking it may seem messy to judging types.

Based upon the foregoing, Sue and Bob have close to a first-pass estimate of their Best-Fit Types, as shown in Figure 5.9.

The key to Best-Fit is that knowing it helps you understand when you are in your comfort zone or not. It allows you to recognize that gaining access and comfort to the nonpreferred is effortful. It also provides insights into others as you listen, watch, and observe them behaving consistently with their preferences. This knowledge allows you to

Figure 5.9. Indicated Best-Fit Type

ISTJ **Bob**	ISFJ	INFJ	INTJ
ISTP	ISFP	INFP	INTP
ESTP	ESFP	ENFP **Sue**	ENTP
ESTJ	ESFJ	ENFJ	ENTJ

Source: Adapted from J. M. Kummerow and N. L. Quenk, *Working with MBTI® Step II Results* (Mountain View, CA: CPP, Inc., 2005). All rights reserved. Reprinted with permission.

improve communications and relationships while leveraging similarities and differences.

One example of how organizations might use Best-Fit is team composition. Two of the challenges faced by a large multinational company were developing new ideas and entrepreneurial behavior. Using MBTI the organization discovered that 75–80 percent of its executives were STJs. Unfortunately for those purposes, STJs prefer stability. The difficulty was exacerbated by an economic downturn when hiring was frozen, so new hires were not the answer. A solution was found when the STJs agreed to designate one team member in each meeting to be the designated NFP and propose new ideas, consider the more subjective aspects of issues, and keep options open. This actually worked! The managers noted that engaging in nonpreferred behavior was exhausting but useful.

A caveat is in order: even if organizations are able to assemble teams with the right mixture of preferences given the need, this may be insufficient to ensure success. Leaders still have the challenge of ensuring the team uses a breadth of behaviors consistent with its members' preferences.[15]

5.4. Understanding the Sixteen Types

The sixteen types provide sixteen unique paths to personal and professional excellence.[16] By knowing who we are and valuing our preferences, we can better value and respect differences in others. MBTI theory posits that each preference element is equally valuable in life, but differences at times may lead people to believe certain differences are more valuable than others.[17] For example, for an INTJ, the opposite type is an ESFP. Knowing this allows the INTJ to recognize, appreciate, and respond more appropriately to an ESFP's feelings and behaviors. In a real-world series of sessions with an ESFP where disagreements at first appeared pervasive, an INTJ used type to work effectively and harmoniously with the ESFP by focusing on common goals and leveraging their differences. A starting point for achieving such understanding of others is to learn each of the sixteen types' preferred feelings and behaviors.

Located in the upper left corner of Figure 5.9, the ISTJ is often referred to as the *law-and-order type* due to his or her desire to bring structure to most, if not all, situations. ISTJs typically are serious minded and practical in their thinking, preferring to organize everything—work, home, and life. ISTJs have an institutional memory of many organizations, placing a high value on loyalty and doing things the way they have been done in the past. ISTJs take responsibility seriously and may be aggressive toward those who do not share their approach. ISTJs have a need to find their place in an organization so they can perform responsibly. When ISTJs experience stress, they may become extremely critical to the point of imagining catastrophic events and can become excessively rigid to the extreme detriment of the organization.

The ISFJ is often referred to as the *caring cop*—law and order with feelings. ISFJs are typically dependable and loyal in their organization. They tend to organize everything—life, home, and work. The order of structuring is different from the ISTJ in that the ISFJ usually starts with life, next family, and then work. If the organization becomes a substitute family, then the ISFJ is a keen organizer of this new family. ISFJs take their responsibility to others very seriously but are less interested technically in situations than ISTJs. As with ISTJs, ISFJs under stress may become extremely critical to the point of imagining catastrophic events and their effects on others. The only way to alleviate this stress becomes a rigid focus on others, possibly to the detriment of all.

The INFJ is known as the *personal innovator for people*—an insightful futurist with his or her eyes on the future possibilities for people. Intuitively understanding human relationships, INFJs are typically quietly empathetic. Their empathy, combined with a reflective approach, provides opportunities for improving others' lives in an orderly manner. Under stress, however, INFJs may become extremely focused on sensing and gathering data, perhaps becoming stubborn to the exclusion of empathy.

The INTJ *system builder* conceptualizes a future and builds a system for achieving it. Sometimes this is so subtly intuitive that other types don't recognize it has happened. INTJs so prefer complex challenges that the unsolvable is sometimes interesting to them. They may be satisfied with visualizing a solution regardless of whether it is implemented, but INTJs will implement relentlessly if necessary, even excluding others. They often need reminding of the people aspect of their vision. Under stress, INTJs may become distant and excessively stubborn about superfluous details.

The *quiet firefighter* ISTP is a troubleshooter with reservations about being loud. ISTPs are efficiency oriented in finding and solving problems to the point of quickly wanting to move on to the next problem. ISTPs do not want to be told how and when to solve problems. The phrase "no fuss, no muss" is descriptive of their attitude. Because they value freedom in problem solving, ISTPs typically do not perform well in regimented situations. Under stress, they may become focused outwardly to the point of exhibiting anger and outbursts against others.

Known as the *sensitive troubleshooter,* ISFPs are oriented to solving problems while maintaining harmony. Similar to ISTPs, ISFPs want to immediately contribute to solutions and facilitate people being happy. For ISFPs, trust and relationships are the foremost components of their solutions. ISFPs are often noted as gentle and caring with no real desire to lead or dictate. Under stress, however, they may become almost violent in their vocabulary and critical comments toward others.

INFPs as *friendly idealists* have a goal orientation going far beyond a paycheck. INFPs care for people, desire harmony, and have strong personal values that drive their behaviors. INFPs enjoy working on numerous topics, projects, and ideas simultaneously to the point that the NP in INFP may come to mean "new project, new product, new people, and now panic."[18] INFPs seek to understand human development and help others achieve their potential. When INFPs experience stress, they may not contribute to projects, especially those in which they have lost interest.

The *independent thinker* INTP's thinking process may offer insight into problem finding and problem solving, but INTPs typically are not interested in the solution implementation. Solving the conceptual problem is critical to the INTP. INTPs offer insights without reservation and have no desire to organize to solve problems. INTPs do not appreciate the need for routine tasks that may threaten their independence. When INTPs experience stress, they may abandon their reserve and engage in emotional outbursts that seem so out of character that others are disturbed.

ESTP *energetic troubleshooters* exhibit extraversion and an energetic approach to bursts of providing problem solving. ESTPs prefer to move fast, be active, respond creatively, ignore bureaucracy, and enjoy their work while solving the problem quickly so they can move to the next problem. Aside from the abstract and conceptual, ESTPs are enthusiastic about most topics including nature, fashion, food, people of all types, and anything that offers new experiences. When ESTPs experience stress, they may become frustrated to the point of losing interest in these experiences.

Extra special friendly person ESFPs exhibit extreme extraversion and energy that are often contagious to others. Like ESTPs, ESFPs prefer to move fast, be active, respond creatively, ignore bureaucracy, and have a good time while working with people on solving the problem quickly so they can move to the next group of people and the next problem. Their gregariousness lends itself to their being an excellent team member with the intention of helping people avoid routines by using common sense instead of procedures. When ESFPs experience stress, they may become overwhelmed by having unrealistic expectations of themselves and others.

The ENFP *friendly entrepreneur* combines extraversion and intuition, resulting in creative innovation. They prefer to imagine possibilities resulting in organizational entrepreneurship. ENFPs prefer freedom to explore and want to be appreciated for their work. Not receiving appreciation, they may exit the organization rather than exhibit perseverance. When ENFPs experience stress, they may become distant and focused on trivial details to the point of ignoring possibilities.

ENTPs are *thinking entrepreneurs* displaying extraversion and intuition combined with objectivity, which makes them thoughtful risk takers. ENTPs think of the future in terms of systems and interactions that others may not see as quickly or at all. Their objectivity and flexibility provide them with resilience in the face of failure. ENTPs display positivism in most uncertain situations due to confidence that their intuition will lead to a solution if they just press forward. As with ENFPs, when ENTPs experience stress they may become distracted by details, but their more typical response is to focus on details and become defensive.

The ESTJ or *take charge cop* often exhibits an extraverted, law-and-order approach, taking control of situations, organizing, and implementing solutions. This approach usually manifests itself in situations where problems are relatively well defined and solutions have been proven to work in the past. ESTJs are administratively inclined, using analytical talent to form objective solutions. ESTJs appreciate others as long as they deliver on time and under budget. They are conscientious and reliable to a fault, often not imagining alternatives to their approach exist. Under stress, they may exhibit feelings of desperation and behave out of the norm in such ways as becoming uncommunicative and angry at others because circumstances do not respond according to plan.

The *people's patrolman* ESFJ displays extraversion combined with a desire to help others constantly and repetitively resulting from his or her preference for feeling and sensing. They value others, security, and appreciation (both given and received). ESFJs prefer to organize and solve problems with harmony and commitment and celebrate when successful. They tend to default to a people perspective when examining options for solutions and seek people-oriented solutions that have worked successfully in the past. When ESFJs experience stress, they tend to anchor to an impression, point of progress, or position regardless of additional objective evidence. In such situations they may become so critical that they become a detriment to the organization despite their normal preferences for assisting others.

The ENFJ or *leader's leader* is an extraverted visionary who prefers people-focused solutions and often earns the followership of other types. ENFJs prefer to get the job done on time and under budget with a cooperative approach, prizing harmony and priding themselves on getting others to accept their position. They join in group activity joyfully to ensure the goal is reached. ENFJs are committed to helping others maximize their potential and communicate this with passion to those who choose to follow them. ENFJs prefer the orderly life but, if their personal needs interfere, they will seek a way to accommodate those needs. When ENFJs experience stress, they may become overtly hard headed and find fault with others.

Loud leader ENTJs provide visible and vocal leadership, preferring order and a systematic roadmap for both short-term and long-term objectives. ENTJs trust in systematic plans to provide guidance as needed, and they tend to not be disturbed excessively by people problems. ENTJs tend to challenge others, leading to mutual learning. At times, this challenging aspect can be seen as overpowering. When ENTJs experience stress, they may become condescending to the point of arrogance, believing they had the plan but others could not implement it.

Having read these brief descriptions of the sixteen types, perhaps you have noted that one or two seem to represent your preferences and behaviors. Keep in mind that not all people have equal fit with respect to a Best-Fit Type, and more self-examination may well be required to arrive at Best-Fit Type even if a single type exists. For example, one of the coauthors has repeatedly identified as NTJ but is consistently evenly split on the E versus I preference. Also keep in mind that types refer to preferences and do not preclude people operating effectively outside their preferences. When they were Best-Fit Typed in the 1990s, the majority of faculty consisting mainly of senior military officers at the U.S. Marine Corps Command and Staff College were introverts despite their backgrounds as commanders and the requirement that they often lecture to large groups of other military officers. They had to behave effectively in a manner inconsistent with their preference for introversion because their jobs dictated that they do so.

One very beneficial aspect of studying one's own type, however, is that it sensitizes us more to the behavioral patterns associated with all other types. You might think of your Best-Fit Type as a passport that allows you to visit other types; but, after visiting, you eventually return to your own Best-Fit Type.

5.5. Using the Keirsey Temperament Sorter

Since leadership is often about the reconciliation of differences, personality differences expressed by type merit strong consideration. The **Keirsey Temperament Sorter** can be useful in this regard.[19] Keirsey takes a collection of elements in type, combines them such that similar behavioral patterns emerge, and provides a way to identify each collection. These elements are based upon what we say and do. **Communication** is divided into *concrete* and *abstract,* wherein concrete is about some aspect of reality and abstract relates to ideas. Keirsey divides **actions** into *utilitarian* and *cooperative,* wherein utilitarian is a *results-oriented perspective* and cooperative is a *process-oriented perspective.* The next step involves creating four combinations using communication and action: *concrete cooperators,* *abstract cooperators, concrete utilitarians,* and *abstract utilitarians.* With these in place, Keirsey then identifies the sixteen types into one of the four combinations into which Best-Fit assessments can be placed (see Figure 5.10).

A few general observations about the four general categories are appropriate prior to taking a more in-depth look at the sixteen types.

Guardians (concrete cooperators) are often the foundation of organizations, providing loyalty, responsibility, and continuity. Their leadership orientation is typically one of stability in an uncertain world. This orientation can be comforting to those followers needing stability and structure with a plan to get through the uncertainty, but it can be stressed when confronted with uncertainty requiring guardians to exhibit nonpreferred behaviors. Leadership intervention, along with support of others with different temperaments, may then be necessary to restore the guardian's sense of stability and self-confidence.

Figure 5.10. Keirsey Temperament Sorter with Leadership Elements

Concrete Cooperators **GUARDIANS**	Concrete Utilitarians **ARTISANS**
ESTJ supervisor ISTJ inspector ESFJ provider ISFJ protector	ESTP promoter ISTP crafter ESFP performer ISFP composer
Abstract Cooperators **IDEALISTS**	Abstract Utilitarians **RATIONALS**
ENFJ teacher INFJ counselor ENFP champion INFP healer	ENTJ field marshal INTJ master mind ENTP inventor INTP architect

Source: Adapted from www.keirsey.com.

For example, a guardian manager in a woodworking plant in the Midwest had provided excellent leadership and managerial skills for two decades. The guardian was a pillar of the community and well respected in the industry as well in the company. When a significant exogenous economic event destabilized the work environment, the guardian under great stress sought unsuccessfully to restore stability. In this process, the guardian lost self-confidence and asked to be replaced. The company's board of directors encouraged the guardian to more objectively assess the situation and determine places where control was possible. The guardian was then able to achieve some success by calling on others of different temperaments in the management team for assistance.

Artisans (concrete utilitarians) are adventure seeking, often providing rapid-response leadership in troubleshooting problems. These "firefighters" find leadership in crisis situations to be invigorating. Whether universally true or not, some maintain that if no crisis is immediately available artisans may create one. Artisans' eagerness to solve problems sometimes manifests itself in a reckless, ready-fire-aim manner.

For example, a manager in a multinational corporation had a reputation for often thriving in faraway and potentially dangerous locations to solve production problems. He worked in six countries over 13 years. While in attendance at an executive-development program for high performers, a senior executive asked him to go to yet another country to solve yet another problem. His response was without hesitation, "YES."

Idealists (abstract cooperators) provide friendly, supportive leadership in most situations. Idealists' leadership orientation is to help others self-actualize, and their approach is to soften the blows of adversity so that human potential may be achieved. Idealists are often the most inspira-

tional and authentic leaders in an organization. Once inspiration has occurred, however, idealists may need to call on nonpreferred behaviors and leaders with other temperaments to implement the ideal.

In one example of an idealist serving as a buffer, the idealist was placed on a research and development team of rationals in order to attempt to foster cooperation. At first, the rationals not only fought among themselves but fought the idealist as well. Over time, however, the idealist brought some smoothness to the team's interactions by causing the rationals to realize other rationals' ideas had merit.

Rationals (abstract utilitarians) are problem solvers and system builders, finding ways to solve problems and then to improve upon the solutions. With laser-like focus, rationals provide logical leadership, leaving little room for doubt and generation of alternative courses of action. Once a solution is designed, their leadership orientation is to move on to the next problem if possible. If there is no new problem to solve, rationals will focus upon implementing their solution for the last problem; however, rationals often need other temperaments to accomplish their visionary plans. At times, rationals left out of a planning process may resist buy-in as a result.

For example, a rational C-level executive in a large multinational company had, along with senior staff and consultants, created a 5-year strategic plan that substantially redirected resources. The program had specific resources assigned to it: people, pamphlets, brochures, website, and numerous reminders. Eighteen months into the 5-year plan, several rationals who had not participated in the design and rollout of the plan surprised the C-level executive by saying, "We are not convinced about the plan's efficacy, and we must be convinced to convincingly lead our subordinates."

5.6. The Sixteen Types as Leaders

Path-Goal Theory emphasizes leader/subordinate relationships in employing an appropriate style to fit subordinates' characteristics and work settings. Using type in conjunction with these styles can lead to insights for leading others in challenging situations. A deeper understanding of the sixteen types can provide insights into leadership styles because different types gravitate toward different leadership behaviors.[20]

ISTJs are sometimes referred to as *responsible executor* leaders who set direction by planning ahead with clear milestones leading to end goals. ISTJs inspire and mobilize by clear definitions of roles and also by being a role model. ISTJs are sometimes challenged in leadership roles because their desire to cling to the past results in attitudes expressed as, "We do not do things that way here," or "We tried that once and it didn't work." ISTJs also have a tendency to micromanage.

ISFJs are often referred to as *dedicated steward* leaders, setting direction by quietly assessing what is achievable and gaining people's trust for implementation of plans. ISFJs inspire and mobilize by their concern for others being integrated into planning to the point of possibly even modeling work–life balance. ISFJs are typically challenged in leadership roles by an excessive reliance on the goodness of people to implement. Their quietness in their approach to leadership may make them appear to be slow in making decisions.

Insightful motivator INFJs set direction by leveraging their internal value system in such a way as to show the benefits to others clearly and concisely. They inspire and mobilize others by offering a plan to achieve goals with passion and commitment that are operationalized mutually. Since conflict avoidance is a value of NFs, INFJs find it difficult to separate the personal from the professional. INFJs are typically challenged in leadership

situations in which conflict might help clear misunderstandings and provide needed direction.

INTJ *visionary strategist* leaders set direction by building a comprehensive system of subgoals, goals, and a metagoal so that the full picture is available to followers. INTJs inspire and mobilize others by clarifying the plan with ample evidence of why and how this vision will work. INTJs typically are challenged in leadership roles when they fail to communicate details that others need to accomplish the mission.

Nimble pragmatist ISTPs set direction quickly and efficiently and are willing to switch direction as more evidence becomes available. They inspire and mobilize with informality combined with flexibility. ISTPs are typically challenged in leadership roles when their flexibility is interpreted as a lack of decisiveness and their fast action results in some aspects of their problem solution being missed.

ISFP *practical custodian* leaders set direction by quickly integrating others' values with their own. They inspire and mobilize with people skills, helping others to achieve their optimal performance without getting in their way. ISFP-led teams tend to develop good cohesion. ISFPs are typically challenged in leadership roles when their values are unable to integrate with those of others and when directive leadership behavior is needed.

INFP *inspired crusaders* set direction with their excitement for helping people do what is right. They inspire and mobilize by rapidly reading other people's type behaviors and trusting others. INFPs are typically challenged in leadership roles where a definitive plan is needed with milestones in place. INFPs are also challenged in giving and receiving feedback, especially corrective and negative feedback.

INTP *expansive analyzers* set direction by identifying a causal chain of action to goal achievement. They inspire and mobilize by showing the sophistication of their solution and welcoming criticism to improve it. INTPs are typically challenged in leadership roles when their independence and detachment are not understood. This may result in some defensive posturing.

ESTP *dynamic maverick* leaders set direction logically and energetically in sometimes aggressive ways given the costs and benefits of a mission situation. They inspire and mobilize with their charismatic personality and resourcefulness to induce others to accomplish tasks. ESTPs are typically challenged in leadership roles when they move too fast for others to follow.

ESFP *enthusiastic improviser* leaders set direction rapidly and attempt to reach mutual agreement with others on ends/ways/means. ESFPs inspire and mobilize with their gregarious behaviors, including encouraging others, celebrating successes regularly, and generally having a good time. ESFPs are typically challenged in leadership roles where a greater degree of seriousness is required or a more visionary approach is expected.

Impassioned catalyst ENFPs set direction with a positive outlook to achieve stretch goals, including goals for people. ENFPs inspire and mobilize with their inherent concern for others and willingness to dialogue at both personal and professional levels. ENFPs are typically challenged in leadership roles when the followers require structure and accountability.

ENTP *innovative explorer* leaders set direction with their opportunistic approach, even to the point of viewing problems as opportunities. They inspire and mobilize others with their intense interest in seizing opportunities with their teams. ENTPs are typically challenged in leadership roles when teams need to be trusted to execute. ENTPs may also tend to explore other projects prior to completing a current one.

Efficient driver ESTJs set direction logically with clear and achievable goals and milestones. They inspire and mobilize using clarity to identify roles, resources, and requirements for implementation. ESTJs typically are challenged in leadership roles when new directions are needed or when others' needs are not the priority but others believe they should be.

ESFJ *committed builders* set direction by leveraging their values in helping others in a pragmatic way using detailed plans and milestones. ESFJs inspire and mobilize by encouraging others to build sustainable results that help people. They are typically challenged in leadership roles when questions are raised, in which case their responses may be defensive to the point of making personal criticisms of those asking questions.

ENFJs are *engaging mobilizer* leaders who set direction with their commitment to the organization and others by communicating the meaning of the overall work effort. They inspire and mobilize with authentic concern for others and a readiness to appreciate all contributions. In leadership roles they may overlook challenges and fail to take corrective actions.

ENTJ *strategic directors* set direction with decisiveness in facing situations and an ability to clarify each aspect of a project. They inspire and mobilize with their charisma and inherent enthusiasm. ENTJs typically are challenged in leadership roles when their charisma and enthusiasm overwhelm and even intimidate others.

5.7. Type Development, Leadership, and Emotional Intelligence

Current leadership conversations often include the terms **emotional intelligence** (EI) and **emotional competence**.[21] Irrespective of the exact expression, the associated abilities include the following:

1. Self-awareness: leaders know their strengths and opportunities for improvement, are aware of others' emotions, and understand the interaction of their emotions with those of others.

2. Self-managed: leaders have the humility to recognize others' contributions and to learn from mistakes.

3. Self-motivated: leaders are intrinsically motivated to succeed and persevere through difficulties.

EI is an indicator of courageous leadership. Behaviors involve activities wherein patterns are developed and practiced; by implication EI may also be developed.[22] Once their Best-Fit Type is assessed, leaders can begin the path to EI through an understanding of how the components of type function together. Individuals use these components with differing intensities, frequencies, and competencies. Self-awareness involves using the less preferred and less used behaviors in a competent way. Jung referred to this phenomenon as using less preferred functions in a differentiated manner. **Differentiation** in human behavior suggests that the person has sufficient understanding of self to grasp the effort needed to gain expertise in the less preferred behaviors.

In some ways type development mirrors current discussions about developmental leadership from Level 1 to Level 5.[23] **Level-5 leadership** is built on the premise of building from individual talent to team member, member to manager, manager to leader, leader to executive with two key elements: humility and will.[24] Gaining competence in the various components of type is critical in understanding ourselves and others as we move toward a degree of EI. Just as Level-5 leaders seek to go beyond the other levels to lead others by gaining confidence and trust in themselves so that their humility and will are properly used, courageous leaders seek to understand the more complex nuances of type through type development.

Type development begins with the idea that humans have E, I, S, N, T, F, J, and P mental processes available at all times. Early in life, each process is used, tested, and reused. Accepted patterns are built in a manner analogous to building muscle memory except that practice does not make perfect. In type development, practice makes **preferred**.[25] As the preferred processes are practiced, greater facility, comfort, and confidence are gained. An analogy would be signing one's name with the usual hand and then signing with the other hand. Few if any people are equally competent with both hands. The same idea applies to each of the eight components of type. A signature exercise usually generates comments such as those in Figure 5.11.

The preferred hand column is the **GREEN** zone for **GO**; the nonpreferred hand column is the **RED** zone for **STOP** and **THINK**. This exercise

Figure 5.11. Hand-Exercise Descriptions

Preferred Hand	Nonpreferred Hand
Easy	Difficult
Fluid	Awkward
Comfortable	Uncomfortable
Did not need to think	Had to think a lot
Could do this all day!	Exhausting—would not last long doing this

Figure 5.12. Determining the Ordering of Preferred Behaviors for an INTJ

The introverts let you only see the second preferred way of gathering information or making decisions

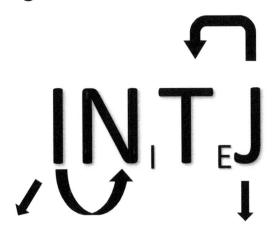

The **J** point towards the judging function **T**.

Because this type prefers introversion, the dominant function is intuitive perception, and it is introverted.

Orientation towards the outer world.

> **The Dominant is Introverted Intuition (N$_I$).**
>
> **The Auxiliary is Extraverted Thinking (T$_E$).**
>
> **The Tertiary is Feeling.**
>
> **The Inferior is Extraverted Sensing (S$_E$).**

helps illustrate how type development emerges from practice. The most preferred process with practice becomes the *dominant function.*[26] For example, the dominant function might be introverted intuition. Because of the trust, competence, and comfort in the dominant function, it forms the core of people's behaviors. The dominant function acts as a compass for many behaviors and decisions. The second most preferred function becomes the *auxiliary function,* which functions in the opposite way from the dominant. The auxiliary function acts as second-in-com-

mand to help balance behaviors and decisions. For example, if the dominant function is introverted intuition, then the auxiliary will be extraverted thinking. The third most preferred function is called the *tertiary function* and is the opposite of the auxiliary. So, if the auxiliary is introverted intuition, the tertiary is feeling. The fourth most preferred function is called the *inferior function* simply because it is least preferred. The inferior function is opposite of the dominant. For example, if the dominant function is introverted intuition, then the inferior function is extraverted sensing. Although a bit complex, the key point is that these preferred functions assume a hierarchy that forms the basis of type development with links to EI. Figure 5.12 illustrates this process for an INTJ.

Examination of Figure 5.12 offers insight into a challenge facing INTJ-type leaders in extraverting their thinking while keeping their most preferred, most practiced, and most proficient function, intuition, in their internal world. Stated differently, INTJs tend to internally form an intuitive view of complexities that are then burst on the world in the form of a logical conclusion—logical at least to the INTJs but not necessarily to others who are not privy to the INTJs' intuition and thought process. Consequently, for INTJs to practice courageous leadership and EI, they need to develop their awareness of others' preferences and emotions; otherwise, their inner model clarity (to the INTJs) becomes a stubborn insistence on having their way. To accomplish this, INTJs must engage their less preferred functions. This requires personal courage, as the tertiary and inferior functions are feeling and sensing. Specifically, EI improvements include being more empathetic, more supportive of others' needs, and more cooperative in information sharing—indeed, the nonpreferred red zone for an INTJ.

Figure 5.13 illustrates this same process with another type, an ESFP. The hierarchy is exactly the opposite of the INTJ. In other words, both types have developed worldviews with opposite perspectives. What this likely means is that their communications and interactions will require continual effort to clarify their views to each other. This provides insight into the challenges facing ESFP-type leaders when dealing with INTJs. These two type-interacting-with-type comparisons illustrate the use of EI as a product of type in better understanding the challenges of very different types interacting with one another and how these challenges might be met. Some reasons leaders derail

from a career perspective are difficulty in adapting to change and interpersonal relations issues.

The key elements of EI—empathy, energy, social competence, acceptance of others, convincing skills, and helping others—fit nicely into the framework of courageous leadership. As one author notes, "managers who don't feel a responsibility to others, can't handle stress, are unaware of their own emotions, lack the ability to understand others, or erupt into others are easily viewed as likely to derail due to problems with other people . . . Self-Awareness is key to leadership development."[27]

5.8. Anecdotal Examples of How Type Affects Real-Life Decision Making

The following anecdotes are exemplary of how type plays out in real-life settings. The first anecdote involves career change. Consider the case of a successful cost accountant with 16 years of experience working for an industrial products manufacturer. After exposure to MBTI, the accountant first noted parallels to the accounting equation in its simplicity yet complexity. As the accountant gained more experience with MBTI, he realized why he was growing less pleased with his accounting work and liked being chosen to explain the cost accounting elements to nonfinancial personnel. In time, he requested a move to the HR department with specific assignments in training others. During his first 2 years in the HR department, he became MBTI qualified so he could teach using MBTI materials. It was no surprise that his Best-Fit Type was ISFJ. This story suggests that, as people assess themselves more completely, they may find the need to clarify personal goals—even to the point of switching jobs, careers, or companies.

Consider a conflict-resolution situation in which sales growth was at issue. The executive was a hard-charging, no-nonsense INTJ, and the

Figure 5.13. Determining the Ordering of Preferred Behaviors for an ESFP

The extraverts display their most preferred way of gathering information or making decisions

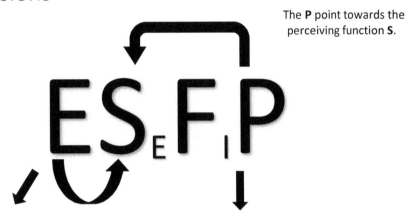

The **P** point towards the perceiving function **S**.

Because this type prefers extraversion, sensing perception used in the external world is the dominant function.

Orientation towards the outer world.

> **The Dominant is Extraverted Sensing (S$_E$).**
>
> **The Auxiliary is Introverted Feeling (F$_I$).**
>
> **The Tertiary is Thinking.**
>
> **The inferior is Introverted Intuition (N$_I$).**

sales leader an ESFP. Neither recognized the other's personality as a factor in their conversations—which were in reality monologues going by each other. Years later after the two became exposed to MBTI with different employers, they reminisced about their inability to grow sales with their previous employer. The INTJ noted a better approach to the sales leader would have been to ask, "What can I do to help you increase sales?" Instead of asking that, the INTJ continuously exerted more pressure on the ESFP to grow sales. For his part, the ESFP noted that he had not listened carefully to the INTJ because, since his preference was to talk rather than listen, he was preoccupied with his beliefs about why sales could not be increased. As we understand our own personality more completely, we may find the need to contemplate the effects of type on ourselves and others. This is not to suggest that type explains everything but that type helps where used properly.

Next, consider how a given type can influence a career decision. In this anecdote a high-performance, high-potential manager made a summary judgment about a potential employer based upon interactions with two interviewers from one prospective employer, choosing another employer instead. His decision was based upon his assessment that the two interviewers were too inflexible, and he extrapolated this assessment to the employer, assuming it, too, was inflexible. After exposure to MBTI, however, his perspective changed. He came to believe that he had possibly overstated the interviewers' inflexibility by not recognizing they were probably SJs and consequently rules oriented. He also thought that had he interviewed with other company representatives having different types his conclusion might have been different. By assessing ourselves and others more thoughtfully and completely, we may be less inclined to rush to judgment. This is a part of good type development and EI.

In another case a team leader was an introvert who had failed to understand the need for the team to discuss issues more than once in order to acquire a firm perspective. As a result of considering type, the team and its leader eventually understood that extraverts need to discuss ideas and plans more than once, even though this may seem wasteful to introverts. It also came as a surprise to the introverted team leader that the extraverted team members preferred for the leader to interact with them in informal ways, such as having coffee with them. This is illustrative of how self-assessment can reveal the danger of leaders implicitly assuming their own personality preferences are shared by subordinates.

Busy managers often rely on assistants to keep track of schedules and details, sometimes neglecting to take time to express appreciation. Typically, the Ts are objective and require little, if any, appreciation other than the job is done well. Fs are more subjective and want to feel appreciated. In one case during a second perfect performance review, an F-type assistant asked the T-type manager three times, "Do you appreciate

what I do?" Despite the manager's affirmative responses, the assistant asked a fourth time with tears in her eyes! From that point on, the manager would write the code TY meaning thank you at the bottom of her work. After several months, the T manager asked, "Does my doing this seem trite to you?" The assistant responded, "No, I love hearing those words." As leaders gain understanding of themselves and others through assessment, they become more aware of opportunities to leverage knowledge of type and, often with minimal effort, foster greater job satisfaction in their followers.

Sometimes without realizing the extent of their differences, leaders of different types may have diametrically opposing perspectives despite having the same facts. For example, in a graduate program approximately ninety students are exposed to a luncheon involving a panel of senior professionals providing an overview of the factors they believe led to career success, followed by several minutes of questions. The INTJ was reasonably satisfied with the results and wanted to improve the question preparation. The ENTJ was dissatisfied and preferred to cancel the lunch panel. The E argument was that there were too few questions and the question quality was lacking. The E maintained that the questions had to be forced out of the students and that sometimes the students' questions did not fill the time allotted. The I argued that the questions asked were only indicative of the tip of the iceberg of possible questions, recognizing the challenge that introverts have in asking questions immediately. This is illustrative of Type Talk—that is, each person perceiving facts through his or her own type.

Sometimes type differences are mistaken for gender and cultural stereotypes. Consider the case of a German male ESTP and a French female ISTJ driving from their home in Germany through France on a holiday trip to Spain. The ISTJ had meticulously scheduled the trip and was driving. The German male saw a sign showing Florence, Italy, and a variety of attractions that enticed him, so he suggested a change in plans. The resulting discussion was intense, personal, and indicative of Type Talk. The J preferred well-thought-out schedules, while the P preferred not to be relegated to a fixed schedule. Because the partners were alert to type differences, they were able to reach a compromise whereby the return trip was modified to accommodate an excursion to Florence. This story is exemplary of how type knowledge can be used to remedy disagreements arising in everyday communications.

5.9. Some Final Comments and Caveats

Best-Fit Type can be a powerful tool assisting leaders in such tasks as selecting members of task groups, resolving conflicts among employees, and better understanding their own and employees' behaviors under varying conditions. Like all tools, however, type knowledge has its limitations. At a general level, human beings are complex, and knowledge of personality preference does not explain all beliefs and behaviors. Moreover, MBTI requires effort to implement effectively, and it may become tempting to leave the tool in the tool shed, forgetting its power. At the other end of the spectrum, in an ends/ways/means sense MBTI is a way, not an end. It is possible to become so enamored with your tool that you forget that it is only a tool and that it has limitations.

Recall that in chapter 1 we began with a prioritization of concerns for courageous leaders. The welfare of the pack comes first, followed by that of other members of the pack, and with the leader being concerned for him- or herself last. There are times when accomplishing the organizational mission must override excessive leadership sensitivity to type preferences when those preferences are manifesting themselves in behaviors contradictory to mission accomplishment. Type should therefore be considered just one tool—albeit a

powerful one—that guides leaders to engendering more effective organizations and higher-performing and more-satisfied employees, not a fixation.

At a more specific level, leaders should keep in mind certain specific attributes of Best-Fit Type:

1. Knowing your type should not lock you into a behavioral box but rather provide confidence emanating from knowing yourself that assists in self-development.

2. All types have great potential value in organizations. Each type has excellence possibilities.

3. Each type is unique, and each person within each type is unique. Thus, a given INTJ may bear strong semblance to some INTJs but some dissimilarity to others.

4. In the end, each person needs to work toward confirming his or her own Best-Fit Type. No leader can know a subordinate the way the subordinates know themselves.

5. Leaders should be aware of type biases. A certain Best-Fit Type leader many feel more positive toward certain other types and more negative toward others. Properly used, type should guide leaders to overcome these biases rather than perpetuate them.

6. Type clarification is just one step toward excellence, and a clarity of preference does not automatically suggest excellence in type behaviors.

7. Properly used, type opens doors instead of closing them. People are capable of operating effectively outside their preferences. Accordingly, from a leadership perspective type should not be used to exclude employees from opportunities but rather

to better understand and guide their actions and reactions.

8. Type is learned first for yourself to enhance your own relationships, then applied to others.

This chapter represents only a cursory exposure to MBTI and its usefulness in leadership. We have barely touched the tip of the type iceberg. Our intent has been to create awareness of the tool and explore its utility further. There is a vast array of materials regarding type and its impact on individuals, teams, learning, organizations, selling, conflict resolution, coaching, careers, change, project management, leadership, innovation, decision making, communication, EI, reintegration, and navigating midlife.[28] In each of these topics, knowledge of Best-Fit Type allows leaders to further their journey along the path to becoming courageous leaders.

CHAPTER 6

Business Ethics: The Organization's Inner Self

> **"I do not love for silver, I do not love for gold.
> My heart is mine to give away, it never will be sold."**
>
> —Glenn Yarbrough, "Baby the Rain Must Fall"

When you read the above quote, did you say to yourself, "Yeah, that's me all right. I would never sell out for money. I'm my own person." If so, consider what distinguished jurist, legal theoretician, and economist Richard Posner has written:

> People systematically misrepresent their motivations to themselves. Almost everyone pretends to himself that he is less concerned with money and status, less selfish, more courageous, more ethical, than he actually is.[1]

Our former colleague and accomplished law and ethics professor Mike Metzger sometimes encountered students in his MBA ethics course who would ask, "Why do I need to take a course in ethics? I'm a good person." If Posner is correct—and if we are capable of a modicum of honest self-examination—most of us will come to the conclusion that the temptation is frequently there to place personal advantage over righteous moral action. Ask yourself, "Would I murder someone?" If you're not a sociopath, your response is likely to be, "Of course not." Rephrase that question in the following manner, however: "Would I murder someone who is out to murder my family if I knew for sure I could get away with it?" Now, despite the illegality of the preemptive act of murder on your part, you may begin to ask yourself questions such as,

"Can't law enforcement prevent him from murdering my family?" "If not, are you sure I won't be caught if I kill him before he murders?" Next may follow rationalizing statements such as, "After all, this is his fault, not mine. He's the murderer, not me. I didn't ask for this problem. It's really self-defense for my family on my part, not murder."

The point is simply this: given the right set of circumstances, many who otherwise abhor violence might consider preemptively killing someone—even if it's illegal—in order to protect those whom they love and call it self-defense. This calls to mind an old joke. A man asks a woman if she will engage in a sex act for a million dollars. She thinks about it, weighing her morality against the prospect of obtaining such an egregious sum for an immoral act lasting only a few minutes, and finally says yes. He then asks her if she would do the same thing for $20. Indignantly she responds, "Of course not! What do you think I am, a prostitute?" To which the man replies, "We have already established that. Now we are merely trying to arrive at a price." Some philosophers have argued everyone has a price at which they will violate their moral principles. Do you believe that? The answer to this question is more complex than perhaps it seems, and one we'll explore in a subsequent section of this chapter. However, we should be continually wary that once we have decided there is a price at

> **"Truth and moral identity are linked. As self-deception feeds on itself, there is less and less to stop beliefs about one's moral identity becoming systematically false. The growth of such a system is a personal moral disaster."**
>
> —Jonathan Glover, *Humanity: A Moral History of the Twentieth Century*, as cited by Michael B. Metzger, *Ethical Responsibilities of Managers* (L533 course notes), Spring 2008, Indiana University, Bloomington, p. 47

which we are willing to violate our moral principles for the sake of expediency or reward, the question becomes the price point at which that can occur.

That leads us to another point. When we take a high-minded, self-righteous position regarding our own moral superiority, we are perhaps in the most danger of succumbing to ethical fallibility because we assume ourselves to be invulnerable. When we think ourselves above temptation we may well succumb to it, not even realizing we are rationalizing away our weaknesses, because we are insensitive to our own thought processes. As with entertaining rationalizing thoughts about the morality of committing a preemptive murder to protect our loved ones from someone intent on harming them before he can attempt to act, it is all too easy to allow the issues of ethical traps such as relativist thinking to enter our thought processes when confronted by difficult ethical dilemmas.

This is true in our professional lives as well as in our personal lives. Consider the following situation. You work for a large company that is doing business in a country in which bribery is an accepted way of getting business. You watch as your company repeatedly loses business to companies headquartered in other developed countries that do not have laws such as the Foreign Corrupt

Practices Act, which makes bribes to obtain business illegal. You are under extreme pressure from your boss back in the United States to increase business. When you raise the issue with him you get the distinct impression that he could care less how you meet your sales targets as long as you do it. Paraphrasing from *Tales of Hoffman,* he uses one of his favorite expressions, "The world cares not what storms you encountered, but did you bring in the ship?" He then adds, "We sent you over there to do a job. If you can't do it, just say so, and we'll get someone who can."

How would you respond in the above situation? Would you become a whistle-blower and report your boss? Perhaps you recall that the last incidence of whistle-blowing in the firm did not go well for the whistle-blower. The company denied her allegations, and she was demoted and placed in a job with no future. She ultimately resigned in frustration and filed a lawsuit that has been pending in the courts for several years. You heard that she has exhausted her personal resources paying legal fees, and the case is nowhere near a final decision. Would you resign and not report your boss? Might you worry about the recommendation you would receive from the company when you attempt to obtain another job? Would you ask to be transferred, knowing that you will likely experience the same initial fate as the whistle-blower—demotion to a no-future job? Would you engage in bribing foreign officials, telling yourself this is, after all, the company's fault, not yours, and who will know anyway? Would you quietly go looking for another job but not report your boss's attempts to seduce you into engaging in corrupt practices, knowing that proof of your boss's behavior would be very difficult if not impossible to provide?

You know your boss is on bad moral and legal ground, but you can't really prove it. If you take a vocal stand, your career may suffer extensive damage. Your family will suffer if you don't bring home a paycheck. American politician and minister J. C. Watts once said, "Character is doing the right thing when nobody's looking. There are too many people who think that the only thing that's right is to get by, and the only thing that's wrong is to get caught." But often people are looking, and some of them may want you to do the wrong thing. Where did you go wrong in the above situation? Was it when you first observed how your employer treated the whistle-blower, suspected that your company had a bad ethical culture, but didn't seek other employment? Did you tell yourself at the time you didn't know whether the whistle-blower was telling the truth or just a disgruntled employee seeking retribution? Was your decision to stay influenced by the fact that you had been with the company for 25 years and were only 5 years from being able to retire? Suddenly, an ethical dilemma does not seem so clear-cut anymore.

There are ethical gray areas in business that defy easy resolution. Finding your way through such moral mazes takes more than just a personal belief that you are a moral person. It takes self-understanding, an ability to think your way through the maze, and the courage to act. It is too easy for unacknowledged cowardice to lead people to characterize difficult and potentially costly situations as ones in which they are powerless to act and therefore have no responsibility to do so.[2] This is why we devote a chapter to values and ethics—not that we will be able to do the topic justice, but rather that we hope to create an awareness of your need to know yourself and your values and to anticipate early on when events are drifting in the wrong direction—and, when possible, to be able to deftly maneuver so as to stay on the moral high ground while not destroying your career. If you are in a leadership position, your responsibilities go even further. As a courageous leader, you should be capable of nurturing an ethical environment inside your organization and be able to spot evidence of ethical problems early on and fix them before they explode into something really ugly.

> **"We do not go to work only to earn an income, but to find meaning in our lives. What we do is a large part of what we are."**
>
> —Alan Ryan (quoted in *If Aristotle Ran General Motors*, by Tom Morris)

One caveat is in order, however. Sometimes you may not always be able to anticipate and maneuver deftly to forestall ethical problems. Then you may find yourself needing to take a strong, open stand for what is morally right, but which is more problematic, knowing the right thing or doing the right thing? At those moments will you have the courage to do the difficult right thing instead of the easy wrong thing and persevere in this course of action when things get rough? And if the answer is no and you succumb to temptation, what will you see when you look at yourself in the mirror? If you take that difficult right path you can expect pain. At what may well be a strategic inflection point in your life where your choice will send you down the right or wrong path—a choice between temporary career pain versus slowly sliding down the slippery slope into a moral quagmire—you might take some solace in the words of the savior of Great Britain during World War II, Sir Winston Churchill: "You have enemies? Good. That means you have stood up for something, sometime in your life."[3]

6.1. Why Ethics in Business?

Some might ask why one should be so concerned about ethics in business. "After all, it's just business. We aren't talking about killing someone." Setting aside the fact that people have been killed because business leaders have failed to exercise sound moral decision making, there are a number of economic reasons—in addition to "it's the right thing to do"—that businesses and their leadership are well served by creating and nurturing a culture of ethical practices inside their organizations.[4]

Among these reasons are both protecting corporate assets and projecting a public image that encourages socially conscious consumers to buy the company's products.[5] Employees who subscribe to a code of ethical conduct are less likely to misappropriate corporate assets and overconsume perquisites. Also, ethical corporate conduct makes the organization less likely to become a defendant in lawsuits.[6] Corporate social responsibility enhances a firm's image in the eyes of the public and makes it less likely that it will experience adverse publicity and boycotts that adversely affect the top line. Despite these and other benefits we'll discuss in a moment, if you take ethics seriously it makes claims on you because your pursuit of worldly success may be impeded by paying a worldly price for taking an ethical stand. This price

"People slide by degrees into doing things they would not do if given a clear choice at the beginning. Each of the early stages may seem too small to count, but later anxiety about the moral boundary may only suggest the uncomfortable thought that it has already been passed."

—Jonathan Glover, Humanity: *A Moral History of the Twentieth Century*, as cited by Michael B. Metzger, *Ethical Responsibilities of Managers* (L533 course notes), Spring 2008, Indiana University, Bloomington, p. 59

is one of the reasons that unethical behavior passes for normal in many businesses.[7]

One would be tempted to believe that the foregoing two reasons would be sufficient to compel businesses to be ethical, but apparently this is far from the case. The *Wall Street Journal* once compiled a list of nineteen large companies whose business practices had been recently questioned. Eighteen of the nineteen companies had experienced precipitous stock-price declines following revelation of their misdeeds. Moreover, it is not as though these companies should not have been forewarned by precedent. Previous decades had evinced numerous instances of companies having suffered similar fates.[8] Because neither financial nor reputational incentives with their adverse economic consequences were sufficient to prevent serious ethical lapses in these companies, perhaps we need to look deeper into why ethics are so important in business.

Take, for example, the well-known case of Enron, a business that began as a natural gas pipeline company and grew to become the nation's seventh-largest publicly held corporation. Enron ultimately collapsed due to unethical practices, bringing down with it one of the largest public accounting firms in the world, Arthur Andersen, Enron's auditor. The influence of unethical practices in companies often radiates toxically far beyond corporate boundaries.[9] When Enron collapsed many people suffered, including its own innocent employees who lost their jobs and pensions, its shareholders, and pension funds that had invested in Enron stock. But the fallout from Enron's sorry debacle did not end there. Because of a small number of Arthur Andersen personnel who were complicit in covering up Enron's unethical business practices and attempted to cover up their own involvement as well, many partners and employees of what had once been one of the most highly regarded firms in the world also lost their jobs, partnership equity, and retirement dreams. Although some top executives at Enron suffered criminal prosecution, sadly the situation was not exactly an anomaly. Those prosecutions had been preceded by similar ones at companies such as Adelphia Communications, Tyco International, and WorldCom. Consequently, the cost of unethical practices goes well beyond those responsible and extends to society as well. A myopic focus on earnings that leads to financial manipulations in attempts to deceive the equity markets has to be balanced against a much larger constituency outside the company.[10]

Some of the benefits of running businesses ethically are less obvious than the financial impact of protecting corporate assets and avoiding adverse economic consequences from a bad reputation. One of the major benefits is that having a sound ethical culture reduces the requirement for costly policies and regulations designed to prevent unethical behaviors. Such behaviors seem to inevitably lead to a codification of permissible and impermissible workplace behaviors designed to prevent bad behavior and also to protect bosses from blame when something goes wrong. When violations then occur, bosses can say that rules were already in place proscribing the behaviors.[11] The problem with the proliferation of detailed codes of conduct is at least twofold. One, such excessive proscription inhibits often needed latitude of discretion and, concurrently, innovation. Creative employees who feel they must always check with some written authority before acting eventually grow weary and either fail to act or find a workplace environment more to their liking. Two, as mountains of codification pile higher and higher, eventually they collapse under their own weight as employees stop paying attention to them because of the impracticality of checking every action. All the policy manuals in the world won't help prevent unethical behaviors if they go unread because the volume of reading is simply too cumbersome to be of practical force. It is far better to cultivate an environment in which employees have an intuitive sense of permissible and impermissible behaviors than to rely upon volumes of regulations.[12]

Too often, honesty and decency get lost during business dealings. It takes constant vigilance by leaders at both the personal and organizational levels to maintain a culture of ethical conduct.

> **"Cowardice asks the question, 'Is it safe?' Expediency asks the question, 'Is it politic?' Vanity asks the question, 'Is it popular?' But conscience must ask the question, 'Is it right?'"**
>
> —Martin Luther King, Jr.

But business ethics don't just involve integrity in a company's financial transactions. Unethical nonfinancial behaviors in organizations can have a decidedly deleterious effect on employee productivity, teamwork, morale, and retention.[13] Unethical practices come in many varieties, large and small. Consider the following examples:

1. Married co-workers engage in sexual affairs with one another, but one of their spouses discovers this infidelity and begins making accusations that disrupt the workplace.

2. Bosses consistently say they will attend training and then fail to show, always citing some excuse about being too busy. Eventually employees pick up on this poor leadership example, and training suffers.

3. A boss has a relationship with an employee outside work and shows favoritism toward that employee as a result.

4. Employees take office supplies home for their kids to use at school.

5. Employees spend hours each day surfing the Internet for shopping bargains, taking personal phone calls, and exchanging e-mails with friends using their company e-mail accounts.

6. Employees claim credit for the work of other employees.

7. Employees take part in malicious and destructive gossip about other employees.

8. Sales personnel misrepresent their position with the company in order to sound more important to prospective clients, and then they say the client must have misunderstood when their misrepresentation is discovered.

9. Sales personnel misrepresent the company's products to gain sales.[14]

> **"The question of what sort of person you want to be is central to the argument given by Socrates against the view that it is in our interest to seem moral but not to be moral."**
>
> —Jonathan Glover, Humanity: *A Moral History of the Twentieth Century*, as cited by Michael B. Metzger, *Ethical Responsibilities of Managers* (L533 course notes), Spring 2008, Indiana University, Bloomington, p. 59

The foregoing list is by no means all inclusive. Business ethics reflects the philosophy of how a company does business and, as such, touches upon many aspects of the company, including the rights and duties between the organization and its members, suppliers, customers, shareholders, and society.[15] Fairness in employment practices, trade practices, contracting, tax payments, avoidance of insider trading and illicit sales transactions, and safety and concern for users of products and services are just some organizational activities with ethical implications.[16] This expansive scope is suggestive of the depths of complexity associated with business ethics. Far more than good intentions are needed for leaders to be able to deal effectively with this complexity. Consequently, we now examine some of the foundations of ethical practices in the following section.

6.2. Foundations of Ethics

"Ethical leadership is leading by knowing and doing what is right. The problem with ethical leadership is that it is difficult to define 'right.'"[17] As this quote suggests and as noted previously, ethical dilemmas are not always black and white, and their complexities can lead to consternation about how best to handle them.[18] Leaders must sometimes choose among options that vary in terms of their ethical implications, sometimes due to competing priorities. A starting point for leaders wanting to prepare themselves to deal with ethical complexities is to have a sound grounding in the foundations of ethics. The underlying principles of ethics have been part of human reasoning for thousands of years because ethical practice is fundamental to human beings' relations with one another.[19] Despite this long history and the importance of ethics to human well-being, it is often surprising how few people can articulate even the most basic forms of ethical reasoning, much less the ethical traps into which humans can so easily fall. Although we cannot begin to do this topic justice in one section, hopefully we can establish a basic framework based upon some philosophical underpinnings and provide a starting point for further study.

The word "ethics" in English can have different meanings, ranging from philosophical to concerns about moral behavior to an individual's values. This, in part, results from the fact that there are four major areas of ethics study: **meta-ethics** is concerned with moral propositions, what they mean, and how one determines their truth. Meta-ethics deals with the fundamentals of what we mean by good and bad moral behavior. It can be divided into *cognitivism* (right or wrong is a matter of fact) and *noncognitivism* (right or wrong is a matter of opinion). **Descriptive ethics** compares different beliefs about ethics. It examines the way in which people behave and draws conclusions based upon patterns of behavior. **Normative ethics** pertains to how one goes about determining a moral course of action. What questions arise when faced with a given ethical dilemma is the ground of normative ethics. **Applied ethics** uses ethical theory to determine what one should do in a given situation with ethical implications. It attempts to apply ethics to real-world situations such as business ethics, healthcare ethics, and so forth.[20] Although most leaders might intuitively gravitate toward normative and applied ethics as a practical matter, all four categories in varying degrees may be of value to business leaders to the extent they inform one another. Nonetheless, due to paucity of space, it is primarily normative and applied ethics to which we devote our attention in this section.

One branch of normative ethics is **virtue ethics**, that of the early Greek philosophers. In keeping with the emphasis of the Greeks of that time on the acquisition of knowledge, knowledge of self enjoys a primacy in this branch that focuses on the human condition. Self-realization in accordance with one's natural attributes leads to happiness, the ultimate goal. Man is not supposed to just live but to live well. In this mindset, "virtue denotes doing the right thing, to the right person, at the right time, to the proper extent, in the correct fashion, for the right reason," a lofty, but obviously very difficult, standard to meet.[21] Nonetheless, despite its impracticality, it is difficult to argue with that particular set of criteria, assuming one can discern what constitutes "right" in each criterion.

Stoicism is perhaps slightly less idealistic in that it trumpets contentment and security through a mental equilibrium achieved by self-mastery of one's emotions and desires as the ultimate goal. Despite this somewhat more self-serving philosophy in comparison to virtue ethics, stoicism has its positive points. To a stoic, one should not become upset about something one cannot change. Difficult problems should be embraced because they lead to a healthier spirit, and resisting temptation is deemed a personal triumph to a stoic.[22]

Hedonism is an even farther step away from virtue ethics in terms of placing others over self, positing that humans' primary goal should be avoiding pain and maximizing pleasure. There is some variance among hedonists as to how far this mandate should be taken to include its pursuit even at the expense of others. One might postulate that the senior officers of corporations that are the object of scandals might have embraced extreme forms of hedonism. While embracing hedonism, however, the *Epicureans* rejected such extremism, advocating moderation and prudence in one's behavior. [23]

Consequentialism, often referred to as an *ends-justifies-the-means* philosophy, argues for basic possessions such as shelter and clothing in the belief that violence and discord might be avoided if people have sufficient amounts of wealth. Consequentialists believe in a cycle in which wealth produces more people and more people produce more wealth.[24] Although some might justifiably reject the end-justifies-the-means approach, the notion of all members becoming wealthier and thereby resulting in improved overall relations may have efficacy in some situations. This might be analogous to what are often called "win-win" situations in business. *Utilitarians,* consequentialists by nature, form yet another branch of the normative school. They argue that the best course of action is one that results in the greatest good, with "greatest good" defined in various ways, such as general welfare and personal happiness. Some utilitarians, such as John Stuart Mill, posit a hierarchy of pleasures in which some are more highly valued than others.[25]

Deontology posits virtue as stemming from adherence to rules and responsibilities to which humans should strive to adhere and fulfill. Deontology is often contrasted with consequentialism because under deontology a course of action might be the right one even if the result is bad.[26] For example, suppose police have captured a terrorist who has placed a bomb on one of 500 school buses in a major city, but the terrorist refuses to say which bus, only that the bomb will go off in minutes. There is no time to track down all the buses currently carrying school children and evacuate them. It is therefore imperative that the terrorist disclose which bus the bomb is on or many innocent children will die. A consequentialist would likely say that torturing the terrorist in an effort to extract the answer is justified to save the lives of the children. A deontologist would likely argue that saving the lives of the children does not justify resorting to an illegal and immoral course of action to rectify another illegal and immoral course of action. Incidentally, into which camp would you fall? Would your answer change if you knew for certain that your child was or was not on a bus?

As its name suggests, applied ethics extends theories of ethics to real-world settings such as business, medicine, government, and law. In such settings the right answer is sometimes difficult to discern.[27] For example, should a criminal defense attorney charged with providing the best defense possible for a client he or she knows is guilty file spurious motions solely in the hope that the prosecution will make a procedural error such that there are grounds for appeal if the client is found guilty at trial? Such a practice was once advocat-

"Count it the greatest sin to prefer mere existence to honor, and for the sake of life to lose the reason for living."

—Juvenal, 60–130 AD

ed by the criminal law professor of one of the co-authors. If he or she fails to act in this manner, is the defense attorney not providing the best possible defense and therefore failing the client? Or is he or she attempting to game the system in unethical ways? Would a consequentialist view this differently than a deontologist, and how?

Business ethics is a professional application of ethics theory, both normative and sometimes descriptive, as with academic studies. It is primarily normative from a practitioner perspective, with the purpose of deterring errant corporate and employee behaviors.[28] Unfortunately, concern for the adverse consequences of a failure on the part of companies and their employees to act ethically often surpasses practitioners' understanding of what "ethically" means. "Unethical," like "unjust," is a word most people carelessly throw around but can't define. When you ask, "Why is that unethical, you get a blank look and a response like 'because it is.'"[29] Perhaps one reason is that people are often confused in today's world about where they stand personally on important moral issues. In essence they are asking, "Who should I be?" but often there is no sustained reflection on that question. Many have never stopped to examine how their basic beliefs regarding right and wrong hold up as they wander the moral mazes of the business world—the subject of the next section.

6.3. Values, Morality, Ethics—and the Relativism Trap

"Values," "morality," and "ethics" are words sometimes used interchangeably. What exactly does each word mean? Although some might be inclined to make semantic distinctions, when one examines various definitions the three words are often used to define one another. **Values** are important and lasting beliefs about what is right and wrong, that is, morality. **Morality** is accepted standards based upon values defining right and wrong, and **ethics** is a system of moral principles. Therefore, any semantic distinctions aside, obviously the three are inextricably entwined because each helps define and impacts upon the others.[30] Perhaps the more salient question for business leaders is whether bad personal values lead people to commit ethical violations or whether people with good values are somehow corrupted by immoral systems and practices inside their businesses or industry. In other words, do ethical problems result from bad people or bad cultures?

The answer would seemingly be both. Unethical or limitedly ethical leadership allows unethical cultures to grow, which in turn encourages unethical behaviors on the part of individuals experiencing the culture who lack the knowledge, understanding, and courage to resist engaging in those behaviors. In a world in which people's perceptions are often formed by 20-second sound bites containing half-truths and lacking factual context, it is easy to find someone purporting to be authoritative who supports our a priori position on some ethical issue. Even if one is sufficiently aware of the dangers of this frequently biased noise presented as information and has the intellectual appetite to search for deeper, more reflective truths, finding some apparently learned authority who supports a particular course of action is not difficult. Consider the following quotation:

> The reason why morality is such a confusing subject (even, or especially, in our universities) is because some key philosophers have led folks' thoughts away from what it really means to be moral. There are 4 main theories of morality which have surfaced in our culture due to the influences of these key philosophers: (1) An ethic based on building one's character via virtue—e.g., Aristotle's Nicomachean Ethics; (2) An ethic based on one's widest and highly-variable personal feelings; rather than an ethic based on any reasoning, per se—e.g., David Hume's noncognitive ethics; (3) An ethic based on the adoption of universal rules; rules that are never meant to be broken, regardless of specific consequences—e.g., Immanuel Kant's deontology; (4) An ethic based on a supposedly-defined "good" and on the supposedly-knowable and widest—i.e., individual and social; present and future—consequences (regarding this

supposedly-defined "good") of each of our chosen actions—e.g., Jeremy Bentham's utilitarianism. Depending on which moral view you currently adopt, morality can feel somewhat easy or it can be very, very hard—if not, impossible—to do. It can be something that makes you feel deeply satisfied with how your life is going on Earth; or something that makes you feel fatally ashamed of your own existence or being. Critical reflection on these issues reveals much insight to inform our moral evaluations.[31]

This author goes on to say the following: "Apparently, we had it 99% right the first time—with Aristotle—and we have mucked it up ever since (until Ayn Rand's thoughts emerged on the ethical scene). Upon a closer inspection of how it is that these 4 views can arise in one's mind in the first place, it is found that they arise from a selective focus."[32] Basically, the author is making an argument that the ancient Greek philosophers actually were correct, and that philosophers have subsequently served to confuse people by moving them away from Aristotle's belief that virtue is doing the right thing, to the right person, at the right time, to the proper extent, in the correct fashion, for the right reason. The point is that one need only look to academic "experts" to find support for some course of action.

"If relativism signifies contempt for fixed categories and men claim to be the bearers of an objective, immortal truth . . . then there is nothing more relativistic than Fascist attitudes and activity . . . From the fact that all ideologies are of equal value, that all ideologies are mere fictions, the modern relativist infers that everybody has the right to create for himself his own ideology and to attempt to enforce it with all the energy of which he is capable."

—Fascist dictator Benito Mussolini, *Diuturna* (1921)

Aristotle's standard is a very high one, as previously noted. Perhaps that is why human beings have subsequently searched for lower standards by rationalizing their cognitive dissonance problem of virtuous values in contradiction to desires for self-enrichment, power, and fame. We can embrace Hume's notion that if a practice is widely acknowledged as acceptable, then it is also ethical. Or, we can comfort ourselves by saying that rules are rules and never to be broken, but we are ethical as long as we comply with the rules. Or, we can take a utilitarian perspective and maintain that whatever does the most good for the most people is the right standard even if some people are harmed along the way.

The problem with the latter three approaches is that none works well in many situations. Consider, for example. a corporation that runs a mining operation in a third-world country with very low health and safety standards that result in low-paid workers sometimes becoming ill or even killed. The company's top leadership might argue that the company is only doing what other companies do all around the world and it must do as it does to be competitive. Or, it might argue that it is in compliance with the laws of the country in which it operates, and any deficiencies are therefore the fault of the host-nation government's rules. Or, it might argue that as a result of its operations thousands of workers have jobs they would otherwise not have and therefore, despite the issues of health and safety, the greater good is being served by feeding indigent peoples, pumping more money into the local economy, and raising the overall standard of living of the host nation.

Perhaps a second problem with embracing Aristotle's high standard for ethical conduct is that it requires considerable cognitive effort to determine the *right* thing, to the *right* person, at the *right* time, to the *right* extent, in the *right* fashion, for the *right* reason. One wrong is easier than six rights, especially if it can be easily rationalized. Caught up in the exigencies of the moment of running a business, it is easier to fall back on relativism, utilitarianism, or compliance with rules than to think our way through the moral mazes to come up with all those *rights.* Shortcuts are faster than following the longer race course, but in the end the semi-ethical runner who takes shortcuts has to live with the self-knowledge that whatever was gained in winning using shortcuts is greatly diminished *ex post* by the knowledge that people were harmed along the way.

What should business leaders therefore do to steel themselves against the temptations of succumbing to lower standards of ethical behavior? A starting point is to be aware of common cognitive traps that distort our thinking. One of these is **relativism**. Consider the following statement (now somewhat discredited) by anthropologist Ruth Benedict: "Morality differs in every society, and is a convenient term for socially approved habits."[33] If one were seeking a rationale for cannibalism, this statement might provide some comfort. In what is admittedly a bit (but a big bit) of an exaggeration, if it is acceptable in a cannibalistic society to kill humans for food, then as long as one finds oneself in that society, feel free to order up a shrunken head for dessert. The essence of the relativist argument consists of five tenets:

1. Different societies have different moral codes.

2. Ergo, there is no definite standard that can be used to decide the relative merits of a given code.

3. One society's moral code is one among many and has no special status.

4. What's right in that society is determined by that society's moral code.

5. We are guilty of arrogance when we judge other societies' moral codes.

Does this sound like a great way to rationalize the aforementioned mining corporation's unhealthy and unsafe working conditions because it happens to be located in a country where the standards are low? The problem with relativism does not stop there, however. Some relativists take this argument even further, to say, "If morality is just what my society thinks is right, who says my society is right?" Now, we are obviously on a very slippery slope, the bottom of which is, "I can do as I like because there is no definitive code of conduct." In *Is Reality Optional?* (1993), Thomas Sowell stated, "Much of the advancement of the human race has occurred because people made the judgment that some things were not simply different from others, but better."[34]

Relativism is a common technique for evading doing the difficult right thing and opting for the easy wrong thing. It essentially deconstructs the conditions of self-condemnation by undermining ethical standards using a strategy of arguing that the particular set of standards impeding a person

> **"Hire and promote first on the basis of integrity; second, motivation; third, capacity; fourth, understanding; fifth, knowledge; and last and least, experience. Without integrity, motivation is dangerous; without motivation, capacity is impotent; without capacity, understanding is limited; without understanding, knowledge is meaningless; without knowledge, experience is blind."**
>
> —Dee Hock (quoted in Tom Morris, *If Aristotle Ran General Motors*)

from doing what he or she wants is derived from a particular set of circumstances and not universal principle. This, in turn, implies that the authority of the impeding moral principle is limited and may not apply to the situation in question.[35] Relativism is one of the main ethical traps to which leaders should be attuned when listening to employees explaining their actual or proposed behaviors. It is illustrative of one of the many challenges leaders face in attempting to ensure ethical standards are met in their organizations. The following section discusses some of these challenges.

6.4. Applying Ethics as a Leader

A greater knowledge of business ethics does little good if leaders do not apply that knowledge effectively. This seemingly obvious truth can get lost in the complexities of businesses. In the previous section we mentioned the interrelationship between individual values and organizational ethics, each impacting upon the other. Obviously, hiring practices are of extreme importance in creating and maintaining an ethical culture inside organizations. Imagine the illogic of having an ethical organization staffed with unethical employees. George Herbert has said, "Associate not with evil men, lest you increase their number."[36] One of the coauthors states this less eloquently: "You can't keep rattlesnakes for pets. One toxic snake running loose in your house is all it takes to create chaos." A starting point for organizational ethics, then, is hiring ethical people. Consider the following anecdote experienced by one of the coauthors:

> The Department of Justice (DOJ) was suing a division of a large healthcare provider for violations of Medicare laws. Our firm was hired by DOJ to be consulting experts to the case. The healthcare provider had previously hired a new CEO prior to events that lead up to DOJ's lawsuit. As the case unfolded we learned that the CEO had been terminated by his previous employer for similar practices. To our amazement, the provider's board of directors not only had failed to perform an adequate due diligence prior to hiring the CEO but had subsequently failed to monitor his actions with regard to the practices that gave rise to the lawsuit. The board member who chaired the audit committee was completely unaware of her responsibilities as chairwoman of that committee as required by laws governing corporate governance.

As Thomas Ricks has said, organizations need to be truly relentless in focusing on people, "getting the right people into the right jobs and the wrong people out of them."[37] But what can be done to ensure hiring ethical employees besides performing the normal background and reference checks and due diligence that, given past employers' fears of being sued for defamation, may reveal little of people's inner nature except that they may not have been caught and successfully prosecuted? There are three questions to ask before hiring someone: (1) Is your hiring this person consistent with company guidelines and polices? If you are making an exception, can this be justified on ethical grounds? Although this might seem like an obvious consideration, it has been violated. This consideration may preclude you hiring someone as a favor to someone else. (2) Is it a win-win decision for the organization and the candidate? (3) Is it right? How do you feel about the fit? Does the candidate seem like someone who shares the same values as the organization? Consider the following real-world scenario.

A financial services company has rules against nepotism—that is, hiring members of the same immediate family such as spouses and children. Two outstanding employees decide to get married. Even though the employees did not work in the same unit, they were told by human resources that one would have to resign because of company policy. The couple appealed to the CEO for an exception to policy, but he refused. One was forced to find a job with a rival company, costing the organization an outstanding employee. A short time later the CEO had the nepotism rules changed, so that the company could hire his two sons, neither of whom was qualified on paper for the job to which he was hired. Many in the company were indignant, but there was little they could do.

What's the ethical message in the foregoing example? The message is that the CEO refused to waive the rules against nepotism to accommodate two excellent employees already working for the company who decided to marry, but he was quite willing to change the rules to accommodate members of his own family and attempted to justify doing so with a superficially weak intergenerational argument that fooled no one. This suggests that the CEO believed that rules applied to others but not to himself. Although he managed to get away with unethical practices in that position, his ethical problems caught up with him in his next and much higher position, from which he was forced to resign. Even worse, the unethical culture

> "When you dissect the research, the most important set of values to drive organizational commitment is clarity of personal values as opposed to organizational values. With personal values clarity, organizational values are, at best, memorized, not internalized. The more clear I am on my personal values, the more I can use them in my association with those of the organization."

fostered under the CEO brought external scrutiny and shame upon the financial services company he left behind.

People's values are their core beliefs, so these values are paramount in determining their starting point for viewing ethical issues.[38] If you simply ask someone to respond to the question, "Are you honest?" don't expect "No" for an answer. During the interview process, we recommend presenting applicants with various work scenarios having embedded ethical implications appropriate to the job level for which they are applying, asking how they would go about determining a course of action, what decision they would make, and their rationale for that decision. Can applicants spot the more obvious ethical issues and respond appropriately? Less obvious issues can be food for further exploration using questions such as, "Did you take a course in ethics in your program, and, if so, how would you apply what you learned to the issue in the previous scenario about the supposed whistle-blower?"

Despite the best filtering systems, employees with questionable ethics will likely still find their way into organizations sooner or later. Vigilance is therefore needed to spot ethical problems before

they can manifest themselves in disasters. Common ethical issues can be categorized into five general types: (1) human resources, (2) employee safety, (3) conflicts of interest, (4) customer confidence, and (5) misuse of corporate resources.[39] A starting point for preventing questionable ethical practices from manifesting themselves into destructive violations is developing vigilance guidelines for each category based upon the organization's code of ethics—the subject of the next section—if one exists. Even if the organization does not have a code of ethics, individual leaders can benefit by compiling their own list for each category of potential unethical practices and informing employees of the list's contents to help employees understand what are regarded as ethical violations. Here's one example of a partial list for misusing corporate resources:

Employees are cautioned against using company resources for personal use. The following guidelines are intended to help avoid this becoming a problem:

1. Organizational supplies are not to be removed from the office. If this occurs inadvertently, please return the supplies when you realize you have removed them.

2. Please do not use the copy and fax machines for personal use.

3. Except for emergency phone calls, please restrict company phone usage for company business.

4. Employees should not use company computers for personal use except that personal (not corporate) e-mail accounts may be accessed provided this practice does not become too time consuming. Respect for this privilege will help ensure that it can continue.

5. Etc.

Beyond the foregoing, there are some general steps leaders can take to apply ethics in their organizations:

1. If there are rules regarding such matters as conflicts of interest imposed as a result of professional certifications, ensure that all employees are aware of the rules and are periodically tested on them.

2. Ensure that all employees are aware of your own organization's codes of conduct and know how to look up the answers to questions.

3. Keep an open door about ethical problems for your subordinates. Encourage them if in doubt to seek advice but do not allow this access to degenerate into subordinates coming to you routinely to avoid taking responsibility for making ethical decisions.

4. Acknowledge the sometimes gray areas and complexities associated with ethical decisions. Openly discuss this with subordinates to help them learn and take responsibility for their actions and those of their subordinates. Be sure to emphasize, however, that the fact that gray areas exist does not mean there aren't good and bad choices.

5. Keep ethics part of everyday business, not something that gets discussed once a year. Make it clear that ethical practices are the rule in the organization. When a complex problem surfaces that requires considerable thought to find the right way through the maze, if circumstances and the need for confidentiality permit, use this problem as a learning tool for subordinates.

6. Don't think and act as if business ethics is simply a requirement for dealing with laws, regulations, and policies. Talk to subordinates about how ethics influences organizational performance, teamwork, morale, job satisfaction, and a sense of pride in the organization.

7. Make it clear that no one—especially you—is exempt from meeting ethical standards. Hold everyone, including your best performers, to those standards. As discussed in a previous chapter, ensure everyone understands what types of mistakes may be forgiven if not repeated and which constitute mistakes involving moral turpitude leading to virtually certain immediate termination.

8. Continuously champion good ethical conduct and give concrete examples of it when possible and appropriate.

9. If you are working in a profession or firm that requires annual ethical training, talk about ethics as an ongoing process, not a check-in-the-box that your organization performs once a year.

10. Above all, do not allow questionable personal behaviors to destroy employees' trust in the organization and its leadership. Practice what you preach and always be on guard in your own behaviors against sending the wrong signals to employees. Subordinates may not always be able to distinguish between actual behaviors that are questionably ethical and behaviors that are only perceived that way. Always be sensitive to how your behaviors are being perceived, and, if necessary, clarify them if you believe a misperception has occurred.[40]

6.5. Ethical Codes of Conduct in Business Organizations

Corporate cultures must reward ethical conduct and be constantly on the lookout for violations.

One commentator has noted, "The key to creating a just and ethical corporate culture is to breed fair and lasting business principles."[41] Many companies have created **ethics codes of conduct** to this end, and an increasing number require employees to attend ethics training. Some large businesses have gone so far as to appoint **ethics officers** who often report to the CEO and are responsible for overseeing organizational efforts to ensure adherence to ethical standards. The trend has been furthered by the Sarbanes–Oxley Act in the United States, enacted in reaction to a series of corporate scandals involving unethical behavior.[42] One might therefore conclude that leaders' efforts to apply ethics in business are greatly facilitated by an organizational code of ethics. We, in turn, might retort, "Not necessarily" and "It depends."

Business codes of conduct have their critics for the following reasons. First, it is argued that many ethical codes are really intended to limit legal liability as opposed to actually curb unethical practices. This argument is underscored by the fact that under federal guidelines businesses convicted of crimes are eligible for reduced sentences if they have ethical codes in place. By showing that they have an ethics code of conduct, businesses can hope to convince courts and juries that they were not negligent in failing to articulate the need for ethics and in their efforts to prevent unethical behaviors. If the motivation for having ethical codes says anything about how seriously companies take the importance of ethics codes per se as opposed to merely concerns over mitigating legal risk, then having codes with the purpose of mitigating legal risk may say little about their effectiveness. Otherwise, why do we observe companies such as Enron, which had an ethics code, engaging in illegal activities?[43]

A second criticism of ethics codes is that they are more often a form-completing exercise unconcerned about real ethical dilemmas—in other words, perhaps an exercise in self-deception on the part of business leadership that soothes leaders' consciences that they are doing the right thing without actually doing the right thing. As one commentator has noted, "Ethical failures are usually not the result of people not knowing the law or regulations. It is because they felt a variety of other pressures."[44] A third criticism is that most codes are common sense, and emphasizing the use of sound judgment by employees is equally effective. This might be construed as an argument that employees know what the right behaviors are instinctively, and the extent to which they behave that way or not depends upon their personal values.[45]

Similar to codes of ethics, the effectiveness of corporate ethics officers remains an open issue. Ethical practices of business are primarily the result of culture, and it is difficult to imagine that a single ethics officer in a very large organization can do much more than ensure that documents are present and training takes place.[46] As a staff person, an ethics officer likely has no line authority, must derive any authority to intervene from line management, and can be only as effective as top leadership allows him or her to be. Periodic ethics training has also been questioned. Arthur Andersen, which failed because of ethics problems, had for years provided consulting services on ethics to clients.[47]

Do the preceding criticisms suggest that companies should forego codes of ethics, ethics training, and ethics officers? Again, we respond, "Not necessarily," for several reasons. First, formal ethics initiatives help provide some legal protection and may be required in some professions and businesses. Second, formal initiatives can draw attention to the need for ethics, and requirements for periodic training can serve to refresh organizational members' understanding of such matters as complex conflict of interest rules imposed on such professions as public accounting that limit investments by firm members in clients. Third, formal ethics codes, ethics officers, and training can be a very useful complement to a sound ethical culture if they do not become merely token efforts.

How does a business go about ensuring that its code of ethics and attendant oversight and employee training do not become mere boilerplate facades? The Josephson Institute Center for Business Ethics lists the following characteristics of successful formal business ethics initiatives:

1. Guidelines are explained clearly using common scenarios. Using words, videos, and even skits during ethics training, create mental pictures of ethical dilemmas and how they might be resolved. Teach employees how to analyze situations and make good choices. Present ethical dilemmas using training aids such as videos followed by guided group discussions.

2. Avoid legalese, vagueness, jargon, and platitudes. Instead of phrases such as "Avoid improper use of equipment," explain precisely what is meant with examples and unambiguous language. Make guidelines readable for the lowest level of employees. Avoid complex sentences. Translate dense, complex paragraphs into lists with bullet points.

3. Make guidelines realistic. "Absolutely no personal phone calls" is unreasonable. "Accept no gifts or gratuities" is vague. Can an employee accept a client buying her lunch? If so, is there a dollar limit? Are holiday gifts from suppliers acceptable? If so, is there a limit on the value of the gift?

4. Ensure the guidelines are enforceable and enforced. Do they comply with existing laws and regulations? Are they free from conflict with other organizational guidelines? When obvious disconnects present themselves or unrealistic requirements are exposed, revise the guidelines. Are vi-

olations acted upon once revealed? Is the ethics officer fully engaged in advising and assisting line management in handling violations? Is the ethics officer a trustworthy resource to whom line leaders can go for advice about nebulous situations?

5. Ensure that there is one code, not two. Recall the aforementioned nepotism episode when the CEO hired his sons after refusing to make an exception for two employees wanting to get married. There is not one code for employees and another for top management. All leaders from the top down must adhere to the codes and policies if all organization members are to internalize the importance of ethics.[48]

In the end, no set of formal ethics initiatives will be effective if the organization's culture is toxic. Despite Enron's ethics code its top management created what has been termed a "cowboy culture" of pushing and sometimes exceeding ethical and legal limits in both business practices and the personal behavior of top management, to include overconsumption of job perquisites. This culture of excess drove Enron's temporary but unsustainable high rate of growth that created ever-growing expectations of more growth. The pressures to maintain this high growth were both powerful and ultimately destructive.[49]

Any formal ethics initiatives such as codes, ethics officers, and ethics training need to be juxtaposed against the organization's ethics culture. Does the culture reflect what is in the code? If not, what are the differences? Is the culture deficient, or is the code deficient? Does ethics training reflect a wholehearted attempt to correct deficiencies, or has it become a routine that has lost much meaning? Is the ethics officer a viable organizational resource for leaders or just a staff person tucked obscurely out of sight on the organization chart? Answers to these and related questions are needed to assess the overall health of the organization's ethics culture, the topic of the next section.

6.6. Assessing the Health of Organizational Ethics Cultures

Organizational high performance can be temporarily attained but not maintained without a strong ethical framework. Enduring, high-performing organizations have such frames. For example, the United States Marine Corps has as its motto "Honor, Courage, and Commitment." These three simple words sum up much about what has made that organization an enduring one since 1775. These words help strengthen a complex culture that strives for effectiveness, efficiency, and sustainability, all accomplished in an ethical manner—ethics being paramount in professions like the military and healthcare dealing in life and death situations wherein time can be of the essence and decisions unable to be deferred pending further deliberation. In effect, that culture becomes a control mechanism, often guiding both leaders and followers in nebulous situations in which organizational members are asking themselves, "What is the right thing to do now?" Although reams of laws, regulations, and policies govern what military personnel may and may not do under varying conditions and circumstances, no marine can remember those volumes of words when the time comes to act decisively at a given moment. But every marine knows that he or she is supposed to act honorably, courageously, and with total commitment in accomplishing each mission.

The benefits of cultural control are obvious here, but perhaps less obvious is what it takes to build and maintain a healthy culture that enables organizational members to act with the necessary latitude in myriad situations. Ethical cultures take a long time to build and, like trust, are easily destroyed. Constant vigilance is required by leadership to ensure the continuance of ethical health in their organizations. This is perhaps nowhere more evident than in the armed forces, whose member

organizations have long made extensive cultural control. Despite its long-standing and powerful culture, the top leadership of the Marine Corps has recently deemed it necessary to intervene powerfully to address what it believes to be an erosion of ethical culture evinced by unethical behaviors.[50] The U.S. Army, another storied institution, is currently undergoing a similar self-examination of its own culture.[51]

If an organization's ethics are no better than its ethics culture, then how should leaders go about exercising this constant vigilance in ensuring a healthy culture? There are some macrolevel areas that leaders can examine to assess organizational ethical health:

1. First of all, are laws and regulations being followed? If the answer is "Not always," this obviously suggests trouble. In essence, this represents the minimum standard for ethical behaviors. For example, are corporate governance requirements, such as an independent requirements audit committee of the board of directors, being met?

2. Are the words, deeds, and thoughts exhibited by leaders aligned? Do top leaders exhibit moral awareness?

3. Does the organization exhibit caring and concern for people, in particular those who lack power and influence?

4. Does the organization strive to improve the communities in which it operates? Is it sensitive to the impact of its operations on those communities?

5. Does the organization show concern and awareness for being a good steward of environmental resources wherever it operates?

6. Does the organization have a sense of responsibility for developing future generations of ethical leaders?[52]

The problem is that, even if businesses practice sound ethics at the macrolevel, some ethical failures are nearly invisible in the everyday workplace environment at lower levels.[53] At a more microlevel, one of the keys to maintain a healthy ethical culture is being alert to the attitudes of organization members in resolving ethical dilemmas. The Josephson Institute Center for Business Ethics offers the following warning signs of toxic ethical attitudes:

1. *It's ethical if it's legal and permissible.* Loopholes, lax enforcement, and/or personal moral judgment do not outweigh what's right.

2. *It's ethical if it's part of the job.* Separating personal ethics from work ethics can cause decent people to justify doing things at work that they would never do at home. Everyone's first job is to be a good person.

3. *It's ethical if it's for a good cause.* People can be vulnerable to rationalizations when advancing a noble aim. This can lead to deception, concealment, conflicts of interest, favoritism, or other departmental violations.

4. *It's ethical if no one's hurt.* Ethical values are not factors to be *considered* in decision making; they are ground rules.

5. *It's ethical if everyone does it.* Treating questionable behaviors as ethical norms under the guise of "safety in numbers" is a false rationale.

6. *It's ethical if I don't gain personally.* Improper conduct done for others or for institutional purposes is wrong. Personal gain is not the only test of impropriety.

7. *It's ethical if I've got it coming.* Being overworked or underpaid does not justify accepting favors, discounts, or gratuities, or abusing sick time, insurance claims, or personal use of office equipment. These are not fair compensation for one's services or underappreciated efforts.

8. *It's ethical if I'm objective.* By definition, if you've lost your objectivity, you don't know you've lost it. Gratitude, friendship, or anticipation of future favors can subtly affect one's judgment.

9. *It's ethical if I fight fire with fire.* Promise breaking, lying, or other misconduct is unacceptable even if others routinely engage in it.

10. *It's ethical if I do it for you.* Committing white lies or withholding information in professional relationships (such as performance reviews) disregards the fact that most people would rather know unpleasant information than soothing falsehoods.[54]

Involvement of more than just top leadership is required to maintain organizational ethical health. Some of the toxic behaviors in the Marine Corps and the U.S. Army are alleged to be the result of failures on the part of middle-level leadership. This is true in business as well, as suggested in the following quote:

What is needed in every organization is an understanding by the top management and by the ethics/compliance professionals that they are seeking to influence specific behaviors of middle managers, just as they have focused in recent years on specific behaviors by top executives. The problem of motivating middle managers, however, is in many ways more difficult. Middle managers are given explicit and often unyielding financial, sales, and cost control goals to achieve. At times, they may perceive that top management is actually giving them the message to focus on the quantifiable business goals and not on the "softer" ethical goals, that the ethical messages were "for the record" and not real. At other times, they may perceive that top management simply does not realize they cannot meet the stretch performance goals without "stretching" the ethical standards of the organizations. In these cases, many middle managers decide for themselves to take the expedient path.[55]

How can top managers coach middle managers to become effective stewards of the organization's ethical culture in the subunits they lead? One commentator writing for the Markkula Center for Applied Ethics at Santa Clara University indicates that top leadership should insist that middle-level leadership do the following:

1. Make ethical decisions consistent with organizational values and ethics.

2. Report concerns about ethical and unethical actions to top managers.

3. Talk frequently to subordinates about the organization's ethical code.

4. Recognize and anticipate ethical issues when they arise and act to resolve them before they become larger issues.

5. Talk with subordinates about how ethics apply to specific work situations.

6. Talk with higher-level leaders about concerns regarding how ethical values apply to specific decisions in which the middle-level leader participates and ask questions and for clarifications when the appropriate ethical action is unclear.[56]

In the coaching process, it is very important that senior leaders "walk the walk," ensuring their own words and behaviors are consistent with the ethics culture. It is necessary to repeatedly reinforce top leaders' belief in the importance of the

> "There are some that live without any design at all, and only pass in the world like straws upon a river. They do not go, but they are carried. Others only deliberate upon parts of life and not upon the whole, which is great error; for there is no disposing of the circumstances of it unless we first propound the main scope. How shall any man take his aim without a mark?"
>
> —Seneca, 4 BC–65 AD

ethics culture at employee meetings and provide guidance about applying the ethics code. Ethics issues that arise should be discussed consistent with confidentiality concerns at meetings of subordinate/leader peer groups. Senior leaders need to delegate responsibility for handling ethical issues to subordinate leaders but follow up, inquiring about outcomes and being available for advising. How subordinate leaders handle ethical issues needs to be made explicitly part of their performance reviews. Senior leaders need to use performance reviews and other one-on-one meetings regarding subunit performance to ask about any ethical problems subordinate leaders face.[57]

In the end, business ethics is not a necessary adjunct to running a high-performing business. Rather, it is at the very core of creating a sustainable, winning organization whose members share in the pride of being part of something admirable, something larger than they are, something of which they can proudly claim to be part. We end this chapter with the above quote by the great Roman philosopher Seneca. Are you a courageous, ethical leader—or a straw upon the river?

Profiles in Courageous Leadership— Mike Metzger

Mike Metzger is professor emeritus of business law and ethics at the Kelley School. Formerly associate dean and Foster Chair in Business Ethics, and prior to that chair of business law and ethics, he pioneered ethics instruction at the Kelley School, winning twenty awards in the process, including the President's Award for Outstanding Teaching. He has been noted in *Business Week* on several occasions for his outstanding teaching. As a leader in the Kelley School, Mike faced many situations that required the courage to address questionable behaviors, and his extensive knowledge of ethics and critical thinking served him well. A few of his many thoughts about business ethics follow:

> One of the major limits of practical ethics instruction is that, to be effective, it must presume that those being instructed are *intendedly ethical*, that is, they see themselves as the kind of people that want to do the right thing. Philosophical ethics theories can help the morally motivated reason through the difficult problems with which life confronts us, and can help decision makers justify their ultimate decision, since they should understand that some of their crit-

ics' criticisms will originate from these perspectives. But, unless decision makers see their own character and what they make of themselves as their life's work, they're unlikely to find the courage to do the right thing. That's because the real message communicated to people in business organizations often is: "Only results matter—produce results or else; if you produce them we'll not look too closely at how they're achieved, but if you get caught we'll hang you out to dry."

People who want to be leaders should understand that they're also teachers—modeling appropriate behavior for their followers with every action they take. They're always watching you, so you should constantly be asking what signals to send them. I think most of us want to follow someone whose knowledge and skills we respect, someone we trust, and someone who puts the greater good of the organization ahead of his or her personal interests. If you're not that kind of person now, then why should anyone want to follow you? What are you going to do about making yourself the kind of person others want to follow? If you don't, you can have all the leadership training in the world, and you may as a result be able to "talk the talk" of leadership but you'll never be able to "walk the walk." Let me finish by observing that it's not just those out front leading the charge who set the organization's tone—the opportunity for ethical leadership exists at every level—people who are committed to honesty and excellence on a daily basis lead by positive example. Every day.

CHAPTER 7

Motivating Others and Yourself

"Really great people make you feel that you, too, can be great."

—Mark Twain

Recall our earlier definition of leadership as getting followers to *want to do* what the leader wants them to do. Given that wanting to follow is essentially a voluntary reaction in response to some intrinsic or extrinsic stimuli, motivation is obviously a critical component of getting people to want what the leader wants. In turn, evidence suggests that satisfied employees are more likely to be motivated toward accomplishing ends sought by leaders than are dissatisfied ones.[1] Consequently, job satisfaction also influences employees' willingness to follow. Further, there is evidence that employers overestimate their employees' job satisfaction. A recent employee satisfaction and retention survey reported that employers believed that approximately 77 percent of their employees were satisfied with their jobs, whereas approximately 65 percent of the employees reported job satisfaction.[2]

Recall that with the Path-Goal Model, the role of leaders is to remove obstacles representing barriers to employees reaching their goals. Leaders desiring to influence employee performance have certain fundamental levers over which they have some control: (1) extrinsic rewards, (2) leadership style, (3) organizational environment, and (4) job characteristics. By adjusting compensation and benefits, improving interactions with employees with an appealing style, fostering a more fulfilling organizational environment, and structuring jobs

to be more satisfying, leaders can hope to foster a workplace environment in which employee job satisfaction and motivation are encouraged.

As basic as it seems, implementing these four seemingly simple levers can be quite complex. Human workplace behavior is a very complex phenomenon and has proven somewhat difficult to unravel despite decades of research, but there are nonetheless some research findings that fit well with real-world observations and have implications for leaders attempting to improve employee performance. This chapter deals with leaders motivating employees, in part by enhancing their job satisfaction, and motivating themselves because it is far more difficult to motivate others if leaders are unmotivated. Because of the interrelations between motivation and job satisfaction, we cover these topics together, first examining some complexities of motivation, next theories of causality, and then theories of job satisfaction, before moving into the implications of this research for practice and practical guidance for leaders on motivating others and ourselves.

7.1. Complexity in Assessing Motivation

A starting point is to understand exactly what the word "motivation" means. "**Motivation** is the force that initiates, guides, and sustains goal-oriented behaviors . . . The forces that lie beneath

> **"Bosses are not necessarily good leaders; subordinates are not necessarily good followers. Many bosses couldn't lead a horse to water. Many subordinates couldn't follow a parade. Some people avoid either role. Others accept the role thrust upon them and perform it badly . . . our preoccupation with leadership keeps us from considering the nature and importance of the follower. What distinguishes an effective [follower] from an ineffective follower is enthusiastic, intelligent participation."**
>
> —Robert E. Kelley, Graduate School of Industrial Administration, Carnegie Mellon University

motivation can be biological, social, emotional or cognitive in nature."[3] A large amount of research has been conducted on motivation, resulting in a number of theories. There are two general types of theories, nonpsychological and psychological, with the latter receiving by far the most attention and credibility. Many theories attempt to distinguish between conscious (aware) and unconscious (unaware) motivation. Some believe that much motivation causality is actually unconscious and not necessarily directly connected to conscious causes of motivation. Business leaders are obviously interested in **work motivation**, defined as "a set of energetic forces that originate both within as well as beyond an individual's being, to initiate work-related behavior, and to determine its form, direction, intensity and duration."[4] In other words, work motivation is concerned with what employees do, why they do it, how long they do it, and how much energy they expend in the process.

Although such definitional issues may seem obvious at first glance, there is hidden implication for leaders in assessing subordinates' performance. For example, suppose a performance review contains the following statement: "John needs to improve his motivation." Does such a statement convey enough information to be helpful or to be dangerous? Is the writer speaking about John's effort level or his inability to stay focused on desired objectives? Is the problem that John does not follow through on assignments or that he goes about it in the wrong way? Will John interpret his inadequate motivation the same way as the manager who wrote the report? Employees can be motivated to do the right things but in the wrong manner, or they can be motivated to do the wrong things but be very energetic about doing them. The point is that leaders often use terms like "motivation" loosely, assuming implicitly that subordinates will interpret them in a similar manner. What if John believes he is not working hard enough to please the supervisor when, in fact, the problem is he's working in the wrong manner? If John doubles down on his wrongly directed efforts, results will be worse rather than better. Inadequate direction for subordinate improvement can therefore lead to confusion and even be dysfunctional. This illustrates some of the complexities of dealing with motivational issues in the workplace.

Consider the attributes in Figure 7.1, previously discussed in chapter 5. It is immediately apparent that many attributes we might intuitively associate as fostering job satisfaction and motivation in employees at managerial levels such as creativity, critical thinking, and problem finding and solving are high in importance but difficult to measure. Notice also the clustering toward the upper right-hand corner of the figure. What this implies is that understanding and assessing motivation becomes more and more difficult as we ascend the organizational hierarchy. Unfortunately, consistent with the sidebar quote,

Figure 7.1. Relative Difficulty in Assessment of Different Aspects of Learning

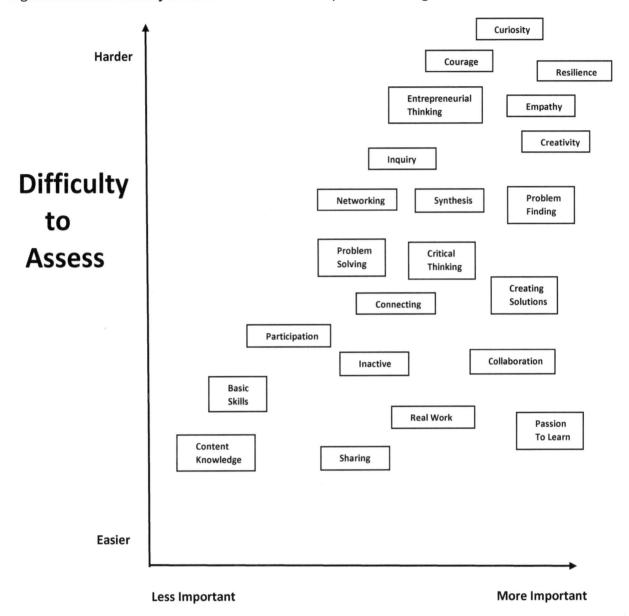

Learning in a Networked World

in our experience few leaders seem to have a good grasp of these motivating factors, often attributing a lack of motivation to incorrect causes.

Recall an anecdote presented earlier when one of the coauthors as a young management trainee decided to leave his employer because of insufficient intellectual challenge and an immediate supervisor who stifled motivation by refusing to delegate authority and insisted upon exercising his power in demeaning ways. When the young management trainee met with two senior managers inquiring why he was leaving, their first question was, "Is it about money?" The first potential causal factor that came in the senior managers' reasoning was that the problem emanated from insufficient extrinsic rewards. Yet, not only was that not the case with the management trainee, but research indicates that often employees resign because of inadequate intrinsic, not extrinsic, rewards. It might be comforting to believe that incidents such as this one occurred before researchers began to understand the complex nature of workplace motivation, but that would be self-deception. The foregoing incident occurred over a decade after MIT's Douglas McGregor's pioneering work in which, contrary to the prevailing thinking at the time, he proposed that external control and threat of punishment are not the only sources of employee motivation. Instead, McGregor posited that under proper conditions people often seek responsibility and that in work environments the intellectual capacities of employees are only partly utilized.[5]

It is much more difficult to improve employee motivation if leaders do not understand why employees are limitedly motivated. Leaders often develop their own heuristic beliefs about motivation based upon limited experience with a few subordinates without considering, much less understanding, differences in motivational factors across a much wider range of subordinates. Therefore, some understanding of motivational theory may assist in raising leaders' awareness of how different employees respond to various attempts to encourage their motivation.

7.2. Theories of What Motivates Employees

A number of motivation theories have been posited. This section presents six broad theories in brief, some with subordinate variations. Individually, none of these theories is sufficiently rich in predictive ability to suggest a perfect formula for motivating employees. All contain useful insights, however, and in the aggregate can serve to better inform leaders about what motivates subordinates. Some believe that leaders cannot motivate subordinates but rather that subordinates motivate themselves. At the anecdotal level, many leaders can no doubt recall a subordinate who, despite the leader's best efforts to facilitate motivation, refused to become so. We do not believe this is a useful semantic distinction, however. Even if it is true that motivation only comes from the inner self and cannot solely be externally driven, leaders can certainly help shape a work environment and set of conditions that is more conducive to self-motivation. There is no shortage of both systematic and anecdotal evidence that followers generally believe that leadership affects their motivational levels.

Generally, motivation is thought to involve three processes. **Arousal** happens when a person realizes a desire for something and initiates action to obtain it. Arousal can result from positive (rewards) or negative (punishment) causes. **Direction** entails the goals people set and how they go about obtaining them. **Intensity** is the energy expended in the process of taking action to reach the goals and is a function of the importance a person places on achieving a goal and the degree of difficulty in reaching it.[6] Is there a benefit for leaders in understanding this trio of psychological processes? Doubtless, most experienced leaders have experienced situations wherein a subordinate seemed both aroused and directed toward goal attainment but lacked the intensity to achieve it. Alternatively, subordinates may exhibit intensity but misunderstand the intended goal. Consequently, when seeking to motivate subordinates, leaders are well served to assure themselves that all three processes are operating as intended. Awareness of these three processes can serve to remind leaders to seek evidence that all three are operative.

First, **organizational behavioral modification theory** deals simply with positive and negative reinforcement. Good behaviors are rewarded with extrinsic rewards and/or praise and poor behaviors with punishment. Frequency of reward is believed to increase performance, and the less time between occurrence of a behavior and reward the more effective the reward is expected to be in encouraging that behavior. One caution is that overuse of punishment can lead to perceptions of unfairness.[7]

Second, as their name suggests, **need-based theories** focus on subordinates' drive to satisfy a variety of needs ranging from basic survival (e.g., eating) to the need to create something. An early need-based theory was **Maslow's hierarchy of needs**, which created a ladder of needs ranging from basic physiological needs (e.g., food, shelter) at the bottom, to safety, followed by love and belonging, then self-esteem, and finally self-actualization (e.g., morality, creativity, problem solving) at the top. Maslow's original idea was that human beings would not strive to meet needs farther up the ladder unless lower needs had been satisfied, but this has not been supported by research on work environments. **ERG theory** collapsed Maslow's hierarchy into three components—existence, relatedness, and growth, but with only mixed empirical support.[8] Consequently, although we have known of these need-based theories being used in executive education programs, their predictive usefulness for work settings is dubious.

On the other hand, another need-based theory, **achievement theory,** may be more useful. It posits three types of motivation to achieve that can vary in proportions: *achievement* (drive for accomplishment), *authority* (drive to lead, make an impact), and *affiliation* (drive to belong to group and have social interactions). Individuals possessing these three motivations are believed to be more effective employees. Consequently, of the three foregoing need-based theories, achieve-

ment theory may be the most useful to leaders by providing a set of criteria for assisting in identifying subordinates with high-performance potential.[9]

Social cognitive theory is a need-based theory that emphasizes the concept of *self-efficacy,* an employee's belief in his or her ability to achieve the desired results. This belief can affect how much effort an employee puts into task accomplishment and how persistent the employee is in task completion. Self-efficacy can be increased by additional training and experience in task proficiency, particularly training that is focused on mastering skills as opposed to delivering outcomes. (A baseball analogy would be improving hitting by spending more time in the batting cage.) Importantly, setting goals that are too low can have a negative effect on self-efficacy, so leaders should be cautious about continuously assigning tasks that are too low level for employees.[10] Third, **cognitive-process theories** focus on how individuals assess work conditions and outcomes. **Equity theory** posits employees seek to balance effort versus outcomes. It has proven more useful in predicting demotivation than motivation through its focus on factors giving rise to injustices. Organizational justice has four aspects: (1) Distributive justice—are outcomes fair given the effort required to achieve them? (2) Informational justice—has an employee been given the requisite information and data required to perform well? (3) Procedural justice—is the manner in which outcomes are measured fair? (4) Interactional justice—is the employee treated with sufficient respect? The theory's implications are that leaders desiring to reduce demotivating factors should focus on (1) ensuring that policies are applied consistently, (2) outcome measurement is reasonably accurate, (3) rewards are as free from bias as possible, and (4) flaws and inequities in policies, outcome measures, and rewards are corrected as they are identified.[11]

Another cognitive-process theory is **expectancy theory**, which can be useful in guiding the design of reward systems by predicting how a given employee selects among alternative choices of effort versus reward. Equity theory, expressed as $F = E(\sum I \times V)$, posits that work effort, F, is a function of three variables: (1) E, the belief that the effort will deliver desired performance, (2) I, the belief that the desired level of performance will result in the desired outcome, and (3) V, the value of the outcome to the employee. In this model, job satisfaction is a function of the outcome rather than the other way around.[12]

Yet another cognitive-process theory, **goal-setting theory**, is based upon arguments that goals should be specific, measurable, attainable, relevant, and timely, known as SMART criteria. How committed employees are to goal attainment is a function of three types of influences: (1) *internal influences* involving intrinsic rewards, (2) *external influences* such as extrinsic rewards, punishments, and peer pressure, and (3) *interactive influences* such as competition with others and participation in goal setting. The theory has received good empirical support.[13] Goal-setting theory can be helpful in increasing subordinates' focus on achieving goals by drawing leaders' attention to the overt manipulation of influence factors. For example, if the leader is limited in his or her ability to apply external influences because of resource constraints, then the leader might wish to increase participation in goal setting or perhaps set up a competition between teams striving for the same goals.

Fourth, **job-based theories** focus on the design of job characteristics as the source of employee motivation. **Motivation-hygiene theory** posits job content to be the primary source of employee motivation. Under this theory, what are termed "hygiene factors" (e.g., compensation, job security, workplace environment and conditions, benefits, colleagues) only reduce dissatisfaction.

Rather, it is a set of intrinsic factors associated with the nature of the job tasks that motivate (e.g., challenge, responsibility, promotion, opportunities for creativity). Motivation-hygiene theory is also related to *job enrichment*, which involves employees being more involved in designing their tasks and increasing their levels of skills and knowledge. Although aspects of the theory seem intuitive, it has only been weakly supported by empirical research.[14]

Job-characteristics theory is a job-based theory having at its core the *job characteristics model* (JCM). The JCM has five key elements: (1) the skill variety required, (2) the extent to which the task is identified with the larger objective, (3) how significantly the task impacts others, (4) how much autonomy the employee enjoys, and (5) the nature of the feedback, such as whether it is clear, timely, sufficiently detailed, and can be acted upon. The theory also posits that employees' *growth-need strength* affects outcomes by its impact on the foregoing elements. A *job-diagnostic survey* (JDS) based upon the theory is often used to measure the level of growth needed by an employee along with his or her job satisfaction and perceptions of the job characteristics.[15]

The fifth and sixth motivation theories are more recent: **self-regulation theory** and **work-engagement theory**. The former assumes that employees are self-governing to a large extent and is based upon employees setting their own goals, receiving accurate feedback, and monitoring and evaluating themselves. The latter posits employees seek intellectually fulfilling tasks based upon three work-engagement factors: (1) personal energy devoted to work, (2) challenge and pride in work, and (3) a capacity to immerse in and experience a sense of flow from their work.[16]

There are some general takeaways from surveying the foregoing theories. First, motivating employees is a complex issue that defies simple categorizations. Second, think critically, therefore, of simplistic, formulaic solutions to such a complex problem presented by motivational gurus who peddle off-the-shelf, one-size-fits-all answers. Learning to craft a work environment conducive to nurturing employee motivation takes some in-depth thinking. Third, if you want to become a great leader, one important tool in your toolbox—one that will differentiate you from many if not most leaders—is mastering the art of fostering motivation in your subordinates.

7.3. Job-Satisfaction Theories

Overall, **job satisfaction** is defined simply as how content an employee is with his or her job, but it has two somewhat distinct constructs, albeit ones that can impact upon one another. **Affective job satisfaction** is the degree of pleasure an employee derives from his or her job. **Cognitive job satisfaction** pertains to how the employee perceives one or more of the job's characteristics, such as compensation and challenge.[17] As with motivation, several theories exist with respect to job satisfaction.

Affect theory posits that job satisfaction is determined by the difference between what an employee desires in a job and what the job delivers, and that the value an employee places on some aspect of the job affects the employee's dissatisfaction if expectations are unmet. **Dispositional theory** holds that employees' outlooks and dispositions largely drive job satisfaction regardless of job conditions. This is somewhat supported by evidence that job satisfaction tends to be relatively stable over time.[18] To the extent that dispositional theory has some predictive power, this underscores the need for self-assessment as discussed in chapter 5—that is, if employee self-assessment helps employees better understand their sources of job satisfaction and dissatisfaction. That would seemingly lead managers to better design work environments conducive to satisfaction. **Opponent-process theory**, however, argues that such efforts often backfire. Efforts to enhance employees' moods, such as creating positive events, can sometimes give rise to feelings of anxiety.[19] For example, suppose you celebrate one employee's accomplishments but in the process make another employee feel as if he is not performing well because he wasn't similarly recognized. You may have increased one employee's satisfaction while decreasing that of another. This raises yet another possibility, one posited by **equity theory**, that deals with how different employees perceive what is fair in the workplace. Distress is created when an employee perceives inequities in rewards versus performance. Extension of this theory considers three response patterns, as shown in Figure 7.2.

Benevolent/satisfied employees are relatively indifferent to perceived inequities. Equity-sensitive employees believe that rewards should be fair in terms of being performance driven. Entitled employees assume that they deserve any rewards coming their way and that they are not overrewarded even if that is the case.[20] On the other hand, **discrepancy theory** is focused upon self-guidance and addresses employees' anxiety

Figure 7.2. Equity Theory Behavioral Response Patterns

Behavioral-Response Pattern	Employee Feelings about Equity
Benevolent/satisfied	Even if under rewarded compared with others
Equity sensitive	Everyone should be fairly rewarded
Entitled	Employee deserves everything he or she gets

resulting from feelings that they have not fulfilled their responsibilities well and regret experienced for not having achieved their goals.[21]

Factors that influence job satisfaction have been classified into three categories: environmental, individual, and psychological well-being. **Environmental factors** include **communications overload and underload**, **leader/subordinate communication**, and **employee recognition**. Too much or too little communication about a task is believed to give rise to dissatisfaction. Both verbal and nonverbal communication between leaders and subordinates influence satisfaction. Employee satisfaction is enhanced if leaders are perceived to be positive, friendly, and supportive, whereas unfriendly, disapproving, and negative perceptions increase dissatisfaction. **Strategic employee recognition** posits that job satisfaction is enhanced when employees perceive they are able to influence their employers' strategic outcomes.[22]

Individual factors thought to influence job satisfaction include emotion, genetics, and personality. Attempting to self-manage one's emotions can have both positive and negative outcomes in terms of job satisfaction. Amplification of one's positive emotions may contribute to job satisfaction and vice versa. The impact of emotion on job satisfaction has been modeled two ways. **Emotional dissonance** describes the difference between how emotions are displayed to others and the way an employee actually feels and can lead to emotional exhaustion and low job satisfaction. The social interaction model posits that an employee's favorable interpersonal interactions can enhance job satisfaction and vice versa.[23] **Genetics** is also believed to play a minor role in the intrinsic aspects of job satisfaction. **Personality** is related to job satisfaction through affectivity (how people experience emotions and interact with others). Employees having positive affectivity have a greater likelihood of job satisfaction.[24]

Research has indicated that **psychological well-being** is positively related to job satisfaction. The interrelationships are complex, however, because positive well-being has been associated with other variables related to job satisfaction, such as feelings of positive emotions. One potentially important note is that psychological well-being refers to one's total life, not just employment. The import is that job satisfaction may be affected by employees' lives outside work.[25]

Keeping the foregoing theoretical underpinnings from this and the previous section in mind, in the following section we critically examine advice from practitioner literature about motivating employees. There is no shortage of such advice, especially various lists of do's and don'ts. One limitation of this type of advice—an issue to which we will return in section 7.5—is that it often treats employees as being the same in what motivates them and what provides job satisfaction, an implicit assumption that we know from research findings to be somewhat perilous. Although heuristic approaches can sometimes be helpful to busy leaders, employee motivations are too complex to be easily defined by checklists. Consequently, it behooves leaders to think more deeply before uncritically adopting a checklist approach.

7.4. Implications for Leaders

Recall our previous admonitions regarding uncritical acceptance of simplistic solutions to the complex challenge of nurturing motivation among subordinates. Although, like most business leaders, we love easy solutions to complex problems, there is usually a reason complex problems are still problems. To wit, if simple solutions existed, the problems would no longer be problems. We are therefore rather suspicious of one-size-fits-all motivational formulas. This is not to say, however, there is nothing to be gained from surveying practical advice proffered in popular literature on this topic. What may prove useful is to examine several of these more simplistic formulaic approaches, look for common threads among them, and then critically test these threads against both common sense and what empirical evidence from research has to say about them.

Let's take this path using an article titled "5 Easy Ways to Motivate—and Demotivate—Employees."[26] This article lists several do's; the first is to *align individual economic interests with company performance.* The recommendation is to "create incentive programs at all organizational levels to benefit when the company prospers." Although the article doesn't advocate some sort of employee stock option plan or profit-sharing plan, those would seemingly be ways in which to attempt to accomplish this. On the surface this proposal seems quite rational, but it has its limitations. Our experience suggests that such plans work well for many employees, especially long-term employees, but not so well for other employees, especially those whose time horizons are shorter term.

A commercial bank where one of the coauthors worked implemented two incentive programs designed to motivate employees to solicit business from retail customers. Although all employees were eligible, the programs were particularly intended to involve employees at the clerical level to become involved in cross selling the bank's services. The more sophisticated program involved paying any employee who enticed a customer into opening deposit accounts and paid the employees very small amounts for each account over time for as long as the accounts remained open and the employees remained with the organization. The payments were somewhat similar to the manner in which life insurance salespeople are remunerated for life insurance policies over longer periods of time as long as the policies remain in effect. The second program paid each employee $100 for each customer solicited who within 6 months following the solicitation leased an automobile through the bank.

One commenter on "5 Easy Ways to Motivate—and Demotivate—Employees" makes the following astute observation: "Many people have the belief that money does not motivate because they have not seen it work. This is mostly because it is rarely done right."

The first program had little impact, but the second was a huge success. Why? Many clerical employees had short time horizons with little idea how long they would remain with the bank. Future possible events such as marriage, spousal transfer, better job opportunities, and so forth contributed to this short-term focus. Moreover, the compensation system was too complicated for employees to form any reasonable idea of future payoffs. On the other program, $100 next month if a friend or relative leased a car was far more immediate, quantifiable, and appealing to rank-and-file employees. The point is that, while incentive programs based upon extrinsic rewards can be positive motivators, they must be designed with an understanding of the type of employees involved, their time horizons, and their understanding of the costs in terms of extra effort versus the apparent benefits. One size does not necessarily fit all when it comes to incentive programs.

The article's second recommendation is to *take an interest in the future growth of employees' careers* through mentoring and coaching. This one is difficult to find fault with at a general level because both mentoring and coaching, properly implemented, can be very effective tools for performance improvement, which, in turn, can have a motivating effect upon employees. But leaders are well advised to enter into coaching and mentoring employees with a solid understanding of the roles of each, which are different, and how to go about effectively filling these roles. This topic is discussed extensively in chapter 8. Not so easy.

A third recommendation is for leaders to *take an interest in employees' work–life balance,* with such compassionate acts as offering schedule flexibility and being sympathetic to family commitments. Compassion is often a good thing but not necessarily for everyone all the time. The boss who allows John to leave work early to attend his child's soccer game may inadvertently affect others who are depending upon John on collaborative work. Recall also that equity issues are an import-

We like the advice given by one author of a practitioner article offering advice on motivating employees: "Do more than read this article."

—Carter McNamara, "Steps You Can Take to Support the Motivation of Others"

ant part of motivation. If Jane, who has no children, sees John leaving work early for a family reason with some frequency, she may perceive it as an equity issue. What would be your response as Jane's and John's boss if Jane came to you and asked to get off early to go shopping? Would you draw a line between leaving for family reasons and reasons of purely personal enjoyment? If you did, how would Jane's motivation be affected? If you allowed Jane to leave early as a matter of equity, where would you draw the line between valid and invalid reasons for employees leaving early routinely? The point isn't that compassionate flexibility shouldn't be allowed—in fact, the contrary is usually true—but rather that there are pitfalls for the unwary leader in how to apply this equitably and how to balance an employee's personal needs with those of the organization. In our experience, hiring employees who express higher levels of internal motivation based upon job fit to preferences can be very helpful here. Our experience is that employ-

ees who engage in work transactions they enjoy are more motivated and less likely to take advantage of a leader's compassion. Again, not so easy.

A fourth recommendation is to *listen,* a topic to which we later devote much of a chapter. The article touts this as "an easy one." Leaders are advised to "just listen thoughtfully." We respectfully disagree. Listening, like writing and speaking, is a skill that requires considerable development and self-discipline. One professional counselor and listening expert argues that there are two levels of listening. The first level is simply an exchange of information, such as, "Where is the stapler?" "It's on the table." The second level involves a much deeper form of communicating in which feelings are communicated, intentionally or inadvertently.[27] If that same question interrupts your train of thought and you respond with, "It's on the table," but your tone of voice and mannerisms communicate, "I'm busy, go find it for yourself," then you have communicated on the second level. Consider also that thoughtful listening has its perils. John Hill says this about Terry Campbell:

> Terry is a very deep thinker, an INTJ in Myers-Briggs terms. When I listen to him, his thinking almost always evokes new thinking on my part. Ideas and possibilities pop into my mind. Before I realize it, I'm off on a mental tangent and no longer listening to Terry. I have to keep disciplining myself to jot a quick note about an idea, refocus, and concentrate on what he is saying, not allowing my mental drift to persist. But it recurs, and it's not easy to stay focused. I know I need to improve my listening skills.

The fifth recommendation is to *do unto others as you would have done unto you.* Biblical in its origins, this advice has lasted 2,000 years, so it must have efficacy. But, in the context of leader/subordinate relations in business, it may benefit from some clarification. As previously discussed, leaders sometimes have the responsibility of confronting employees with unpleasant corrective measures. Quite often the employee would prefer not to be confronted and corrected. We think what the article's author is really getting at is the need to treat others with respect, regardless of whether an exchange involves pleasant, neutral, or unpleasant discussion. A leader might ask him- or herself, "If I were being counseled about a job-related deficiency, how would I like my boss to address this with me?" Correcting employees using firm but compassionate respect can often keep what is a potentially discordant exchange on a professional plane. But, again, as we have discussed previously, it's not all that easy.

The article enumerates five demotivating practices that include (1) disrespecting employees by misuse of power, (2) taking credit for work your employees did without giving credit to them, (3) losing self-control, (4) being unwilling to stand up for your employees when you should, and (5) failing to praise employees. Obviously, these are generally unhealthy leadership practices, but there are a few caveats. For example, although losing self-control is not a good thing, there are times when a leader *should* express righteous anger over unacceptable practices. Sometimes unhealthy cultures can grow inside organizations, and a carefully controlled display of anger can send a much-needed message that such practices are intolerable. Employees whose sensitivity to unacceptable practices has been dulled by a bad culture sometimes need to be awakened in an unmistakable manner. The point is that leaders' management of potentially demotivating behaviors is not always that simple or easy.

On the whole, the recommendations contained in this particular article represent reasonable advice for the most part but miss a number of important complexities and nuances. As one savvy commenter on the article remarked, "Employees are individuals and you really need to find the

Many years ago the CEO of a very large international company was dealing with an unacceptable volume of customer complaints about its service. When he addressed this with the company's senior officers, they all had large volumes of computer-generated paper in front of them explaining why their units were not responsible for the problems. Realizing that an unhealthy culture had grown in the company, the CEO swept the paper off the table and told his senior officers that he was seeking solutions, not excuses. The attitude changed, and the company became known for its outstanding service.

unique things that motivate each employee... The key to motivating employees is finding the unique things that they are looking for in the employment relationship." That takes hard work on the part of leaders. So, are there some practical guidelines supported by research to assist leaders in motivating employees? Thankfully, yes, and these can be broken down in the following categories: (1) extrinsic rewards, (2) intrinsic rewards, (3) individual job structuring, (4) team structuring, and (5) development of a healthy work culture.

Extrinsic rewards can take various forms including salary, commissions, bonuses, profit sharing, and equity-based (e.g., stock options, phantom stock, stock appreciation rights) and fringe benefits. Evidence on the motivational impact of fringe benefits is somewhat murky, but, as previously discussed, direct financial incentives can positively impact motivation provided they are carefully tailored to conform to the extent possible to organizational goals. Equity theory suggests pay-for-performance is a reasonable motivator if one considers the employee to be someone who believes in employees receiving rewards commensurate with value contributed. It may be less so for employees who believe they deserve anything they get and employees who are rather indifferent to inequities.[28] Also, as suggested earlier, employees' time horizons and the time before rewards are realized may also play a role in the extent to which they enhance motivation.

Intrinsic rewards in the form of recognition and praise have the greatest motivational impact when they closely follow the desired behaviors and acknowledge aspects of performance over which the employee exercised significant control.[29] It has also been our observation that physically commemorating acknowledgement of outstanding performance has an impact. The military and law enforcement are perhaps best known for awarding medals and ribbons for accomplishment. These awards are then worn on uniforms for all to see. Although businesses may not have these same opportunities, wall plaques hung in employees' offices may achieve an analogous effect of memorializing employees' contributions that might otherwise be long forgotten.

Individual job structuring can contribute to employee motivation.[30] For example, job rotation and enrichment may be helpful in avoiding simple, repetitive jobs becoming routine and boring. Making jobs more intellectually challenging and giving employees more control over decisions involving their work may also improve motivation for employees who value challenge and control. Some employees are not motivated by job enrichment, however, and may even be threatened by the requirement to meet new challenges. Other ways to enrich jobs include increasing task significance, task variety, and task identification and visibility of benefit to customers; providing good two-way feedback; and combining tasks into larger units of work and responsibility.[31] Some leading-edge research involves the simultaneous examination of motivation with creativity. Apparently, some of the same variables associated with creativity are associated with higher levels of motivation. The implication is that for employees who seek creative work, motivation may be enhanced by structuring jobs involving more creativity.[32]

Team structuring research suggests that semi-autonomous teams exhibit higher levels of organizational commitment and intrinsic and extrinsic motivation. Developmentally mature and voluntarily formed teams also exhibit higher levels of motivation. There are mediating variables involved, however, such as team cohesion, so it is difficult to draw firm conclusions.[33]

A **healthy work culture** may contribute to motivation by reducing the need for formal controls that may demotivate creative employees. There is evidence that strategically appropriate, adaptive cultures are associated with higher performance due to higher motivation, better goal alignment, and better-performing team structure. Four different types of cultures have been identified: (1) *Hierarchical cultures* tend to result in control, efficiency, and predictability. (2) *Market cultures* are competitive and aggressive, with success measured in market-based outcomes. (3) *Clan (familial) cultures* are collaborative and characterized by open communication, employee engagement, and individual development, somewhat similar to the way in which family members might be inclined to assist one another because they are family. (4) *Ad hoc cultures* result in more innovation and creativity.[34] Employees are motivated by being agile in responding to problems and creating solutions. The type of culture greatly affects success and employee motivation. Having the most appropriate culture for the environment in which the organization operates is critical. For example, a manufacturing operation engaged in producing a high volume of the same commodity products year in and out might be best served by a hierarchical culture. A small company in which employees may be required to identify and perform a variety of tasks as they arise without direction might benefit most from a clan culture. A real estate sales company in which the revenue stream is greatly enhanced by home sales and purchases might be best served by a market culture. A semantic-software development company might benefit from an ad hoc culture.

7.5. Using Preferences to Help Motivate Subordinates

From the foregoing sections it is obvious that motivating employees and enhancing their job satisfaction is not as easy as is sometimes represented. Further, another obvious point is that what motivates and satisfies one employee may not be the same for another. Leaders make a mistake if they assume their subordinates are all motivated by the same things that motivate the leaders.[35] To what, then, can leaders turn for help in tailoring motivation and satisfaction influences to best serve their organizations? The starting point begins with understanding who your subordinates are inside. Yes, employees will often step outside their preferred roles and serve their employers well, but having employees continuously engage in transactions they don't enjoy can be demotivating and dissatisfying. The previous section discussed in general how leaders may be able to structure employee tasks to improve employee motivation and job satisfaction. One thread throughout this section and in chapter 5 is that employees are individuals with definite work preferences that differ greatly from employee to employee. Consequently, to the extent leaders understand their subordinates' work preferences they may be able to better structure tasks and teams and thereby increase motivation and satisfaction—and organizational performance as well.

Hopefully, your employer has performed some sort of preference assessment to help employees and leaders identify preferences. In chapter 5 we learned about using Myers-Briggs

for that purpose. But even if that has not been accomplished, you may be able to make useful observations yourself. In this section we refer back to chapter 5 and use Myers-Briggs to exemplify how task assignment may be used effectively to structure individual employee tasks to better coincide with preferences. In chapter 14 we will apply this to team selection. The following are examples of situations in which leaders might benefit from carefully considering matching employees with task characteristics.

Suppose your corporation has a complex project with a tight, definite timeline that currently lacks exact strategic definition, requires considerable planning, and has drifted off track to the point where the first project manager has asked to have the project reassigned to someone else because of the stress it is creating for him. What work-preference profile might work best in such a situation as his replacement? You might consider assigning an employee with an ENTJ profile to lead the project. ENTJs are goal and results oriented and they take charge quickly, logically analyzing and controlling situations. They are resourceful, good planners, and like designing structures leading to goal accomplishment. ENTJs are willing to deal directly with problems caused by confusion and inefficiencies and like challenges. Their management style is often hands on, direct, and decisive—even tough when necessary. Failure is often not an option for ENTJs. They want the facts summarized for them and have a low tolerance for excuses. If your project is currently in the ditch, consider using an ENTJ to help get you out.[36]

On the other hand, suppose you are the partner-in-charge (PIC) of the forensic services group in an international public accounting firm. On behalf of your firm, you have just agreed to be a testifying expert on the plaintiffs' side in a complex civil litigation case to estimate damages from an alleged misappropriation of a trade name. The client agreed to hire you after being referred by a large law firm from which you have been hoping to get referral business. If you do an exceptional job on this case, it will likely lead to future referral business. Unfortunately, the case facts are messy, in part because the client failed to follow state

> ## "A great place to start learning about motivation is to start understanding your own motivation."
>
> —Carter McNamara

law in appropriately registering the trade name. There are three different legal theories that might form the basis of a damages calculation, each with a different method of computing damages. Developing the damages estimate will therefore take considerable research and some creative thinking. To which preference profile might you assign the task of developing the damages estimate? In such a situation an INTJ type might be a good candidate. INTJs tend to be hard-driving creators with theoretical insights that they then turn into strategic vision followed by an action plan. They get the big picture first and then move into details. INTJs can conceptualize and build new models. They are task-focused and efficient problem solvers who work independently and act strongly and forcefully on their ideas.[37]

You are PIC of a large international consulting firm. One of your units, healthcare advisory, has been struggling somewhat completing projects. As a result, the unit has recently been losing clients. When the current PIC announces his retirement, you consider two younger partners in the unit as replacements and review their personnel files. Although your firm has not used Myers-Briggs as a means for employees typing themselves, taking comments from these files you draw up the chart in Figure 7.3 to get a better idea of which partner is the better fit for leading the unit. Based on this comparison, which partner seems to be the better fit based upon what rationale?

So, who is the better fit to lead the unit, Jane or Mary? If you are having some difficulty in deciding, you are not alone. Both appear to have commendable attributes. For example, on one hand, Jane sounds like a leader who gets things to closure, currently a big problem with the unit. On the other hand, Mary sounds like someone who could better deal with client relations issues. Mary's leadership style might contribute to higher overall unit morale, but Jane's might result in more efficiency and output. Jane sounds like a leader whose employees are less likely to cause problems, but Mary's ability to assess people well and use people synergistically could serve the unit well. In the end, whether you chose Jane or Mary is not the most important issue. Both have strengths that might improve unit performance and weaknesses that could get in the way. If it is possible to mend fences with lost clients, Mary's extroversion seems encouraging. That said, her difficulties getting to closure may cost clients, especially clients that give the firm another chance, only to see the same problems repeated.

One obvious potential use of the information in Figure 7.3 is discussing the possible issues you see with both candidates prior to making a selection and then deciding which provides you with the greatest comfort in her responses. Another use postselection is to carefully monitor the unit's performance for evidence of problems such as sinking morale or difficulty getting to closure suggested as possibilities by Figure 7.3. By the way, in case you are wondering, Jane is an ISTJ and Mary an ESFJ.

7.6. Self-Motivation

Motivating ourselves is a starting point for motivating others.[38] It is far more difficult for leaders to motivate others when they are not motivated themselves, so one way to foster motivation among subordinates is to ensure you maintain

Figure 7.3. Comparison of Behaviors of Two Partners as Suggestive of Work Preferences

Attribute	Jane's File Comments	Mary's File Comments
Leadership Style	Uses experience and knowledge to make decisions. Rewards those who follow rules while getting job done. Pays attention to immediate and practical organization needs. Respectful of authority. Expects others to display the same commitment to the organization she does.	Casual, easygoing, friendly, likes action. Fun loving and generous. Well-liked by unit members.
Problem-Solving Style	Always thoroughly grounded in facts. Works within the organizational structure.	Makes realistic and concrete assessments, especially about people.
Strengths	Can always be counted on to honor commitments. Gets things done on time. Detail focused and manages details carefully.	Energetic, enthusiastic, positive, focuses on most immediate problems. Good at defusing tense situations and facilitating interactions among unit members. Good at getting projects started.
Possible Weaknesses	Sometimes distracted by job to point of neglecting interpersonal relations. Does not always keep big picture in mind.	Difficulty sometimes getting closure on projects. Tends to socialize a lot in the office, sometimes distracting staff members.

Source: Adapted from S. K. Hirsh and J. M. Kummerow, *Introduction to TYPE in Organizations: Individual Interpretive Guide,* 3rd ed. (Mountain View, Calif.: CPI, 1993), 10, 17.

your own motivation. Personality type can help with self-motivation in assisting people in choosing the careers that best suit their preferences. We believe that it is far easier to be self-motivated if we enjoy our daily transactions. For years, one of the coauthors has been fond of telling students seeking career advice things like, "Being a gastroenterologist can be a satisfying and financially rewarding career, but don't become one if you're going to hate spending whole days doing colonoscopies." We know of no career that offers 100 percent transactions you'll enjoy, but getting as many of your transactions as close to your preferences as possible will go a long way toward you being self-motivated.

Knowing your personality type's preferences can help with this. A neuroscientist at UCLA has demonstrated by using EEG electrodes attached to test subjects' brains that each of the sixteen Myers-Briggs types uses sections of the brains in somewhat different ways.[39] Extrapolating a bit upon this evidence, we might conclude that work transactions compatible with preferred brain activity comprise a better fit and lead to higher motivation One career coach's anecdotal evidence somewhat supports this position:

I've been using personality type long enough that when I get a new career counseling client, I can usually look at their resume and their four letter personality type code and pretty accurately guess what they liked about their jobs and disliked. I can see the underlying conflict if they were in the wrong career for their personality type.[40]

Aside from picking careers and jobs with transactions we mostly enjoy, there are things leaders can do to remain motivated. One source cites three primary reasons we lose motivation: (1) lack of self-confidence, (2) lack of focus, and (3) loss of direction.[41]

Self-confidence concerns are natural when we are confronted with daunting tasks, particularly one with which we are unfamiliar. This is one reason leaders often benefit from accepting new responsibilities that provide challenges. Experience in successfully dealing with one set of unknowns can provide assurance of our ability to deal with other unknowns. Reflect back on past challenges that required you to "bootstrap" yourself up to success. Think of what made you successful in addressing those challenges. Was it your ability to research a topic using your connections and getting advice from friends? Was it your ability to organize a group, develop a plan, or gather resources? Remember the **ends/ways/means model**. Get a clear vision for what success will look like. If you lack such an understanding, ask for clarification. If the assignment is such that even your boss has no clear vision of the end state, then ask for his or her intent. The military calls this **commander's intent**. Battle and business share the common characteristic of often being dynamic. As leaders engage in problem solving, often knowledge grows and circumstances change, requiring changes in plans and sometimes objectives. Nonetheless, if leaders have a clear understanding of the end state—that is, what constitutes "victory" in the organization's eyes—then ongoing adjustments can be made to reflect this dynamism. This is something to keep in mind when you are assigning tasks to subordinate leaders. Assuming you believe them capable, informing them of your intent, issuing **mission orders** that state the desired end state, and then allowing your subordinate leaders latitude to make adjustments in carrying out the mission all improve morale. Therefore, when you get the commander's intent and mission orders, you should regard it as a statement about your boss's confidence in you and not as vagary to be feared.

Lack of focus is a second reason for losing motivation. This occurs when leaders focus their energies on the wrong things, only to find themselves off track and feeling lost. Again, ends/ways/means thinking helps. It is too easy to get lost in the complexity of the ways and lose sight of the desired end state. Keep in mind the desired end state, revisiting over and over again to be sure you are still headed for the right end. Do not allow fear-based thinking to sidetrack you. Identify the obstacles that threaten successful attainment of the end state and develop step-by-step plans for removing them. For example, if what is deterring you is a lack of knowledge of some aspect of a problem and you don't know whom to contact to help, think of other people you know who are well connected and might be able to connect you with a person with the answers you seek. Ask these people to introduce you to get your foot in the door. Once you begin to take positive steps, the fear emanating from lack of focus and its destructive effect on your motivation start to disappear.

Loss of direction is yet another self-demotivator. The feeling of suddenly realizing all the efforts put into a project over the past week were misdirected can quickly take the wind out of one's sails. Once again, the hopefully familiar ends/ways/means tool can help. Just as lack of focus on the desired end state is demotivating, getting lost in the ways of getting there is too. Without checkpoints, projects can drift off course. Milestone plans with intermediate objectives can provide guideposts to measure progress to the end goals and signal when efforts are becoming misdirected.

Recall that the perseverance to weather life's storms is one of three subthemes of courageous leadership. There are ways in which leaders can exercise what some call "grit" in getting through storms at work that might demotivate.[42] The United States Marine Corps, along with many other organizations and teams, recite the mantra that "pain is weakness leaving the body." This is as true in the business world as it is with physical exercise. Pain of failure should teach us and make us better. We often learn far more from our failures than our successes. When one of the coauthors became a commercial lender, a sage older banker told him, "Ask to help collect a few bad loans other officers have made. You'll learn more from one bad loan than you will from ten good ones." The sage banker was right. If leaders count failures as learning experiences, this tends to lessen the blow of making mistakes to their motivation.

When agonizing over a demotivating mistake, take a longer-term perspective. One of the coauthors asks himself, "Is this going to matter 5 years from now?" If the answer is "No," then he asks himself why he's agonizing over it. A somewhat similar tactic when confronted with a perplexing problem that defies immediate solution is to take a break and step away from the problem. Then, after clearing your mind, take a step back from the problem in a figurative sense and try to examine it from a larger perspective. There may be ways to circumvent it you have been unable to see because you were too immersed in the details.

In summary, the iconic Steve Jobs of Apple fame had some interesting advice on motivation: "Do what you love to do. Find your passion. The only way to do great work is to love what you do."[43] We're not sure whether that last sentence is 100 percent accurate, but we believe that Jobs was on the right track.

CHAPTER 8

Fostering Growth in Others and Yourself

> **"Tell me and I forget, teach me and I may remember, involve me, and I learn."**
>
> —Benjamin Franklin

One of the greatest responsibilities of leaders is to grow their followers and themselves by engaging in new challenges. This entails coaching subordinates, mentoring others, and becoming your own mentor regardless of whether you have a coach or mentor. **Coaching** takes place within the context of the leader/subordinate relationship and often ends when the subordinate or the leader moves on to another position. **Mentoring** is defined as "a professional relationship in which an experienced person (the mentor) assists another in developing specific skills and knowledge that will enhance the less-experienced person's professional and personal growth."[1] **Self-mentoring** is highly desirable for several reasons. You can augment your mentor if you have one, be a mentor for yourself if you don't, and become a better mentor for others. Although all three of these activities can make you a better leader, it takes effort, and success often does not come easily. One critical element in all three is involvement. It takes real engagement to improve one's subordinates and oneself and grow both into leaders of the future. This can sometimes mean going it alone to some extent because businesses often fail to provide as they should for development. The Drucker Foundation has stated the following:

> Many believe that 80 percent of a typical executive's development is the result of on-the-job experience. Unfortunately, on-the-job experience has historically fostered management skills rather than leadership skills, For the most part, our managers develop leadership skills by chance, through the school of hard knocks. Also, they are products of a system that provides few on-the-job opportunities to develop leadership skills. These executives are part of a system that confuses management with leadership.[2]

One of the difficulties we have observed with learning leadership exclusively through experience is that experience can be a fickle mistress. For example, leaders who experience success using one style of leadership in one setting or situation may attempt to extrapolate that style to other situations and settings in which it works far less well and may be dysfunctional. If we buy into the quote by Benjamin Franklin above that experience is the best teacher, the real question organizations face is whether to allow that experience to just occur by chance opportunity or whether to create and structure opportunities for leaders to grow. The problem is that such structuring is not free even though, properly done, it can sometimes provide a high return on investment in the long run, as noted in chapter 3 when one study correlated leadership style to 30 percent higher profitability. You are fortunate if you happen to work for an enlightened organization that believes in systematically structuring opportunities for leadership growth and programs for developing leaders. If you are not so fortunate, you can still make a contribution to your employer and subordinates and benefit yourself in the process by becoming a coach and a mentor and by mentoring yourself.

8.1. The Need to Foster Growth and Develop Leaders

One of the foremost and important responsibilities of courageous leaders is to nurture and foster growth in their subordinates. Many employees stay with employers not because of financial incentives but rather because of continual learning opportunities and professional and personal growth. When leaders nurture growth in their followers they strengthen the latter's commitment to the organization, increase their value, and foster greater job satisfaction and loyalty. The result is often higher productivity and service levels. Not treating the growth of employees as a priority can lead to higher employee turnover. Hiring from outside is more expensive and riskier than promoting from within. Not only is there the cost of acquiring and training a new employee, there is the production lost as the new employee learns the organizational culture, key points of contact, and informal ways of getting things done. In addition, as an unknown entity, the new employee has a higher risk of not working out as well as hoped.[3]

Unfortunately, many business organizations treat nurturing employee growth as a collateral responsibility to be dealt with as time and financial resources permit. Three common poor leadership practices smother employee development. One is failing to acknowledge the importance of employees. Leaders frequently take credit for successes but fail to share credit with those subordinates who contributed to success. A second is not asking the opinions of employees when structuring

> "Business is a complex system whose facets include inspiration, people, finances, goals, logistics, strategy, the market, stressors, and glee (among other things). One of the primary sources of this complexity is employees . . . Overlay this topic onto the business plan and it's easy to see where 'the employee factor' requires nimble—but assured— footing in the bottom line and vision of your business."
>
> —Jamie Walters

solutions to problems. It is tempting for leaders in a hurry to consider it a waste of time to ask for employee input. After all, isn't the reason they are the leaders to set the course for others to follow? This confuses ends, ways, and means. The leader may well be the one to set the end goals, but how a unit achieves these goals and with what resources can be decisions benefitting from employee input. Third, leaders who start by giving their opinions about ways and means often and forcefully discourage feedback. Subordinates assume the leader knows what he or she wants and consider it a waste of time and possibly a personal risk to offer suggestions.

Why do leaders not pay more attention to nurturing their followers? We believe that two primary reasons are time constraints and the lack of good guidance on how to go about it. Some relegate most of the responsibility to the training unit in the HR department. Some believe they satisfy this requirement by sending employees off on external programs or by having an occasional internal seminar with a guest speaker. Although such training may sometimes be helpful, our observation is that, without consistent follow-up and guidance on how to actually implement growth nurturing, it frequently becomes a check-in-the-box on a leader's to-do list rather than a significant cause of employee growth. Astute senior business executives understand that an outstanding employee-development program can mean the difference between success and mediocrity. Business growth and employee development are closely related. Future leaders are critical to the lifeblood of medium-sized and larger firms. A well-executed, multipronged program can have a major impact.

First, businesses can create effective **employee-training programs** that provide ongoing training pertinent to current jobs, including coaching, instead of the "one and done" training that is all too pervasive. This includes a development plan for each employee. The development plan does not have to be voluminous. It can be one sheet

"It doesn't matter whether your business is a small manufacturing shop or a multi-store aftermarket retailer, the employee remains your front line in combating the hurdles of the economy."

—Dick Dixon

of paper that outlines the employee's aspirations for progression, the skills required for the next upward move, skills gaps that need to be closed for that progression to happen, and how the supervisor and employee plan to close those gaps. The plan can but does not need to be on file with HR. Instead it is a contract between the supervisor and employee. Coaching should also focus on creative learning processes whereby employees can provide input that assists the business in improving. Although formal suggestion programs with financial rewards tied to increasing revenue or cost savings can be productive, having supervisors

routinely ask for suggestions during meetings and performance reviews can yield good ideas while fostering creative thinking among employees.[4]

Second, in conjunction with coaching, the firm can **reimburse tuition costs** for external education and training. Some types of businesses (e.g., banking, healthcare, public accounting) have their own courses developed by a professional association that are directly applicable to that type. Often clerical-level personnel have difficulty affording tuition. Tuition reimbursement for employees to attend local universities during off-hours can sometimes mean the difference between promising clerical employees ascending to the ranks of management and leaving the firm for better opportunities. Providing tuition assistance can also be useful in attracting good candidates, and employees who successfully complete such programs demonstrate high motivation and self-discipline that helps signal their future potential.[5]

Third, businesses can implement **formal mentoring programs** pairing new employees with more experienced and successful leaders. Mentors can assist in providing career advice and be sounding boards, enabling their mentees to grasp the "big picture" of how the organization functions. For example, in a professional services firm a new hire may report to a junior manager who may assume coaching responsibilities. Having a partner for a mentor can provide a different and higher-level perspective for the new hire.[6]

Fourth, it is essential to **acknowledge and reward star performers**. One of the best ways to accomplish this is by hiring and promoting from within the organization.[7] Sometimes it is necessary to hire externally in order to immediately obtain skills the business lacks or to bring in fresh perspectives. This should be the exception, however, not the rule. Hiring and promoting from within signals that the organization rewards good performance and loyalty. It is disheartening to hear an employee say, "The only way to get promoted here is to go somewhere else." It is especially important to recognize achievements that require employees to go well beyond their normal duties. Recall from chapter 2 that part of a courageous leadership philosophy is celebrating special accomplishments of pack members. One of the coauthors notes, "I obtained three of my degrees while working full-time helped by employer tuition assistance. Those degrees represented 8 years of continuously working long hours. Not once did my employer make any announcement of my having received these degrees. It puzzles me that my employer thought it important enough to pay for my additional education but not important enough to acknowledge it." In the sidebar, another of the coauthors tells a different story.

Often the person in the best position to nurture employee growth is the employee's direct supervisor because the supervisor usually spends more time than anyone else observing the employee at work and has a substantial stake in the employee's performance. Coaching should not be a secondary responsibility. It is fundamental to ongoing improvement of the business. Leaders' performance as coaches and mentors should be made part of their performance review process, and for leaders who have been with the organization for a long time in leadership roles, one aspect of performance is the progression made by those who have served as their subordinates. This assessment should be somewhat subjective and not become a nose-counting exercise, however, because one subordinate who turns out to be a superstar may have more organizational impact than a half-dozen good-but-not-great others.

Recognizing the need for growth requires a balancing act on the part of employers. Growth takes commitment and, importantly, time. For example, Kelley alumnus Derek Bang, partner-in-charge of Crowe Horwath's national healthcare

> **Coauthor comment**
>
> "When I earned my CPA certification it was announced at a monthly meeting. Afterward many fellow employees queried me about it. Perhaps inspired by seeing me recognized, several went on to get their own certifications."

practice and the firm's chief innovation officer, takes a day once every couple months to meet with his direct reports for purposes of training, development, and obtaining feedback. Leaders have to balance the time required to meet the needs of the ongoing business with that required to develop subordinates. If certain subordinates are targeted for special development, part of this balancing act is to ensure that the workload does not become unevenly distributed as a result of training time. There is also a balancing act in terms of short-term needs versus higher performance long term.[8] It is often difficult to envision much less quantify just how valuable employee-development efforts can be, especially when the value can vary greatly with the quality of the efforts. For this reason it is important to ensure that employee-development time is used optimally and is not allowed to become a check-in-the-box activity that merely allows a firm to say to a prospective recruit, "Sure, we have a great employee-development program here at XYZ." Nonetheless, by allowing employees to flourish and develop their talents, businesses strengthen employees' ties to the organization and increase the value they offer.[9]

8.2. Creating a Growth Culture

Employee-development programs such as those discussed in the previous section are highly conducive to growing leaders in businesses, but to be effective they need to be supported by a strong culture that nurtures professional and personal growth.[10] What are the characteristics of such a culture? This section presents some of the more important of these characteristics.

Start by *acknowledging the importance of employees* to the firm's success. Surveys indicate employees leave businesses more often because of the lack of recognition than because of inadequate compensation.[11] One way to do this is by honoring the firm's heroes, those legacy employees whose contributions paved the way for its success today. Another is to provide anecdotal evidence of how current employees' efforts have enhanced success of projects. An excellent time to do this is when celebrating victories. During a group meeting, don't just present a subordinate for being the employee of the month. Take the time to explain why the employee earned that honor. If you can't explain why, it is time to question whether you are cheapening the "employee of the month" idea by automatically rotating it among employees, a practice we have observed. In fact, instead of an employee of the month, consider having an "outstanding-employee-performance award" given only when a performance is truly deserving. Know your people and call them by their names. Know their birthdays, their spouses and children's names, their educational backgrounds, and so forth. Keep these on a 3×5 card, in your Outlook contacts list, or on your iPad for handy reference, and glance at them before engaging the employee in conversation.

Set clear expectations and milestone objectives and ensure each subordinate knows what is expected of him or her and what constitutes superior and minimally acceptable performances. Provide context for these expectations, meaning communicating an understanding of how the subordinate's efforts contribute to organizational success. Explain how routine job functions represent growth opportunities. Discuss the rewards for the organization and the individual that come

from success, but keep the focus on growth and achievement instead of profits and individual monetary incentives.[12] Focusing on the latter has a tendency to create a piece-rate mentality and tie people to the organization only until some other firm offers more.[13]

Next, *open the lines of communication,* offering honest, positive, caring feedback, and seek input.[14] A good way to do this is by helping subordinates to find their "familiars," those feelings that we unconsciously reproduce that emanate from our backgrounds.[15] Be friendly, approachable, and continuously solicit feedback and suggestions. Sometimes it is best to share your feelings first if doing so does not prejudice subordinates' responses. In one-on-one conversations ask for opinions on such things as how new programs are working out. Ask what problems employees are experiencing and why these are problems. Ask for recommended solutions. Then take the opportunity to offer praise. Seeking feedback requires leadership courage because, as Stephen Covey notes, "Many business executives lack the internal security to seek and take feedback from stakeholders—they are threatened by it."[16]

Accountability groups can be quite useful in opening the lines of communication. Such groups serve to "give and receive feedback, create action plans based upon the feedback, and hold group members accountable for implementing their plans . . . Done correctly, they can lead individuals and organizations of all sizes to transform themselves from the inside out."[17] It is good to offer subordinates opportunities for leadership, even if on a spot basis. For example, a leader might offer a promising subordinate the opportunity to lead a meeting of the accountability group.

One of the coauthors tells the following story:

> In the company of a senior vice president, I was once touring the plant of a medium-sized, highly profitable manufacturer

of automotive parts. The plant was organized in assembly line fashion around large, complex machines, each of which was manned by a team. Interestingly, the teams were mostly constituted around ethnicity, with employees of one team being of Korean extraction, those of another being Hispanic, and so forth. Two things jumped out at me. One was that the SVP knew the name of every employee and asked about family members. The feedback he received from being so engaged with his employees was simply amazing. He laughed and joked with them, but there was no question they respected him and felt at ease communicating with him. He would ask if anything could be improved and get responses such as, "The gozorkinflickin on the machine is getting old and needs to be replaced soon. It broke down twice last week and cost us 4 hours of overtime to meet the production schedule." Would production managers have noticed the small amount of overtime and linked it to the maintenance report? Maybe not.

A second surprising thing was his description of the familial culture within each team. Candidates for job openings within each team mostly came from people the workers in the units knew and recruited. The workers within the team assumed responsibility for training each new worker and also for ensuring that the worker performed well. No worker wanted a poorly performing employee to detract from the unit's reputation for high performance. For my benefit, the SVP would say things such as, "Our team leader, Sung, has been with us for 20 years, and I've never known him to miss a day of work. His nephew Kang just joined the team. How's Kang working out?" To which Sung might reply something such as, "He makes too many mistakes, but he is learning. I am on him hard to improve." In effect, each team was its own accountability group. Although one might

find reasons to criticize such a system, the familial culture functioned as a vehicle for recruiting, training, growth and development, ensuring high performance, and retention—and the esprit de corps of each team was amazing!

8.3. Growing with Understanding

One of best things leaders can do to help their subordinates grow is to recognize what motivates them. Too often there is the implicit assumption that compensation is the foremost motivator. As noted previously, that is often not the case. Subordinates are motivated when they feel self-fulfillment, and fostering self-fulfillment requires setting aside tacit blanket assumptions that subordinates are alike. As the box quote on the left suggests, the degree that leaders get what they

> ## "A leader is a leader only as he has followers. A follower is a follower only insofar as he does what a leader wants in order to please the leader."
>
> —David Keirsey and Marilyn Bates

want is a measure of their leadership. Followers, in effect, present their work to their leaders in a sense as gifts, which makes leaders imprudent if they do not thank their followers. Paychecks are not enough. Followers want to be thanked for their contributions and want the appreciation proportionate to the contributions. Many leaders may resist thanking followers for doing what they are paid to do, and, given what we've said previously about avoiding cheap, hollow praise, that might seem reasonable. But, if leaders are doing a good job, they hopefully have spawned followers who are so engaged that their contributions exceed what is contemplated in their compensation. In fact, if followers are adhering to the advice we offered in chapter 1 about building the balance in the credibility accounts, they are doing more than

Figure 8.1. Follower Likes and Dislikes by Style

Style	Appreciates Leader Recognizing	Implications for Leader Behaviors
SP	Cleverness, flair, recognition of risky nature of work, boldness, endurance	Companion in celebrating success, reassurance when unsuccessful
SJ	Quantity of production, exceeding standards, responsible	Abundance of appreciation for loyalty, responsibility, and industriousness
NT	Great ideas, intelligent listening, complexity of work, capabilities	Appreciation for routine tasks disdained, wants leader credibility
NF	Uniqueness as individuals, unique contributions	Least likely to respond positively to negative criticism

required, often much more. If those contributions go continuously without being rewarded by praise and recognition, the odds of an employee leaving the organization increase substantially.[18]

How can leaders best thank their followers? Start by caring enough about followers to understand them. Jung's theory of psychological types posited that much of the seemingly random variation in human behavior is actually orderly and consistent with differences due to the way people prefer to become energized, receive information, make decisions, and approach life. These preferences are more or less hardwired.[19] Achievement creates a hunger for approval by the leader, but, even if the leader does thank his or her followers, the leader may fail by imposing his or her own style upon followers who have a very different style. To get the most from showing appreciation to their followers, leaders not only have to understand themselves but their followers as well. Fortunately, there are tools available to assist in this understanding, as discussed in chapter 5. Consider the following information in Figure 8.1 that reveals how four different

styles react to appreciation and what irritates each.

As Figure 8.1 indicates, each of the four styles is likely to desire different types of recognition and to respond somewhat differently to a given type. For example, the leader's title means little to an NT, but his or her credibility in the chosen field means a great deal. In dealing with an NT over some matter at work, the leader might begin with a discussion designed to demonstrate technical competence, such as an understanding of financial reports. Each style also differs with respect to what annoys. Rules and standing operating procedures create impatience in SPs, whereas SJs are annoyed when others do not follow such procedures. A leader handling a complaint from an SJ about an SP missing an important deadline because of his or her unstructured approach might wish to assure the SJ that deadlines are important and the leader intends to take the matter up with the SP. NTs insist on getting maximum results from their efforts and are annoyed when asked to do something that seems illogical to them, so a leader attempting to respond to a complaint about a new corporate policy requiring paper clips to be recycled (yes, that one is real) might be forewarned to not make light of the NT's concern. NFs are irritated by what they perceive as impersonal treatment, so leaders who might be otherwise inclined to be somewhat impersonal when very busy should be sensitive enough to show personal attention by such seemingly minor behaviors as smiling and calling the NF by name.[20]

It is tempting to ask, "How can I possibly be aware of all the likes and dislikes of my followers and respond in kind to each?" Two other tempting questions are, "Why should I do all the adjusting?" and "Can't followers adjust, too?" The answers are, "You can't know all of every follower's likes and dislikes," "You won't have to do all the adjusting," and "Yes, followers can often adapt to situations when required to do so." For example, as discussed in chapter 5, when the Myers-Briggs Type Indicator was administered to faculty consisting of senior military officers and professors with PhDs at the U.S. Marine Corps Command and Staff College, it was discovered that the majority of the faculty members were introverts by nature. Yet they routinely gave lectures to groups of experienced military officers in a manner that suggested they were quite extroverted. These introverts-by-nature had simply trained themselves to respond to a professional requirement imposed by their work environment. But forcing followers to use their nonpreferences more than their preferences increases their stress levels. Leaders can reduce miscommunication with employees and concurrently employee stress by knowing at least some of employees' preferences and guiding communications accordingly.

Growing employees with understanding takes effort. Remember the SVP of the automotive parts company who knew every employee by name? That took effort, but it paid real dividends for the company. Recall also the suggestion of the deck of 3×5 cards (physical or virtual) containing your

thumbnail sketch of each employee. Courageous leadership is not easy, but the payoffs are huge. Tools such as the MBTI, which has been used for over 50 years, are very useful for understanding individual differences and becoming a better communicator, coach, and mentor.[21]

8.4. Coaching Subordinates

The front lines in employee performance improvement involve counseling and coaching and should be part of the day-to-day interactions between leaders and subordinates. Coaching is ongoing and ends only when the employee becomes some other leader's subordinate. It involves providing both positive and negative feedback with follow-up actions regarding improvement or lack thereof. The goal is improvement of both good-but-not-great strengths as well as weaknesses.[22] Hopefully you will enjoy the benefits of a formal coaching program implemented by your employer, but even if your current or future employer doesn't have a program, you can still make an impact by becoming a coach and applying the same principles. Coaching often takes courage because there are risks involved, but the rewards can be great if coaching is done consistently and well. One of the risks is that those being coached will make mistakes when handling new responsibilities. Another is that sometimes coaches will lose their subordinates because the latter grow beyond the challenges the coach can offer them and migrate elsewhere. Enlightened organizations will treat such progression explicitly as a positive factor in leaders' performance evaluations.

It may be helpful to think in **progressive phases** when coaching. Consider the sport of American football and what is necessary to prepare a team to play a game. First, learning must take place. Football plays are diagrammed in what is known as "skull sessions," where players see the plays drawn in some medium to learn their individual roles. Next, the plays are walked through on the practice field, followed by being run without contact with opposing players. Then, plays are run with opposition in light contact, followed by full contact drills. Finally, the plays are run against opposing teams. During each phase coaches observe, critique, and correct players. After a game, the cycle starts all over again with an **after-action critique** of the past game and necessary improvements.

Taking the above analogy to business settings, some *general guidelines for effective coaching* are helpful:

1. Conduct an *initial assessment meeting* with the subordinate. Describe clearly the performance issues, whether the nature is improving upon a good performance or correcting a poor one. Focus on behaviors, not the employee personally. Use factual data and information and cite specific examples of behaviors and when they took place. Ask for the employee's input on the situation. Does the employee agree with your assessment? If not, what are the points of difference? Determine if any issues are impeding the performance (e.g., time, workload, lack of tools, interpersonal conflicts with other employees). Discuss possible solutions and ascertain how to mitigate these issues. Ask for the employee's ideas for improving, and show confidence that improvement is possible and concern for the employee's well-being.

2. Create an *informal contract* with the subordinate. State the ends (improvement goals) and include milestone objectives, dates for achieving these objectives, and specific measures indicating if these objectives are being maintained. Be explicit to avoid a lack of clarity. Outline the agreed-upon ways for meeting the objectives and any means (resources) required to assist the employee and how these means will be obtained. Create a list of action items to be followed up. Once the document is drafted,

establish that the employee understands the document's contents and clarify any misconceptions by obtaining answers to the following checklist questions:

A. Is the employee's vision of success the same as yours?

B. Have you identified all the major obstacles to improvement?

C. Does the employee have a clear understanding of the goals and objectives and exactly what he or she needs to do to attain them?

D. Does the employee have the necessary self-confidence to carry out the plan? Does the employee seem overwhelmed by the magnitude of the task? Procrastination often results from lack of self-confidence. If there is a self-confidence problem, is there anything you can do to bolster the employee's self-confidence, such as additional training?

E. Is the employee practicing good work management, such as breaking large tasks into smaller ones, keeping lists of action items, and tracking progress on projects? If the answer is no, you may need to demonstrate how to use these tools to better manage workflow.

F. Have you identified all necessary resources and how the employee will obtain them?[23]

3. Do your part and *keep your end of the contract.* Your job is not over when you have reached agreement about an improvement plan. You must demonstrate at least the same diligence and attention to detail that you expect from your subordinate. If you promised resources, follow up to ensure the employee received them. If you promised written guidance (e.g., reading materials), produce it in a timely fashion. If you promised tuition reimbursement for

signing up for professional development, follow up to ensure your subordinate is being reimbursed.

4. Conduct *follow-up meetings* (plural) to discuss progress against the milestone objectives by reviewing the plan. Be compassionate but candid in your after-action assessments. If objectives are not being met, ascertain why. If objectives are being met, praise the employee's efforts and encourage him or her to continue to improve while warning against complacency.[24] Follow up to ensure suggested work management tools are being used and find out if there are any resource availability difficulties. If progress is not being made as anticipated, try to differentiate and reach agreement on what is and is not the fault of the employee. If there are significant issues that were unanticipated at the initial assessment meeting, the contract may need to be adjusted, but avoid being talked out of the desired end state simply because the employee is having difficulty reaching objectives. Instead, modify the plan to provide more assistance.

You can apply a similar phased approach in situations involving coaching nonperformers called **progressive discipline**. The "three-strikes rule" discussed in chapter 4 embodies the notion of progressive discipline. Assume you have already conducted an informal, oral counseling session with the employee without positive results. It is now time to formalize the corrective coaching process using progressive discipline, which represents an opportunity to apply the Zig-Zag Model. This entails the following: (1) Gathering information to determine the underlying reasons for the poor performance. (2) Holding an initial assessment meeting with the employee to obtain his or her input. Consider alternative courses of action recalling that in the Path-Goal Model your role is first and foremost to remove obstacles impeding your subordinates' progress. (3) Decide on

a course of action and memorialize this in a document as discussed previously in this section using a milestone plan. Ensure the contents are clear and contain the relevant information noted previously. (4) Using the document as a basis for counseling the employee, obtain agreement with regard to ends (goals), ways (objectives and action items), and means (resources). (5) Monitor the employee's progress against the plan and coach continuously, providing both positive and negative feedback as appropriate.[25]

You may have been wondering whatever became of Susan.

Recall that Susan was the bank administrative assistant who received a bad performance report from her former boss after he sexually harassed her. Susan told her current boss that she wanted very badly to make it to management ranks and would work hard if given an opportunity to prove herself.

We return now to the real-world story of Susan, your administrative assistant at the bank, discussed in chapter 4. You have a fine, loyal employee who has suffered an injustice, one who goes well beyond her job description responsibilities to provide a superb, unselfish performance—and, importantly—one who wants to become a manager. But she feels her growth is blocked at the bank. You realize that sooner or later the bank will lose Susan unless she is able to grow in her professional life. You recall that the Path-Goal Model of leadership holds that it is your responsibility as a leader to remove blockages that prevent your followers from reaching their goals, so you return to the Zig-Zag Model and consider alternative courses of action. As one possible course of action (COA), you consider whether to attempt to

Fostering Growth in Others and Yourself

undo the damage caused by her previous boss to her performance record by encouraging Susan to file a grievance along with a request to have the adverse report expunged from her employment record. After carefully considering this COA, you conclude that it will likely cause more harm than good, drawing unwanted attention to Susan and perhaps resulting in no positive result at all. Making accusations of sexual impropriety without sufficient evidence to back them up could backfire on Susan and you. Consequently, despite some per-

> **Coauthor comment:**
> **coach to mentor to coach**
>
> "My mentor started as my boss. He was a leader who took a keen interest in his followers' development, championing their accomplishments at every opportunity. In my case, he went from coach to mentor as I migrated to another organization, and then back to coach when he rehired me years later. He never lost interest in me and right up until his death he was still advising me. At his funeral the church was so full of his followers that it was standing room only. No single person had such a great impact on my career."

sonal feelings about leaving the injustice unremedied, you turn to another COA involving helping her to gain entry into management through her hard work and a very visible display of her talents.

You tell her no promises, but together you come up with a training plan involving additional work and learning on her part. She never complains about the additional effort the plan involves. Later when your unit's assistant manager is transferred, you ask Susan if she would like to fill in until

another one is assigned. She accepts enthusiastically and never asks, "Will I get paid more?" In turn, you never ask for a new assistant manager to be assigned. A few weeks later after Susan performs well in her acting-assistant-manager role, you are able to have her promoted to assistant manager permanently with a big pay increase after showing how she has fully embraced her plan for self-improvement and made an impact. In discussing her recommended promotion with your own boss, who has the ear of top management, you confidentially mention there is another side to Susan's difficulties with her previous boss, but one perhaps best left untouched for the benefit of all concerned. By now a dramatic improvement in your unit's performance—thanks, in part, to Susan—has greatly increased the balance in your own credibility account. Consequently, your boss respects your opinion highly and gets the subtle message, asking no questions. Susan continues to perform well and is eventually promoted to manager of another unit with another big raise, becoming an officer of the bank. Her former boss retired early. No reason was announced, but performance issues were rumored.

There are some takeaways from Susan's story. Problems can sometimes be turned into opportunities through coaching, and having guidelines to follow helps. Although Susan's boss was unaware of the Path-Goal and Zig-Zag Models at the time, he nonetheless followed their principles with good results. Life is often unfair, as was the case with Susan's treatment by her former boss, but by knowing how to grow employees, leaders can sometimes turn dead ends into opportunities and serve their pack and followers well.

8.5. Mentoring

Mentors are often critical to career success, and many organizations attempt to establish formal mentorship relationships. Although some highly tout formal mentorship programs, saying they are easy to establish and take little time, our experience has been more mixed.[26] It takes more than a cursory effort for mentorship relationships to blossom into valuable tools for developing talent. If not implemented well, formal mentorship programs can create unmet expectations, foster disillusionment, and waste time with mentor/mentee meetings that achieve little. Well done, however, the rewards for the organization can be great. Mentorship differs from coaching because there is no boss/subordinate relationship, but in some respects the roles can overlap greatly. One source lists six possible functions for mentors:

1. Teaches mentees about specific issues.

2. Instructs mentees on particular skills.

3. Facilitates mentees' growth by sharing resources and networks.

4. Challenges mentees to growth beyond their comfort zones.

5. Creates a safe learning source that better enables mentees to take risks.

6. Focuses on mentees' total development.[27]

In other words, a mentor may engage in coaching, but a coach is not a mentor, at least not simultaneously. Coaching by managers is often more of a function of job responsibility, whereas mentoring is usually relational. Whereas managers have a responsibility to coach all their employees, a mentor assumes responsibility for guiding someone junior in experience and knowledge outside of a formal boss/subordinate relationship.[28] As the sidebar on the previous page indicates, mentor/mentee relationships can begin with coaching relationships when the mentee is a subordinate and last for many years, spanning various organizations after the mentee is no longer a subordinate. This entails a completely voluntary relationship on the part of both parties and implies that both

parties derive some benefit from the relationship—even if that benefit is simply the mentor's satisfaction in observing the mentee's growth. On the other hand, we are less hopeful about the

Coauthor comment

"I see a subtle conflict in the mentoring process with volunteers involved on an informal basis versus programmatic processes. This holds the possibility of engendering potential conflicts. This is perhaps resolvable in an enlightened organization, but in one less enlightened it has the potential for negative consequences."

benefits of being assigned a new "mentor" every time one is transferred from one locale to another. Real mentorship is a labor of love that takes time, thought, effort—and, importantly, compassion.

One way to differentiate the coaching that takes place in a boss/subordinate relationship versus that in a mentor/mentee relationship is that the former involves what has been called **instrumental coaching**, whereas the latter involves **compassionate coaching**. By necessity of their responsibilities, managers usually engage in instrumental coaching. Instrumental coaching encourages employees to change to better fit the goals of the organization and/or their managers, such as improving performance, accepting additional responsibilities, or acting more consistently within organizational norms, all primarily to benefit the organization. This means a primary focus on what some researchers have termed **ought self**—that is, what an employee ought to be in the eyes of the employer. Instrumental coaching is often focused on deficiencies, whether they result in poor performance or simply barriers to progression, as was the case with Susan needing to acquire new knowledge. On the other hand, with compassionate coaching the focus is principally on assisting the mentee to focus on **ideal self**—that is, the mentee's vision of who he or she wants to be—and accentuates the positive.[29] Even though Susan's boss was compassionate in considering her goals and aspirations, his primary motivation was improving his unit's performance. If Susan's goals and aspirations had differed from those he felt were in the organization's best interests, his primary allegiance would have been to the organization in furthering its interests even if those conflicted with Susan's. In that case, his advice to Susan might have been to seek a situation more to her liking while he sought a new administrative assistant.

What does compassionate coaching in mentorship entail? **Compassion** involves noticing another person as being in need, empathizing with him or her, and acting to enhance his or her well-being in response to that need. Compassion is present when the mentor responds empathically to the mentee's need to develop and grow, experienced by the mentee when he perceives such concern. Focusing primarily on the ideal self can create conflicts with the ought self.[30] For example, suppose Sung Kang works in the New York office assurance unit of an international public accounting firm that has assigned him a partner as his mentor who is not in Sung's chain of command. Sung's boss thinks highly of his performance and, because of an unexpected opening due to a serious illness, is encouraging him to join the audit team of a major client in the United States. Stating the need for continuity on the team, the assignment would be for 2 years. The boss explains the critical nature of the need and that such an assignment will be a boost to Sung's career. On the other hand, Sung misses his home country of Korea and has been hoping to be reassigned to the firm's Seoul office soon in order to be nearer his family. How should Sung's mentor react when approached by Sung for advice? Whose preferences should be foremost, Sung's or his boss's?

The foregoing example illustrates the tension that can exist between a boss and a mentor even though both have an interest in the development of an employee. Note that compassionate mentorship need not exclude the mentor considering what is in the best interests of the organization. After all, the firm assigned the mentor to help facilitate Sung's development so that he can better serve the organization. The real question is whether the primary focus is on the immediate need of Sung's unit or Sung's willingness to stay with the firm longer term. Whereas the manager is seeking to fill a critical current need, the mentor can view Sung's situation from a more compassionate, less utilitarian, and longer-term perspective, recognizing that assigning Sung to the U.S.-based client may solve an immediate need but could result in losing Sung's services down the road because his ideal self and ought self are seriously mismatched. The mentor might suggest that Sung approach his boss with some compromise solution that resolves the immediate crisis but does not require

Coauthor comment

"Even if you have a formal mentor, having other informal mentors can be very helpful. You may have one who can help you specifically within your service line but may have another who is better dealing with cultural and personal challenges.

In one office where I worked we had a very informal mentoring group consisting of six employees with young children. We would go to each other about everything from how to get the kid to sleep to how to meet clients' needs while spending more nights at home."

a 2-year commitment, but that may not satisfy Sung's boss. Further complicating matters, what if Sung's boss and mentor are good friends? How might that change the mentor's advice to Sung? Typical goals of a mentoring program are improving recruitment, retention, professional development, and development of a multicultural workforce.[31] How does Sung's mentor balance these somewhat conflicting (in this case) goals when his mentee's professional development must be weighed against retention and the need for a multicultural workforce?

Despite such potential conflicts, formal mentoring programs can have additional benefits beyond those just mentioned. These include improving productivity, improving interunit cooperation and information exchange, elevating knowledge transfer to a lessons-learned level, and breaking down "silo" mentality in problem solving.[32] Formal mentoring programs can also help get new hires up to speed faster, improve the rate of application of newly acquired skills, assist employees in adapting to major organizational changes such as mergers, help bridge generational gaps, build trust among employees, and show commitment to employees.[33]

Formal, structured mentoring programs require attention. A **mentoring program manager** is the organization's internal mentoring expert, coordinating the mentoring process, attending to seeing that mentors receive training in how to mentor, often assigning mentors to mentees, and monitoring ongoing mentoring activities for effectiveness. Structured programs can be patterned around one of several models. **One-on-one** is most common, matching one mentee to one mentor. Many prefer this model because it better fosters a one-on-one relationship in the pairs. **Resource-based mentoring** differs from one-on-one mentoring in that the program manager does not assign pairs. Instead, mentees pick mentors from a list of available mentors. Mentees initiate

this process, which can often result in mismatched pairs. In **group mentoring**, mentors work with several mentees often meeting at one time. This model has the advantage of mentees helping to mentor one another but presents disadvantages in difficulty in scheduling meetings and being less personal. Some firms combine one-on-one and group mentoring. **Training-based mentoring** is narrow in scope and assigns mentors to mentees to accomplish a specific objective. **Executive mentoring** is a top-down model that cascades mentors and mentees such that a C-level officer might mentor someone just below him or her who, in turn, mentors someone just below him or her. This can become an effective management-succession-planning tool.[34]

Mentoring can be a powerful tool for personnel recruiting, development, and retention, but it requires careful attention and monitoring. Assigning a mentor/mentee relationship that is ineffective can be disillusioning for the mentee. Mentors too busy to meet mentees with some reasonable frequency make a mockery of the program and can breed mistrust stemming from failing to fulfill mentees' expectations. On the other hand, if mentees are unwilling to engage meaningfully with mentors, a formal program becomes a waste of resources. Consequently, if you find yourself in a mentor/mentee relationship that is not meeting expectations, try to ascertain why this is and seek assistance from the mentor program manager.

8.6. How to Be a Good Mentor and Mentee

In the end, no matter how well orchestrated an organizational mentoring program may be, it is up to each mentor and mentee to make it work for the pair. The foundation for a good mentor/mentee relationship rests upon three attributes on the part of both. **Mutual respect** exists when both parties demonstrate professional and personal appreciation for each other, each respecting the other's professionalism and personal character. **Responsiveness** entails the mentor's willingness to respond to the mentee's questions and needs for information and the mentee's humility in being willing to learn from the mentor. **Accountability** refers to keeping agreements regarding mutually established goals and expectations. The following steps will help assure that these attributes are present in the mentor/mentee relationship:

> 1. Be a willing participant and enjoy the relationship while being willing to learn from each other.
>
> 2. Foster and protect trust through a culture of honest communication with reciprocal feedback.
>
> 3. Establish agreed-upon standards, goals, and expectations.
>
> 4. Be flexible, tolerate occasional mistakes, and consider each other's time constraints but meet regularly, as frequently as weekly but at least monthly.[35]

Listening is vital in a mentoring relationship for both parties. Ensure advice is relevant, recognizing that it is often cheap to give but expensive to implement, especially if wrong. Mentors need to consider alternative courses of action and assist mentees in understanding trade-offs between them. Sometimes being a great mentor is not so much about giving great advice but rather asking great questions. Both mentors and mentees should respectfully challenge each other's ideas and advice. Mentees should recognize that mentors, like all of us, are to some extent prisoners of their experiences. This may lead them to make assumptions and have biases that do not necessarily reflect the best course of action for all people and situations. Mentees should not be afraid to ask mentors why they believe a course of action to be best. In the end, it is the mentees' responsibility to listen carefully to what they hear, weigh sugges-

tions against their own knowledge and intuition, and decide what to accept, ignore, and reject.[36]

Why do mentor/mentee relationships fail? Research that focused on mentoring relationships at two large academic health centers suggests that poor communication, lack of commitment, personality differences, perceived or real competition between the mentor and mentee, conflicts of interest that destroy trust, and mentor inexperience were the major causes of failure. The study identified reciprocity, mutual respect, clear expectations, personal connections, and shared values as being important to success. Good mentors were said to be trustworthy and good listeners, with a network of contacts that could open doors for mentees, help jump-start mentees' careers, and explain how systems work.[37] Mentors should not perceive the need to be oracles of information. They need to be aware of and humble enough to admit what they don't know. Mentors should not be too proud to say, "I don't know the answer to that question, but I'll try to get you one." Mentors should also confess their biases, making statements such as, "My understanding of that is based upon one anecdotal experience I had long ago, so my impression may not reflect the current situation."

Mentees, too, need to take actions to make mentor/mentee relationships work well. Don't wait for your mentor to probe for insights into who you are and what needs you may have. Take the initiative. Define your goals and objectives from the relationship. Know what you want and need in the way of guidance and understanding. Attempt to identify obstacles that will prevent you from reaching your goals and objectives and think about how the mentor might help you overcome these obstacles. Be respectful of your mentor and his or her time.[38] Be prepared and on time for meetings with your mentor. Decide in advance on questions about substantive issues concerning you. Provide advance notice of your questions to the mentor, so that he or she can be prepared as well. Don't be obtuse. Open up. Share your goals, ideas, hopes, and fears openly with the mentor. Ask direct incisive questions about what you want to know. Focus on your relationship with the mentor, not on what he or she can do for you. It is not your mentor's responsibility to find you a better job in the organization, although he or she may be able to make helpful suggestions. Follow up on your mentor's suggestions and provide feedback on the results at your next meeting. It can be frustrating for a mentor to take time only to see you fail to take action. Be sure to always thank your mentor for taking time for you.[39]

8.7. Self-Mentoring and Self-Monitoring

Regardless of whether your employer has a formal mentoring program or not, and regardless of whether you have acquired your own mentor through informal channels, you should become your own mentor. There are several reasons why becoming one's own mentor is well advised. First, all mentors are not good ones. Some, being enamored with the sound of their own voices while having little to offer in the way of good advice, derive personal utility from having an audience to whom they can privately pontificate. You should never take what a mentor tells you as being the unvarnished, accurate truth. Using prudent and informed thought, you need to able to critically judge the quality of advice you receive and decide whether to follow it. Second, even if you acquire a good mentor, he or she may not be with you for the long haul. Circumstances such as job changes, illness, or even death may dissolve the relationship. Third, no mentor but you can be with you all the time, constantly providing feedback that helps you continually adjust and improve your behaviors.[40] You will improve faster if you become your own mentor and use other mentors to augment your own efforts, providing an external source of knowledge and validating or invalidating your thinking.

As with being a good mentee, there are several keys to becoming an effective self-mentor. First, understand yourself. Know your likes and dislikes. Decide what types of transactions you enjoy and which you do not. Learn about jobs that offer more of the transactions you enjoy and set your goals on those. Create your own career plan in writing. Writing helps solidify thinking and exposes weaknesses. In all likelihood your plan will change over time as you receive new information and new opportunities present themselves, but have a plan! Include milestone objectives and set rough timetables for achieving these objectives. Don't agonize too much if you miss an objective, but understand why you missed it. Was the cause something you did or didn't do? If so, create a plan to fix the problem. If the cause was some random event, recognize that no one has complete control over events and outcomes. When you do reach an objective, pause for a short while to celebrate your accomplishment, and then get back to working on your plan.

Key on your work environment, and observe how other employees—great and not so great—operate. Attempt to discern what behaviors are appreciated and those that are not. Pay particular attention to those who are best in class. Using high-performing co-workers as a benchmark, assess your strengths and weaknesses and make a list. Challenge yourself to correct shortcoming and reach a higher level of professionalism. Continuously ask questions of others in a polite way. If you see someone doing something really well, you might remark, "You really seem to have that down well. How did you become so proficient at it?" Be alert to forms of professional development that are available; seek them out and decide which ones offer the most promise for improving your performance. Assist others whenever you can even if you don't benefit directly and they show little appreciation. Doing so will help create a network of co-workers who can appreciate your talents at the same time as you are building your leadership skills. Cast your net far and wide to gain knowledge. Use the Internet to build a directory of professional friends and acquaintances to whom you go occasionally for advice. People often enjoy being asked for advice, but don't abuse these relationships by asking too much or too often. Finally, become a mentor to others, formal or informal. In doing so, you will gain leadership skills while having the satisfaction of serving others.[41]

Self-mentors can benefit from **self-monitoring**, a concept that has its origins in expressive controls theory. High self-monitors are concerned with how they present themselves to others. Self-monitoring involves continuously attempting to understand how groups and individuals perceive one's behavior and then making adjustments accordingly to increase positive perceptions and receptivity to behavior. Some self-monitors adjust their behaviors subconsciously, while for others it is a conscious effort. Compared with low self-monitors, high self-monitors typically experience greater receptivity from others. People who refuse to self-monitor are often characterized by higher levels of aggression, less willingness to compromise, and more insistent behavior. Low self-monitors are more prone to condemnation and rejection, in turn leading to consequential feelings of anger, guilt, anxiety, and low self-esteem.[42] Consequently, self-monitoring seems well advised for business professionals, but a word of caution is in order. You cannot please everyone, and attempting to do so can be very frustrating. So don't share your values and beliefs. Some are envious. Some simply don't care about others. Decide on those people whom you especially admire and feel represent outstanding professionalism and gauge their reactions to your behaviors.

The benefits of becoming a self-mentor are several. Your problem-resolution skills will increase over time, along with your ability to think quickly and decisively. With these skills comes new self-confidence in dealing with difficult problems. This self-confidence leads to an increased willingness to take on increasingly complex problems, which increases your experience in solving difficult problems.[43] You are now spiraling upward, creating an ever-growing personal repository of greater and greater problem-resolution skills. This virtuous cycle leads to greater professional enrichment, fewer thoughts of failure, and a newfound boldness in your professional career. You are now less dependent upon others for emotional reinforcement and acclamation and ready to assume ever-higher leadership roles.

PART III
Your Personal Career-Sucess Toolkit

Foreword

Part III deals with some tools you will need to be a successful courageous leader in business. Chapter 9 deals with the business value-adding ability to identify and solve complex business problems using critical thinking. Chapter 10 examines self-learning to accelerate development of knowledge and leadership skills to enable courageous leaders to assume responsibility faster. Chapter 11 discusses communication skills, and Chapter 12 explores combining leadership and technical skills to become a talent that fits throughout career progression.

CHAPTER 9

Critical Thinking in Identifying and Solving Complex Problems

> **"We always hope for the easy fix: the one simple change that will erase a problem in a stroke. But few things in life work this way. Instead, success requires making a hundred small steps go right— one after the other, no slipups, no goofs, everyone pitching in."**
>
> —Atul Gawande, *Better: A Surgeon's Notes on Performance*

Recall our basic statement of belief in the preface about what businesses want in the way of leadership: *What organizations really want (or should want) is courageous, ethical leaders who can* **identify and solve complex problems under conditions of uncertainty**, *motivate others to perform at high levels, and consistently achieve superior organizational outcomes on schedule within resource constraints.* Note also the portion of this statement in boldface. Identifying and solving complex problems is at the heart of what businesses need leaders to be successful in doing. It is a primary way in which leaders add value to businesses. Consider the quote above. Easy fixes are often difficult to find. If problems are easy to solve they usually don't remain problems very long. Instead, complex-problem identification and solving usually requires many steps and often involves coordinating with others, making it a leadership issue. Finally, done effectively, it means being able to do lots of things correctly in the right sequence. This sort of ordered thinking leads directly to critical thinking. But good thinking is hard work and not something many are inclined to do. Even when we're doing it, it sometimes is not fun, raising troubling questions and exposing the world as a more complex place than we believe it to be.

Are you a good critical thinker? Have you had lots of complex-problem-solving experience? Good for you. You're set then, right? Or maybe you should consider Chris Argyris's argument in "Teaching Smart People How to Learn." The smarter you are and the more successful you've been, the harder it is for you to become a more effective person by moving your reasoning to the next higher plane. The smarter people are, the better they are at **defensive reasoning**—that is, rationalizing and defending their ideas even if the ideas are objectively indefensible.[1] One form of defensive reasoning is that everyone is entitled to an opinion. Although we all have opinions, when we're dealing with matters of judgment some people's judgment is more informed than that of others.

9.1. Why Critical Thinking?

Numerous studies have produced evidence that a lack of critical-thinking skills is linked to poor mathematical skills and a lack of understanding of scientific principles. This obviously has import for business leaders who deal frequently with issues involving technology, finance, accounting, and operations management. Inasmuch as these disciplines are continuously growing in complexity, the need for critical-thinking skills is in all probability increasing. A major point of debate among educators is whether critical-thinking skills can be learned and transferred among various knowledge domains, but recent evidence supports this possibility.[2] Some things researchers do tend to agree on are that people tend to have a poor understanding of logic, makes reasoning mistakes in consistent ways, have little awareness of their own mental processes, and are overconfident about their reasoning ability.[3] Business leaders therefore need to be attuned to the need to continuously improve their critical-thinking skills.

This growing need for critical thinking is found in such business activities as auditing, in which skepticism of client financial transactions is important, as well as greater subjectivity in fair value measurements of such assets as early stage intellectual property. As a result, leadership development programs at leading universities have begun including critical-thinking components in their curricula. Some businesses are starting to focus on building cultures that embrace a process demanding critical thinking, to include training senior leadership teams. Decision framing, divergent views, and devil's advocate approaches such as the use of **murder boards** (Friendly but objective reviews of the assumptions and COAs) are components of this culture leading to consideration of the consequences of different courses of action as opposed to single answers. In this culture, the focus is on not just responding to decisions but challenging them. This requires more than just a linear approach to problem solving. For example, businesses often perform poorly in forecasting because linear approaches fail to consider dynamic changes in the business environment. In part this entails having a plan B if plan A is not being achieved. Developing organizational protocols for including critical thinking in decision making can help ensure a more dynamic approach that embodies consideration of alternatives.[4]

> **"Analytical thinking, skepticism and good judgment are increasingly the key ingredients financial executives must add to their intellectual/educational mix to remain competitive in a world economy that now places more emphasis on critical thinking than ever before."**
>
> —Susan Schott Karr, "Critical Thinking: A CRITICAL Strategy for Financial Executives," *Financial Executive*, December 2009

The United States Marine Corps has long used operational planning procedures that force critical thinking. When assigned a mission, operational staffs first perform a mission analysis identifying the precise mission, what constitutes victory, and the expressed and implied assumptions in the mission statement. Once this has occurred, three distinct courses of action (COAs) are developed. Next, individual staff functions such as intelligence, operations, logistics, and communications each develop estimates of supportability for each COA. The COAs are then briefed to the commander who, based upon these inputs, either decides on a COA or sends the staff back to do more planning. Once the commander has chosen a COA, irrespective of whether the COA chosen was its own preference, each staff section then enthusiastically goes about preparing to implement the chosen COA. Other military services have similar processes. Compared to this formalized process that encourages critical thinking, the ad hoc decision-making processes in many businesses seem primitive in comparison.

In summary, the quality of your critical thinking in solving complex business problems has everything to do with your long-term success as a business leader. Above all, critical thinking involves **systematic questioning** of goals and agendas; the precise questions that need answering; the quality and validity of information being used to make decisions; how information is being interpreted and what concepts, models, and principles are being used; what assumptions are being made; and the implications and consequences of decisions.[5] The next section begins our journey into the rich topic of this very important ability.

9.2. Some Assumptions and Cautions

Our explication of critical thinking in complex-business-problem solving is based upon some fundamental assumptions, the first assumption being that *it is better to think well than poorly.* We're not trying to insult your intelligence with this assumption. As obvious as it seems, ask yourself the following questions: If decision-makers really believe it is better to think well than poorly, why do so many put so little effort into thinking well? Why do they not study logic and other tools for thinking better?

This leads us to a second assumption: *To think well we have to think about how we think.* Much of

"The human mind, once stretched by a new idea, never regains its original dimensions."

—Oliver Wendell Holmes

the thinking people do is mindless in that conscious process powers have not been brought to bear upon it. For example, when some stimulus brings something to mind and that triggers a memory, we are engaging in mindless thinking. To think critically we need to engage in **mindful thinking** in which ideas, beliefs, and intuitions are subjected to conscious, systematic scrutiny. Scientific reasoning is one principal mode of mindful thinking, and learning to think more critically, in part, entails applying scientific thought processes

to complex business problems. Leaders with the right mental model, those who see each learning opportunity as part of a process of *self-creation,* are always asking, "What can I take away from this learning opportunity that can help me make better decisions in my professional life?" On the other hand, smart people who are too invested in their own intellectual abilities tend to think of themselves as having something others lack. These smart people become too focused on looking smart rather than challenging themselves.[6]

The third assumption is that *good thinking has certain identifiable, universal elements regardless of the subject matter.* Therefore, when we apply conscious mindful thinking to problems in business we can utilize the same basic elements we might use in academia or the military, for example. This assumption is consistent with the quote on the right. Stretching our minds leaves us with permanently broader perspectives. For example, a chess player who continuously scrutinizes a chessboard with pieces representing different capabilities in that game might also be developing the skills needed by senior military officers examining large maps filled with symbols representing the size, structure, and capabilities of friendly and opposing forces. In turn, the ability to analyze competition in a military setting might be very useful for business leaders attempting to assess competitors' strategies and develop their own strategies for countering the competition.

Our final assumption is that *it is possible to improve our critical thinking by studying the subject.* Although this may seem intuitively obvious, this point has been the subject of debate among researchers, some of whom have argued that the mere study of critical thinking does NOT improve thinking. Fortunately, some recent research offers hopeful evidence to the contrary suggesting that exposure to critical-thinking/problem-solving instruction can result in improved critical-thinking ability.[7] Why should leaders aspiring to success have real hope that this assumption holds? A recent Harvard survey of alumni and recruiters identified individual skills and personal attributes as being far more important that traditional subject-matter knowledge in both short- and long-term career success.[8]

At the most basic level there are only three kinds of questions we can ask: (1) *questions to which there are lots of right answers* (e.g., Which team is America's favorite sports team?); (2) *questions to which there is only one right answer* (e.g., What is the molecular composition of water?); and (3) *questions to which there are multiple possible answers, some of which are better than others* (e.g., What is the best software for a particular purpose?). Almost all of the really important questions business leaders face fall into the latter category. With that in mind, consider the following.

Some cautions are warranted as we embark on the study of applying critical thinking to solving complex business problems. First, be careful in accepting the foregoing assumptions because the implication is that you will be implicitly acknowledging that improving your critical reasoning is a lifelong challenge—a journey, not a destination. Second, one of the greatest criticisms of studying critical thinking is that those who study it often end up becoming hypercritical of others' thinking but not their own reasoning. As a courageous leader humble enough to learn, you must be prepared to take your own medicine. Third, unless you want to disclose that you are an empty vessel waiting to be filled with "right" business answers, beware of the "What's this got to do with business?" syndrome. When CEOs are queried about the kind of person they want in their organizations, they never say, "Send us people who know more cost accounting and corporate finance." Instead they say, "Send us people who can think." Finally, it is tempting for professionals to sometimes to think about the technical skills and knowledge needed for the *next* level, not three levels above their current level. Becoming a better thinker takes time, with definite milestones more difficult to identify than an expanded set of technical skills. This is analogous to undergraduate accounting students asking, "Is that on the CPA exam?" Passing the CPA exam is a necessity for a career with a CPA firm, but no one ever got to be CEO of a CPA firm of any consequence just because they earned a high score on the CPA exam.

9.3. Roots and Components of Critical Thinking

Hopefully it will come as no surprise that critical thinking starts with thought. What may be a surprise is how complex critical thought is and how uncommon it appears to be. The frailties that afflict human reasoning mean there's good reason to suspect many of the things we believe about ourselves and others, and about how the world works, may be wrong.

Eight elements of thought have been identified. A starting point is often a general idea of the **problem to be dealt with** followed by the **desired end state** assuming the problem is solved—and ending with an understanding of the **implications and consequences of the solution** decided upon. Note that the implications and consequences of problem solution include **second- and third-order effects**. Recall that second- and third-order effects are those unintended, adverse consequences to parties directly and indirectly affected by the problem solution, respectively. This is often a consideration overlooked by leaders, to their detriment; leaders all too satisfied with having arrived at what they believe to be a good solution to a complex problem. Failing to consider the unintended consequences of decisions often turns momentary bliss into more hard mental work in solving even more complex problems created unintentionally by the solution chosen for the first problem.

Between carefully identifying the desired end state and understanding the consequences of the solution, five other elements of thought should influence the critical-thinking process. These include (1) **relevant information, data, observations, and experiences** and how these bear upon the problem; (2) applicable **concepts, models, laws, and principles**, (3) **explicit and implicit assumptions** in the mission statement; (4) **the personal points of view** of those tasked with problem solving; and (5) how the proposed solution will be **interpreted by others** and what **inferences** may be drawn from it. Good reasoning based on bad information is unlikely to lead to good conclusions. Bad reasoning based upon good information is also unlikely to lead to good conclusions.

Problem identification and solving are inextricably linked to **critical thinking**, which has been defined as "the use of cognitive skills or strategies that increase the probability of a desirable outcome."[9] Another definition is "the conjunction of knowledge, skills, and strategies that promotes improved problem solving, rational decision making, and enhanced creativity."[10] Irrespective of the precise definition, psychologists and educators have identified six components to critical thinking: (1) **creative thinking**—the generation of new ideas, (2) **decision making**—making an evaluative judgment and choosing an alternative course of action, (3) **problem solving**—recognition and solution of problems, (4) **seeing things in the mind's eye**—organizing and processing symbols, graphs, and so forth, (5) **knowing how to learn**—acquisition and application of new knowledge and skills, and (6) **reasoning**—using a rule or principle to solve a problem.[11] By definition then, problem identifying and solving is but one of several components to the broader skill of critical thinking. It would be a mistake, therefore, to view the six foregoing components as separate and distinct. Recognizing and solving complex problems frequently requires creativity, organizing and processing data and information, acquiring new knowledge and skills, and using sound reasoning to arrive at a decision.[12]

9.4. A Simple Model of How Humans Think

In understanding how the elements of thought and components of critical thinking play out in decision making, it is helpful to have a simple model that describes this process sequentially. Figure 9.1 shows this model.

Figure 9.1. Simple Model of Human Thinking

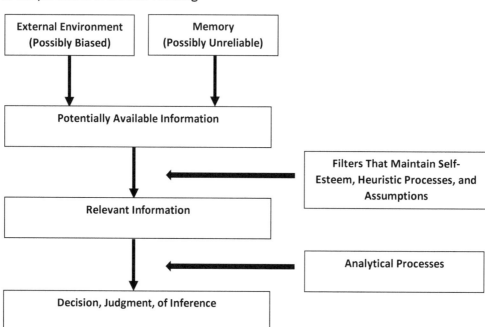

In the model, bad things can happen at each step. Both the external environment and our own memory provide potentially available information as inputs to the decision process. Our attention is selective, resulting in a failure to consider all relevant, available information that may impact the decision. Our memories are also selective and frequently inaccurate, with a consequently negative effect on our ability to bring past experiences to bear in solving complex problems. Heuristics are preconscious mental programs that retrieve information from memory and identify which bits of externally available information seem relevant and therefore subject to further processing. Also, our desire to maintain self-esteem may lead us to accept dubious data, reject compelling data, and persist in behaviors and strategies long after an objective observer would have concluded they were ineffective.

Even if our information is accurate and complete and our selection of it free of bias, we may nonetheless make mistakes during the **analytical phase** of the thought process if our grasp of logic is poor. Mistakes are also possible if certain aspects of the problem prevent us from bringing our full reasoning powers to bear upon it. This analytical aspect of the process should be the portion most susceptible to improvement because it is *conscious* and because most people can improve their logical reasoning abilities. In contrast, the **heuristic aspect** is more difficult to improve because it is *unconscious*. Often people are more unaware of biases at the unconscious and nonverbal levels. There is some hope of lining the conscious to the unconscious, however, because logic may be an antidote for some kinds of unconscious biases.[13]

One of unconscious characteristics of the thinking process is that of **mindless assumptions**. By necessity arguments about complex matters almost always contain embedded assumptions because there is no way for the human mind to think of everything. Assumptions therefore al-

low us to function when otherwise we couldn't. Consider, for example, an assumption you make virtually every day driving. As you approach an intersection you see that the traffic is green in your direction, so you go through the intersection without stopping, assuming that the lights are red for traffic crossing the intersection at right angles to your directions. This is an assumption because you can't actually see those lights. You don't actually know the light hasn't malfunctioned and is green in both directions. Imagine what would happen to traffic if drivers decided not to trust the light and stopped to check it was red for crossing traffic. Like this one, many of our assumptions are made mindlessly.

These mindless assumptions play out every day in business settings in ways that influence attitudes and predispositions to problems and their solutions. Suppose, for example, you are in corporate accounting and have been assigned as a member of a multidisciplinary task group to review a major capital expenditure (CAPEX) proposal to expand manufacturing facilities. At the group's first meeting you mention that the projected rate of return on investment (ROI) on the project is very close to the company's hurdle rate for CAPEX projects. Another task-group member with a production background comments, "Bean-counting isn't going to get us where we need to go. What is needed here is strategic vision." What are the likely assumptions implicit in this statement?

The first is that your concern about the project ROI is an excessively detailed focus on numbers. Perhaps underlying that is an assumption that corporate accountants are bean counters. Another assumption is that focusing on project ROI is inconsistent with a strategic vision. Dismantling these assumptions is fairly easy. A CAPEX project portfolio with an ROI higher than the company's cost of capital is necessary for the company to create shareholder value, so concern about a project's ROI is a valid consideration, al-

Critical Thinking in Identifying and Solving Complex Problems

beit not the only consideration, in project approval. Further, CAPEX projects entail step costs that are largely fixed, making it difficult to recover an investment once it is made. All CAPEX projects involve assumptions about certain factors, such as expected future demand for products. The closer the projected ROI is to the hurdle rate, the greater the risk of failure if the demand assumption doesn't hold. Consequently, it does not necessarily follow that careful examination of the projected ROI is inconsistent with strategic vision. At a more fundamental level, the production chap may be highly desirous of making the CAPEX expenditure because he is enamored with the technology, and his characterization of accountants as bean counters may be a self-serving attempt to convince other members of the group that you are taking an excessively narrow focus by appealing to stereotypes. The assumption that the CAPEX project should be approved may therefore underlie his approach to the project.

One technique that is useful in unearthing assumptions is **constraint analysis**, which entails attempting to identify certain key "givens" that underlie thinking. For example, in the foregoing example perhaps the current HR structure of production forms a constraint on advancement for production personnel. Expansion of the company's manufacturing capabilities likely means growing both the domain of those charged with overseeing production and opportunities for job enhancement and greater compensation. Production personnel may therefore view the proposed expansion as highly desirable from a personal perspective.

This brings us to another difficulty with the human thinking process—**points of view**. Putting aside assumptions resulting from private gain, "where we sit is often where we stand" when it comes to how we look at a problem. An architect views the same house differently than an interior decorator, who, in turn, views it differently than a

realtor. It is helpful when wrestling with a business problem to ask whether you are viewing the problem through the lens of your own expertise. Sound judgment requires multiple perspectives in problem identification and solving, which is one reason that multidisciplinary approaches are often warranted.

Finally, there are the **implications and consequences** of a solution decision to consider. Even if we agree with the conclusions about what a problem really is and how to solve it, what are the financial, legal, moral, and practical implications of implanting a solution? In one real-world example, suppose you work for a large, privately held manufacturer that has long had a familial culture. Consecutive generations of the same families have worked loyally for the company. The new CEO, who came from an investment management firm, wants to reduce the workforce by 30 percent in order to enhance the return to shareholders, who are mostly from one local family. What is the likely impact on employee morale, productivity, and trust? In this actual decision, the downsizing backfired, the CEO left the company, and a senior vice president told one of the coauthors, "It will be at least 10 years, if ever, before we can restore the employee loyalty we once had."[14]

9.5. Logical Reasoning

As the preceding section suggests, taking an objective look at situations, others involved, and ourselves is essential to thinking effectively about complex problems. But even if we are able to do this we won't do it well if we don't have a basic understanding of how to think logically. Logic is the basic formal tool underlying good complex-problem identification and solution. It is a tool that has a variety of important uses. First, we can use it to persuade others. Second, we can use it to resist the misguided attempts of others to persuade. Third, we can use logic to improve the quality of our own decisions.

Figure 9.2. Importance of Order of Statements When Making Arguments

When the CEO is abrupt, he usually offends people unnecessarily.	The CEO is usually a very pleasant person.
Despite being basically a pleasant person, the CEO can at times be abrupt.	Despite being basically a pleasant person, the CEO can at times be abrupt.
The CEO is usually a very pleasant person.	When the CEO is abrupt, he usually offends people unnecessarily.
Therefore the CEO has some questionable leadership skills.	Therefore the CEO has some questionable leadership skills.

Logic is a process for effective thinking that has been refined by mathematicians, philosophers, and scientists over the past 2,500 years. The first step in applying logic is understanding what is and is not an argument. An **argument** is a related group of statements in which one or more of the statements (called **premises**) is alleged to be a logical reason why we should believe another statement (the **conclusion**). **Statements** are sentences that are either true or false. Questions, commands, slogans, assertions, beliefs, and exclamations are not arguments. Consider the following three statements.

1. The Lexus will never sell.

2. Americans will never pay luxury car prices for a Japanese car. Therefore the Lexus will never sell.

3. Americans will never pay luxury car prices for a Japanese car. Toyota's Lexus will be luxury cars. Therefore the Lexus will never sell.

Statement 1 merely asserts a claim. Statements 2 and 3 argue for the claim (*conclusion*) stating why we should believe it (*premises*). Often we observe people trying to persuade others by piling on assertions and mixing in rhetorical appeals in attempts to sway others to their viewpoints. In the Lexus example, prior to the introduction of the Lexus line competitors might have made exhortations such as, "Toyota doesn't compete fairly." "We need to stand up for

American automobile manufacturers." "Everybody knows our cars are as good as Toyota's." Even if the competitors acted as though they had made convincing arguments, those who were fooled by such exhortations failed to think critically using the tools of logic. Further, as evinced by the subsequent success of Lexus, just because arguments as in statements 2 and 3 are made in a logical form does not make them valid.

The order in which statements are presented may affect an arguments' persuasiveness. Consider, for example, the two streams of statements in Figure 9.2 and decide which is the most persuasive.

If the purpose of the argument is to convince someone that the CEO has questionable leadership skills, the argument sequence on the left is probably less persuasive than the one on the right because it starts with the most unfavorable statement and ends with a favorable statement prior to the conclusion. The sequence on the right takes the opposite approach.

Sometimes it is difficult to separate a person's arguments from her assertions, exclamations, exhortations, and professions of belief. Arguments are often buried in paragraphs of statements and mountains of so-called evidence. Before leaders can evaluate an argument they have to understand the argument. It is critical that leaders be able to read reports, listen to presentations, and identify key points before deciding whether or not to be convinced.

There are times when the subject matter of an argument touches one of our "hot buttons"—that is, the problem content, the situation context, or the person presenting affects leaders' ability to reason about it. This is known as **content bias** and may result because we like or dislike the person presenting or the situational context. Suppose a subordinate is recommending harsh punishment for an allegedly errant employee, and you have personally experienced an almost identical situation as being alleged with a different employee. Your intuitive reaction may be, "I've seen this before, harsh discipline was warranted with that case, so I agree that harsh discipline is warranted in this case." Care needs to be taken to first verify that the circumstances are indeed analogous before extrapolating from our own experience to that being asserted about another. This surfaces another important point. The most extreme version of the negative impact of our favorable or unfavorable predisposition to an argument occurs when the argument is our own or triggers an argument similar to one we have made. Humans are not inclined to examine their own beliefs and positions with the same rigor with which they examine those of others.

One device that can assist us to better understand the nature of an argument is to put the argument into a **standard form** using the following steps,

1. Put each premise and its conclusion on separate lines with the premise stated first and the conclusion stated last, omitting all words that do not contribute to the content of the statements.

2. Draw a horizontal line between the conclusion and the premises listed above it.

3. Place "therefore" in front of the conclusion statement.

Take, for example, the argument that Lexus automobiles would not sell.

Americans will never pay luxury car prices for a Japanese car.

Toyota's Lexus line will be luxury cars.

Therefore the Lexus will never sell.

People often omit premises when they're making arguments for a number of reasons. One is that the arguments are not well thought out. A second is that they have decided to omit the weakest premises in the hope this omission is not discovered. Sometimes it is done because requiring the audience to fill in the blanks may make the audience take ownership of the argument. Omitting premises has risks, however, because the audience may not understand the argument or may decide that the argument lacks credibility because of the omission.

A useful technique for evaluating arguments is to consider their purposes or objective. Arguments can have three basic purposes: (1) **Demonstration**—arguments designed to support the truth of a particular conclusion. For example, "Our competitor XYZ is the industry leader that always launches successful products, so we should emulate it and create our own widget line because XYZ has a widget line." (2) **Critique**—arguments designed to challenge another argument. For example, "ABC recently launched a widget line that flopped, so we should not emulate it by launching a widget line." (3) **Defense**—arguments designed to respond to someone else's arguments by showing its flaws. For example, "Arguing that we should or should not launch a widget line based upon what ABC is doing is fallacious because its success in launching new product lines has been a coin toss." Amid the confusion of a cacophony of debate as occurs in many business meetings, placing each person's argument(s) into one of these three categories and putting it in standard form helps leaders clarify participants' positions on a topic as well as the persuasiveness of each argument.

9.6. Inductive versus Deductive Reasoning

There are two basic ways to reason, **inductive** and **deductive**. When we attempt to draw general conclusions from specific data, facts, or behaviors we are using inductive reasoning. For example, "*Many* bank customers use ATMs and bank online, so *bank customers prefer convenience to personal service*." When we reason from a general rule or proposition to a specific conclusion we are using deductive reasoning. For example, "*Bank customers prefer convenience to personal service. Bob is a bank customer, therefore he prefers convenience to personal service." People regularly use both forms of reasoning, and the two are interrelated. In both examples of inductive and deductive reasoning we are immediately suspicious that they contain a logical error in jumping from *many* to *all*. This is obvious if we insert the word *all* in both cases where an asterisk is shown.

Since inductive reasoning always involves reaching conclusions that are broader that the premises, we can never be absolutely certain the conclusion is correct. It is important to recognize that the most inductive reasoning can ever tell us is that if the premises are true, then the conclusion is probably true. Therefore, when we're attempting to separate good inductive-reasoning arguments from bad we judge the quality of these arguments in terms of strength or weakness, not in truth or falsity. But how do we judge strength or weakness? One way is by the **scope of the conclusion**. The shorter the logical distance between the conclusion and the premises the stronger the conclusion is likely to be. If we substitute *most* instead of *all* for the asterisk in stating "*bank customers prefer convenience to personal service*," we can be somewhat more confident that the statement is correct. For one thing, we would have not to query every bank customer for *most* as we would in the case of *all*. If we insert *some* rather than *most* we could be even more confident.

Two other criteria on which to evaluate the strength or weakness of inductive reasoning are **quantity and quality of the observations they contain.** Suppose we are contemplating launching a new product, the gazorkinflickin, and interested in how many consumer households would be interested in purchasing these wonderful robotic devices designed to vacuum homes when no one is there for $1,500 each. Accordingly, your company conducts a random telephone survey of a sample one hundred households with the result that only 2 percent of these households indicate they might be willing to purchase a gazorkinflickin. An internal opponent of the product touts this survey as a reason not to produce it, but how strong is the argument for moving forward with producing the product?

Granted, the quantity of affirmative responses appears low, but there are many reasons to lack confidence in the results. First of all, is one hundred a sufficiently large sample? The law of large numbers suggests that you need a reasonably large sample to ensure a random draw representative of the population. How random was the sample? Properly done, random selection can eliminate unsystematic bias but not systematic bias. Was there a systematic response bias because members of some types of households weren't home during the survey? Were those households of the type most likely to purchase a gazorkinflickin? Is there reason to expect a self-selection bias? Perhaps many consumers affluent enough to purchase a gazorkinflickin are sophisticated enough to place their phone numbers on the no-call list. Who are the likely purchasers? What households represent the real target market? Given the price of the robotic vacuum, it seems likely that the target market should be affluent households in which time is often more important than money. One might argue, therefore, that the target market should be affluent, single households or ones where both spouses work long hours as executives with little time to vacuum but adequate financial

Figure 9.3. Comparative Deductive Reasoning Arguments

Persons practicing public accounting must be licensed CPAs.	Persons practicing public accounting must be licensed CPAs.
Persons practicing public accounting must pass the CPA exam to be licensed.	Persons practicing public accounting must pass the CPA exam to be licensed.
Tom has not passed the CPA exam.	Tom has passed the CPA exam.
Therefore Tom is not a practicing public accountant.	Therefore Tom is a practicing public accountant.

resources to purchase. How many of those types of households are there in total, and how many were captured in the sample? It would be folly to believe that adequate evidence exists for not producing the product based upon the survey.

The nature of deductive arguments permits saying that some alternatives are better than others. The basic standard for evaluating deductive arguments is *whether the premises logically support the conclusions.* Listing the premises can often be beneficial in helping to make this determination. For example, compare the two arguments in Figure 9.3.

Which of the two arguments is best supported by the premises? Obviously the answer is the one on the left. If practicing public accountants must be licensed and must pass the CPA exam to be licensed, and if Tom has not passed the CPA exam, then he cannot be a practicing public accountant. On the other hand, the fact that Tom has passed the CPA exam does not mean he is a practicing public accountant. The essential difference between valid and invalid deductive arguments is that a valid deductive argument is one in which the conclusion must be true if the premises are

true. There must be no possible circumstances in which the premises could be true and the conclusion be false. This is sometimes called the **principle of necessity**. The foregoing example illustrates the important difference between **necessary and sufficient conditions**. If the first and second premises are true, then Tom cannot be a practicing public accountant unless he has passed the CPA exam. However, again assuming the first two premises are true, just having passed the CPA exam is insufficient to conclude he is a practicing CPA because Tom may have passed the exam but be employed in some capacity other than a practicing public accountant.

One of the most important aspects of deductive logic is that it enables discerning leaders to detect invalid or weak arguments even if they don't understand much of the technical gobbledygook in the arguments. This is increasingly important in the business world where technology is becoming increasingly complex and leaders cannot be experts in all the technologies about which they must pass judgment. A word of caution is in order, however. Deductive arguments can be totally logical and totally wrong. Consider the four following possibilities in Figure 9.4.

Figure 9.4. Possible Varieties of Deductive Arguments

Form of Argument	Premises	Validity of Argument
Valid	True	Valid
Valid	False	Invalid
Invalid	True	Invalid
Invalid	False	Invalid

A final point is that asking whether or not an argument is sound is not the same as asking how persuasive it is. Sadly, sound arguments often fail to persuade many people, and history is replete with awful examples of people who were persuaded by unsound reasoning. Consider the following example in Figure 9.5 that provides a real illustration that resulted in the persecution of humans for their scientific beliefs.

Figure 9.5. Illustration of Invalid Deductive Logical Argument

Both the sun and the earth
are orbital spheres.

The sun moves across the sky
from east to west each day.

Visually it's obvious the sun moves
relative to a particular spot on the earth.

Therefore the sun revolves
around the earth!

9.7. Problem Identification—the Starting Point in Complex-Problem Solving

Assume you are a high-performing junior partner in the healthcare consulting practice of a large CPA/consulting firm. Last week the partner-in-charge of the practice informed you that she is appointing you as head of a task group consisting of you and five of your colleagues to recommend ways to improve the practice. She noted that there are lots of regulatory changes going on in healthcare that are causing disruptions and consolidations of healthcare providers (HCPs). There are also issues of costs and affordability of care for both patients and HCPs. Additionally, there are new competitors entering healthcare consulting offering new technological solutions. This turbulent environment has her concerned about defending the firm's current clientele, but it also

excites her about the prospects of making new inroads with existing clients and creating new ones. Today you are in the process of chairing the first meeting of the task group. Being a proponent of participative management, you begin by asking the members for their ideas, resulting in the following dialogue:

> **Bob:** "I think we need to consider providing clients with more financial information to better manage their businesses."

> **Ying:** "I disagree. Based on client feedback we are doing a great job of that. I think we need to focus on getting more into the operational side of healthcare."

> **Jason:** "It's all about information technology these days, particularly electronic medical records. We aren't doing anything with EMRs."

> **Sarah:** "EMRs are a black hole. That business is dominated by two very large firms. We'd be crazy to try to compete with them."

> **Jason:** "I'm not saying compete with them. I'm saying we need better linkages of financial data to patient data."

> **Ying:** "How do we do that without getting deeply into EMRs? That's a giant step and would cost a fortune in R&D. Are we ready for that? Will the firm even pay for it?"

What is happening here? The task force is in the process of doing what similar groups do every day in a multitude of organizational settings. It has launched into the ways of doing something, overlapping into discussion of means, without a clear understanding of the desired end state(s). In other words, the task group has launched into its deliberations with only a vague understanding of what constitutes success. Albert Einstein argued that "the formulation of the problem is often more essential than its solution." Ends/ways/means thinking reveals the inherent veracity in that statement.

"The manager's job is not only to solve well-defined problems. He must also identify the problems to be solved. He must somehow assess the cost of analysis and its potential return. He must allocate resources to questions before he knows the answers. To many managers and students of management, the availability of formal problem solving procedures serves only to highlight those parts of the manager's job with which these procedures do not deal: problem identification, the assignment of problem priority, and the allocation of scarce resources to problems. These tasks, which must be performed without the benefit of a well-defined body of theory, may be among the most critical of the manager's decision making responsibilities."

—William F. Pounds

It is far more difficult to solve a problem without knowing precisely what the problem is. As previously stated, the tendency to jump into developing a problem solution without first understanding what the problem is and what constitutes victory in solving it is rampant in all sorts of organizational settings. Moreover, the discussion is mostly focused on the firm without first considering the **client's pain**. Complex-problem solving begins with complex-problem identification.

What should you as task-group leader have done? A better beginning would have involved having the group perform a **mission analysis**. What precisely is the deliverable in this situation? Granted what the partner-in-charge (PIC) wants is one or more recommendations to improve the healthcare practice, but precisely what are her concerns? Further, what are the explicit and implicit assumptions? One explicit assumption is that healthcare is in a very dynamic state. Another is that the PIC is concerned about preserving current client relations. Yet another is that she believes opportunities exist for expanding the practice. Implicit assumptions include the following: (1) Healthcare will continue to offer profitable opportunities for consulting despite—or maybe because of—client cost pressures. (2) The existing client base can be leveraged to create new opportunities. (3) One or more meaningful differentiable value propositions to clients is necessary to allow for sustainable competitive advantage. (4) The firm is not acting in a vacuum. That is, some competitors are also moving in the same space, and we need to develop ways of differentiating our firm that will provide sustainable competitive advantage. Using these assumptions, can you formulate a clear, precise, and reasonably concise mission statement?

How does the following mission statement sound? *The mission of the task group is to recommend alternatives for both preserving and expanding the existing healthcare client base that offer* **value-adding solutions for solving client pain** *while providing our firm with a* **sustainable competitive advantage** *in the healthcare consulting market that will preserve and grow our client base.* Assuming you run this mission statement by the PIC and she agrees with it, how does it help guide the group? Let's return to the task group to see the benefit.

Leader: "Now that we have a precise, agreed-upon mission statement, let's begin by focusing on the most critical element—**our value proposition** *to existing and prospective clients.* I'd like to start that discussion by first surfacing, understanding, and articulating clearly the current pain being experienced by existing and prospective clients before turning to a discussion of how that pain might be cured. Once we are satisfied we have accomplished those steps, then we can turn to our possible roles in curing client pain, how we may be able to develop sustainable comparative advantage over our competition in doing that, and lastly, the resources each solution will require in people, expertise, time, and money."

The leader is now doing what leaders should do—providing structure and establishing a logical process for problem solving that offers a better hope of ends, ways, and means being clearly identified and aligned at the end of the group's deliberations. The leader is not prejudicing the team members' decisions. Members are free to put forward ideas, but they are encouraged to do so in a manner consistent with not losing sight of clients' needs and staying on a logical path. Take, for example, the following subsequent conversation:

> **Jason:** "I'd like to move the discussion forward and talk about linking EMR data to financial data."

> **Sarah:** "There you go again on your EMRs. I keep telling you EMRs are a black hole, Jason. EMRs are too complicated and messy—and not in our core competencies."

> **Leader:** "Regardless of whether or not linking EMR data to financial data represents an area in which we may be able to help our healthcare clients resolve their pain, I think we first need to gain a better understanding of exactly what that pain is. Let's go back to the issue of physicians spending too much time extracting information from existing systems and how much pain—and cost—that is creat-

ing. If we decide that sufficient pain is caused by a data disconnect such as Jason has previously suggested, then we can return to that as a possible solution when we discuss ways in which to solve our clients' pain."

In the foregoing dialogue the effect of ends/ways/means thinking is to keep the discussion on track in terms of problem identification before the group launches into problem solving. Having a clear mission statement in mind helps the leader keep deliberation and discussion on a logical path rather than degenerating into a morass of confused and competing monologues as individual members attempt to "walk their pet rocks," as Jason may be doing. In stating he wants to "move the discussion forward," Jason is doing something typical of people seeking to promote a pet agenda. Although couched in words that make it sound as though he seeks to help make progress, what Jason is really doing is attempting to throw the group off the track and redirect its focus back to a possible *way* that he happens to favor.

We anticipate someone asking, "But didn't you previously tell us that each of the sixteen different personality preference types fires various parts of the brain in different sequences? Aren't we stifling people's creative genius if we more or less force them to think in terms of ends/ways/means?" The answers are yes, brains do fire differently, but no, we are not suggesting stifling creativity. If time and energy were meaningless and all human beings had an appetite for endless unfocused discussion, then free-form problem exploration would perhaps be more acceptable, assuming it actually led to precise problem identification and efficacious solutions. But organizational constraints rarely allow for endless free-form discussions that often lead to frustration with a lack of real progress. Astute leaders need to guide and direct group debates while at the same time capitalizing on the benefits of diversity of thought among group members.

Moreover, although ends/ways/means thinking seems linear, it is in reality often *circular,* doubling back on itself as discussion unearths greater clarity of thought and new ideas. Suppose one point of pain the group decides upon initially involves the inability of physicians to get the information required at the patient point of contact in an efficient manner. As discussion moves from ends to ways and ultimately to means, it may become obvious that the problem is really most prevalent for primary care physicians, and the means required to solve the problem for PCPs seem more viable economically. Now the desired end state is revisited and refined to be providing materially more efficient access to online information for primary care.

9.8. Bridging Problem Identification and Problem Solving

Ends/ways/means thinking offers a discipline for bridging problem identification to problem solving, but it is helpful to dig more deeply into the cognitive mechanisms that underlie the process and show its **iterative circularity**. Iterative circularity means that the process loops back upon itself such that, as problem solvers move through the process of problem identification and problem solving, new information is often obtained that causes them to revisit their initial conclusions about what the problem actually is. This may result in refining the mission (problem) statement or sometimes a new statement altogether. Figure 9.6 represents a schematic of how this circularity operates using the healthcare consulting example in the previous section.

In executing this iterative process there are several core questions that problem-solving leaders should ask of themselves and others.

1. Are we clear on the problem? Is this the central problem to focus upon? How precise is our understanding of the desired end state? Is this the most important problem we should consider?

2. How accurate and relevant are our data and information about the problem? Which facts are most important to focus upon? How can we test the accuracy of these inputs to our problem identification and solving process? How directly do these inputs into our decisions bear upon the problem?

3. What factors make this a difficult problem? What are the major complexities? What are the major obstacles that must be dealt with?

4. What are the different perspectives on this problem? Does perspective change the problem and how? Are these perspectives (including my own) biased? Am I giving full consideration to others' perspectives rather than focusing mainly on mine?

5. Does our thinking stand the test of logic? Are our ends, ways, and means aligned?

Plunging even deeper into complex-problem solving, the foregoing approach represents a **rational approach** to complex-problem identification and solution. An alternative to the rational approach is the **organic approach** as described in the following quote: "Some people assert that the dynamics of organizations and people are not nearly so mechanistic as to be improved by solving one problem after another . . . The quality comes from the ongoing process of trying, rather than from having fixed lots of problems." In other words, it is the method of problem solving that enriches and distinguishes the organizational environment rather than merely arriving at a solution in a logical manner. A major advantage of the organic approach is that it is highly adaptable to understanding and explaining chaotic change and fits well into organizational situations in which

Figure 9.6. Problem-Identification/Problem-Solving Circularity

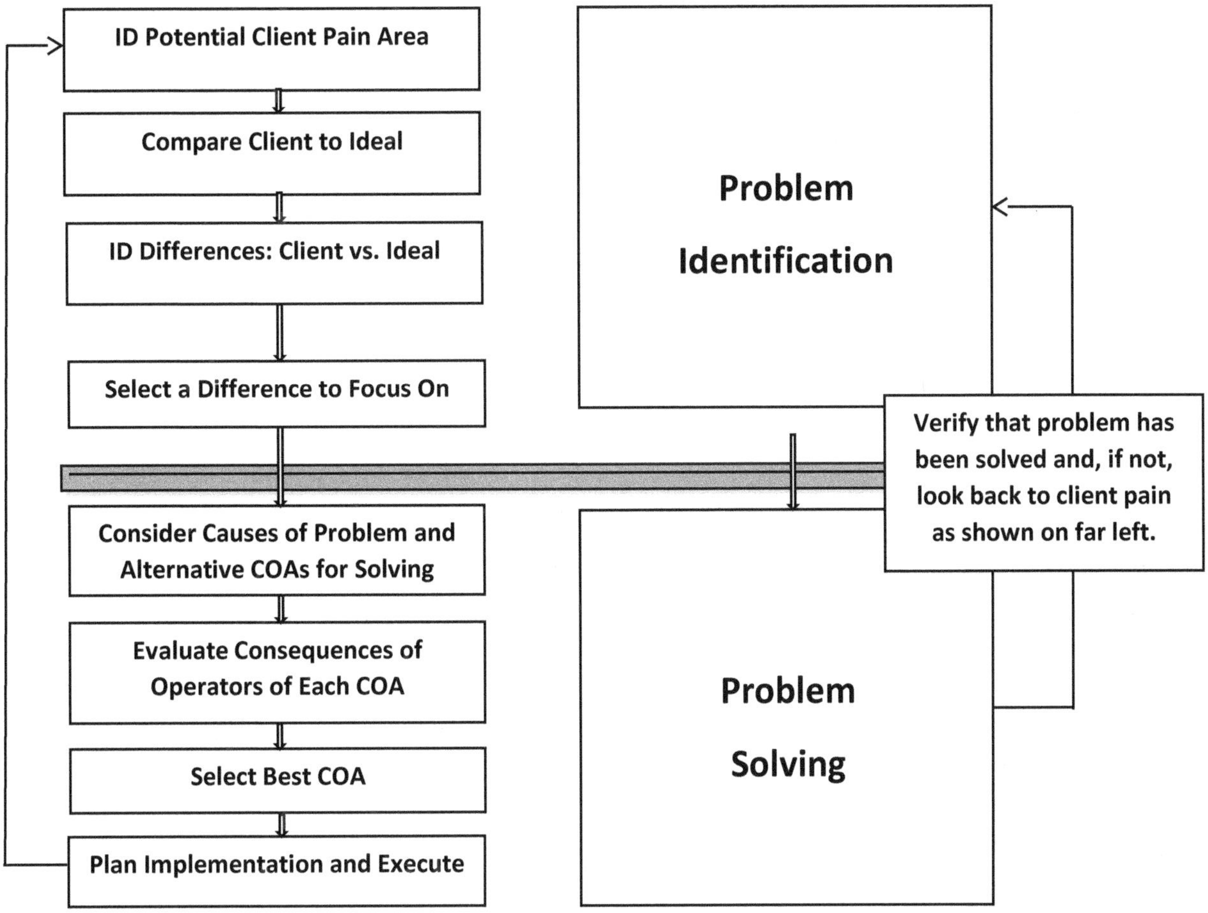

ID Potential Client Pain Area		Problem Identification
Compare Client to Ideal		
ID Differences: Client vs. Ideal		
Select a Difference to Focus On		
Consider Causes of Problem and Alternative COAs for Solving		
Evaluate Consequences of Operators of Each COA		Problem Solving
Select Best COA		
Plan Implementation and Execute		

Verify that problem has been solved and, if not, look back to client pain as shown on far left.

Source: Adapted from W. F. Pounds, "The Process of Problem Finding," *Industrial Management Review* 11 (Fall 1969): 8.

out-of-the-box thinking is highly valued because it disdains a linear, mechanistic approach to problem solving. A major disadvantage is that it provides no clear frame for decision making and no definitive metrics for measuring progress toward problem solution. The implication is that an organic approach may be best used when free-for-all brainstorming is more likely to result in new and innovative ideas than the more orderly rational approach. For example, an organic approach might be used during an executive retreat in which leaders are expressly asked to think differently and more innovatively than normal. It is probably not the choice for ongoing problem-solving activities.

9.9. Pros and Cons of Reductionism as a Complex-Problem-Solving Tool

Complex problems are often daunting because it is difficult to comprehend and massage mentally many ideas, concepts, and models at once. This makes getting to the roots of a problem far more difficult, so people are often tempted to break complex problems down into components so that it is easier to deal with them. This is called **reductionism.** Although reductionism used properly and under certain conditions can be an important complex-problem-solving tool in leaders' critical-thinking toolkits, it can be insidiously dangerous as well. Often people attempting to solve complex problems engage in reductionism without realizing its potential benefits and dangers. Consequently, it behooves leaders to be both aware of when and how to use reductionism and when to be wary of its dangers.

Reductionism is a technique that takes complex problems and simplifies them by breaking them down into smaller units.[15] People often use reductionism without realizing it. Suppose, for example, one very cold morning your car won't start, and when you turn the key a thousand lights come on on the dashboard. You might go through a mental process something along the lines of the following.

1. Does the engine turn over when I turn the key? If the answer is no, then the problem may be a dead battery. Check the fluid lev-

el in the battery and try jump starting the engine.

2. If the engine turns over, is the gas tank empty? If the answer is yes, put gas in the tank.

3. If the engine turns over and the tank contains gasoline, then the problem may be ice in the fuel line. Try adding gas line antifreeze or pushing the car into a warm garage.

In the foregoing example the problem of the car not starting is broken down into component parts: (1) dead battery, (2) no fuel, (3) ice in the fuel line, and so forth. Each of these propositions can then be tested sequentially to provide evidence about the cause of the mechanical failure.

Figure 9.7. Example of Reductionism in Solving a Business Problem

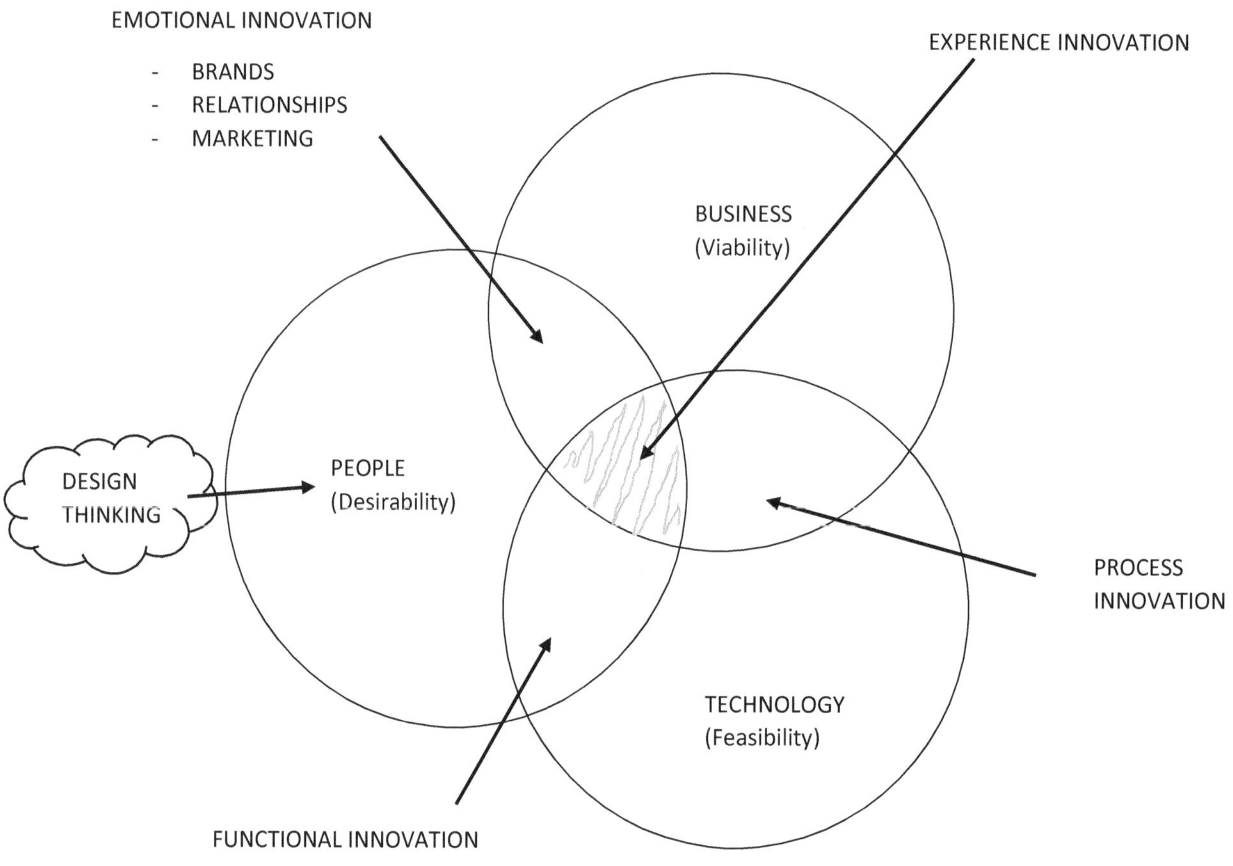

Source: Adapted from http://www.davidgilbert.de/blog/wp-content/uploads/2010/05/design_thinking_ideo.jpg (accessed February 16, 2015).

Good idea, right? So what's the danger? What if one or more of those lights on the dashboard mean that you have also an oil pressure problem? If that's the case, then attempting to crank the vehicle may result in serious damage. This exposes the danger of reductionist thinking. When applied mindlessly to complex systems—and if you don't think your car is a complex system you haven't paid a repair bill lately—reductionism can create more problems than it solves. Why? "With dynamic systems the concern is for the functioning of the whole and its [e]ffect on the constituent parts, and not merely the separate parts locally transacting."[16] An analogy is a physician treating a patient's overall well-being as opposed to one specific problem.

How to use reductionism without shooting yourself in the foot may be best explained using an example. Figure 9.7 presents a diagram of the use of reductionism in an attempt to solve a complex business problem without losing sight of the relationships of the parts to the whole. Assume that the problem being considered is whether the international technological giant, Goggles, Inc., should offer a revolutionary new personal computer known as a Zygate that would be worn like a hat. Assuming the Zygate performs as envisioned, it will enable users to communicate orally with the internet and other users while conducting everyday activities such as walking, driving, scratching, and so on. The team charged with developing a feasibility study on the Zygate has broken the problem of determining Zygate's feasibility into three major components: consumer acceptance, technological feasibility, and business viability, as represented in the Venn diagram in Figure 9.7.

The overlapping circles enable the feasibility team to better conceptualize the intersection of the three major components of the Zygate problem. For example, consumer acceptance is likely to be influenced by business activities such as brand name (almost everyone except Yahoo and Microsoft thinks Goggles is a cool outfit, right?), distributor relationships, and a marketing campaign to convince everyone that Zygate will not only make wearers slicker than black ice on an interstate, but will also protect them from harmful ultraviolet rays. As represented by the intersection of all three circles, this is all dependent upon coming up with a very fashionable design coupled with super-cool marketing using ethereal-appearing people that makes Zygate users feel as though they are on an avant-garde technological adventure—and therefore the envy of their 500 closest friends on Facebook.

9.10. Concluding Thoughts

In summary, identifying and solving complex business problems are critical-thinking activities. Critical thinking, in turn, is the art of analyzing and evaluating thinking with the aim of improving it. It is self-directed, self-disciplined, self-monitored, and self-correcting, requiring rigorous standards of excellence. It involves effective, mindful problem-solving skills and an ability to overcome the hubris resulting from thinking ourselves superior as we continue to develop and refine our critical-thinking skills.

What characterizes a great problem-solving leader? (1) Truly accomplished problem-solving leaders are great critical thinkers who identify important problems and formulate them clearly and precisely. (2) They gather relevant data and information and assess these inputs to decisions using abstract concepts and ideas to interpret and think open-mindedly to assess the inputs in a logical and orderly manner. (3) They are consciously aware of their assumptions and possible biases and those of others. (4) From this assessment they develop well-reasoned, logical conclusions about alternative courses of action and make estimates of the potential efficacy and supportability of each. (5) They assess the consequences and implications of the different courses of action being attuned to their second- and third-order effects. (6) They choose the best course of action and communicate effectively with their followers, steering them toward successful implementation. (7) Ever sensitive to the arrival of new information that may change the problem definition and choice of solution, when necessary they loop back through the problem-identifying and -solving process.[17]

Perhaps these attributes are well summarized at a more general level in the following quote:

> Accomplished thinkers not only have systematically taken charge of their thinking, but are also continually monitoring, revising, and re-thinking strategies for continual improvement of their thinking. They have deeply internalized the basic skills of thought, so that critical thinking is, for them, both conscious and highly intuitive. They regularly raise their thinking to the level of conscious realization. Through extensive experience and practice in engaging in self-assessment, accomplished thinkers are not only actively analyzing their thinking in all the significant domains of their lives, but are also continually developing new insights into problems at deeper levels of thought. Accomplished thinkers are deeply committed to fair-minded thinking, and have a high level of, but not perfect, control over their egocentric nature.[18]

Management guru Peter Drucker is known for his disciplining-the-mind approach to problem solving that identifies key assumptions, establishes their mutual relations, and evaluates alternatives. Given the kaleidoscopic business landscape characterized by an explosion of new technologies, increasingly global nature of business, and growing view of business as a process, Drucker applies his critical-thinking skills in problem identification and solving such that a holistic mindset emerges, holding out the promise that even the most complicated problems are malleable to orderly thought.[19] Courageous leaders can use this same orderly thinking to inspire and develop courage in their subordinates to tackle complicated problems.

CHAPTER 10

Self-Learning

> ## "I never flunked anything in my life.
> ## I was given a second opportunity to do it right."
>
> —Winston Churchill, remarking about having to repeat a grade in school

You might deduce from the quote above that Winnie had a way with words. What might be surprising to many is that, despite his occasional erudite glibness, for much of Sir Winston's life words were an impediment for him. You see, Churchill suffered from a lisp throughout his career that he worked hard to overcome, so learning to speak had a special meaning for him in that it was a journey, not a destination.

As was the case with Churchill, leaders are always faced with the need to learn, and failing to do so can have seriously adverse consequences. We are all given second and often more opportunities to "do it right." Whether we "do it right" or not, however, has a great deal to do with whether we recognize and learn from our mistakes and work to correct them—or whether we just continue to repeat them. High-performing leaders are often acutely aware of their weaknesses as well as their strengths and try to correct the weaknesses. Expressed differently, they are continual learners.

Continual learning for leaders is especially important for two reasons. First, CEOs in every industry rate leadership development as one of their top three priorities.[1] Second, leaders fail at alarming rates. Studies indicate that 40 percent of new leaders fail within the first 18 months of promotion and appointment, a rate that is apparently increasing. Compounding this is the reality that businesses are facing increasing dynamism on an unprecedented scale. Four types of leadership skills are thought to be critical for leaders to succeed in this dynamic environment: (1) cognitive skills, (2) execution skills, (3) relationship skills, and (4) self-management skills. Included in this latter category are intellectual curiosity and a *love of learning*.[2] The implication for business leaders is that, if they do not already possess this love of learning, they need to develop it to become and remain successful.

10.1. Navigating the Passages

Some have argued that leaders learn most when they transit thirteen potentially traumatic "passages" occurring in life as shown in Figure 10.1 on the following page.[3] These life passages require the leader to work through them. Too often, however, leaders don't talk about them because discussing personal failures is seen as an admission of their fallibility. The reality of courageous leadership as a difficult process that leaders often get wrong is denied. This denial includes hiding the self-questioning, self-doubt, and feelings of vulnerability leaders often feel as they struggle to deal with life's passages.[4] One of the coauthors tells the following story:

Once I was charged with commanding a major military training exercise involving over 20 ships, 6,000 troops, and approximately 60 aircraft. The exercise was highly complex involving everything from amphibious operations to mine countermeasures, air defense to large-scale medical activities, missile defense to air logistics. When I learned statistics developed from similar exercises indicated we would kill or seriously injure about a dozen participants during the exercise, I was shocked. This was completely unacceptable to me and those above me. The moral implications came down upon me like a ton of bricks. In the months leading up the exercise I was filled with self-doubt, worrying that my staff and I might have overlooked some detail in our planning that would result in someone being harmed. It was one of the greatest and most humbling psychological challenges I ever faced, but as the commander I felt I was obligated to wear the "mask of command," the face of infallibility, so I spoke to no one about my fears. The morning the exercise kicked off, as I flew in my helicopter above the ocean watching myriad activities below me, I turned to a subordinate commander sitting beside me and said, "Jack, I feel like we just took the brake off a huge freight train that's barreling downhill. I just hope we've laid the track well." Did I handle this challenge as well as I might have? No, certainly not; but I learned a lot, and thanks to the hard work of many outstanding subordinates the exercise was a complete success—and, most importantly, not a single participant was killed or maimed. That experience represented one of life's passages, stretching me as a leader and making me humbly aware of my own fallibility.

Courageous leaders need the humility to admit mistakes and learn from them, and learning is a never-ending process for as long as we remain leaders. The problem is that many professionals don't begin their careers with that mindset. Instead, they feel a great relief when they receive a university degree, thinking, "I'm glad that's behind me. Now I can get about applying what I've learned instead of having to worry about being a student." For some professionals the falsity of that belief becomes apparent quickly. Others drift along, ignoring or even resisting the difficult truth that their time as a student has only just begun. Worse yet, for the most part they will no longer be spoon-fed knowledge that some professor has identified as important and distilled into easy-to-swallow bites with periodic measurement administered in the form of exams to encourage study. Instead, they face the requirement to identify for themselves the gaps in their knowledge and skills required to progress as professionals and set about acquiring them. This entails self-learning, and failure to self-learn usually means these professionals topping out early in their careers.

10.2. A Cyber What?

Courageous leaders need to develop tight **cybernetic loops**. This has nothing to do with the Internet. Instead, think of a thermostat that continuously senses room temperature and initiates action to keep the room at the desired temperature. Courageous leaders are continuously monitoring their environments, others, and their own reactions to the environment and others—assessing these reactions and modifying their behaviors based upon the assessments. The *tighter* this feedback/adjustment loop—that is, the better the sensing and faster the adjustment is made—the better leaders are at learning from their successes and failures. To understand this, compare thermostat 1 that measures room temperature every half an hour and takes five minutes to process this datum with thermostat 2 that continually senses temperature and takes less than a second to process data. Which would you prefer in your home?

Figure 10.1. Traumatic Passages Occurring in Life

- Dealing with significant failure for which you are responsible
- Coping with a bad boss or competitive peers
- Derailing (losing your job or being passed over)
- Being acquired or merged

- Enduring the end of a meaningful relationship through death or divorce
- Surviving a debilitating illness or physical challenge
- Losing faith in the system
- Facing retirement or end of career

Failure or difficulty at work or in leading others	Personal upheaval, death, divorce, loss of meaning
Range of interesting, stimulating projects, assignments, and roles	Breadth or life experience; living in unique places, family, culture

- Joining a company
- Moving into a leadership role
- Accepting the stretch assignment or test assignment
- Moving across functions
- Working internationally
- Stepping into senior management or responsibility for a business

- Living abroad or in a different culture
- Blending work and family into a meaningful whole
- Letting go of ambition or relishing the success of others
- Developing and living a meaningful credo
- Understanding and accepting your legacy

Source: Adapted from D. Dotlich, J. L. Noel, and N. Walker, "Leadership Passages: The Personal and Professional Transitions that Make or Break a Leader," *The CEO Refresher*, 2005, http://flylib.com/books/2/289/1/html/2/images/c01f002.jpg (accessed February 16, 2015).

Figure 10.2. Example of OODA Loop

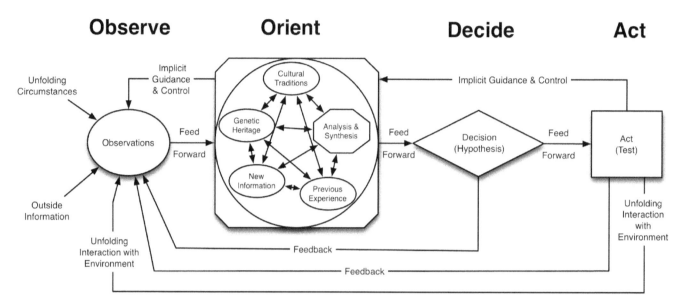

Source: Adapted from http://4.bp.blogspot.com/-tpMvKrY54sc/UkdBTVqi59I/AAAAAAAAMdA/sK9_UeXaOl4/s1600/OODA_Loop.png (accessed February 16, 2015).

The military and increasingly business talk about OODA loops—observe, orient, decide, and act. Figure 10.2 provides a schematic representation of an OODA loop.[5]

This schematic reveals that a decision maker first observes circumstances and assimilates information about his or her observations. This results in a feed forward to orienting on the decision problem, considering the interactions among several factors including the decision maker's previous experience, the organizational culture, and the genetic heritage (history and type) of the problem being analyzed and synthesized. This synthesis forms the basis for a decision that is acted upon. Results of the actions are received and fed back, forming new observations, and the process iterates. The entire process is guided and controlled by the decision maker.

On a battlefield, the side that is able to gather intelligence, orient on a developing problem, decide on a course of action, and act upon it faster than the opposition has a distinct advantage. The effect is to keep the enemy reacting to your side's decisions rather than it reacting to the enemy's decisions. This is known as being inside the enemy's loop. The same is true in business, where the nature of competition often determines success or failure. Business organizations that have tighter OODA loops are better able to respond to competitive pressures and take advantage of opportunities. Further, having a tight OODA loop does not necessarily mean always being the first mover.

For example, during discussions with the consumer products division of a Fortune 50 company, one of the coauthors learned about a large, family owned, consumer-products competitor that was usually a second mover, but one with a very tight loop. The family owned company would wait until the Fortune 50 company performed the research and development and marketing necessary to launch a new product and create customer awareness. Then it would quickly analyze the new product, develop a similar-but-better product of its own, and then launch it with advertising explaining why its product was superior. One example was a tube containing stain remover in a bright green container similar to personal deodorant that could be rubbed on stained clothing prior to washing. The family owned company took advantage of the Fortune 50 company's R&D and consumer-awareness advertising before launching its own product in an even brighter orange and displayed it more prominently on store shelves to better attract shoppers' attention. Astute leadership pays attention to the tightness of the organizational OODA loop and uses it to advantage.

At the individual level, leaders need to develop their own tight loops in addition to tightening their firm's loops. But how does one develop a tighter loop? The answer is that it starts with the leader sensing his or her environment and the behaviors of others and him- or herself. We have already begun the process of self-understanding by identifying what we believe to be our Best-Fit Type, so leaders can use that as a starting point in tightening their OODA loops.

10.3. Using MBTI to Tighten Leaders' Loops

A fundamental premise on which Myers-Briggs Type Indicator (MBTI) development is based is the need to be sensitive to the strengths and weaknesses of ourselves and others. This sensitivity provides a good starting point for tightening loops. Given space considerations we cannot deal with the strengths and weaknesses of all sixteen types, but we can illustrate how type can be used to develop a tighter loop in the following two examples.

Consider ESTPs who are *adventurous leaders* (see chapter 5). ESTPs are enthusiastic, action oriented, straightforward, and logical problem solvers. They are resourceful and adaptable, meeting practical needs in the most efficient way. They are willing to negotiate and compromise, working best in environments where goals are clear but there is flexibility in how they are achieved. ESTPs lead by focusing on required actions, establishing logical

processes for task accomplishment, and finding the most efficient way to bring people together. But ESTPs can become stressed when they feel they lack adequate control over such resources as people, time, and money. Failure to make progress and dealing with too much structure in problem solving are also frustrating to ESTPs.

When are leaders most likely to behave in less desirable ways? The answer is often when they are under stress. One way for leaders to tighten their cybernetic loops is to observe the environment for factors that are likely to stress them, orient on behaviors that indicate they are becoming stressed, decide on ways to mitigate stress, and implement these ways. In the case of the ESTP leader, this might involve the following: (1) imagining the worst possible outcomes and developing contingency plans for dealing with these outcomes; (2) keeping long-term goals in mind and not allowing temporary setbacks to deter efforts; (3) recognizing that when under stress they are more likely to be insensitive to others and avoid saying and doing things that suggest insensitivity; (4) behaving with enthusiasm to avoid deflecting stress and disappointment to subordinates; and (5) seeking new strategies to overcome obstacles causing stress. Over time, as the ESTP learns to sense the onset of stress and make conscious responses to reduce it and avoid undesirable reactions and behaviors, their OODA loops will become tighter and tighter.

Now consider INTJs who are *inventive leaders.* INTJs are excellent at envisioning ideas, shifting others' thinking to new paradigms, seeing individual characteristics or relationships as part of a whole, and thinking independently about design issues and future needs. They work best in situations where autonomy and out-of-the-box thinking are encouraged, efficiency is appreciated, people are willing to implement new ideas, co-workers are intelligent, and they can work in private space. INTJs can become stressed when confronted with details that don't make sense, when there is

> "In the new global economy, the value of organizations is no longer determined by product inventory or market exclusivity. When information can be disseminated in nanoseconds, competitive advantages derived from technological innovation are short lived as well. This means that the sustained competitive advantage of any organization in the 21st Century is its people . . . The shrinking world makes interpersonal communication and teamwork essential, as regional and continental barriers disappear for both a company's workforce and its market."
>
> —Center for Applications of Psychological Type

insufficient time to adjust their models to changing conditions, and when poor results are experienced in spite of careful planning and execution. INTJs should be sensitive to the following clues that they are becoming stressed and therefore more likely to engage in undesirable behaviors: (1) obsessing over details, (2) withdrawing from team activities, (3) showing overt hostility, and (4) engaging in nonproductive activities. Upon observing stressful conditions forming in the environment and sensing and orienting of stress indicators, INTJs can take action to mitigate undesirable stress-induced behaviors by focusing on a concrete task that can be accomplished relatively quickly, exhibiting more patience with colleagues and subordinates, listening more carefully to others' ideas, and balancing any necessary criticism of subordinates with positive feedback.

10.4. Using MBTI to Tighten Team Loops

More and more business activity is carried on at the team level. The growing complexity of business necessitates assembling teams with multifaceted knowledge and skills. This is especially true in professional services firms where teams of auditors, attorneys, and consultants work on client engagements. Teams have learning loops just as individuals do, and, as with individuals, tightening team learning loops can have very beneficial consequences in terms of nimbleness in dynamic environments. As indicated in the quote on the left, the business world today is increasingly people focused, as knowledge provides the real sustainable competitive advantage in product and service delivery. With the pace of technological change ever increasing, no longer can many business organizations be content with a product that today enjoys market dominance but can be rapidly overtaken and passed by a new technology. Organizational nimbleness is required, and since much of what is accomplished in business is accomplished by teams, teams need tight learning loops to enable them to react to change.

MBTI can be a useful tool for teams in establishing a framework for improving team members' awareness of their teammates, providing a vocabulary for different types to improve intrateam communications, in relationship building, and as a method for identifying and mitigating stressors. Properly used, MBTI can assist team members in understanding team dynamics and each other, understanding the team leader and the impact of his or her type on the team, discerning ways to communicate more effectively, and enabling team members to navigate through inevitable conflict. One lesson from the battlefield is that conflict can bring out the best or worst in people. On one hand, conflict can destroy an initiative. On the other hand, the clash of ideas gushing forth from nimble minds can result in breakthrough concepts.

Before embarking on a more detailed look at using MBTI in tightening team learning loops, consider the following quote:

> Learning may be defined as the detection and correction of errors. Single-loop learning occurs when errors are corrected altering the underlying governing values. For example, a thermostat is programmed to turn on if the temperature in the room is cold, or turn off if the room becomes too hot. Double-loop learning occurs when errors are corrected by changing the values and then the actions. A thermostat is double-loop learning if it questions why it is programmed to measure temperature, and then adjusts the temperature itself.[6]

Why is this distinction important in a business context? If one replaces the word values with parameters in the above quote, the answer becomes more apparent. As indicated by the quote on the right, in the increasingly dynamic business environment in which nimbleness is important, both external and internal factors may change during the course of the project. This may require refining the project's parameters, which entails double-loop learning. Consider the following example.

A software company has developed a new technology that holds promise of increasing the likelihood of drug discovery by improved portrayal of associations among various molecules. However, the marketing team is frustrated in its efforts to penetrate the research and development organizations within major pharmaceutical companies due to internal upheaval in those organizations resulting from downsizing, outsourcing, and acquisitions. As a result, the marketing team redirects its focus toward the safety and drug efficacy organizations inside the pharmaceutical companies because that is the direction in which these companies' emphasis seems to be moving. The new pitch to the pharmaceutical companies is that the

"The process of managing and implementing a project is typically more dynamic than what an initial project plan would indicate. Projects exist within organizational as well as economic contexts and are designed and executed by human beings. When such influences are considered collectively, chances are that a successful project will have required a series of reassessments and adjustments throughout the project's duration."

—Drs. Karla Black and Robert Seaker, University of Houston

speed of the due diligence process for approving outsourced drugs can be increased through the use of the software. The original project parameters that emanated from a focus on drug discovery have now changed in two ways: (1) the software will be marketed to a different portion of pharmaceutical companies, and (2) adverse-drug-event data will be analyzed.

Double-loop learning is predicated upon the understanding that plans, processes, and technologies must be continuously modified based upon environmental feedback. This means more than just new decisions. It also entails *new methods for deciding.* In the foregoing example the assumption had been that pharmaceutical companies would leap at the prospect of a tool that held promise of increasing the likelihood of drug discovery and simultaneously reduce research and development costs. The difficulty was that these companies have been in turmoil with a broken business model. Because of the long drug-approval process and finite patent lives, for many years pharmaceutical companies depended upon new breakthrough drugs being developed to maintain their revenue streams. As discovery of new breakthrough drugs declined, the companies came under increasing pressure to find a new business model and considered such possibilities as partnering with genomic and proteomic research firms. Unfortunately these efforts failed with the result that pharmaceutical companies began to increasingly outsource drug discovery in order to reduce fixed costs. Combined with the turmoil of downsizing, this made them much less interested in new discovery tools. For the software company this meant a new method for approaching phar

"Self-education is, I firmly believe, the only kind of education there is."

—Isaac Asimov

maceutical companies, focusing on very specific units with the companies and very specific ways in which value could be created. Moreover, the method of deciding how the marketing approach should be made became more complex.

Double-loop learning in teams is inhibited when individuals use what Chris Argyris termed **Model I** behaviors. Using Model I, leaders need to be in unilateral control, strive to always win in the sense of being in control, suppress negative feelings, and always act rationally. Model I governing behaviors are problematic in that they are defensive in nature, creating misunderstandings and self-fulfilling processes. This defensive behavior is intended to prevent the leader being embarrassed or threatened. The result can be mixed messages such as, "You are in charge of your group but check with me," or "Be innovative, but be careful." **Model II's** governing behaviors, on the other hand, promote double-loop learning in teams. These involve team leaders nurturing team members by

providing valid information, promoting free and informed choices, and fostering an internal commitment to team choices.[7]

Can MBTI assist leaders in developing a double-loop learning capability in teams? Recall that the one category of preferences involves how individuals prefer to absorb information, focusing on the actual (sensing) or on patterns, ideals, and meanings (intuiting). Another category involves whether people prefer to make decisions objectively (thinking) or based upon the impact of decisions on others (feeling). A third describes whether the environment is understood and perceived in an orderly way (judging) or with openness and spontaneity (perceiving). Because double-loop learning requires a broad vision, rationality, and flexibility, types favoring intuition, thinking, and perceiving are expected to engage more frequently in double-loop learning, and there is some evidence to support this position. Consequently, in complex, dynamic projects placing members who exhibit some or all of these preferences on teams may result in more double-loop learning. Aside from team membership selection, the use of techniques such as role-playing sessions, brainstorming, and table-top exercises may be useful in promoting double-loop learning.[8]

10.5. Self-Directed Learning

Throughout their careers leaders will be challenged by gaps between what they know and what they need to know. Leaders' ability to identify and close these knowledge gaps is critical to long-term success. This challenge is made greater by the already fast and growing rate of change in the business environment. No organizational training program alone is likely to be sufficient to enable leaders to close their knowledge gaps. In fact, although employers can provide material assistance in promoting self-learning, the bulk of the instructional responsibility will, in many cases, fall directly on the leader's shoulders. This requires a very different approach to thinking about learning than most people have been accustomed to.

Beginning in early childhood learners are spoon-fed bits of knowledge by instructors who have predetermined what knowledge is important. Students are often passive, not just in the way they receive knowledge but just as importantly in assessing what they need to know. Stated slightly differently, most people are accustomed to someone telling them what they need to know. Employers sometimes perpetuate this inculcated passivity by loading new recruits down with manuals and classes designed to instill "the way we do things here at XYZ Company." This passivity is both comfortable and insidiously harmful. Professionals desirous of getting leadership traction early in their careers and progressing rapidly need to reprogram their own beliefs and instincts about how to learn. They need to become self-directed learners.

An important part of this reprogramming involves understanding that self-directed learning is not just about the acquisition of knowledge but also about developing cognitive abilities. Students at all levels think the primary purpose of education, self or institutional, is to gain knowledge of some subject matter. Consider the following statement by one of the coauthors:

> I took twenty-seven courses in law school, ranked high in my class, and probably don't remember 10 percent of the facts learned for those courses. Although I passed the bar exam, I never practiced law. For many years the primary benefits I derived from 3 years of law school were becoming a better critical thinker and oral and written communicator. But then as a business professor 30 years after finishing law school I embarked on a research agenda that involved law. It was not the knowledge of law per se but rather how to think about law that was a great benefit in my research.

The import of this is that leaders often do not know how their learning experiences are going to play out later in life and are often unaware of how various learning activities benefit them. Does playing chess as a child make a person a better military officer because of the ability to look at symbols on maps and see capabilities and threats? Perhaps only when a learning experience of 30 years suddenly becomes integral to something today do we often grasp its significance. In one sense this constitutes a violation of ends/ways/means thinking discipline. We often engage in learning with no clear vision in mind of how its usefulness will play out, the process frequently being more important than the knowledge product. That said, once we are on the far side of school learning and into workplace learning, we often have more definite clues about what we need to know that we don't know to perform better and consequently, using self-directed learning, can focus our learning activities on that need.

Self-directed or self-regulated learning is that "guided by metacognition (thinking about one's thinking), strategic action (planning, monitoring, and evaluating personal progress against a standard), and motivation to learn."[9] Beyond school self-directed learning takes on significant importance because of several trends:

1. Growing need to work smarter instead of harder.

2. Increasing frequency of people changing jobs.

3. Diminishing number of quality versus lower-level jobs.

These trends are exacerbated by the failure of educational institutions and employers in many cases to adequately support the school-to-work transition.[10]

189

Evidence suggests that self-directed learners feel more empowered, take more responsibility for decisions, and are better able transfer the knowledge gained from one situation to another. Self-directed learners are thought to be successful because they better control their learning environments, with much of the learning taking place at the learner's initiative. Learners take the initiative and responsibility for learning, exercising independence in setting goals and defining what is worth learning. Self-directed learners are often highly motivated by both extrinsic and intrinsic rewards, demonstrating persistence, self-discipline, confidence, and goal focus.[11]

To be successful, however, self-learners must develop their own personal feedback loops that enable reasonably accurate assessment of the improvement or lack thereof of their knowledge and cognitive abilities. They must also hold themselves accountable for any failure to make progress against their learning objectives. Finally, they often must identify, recruit, and engage their own part-time "instructors" who may consist of mentors, colleagues, external resources, or even subordinates. If this sounds more difficult than you might have previously imagined you're on track. Like any complex cognitive ability, becoming a good self-learner takes time, effort, and ex-

perimentation. With perseverance, however, the results can be enormous in terms of career progression, often opening doors that would have remained closed but for new skills and knowledge.

One reason that self-directed learning is so important for leaders is the differences between learning in school and learning in the workplace. Figure 10.3 compares and contrasts these differences.

Merely glancing at the figure reveals many differences between learning at school and at work. One major difference is that workplace learning is far less structured, less unidirectional, and far more contextual with respect to specific problems faced by the employer. This enhances learning, as evidence indicates that learners perform better when dealing with problems in authentic contexts and embedded in intrinsically rewarding activities. Given the rather stark differences in school versus workplace learning and the aforementioned failure of many educational institutions and employers to adequately support the school-to-work transition, self-learning becomes an imperative for aspiring leaders. The good news is that overall the evidence suggests that self-directed learning works.

Figure 10.3. Comparison of School and Workplace Learning

Differences	School Learning	Workplace Learning
Emphasis	Basic skills	Learning embedded in work
Drawbacks	Largely decontextualized	Context more important
Problems	Given	Have to be constructed
New topics	Define by curricula	Arise from needs of employer
Structure	Generic and logical	Circumstances determine
Roles	Expert novice	Reciprocal learning
Instructors	Expound on subject matter	Evolve from work practice
Mode	Knowledge absorption	Knowledge construction
Answer and method	Given	Must be devised

Source: Adapted from G. Fischer and M. Sugimoto, "Supporting Self-Directed Learners and Learning Communities with Sociotechnical Environments," *Journal of Research and Practice in Technology Enhanced Learning 1, no. 1* (2006): 37.

10.6. Developing Your Own Learning Plan

So, how should aspiring leaders go about designing a self-directed-learning program? The following steps offer one approach.

1. *Discover your strengths and weaknesses.* A starting point is self-understanding. MBTI Best-Fit Type is a first step in self-understanding because it provides a framework for knowing your preferred behaviors and behaviors you prefer to avoid.

2. *Get clear on your vision.* Armed with knowledge of yourself, assess your professional goals. What are your goals for 1, 3, 5, and 10 years from now? Consider carefully what transactions you particularly enjoy and those you do not enjoy, and select goals as consistent as possible with enjoyable transactions. This may well require research into various other organizational units or even other industries.

3. *Identify your gaps.* Select a handful of leaders who appear to be successful doing what is represented by each of your goals. These can be in your current or other businesses. Assess what knowledge, attributes, skills, and abilities these leaders possess. Look up their resumes online and examine them carefully for evidence of their qualifications. Make a realistic assessment of your current knowledge, attributes, skills, and abilities against your comparison group and identify each significant deficiency.

4. *Set your learning goals.* Research your learning needs and how to go about meeting these needs. Consider degree programs, nondegree programs, single courses, or home study as appropriate. Distance learning represents one of the most powerful tools enabling self-directed learning. It is now possible to take classes, courses, or even entire degree programs online from a wide variety of educational resources varying greatly in cost and quality.

5. *Design your learning plan.* Ascertain what it will take in time, money, and other resources to resolve each deficiency. Decide on your priorities. What deficiencies need to be rectified first? What can you afford in time and money? Recognize that sometimes getting where you want to be means taking more than one step. For example, if your goals involve an in-depth knowledge of econometric analysis and your mathematical skills are weak, it may be necessary to take some math courses before tackling econometrics.

6. *Schedule regular reviews.* Develop a detailed, personal self-learning plan with benchmarks for tracking your progress against plan. Challenge yourself, but don't over program your self-learning such that you induce multitasking paralysis.[12] Don't over agonize if you miss an objective occasionally. Instead, develop the ability to shift between two mindsets. Use a deliberative attitude when assessing the feasibility of a learning action, but maintain a positive attitude when implementing the action.[13]

Parts of your self-learning program may entail acquisition of knowledge, but other parts may relate to skills. For example, suppose you have identified public speaking skills as a deficiency. Reading about how to be a better speaker may be helpful, but there is no substitute for **deliberate practice**. You might, for example, join Toastmasters to gain actual practice experience speaking in front of a group that provides clear and immediate performance feedback. Although not all skills learning is amenable to deliberate practice, there is evidence

Figure 10.4. When to Use Deliberate Practice

Criterion	Well Suited	Less Well Suited
Duration	Short	Long
Feedback	Immediate	Slow
Order of tasks	Sequential	Concurrent
Performance	Absolute	Relative

Source: Adapted from P. Rosenzweig, "Making Better Decisions Over Time," *Strategy+Business,* January 6, 2014, www.strategy-business.com/article/00227?pg=all&tid=27782251 (accessed February 15, 2014.)

many skills are improved by it. Deliberate practice means "practice that conforms to a clear process loop of action, feedback, adjustment, and action once again. Deliberate practice functions best when learners receive explicit feedback soon after practice."[14]

Although it can result in the creation of expertise, not simply experience, all skills development is not well suited to deliberate practice. Figure 10.4 indicates those conditions under which deliberate practice is more likely to succeed.

Deliberate practice works best with skills-related tasks that are short lived, provide immediate feedback, are sequential and not current in nature, and for which success or failure can be measured in absolute terms. For example, programming Excel for purposes of corporate valuations might be well suited to deliberate practice. More complex projects requiring concurrent actions with less well-defined measures of success or failure are contraindicated. An example would be using the market, discounted-cash-flow, and asset-based approaches to value a company.[15]

One of the most powerful tools for self-learning can be joining a self-learning group. There is evidence that group self-learning can lead to more direct engagement with the subject matter, increased exposure to different ideas, and higher levels of information processing.[16] One of the co-authors relates the following story:

For the first 2 years in law school I was a member of a group that had been in existence for many years called the Legal Studies Society. It consisted of twelve members who met weekly for 3 hours. Each student was handpicked and highly disciplined. Each of us would brief the same six cases prior to meetings. One person would be selected at random to present his brief of a particular case. This was followed by the other members attacking his brief. Any tardiness or lack of preparation resulted in a warning to the member. If repeated the member was kicked out of the group. It was great critical thinking and debate experience. At the end of 2 years, those of us who were seniors were required to find replacement members. The outgoing seniors then formed another group that met weekly for 3 hours to study for the bar exam. The discipline enforced in the first group carried over to the second. The first-attempt pass rate on the bar exam for former Legal Studies Society members was 100 percent.

The story reveals the power of group self-study, but it also reveals the importance of one other aspect. Effective self-study in groups requires self-discipline and group-discipline. In this case, the group members were carefully selected based upon academic achievement, there were concrete objectives in terms of coverage of materials for each meeting, and a strict discipline about punctuality and preparedness was enforced. In addition, a looming performance measurement at the end of the study in the form of a difficult professional examination helped encourage the members. Those structuring self-learning groups should therefore give careful consideration to group member selection, rules, and accountability standards because self-discipline reinforces group discipline and vice versa.

Group member selection can sometimes be tricky for various reasons, but there are some helpful guidelines. Team formation starts with the subject matter of a learning project. To be most effective, teams should have a common body of knowledge related to the project that enables them to assist one another. In the previous example involving law students, despite a diversity of backgrounds, their experience in studying law for 2 years provided a common body of knowledge. This knowledge need not be exactly the same in amount, content, or quality, but it should be related to the same subject matter. For example, a group of learners studying management accounting might not all be accountants, but ideally all should have knowledge of the business circumstances under which cost accounting is being studied. To see why this is so, consider a self-study group consisting of a marketing manager, a production engineer, and a high-school English teacher. The marketing manager (who perhaps provides product pricing input based upon unit costs) and the production engineer (who may pay a great deal of attention to budget versus actual cost variance reports) are likely to have a far greater understanding of the ways in which cost accounting is applied in business than an English teacher.

With self-study groups it is useful to have an agreed-upon curriculum with milestones to guide progress. Without such guidance, self-study groups can wander off topic and consume time engaging in unproductive conversation. In the case of the law study group, a bar examina-

tion preparation course formed the basis for the group's study, which included written materials to be read in advance of meetings, tapes with lectures covering the materials to which the group listened as a body with the option to stop and discuss points as needed, and self-examinations to gauge the extent of learning.

Businesses can facilitate self-learning among employees in a variety of ways to include making special provisions for group study. Allowing use of spaces such as conference rooms after hours for meetings, purchasing study materials, and providing access to resources such as video equipment can encourage study regime. Often a particular industry will have an association of professionals, one function of which is to promote education about industry issues. An example is the American Institute of Banking and American Institute of Certified Public Accountants, which sponsor training courses and seminars for employees. These courses represent an excellent form of guided group study with the costs often paid by the employer. Savvy employers also find ways to recognize employees who make progress in their self-study plans. Mentioning self-study efforts in performance evaluation reports and employee meetings are two ways of recognizing these accomplishments.

10.7. Too Young to Lead?

Many U.S. businesses today are confronted with a demographic problem without an easy solution—a middle-management workforce of baby boomers, many of whom are retiring. These businesses face what one author has termed an "impending worker drought."[17] Confronted with insufficient supply, rising expectations, and declining loyalties, in the case of business professionals there are only three apparent solutions to this problem: (1) prepare younger professionals to move into leadership positions sooner, (2) retain some older professionals who demonstrate an ability and willingness to keep themselves at the edge of their professions, and/or (3) buy talent.[18] All three solutions are challenging and very likely to depend to a significant extent upon self-learning. The third option, buying talent, rests largely outside our discussion of self-learning. Suffice it to say that it is fraught with various risks, including paying a high cost to hire apparent stars that don't fit for one reason or another and an insufficient supply of stars to meet demand. Consequently, subsequent discussion deals with options 1 and 2.

The challenge with younger leaders is often their having the courage to step into unfamiliar situations fraught with uncertainty about how to proceed, and fear of failure. Consider the following:

> According to the "2010 Best Companies for Leadership Survey" (conducted by Bloomberg, BusinessWeek.com and Hay Group), the quality most valued by top companies in their leaders is strategic thinking. Most of us clearly recognize the benefits of more strategic thinking as a way to seize more profitable growth in our companies. The challenge is how difficult it can be to quickly build this skill among managers and leaders, who are often focused only on tactical execution.[19]

Many organizations talk about leadership development, but not many follow that talk up with real action by creating the "underlying framework, brand, and holistic development system to support their claims. This approach is especially likely to backfire with next-generation leaders who typically become frustrated by the disconnect between actions and words."[20] What is required is an integrated approach that identifies high-performance-potential leaders and accelerates their growth by affording them (1) opportunities to gain both depth and breadth of experience through stretch assignments, (2) greater exposure to senior leaders from whom they can learn, and

(3) learning programs—sometimes experimental—that bridge the classroom with the real world.

This opportunity triad is emblematic of the entire issue of accelerating development of young, high-performance-potential leaders. Accelerating leader development requires an integrated approach. Not only must businesses identify these future stars, but the development process requires *joint ownership* by both the young leaders and the organization. For its part, the organization must provide guidance and templates for progression while allowing young leaders considerable latitude to plot their own paths. For the leaders' part, they must commit themselves to doing more, learning more, and taking more challenges.[21]

Although people with the attitude that failure is not an option are often great to have around, even leaders for whom failure is an anathema will sometimes fail in stretch assignments. Properly seized upon as a learning experience, noncataclysmic failures not resulting from moral turpitude can be turned into positive learning experiences. Leaders usually learn much more from a single failure than they will from several successes because learning often stops when success is achieved and people move on to the next project. Not so with failure. When leaders fail, the pain causes reflection. They should want to know why they failed, when exactly in the process failure occurred, and how to plan better to avoid future failure. They learn about taking responsibility for their failures and that they can recover from failure.[22] With the caveats that, as long as failures occur within the bounds of acceptable organizational values and losses—and failures of a type are not repeated—organizations desiring to accelerate leadership development need to accept failure in stretch assignments. The good news is that "failure" probably will not mean complete failure most of the time. Rather, it means a failure to perform to some desired level.

Managing failure can be difficult for both the leader and the organization. Failure can cripple leaders if not handled properly by the organization. Often the key is the manner in which older leaders react after a young leader fails. Are older leaders able to relate their own experiences with failures in ways that encourage learning and build confidence, or do the older leaders dwell on the failure itself rather than the lessons it provides? This should not be interpreted as coddling failure but rather as a level-headed response that focuses on applying lessons learned to future challenges.[23]

One reason that developing young leaders is so difficult is that it requires a pack mentality on the part of the leaders' leaders. Leaders of young leaders must resist the strong temptation to hold onto talent too long. To acquire the breadth of experience necessary to fulfill their promise as stars, high-performance-potential leaders must move not only up but out, sometimes making lateral moves to gain experience. This often runs counter to the needs of a particular unit whose leader naturally desires to hold onto high-performing talent as long as possible. What is needed to unfreeze talent is top-down governance and guidance that places a priority on leadership development backed up with attention and funding.

Recalling Dave Roberts's story about being forced to assume the responsibilities of an officer as a corporal at the age of 19 in combat, for young people with the courage to lead, being thrust into a leadership role early in their careers can become a launching pad to an accelerated career. Mistakes will be made, but if these mistakes are of the forgivable variety, not catastrophic or immoral, and used to tighten their learning loops, young leaders and their organizations can benefit greatly.

10.8. Too Old to Learn?

In essence this section deals with a potential reciprocity that too few businesses in the coauthors' opinions truly understand and use to their advan-

> ## "Intellectual growth should commence at birth and cease only at death."
>
> —Albert Einstein

tage. This potential reciprocity exists between young and seasoned leaders. It involves mentoring and **reverse mentoring**. We've previously discussed mentoring, but what is reverse mentoring? Reverse mentoring occurs when younger leaders mentor older, seasoned leaders. To better understand this let's begin by revisiting the problem looming for many businesses. Recall that the second option for businesses faced with future leadership shortages is to retain *some* seasoned leaders who exhibit both high-performance ability and a willingness to engage in learning themselves. Part of accelerating young leaders' development is coaching and mentoring by older leadership. There is a wealth of experience that these leaders in what has been called the "magnificent middle"—those who make things happen in many organizations—can impart to younger leaders. How can businesses retain enough older leaders who will continue to find work challenging and who, at the same time, are willing to take the steps necessary to stay at the cutting edge of their professions in order to continue to add real value?

Many baby boomers are experiencing the confluence of three factors. First, they have the means to retire comfortably. The children are grown and out of college, the house and the Florida condo are paid for, and the retirement account looks robust. Second, they no longer feel as challenged as they once did in their professional lives. They weary of the same old transactions year in and out, dealing with the same client and employee problems, and perhaps feel they've climbed their mountains. Third, there may be an often-unspoken-but-growing feeling of inadequacy that they are no longer on the leading edge of technology in an age when technology is becoming more and more import-

> **"Those people who develop the ability to continuously acquire new and better forms of knowledge that they can apply to their work and to their lives will be the movers and shakers in our society for the indefinite future."**
>
> —Brain Tracy

ant. How can some of the best of these senior leaders be convinced to stay and nurture younger leaders while keeping their skills sharp enough to stay abreast in the midst of business dynamism? The answers rest with (1) making them feel needed and respected, (2) challenging them with new opportunities, and (3) engaging them in learning.

For those organizations with the aplomb to make it work, bilateral mentoring offers a unique-but-rarely-attempted partial solution to this problem. Consider Figure 10.5. The organizational pain is a looming shortage of high-performing leaders. The older leader's need is for new challenges to maintain interest in professional life.

"Education is the kindling of a flame, not the filling of a vessel."

—Socrates

The younger leader's need is for guidance that will facilitate accelerated growth. By pairing older leaders with younger leaders with respect to interest, intellect, and personality the interests of the organization and the leaders can become more aligned.

One of the difficulties with establishing a bilateral program of mentoring and reverse mentoring is that mentoring relationships are usually best when they evolve over time on an informal basis

through a shared interest in professional development.[24] The coauthors are convinced that a major reason that many mentorships are mediocre at best is an asymmetry in that the benefits accrue mostly to the mentee. Normally, only if the mentor has a personal utility for assisting junior personnel is there benefit to the mentor. Properly paired and managed, however, the creation of a shared interest in professional development between older and younger leaders has the potential to be a positive force for all three parties. Consider the following testimony from one of the coauthors:

> In my late 50s while still active as a professor, I began working on a part-time basis directly for the chief advisory services officer for a national CPA/consulting firm who had climbed very rapidly to a senior level at a young age. My role was to assist him with some of his more complex valuation case work, in part because he had become increasingly busy with his administrative responsibilities as he progressed rapidly in his career. Although a quarter century younger than me, he was highly regarded nationally as an expert in the business-valuation field and often coached me in the intricacies of complex litigation-related valuations you might call stretch assignments. In return, because I had extensive leadership experience in business, academia, and the military, I became an advisor to him regarding the handling of difficult organizational leadership problems similar to those I had experienced in these other domains. This symbiotic relationship worked well, with both of us sharing our diverse expertise. One of the important contributors to the success of the relationship was that we both were willing to humbly admit the gaps in our knowledge and ask each other for advice. A friendship blossomed from this relationship that continues to this day.

Your Personal Career-Success Toolkit

Figure 10.5. Needs and Offerings

Organization	Older Leader	Younger Leader
Capable high-performance leadership in light of leader shortage	New challenges to induce retention New technological and methodological skills	Accelerated growth as leader coming from stretch assignments Seasoned mentorship
Innovative training and retraining Support for learning Challenging opportunities	Mentorship of young leader in handling leadership problems Project management Organizational savvy Continuing to add value	Mentorship of older leader in new technologies and methodologies Continuing to exhibit high performance potential

After 55, the number of business professionals engaged in formal corporate training drops dramatically. One reason is that such programs are often viewed as increasingly irrelevant, a rehash of lessons already learned. This older group prefers a do-it-yourself approach to learning that allows them to choose how best to fill knowledge gaps. Providing seasoned leaders the opportunity to learn new skills from younger leaders while imparting leadership wisdom to them creates a reciprocal mentoring asymmetry. Both parties have reason to feel valuable and respected for their knowledge and skills. It also plays to the proclivities of seasoned leaders, who often prefer training that is less abstract and more about workplace tasks. Although creating such relationships is not as easy as simply assigning seasoned and younger leaders to work together, with its aging leadership problem, businesses must do something to retain some well-performing seasoned leaders or face losing their experience-based knowledge and mentoring potential. By carefully pairing seasoned leaders with younger leaders in symbiotic relationships, both the parties and the organization can benefit.[25]

10.9. Concluding Thoughts

In recent economic crises, many organizations found that they lacked the depth of leadership necessary to navigate the troubled waters of challenging business conditions. They also lacked accurate means of measuring performance in order to identify those high-performance-potential leaders worth investing in to accelerate their progress as leaders. Which potential leaders have those critical leadership attributes that enable them to create value by helping to drive organizational growth and profitability? High-performance leaders must have tight learning loops, adapting quickly to global change to meet aggressive growth targets in converging markets. Although expected to do more with less, tomorrow's leaders are often

> **"Anyone who stops learning is old, whether at twenty or eighty. Anyone who keeps learning stays young."**
>
> —Henry Ford

insufficiently challenged today with a diverse set of experiences that tighten their loops rapidly.[26] Instead, five years of experience often means one year of experience repeated four times.

In the end, as Socrates believed, learning is a journey, not a destination, and the real responsibility for self-learning falls upon the individual. Learning is a lifelong process, and the individual's desire to learn is likely to be the one continuity during a lifetime. Leaders, both young and old, need to commit to continuous learning in order to stay abreast of the increasing dynamism of global business. "The single most important thing within any organization is leadership," and "the importance of leadership development programs cannot be overstated."[27] Due to an aging population, businesses are facing a critical leadership shortage when leadership succession is especially critical to future success. Figure 10.6 shows just how daunting this problem is for firms.

Figure 10.6. The Looming Leadership Problem in Business

Concern	% Firms Reporting	Concern	% Firms Reporting
Employment levels expected to rise over the next 10 years	71%	Very or somewhat difficult to hire good leaders	63%
Very or somewhat difficult to retain good leaders	46%	Very or somewhat difficult to develop good leaders	53%
Formalized succession plan	< 40%	360-degree assessment	< 40%
Personality assessments	< 50%	Formal executive coaching program	40%
Knowledge retention a serious challenge	86%	Changing competitive environment and cost pressures challenge leadership development	80% +

Source: Adapted from "Workforce and Succession Management in a Changing World," *CPP Global Human Capital Report*, November 2008, https://www.cpp.com/Pdfs/Workforce_and_succession_mgmt.pdf (accessed February 27, 2014).

CHAPTER 11

Effective Communication

> "To succeed, you will soon learn, as I did, the importance of a solid foundation in the basics of education—literacy, both verbal and numerical, and communication skills."
>
> —Alan Greenspan

As the quote above suggests, good communication skills, like leadership, are something leaders must learn. We are not born good communicators. Difficulties in communicating with others are ubiquitous in most aspects of our lives, from family to work to social life. Whether we progress over time as communicators or languish in the often mistaken belief our messages are received and understood is largely a function of how sensitive and savvy we are to the responses and behaviors of those with whom we are attempting to communicate.

What is communication? One definition that seemingly captured much of its totality is "the act or process of using words, sounds, signs, or behaviors to express or exchange information or to express your ideas, thoughts, feelings, *etcetera* to someone else."[1] Note our emphasis on the word *etcetera,* implying elements left unmentioned. This definition relegates to the unmentioned what is often the most problematic aspect of communication for leaders. Most communication experts define communication more specifically as what is *understood* by the recipient of the message and not what is *intended* by its sender. The delta between *understood* and *intended* is something we have all experienced in one way or another. Examples include attempting to get directions to a restaurant in a foreign country where we don't

speak the language, deciphering what our tax accountant is telling us about the recent changes in the tax code, or trying to understand why your newborn is screaming—is she hungry, tired, hurt? Sometimes unintended miscommunication is even comical. One of the coauthors was in France and asked an office receptionist if the latter spoke English. "Je m'appelle English" was repeated several times until he realized that what he was saying was, "My name is English." Unfortunately the business world is full of examples of communication mistakes with much greater impact.

Every day we are literally bombarded with thousands of messages in various ways, all competing for our attention. A small portion of this communication is directed right at us, such as letters, e-mails, and phone calls; but many of the messages we receive come via more indirect means, such as mass advertising. Then there is communication received but never intended for us, such as overheard conversations of people nearby. Regardless of the intent of the communication, we can be easily distracted by this cacophony. This is something leaders should be aware of when attempting to communicate. In getting their intent across to followers, leaders are competing with all manner of messages, including messages followers themselves are sending to the leaders.

This problem is exacerbated by the growing prevalence of technology, particularly cell phones and messaging devices. You have doubtless been to numerous meetings where participants sat

> ## "The single biggest problem in communication is the illusion that it has taken place."
>
> —George Bernard Shaw

fiddling with cell phones, iPads, and other mobile messaging devices, perhaps messaging during the meeting with their 300 closest friends on a social media site, some of whom they've never met. Against this distractive, cacophonous background, the challenge for leaders to have their messages received and understood by followers is greater than ever. People may appear to be listening, but their minds are often far away. As a result, the need for leaders to master good communications skills is greater than ever. This mastery begins with simple communications—clearly communicating who we are and what we want. Although this should seemingly go without saying, many leaders still manage to botch it.

11.1. The Importance of Clarity in Simple Communications

Much day-to-day communication is easily sent and easily understood. We say "good morning" to a neighbor at the coffee shop or we order lunch at the local deli. This is, in part, due to the fact that most everyday conversations are repetitive and with people we know, but also because both the roles of the sender and receiver and the objective of the conversation are generally understood. This may lead to the unfortunate habit of assuming implicitly this is always the case.

Imagine a person who walks into a retail store and approaches a sales associate who asks, "How may I help you?" The associate is assuming the person is a potential customer and will most likely have a question about products and services the store is selling. Even if the "customer" asks about something else, such as the time of day or directions, he or she still desires the associate's assistance. What if instead the customer asks if the sales associate needs assistance planning for his or her retirement? Everything changes. The sales associate was prepared for one conversation but finds him- or herself engaged in a very different one, probably to confusion and perhaps distress. Most of us have experienced somewhat analogous situations in which we were expecting one conversation but found ourselves engaged in a quite different one. These situations can easily lead to discomfort and miscommunication. In the preceding example, the sales associate is now torn between the need to be nice to someone who may be a customer if not now at another time, and his or her employer's expectation of serving customers rather than discussing personal business while on the job.

Two basic rules for effective communication are (1) clearly understanding who you are and (2) understanding your objective in an interaction. Both help clarify the roles of the sender and the recipient as well as providing context for the message. A leader might think of e-mail as an analogy. Business e-mail messages usually show the sender's and recipient's identities and the subject. Business phone conversations often follow the same rules, with callers announcing who is calling, with whom they wish to speak, and often the reason for the call. Both means of communication are sometimes accompanied by some indication or statement of the importance of the message.

In cases where we are unfamiliar with the person with whom we are communicating, it often helps to not only clarify who we are and our role but also provide some context. For example, after stating his name, one of the coauthors may also state, "I am with the Accounting Faculty at the Kelley School of Business and our common acquaintance Dean Fisher recommended that I reach out to you directly regarding our MBA program." Not only has this statement clarified the *who* and the *why* of the communication but it has also generated some degree of trust because of the common acquaintance. There is also now an implicit incentive for the person being contacted to not only pay attention but to provide valuable feedback, if applicable; or, failing that, run the risk of the common acquaintance learning that the person was not helpful.

Even when we believe that we are communicating our identity and purpose clearly, it is sometimes easy for others to misinterpret the caller or purpose of the call. Consider the amusing anecdote of a dean who called his associate dean, who also happened to be a commanding general at the time on active duty with the marines. When the general's headquarters answered, the dean announced that he was Mr. Dalton and asked to please speak with Mr. Hill. Chaos ensued. By coincidence the dean's last name was the same as that of the then secretary of the navy, a very high-ranking government official. Believing that the secretary was calling, headquarters personnel scrambled all over the building in an attempt to find the general, who was not in his office at the time, with the phone watch all the while apologizing profusely to "Mr. Secretary" for keeping him on hold.

Other keys to effective communication include ensuring you have the other person's attention, being direct and honest, and asking for and providing feedback to help ensure messages are sent and received properly. Although this may seem like common sense, we often become careless when we are in a rush or taking a particular conversation for granted. It is also very important to keep in mind the nature of the subject matter when we are communicating. Polite conversation is relatively easy because we spend much of our lives engaged in this type of communication. On occasion, however, when we are communicating about sensitive matters such as convincing someone to think differently or correcting undesirable behaviors, careless casual words may materially exacerbate a problem if the listener misinterprets the message.[2] Once communicated, erroneous information sometimes requires considerable time and effort to retract.

One of the fastest and most destructive means of miscommunicating is e-mail. Once misinformation has been sent, the sender has lost control over who receives the message. Forwarded e-mail can result in a very large audience receiving the misinformation in a short period of time. Even something as simple as a wrong meeting time sent to several addressees can easily result in a botched meeting. A subsequent e-mail sent to correct an erroneous e-mail may not arrive to the original addressees before it has been forwarded to others, who in turn forward to others. Eventually, some recipient may recognize the errors, but the original sender may not know all the forwarded recipients. What sometimes ensues is exemplified by hallway conversations such as the following:

> **Sue:** "Are you coming to the meeting describing the division reorganization tomorrow?"
>
> **Bob:** "I thought that meeting was on Thursday."
>
> **Mary:** "I received an appointment e-mail canceling an e-mail that said Wednesday, so I assumed the meeting was canceled."
>
> **Bob:** "There was a follow-on appointment e-mail that said Thursday."
>
> **Tom (just walking up):** "Bob's right about the day of the week, but the meeting was last Thursday, not this week."

One technique that helps eliminate confusion in simple business communications is summariz-

"If you can't explain it to a six year old, you don't understand it yourself."

—Albert Einstein

ing what was decided in a conversation and asking for questions and feedback. This helps ensure all parties have understood details correctly. For example, a summary such as the following can go a long way toward avoiding subsequent problems resulting from unclear statements and faulty memory: "Okay, let me see I can briefly summarize what we've decided. We will meet again at the same time and place next Tuesday. At that meeting we will discuss what progress we've made since today. All department heads should attend. I will send out a detailed agenda prior to the meeting. Are there any questions?"

By becoming more aware of the value of communicating in clear, simple terms in everyday interactions, leaders can save themselves time and grief, avoiding problems that result from communicating misinformation. Perhaps one of the best examples of this rests with the benefits of explanation rather than assuming implicitly that the understanding of those with whom leaders are communicating is the same as that of the leaders.

11.2. The Importance of Explanation in Communication

One of the coauthors had just broken his arm. This injury was complicated by the same arm having been severely injured years earlier. Initially medical staff failed to communicate accurately the nature and extent of the damage because they provided no clear explanation, only veiled prognoses. Subsequently, an orthopedic expert for professional sports teams was consulted, and the expert asked, "What is your level of medical knowledge? What do you know about how your body works?" Thus began an in-depth explanation that formed the beginning of the coauthor

understanding the extent of damage, what alternative treatments were available, and the pros and cons of each.

For business people explanation constitutes a great deal of routine professional communication, but making facts more understandable is at times far more difficult than it sounds. One reason explanation is difficult is that it often requires empathy in that the person doing the explaining needs to understand the other person's perspective.[3] This starts with understanding others' points of view by listening and responding to questions. When presenting and responding to questions, attempt to assess the audience's level of understanding by asking questions occasionally, and pitch the level of complexity accordingly. After answering a question ask, "Does my response fully answer your question?" Avoid talking over people's heads or sounding condescending by oversimplification. It is also helpful to avoid acronyms and jargon unless you are sure the listeners are familiar with them and know exactly what context you mean.[4] For example, the acronym AMR can mean any of the following: arithmetic mean return, AMR Corporation (American Airlines's former parent company), automated medical record, or any one of approximately seventy other organizations, events, physical phenomena, or capabilities.

In most business presentations to prospective clients, one critical point to keep in mind is to focus first on the **benefits to the client**, not the features of your product, technology, or service. Consider the following simple example.

> A feature is some inherent property of an object. A benefit, on the other hand, is a way the feature helps the person. For example, one of the features of a Styrofoam cup, because of the material used, is insulation. Someone planning a party doesn't care how the cup provides insulation. That

person is more interested in the fact that such a cup keeps hot things hot and cold things cold.[5]

As obvious as the foregoing example of a cup may seem, when complexity is added in the situation of selling to clients, presentations often wander into product, service, and technological attributes instead of beginning with client benefits in order to hook the listeners. But the first step of hooking with a benefits focus alone usually isn't sufficient. It is often helpful to use **analogies** to make concepts clearer. Think carefully about the central benefit principle to the client and then choose something from ordinary experience that illustrates the principle. The foregoing cup analogy is an example. Then draw a comparison between the benefits provided by your proposed product, service, or technology to those currently in use. A simple graphic showing a **side-by-side comparison** is often helpful in communicating the superiority of your proposal. In this comparison **subsets** and **supersets** are sometimes useful in explaining relationships. For example, a certain software capability may be a subset of a larger set of capabilities, but that same capability may be a superset of the software currently used by the client in that the proposed capability does everything the existing capability does and more.[6]

The old saying "A picture is worth a thousand words" often proves its truth. For example, in his bestselling books, Dr. Brian Greene of Columbia University uses analogies, such as Bart Simpson on a nuclear-powered skateboard to help explain complex subjects like particle physics. Pictures need not be only visual, however; they can also be verbal. In writing a performance review you can paint a helpful mental picture of an employee for other readers. Consider the following paragraph.

Jack displays extraordinary enthusiasm for his assignments, often tackling difficult tasks that others are reticent to take on.

His eagerness sometimes leads to starting tasks without a complete understanding of the precise outcomes desired with the result that others have to tie up loose ends. His intense focus on task completion can sometimes result in skipping some planning steps. That acknowledged, he rarely repeats a serious mistake once he is aware of its consequences. Jack functions best on teams comprised of members who possess his imperative for rapidly accomplishing tasks, sometimes showing impatience with team members who prefer a more thoughtful approach to problem solving. Jack is at his best when assigned urgent tasks that are not overly complex and can be accomplished quickly.

What mental picture of Jack do you form from reading these comments? Is it one of an employee who (1) is enthusiastic but perhaps overconfident who rushes into difficult tasks, (2) does not like to spend much time thinking about complex problems and has little patience with others who do, (3) is in a hurry to complete tasks and does not always follow prescribed procedures and see tasks through to completion requiring others to step in, and (4) sometimes makes serious mistakes even though he may learn from these mistakes if and when he becomes aware of them? If you had a critical assignment involving significant client sensitivity to outcome success, Jack might not be your choice for that assignment.

In summary, some general guidelines for better explanations are (1) use explanation in problem solving—by helping someone solve a problem by explaining it, the other person becomes more communicative; (2) keep explanation short and to the point while minimizing distractions; (3) pace your explanation to the speed of your audience's understanding; and (4) use language that your audience can understand.[7] The latter guideline makes a clear statement about choosing the words we use.

11.3. Choosing the Words We Use Carefully

Good leaders choose their words wisely when they communicate. Who is the intended recipient of the message? Are there cultural, experiential, or educational differences that should be considered? A memo on a given subject to lower-level employees may be quite different than one intended for a peer group. An internal corporate communication with personnel in a foreign subsidiary may need to be devoid of colloquialisms with which foreigners may be unfamiliar and that may cause confusion. Many electronic communications are filled with shorthand expressions. Common current expressions for someone in his or her 20s used to e-mailing and texting friends may have no meaning for someone in his or her 50s.

Many industries and professions have their own distinct language that people within the profession use to communicate with each other more effectively and at a finer level of detail. Problems occur, however, when acronyms, jargon, colloquialisms, and industry-context-specific terms overflow into communications with people unfamiliar with the language. This not only includes those employed in other industries and professions but also those new to the organization. Consider (and, those of you with refined taste, please forgive) the following anecdote that illustrates this point rather graphically.

> Years ago during wartime soldiers used latrines with open drums underneath as waste receptacles. Each morning the drums were removed, diesel fuel poured into them, and they were set on fire in order to destroy the waste. This became known in the soldiers' jargon as "burning the latrine." Once, an inexperienced solider who had just arrived in combat was ordered by his sergeant, "Get some diesel fuel and burn the latrine." Being unfamiliar with the jargon, the soldier proceeded to burn the entire structure to the ground.

Choosing words wisely often means knowing your audience. Business professionals frequently use financial information to communicate. According to one source, the objective of financial reporting is "to provide financial information about the reporting entity that is useful to present and potential equity investors, lenders, and other creditors" and "may also be helpful to other users of financial information."[8] In short, accountants prepare financial statements primarily for people who are accustomed to using financial information but secondarily for consumers of that information who may or may not be as familiar with financial reports, such as marketing and operations personnel. Consequently, financial reports may need to be tailored to meet the needs and relative financial sophistication expertise of the target audience.

One of the situations leaders will sometimes confront is that of the angry employee, colleague, or boss. The result of responding to anger with anger is often greater anger. Choosing words carefully when confronted by angry individuals can often defuse volatile situations. One way to do this is to ask questions rather than responding to accusations with statements of your own. Consider the following possible response to an angry employee who chronically has difficulty getting along with other employees:

> **Employee:** "I'm upset! I'm sick and tired of Bill's refusing to cooperate on this project. He doesn't get his stuff done on time, and when I ask him about it he clams up and won't talk. I'm done. If you want this project finished, get someone else to do it!"

> **Leader (frustrated):** "Joe, I've been meaning to talk to you. If you didn't fly off the handle every time somebody does something you don't agree with your colleagues would

cooperate better. I know for a fact Bill has worked hard to get this project completed on time, and he got behind last week because he had to fix a mistake you made."

Although the leader's response may be entirely accurate and the problem may rest with Joe, not Bill, the nature of her response is likely to lead to more anger. Now consider a different response:

> **Leader (calmly):** "Joe, I'd like to hear more before responding. Please have a seat and explain the details of the problem."

By adopting neutral instead of accusatory words in responding initially, the leader has begun to defuse rather than exacerbate Joe's anger, allowing Joe time to calm down, and perhaps opening to door to a conversation that will afford opportunities to help Joe understand his own role in his negative interactions with Bill.

A similar principle of caution can be effective when it is leaders themselves who are upset. One mistake leaders can make is responding in anger, regardless of whether the response is oral or written. Drafting a terse e-mail in response to someone's misfeasance may evoke unnecessarily and even destructive feelings on the part of the recipient. Sometimes in haste leaders fail to see some aspects of problems, prematurely making incorrect conclusions about fault. Assuming circumstances permit, leaders are often well advised to wait until the following day before responding in anger to employee problems. The result of waiting will frequently be a calmer, more thoughtful response that calms rather than inflames emotions.

But how can leaders discourage the excitable employee who is constantly trying to get the leader's ear with rumors of disaster, questionable proposals, and offbeat recommendations? One former dean had a standard response for that type of situation that seemingly worked well. After listening silently to the latest emotional diatribe, in a neutral tone he would simply utter one word, "understood"—a word that said a great deal by saying little. "Understood" did not signify concurrence, contained no express or implied promise of any action, but likewise contained no criticism. Importantly, it contained no encouragement for continuance of the communication, effectively discouraging future such attempts. Perhaps the dean had taken to heart a quote attributed to former President Dwight D. Eisenhower: "I have been sorry more often for things I said than things I didn't say."

11.4. Choosing a Medium of Communication

The method we use to communicate may enhance or detract from our ability to clearly convey our messages. Written, oral, and electronic communication methods each have their own strengths and weakness. In some cases the method is irrelevant, such as when asking a clarifying question like, "Is the monthly review on the 14th or 15th?" In other instances, however, one method may be preferable over others. For example, when communicating with a colleague in a busy airport, a text message may be preferable to a phone call to eliminate background noise. As information becomes more complex and detailed, more care is required in selecting the method of communication.

> **"Words mean more than what is set down on paper. It takes a human voice to infuse them with deeper meaning."**
>
> —Maya Angelou

The choice of communication methods is often dependent on the amount of information that needs to be sent and the importance of the information. A general announcement to the entire organization regarding the availability of support staff during the holiday season is often very factual. An e-mail to the entire organization is straightforward and easily understood. Senders would not expect a need for clarification. Written communication provides a permanent record of the message and is a good medium to convey more complex ideas, but it often takes longer to prepare. Oral communication is much faster, more personal, and provides each party the opportunity to give and receive immediate feedback, but it provides no record of the conversation, with the result that recipients may forget important elements. In many ways e-mail provides a balance between written and oral communication, but often senders do not take care to prepare a well-written message with the result that context and tone can be easily lost. As topics become increasingly complex, so does the need for explanation. For example, a system-wide software upgrade would naturally evoke questions by the staff, many of which might be prevented by the inclusions of an FAQ page and a helpdesk number.[9]

As a general rule bad news should be communicated in person when possible. As the information becomes more sensitive, such as conveying informal performance feedback, face-to-face conversations are often more appropriate, providing a more personal venue and opportunity for immediate response and exchange. Formal performance reviews should be in writing but delivered in person with appropriate time for discussion. This allows leaders to explain the reasons for the evaluation, what it means for the employee in terms of compensation and career advancement, and an opportunity for the employee to ask questions. Once the employer and employee are satisfied with the results of the conversation, then a written statement is often used to document the conversation, indicate the employee has read the report and been counseled, and afford the employee the opportunity to dissent.

In some instances the way a message is communicated is more important that the message itself. Civil defense sirens are used to warn a large population of an impending threat such as a tornado. The reason the siren has been sounded is initially less important than the message to "Take shelter now!" Only when properly sheltered should those warned seek further information.

When sending mass e-mail, the important traits of a particular group may be as broad as all European staff. In such cases, sensitivity in avoiding colloquialisms that do not translate well into other languages is important. In cases of e-mail to individuals such as performance and compensation information, the ramifications of sending the data to the wrong person may have serious implications. The same is true for sensitive client information.

As a first-year consultant, one of the coauthors learned that in the worldwide organization consisting of several thousand people there were three other employees who shared the same first and last name. Although each worked in a different practice area and in different offices, each would regularly get e-mails meant for another. It was not uncommon for the coauthor to get an e-mail about ongoing issues with employees who had been accessing inappropriate websites that was meant for the similarly named employee who worked in IT security. At other times he would get confidential client e-mails that were intended for the senior partner in Australia. Often the culprit is auto-address provisions in e-mail systems whereby when the sender begins to type a name several addressees beginning with the same letters are shown. If the sender points and clicks on the wrong name, the e-mail then goes to the wrong party.

We use e-mail so frequently that we become inured to its dangers. Many firms have strict policies proscribing the use of company e-mail for personal communications. One reason for this is to reduce the possibility of sensitive information being sent outside the firm. Many e-mails are sent with an automatically inserted signature line showing the name, title, and contact information of the sender. This is another reason to be careful with recipients of e-mail. E-mail is easily altered and forwarded, creating an impression that false information was sent by the originator. One of the coauthors learned this the hard way when his signature line was used to create the appearance of credibility to a politically motivated, false message and then forwarded via mass e-mail by an unscrupulous person. The result was so many inquiries from people upset about the contents of the message that the coauthor was forced to change his contact information, as was a member of another organization treated in a similar manner.

11.5. Nonverbal Communication

Sir Arthur Conan Doyle's Sherlock Holmes may be the world's most well-known fictional character with respect to interpreting **nonverbal communication**. An example is the episode in which Holmes correctly deduced that one of his clients was a cyclist by observing that his feet had "the slight roughening of the side of the sole caused by the friction of the edge of the pedal." Although most of us will never acquire the extreme powers of observation of the famous detective, nonverbal communication is nonetheless very influential. Dr. Albert Mehrabian at UCLA performed extensive research into the impact of communication and determined that only 7 percent of the impact of direct, person-to-person communication is due to the words we use; 38 percent is based on the voice and the confidence we project; and the remaining 55 percent is based upon nonverbal communication including eye contact, posture, expressions, and gestures.[10] In addition, words can convey one meaning while body language conveys another. Based upon the above percentages, it is more likely a person will believe the communicator's body language than his or her words.

> ### 7 percent of meaning is in the actual words spoken (verbal).
>
> ### 38 percent of meaning is in the way words are spoken (vocal).
>
> ### 55 percent of meaning is derived from what we see (visual).
>
> —Albert Mehrabian, *Silent Messages: Implicit Communication of Emotions and Attitudes*

Timothy J. Koegel's *The Exceptional Presenter* provides numerous examples of how a person's body language impacts the way in which a communicator is perceived by others.[11] From the moment eye contact is made, people begin to form impressions about each other. These impressions are often lasting ones. Posture alone may send strong messages. For example, the placing of hands on hips is often interpreted as a defiant pose, while hands hanging along the side of the body is a relaxed and confident pose. In a seated position, keeping one's hands on the table is recommended by Ann Marie Sabath in *One Minute Manners: Quick Solutions to the Most Awkward Situations You'll Ever Face at Work*.[12] This is especially important outside of North America, where not showing a hand is considered bad form.

Gestures can be an effective tool for improving communication. One research study provided evidence that "We're born with a propensity to move our hands when we speak," and even blind people will gesture when describing objects.[13] Well-trained traffic officers often use nothing but hand gestures to control traffic at busy intersections. Gestures can add a certain amount of drama to communications. When speaking about a change in financial markets, a presenter may use sweeping hand gestures to indicate magnitude of change. Appropriate gestures can assist audiences in retaining information as well, but presenters should be careful to make these gestures neither too fast nor too slow and not overexaggerate the motions to the point of distracting the audience.

One of the best ways to convey confidence and a friendly disposition is also the easiest gesture to master—**smile**! The simple act of smiling will help both the presenter and the audience to relax. Smiling people are usually thought to be more likeable, and likability influences receptivity to their messages.

11.6. Another Meeting

Much formal, in-person business communication involves meetings. Unfortunately, formal meetings themselves have become greatly overused and ineffective, but when conducted properly they can be a valuable business tool. Michael Doyle and David Straus identify two ways of evaluating the successfulness of meetings. The first is evaluating the results of the meeting. Were the meeting objectives met, and why or why not? The second is evaluating how those results were achieved. We have all been in meetings where a good solution was achieved, but the atmosphere was contentious and participants left frustrated and angry. In other cases there are meetings where the goals and objectives were not met, but the team left energized and positive.[14]

As long as the desired results are attained, is that not the point of the meeting? Such a hard-line approach may sometimes be necessary, but it can often have what Doyle and Straus refer to as a ripple effect. Employees who return to work resentful and disillusioned can exhibit negative emotions to co-workers and clients. One researcher has estimated that ineffective meetings can cost a firm $800,000/year for every 1,000 employees. There are two key steps to improving meetings. (1) Meetings should have agendas sent to all participants prior to the meeting. Agendas need not be formal documents but can be as simple as, "Eric, if convenient, I would like to meet with you Monday from 1:00 to 2:00 PM in your office to update you on the new marketing campaign." In one sentence everything Eric needs to know about the meeting is provided, including who, what, when, where, and why. (2) The roles of the participants are also implied. Clarifying these basic points is important. Too often we are asked to attend a meeting unsure of why we were asked and what we will be responsible for.[15]

As meetings become larger, formal roles are often assigned, allowing advance preparation. However, providing attendees with role assignments and agendas is insufficient to ensure successful meetings. Those responsible for conducting meetings must often strike a delicate balance between ensuring attendees participate and incorporating that participation into the decision process. They must ensure that one person or subgroup does not dominate the meeting or throw it off schedule. It is also important for meeting moderators to help protect group members from personal or professional attacks should the meeting become heated. At the end of the meeting it is important to recap the goal of the meeting, the events that occurred, what was achieved, and what still needs to be done. At this point group members are sometimes assigned specific tasks and follow-on meetings planned as necessary. After meetings are adjourned, it is frequently a good idea to send a summary of the meeting results and next steps to applicable parties to reinforce any decisions, outcomes, and follow-up responsibilities.

11.7. Listening

Most business people find themselves recurrently in situations such as the following. Fifteen minutes from now you have a short-but-important meeting with a senior officer of a major client. As you wait for the meeting to begin, you make a final run through your preparation checklist for the meeting. You've researched the client, its operations, its history with your firm, and assessed what you believe to be its needs and current satisfaction with your firm's services. You're up to speed on the client's financial performance and operations. You've talked with others who know the officer you're seeing and gotten their take on her likes and dislikes. You've reviewed your goals and objectives for the meeting, the message you are attempting to convey about how your firm can add additional value for the client, and what constitutes victory for your firm coming out of this meeting. You've even practiced the words you wish to use and the hot-button items you want to avoid. What have you forgotten? Nothing. You've taken care of every item on your meeting preparation punch list. But have you fully prepared?

How often do business people prepare for listening? Most rarely do. A major reason is that we haven't been trained in listening. Instead we concern ourselves with such things as mentioned in the previous paragraph. As shown in Figure 11.1, the book *Are You Listening?* indicates there is an inverse relationship between the amount of time we utilize the four main modes of communication—reading, writing, speaking, and listening—and the formal training we receive in each.[16]

In chapter 5 when we explored how the 16 different **Best-Fit Types** prefer to function, we learned each type uses different areas of the brain in different sequences. Yet when we prepare for encounters such as the imaginary one above we usually prepare as though every appetite for information is the same. Further, we enter such encounters intent on presenting, not listening. Consider the following real-world situation that occurred recently.

> ### "Courage is what it takes to stand up and speak; courage is also what it takes to sit down and listen."
>
> —Sir Winston Churchill

A leadership consultant entered a meeting in which he expected to make a presentation about employee training to the training director for a large CPA firm. Despite having carefully prepared a slide deck in a logical sequence describing his group's capabilities, qualifications, and approach, from the onset it was apparent that the director preferred to immediately plunge into a discussion of the firm's needs. Instead of pushing his presentation, the consultant immediately deviated from the slide show and changed first to a listening mode and then interactive mode, only occasionally referring to a slide if it contained information relevant to a particular point. The lesson is to not become so focused on presenting our carefully prepared pitch that we forget to plan to listen. But what does planning to listen entail? Perhaps an example best answers this question.

The chief operating, scientific, and technical officers of a software company were preparing for an important upcoming meeting with the vice president of drug safety and efficacy for a major pharmaceutical company. They were uncertain exactly what the value proposition of their software was for the pharma in the opinion of the vice president. Was it earlier discovery of the interaction of a proposed drug with existing drugs for the purpose of eliminating the proposed drug from consideration? Was it to detect adverse drug reac-

Figure 11.1. Usage of the Four Main Modes of Communication

Mode of Communication	Years of Formal Training	% of Time Used
Writing	12 years	9%
Reading	6–8 years	16%
Speaking	1–2 years	35%
Listening	Less than 1/2 year	40%

tions and mitigate them during the drug approval process? Was it more generally to shorten the normal diligence cycle for drug approval? In planning the presentation, the decision was made to plan for all three possibilities by listening to the vice president's reaction when each value proposition was presented early in the presentation. Depending upon her reaction the presentation would then take one of three different courses. Thus, listening was made an explicit part of the presentation.

In many business situations people need to hear what we to say, but there are many barriers to effective listening. Being a good listener can take lots of effort. One of the biggest challenges is **physiological**. Studies indicate that the average a person can speak 125–200 words a minute, but the human brain can process between 300 and 500 words per minute. This means listeners' minds are prone to wander while we speak. Sometimes listeners are focused on trying to understand, but at other times they may be thinking ahead, trying to formulate responses, take detailed notes, or attempting to discern what is not being said. Wandering thoughts often result in misunderstandings. This implies the need for self-discipline on the part of listeners and attention on the part of presenters to whether effective listening is occurring.

The rate at which our brain processes information is not the only physiological barrier to effective listening. Another barrier is **biased listening**. Because our first impression of a person is often lasting, these impressions can create bias toward the person's message. Listeners can also be biased by their own perspectives. This bias can be exacerbated by stereotyping. When listening is biased, the listener's understanding becomes skewed toward confirming the bias. Consider a financial officer listening to a capital expenditure proposal being made by an operating division of his company. The financial officer grows weary hearing about the wonderful market growth po-

tential that will result from spending a substantial sum to create and build a new product and gravitates toward thinking that he has yet to hear about the underlying assumptions in the financial modeling. The financial officer is now attuned to anything that might suggest those assumptions are unrealistic. He may then begin to think in terms of stereotyping, thinking to himself that marketing and sales types are frequently not focused enough on the numbers.

It is typical for listeners to form judgments about what is being said prior to the end of presentations. Does the speaker have his or her facts straight and are the assumptions realistic? This is often referred to as **evaluative listening**. Listeners' subsequent responses are then a function, in part, of the extent to which they agree or disagree with the presenter. Unfortunately for presenters, this bias may negate presenters' subsequent points in listeners' minds as the latter anchor on their earlier conclusions about facts and assumptions.

Another factor that may impede effective listening is **physical discomfort**. Perhaps the room is too hot or cold or too large or small. Some studies suggest that natural light often improves learning, but windows may offer visual distractions, reducing attentive listening. In *Are You Listening?* Ralph G. Nichols, suggests "if we define the good listener as one giving full attention to the speaker, first-grade children are the best listeners of all," and that as a person ages focus on listening decreases.[17]

Becoming a better listener starts with keeping an open mind and setting aside one's own agenda, focusing on the meaning of words and the speaker's intent. A useful technique for better listening is using **gap time**, the difference between the rate of speech and the rate at which the brain processes speech, to mentally review key points about what is being presented.

Listening etiquette is part of becoming an effective listener. Savvy presenters will likely be attuned to the audience's body language, just as the audience is reading nonverbal cues from the presenter. When an audience is signaling a lack of interest to a speaker, the fact that they are not interested makes it that much more difficult for the speaker to be effective. An attentive and engaged audience will help motivate the presenter to be that much better. Good listening etiquette involves being an active listener, focusing on what is being said, making eye contact with the speaker, and avoiding negative gestures such as frowning and folding arms. Sidebar conversations with other listeners can distract other listeners and detract from a speaker's ability to communicate effectively.

11.8. Disruptions and Noise

One of the most challenging situations in communication is dealing with **disruptions**. One of the coauthors was leading an engagement team working at a client site when numerous state and federal law enforcement agents came into the offices. Although it became clear that the agents were focusing on one particular client employee, someone with whom the team had worked regularly over the course of the project, their presence was sufficient to seriously impede communications. Had anyone on the engagement team unknowingly assisted the suspected client staff? Neither the client nor the consulting firm had a protocol in place to deal with this type of disruption resulting in fear, speculation, and concern over what could be said to whom. How leaders deal with disruptions can often have a material impact on organizational effectiveness. Consider the following scenario.

Suppose you are leading a team of consultants at a client site with a tight deadline for project completion. Suddenly one of your team members rushes into the conference room where the rest of the team is working and announces excitedly, "I just heard that our firm is merging with Great White Shark Consulting! I wonder what this means. I've heard their culture is very different from our firm's culture, and when they acquired Remora Consulting that a bunch of Remora people lost their jobs!" Suddenly the entire team is engaged in speculating what their futures might hold.

> **"Don't let the noise of other's opinions drown out your own inner voice and have the courage to follow your heart and intuition."**
>
> —Steve Jobs

As team leader, how would you go about reestablishing order and getting the team to refocus on the project? Do you simply order the team back to work? Doing so may result in a poor work product as team members continue to mentally focus on the pending merger. Resolving the leadership dilemma caused by this disruption and getting your team back to work instead of worrying about their futures requires careful communication. Careless words could actually make matters worse. You might consider offering to call the home office and gather more information to be communicated to the team. You might also remind the team that, regardless of whether the rumor is true and even if the merger does occur, failure to complete a project on schedule with a high-quality outcome will not look good for the team regardless of what happens with the firm.

Obviously extraneous physical noise can reduce the effectiveness of communication, but there are other forms of noise. **Semantic noise** is confusion created by words having different meanings and definitions that detract us from the intended meaning of the communication. Many of us commit the error of sematic noise without

> "Your purpose is to make your audience see what you saw, hear what you heard, feel what you felt. Relevant detail, couched in concrete, colorful language, is the best way to recreate the incident as it happened and to picture it for the audience."
>
> —Dale Carnegie

realizing it. The danger is that it can quickly destroy a communication. An example is a word interpreted as a racial slur even though the speaker didn't intend that and may not even be aware that a word had that connotation.[18] Yet another form of communication noise is **syntactical noise**, which involves grammatical errors, inconsistencies, or ambiguities that can degrade communication. Consider the following statement: "The boss said on Monday we'd have a meeting." Does the speaker mean that the boss spoke those words on Monday or that the boss intends to hold a meeting on Monday?

The key to reducing semantic and syntactical noise is to carefully consider words. In written communications one tool is using the **Napoleon's corporal technique**. When Napoleon's staff would brief him on a plan for a forthcoming battle, the emperor would have a corporal listen. After the conclusion of the briefing, the emperor would ask if the corporal understood the plan. If the corporal could not understand the plan clearly, the emperor would have his staff rewrite the plan until the corporal could understand it.

11.9. Knowing Your Audience

No matter how well we know the topic of conversation, carefully choose our words, and manage nonverbal communication and distractions, our attempts to communicate may fall short if we fail to take into account the audience.[19] This is true re-

gardless of whether the audience is one person or a group, and it also includes being careful not to distribute sensitive information to recipients who are not entitled to receive it. That said, knowing your target audience is paramount. Consider the following quote:

> Where average performers fail most is in making the leap from basic-level dispensing of information to higher-level influencing through the message. Their style and delivery does not change from audience to audience, even though the makeups of these groups can be very different.[20]

When making presentations or meeting with clients, it is highly beneficial to learn as much as possible about those with whom we are communicating. The first question is, "What is the audience seeking to gain from this?"[21] People are continuously bombarded with messages trying to sell or convince them of something. Amid this cacophony of messaging, consider what it is about your particular message that should gain audience attention—what is the **value proposition** for this particular audience—and focus on that value proposition. This begins with knowing the background of the audience. For years one of the coauthors taught short courses at the Center for Corporate Financial Leadership, an activity sponsored by the Illinois CPA Society. Despite the fact that the audience mainly consisted of certified public accountants, their interest had little to do with public accounting. Consequently, the value proposition for that audience lay with such concerns as improving cash flows.

In **client presentations** it is especially important to know the audience's role within their organizations. Different audiences in the same organization will have different value propositions. For example, financial executives at the corporate level may be very concerned with providing value to shareholders, whereas divisional-level financial personnel may be concerned with reducing costs through the use of activity-based management. When possible, it is also helpful to ascertain if the audience has preconceived ideas on the subject matter of the presentation. One of the best ways to hook the audience's interest is to focus on its current problems and demonstrate a solution. Provide clear examples of problem situations and how your solution has resolved those. Use graphics that contrast your solution with other solutions and show where and how yours is better. Identify the buzzwords that resonate well with the group and hot-button topics that should be avoided.

Understanding the audience's point of view often provides valuable insights for crafting a compelling message. A message crafted for lower-level employees of a client might focus on bite-sized chunks of information using clear, easy-to-read handouts. Conversely, a message for top-level executives on the same subject might contain the same basic information but delivered in a no-nonsense manner and backed up with detailed reports with logical reasoning for conclusions. The import of this is simple: know your audience and shape your message accordingly.[22]

It is also important to understand the audience's level of knowledge. If the audience consists of business executives with little technical expertise, the message should be nontechnical, focusing on capabilities (ends) that create value for clients as opposed to delving deeply into how the technology works (ways). Conversely, if the group consists of technical personnel with PhDs in the subject matter, then that audience may be very interested in details regarding how the technology works compared to existing technology. In either case, the presentation should use language the audience understands. A primary source for information about an audience is usually people who have direct experience with that type of audience. Previous client teams, meeting organizers, and prospective audience members whom the presenter knows are all possible sources. Client websites often have biographies of key staff. External websites such as LinkedIn, university alumni associations, or regulatory documents can yield useful insights about individuals.

11.10. More Thoughts on Preparing for Communication

To avoid unpleasant surprises it is best to gain knowledge of the room where presentations to large audiences will take place beforehand. Size and layout are especially important when the speaker wants to be down with the audience instead of presenting in auditorium style from a lectern. Other logistical considerations include audio and visual equipment to include testing it beforehand. One expert recommends what he calls the 60/20 rule: "Arrive 60 minutes before you are scheduled to present. Use the first 40 minutes to prepare: the room, seating notes, AV Equipment, handouts and props. The 20 minutes prior to your presen-

> **"If you prepare yourself at every point as well as you can . . . you will be able to grasp opportunity for broader experience when it appears."**
>
> —Former First Lady Eleanor Roosevelt

tation is prime time for introductions, information gathering and rapport building."[23] This rule may not be necessary for routine staff meetings, but its usefulness has been demonstrated repeatedly when presenting to larger audiences and clients.

Toastmasters International recommends that a presenter meet all of the meeting participants if practical. Name cards allow the presenter to call participants by their first names, which helps engage the audience. For smaller group settings seating charts are useful for this purpose. If time and audience size permit, asking participants to introduce themselves and describe their organizational roles breaks the ice and provides greater familiarity.

Care given to seating arrangements in client meetings can help avoid us-versus-them settings. One of the coauthors and his consulting colleagues would often sit in every other or every third seat. This arrangement also allowed for better interpretation of the body language of client personnel. In one client engagement, one of the client's personnel continuously sat in the corner of the meeting room and occasionally made negative comments without providing productive insights. In response, the consulting team eliminated corner chairs in meeting rooms. This forced the dissenter toward the middle of the room and encouraged him to engage in discussions with less dissent as the result.

Revising and rehearsing client presentations are paramount, especially for larger groups, complex subject matter, and more discerning audiences. A useful technique for especially critical presentations is to hold a **murder board** consisting of colleagues whose job it is to find all the flaws in the presentation so that they can be corrected prior to presenting to the client. This critique should include any criticism of vocal and visual messages as well as handouts. Facing an audience that is deliberately attempting to find every flaw not only exposes these flaws but also can make the presenter feel more confident about the presentation, resulting in less anxiety and stress during the presentation. This leads to the next topic, managing stress and emotion when communicating.

11.11. Managing Stress and Emotions

Stress and heightened emotions can affect the content and delivery of presentations, including accompanying nonverbal cues. Stress and a heightened emotional state can also lead a person to say or do something later regretted. Consequently, although communicators may not be able to eliminate all stress, they are well advised to control it. Stress reduction starts with communicators recognizing the events or situations that generate stress and taking actions to prepare for these events. For example, if an employee meeting regarding a new, contentious policy promises to be stressful, it is helpful to anticipate employees' questions and concerns and prepare well-thought-out answers and explanations in advance of the meeting. If a meeting involves discussion about a client's complaint about service with a senior client official, the problem should be researched as thoroughly as possible and possible solutions formulated in advance. The example below illustrates what can happen in a poorly handled communication in which the communicator failed to read accurately his audience's signals and obvious stress.

Stress reduction also involves being sensitive to the onset of stress—both the presenter's and that of the audience—and taking steps to control it. Sometimes taking a short break may reduce stress. Sometimes pausing to take a few deep breaths and gather thoughts can be helpful. On occasions when a meeting has gone on a long time with little progress toward its objective, resulting in mounting stress for participants, it may be desirable to reconvene at a later time. At times asking participants to enumerate points on which they agree or are willing to compromise may defuse some stress even if they cannot agree on all points.[24]

One of the coauthors was CFO of a bank whose independent auditor was a large, international public accounting firm. Another auditor firm had been heavily courting the bank for its business, and there had been some dissatisfaction on the part of senior management and the board's audit committee with the current auditor's complacency with what had been for many years

214

a very clean audit client. The partner-in-charge of the audit was late appearing for the meeting of the audit committee when he was to report the results of the bank's annual audit. By the time he arrived, the stress level in the room was already high and growing, with several members of the board expressing unhappiness with what they interpreted as more evidence of the relationship being taken for granted. For his part, the partner seemed oblivious to the cold reception he received from his audience and the obvious stress in the room. He never stopped to ask for questions or concerns until completion of his presentation. Met with an uneasy silence, instead of exploring reasons for what had by then become hostile stares, he uneasily thanked the client for its business and excused himself. Once he exited, the chairman of the audit committee rose, closed the door, and asked of the CFO, "Is there any reason we should retain this firm as our auditors?" Changing auditors is not an easy decision for a banking client for several reasons, but the next month the bank had a new auditor.

It is important to recognize that not all stress resulting from communication anxiety is detrimental. A reasonable level of stress can encourage better preparation. The adrenaline generated by stress may make a speaker more animated and appear more motivated. However, speakers should be aware that adrenaline may cause the presentation to be more hurried than in rehearsal, resulting in finishing before the anticipated time.

11.12. Concluding Thoughts

The ability to communicate clearly and effectively is an essential leadership skill for success in business. An inability to communicate well can be a career-long handicap limiting progression. Having taught thousands of students and executives over many years and experienced virtually every conceivable form of business as members of organizations, our observation is that there is a definite bias toward business people believing they are better communicators than is actually the case. We frequently see unclear statements in executive summaries, an absence of relevant information in presentations, illogical organization of materials, a tendency to dwell on the obvious, an insistence on slogging through several slides reciting a history of past events when audience questions clearly indicate a desire to discuss the future, and other analogous forms of ineffectively communicating.

It is also our observation that this overconfidence about an ability to communicate well is so great that leaders often to fail to take such basic steps as having third parties review important documents and presentations prior to their delivery. In other words, they fail to hold what we called a "murder board" as described earlier in this chapter. Even prior to that stage, leaders sometimes fail to carefully consider their audience, its appetite for information, its level of understanding of the materials, and the overall desired impact and outcome of the communication. Too often we observe leaders failing to ask themselves the simple question, "What is victory with respect to this communication?"

In business communication there is no single style or methodology for being a good communicator that works in all situations. Different styles may be effective depending upon the circumstances. It is important for leaders to determine a style that fits the circumstances that will work well for the communicator and tailor the message to the audience. There is no substitute for knowing the audience, having a clear understanding of the desired outcome of communicating, and rehearsing and reviewing to ensure clarity and impact. There is no more room for laziness in business communication than there is for it in other aspects of leadership.

CHAPTER 12

Becoming a Talent That Fits:

Combining Leadership and Technical Skills

> **"If you want to compete in today's business world, then it's important to keep up with technology in order to get the most out of the technology you have, to keep abreast of new technology, and to find the information that will help you make the right . . . decisions."**
>
> —Brian J. Nichelson

A question that often arises when discussing career success skills is the balance between the need for so-called "soft skills," such as leadership, and technical skills. It is unsurprising that this remains a question inasmuch as the answers one hears often seem conflicting. Consider the following quotes:

> A twenty-year study of leadership effectiveness conducted by Stanford University's School of Business concluded that about 15% of one's success in leading organizations comes from technical skills and knowledge, while 85% comes from the ability to connect with people and engender trust and mutual understanding.[1]

> Technical skills are the most important selection criterion which is taken into consideration by various companies when fulfilling their recruiting requirements. To put it simply, technical skills simply refer to acquisition of technique to do a particular work which can't be done by a layman and needs specialized training in the form

of practical and theoretical knowledge . . . Being weak at technical skills can lead to a person losing his/her chance to get the dream job.[2]

It is essential to remain technical no matter what level you achieve in the management hierarchy . . . What I saw in the latest recession was, managers who were making very good salaries when the market was doing well were now willing to take positions paying as low as a quarter or a third of their previous salaries. When asked why, the response was almost resoundingly the same: "I became so removed from the technology that all I do is manage, and my firm has laid off so many people that my management skills are less warranted than before."[3]

Over 96% of executives today believe they have "above average" people skills. This is a statistical improbability . . . Studies confirm that 75% of North American CEOs believe they are "better" than other leaders in their industry . . . To illustrate the importance of process skills as an imperative for leadership success, it is surely a truism in organizations today that people are far more willing to act on their own ideas before they are likely to act on yours . . . [Research] suggests an individual with an analytical predisposition "acquires his professional designation and then coasts on his laurels for the next 30 or even 50 years."[4]

With seemingly conflicting statements such as the foregoing, it is easy to understand how aspiring leaders can become confused about the relative importance of leadership skills *versus* technical skills. It is also easy to incorrectly dismiss this confusion with arguments such as the following:

> Katz (1955) identified technical skills related to the field, human skills related to communicating with people and conceptual skills related to setting vision as the major areas that leaders need to develop. Higher-level leaders need to be stronger on conceptual skills, whereas more hands-on leaders need to have stronger technical skills.[5]

Although this may have been true in 1955 and the notion still persists today to some extent, increasingly both skill sets are necessary at all levels, but the nature of those skill sets does change over time and with hierarchical ascendancy. The word "versus" is therefore misleading when talking about the two skill sets. Both skill sets become increasingly important as leaders ascend organizational hierarchies and as technological, geographical, and regulatory complexities continue to mount. Because no executive can possibly be technically proficient in all technologies, savvy leaders need to understand what technical skills are required at what level of leadership, what levels of knowledge and understanding are necessary, and where trends are taking require-

ments for technical skills. The right combination of leadership and technical skills is the best way to assure organizational and personal success, as captured in the following quote:

> *Technical leadership skills* [emphasis ours] are the most important tool you have at your disposal for becoming indispensable and maintaining a healthy level of job security.
>
> . . . When I talk about technical leadership skills, I'm referring to the *application of leadership principles to technical environments* [emphasis ours], be that a project, process, or service . . . When I refer to leadership, I'm talking about your ability to bring about positive change, and influencing others to adopt that change.[6]

This chapter explores this issue and attempts to provide meaningful guidance about the important issue of leadership versus technical skills. The increasingly dynamic business environment gives rise to rapidly changing demands upon leaders. As is the case with leadership skills, being technically proficient should be a lifelong journey for business executives.

12.1. The Changing Business Environment

In 1949, following a cataclysmic global war in which the fall of one world-threatening totalitarian state observed the rise of another, George Orwell wrote his classic, seminal novel, *1984*, in which he imagined a dark, totalitarian world dominated by dictatorships in which individual liberties were highly restricted. By the time 1984 eventually arrived, much of the world was very different than the one Orwell envisioned in that novel. Somewhat analogously, a businessperson in 1984 attempting to imagine what the business world would be like 30 years later in 2014 might have missed the mark just as widely. What is different today from business in 1984? The answer is several things, many of which can be grouped into the three following categories: (1) **globalization**, (2) **complexity**, and (3) **technology**.[7]

Today, many businesses are increasingly **global**, not local. Once global business was the domain of large firms. Today, even many small to medium enterprises (SMEs) conduct business internationally and are becoming increasingly important, impacting business models and future needs due to greater fragmentation and diversification of value chains.[8] Global business requires an understanding of such matters as different business cultures, country risk stemming from political

> **"The financial skills sets you've developed and refined throughout your career remain as important as ever to helping businesses succeed financially. But what happens when the intellectual capital you possess doesn't easily apply to the business challenges at hand— not because you don't have the right experience but because you don't have the right tools to enable the things you need to get done?"**
>
> —Benjamin Kang, "Managing the Strategic Finance Gap," *Strategic Finance*, February 2014

upheaval, how to mitigate risks when dealing in different currencies, and country-specific legal requirements. Such understanding requires a combination of both leadership and technical skills.[9] National economies are now inextricably linked, and a slowing or growing global economy affects not only larger firms but SMEs as well. The result is that economic cycles are becoming more complicated.[10]

Business **complexity** is also rapidly increasing with consumers demanding newer and more superior but less expensive products and services. Concurrently, there is growing demand for business to become more socially responsible, with a smaller environmental footprint and more engagement in good citizenship. These forces create a variety of strategic, environmental, social, and organizational governance challenges that are requiring businesses to become more adaptive and efficient. These requirements, in turn, necessitate greater access to timely and accurate information, more knowledge, and an ability to develop and implement innovative solutions that deliver fast results at costs that permit acceptable rates of return for investors.[11]

Technology is having a profound impact on business. Technological evolution and rapid technology turnover afford both opportunities for growth and greater market risk. An increasing volume of new products and services are being delivered through new methods of research, development, production, marketing, and distribution. As a result, on the Internet consumers have more choices of where and how they shop as well as a much broader array of products from which to choose. Information about new products and services travels fast via blogs, e-mail, and social media, and news of a customer fiasco can spread rapidly to many consumers. Technology permits greater decentralization in some industries and centralization in others. For example, some retail bank customers can now make deposits from home in a very decentralized manner, while automobile loan applications are often approved centrally via electronic means. Technology also permits collaborative intercorporate alliances and relationships as well as intracorporate teamwork involving widely dispersed personnel. Business intelligence fostered by expanding technological capabilities in data mining and analysis is increasingly driving the need to be nimble in adapting to new market threats.[12]

The growth of globalization, complexity and technology means that business leaders are experiencing new demands for technical knowledge in order to guide, direct, and oversee business activity. For example, a partner in a CPA firm providing healthcare consulting services may need to have some level of understanding of machine learning and data analytics in order to accommodate the needs of healthcare-provider clients in what has become a data-overloaded industry. As more and more regulatory complexity combined with cost pressures, electronic medical records, and demands for evidence-based medicine give rise to the need for technologies to manage their attendant informational requirements, professionals providing consulting services to healthcare must gain a working knowledge of these technologies. As the quote on the left suggests, not having the right technology tools to meet the challenges of your clients can hinder productivity and business retention. And having the right tools also means knowing how to use them.

Some aspects of change are reasonably predictable. Market forces will always react to supply and demand. Regulators will always generate new regulations at a faster rate than existing regulations will be retired. Other changes, however, are more difficult to predict, and it is often hard to know their impact in advance. Many business performance measurement systems are not always able to accommodate rapid change, and workloads can suddenly increase dramatically, straining organizational resources. Astute leaders therefore plan for growth and change, are proponents of a data-driven culture, and champion real-time information access to business intelligence.[13] All of this means a growing need for technically savvy leaders.

12.2. How Skill Sets Can Change with Hierarchical Ascendency

In general, how do leadership and technical skills

change with hierarchical ascendency? Figure 12.1 answers this question, in part, by way of example using insurance claims managers at three levels, supervisor, middle manager, and upper-middle manager, with a sample of skills taken from job descriptions. Three insights can be gleaned by examining the relative skills required from position to position. First, *leadership skills become increasingly broader* and more involved moving from supervisor to vice president. Second, with some technical skills such as legal knowledge, the need actually *increases* with hierarchical ascendency, contrary to the belief that the need for technical skills diminishes with organizational rank. Third, whereas a claims supervisor is concerned with tactical-level technical issues such as overpayments, the vice president requires broader-based leadership and technical skills and is concerned with operational-level issues, such as whether systems are in place and functioning to ensure that overpayments are caught and rectified.

12.3. Drivers of Sustainable Success in the Changing Business Environment

One key to better understanding of combining leadership and technical skills to achieve career success in this new business environment is knowing the drivers of sustainable organizational success. Drawing upon multiple sources, a 2011 study by the International Federation of Accountants identified **eight drivers of organizational success** in the changing business environment. These drivers, stemming from the megatrends of globalization, complexity, and technology, were reflective of areas or functions in which highly successful organizations seek to attain high performance. The drivers are summarized in Figure 12.2, along with some of the major requirements for managing the drivers.

The remainder of this chapter is devoted to the examination of these drivers and the skills

Figure 12.1. Sampling of Skills Requirements for Insurance Claims Jobs

Level	Leadership Skills	Technical Skills
Claims Supervisor[A]	►Direct, coordinate, and supervise adjusters ►Make presentations ►Communicate technical information so that it is understandable ►Exercise sound judgment in resolution of claims ►Use good interview techniques	►Examine claims and determine whether to authorize payment and recommend other claim actions ►Detect overpayments ►Conduct detailed bill reviews ►Adjust reserves and provide reserve recommendations ►Confer with legal counsel
Claims Manager[B]	►Motivate, develop, direct subordinates ►Identify best people for jobs ►Communicate effectively in writing ►Use logic and reasoning to identify alternative courses of action ►Understand human behaviors ►Guide and advise subordinates ►Manage programs or projects	►Comprehend legal documents ►Analyze reports submitted by claims supervisors ►Principles and procedures for personnel recruitment ►Understand laws, legal codes, court procedures, precedents, government regulations ►Supervise claims investigations
VP Claims[C]	►Listen, read, write, speak well ►Negotiation, persuasion, social perceptiveness ►Exercise stress tolerance and self-control ►Manage personnel resources using coordination skills to adjust actions in response to others' actions ►Manage subordinates' time ►Instructional skills ►Attention to detail ►Identify complex problems and review related information to develop and implement solutions	►Know learning strategies and implications of new information for problem solving and decision making ►Systems analysis to include how systems should work and how changes in conditions, operations, and environment affect organizational outcomes ►Have a knowledge of laws, legal codes, court procedures, precedents, government regulations, agency rules ►Review cost/benefit assessments

Notes: A. "Claims Examiners Property Casualty Insurance Job Description," http://www.insurancejobs.com/claims-examiners-property-casualty-insurance-job-description.htm (accessed March 15, 2014).
B. "Skills, Knowledge, Abilities and Tasks," *Career Guide for Insurance Manager,* http://jobs.virginia.gov/careerguides/InsuranceMgr.htm (accessed March 15, 2014).
C. "Career: Claims Vice President," *MyMajors.com,* http://www.mymajors.com/skills-and-knowledge/Claims-Vice-President (accessed March 15, 2014).

required for leaders to manage them well. The ensuing discussion is not meant to imply that every leader have a *mastery* of the skills associated with every driver. Our position is that, depending upon responsibilities, an understanding of both the drivers and the requisite skills for their effective management is a highly desirable attribute that will contribute greatly to career success. For younger leaders, this means a general awareness of each driver and the related skill sets with a more in-depth understanding of the requisite skills associated with those drivers with which the young leaders deal directly as part of their job responsibilities. As leaders ascend organizational hierarchies, their knowledge should broaden to a greater understanding of other drivers and deepen with respect to the drivers of most relevance to their jobs. This is necessary in order to accurately assess subordinates' performance with respect to those particular drivers. Leaders should be capable of assessing subordinates' performance with respect to all eight drivers and possess sufficient knowledge of the individual skill sets that make for effective performance to assign capable subordinate leaders to key leadership positions.

Before proceeding a caveat is in order. We do not maintain that our discussion of skill sets associated with each driver is exhaustive of all necessary and desirable skills. Even assuming such a list could be complied and relative weights assigned, space does not permit that depth of examination. Rather, what follows is an attempt to provide aspiring leaders with a flavor for each driver and its related skill requirements. As discussed in chapter 10, learning is a lifelong process, and any attempt to codify all the knowledge and abilities needed for career success is almost certain to suffer to same fate as the Napoleonic Code, a nineteenth-century attempt by France to identify all potential criminal acts and prescribe judicial remedies. In addition to being excessively weighty, eventually new situations arise not contemplated in such a code, rendering it obsolete and giving rise to legal dynamism through common law. The same seems likely true of both the eight drivers and their associated skills. As business continues to evolve globally, new drivers may well become important, old ones less so, and new skills emerge required for managing drivers as both technology and business acumen continue their seemingly inexorable march.

12.4. Key Driver Number One: Customer and Stakeholder Focus

Successful businesses are top-line driven because **growing revenue** is the only way long term to create a growing value for shareholders. To do

USAA's annual report makes its mission to serve its customers and its core values clear:

"The mission of the association is to facilitate the financial security of its members, associates, and their families through the provision of a full range of highly competitive financial products and services; in so doing, USAA seeks to be the provider of choice for the military community."

"USAA's core values of service, loyalty, honesty, and integrity reflect the values of the military and our membership and form the foundation on which USAA employees work and conduct themselves."

—USAA Annual Report 2012

this in an increasingly competitive environment, firms have to first and foremost create value for customers and clients. This means knowing precisely who the customer is in terms of characteristics and carefully defining the value proposition of a product or service for the customer. Entrepreneurs and venture capitalists sometimes refer to this as the "pain" statement. Knowing the cause of customers' "pain" and how to cure it becomes paramount in customer communications.

Not only must the business know customers' "pain" and clearly communicate their cure for it to these customers, they must also ensure that the organization as a whole, not just top leadership and those directly engaged with customers, understands the importance of placing customers and stakeholder groups at the forefront of organizational efforts. This includes everyone from sales personnel to those who manufacture products.[14] This is a longer-term focus than that of many

Figure 12.2. Drivers of Sustainable Organizational Success

	Driver	Major Requirements	
1	Customer and Stakeholder Focus	Understanding and satisfying customer needs Aligning all parts of organization to these needs	→
2	Effective Leadership and Strategy	Ethical and strategic leadership focused on sustainable value creation Key performance enablers including strong values, ethical culture, and highly effective organizational structures and processes	→
3	Integrated Governance, Risk Management, and Control	Deploying effective governance and processes with integrated risk management and controls Balancing performance and conformance	→
4	Innovation and Adaptability	Innovative processes and products to improve product performance and firm reputation Adapting rapidly to changing circumstances	→
5	Financial Management	Ensuring the firm's financial leadership and strategy support sustainable value creation Implementing good practices in areas such as tax and treasury, and cost and profitability improvement	→ Sustainable Organizational Success
6	People and Talent Management	Enabling people and creating talent as a strategic function Applying talent management to various functions to better serve needs across functions	→
7	Operational Excellence	Aligning resource allocation with strategic goals and objectives using drivers of stakeholder value Supporting decision making with timely and insightful performance analyses leading to incisive decisions	→
8	Effective and Transparent Communications	Engaging stakeholders effectively and ensuring they receive relevant information High-quality reporting to support stakeholder understanding and decision making	→

Source: Adapted from "Competent and Versatile: How Professional Accountants in Business Drive Sustainable Organizational Success," International Federation of Accountants, August 2011, 14, http://viewer.zmags.com/publication/b908956a#/b908956a/1 (accessed March 10, 2014).

businesses mainly focused on maximizing earnings per share and other short-term indicators of shareholder value. In effect, the customer-first focus means placing customers on an equal plane with shareholders and recognizing that shareholders' interests are best served over the longer haul by serving customers well. The extent that high-performing businesses will go to to provide outstanding customer-interface experiences is perhaps best illustrated in the following example.

USAA is a highly diversified financial services firm that is member owned—meaning that its owners are also its customers—and consistently earns the highest rankings for insurance and banking services. Mutual ownership means no divergence of interest between customers and shareholders as discussed in the previous paragraph.

Designed to serve members of the U.S. armed forces and their families, USAA has a national reputation for providing superb service while achieving rapid growth and excellent financial results. As of December 31, 2012, USAA reported assets of approximately $183 billion and revenues of approximately $21 billion with a net worth of over $22 billion. Its 2-year growth rate in members was approximately 17.5 percent, with 9.4 million customers and revenue growth rate of 15.5 percent. As reflected in the box on the left, USAA makes clear the congruence between its values and those of its customers, 95 percent of whom indicate they intend to remain customers for life.[15]

To effectively manage a rapidly growing organization such as USAA while attaining service levels leading to an extraordinary customer loyalty—and, at the same time, achieve outstanding financial results—requires an intense customer focus. Consider the following highlights from a recent release by a senior vice president of the association:

> 1. Staffing for demand, hiring 1,000 additional employees to staff customer contact centers.

> 2. Implementing more flexible call options for greater customer convenience with automated callback request if the wait time is longer than two minutes.

> 3. Deploying more efficient and powerful customer support tools to allow service representatives to access customer in-

"My family has done business with USAA for over 4 decades. Our children's families are now customers. My wife and I have several insurance policies with the company and various investment and banking accounts under its management. Over the years the claims service has been exceptional. It's always nice when the collision repair shop says, 'Oh, no problem,' when we tell them who we're insured by. We are constantly solicited by other financial services companies but wouldn't dream of doing business with anyone else."

—Long-time USAA customer

formation more quickly, resume conversations where they last terminated, and provide greater customer insight into products, services, and advice appropriate to each member's individual needs.

> 4. A new convenient online hub where customers and dedicated claims adjuster teams exchange claims-related information and updates.

> 5. A new application that enables iPhone and Android users to uploads pictures of damage and obtain an estimate via mobile device.

> 6. A mobile-repair capability for minor damage eliminating the necessity for customers to rent vehicles while theirs are undergoing repairs.[16]

> "One of the big priorities I had as I moved into sales and marketing at UPS was to make sure that the company listened to its customers in a way we hadn't before . . . It may be that you add value to your customers by facilitating better processes for the people that do face them. Make sure that the financial systems and measures that you have are supportive of effective sales execution and operation . . . Is our managerial accounting relevant in driving value to customers? This stuff can be very powerful if you align financial insight, product design, and customer execution."
>
> —Kurt Kuehn, chief financial officer, UPS

What is quite clear is that USAA makes serving its customers its first priority, while at the same time paying careful attention to its financial condition, which, in turn, enables it to earn the highest rankings for fiscal solidarity in the financial services industry. The company's leadership clearly understands that outstanding customer service and outstanding financial performance go hand in hand.

12.5. Key Driver Number Two: Effective Leadership and Strategy

USAA's customer focus is directly attributable to the second key driver, effective leadership and strategy. With a razor-sharp-focused strategy aimed at a very specific target market, it is imperative that the organization be keenly attuned to how its products and services are perceived. That the association has a pronounced strategy aimed at customer service should come as no surprise when one considers that its top leadership and board of directors comprises mainly retired flag-level military officers. Not only had these senior leaders been USAA customers themselves prior to being employed by the association, but they also know its target market as thoroughly as any senior business leadership possibly could. They know the lifestyles, mindsets, challenges, difficulties, and attitudes of its customers. Moreover, they are acutely aware that in the association's tightly linked customer community, word travels fast and reputation means everything. As a result, a single bad customer experience might cost the business of several potential customers.

Compare USAA leadership's knowledge of its customers with that of most large businesses. How much of the senior leadership of the average large business has the same depth of understanding of its customers? How much difference would it make if it did? Based upon the USAA example, one might be inclined to believe a great deal of difference, for few businesses have been as successful over the long term. Many of its customers are third generation with rights of membership handed down generation to generation. Since sustainable business success depends upon effective and ethical leadership, how leadership views the number one key success driver, customer focus, is critical.

First and foremost, effective leadership must focus business strategy on sustainable results over the long term. The history of business is replete with examples of the demise of businesses that took a short-run approach of maximizing current earnings at the expense of customers or ethics or both. This means maintaining a long-term focus when making various day-to-day decisions, including how these decisions impact operations, customers, employees, and the reputation of the organization. Successful organizations have a deep understanding of (1) customer and stakeholder needs and (2) the organization's capabilities to generate the required products and services, as well as (3) the opportunities and threats that stem from its competitive environment.[17]

Senior leaders have **four critical roles in delivering sustainable value creation**. First, they must be *creators of value* who take leadership roles in the design and implementation of strategies, policies, plans, and business performance controls and measures. Second, leaders must be *enablers of value creation.* They must be extensively involved in informing and guiding activities at the operational level to include planning, monitoring, and continuous improvement of organizational processes. Third, leaders must work to *preserve value* once it is created. This involves protecting the organization against market, operational, and financial risks. It also entails ensuring that organization members comply with laws, regulations, policies, procedures, and best practices. Finally, leaders must ensure the organization is a *reporter of values* disseminating clear, transparent, meaningful, and reasonably complete information to customers and stakeholders.

The box on the left not only underscores the criticality of creating, enabling, preserving, and reporting value creation, it also reflects the broad-based leadership and technical skill sets desirable in top leadership in today's business environment. Note that prior to becoming CFO of UPS, Kuehn spent time in sales and marketing gaining a deep understanding of customer needs. Note also that he carried with him this understanding when he moved to the financial side of the business, suggesting that skills gained in one functional area of business can be brought to bear with good effect in other areas to help leaders become talent that fits well in the new business environment.[18]

12.6. Key Driver Number Three: Integrated Governance, Risk Management, and Control

Ethical failures such as those in the Enron and WorldCom debacles are graphic reminders of the costs of poor corporate governance.[19] The fact that a large, international public accounting firm such as Arthur Andersen could be demolished by the acts of a relatively small number of employees is indicative of how the lack of effective corporate governance can harm many.[20] Even if inferior governance does not lead to corporate demise, the cost in poor customer relations can seriously affect the organization's top line. The reality of this possibility suggests keen attention to governance and control issues to ensure **compliance** with laws and regulations. But the need for sound governance, risk management, and controls goes well beyond simply ensuring compliance.

In order to ensure continuous value creation, businesses must have very effective controls and measures in place, a topic with which we deal in much greater depth in the following chapter. Effective controls and measures depend to a substantial extent on how well leadership is able to design and integrate systems for governance, risk management, and control. Such systems must be more than simply mechanisms to ensure compliance.[21] They must also facilitate customer awareness, gathering business intelligence; relevant real-time information for strategic, operational, and tactical decision making; continuous monitoring and improvement feedback; and transparent financial reporting—all leading to more effective controls.

In order to have more effective **controls**, firms need to align business processes around value creation by eliminating activities that do not demonstrate a clear business need. This alignment needs to be pervasive. Even if best-of-breed, process-improvement efforts are carried out within segments of the organization but disconnected from other initiatives, they will often lack the desired benefits stemming from an integrated organizational-process improvement.[22] The result has been the growth of **business-performance-measurement systems** designed to view business as a system of systems holistically.

Financial risk management had its origins in the 1980s with the proliferation of off-balance-sheet tools such as derivatives and securitization of assets that made many assets more liquid by making them tradable. Along with advances in information technology, these tools combined with changes in management practices enable vastly improved financial risk management, which is broadly divided into three categories:

1. **Market risk**, at least with respect to financial risk, is defined as exposure to uncertain market prices that exists where assets or liabilities can be marked to market. Risk related to assets or liabilities that cannot be marked to market, such as a factory or an entire business line, is called *business risk*.

2. **Credit risk** results from the uncertainty associated with a counterparty or obligor's inability to meet its obligations.

3. **Operational risk** is the risk that failure of internal processes, inadequate control systems, physical events (e.g., natural disaster, fire, etc.), or employee errors, omissions, and defalcations will result in financial losses.

Despite some notable catastrophic losses that resulted in institutional failures, over time market and credit risks came to be far better managed. Although businesses have always attempted to manage operational risks, in the new business environment these risks have become more proliferate, and due to growing business complexity have proven somewhat daunting to contain. Figure 12.3 provides an indication of the nature and extensiveness of operational risks.

From Figure 12.3, it is obvious that a variety of both leadership and technical skills are important in risk management. These technical skills include, but are not limited to, knowledge of laws and reg-

ulations, financial accounting, financial transactions, financial modeling, taxation, data processing, systems security, telecommunications, and human-resources issues. Many businesses are attempting to manage operational risks more systematically in an integrated fashion that incorporates firm-wide efforts into centralized, operational-risk-management departments that use both qualitative and quantitative techniques.[23] The skill sets required for effective governance, risk management, and control require not only good, insightful leadership skills but also a growing set of technical skills.

12.7. Key Driver Number Four: Innovation and Adaptability

In the rapidly changing business world, the ability to adapt to change and innovate with new products, services, technologies, and processes is essential. When one thinks of innovation, the first thing that comes to mind is often a new product or service, but it is not just those concerned directly with researching, developing, and marketing new products who must innovate. Consider the following quote by the CFO of UPS, a company with over 425,000 employees worldwide operating the ninth largest airline in the world:

Just as things began to stabilize around SOX and many of us got our arms around the documentation processes necessary to meet those requirements, our businesses continued to expand and get more complex. The world became global and whether our companies knew it or not, most transactions had some components of non-U.S. content to them. So that began to put incredible challenges on our financial capability—A, just to keep track of the cost, and B, to help understand the new exposures and risks. For example, like having revenues in a foreign currency, cost in another currency, translation issues,

Figure 12.3. Basel Committee Categories of Loss Events

Event-Type Category (Level 1)	Definition	Categories (Level 2)	Activities Examples (Level 3)
Internal Fraud	Losses due to acts of a type intended to defraud, misappropriate property, or circumvent regulations, the law, or company policy, excluding diversity/discrimination events, which involve at least one internal party	Unauthorized Activity	* Transactions not reported (intentional) * Transaction type unauthorized (with monetary loss) * Mismarking of position (intentional)
		Theft and Fraud	* Fraud/credit fraud/worthless deposits * Theft/extortion/embezzlement/robbery * Misappropriation of assets * Forgery * Check kiting * Smuggling * Account takeover/impersonation, etc. * Tax noncompliance/evasion (willful) * Bribes/kickbacks * Insider trading (not on firm's account)
External Fraud	Losses due to acts of a type intended to defraud, misappropriate property, or circumvent the law, by a third party	Theft and Fraud	* Theft/robbery * Forgery * Check kiting
		Systems Security	* Hacking damage * Theft of information (with monetary loss)
Employment Practices and Workplace Safety	Losses arising from acts inconsistent with employment, health or safety laws or agreements, from payment of personal injury claims, or from diversity/discrimination events	Employee Relations	* Compensation, benefit, termination issues * Organized labor activities
		Safe Environment	* General liability (slips and falls, etc.) * Employee health and safety rules and events * Workers' compensation
		Diversity and Discrimination	* All discrimination types
Clients, Products, and Business Practice	Losses arising from an unintentional or negligent failure to meet a professional obligation to specific clients (including fiduciary and suitability requirements), or from the nature or design of a product	Suitability, Disclosure, and Fiduciary	* Fiduciary breaches/guideline violations * Suitability/disclosure issues (KYC, etc.) * Retail consumer disclosure violations * Breach of privacy * Aggressive sales * Account churning * Misuse of confidential information * Lender liability
		Improper Business or Market Practices	* Antitrust * Improper trade/market practice * Market manipulation * Insider trading (on firm's account) * Unlicensed activity * Money laundering

Source: Adapted from Basel Committee on Banking Supervision, February 2003, http://www.riskglossary.com/link /operational_risk.htm (accessed March 17, 2014).

Becoming a Talent That Fits

> **"As we move into a knowledge economy, the number of jobs where people can simply turn up and be told how to do the job and be paid well for it is diminishing rapidly. We need to go on learning throughout our lives. When someone stops learning, now it's like they've stopped thinking, or at least being creative."**
>
> —John Hawkins, author of *The Creative Economy* and chairman of BOP Consulting, as quoted by Catherine Bolgar, *Wall Street Journal Executive Digest*

staffing issues—all the great stuff that being a multinational company brings about. That layered even more challenges on to us, and at least it's got my function at UPS very busy managing the complexity of the global world. There are great opportunities for business—you've got to go global if you want to lower your cost and if you want to find new sources of revenue. But the complexities and the risks from a financial perspective do increase substantially.[24]

In the Internet era, e-business is not simply about electronic transactions but an innovative way of running a business that helps enable rapid adaptation to changing conditions. One example of innovation to increase flexibility and adaptability is that of an information systems service-oriented architecture (SOA), essentially a collection of services that communicate with each other that requires a means of connecting the services such as the Internet. *Service* in this context means "a function that is well-defined, self-contained, and does not depend upon the context or state of other services."[25] Research by IBM's Institute of

Business Value has found that, although the primary motivation for SOA is cost savings, 51 percent of companies using SOA have experienced increased revenue growth as a result of its use and 100 percent reported greater business flexibility. Flexibility is required in order to identify new opportunities and respond quickly by creating products and services in an economical manner.[26]

For example, COSCON is China's largest container shipper with 127 vessels ships with over 320,000 containers worldwide. In order to direct and track this volume of shipping activity, COSCON uses electronic data interchange systems having twenty-one applications integrated by SOA enabling connections among silo databases. This greatly enhanced COSCON's flexibility in responding to continuously changing customs requirements, improved internal efficiency, and increased customer satisfaction. In addition, changes to the IT systems can be accomplished in days rather than the weeks required prior to implementing SOA.[27]

One of the more interesting findings is most CEOs indicate that more of their new ideas come from clients than employees.[28] This can be interpreted two ways. On one hand, it could suggest complacency and/or an inward-looking orientation. On the other hand, it could emanate from a more intense and growing customer focus. Whatever the underlying causes, two points might be made. The first is that having a strong customer focus can be a driver for innovation. The second is that organizational leadership needs to also be focused on encouraging internal innovation as well as seeking external input. Businesses need three critical ingredients for innovation: (1) a repository of intellectual capital convertible into value, (2) the financial means to fund innovation, and (3) the human capital to sustain innovative processes.[29]

What types of skill sets are required for becoming an innovator? Consider the quote in the box on the left. One of the most important skills required for innovation is that organizational members be good learners who not only take advantage of learning opportunities provided by their employers but also engage in **self-directed learning** as discussed in chapter 10. Another important skill is **developing a critical eye about knowledge**, knowing how to sift vast amounts of information to glean incisively critical insights. Yet another is **enterprise development**—that is, building organizations using exercise of good leadership and management. In addition, entrepreneurial skills are important even in large organizations, entailing the ability to create businesses within businesses.[30]

12.8. Key Driver Number Five: Financial Management

Previous sections have already intimated at ways in which financial management is related to other organizational aspects and functions, but a somewhat more detailed understanding of the importance of sound, proactive, incisive financial management in today's business climate comes from considering what one commentator has called the **seven habits of strategic finance**. Even if you are not yet at the level at which you play an active role in strategic leadership, a knowledge of the habits will better inform you about what top leadership is hopefully doing well and allow you to do your best to support their efforts. Alternatively, if top leadership is not embracing these habits, this, too, becomes lesson takeaways to guide you as you ascend the business hierarchy.

1. Understand the business strategy and stay focused on it. This goes back to the *ends/ways/means model* we've emphasized since the beginning of our journey in courageous leadership. Don't lose focus on what constitutes victory in the heat of corporate battles.

2. Ensure the information being provided to decision makers is *accurate, timely, and relevant* to the decisions. Chapter 13 will delve into this topic far more deeply. Suffice it to say that these three information attributes are indispensable to sound decision making.

3. Ensure that the *financial ramifications of important decisions are thoroughly evaluated* prior to reaching a decision. We've previously discussed adverse second- and third-order effects, the unanticipated consequences of decisions on those directly and indirectly affected by the decisions. Time and thought spent in anticipating and mitigating to the extent possible these consequences saves time, money, and grief later.

4. *Be on the leading edge of change,* not behind the change curve. Early movers are often the businesses that really benefit from change. For example, only about 20 percent of acquisitions actually create real value for the acquirer, and these are usually the early acquisitions. After the early targets are picked, the price of the remainder often rises to the point where additional value is nil.

5. *Understand the risks* the business faces and strive to mitigate them to the extent reasonable. As previously noted, global enterprise carries with it many complexities and associated risks. Rapid technology turnover means the risk of a market shift that could adversely affect the all-important top line.

6. *Develop alternative scenarios and courses of action* (COAs). Alternative COAs accomplish several things. First, they force deeper consideration of each COA, therefore avoiding a rush to judgment about a single COA. Second, obtaining estimates of supportability from different functional areas makes it more likely that poten-

tial second- and third-order effects will be unearthed. Third, they improve the critical thinking skills of those involved.

7. Maintain a customer focus and *ensure that cost-saving initiatives do not come at the expense of customer dissatisfaction.* One difficulty here is often that operating cost savings are more measurable, at least in the short run, than the cost of reduced sales. It is therefore important for financial leaders to work with personnel on the front lines of customer relations to identify and, if possible, quantify the cost of lost sales.[31]

What skills and abilities are needed to support these seven habits? Rather obviously, the same soft skills that we have emphasized throughout this manuscript are needed. These include courageous performance-driven leadership and interpersonal skills, championing growth, effective delegation, strategic insight, independent thinking, team skills, complex problem finding and solving, communications, and so forth.[32]

Technical skill requirements include an understanding of accounting such as activity-based costing, modern business performance measurement systems, managing large amounts of data and information, using data analytics, capital expenditure analysis possibly including the use of real options, and triple-bottom-line reporting which includes social and environmental concerns. Additionally, financial personnel should be able to transform financial measurement systems to meet the demands of changing environments and support sales and marketing efforts with financial information. They also should understand the business's broader operations to correlate and analyze data to support strategic decisions. In adverse economic times, it becomes essential that financial personnel be able to participate integrally in decisions about improving core productivity. With business bombarded with a continuing

stream of new regulations, an understanding of compliance and sound corporate governance is critical.[33]

12.9. Key Driver Number Six: People and Talent Management

With the retirement of many so-called "baby boomers" and the attendant demographic bubble creating a shortage of developed leaders to take their places, how organizations manage the development of their members' talents will be a major determining factor in recruitment of sufficient quantities of good leaders, leader retention, and ultimately organizational success. Moreover, given the aforementioned reality that, although ideas often come from outside the company, most value is created internally, developing the talent to create value is paramount for long-term organizational success. Organizations that attract and retain talent outperform competitors by treating personnel development as a strategic function.[34] Talent management usually means managing organizational members' core competencies as well as position-specific competencies. This includes knowledge, skills, experience, and personal traits such as leadership abilities.[35]

Some organizations have gone so far as to establish intraorganizational **talent marketplaces** wherein employees have a voice in choosing assignments and projects they feel are best suited to their needs and desired for knowledge and skills progression. This is the exception rather than the rule, however. One difficulty is that many organizations spend a great deal of time, effort, and money attracting talented personnel but very little time and effort to guide and direct the further development of this talent. Many organizations have yet to develop the kind of depth of leadership with appropriate attendant technical skills to match their efforts to deepen their global footprint. Only 5 percent of businesses indicate that they have

Figure 12.4. Competency Proficiency Scale: Chemists' Oral Communications

Listening to others and communicating articulately, fostering open communication. (Scale progression: increased complexity of messages, audiences, and communication vehicles)				
Level 1 *Listens and clearly presents information*	**Level 2** *Foster two-way communication*	**Level 3** *Adapts communication*	**Level 4** *Communicates complex messages*	**Level** *Communicates strategically*
• Listens/pays attention actively and objectively. • Presents information and facts in a logical manner, using appropriate phrasing and vocabulary. • Shares information willingly and on a timely basis. • Communicates honestly, respectfully, and sensitively.	• Recalls others' main points and takes them into account in own communication. • Checks own understanding of others' communication (e.g., paraphrases, asks question). • Elicits comments or feedback on what has been said. • Maintains continuous, open and consistent communication with others.	• Tailors communication (e.g., content, style and medium) to diverse audiences. • Reads cues from diverse listeners to assess when and how to change planned communication approach to effectively deliver message. • Communicates equally effectively at varied organization levels. • Understands others' underlying needs, motivations, emotions or concerns and communicates effectively despite the sensitivity of the situation.	• Communicates issues clearly and credibly with widely varied audiences. • Handles difficult on-the spot questions (e.g., from officials, interest groups, or the media), • Overcomes resistance and secures support for ideas or initiatives through high impact communication.	• Scans the environment for key information and messages to form the development of communication strategies. • Communicates strategically to achieve specific objectives (e.g., considers optimal "messaging" and timing of communication). • Uses varied communication vehicles and opportunities to promote dialogue and develop shared understanding and consensus.
	Entry Chemist	Working Chemist	Managing Chemist	

Source: Adapted from http://en.wikipedia.org/wiki/Competency_dictionary (accessed February 16, 2015).

a well-defined talent development and management strategy.[36]

During economic downturns one of the fastest ways to reduce cost is to reduce staff. Often this is accomplished through across-the-board staff cuts. One of the coauthors suffered through two mandated staff cuts during which he was ordered to reduce staff by 10 percent each time. A better way to reduce staff would be through a well-defined talent management strategy. Times when many businesses are seeking to reduce personnel costs provide good opportunities to introduce a talent management strategy involving job analysis and individual performance assessment.[37] This sends a clear signal throughout the organization that job security and talent go hand in hand.

Many well-led, innovative organizations take a proactive approach to talent management by developing **competency architectures** and de-fining skills required for various positions in **competency dictionaries** to include the general and specific competencies associated with each job. These competencies include leadership and interpersonal skills as well as technical skills related to specific jobs. In a competency dictionary, **competency proficiency scales** are developed for each skill related to a position. Figure 12.4 provides an example of a competency proficiency scale related to a chemist's oral communications skills.

Such a scale serves several purposes: (1) it facilitates improvement within the current position, (2) it allows for comparisons among employees in the same position, (3) it provides a road map for organization members to see what the required skills are for advancement to higher levels, and (4) it allows comparisons of the skills required across different positions to ascertain how to place organization members in positions best suited to their skill sets.[38] Obviously, developing such a road map for each critical skill associated with each position takes considerable time and effort but can pay great dividends in the long run. Rather than engage in a pervasive, all-at-once effort, organizations might begin by selecting the most critical positions as a starting point.

Unfortunately, given the low percentage of businesses using a real, well-defined, and well-implemented talent management strategy, many aspiring leaders will be left largely to their own devices to come up with their individual strategy for developing their own human capital. This means falling back on the ideas and principles presented in chapter 10 on self-learning. Even if there is an organizational talent management strategy, aspiring leaders are well advised to develop their own parallel strategy based upon their personal goals and objectives, which may or may not always be well aligned with those of their employers. Ultimately, as discussed in chapter 7, getting into a position in which the majority of professional transactions are enjoyable is one of the keys to job satisfaction and success. Although astute organizational leadership recognizes the importance of this, it is obviously not characteristic of many organizations or the adoption rate of talent management strategies would be higher than 5 percent. Leaders taking charge of their own futures is therefore a well-advised strategy.

12.10. Key Driver Number Seven: Operational Excellence

There are many different models of operational excellence. Even general descriptions of operational excellence differ in some respects but contain common elements.[39] Consider the following descriptions:

> Operational Excellence is an element of organizational leadership that stresses the application of a variety of principles, systems, and tools toward the sustainable improvement of key performance metrics.[40]

All work in organizations is the outcome of a system. Systems are either designed to produce a specific end goal or they evolve on their own. Systems drive the behavior of people; or rather they create the conditions that cause people to behave in a certain way. One of the outcomes of poorly designed systems is enormous variation in behavior and thus significant variation in results. Operational excellence requires ideal behavior that translates into consistent and ideal results.[41]

The first description of operational excellence focuses on it as an aspect of leadership, whereas the second takes a more systems-oriented approach, as if its attainment is a function of systems design. In reality, achieving operational excellence requires both leadership and careful design of systems. Operational excellence means a continuing focus on improvement, and continuous improvement is frequently more difficult that it seems. It requires a culture that engages the entire organization. This means continuous emphasis placed by top leadership, engaged middle-level leaders, and concerted efforts backed up by systems that are capable of supporting operational excellence with timely, accurate, and relevant measures of business performance. *Too often operational excellence programs have focused of the program itself rather than transforming organizational cultures.* This has given operational excellence something akin to a fad mantle, as business has seen quality circles, total quality management, business process reengineering, and Six Sigma gain popularity fairly rapidly but lose it gradually in many businesses. Absent real cultural transformation, operational excellence initiatives are infrequently lasting.[42] This does not mean, however, that operational excellence should be dismissed as futile, but rather that it requires something far beyond organizational rank and file viewing it as the latest program coming from a book the CEO read on the corporate aircraft en route to the company's London office.

Figure 12.5. Operational Excellence Map for a Manufacturing Company

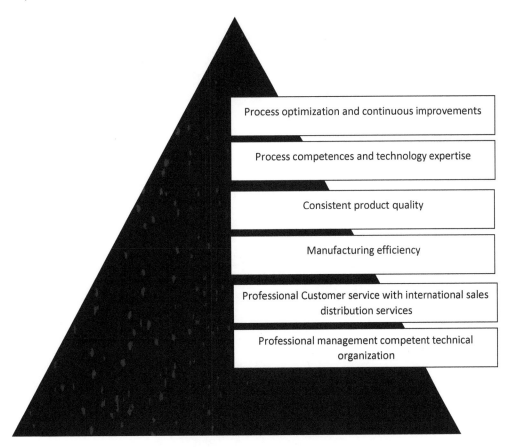

Process optimization and continuous improvements

Process competences and technology expertise

Consistent product quality

Manufacturing efficiency

Professional Customer service with international sales distribution services

Professional management competent technical organization

FTI Operational Excellence

Source: Adapted from http://dict.space.4goo.net/dict?q=operational (accessed February 16, 2015).

How operational excellence programs are designed and implemented tends to be somewhat industry and organization dependent. Consider Figure 12.5, which shows the mapping of an operational excellence program in a manufacturing company.

This particular program has as its foundation technical competency. It attempts to achieve manufacturing efficiency with linkages to customer demand through its sales and distribution activities. It hopes that this improved efficiency will support consistent product quality that translates into process optimization and continuous improvement through process competencies and technological expertise. Note the absence of any explicit reference on the map to organizational culture and the learning aspects necessary to gain total organizational buy-in.

Figure 12.6 depicts an operational efficiency mapping for a telecommunications company. In contrast to the preceding map that implies a somewhat nebulous hierarchical progression, this map presents operational excellence in a circular framework with organizational members at its heart. There is a strong people focus that indicates members need to be well skilled, with talent management explicitly emphasized. Merely looking at the map provides some indication of the technical skills necessary. Also worthy of note is explicit mention of the need for measurement and

Figure 12.6. Operational Excellence Map for a Telecommunications Company

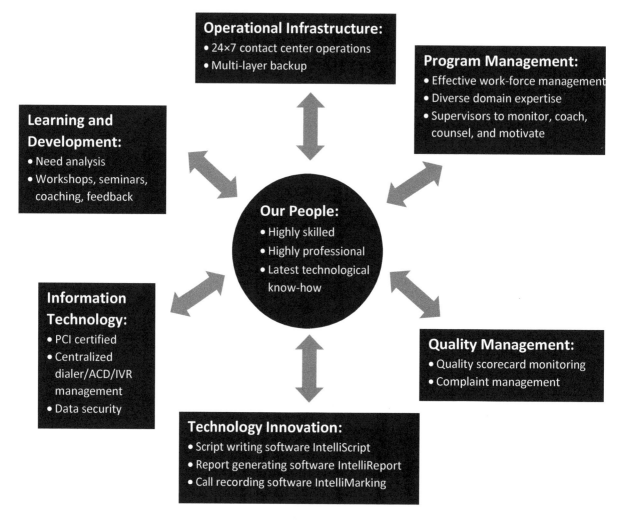

Operational Infrastructure:
• 24×7 contact center operations
• Multi-layer backup

Program Management:
• Effective work-force management
• Diverse domain expertise
• Supervisors to monitor, coach, counsel, and motivate

Learning and Development:
• Need analysis
• Workshops, seminars, coaching, feedback

Our People:
• Highly skilled
• Highly professional
• Latest technological know-how

Information Technology:
• PCI certified
• Centralized dialer/ACD/IVR management
• Data security

Quality Management:
• Quality scorecard monitoring
• Complaint management

Technology Innovation:
• Script writing software IntelliScript
• Report generating software IntelliReport
• Call recording software IntelliMarking

Source: Adapted from http://www.ocurrance.com/operational-excellence.html

monitoring. The overall impression is that operational excellence is first and foremost a function of human capital supported by quality improvement programs, technology and technological innovation, strong infrastructure, continuous learning, and monitoring.

Although it is somewhat hazardous to draw firm conclusions about the two companies' operational excellence initiatives just from studying these maps, maps should be guides that direct people's attention to salient programmatic features. That being the case, clearly the map in Figure 12.6 seemingly captures the notion of an overarching organizational culture of excellence better than that in Figure 12.5, which appears more likely to fall prey to a programmatic rather than cultural focus. Further, the skills demanded for individual success in the organization seem far more apparent in Figure 12.6, thereby providing organizational members with some guidance for skills development. Aspiring leaders in businesses with operational excellence initiatives should be able to gain insights into important skills valued for progression by examining the skills demanded by these initiatives. Even if the initiatives themselves become transitory, changing with top leadership, the skills they demand will likely prove useful in other ways.

12.11. Key Driver Number Eight: Effective and Transparent Communications

The final key driver of organizational success is that of effective and transparent communications. Successful businesses commonly have clear strategies for engaging and communicating with stakeholders to include customers, business partners, shareholders, organizational members, and the communities in which businesses operate. Communications should provide relevant and understandable insight into organizations' vision, strategy, and results. Periodic business reporting mandated by regulation provides one of the principal venues for communication, but savvy leadership should look well beyond required reporting in communicating with stakeholders.[43]

When using the word "transparent" to describe business communications it is important to define what it means. To some, transparent can mean true, to others, sincere, but truth and sincerity are not equivalent. A business can be truthful in communicating facts about itself but at the same time not be sincere about informing stakeholders. For example, reporting a 10 percent increase in revenues over those of the previous year may be accurate but insufficiently informative to investors if much of the increase was due to one-time events.[44]

In reality, transparency in communicating business activities and performance requires balancing three critical needs: (1) the need to disclose facts and results, (2) the need to protect information that is private or could lead to competitive disadvantage, and (3) the need to generate action and desired response. Saying too little or too much can be dangerous from different perspectives. Too much disclosure may provide valuable business intelligence to competitors, but too little may result in derivative action lawsuits by shareholders. "The key is to communicate enough information that is relevant to the audience in order to clarify the situation and support the desired response."[45] This de facto makes transparency not just a communications issue but an ethical one as well, because determining the desired response carries moral overtones. What is more important, being forthright enough that the intended consumer of the information can make an informed decision, or placing the organization in the best possible light under the circumstances? Obstacles to transparency are not just financial in nature but include embarrassment to businesses and their members, who in some circumstances may have failed to exercise appropriate leadership and oversight.[46]

Nowhere has transparency been more discussed than in corporate financial reporting where, despite being ill defined, transparency translates into assurance to investors. One source defines financial reporting transparency as "the extent to which financial reports reveal an entity's underlying economics in a way that is readily understandable by those using the financial reports," while noting some limitations of this definition.[47] Reasons for inaccurate financial reporting include fraud, misaligned incentives, greater reliance on pro forma forecasts, and business complexity. There is a growing body of evidence that business benefits in the long run from transparency. One reason is that investors appear to trust transparent businesses more because the risk of unpleasant surprises is lower. Additionally, more complex businesses that investors find more difficult to understand seem to be discounted.[48]

Despite the emphasis on financial disclosure transparency, the need for transparency is not just external to the organization. Consider the following quote:

> You may rely on an executive dashboard to track and report on various key indicators of operational performance . . . [and] one

of the indicators you monitor is the cost of technical support services. For some reason this month there was a huge spike in the cost of providing that service. Then you send out a red alert to the entire company... [but] no other information is shared. This will likely create chaos and panic . . . If you repeat this behavior, the organization at large will become demoralized.[49]

It is critical to distinguish between transparent disclosure and "spin." Spin usually means twisting negative facts and events to make them more favorable to the organization. Spinning in one instance often leads to more spin as more information about these facts and events comes to the attention of stakeholders. Spin is a short-term strategy that when used repeatedly creates mistrust as stakeholders, both external and internal to the business, discern a pattern of misrepresentation.[50]

There are some general skills required for effective and transparent business communication. These include the cognitive ability to see cause and effect, anticipate adverse second- and third-order effects of decisions, communicate clearly and succinctly, and simplify complexities of business in ways that stakeholders fully understand the information being provided.[51] Additionally, a critical ability is being able to use good intuition and sound judgment beforehand in situations that have the potential to be volatile and then taking appropriate precautions. Consider the following story told by one of the coauthors:

Once I was named to be the officer of record for the main banking account into which all federal election funds flowed for a nominee for president of the United States. When the staff member in charge of the candidate's election finances and I met to discuss how the election funds would be handled, I immediately saw the potential for political scandal and took stringent measures to ensure that all transactions were handled and accounted for properly. These measures went so far as keeping my own log of every transaction in addition to the bank's records. Sure enough, a scandal erupted involving the candidate, and the media were in high gear attempting to find any trace of malfeasance or misfeasance. Because I had anticipated this might occur, taken precautionary measures in keeping clear, accurate records, and was therefore prepared to be fully transparent, there was nothing negative to find in our case.

Some insights can be gained regarding the technical skills required for transparent communications by examining financial reporting as an example. Regulators are desirous of timely, complete, transparent, and quality disclosures that provide investors the ability to see businesses through the "eyes of management." Consequently, they have mandated standards for disclosures regarding the risks and uncertainties firms face, such as the relative importance of each line of business in which they engage, estimates where there is reasonable possibility the estimates will change materially in the near term, and vulnerability to market, customer, supplier, and geographic operations. These disclosures are supposed to be consistent with budgets and business plans, boards of directors, financial analysts, monthly operating results, disclosures to financial analysts, sales to customers, orders from suppliers, and market trends.[52]

Consider the broad range of technical skills that might be required to meet this requirement alone. These skills might include financial accounting reporting, financial risk modeling, statistical modeling, budgeting, market analysis, supply chain, country risk, competitor analysis, and so forth. The point is that financial reporting transparency comes with a skills price tag that can be quite significant.

12.12. Concluding Thoughts

This chapter has examined some of the issues related to leadership and technical skills development based upon eight drivers of organizational success in the new and ever-changing business environment. Leaders who want to be successful over the span of a career must not only be cognizant of these success drivers but must also build their skill sets around them in order to make themselves as valuable as possible to their organizations. They must maintain customers and stakeholders while continuously retooling their skill sets in a never-ending cycle of learn and then lead, learn and then lead. They must be equally aware of both their strengths and weaknesses and seek to rectify weaknesses even as they apply their strengths to organizational decision making and problem solving. They must proactively strive for an ever-broadening vision of the business in order to have the greatest possible impact. They must recognize that one of the greatest risks lies in changing themselves and their businesses as the business climate continues its own inexorable change.[53]

Many, if not most, larger companies have evolved to some extent into some form of a matrix structure because business has become so complicated. The lines between strategy development, finance, accounting, information technology, product development, and risk management are blurring. This structure will take on a new role that allows leaders to collaborate on critical decision points more so than simply around traditional customer segmentation models. This means leaders in various functions need stronger business acumen than that traditionally associated with functionally stovepiped organizations. It means incisive thinking capable of sifting large amounts of data and distilling it into relevant information pertinent to those decisions.[54] Leaders need to be proactive in thinking of the firm's customers as if they are sitting at the table when decisions are made.[55]

Leadership skills alone are absolutely necessary but often insufficient in today's business world. Although essential, leadership skills must be accompanied by appropriate technical skills. One of the biggest mistakes leaders can make is becoming mired in jobs that don't fit their technical skills. To become so makes them less valuable and more vulnerable in downside economic cycles where divestment of underperforming lines of business, cost retrenchment, and downsizing of personnel often occur. In the final analysis, business leadership needs both broadly based soft skills and broadly based technical skills, and the need for breadth is increasing.[56] With hierarchical ascendency the need for leadership skills grows and over time requirements for technical skills morph. This means a career-long journey in learning then leading, learning then leading, in which intellectual complacency has no place.

PART IV
Understanding the Organizational Environment

Foreword

Part IV deals with understanding the organizational environment. Chapter 13 deals with the all-important issues of organizational control and the role measurement plays in it. Chapter 14 talks about the critical issue of teams and how to use—and not use—them. Chapter 15 discusses organizational savvy and how developing it will help leaders navigate the often tumultuous waters of storms that occur in businesses. Chapter 16 explores the client interface based on the premise that in the long run business is all about the top line.

CHAPTER 13

Organizational Control and Measurement:

What Gets Measured Gets Done

> **"What gets measured gets done.
> What gets rewarded gets done well."**
>
> —Unknown

Along with planning, organizing, staffing, and directing, controlling is a basic leadership function designed to be both retrospective and forward looking. Leaders examine past and ongoing results to draw conclusions about employee and systems functioning. **Organizational control** refers to the ability of businesses to direct the activities of employees in ways that are linked toward achievement of the businesses' goals and objectives. It is therefore directly linked to organizational performance. Control is intended to make a business set expectations, govern behaviors, and smooth internal functions though unity of action. Effective control systems also signal leadership when dysfunctions occur and facilitate intervention and corrective action.

Measures are pervasive in business, and it has long been an axiom of business that *what gets measured gets done.* The roots of this axiom lie in the notion that organizational performance is determined to a large extent by the effectiveness of a network of systematic processes that require measurable inputs and generate measurable outcomes. Thus measurement is inextricably related to organizational control. Merely establishing a measure and holding employees accountable for the result is often sufficient to have employees fo-

cus on that measure and the activities that create it to the exclusion of unmeasured activities.[1]

There are often-overlooked difficulties with measures of business activities and results. For example, measures are often imperfect in measuring what is intended. Consider return on investment (ROI). Both *return* and *investment* can be defined in different ways and are often the product of accounting systems that are filled with assumptions and estimates and subject to manipulation. Consequently, the accuracy with which ROI captures actual returns to investors can be situation dependent. Additionally, those who design and implement often fail to anticipate their adverse second- and third-order effects. Recall that a second-order effect is one having an unanticipated effect on those whom the measure was intended to impact, and a third-order effect is one having an unanticipated effect on those whom the measure was not intended to impact.

Measures can be a powerful tool and, like many powerful tools, dangerous if handled incorrectly. Astute leaders need to have a keen understanding of how and when to use measures to organizational advantage and when and how measures become dysfunctional. This chapter ex-

"Management love[s] their metrics. The thinking goes something like this, 'We need a number to measure how we're doing. Numbers focus people and help us measure success.' Whilst well intentioned, management by numbers unintuitively leads to problematic behavior and ultimately detracts from broader project and organizational goals. Metrics inherently aren't a bad thing; just often, inappropriately used. This essay demonstrates many of the issues caused by management's traditional use of metrics and offers an alternative to address these dysfunctions."

—Martin Fowler

plores these issues, along the way dealing with a rising sea of new business performance measurement systems that have gained popularity over the past 25 years. It also touches upon the issues of tying incentives to measures and using culture to help guide employee performance.

13.1. Some Basics of Control and the Role of Measures

Controlling human behaviors to achieve desired organizational outcomes is a basic function of any leadership just like planning, staffing, and organizing. Controlling human behaviors is almost always the greatest control problem leaders face. Dating back to the early twentieth century, control was seen as actions intended to see that operations were carried out according to plan.[2] Recall that human behavior can be governed in three basic

ways: (1) by direct observation and correction, (2) by measures in which people are held accountable for use of inputs and for outcomes indirectly, and (3) by an organizational culture that creates pressure to behave in certain ways consistent with the culture. Each of these ways of controlling behavior has is strengths and weaknesses.[3]

Observation of effort works best when the efforts of subordinates are both observable by leadership and the link between the behavior and the outcomes is obvious. For example, it is obvious whether a subordinate designated to dig a ditch is working hard. The amount of progress is also observable, but importantly, progress is only partly a function of effort. The ground, depending upon whether it is hard or soft, itself may determine the amount of progress for a given effort level. Thus someone supervising the effort might conclude that the subordinate is working hard but slow progress is due to difficult terrain. Any disconnect between quantity of output and quantity and quality of inputs is apparent.

As work becomes unobservable due to lack of physical proximity or the nature of work becomes more complex and mental rather than physical, observation is no longer as effective in controlling behavior. A salesperson who is supposed to be calling upon prospective clients might be on the golf course instead. A subordinate may appear to be thinking about solving a problem, but the quality and quantity of thought may be lacking. Such situations call for **outcome controls** with the requirement that outcomes be measured. Efforts are then judged more by the quantity or quality of outputs and less by the apparent amount of inputs. There are drawbacks to using outcome controls, however, that incur risks for subordinates and additional costs to the organization.

Agency theory suggests a model in which the **principal** (employer) contracts with an **agent** (employee) to do a particular job. When the

Figure 13.1. Agent Risk and Compensation

Compensation Arrangement	Fixed Compensation	Expected Variable Compensation on Average	Total Expected Compensation on Average
X	$100,000	$0	$100,000
Y	$50,000	$50,000	$100,000
Z	$50,000	$75,000	$125,000

agent's efforts cannot be observed by the principal, this creates a moral hazard problem in which the agent can shirk his contractual responsibilities without the principal knowing and overconsume perquisites (e.g., use of company vehicle for unauthorized personal use). To counter this, the agent is often measured based upon the outcomes rather than upon his inputs.

There are two fundamental difficulties with this method of control, however. First, outcomes are often measured imperfectly, resulting in disparities and potential inequities. For example, quantity of sales is easily measured in monetary terms but may not reflect how profitable those sales are to the organization due to an inability to assign costs to sales. Salesperson A making ten sales averaging $10,000 each may create more profit than Salesperson B making one hundred sales of $1,000 each because of fixed transaction costs of processing each sale. Thus, even if B is working much harder than A, A's efforts result in greater profits, and both are compensated equally if compensation is determined as a percentage of dollar sales. Depending upon whether one views the appropriate role of compensation in this case as rewarding generation of profits or hard work, an inequity exists in one direction or the other.

A second drawback to outcome controls is that they place more risk on the agent because the agent often has no control over externalities that affect his or her outputs. For example, an adverse economy may make achieving targeted sales far more difficult. The nature of risk and returns is such that the greater the assumed risk, the greater the expected return. Agents therefore expect to be compensated more when forced to assume the risk of factors over which they have little or no control adversely affecting their performances. To see this relationship, consider the following compensation proposals (Figure 13.1).

First, compare arrangements X and Y. Both have the same expected value, but Y places more risk on the agent. With Y, in some years the agent may earn significantly more than $100,000 and in other years significantly less, making it more difficult to predicate a standard of living on an average annual income of $100,000. Consequently, because risk aversion is the normal human condition, the agent is not indifferent between X and Y even though the expected total compensation is the same. The agent will prefer X to Y, but X carries a much greater risk that the agent will shirk. In order to induce the agent to accept a contract with a variable compensation component that discourages shirking but carries more risk for the agent, the principal must offer a higher total expected compensation package such as in arrangement Z. The more risk that is placed upon the agent, the higher the expected compensation. This can be observed in the often very high CEO compensation packages prevalent in many large companies in which there are a multitude of uncontrollable factors that may affect the overall organizational performance for which CEOs are responsible.

Control in general can be categorized by the nature of the information flow, the type of mechanism used to apply control, and the relationship of control to the organizational decision processes. Information flows can be closed loop or open loop. **Closed-loop information systems** are like those of thermostats set to a predetermined temperature that operate and provide feedback without the necessity of intervention. A business example is a budget versus actual accounting report that shows the deviance from plan. **Open-loop** information flows allow for external intervention and adjustment based upon feedback. A business example might be best-case, worst-case, most-likely case budget scenarios in which forecasts are revised based upon apparent, ongoing scenario realization. Control mechanisms can be **man controlled** or **machine controlled**, which is largely self-explanatory. In business today characterized by a high degree of automated information processing, most control systems involve a combination of both. In **organizational control**, reviews of programs and results emanates from the organizational strategy at a more macro-level. Are the organization's systems in their entirety delivering the desired results, and, if not, why not and what can be done to correct deficiencies? With **operational control**, the focus is at the micro-level on specific systems with day-to-day outputs the concern.

Cultural controls represent a third method in which leaders can influence human behaviors, albeit one involving a great deal of subjectivity. Although rarely a complete replacement for other organizational controls, cultural controls used properly can be powerful ways in which to augment observation and outcome controls. By creating cultures that say such things to members as, "These are our values," and "This is how we handle this type of situation here," leadership can help guide behaviors in circumstances when other methods of control are ineffective and/or when nebulous circumstances arise that have not been contemplated in the design of other controls; for example, with tasks such as development of innovative new products that can be both long

term in nature and difficult to measure. Research and development personnel might work on such products for a considerable amount of time with no tangible results. A culture that values perseverance despite encountering obstacles can be useful in keeping researchers motivated. Another example involves circumstances in which collegiality and mutual assistance are valued but often difficult to measure. A culture that promotes the organization as a family in which "Family members help one another when in need" can help promote these values. Cultural controls usually take a long time to create and are often easy to destroy. They require consistent emphasis and reiteration backed up by matching behavior from the top down. It does little good to advertise "we are family" if top leadership's behaviors don't back that up. The best cultures are those whose basic guiding values and principles are understood and reinforced by all members of the organization and passed on to new members by veterans.

One important behavioral aspect of *the role of measurement in organizational control is that people seem to gravitate toward numbers,* especially those of a summary nature. The result is often the transference of subjective data into numerical form in attempts to quantify the "softer" aspects of performance. This finds its way into all sorts of organizations, including academic institutions. Teaching evaluations are common in universities, with students being asked to fill out many questions and make subjective comments about teachers, most of which is largely ignored in favor of such summary measures as, "To what extent would I rate this instructor as outstanding overall," simply in the interest of leaders' time in evaluating many instructors across numerous courses. This might ignore a tendency for students to give somewhat lower evaluations to highly demanding teachers, reflecting one danger inherent in such summary measures. This same phenomenon can exist in business, where, for example, an excessive focus on the projected ROI of a capital expenditure (CAPEX) project compared to the hurdle rate that must be exceeded for approval of the project may result in not enough attention being paid to the underlying assumptions that went into creating the ROI figure.

Although this section has merely scratched the surface in discussing basics of control, perhaps it has created an awareness of why controlling human behavior is the most challenging aspect of leading organizations. The following section bridges our discussion of these general control concepts to a more specific discussion of the application of controls in business.

13.2. Some Business Measurement Basics

In business, measurement is often the linchpin for performance management and integral to performance improvement. Controls and their attendant measures have the following four major purposes:

1. Making plans and projects *effective* by measuring progress, providing feedback, guiding interventions when necessary, and forming the basis for rewarding members.

2. Improving *efficiency* by measuring outputs against inputs.

3. Ensuring *compliance* with law, policies, and procedures.

4. Creating *business intelligence* to improve decision making by using fact-based support systems.[4]

One of the greatest challenges businesses face is how to align performance measures with business strategy. Because they were already quantified, the tendency for many years was to rely mainly on financial measures that sometimes failed to capture some of the more important elements of business success. Once a firm becomes large enough so that control must largely be vest-

ed in outcome measures, its top leadership faces two salient questions. (1) Do we know the truth or a reasonable approximation of it? (2) What information is it that should move us to act? This leads to the identification of **critical performance indicators**. These indicators can be objective by nature or subjective with an attempt to measure objectively, be leading or lagged, be complete or incomplete measures of objective attainment, and be measures of inputs to a process or of outputs.[5] Measures may be in *absolutes* (e.g., the volume of sales to a customer) or *relative* terms (e.g., the difference between average sales to the ten most profitable customers to those of the ten least profitable). Measures can also be roughly divided into four categories.

1. Measures that provide measures of how well processes are functioning.

2. Measures that quantify outcomes.

3. Measures that help ensure changes to one part of a system are not causing problems with another part.

4. Measures of customer or client satisfaction.[6]

Defining measures in relative terms often provides more useful information, such as size-standardized ratios. That said, ratios can often be deceiving because denominators can be manipulated along with numerators, affording more opportunities to "manage" numbers in ways that make performance appear to be better than actual. Moreover, performance measures denominated in ratios can provide perverse incentives. Consider the simple example of ROI as a performance metric for a division of a company with a cost of capital of 12 percent. The company overall benefits from accepting projects exceeding 12 percent, but the president of a division who is evaluated on his or her division's ROI has an incentive to turn down a project with an expected

ROI of 13 percent because it will lower the division's existing ROI of 14 percent. This incentive would not exist if the president was evaluated on total profit, but total profit can misleading when comparing divisions with disparate investments in earning assets. See appendix E for additional metrics purported to measure economic performance in lieu of accounting performance.

A somewhat analogous conundrum exists when Manager X, assigned to improve a poorly performing unit, is compared to Manager Y, who manages a high-performing unit. On a comparative basis, Manager X's unit may look far worse than Manager Y's unit even though Manager X's job is considerably more difficult. Even measuring the change in performance over time may not resolve the inequities because a 5 percent improvement in performance on some metric in Y's unit may be easier to achieve than a 5 percent improvement on that same metric in X's unit due to disparities in the growth environments of the two units.

These simple examples are only modestly suggestive of the difficulties leaders face when designing control systems for businesses. From a historical perspective, measurements used in controlling businesses have suffered from various shortcomings, such as the following:

1. Backward-looking indicators that do a poor job of predicting future performance, leading to inaccurate forecasts with poor performance prediction.

2. Failure to measure business activities that create failure while directing attention to business activities with little relationship to superior or inferior performance.

3. Failure to measure creation and growth of individual assets in relation to the performance of these assets in creating profits, resulting in asset bloat.

4. Failure to measure innovation, giving rise to intangible assets not reflected on the balance sheet.

5. Failure to measure human resources knowledge, capabilities, and learning that holds the keys to future product development and profitability.

6. Maximization of short-term goals to the detriment of achieving long-term goals.

7. Manipulation by those evaluated using the measurements in ways that make results appear better than actually the case.[7]

Some of the questions leadership must answer when determining how to connect measures to performance include the following:

1. What measures to choose relative to each organizational objective at each organizational level and why?

2. How to measure nonfinancial performance, which can sometimes be subjective?

3. What resources are required to generate the desired information and data?

4. Who are the various parties responsible for each of the results of outcomes measured?

5. At what level and to whom should information and data of various types be communicated?

6. How should measures be connected to incentives in controlling performance at various levels and across various functions?

7. Does the overall system of measures once conceived support the firm's strategy?

8. Are the selected measures internally compatible in that they reinforce as op-

posed to contradicting each other in terms of the behaviors they encourage or discourage?[8]

Ideally, a good performance measurement system allows organizational leadership to distinguish what appears to be happening from what is really happening. It establishes baselines that can be used to measure improvement or lack thereof, make decisions based upon solid evidence, ascertain whether changes have led to improvement, compare performance across units, monitor ongoing process changes, and recognize leaders who are responsible for improving organizational performance.

Hopefully the brief foregoing discussion of some of the basics of measuring business performance provides some idea of the complexities associated with doing it well. These concerns and others have led to substantial disparities in how organizations—often within the same industry—elect to measure performance. That, in turn, led to a need to develop better models for business performance, the topic of the next section.

13.3. The Rise of Business Performance Management

Although only partial lists, the foregoing shortcomings of legacy business performance measurement and the difficulties in arriving at an effective control system provide insight into why many businesses have sought new paradigms for measuring performance that, starting in the 1980s, resulted in what has become known as the **business performance management (BPM)** movement. BPM comprises a set of management and analytic processes supported by technology. The coming of increasingly powerful information systems technology aided this movement as vast amounts of data became available. Warehousing of these data in repositories led to their mining and use for business intelligence purposes. As a result, BPM is frequently misunderstood as requiring ex-

tensive software systems for its use. Sun Tzu, the Chinese philosopher of war, argued that to succeed in battle knowledge of the enemy's and one's own strengths and weaknesses was necessary. Sun Tzu has become oft quoted in business as many have attempted to draw parallels between his writings and business to include collecting data on the firm and competitors, analyzing these data to discern patterns and meaning, and then using this analysis to prompt decision and action.[9]

Because global competition and increasingly rapid technology turnover have led to increased competition and shorter product life cycles, there are parallels between acquiring accurate military intelligence and engaging in maneuver warfare, as Sun Tzu envisioned, and seizing and sustaining competitive advantage in business through business intelligence and nimbleness in responding to dynamic markets. In fact, one definition of business performance is "a state of competitiveness of the organization, reached through a level of efficiency and productivity which ensures a sustainable market presence." Efficiency, in turn, can be defined as achievement of goals with minimal cost.[10] In this environment BPM becomes an integral tool for successful leadership of businesses.

The BPM movement has given rise to various methodologies including *balanced scorecard, Six Sigma, activity-based costing, total quality management, economic value added, integrated strategic measurement,* and *theory of constraints.*[11] Regardless of which BPM methodology is chosen, there are some basic planning considerations in selecting a system.

1. *Goal alignment.*

   A. What are the strategic goal(s) the attainment of which represents organizational business success?

   B. What are the major short-term and mid-term objectives that must be accomplished for goal attainment?

C. How well will this BPM methodology improve performance results?

    i. Consider the firm's core processes. How well does the system capture these processes?

    ii. Do some parts of the business provide intermediate outputs to other parts? If so, does the system provide measures at critical interface points?

2. Assess the *current information and data collection capability* of the firm.

    A. Do the systems exist to capture the necessary information and data?

    B. If not, what are the gaps and how should they be closed?

    C. How much random error is there in the data? Can this random error be measured?

3. *Who are the direct beneficiaries of the system and why?*

    A. Customers?

    B. Top management?

    C. Middle management?

    D. First-line supervisors?

    E. Employees?

4. *What are the information requirements of each of the groups of beneficiaries?*

    A. Decide precisely what information is required at each level and within each function.

    B. Critically analyze these needs and decide:

    i. whether there are too few or many measures in each case.

    ii. how frequently the measures are needed.

    iii. whether some measures should be made optional for parties to receive.

    C. How flexible is the system in providing additional or different information should requirements change?

5. *Once a set of measures is defined for each group of beneficiaries, assess each measure based upon the following criteria. Is each measure:*

    A. Objective and useful?

    B. Understandable to those who will use it and those measured by it?

    C. Controllable even when considering outside influences?

    D. Timely?

    E. Accurate?

    F. Cost effective?

    G. Adequate to motivate the desired behaviors?

    H. Trackable over time with reasonable cost and effort?

6. *Take a step back and look at the dashboard. Does it provide top management with reliable indicators of major areas of concern?*

    A. Effectiveness—outputs realized versus predicted.

    B. Efficiency—inputs consumed to predicted.

    C. Productivity—outputs/inputs.

D. Quality—accuracy, timeliness, customer satisfaction.

E. Innovation—success in creating meaningful change.

F. Quality of work life—strongly related to employee morale.

G. Profitability/return to shareholders.[12]

7. *Make a cost/benefit assessment.*

A. What are the financial consequences if the BPM methodology works as intended?

B. What are the costs of acquiring and implementing the system?

C. What time will be lost due to the need for training?

8. What are the *risks*?

A. Does the milestone plan make sense? What is the risk that the system cannot be implemented as scheduled?

B. What is the risk of disruption of operations?

C. How do we reduce fear and overcome internal change resistance?

D. What do we know about the experiences of other organizations using this system?

E. Will legacy measures that may conflict with the system always be eliminated or negated?

F. What are the adverse, unintended consequences—the second- and third-order effects?

i. How might the system be gamed by employees at various levels and in various functions?

ii. How will we know if the system sends wrong signals that may cause management to make poor decisions?

G. What is the risk associated with vendors being unable to deliver as planned?[13]

As is evident from the above list, there are many considerations involved in making a decision about a BPM system. A system-selection decision affects the entire organization in myriad ways. As with any complex project, even if implementation goes relatively smoothly, leadership can expect a substantial period following implementation to debug problems. Given the cost, time, disruption, and retraining required to select and implement a BPM system, substantial consideration and care need to be given to planning, preparation, implementation, and postimplementation deconfliction of problems.

13.4. The Balanced Scorecard as an Example of a BPM System

BPM systems should be driven by customer requirements and designed to meet real business needs and expectations, promote organization-wide involvement, and foster continuous improvement. Success factors that drive desired outcomes need to be timely, well defined, understandable, and quantified to enable performance assessment and tracking. Emphasis on control measures should be balanced with clear linkages to cause and effect.[14] Given these desirable attributes of BPM systems, the **balanced scorecard** was developed by Robert Kaplan and David Norton in the early 1990s with the goal of creating a more holistic BPM system that addressed the shortcomings of extant systems. The balanced scorecard is characterized by flexibility.[15] Because space considerations do not permit examination of each of the multitude of BPM methodologies, and because the balanced scorecard is the most

Figure 13.2. Balanced Scorecard Framework

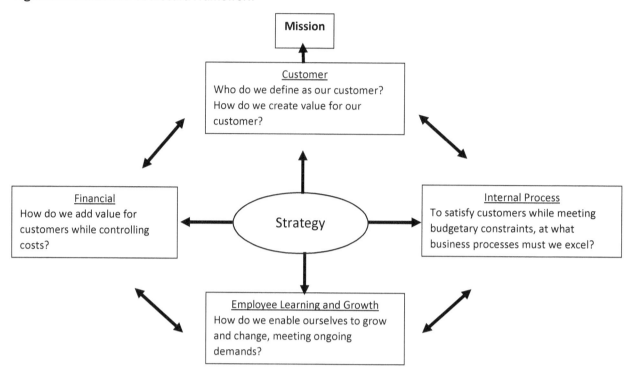

Source: Adapted from http://ventures2b.blogspot.com/2010/11/balanced-scorecard.html (accessed March 6, 2014).

widely used of BPM methodologies, we choose it for more in-depth examination as exemplary of how a BMP system operates.

The balanced scorecard's popularity derives from its more multidimensional perspective that differentiates it from other BPM systems. At its core, the balanced scorecard integrates four categories of activities and their measures, as shown in Figure 13.2.

In this framework, *owners and shareholders* view the business as a financial system that delivers an ROI. Knowing how to add value for customers while controlling costs is essential to delivering the expected ROI to shareholders commensurate with their investment risk. *Clients and customers* see the business as a way to satisfy their needs through its products and services. Knowing precisely who customers are, what their needs are,

and what creates value for them is an essential part of the balanced scorecard. *Leadership and employees* design and implement processes to turn inputs into efficacious outputs efficiently. Knowing what knowledge and skills are required of these members of the organization helps ensure the necessary learning and growth to be able to add value for customers and ownership in the future. The business's *capabilities and capacities* represented by its knowledge, skills, technology, and physical productive infrastructure provide the ways and means to satisfy these three categories of stakeholders. Internal processes must be named to function in ways that create value. At the heart of the entire framework is the *business strategy* or strategies.[16]

One of the most appealing aspects of the balanced scorecard framework is its constant emphasis on business strategy as the driving force

Understanding the Organizational Environment

behind the firm's activities. Although some firms tend to treat BPM systems as simple dashboards of operating performance measures segregated into categories used by managers, the best use of BPM systems is for organization-wide strategic planning with the ability to drill down to operational levels, understand causal relationships among various business activities, and answer the question, "Are we doing things right?"

Strategy is the framework for implementing top leadership's vision for the business and accomplishment of its missions. It exists at different levels ranging from an overarching business strategy in terms of which markets will be served and how to serve those markets to which segments of a particular product or service's value chain to claim and how best to link with other segments of that value chain. Diversified businesses often have more than one macrostrategy that may contain various themes, such as enhanced technology ap-

> ## "I don't fund projects. I fund strategies."
>
> —Sign in CEO's office in a major U.S. corporation

plications, improving speed to market, decreasing response time to customer issues, and so forth. This creates a need to ensure that business strategies are **horizontally integrated**. For example, a public accounting firm may be prohibited by law and regulation from engaging in certain types of business with a client for which it performs the role of independent auditor. As a result, there is a need to coordinate across the attestation and consulting functions within the organization and decide which line of business to pursue.[17]

There is also a need for **vertical integration** such that individual product or service offerings are well linked to the overarching business strategy and activities across all four categories of

Figure 13.3. Strategy Mapping Using the Balanced Scorecard

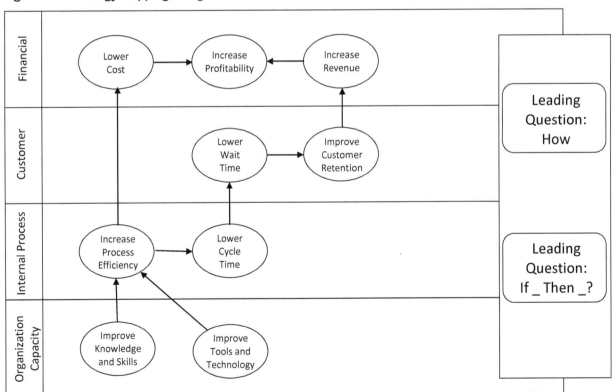

Source: Adapted from *The Institute Way: Simplify Strategic Planning & Management with the Balanced Scorecard,* http://balancedscorecard.org/BSCResources/AbouttheBalancedScorecard/tabid/55/Default.aspx (accessed March 6, 2014).

activities—customer, employee, internal process, and financial—in a bottom-up manner. Given the complexity of many businesses this is a nontrivial exercise requiring careful thought and planning. A very useful tool for dealing with the task of vertical integration to ensure strategic congruence is a **strategy map** as shown in Figure 13.3.

In the example shown in Figure 13.3, knowledge and physical and technology capacities are changed to increase process efficiency, which results in lower cycle time and lower costs. Lower cycle time means less waiting time for customers, improving customer retention. Greater customer retention, in turn, leads to higher revenues, which, along with the lower costs, result in higher profits and return to shareholders. One very beneficial aspect of selecting a balanced scorecard system is that it strongly encourages organizations to examine existing programs, services, and processes to answer questions such as, "Are we offering the right services?" "Are our processes effective and efficient?" and "Are we operating under control?"

In businesses lacking BPM systems that force a strategic focus, for operating management there is often a substantial disconnect between operational decision and the firm's strategic plan because of misalignment between measures and strategy. One benefit of BPM systems such as the balanced scorecard is that they connect critical success factors at the strategic level to operating decisions. This can lead to people being busy in activities that lead to few measurable results in accomplishing the important end states desired by the business.[18]

This importance of maintaining a strategic focus illustrates what the CEO in the box on the left meant by saying that capital expenditures were based upon strategy, not just project analysis. Often intrafirm competition for limited CAPEX funds involves various internal stakeholders presenting analyses based upon forecast ROI against some

hurdle rate that must be exceeded as a prerequisite for project approval. If the ROI exceeds the hurdle rate and is preferable to other projects based upon subjective criteria, then the project may be approved. Along the way, this competition of CAPEX can result in inflated assumptions such that, on average, the firm's portfolio of CAPEX projects fails to return the expected average ROI, a problem once related to one of the coauthors by the CFO of a major European telecommunications company. Balanced scorecard BPM systems help to mitigate such concerns and provide a decision criterion for CAPEX project selection based upon the extent to which proposed projects support the firm's strategy. One implication from this is with a balanced scorecard BPM system measures are appropriately *ways* to arrive at decisions and *not ends.*

13.5. Basic Considerations in Building a Performance Measurement System

Developing a successful BPM system requires consideration of several attributes. BPM systems should be driven by customer requirements, designed to meet real customer needs and expectations. Key success factors that drive the desired results should be clearly defined in terms of cause and effect vertically and horizontally, expressed in ways that are measurable in ways that are understandable to users and not open to multiple interpretations. Measures should be balanced with clear emphasis. The system should provide for timely feedback that allows for rapid intervention and should promote firm-wide involvement in continuously improving operations.[19]

We again use the balanced scorecard as an example of building a BPM system, in part because it is the most popular BPM system with an adoption rate of approximately 40 percent among Fortune 1000 companies.[20] There are nine specific steps involved in its implementation and subsequent assessment as shown in Figure 13.4.

Figure 13.4. Nine Steps in Building a Balanced Scorecard BPM System

It is important to first note the circularity of Figure 13.4. Building a BPM system is a journey, not a destination, requiring continuous evaluation of whether the system and its measures are performing as intended. Given the increasingly dynamic nature of the business environment and shortening of product life cycles, complacency on the part of leadership once a BPM system is in place is hazardous. This raises an important point. Building a BPM system is a pervasive project that first and foremost requires a total commitment by top leadership. Absent this total commitment success is unlikely.

The first six steps in Figure 13.4 are related to building and implementing a balanced scorecard system beginning with an "assessment of the organization's foundations, core beliefs, market opportunities, financial position, short- and long-term goals, and an understanding of what satisfies customers."[21] **Step 1** includes an analysis of the business's strengths, weaknesses, opportunities, and threats (**SWOT analysis**) and the assumptions that underlie all of the foregoing. At this juncture, a BPM team is formed with a *champion* appointed to lead the team. It is best if the champion is some highly respected top leader who has access to the other top leaders of the business in order to break down barriers created by change resistance, resource issues, and other obstacles.

Step 2 is the development of the *overarching business strategy*. **Step 3** entails the decomposition of this strategy to reach organizational

Organizational Control and Measurement

Figure 13.5. Example of Balanced Scorecard

Sourcing & Distribution Pathway		Measurement	Target	Initiative	Budget
Financial Profitability / Revenue Growth		• Operating Income • Sales vs. Last Yr	• 20% Increase • 12% Increase	• Likes Program	$xxx

Customer Product Quality / Shopping Experience		• Return Rate
		  - Quality
		  - Other
		• Customer Loyalty
		  - Ever Active %
		  - # units
			• Reduce by 50% each yr
			
			• 60%
			• 2.4 units
				• Quality management
				• Customer loyalty
					$xxx
					$xxx

Internal "A" Class Factories / Line Plan Management		• % of Merchandise from "A" factories • Items in-Stock vs Plan	• 70% by year 3 • 85%	• Corporate Factory Development Program	$xxx
Learning Factory Relationship Skills / Merchandise Buying/Planning Skills		• % of Strategic Skills Available	• Yr 1 50% Yr 3 75% Yr 5 90%	• Strategic Skills plan • Merchants Desktop	$xxx $xxx

Source: Adapted from http://help.sap.com/static/saphelp_sem60/de/7c/546637a04c2367e10000009b38f8cf/Image94.gif (accessed February 16, 2015).

goals (ends) into objectives that become the basic building blocks of the strategy. **Step 4** involves creating a strategic map for the entire business to connect objectives by identifying causal linkages using if-then logic. **Step 5** deals with the creation of measures to track both strategic and operational outcomes from the perspectives of both external and internal stakeholders. Measures must be developed for each objective developed in step 3 using the strategic map created in step 4. Properly done, this is a significant task because it is far more difficult to develop a few good measures than lots of inferior ones. A common mistake is to rush to judgment and use existing measures rather than putting thought into which measures actually best capture the desired outcomes and result in fewest adverse second- and third-order effects.

Measure selection can be aided by the use of three models. The **logic model** explores associa-tions among four types of performance measures: (1) inputs (resources used), (2) processes (how resources are transformed to produce outputs), (3) outputs (what is produced), and (4) outcomes (how effective the outputs are in accomplishing objectives). The **process flow model** applies flowcharting to identify critical activities and measures that capture them. This model also serves to surface aspects of activities that can be made more efficient and frequently gives rise to new initiatives. **Causal analysis** begins with the desired results and works backward to identify causes and effects of performance. Causal analysis is particularly useful in developing leading indicators of future performance.

Step 6 identifies new initiatives required to achieve the objectives identified in step 3. Such initiatives tend to be more strategic if identified subsequent to steps 1–5 than earlier in the balanced scorecard design process.[22] Step 6 completes the design phase of the BPM system process, so what does a completed scorecard look like? Figure 13.5 shows one example of a division-level scorecard for one division of a retail goods manufacturer.

Steps 7–9 relate to implementing the balanced scorecard. **Step 7** involves creating the information systems necessary to automate and support the BPM system. Information systems issues can range from operating software to spreadsheets to databases to full data warehouses designed to pull together data from disparate applications to create an integrated data source. **Step 8** entails "cascading" the scorecard for the entire business down through subordinate organizational units to teams and even individuals. This requires translating the scorecard for the business into scorecards for business units, divisions, departments, and support units in a manner such that all scorecards are aligned. **Step 9** is evaluation of the strategic success of the business in order to test the validity of assumptions that underlie the strategy and making strategic adjustments as necessary. There are five components to this step: (1) ensuring that organization learning and knowledge is incorporated into planning, (2) making adjustments to existing programs, (3) adding new programs as necessary, (4) eliminating programs that are not cost effective or meeting customer needs, and (5) linking planning to budgets.[23]

Developing and implementing a BPM system is insufficient to ensure success. Leadership throughout the organization is required to ensure that it does not go back to business as usual. There are some specific actions leaders can take to make proper use of a BPM system such as the balanced scorecard. First, the importance of the system and how it will be used must be clearly communicated throughout the organization, and this importance must be continually emphasized. New members joining the organization subsequent to its implementation must be educated

about it and its use. Second, executive meetings can be organized around the elements of the corporate strategy to ensure that strategic goals and objectives remain at the forefront of thinking about decisions. Third, well-defined roles can be assigned to key personnel making them "owners" of specific performance measures. Fourth, teams can be assigned to monitor strategic themes to assess how these themes are playing out. Fifth, the BPM system can be used to drive budgeting and cost control. Sixth, extrinsic and intrinsic rewards should be carefully linked to the measures.[24]

13.6. When Measures Go Wrong

Measures are an indispensable component of business control, but the wrong measures, inaccurate measures, and measures that are linked to incentives in ways that give rise to opportunistic behaviors can be very dysfunctional and even destructive. The history of business is replete with examples of measures gone wrong. Consider the following example experienced by one of the co-authors in which skewed measures led a bank to shift its strategy in a direction that led to reduced profitability and top leadership encouraging lower-level managers to engage in riskier activities some were inadequately prepared to handle.

In the middle 1970s, a bank in a large city hired a new CFO from a public accounting firm who decided to implement a responsibility center accounting system. The announced strategy was to make managers of the bank's branches that handled retail and light commercial business more responsible for performance by turning each branch into a profit center. Unknown to senior leadership, however, there were flaws in the measurement process that caused major dysfunctions at both the strategic and operational levels. The bank's branches could be roughly divided into two categories, those focused on commercial business and those focused on retail. The bank had been heavily slanted toward retail expansion, and most of the retail branches were newer. Due to various unforeseen flaws in measuring and assigning costs, the system was skewed such that the older, more commercially focused branches appeared more profitable than the retail ones. Over time this resulted in a top-level decision to make a strategic shift toward attracting light commercial business rather than retail business, but many branch managers lacked adequate lending skills to successfully propagate this type of business. Further, the bank did not provide the requisite training to improve these skills even though performance evaluations—and therefore ultimately compensation—were tied to a significant extent to loan production. Eventually, after 2 years of charging off bad loans, declining overall profits, and several managers being fired for poor lending performance, the flaws were finally discovered with the result that the measurement system was scrapped. The CFO departed, but the damage was significant, in terms of lost profits, human cost of job loss, and lower morale for those who remained.

The foregoing example is illustrative of how easy it is for management to slip into a trance of believing numbers without questioning the underlying assumptions that go into creating the numbers. This fixation on measures seems to be consistent across various organizational domains, from banking, to industrial organizations, to professional services firms, to even research universities. People seem to gravitate toward summary measures, and the phrase "the bottom line" has become pervasive in business conversation. Too few businesses give due consideration to the potential adverse second- and third-order effects that can arise from implementing measures and then comfortably concluding that the journey is over.

Not only is there a proclivity to fixate on measures, frequently there is also a love for lots of measures—so many, in fact, that the numbers themselves can undermine the fundamental intent behind measuring and holding people accountable for measures. For example, a bank in which one of the coauthors worked had a standard commercial loan analysis process that produced approximately three dozen ratios from the financial statements for each corporate borrower. The difficulty with so many ratios is that human cognition is inadequate to permit their mental processing. Lens model studies conducted by researchers in the 1970s found that, on average, commercial loan officers only used a handful of ratios in their decision making no matter how many ratios were provided. The same phenomenon is observed in business schools that routinely have students complete teaching evaluation forms on instructors containing as many as twenty questions and then normally only focus on one to three of these questions. Consider the following quote in discussing tying measures to individual performances:

> Having too many measures or areas of performance for which individuals must maintain can become an overload and decrease the chances that goals are attained, therefore no more than six or seven goals that represent the greatest potential for positive change in organizational performance should be chosen at any given time to drive maximum performance. Targets are applied to each specific objective to indicate success, each target is then given a specific weight measure with respect to its significance level in an encompassing view of all targets or objectives. This scorekeeping approach can be applied to compensation or incentive programs in different ways.[25]

One difficulty is that "decision-making based upon measurement data is fraught with individual biases."[26] Decision makers suffer from **bounded rationality** in which decisions are often made that make little sense from the perspective of **rational utility theory**. Prospect theory attempts to explain this phenomenon, in part by considering how de-

Understanding the Organizational Environment

cisions are *framed.* Consider, for example, CAPEX projects that require additional investments at various milestones. Decision makers have a tendency to continue to fund unsuccessful projects after it is apparent from a rational perspective funding should be discontinued because they *anchor on sunk costs* rather than making rational expected-value judgments. One retired executive who requests anonymity tells the story of bringing a new technology developed outside his Fortune 50 company to the attention of senior management. The technology could have been purchased for $3 million at the time, but senior management declined because the company had just spent $30 million upgrading its facilities for manufacturing an older technology that the new technology would have made obsolescent. Several years later the company did purchase that same technology from the same developers for $28 million, paying $25 million more because they had framed their decision to decline the technology in light of the $30 million just sunk into a CAPEX project.

Business environments often do not change on an orderly basis. Instead, as the just-mentioned example indicates, in a time when technology turnover is rapid and growing more so, the business environment can shift radically. Sometimes these shifts, though profound, can be subtle enough that old strategies and the measures connected to them are obviated.[27] In the coauthors' opinions, one of the best aspects of a BPM system such as the balanced scorecard is the discipline that goes into creating and assessing measures, ensuring linkages between strategy and strategic goals to operations and operational objectives. As previously mentioned, the circular nature of the development and implementation process means maintenance of the right set of measures is continuous, not a one-time event, and focuses on the right questions: "Are we achieving the desired strategic results?" and "Are our measures performing as intended?"

13.7. Tying Incentives to Measures

Tying incentives to measures is a necessity in order to encourage decision makers to act in ways that top leadership desires and promote organizational well-being.[28] However, as soon as measures are linked to incentives, a **moral hazard** emerges in that individuals whose performances are measured have reasons to attempt to game the measures through ways such as misreporting results and making decisions that benefit themselves but are suboptimal for the organization. Once embedded, dysfunctional behaviors are not always easy to discern. As a result, both measures and

> **"When organizations tie incentives to project measures, people often report the data inaccurately to meet the incentives."**
>
> —David P. Quinn

their linkages to compensation must be carefully thought out prior to implementation. Leadership at all levels needs to engage in what-if thinking, imagining how those held responsible for measures through incentive arrangements might behave in undesirable ways. Once these possible misbehaviors have been identified, ways of mitigating them should be developed. This may involve altering the incentives arrangements, having internal auditors periodically check to ensure they are not occurring, and announcing in advance that such behaviors are contrary to the organization's ethical standards, followed by appropriate sanctions for violations.

A BPM system such as the balanced scorecard is likely as close to ideal as possible for tying incentives to performance in many businesses, but it is still a complex task requiring careful thought and an understanding of human behav-

255

ior. The problem may become particularly acute when both financial and nonfinancial measures are involved. Research based upon agency theory suggests that it is important that scorecard measures not be easily manipulated by those being measured. For example, depending upon the agent's time horizon, an agent whose compensation is predicated upon current profits may benefit from shifting emphasis from future profits achieved through higher customer satisfaction to current profits even if this shifting results in lower customer satisfaction and future profits. Moreover, despite the balanced scorecard's emphasis on leadership understanding and measuring "the various ways in which operational activities interact to create value, these multiple interactions can complicate the use of nonfinancial measures in compensation contracts."[29]

One reason that balanced scorecard is arguably superior to more traditional performance measurement systems is that when a measure is examined in isolation of other measures, management may unjustly attribute good or bad performance to individuals. Suppose, for example, a measure such as effort variance is used to assessment project management, and less effort was expended than budgeted. Should project management be rewarded for this outcome? Many might be tempted to answer yes, but consider the following potential reasons for the favorable variance. Engineers may have padded their estimates. Estimation parameters may have been incorrect. The scope of the project may have been reduced but the effort estimates not updated. Some necessary steps may have been skipped to the future detriment of the project performance. Hours worked may not have been recorded properly, one or more requirements may have been missed, and poor-quality work could have been performed in order the meet a deadline. Obviously, absent linkages to other performance measures it would be easy to misinterpret a favorable variance as a measure indicating commendable management

performance. One measure simply does not provide enough insight.[30]

One measures/incentives issue that can cause problems is the tendency of some individuals to *guard knowledge* as a means of maintaining positions of intellectual superiority over those peers perceived as potential competitors for promotion and thus greater rewards. In one sense, BPM systems attempt to specify, simplify, and quantify interactions of various systems components. A part of these interactions relates to knowledge creation and sharing, but these are difficult activities to measure. Knowledge guarding causes a breakdown in the ability of BPM systems to promote knowledge creation and diffusion in businesses.[31]

One of the most insidious problems involving tying incentives to measures is that of **diminishing marginal incentives**. Take cost-reduction programs, for example. Such programs are often characterized by an inverted U-shaped function. As programs gain momentum the amount of cost savings initially increases, but as time goes on it becomes more and more difficult to save the next marginal dollar of costs. A simple analogy of picking apples from a tree illustrates this phenomenon. The low-hanging fruit is easily picked, but climbing the tree higher and higher to pick additional fruit requires more and more effort in return for the fruit picked. Incentive systems that fail to consider this difficulty begin to lose their potency to motivate cost savings. Another way to illustrate diminishing marginal incentives is captured in the following quote: "Based upon the organizational learning that occurs from doing projects, performance that once provided a bonus for people will no longer result in a bonus as the organization adjusts process performance measures."[32]

Finally, research suggests nonmonetary incentives should not be overlooked when tying incentives to business control systems.[33] Employ-

Understanding the Organizational Environment

ees often appreciate recognition of their performance as much or more than relatively modest financial rewards. Plaques that line the office walls of managers are constant reminders to the managers and those who visit of past performance and may have a far more lasting motivational influence on future performance than one-time incentives. Nonfinancial incentives are best not used in lieu of financial incentives but in conjunction with them. Care should be taken not to create a culture in which organizational members believe that the organization hands out nonfinancial rewards for only modestly incremental performances nor a belief that leadership uses nonfinancial incentives in an effort to avoid paying for financial incentives.

13.8. More on the Role of Leadership in Monitoring and Assessing Performance

Control really begins with leadership because it is leaders who impose the controls designed to shape behaviors of organizational members. Because it is good leaders who propagate good controls, developing good leaders is therefore a prerequisite for good controls. Sadly, many organizations worry more about their control systems than they worry about developing leaders capable of conceiving, implementing, and monitoring good controls. Worse yet, when leadership training is conducted it often does not include any discussion of how leadership and controls relate to one another. Good controls are unlikely to function well under poor leadership, and good leaders encumbered by dysfunctional controls will similarly struggle. To see the need for good alignment of leadership and controls, consider the following real-world anecdote.

A large corporation decided to perform a total overhaul of the manufacture of one of its heavy equipment parts divisions including a switch to state-of-the-art, just-in-time (JIT) manufacturing with inventory minimization as one principal goal.

Despite extensive training designed to instill a JIT philosophy in supervisors, inventory continued to accumulate at various points in assembly lines contrary to plant-level leaders' admonitions to do otherwise. After investigation it was found that the legacy corporate accounting system based upon standard costing was still sending cost-variance reports to supervisors, who were continuing to do as they always had done—maximize their labor efficiency by producing as much as they could in as short a time as possible.

Although the foregoing example demonstrates the disconnect between leadership's strategy and control systems and measures that run counter to that strategy, the answer in that case was simple enough—stop sending labor efficiency variance reports to line supervisors. In some cases, however, disconnects are far more insidious and difficult to discern before serious damage occurs. Many leadership programs fail to consider the role of measures when discussing leadership and organizational controls. Often conducted by trainers whose expertise lies in such activities as coaching, leadership development is frequently regarded de facto as a soft-skills activity divorced from organizational control systems and their embedded measures. Leadership training is often one size fits all and lacks the control-problem context of firm- and industry-specific control issues. Reflection is frequently decoupled from the real work leaders perform, with participants retaining only about 10 percent of the knowledge to which they have been exposed. In training in which leaders become active in dealing with actual real-world problems similar to those they face in the workplace, retention rises to approximately 67 percent.

In some business organizations it is somewhat taboo to speak openly about control issues, giving rise to a failure to address the root causes of these problems. This creates a culture in which organization members fear *the execution of the messenger who brings the king bad news.* A somewhat

Organizational Control and Measurement

less malevolent form of this culture grows when top leaders maintain, "I don't want to hear about problems. I only want to hear solutions." Although it is often a good idea to suggest a solution when presenting the boss with a problem, sometimes complex problems are simply beyond the ability of the organizational member to conceive. Such cultures are unfortunate because behavioral change is often only possible if deep, below-the-surface thoughts and assumptions can be surfaced and dealt with. Astute leadership recognizes the need for open dialogue vertically in the organization when measures aren't working as intended.

Finally, many leadership development programs themselves fail because they neglect to measure their results. Too often instruction begins and ends with participant feedback. Trainers learn to game outcomes in order to make it appear as if behaviors are really going to change. Pre- and posttest measurement using such techniques as 360-degree performance evaluations prior to and 1 year following leadership development training may help provide better estimates of what has been retained and placed into practice. Other longer-term measurement involves tracking leadership training attended, what that training involved, and career progression to determine if leadership training actually correlates in some way to further career progression.[34]

13.9. Concluding Thoughts about Measurement and Control

In the final analysis, *control is first and foremost about engaged leadership.*[35] It is a myth that measurement alone will make the desired difference. Astute leadership knows that organizational controls and the measures used to make them effective need to be aligned with strategy and operations, encouraging desired behaviors and minimizing unforeseen, adverse consequences. Leaders need to understand desired outcomes at various levels, assess how best to measure ac-

tivities that generate these outcomes, gauge the behavioral responses of organization members to potential measures anticipating adverse second- and third-order effects, and then implement and monitor controls. They also need to decide on a set of controls that is broad enough to capture performance without overloading members with data.[36] But who in the organization is specifically charged with ensuring that these leadership functions take place across the entire business? Often the answer is no one. One of the coauthors tells the following story:

> Over many years I've conducted numerous training sessions for large numbers of financial executives. One of my favorite questions to ask at the beginning of each session is, "Who is the chief measurement officer at your firm?" This usually draws quizzical looks but no responses. Some brave soul eventually asks, "What exactly does a chief measurement officer do?" I respond with, "If you had one, the chief measurement officer would be responsible for examining control systems and their associated measures and ensuring that they align strategy and operations, result in desired behaviors, and are as devoid of unforeseen, adverse second- and third-order consequences as possible." I then ask, "If your organization appointed someone the additional duty as chief measurement officer, who would be assigned that function?" After a few moments of reflection one will usually reply, "I guess that would be me." The point is that often no one performs the function of deconflicting control measures prior to their implementation.

CHAPTER 14

Teams and Teamwork

> "What we need to do is learn to work in the system,
> by which I mean that everybody, every team, every platform,
> every division; every component is there not for individual
> competitive profit or recognition, but for contribution
> to the system as a whole on a win-win basis."
>
> —W. Edward Deming

Teams of one sort or another are involved with nearly every aspect of our lives. Although we often rely on teams to help us achieve our personal and professional goals, they can become burdensome when functionally limited. Most business professionals have been part of teams that underachieved or required an inordinate amount of time and effort to achieve their goal and objectives. Sometimes we're required to participate on a team we'd prefer not to be part of but find it difficult to decline for various reasons. Teams can be highly useful or ineffective and wasteful. Some teams are prestigious and some carry the stigma of being a necessary evil. As a business professional, you need to be able to assess which teams are important, which are unimportant and formed simply for purposes of appearance, whether or not team size and composition are appropriate to the team's mission, whether the team has the necessary power and resources to accomplish its mission, and whether or not it has the support of organizational leadership.

Creating and managing teams can be challenging for leaders. What are the rules and parameters under which the team should operate? How much conflict among team members is healthy? When should the leader intervene if the team is not making demonstrable progress toward mission accomplishment, and when should the leaders back off and allow the team to learn from its mistakes? What metrics should be used to measure team and individual performance? If team membership is drawn from organizations other than those you lead, how much of their subordinates' time can you expect other leaders to dedicate to your team? Determining when and why to create a team and how to select its members can be difficult. Despite these challenges, teams are a necessary aspect of business life and can sometimes result in outcomes superior to those possible with people acting individually.

14.1. When to Team and When Not to Team

One of the first questions that leaders should ask before creating a team is whether a team is the best vehicle for mission accomplishment. Consider the following anecdotes.

> Team Anecdote 1: A student team was visiting several companies in various cities.

During one company visit the team had difficulty gaining access to the building due to construction. Repeatedly, team members discussed options and selected a new course of action only to still be frustrated in their attempts to enter the building. Finally, an instructor accompanying the team intervened and obtained a copy of the team's instructions. After examining it he observed, "We're in the wrong place."

Team Anecdote 2: A team of three attorneys and two valuation experts was holding its first meeting to formulate a strategy for defending a client in a civil action involving allegations of fraud. Two of the attorneys, both partners, were late arriving at the meeting, so the law associate began

"The only real purpose of a team is for the strengths of the whole to offset the weaknesses of the individual."

—Anonymous

the meeting. The junior partner arrived 20 minutes later, necessitating a reiteration of what had already been said. The senior partner arrived even later and began a recitation of his beliefs about the case without regard to what had already been discovered. Both the junior partner and associate declined to intercede and inform the senior partner that the points he was raising had already been addressed. Moreover, it was obvious that neither of the law partners had reviewed the case facts prior to the meeting. Eventually, time ran out and the meeting ended without a clear vision of how to proceed or a well-defined strategy.

Team Anecdote 3: A team of faculty members teaching in an MBA program core were participating in an outdoor team-building exercise. The idea behind the exercise was to develop a sense of teamwork among the participants. One particular event required participants to pass each other through a web of rope one at a time without touching the ropes. The team repeatedly failed to accomplish this because during each attempt several of the participants insisted upon giving different directions. The day ended in frustration.

The foregoing anecdotes surface several questions: (1) When do circumstances indicate teams are preferable to individuals in problem solving? (2) How can the use of a team approach detract from mission accomplishment? (3) When teams are appropriate but not well managed, what are the implications for the use of teams in the future? In anecdote 1, the task at hand was actually complicated by taking a team approach that masked the underlying problem—the team being in the wrong place. Getting people to the right place is the task of one detail-oriented leader, not a team. In anecdote 2, a team was called for because of the complex interplay of legal and financial issues, but the poor handling of the team interactions by the senior law partner resulted in a poor outcome. In anecdote 3, because the purpose for the outdoor exercise was team building, the implicit assumption was that each event required a team approach. A better approach would have been for the team to reach the conclusion that some events required electing a team leader for that event, deciding upon a strategy, and then following the leader's instructions during the execution phase.

Often teamwork results in better outcomes than individual, uncoordinated efforts, but teams are not always preferable. The Federal Aviation Administration's training program states that, "Despite the potential contributions of teams, it must be realized that not all tasks are suitable for team use. Teams should be used only when there is a 'fit' between the task and the strengths of a team."[1] An example of team-preferred situations is complex problem solving requiring different skill sets, knowledge bases, and/or high levels of creativity. Another example is when achieving the desired objective requires significant and continuous interactions with other teams such that common skill sets enable improved communication across the different teams.

Conversely, individuals generally outperform teams with routine, straightforward tasks and when deadlines are tight. Assigning tasks to teams rather than individuals can slow productivity when the individuals possess the requisite subject matter expertise and information necessary to make informed decisions and execute tasks. Teams require time to learn to work together and reach agreement, so teams are sometimes contraindicated in situations when time and resources are limited. Using teams can also result in lower employee morale if team decisions are not supported by management.[2] Consider the following anecdote supplied by a coauthor:

> Once I was assigned to cochair a large team with the mission of developing a plan for restructuring and downsizing a large organization. The team was sequestered offsite and given guidance by the chief executive to come up with the best plan for reorganization. The situation was fraught with internal politics, with senior officials fighting to retain their human and other assets. Knowing the delicate nature of the climate and culture, the team used a sophisticated methodology designed to ensure both efficacy and fairness in its planning. Periodic briefings were held for senior officials to keep them informed. Based on guidance from the chief executive, these briefings were tense at times, as senior officials learned that parts of their units would be recommended for restructuring. Despite the political pressure, after weeks of work the team delivered a set of comprehensive recommendations that were derived fairly and served the best interests of the organization. Unfortunately, the chief executive, succumbing to lobbying from various senior officials, proceeded to strike many of the recommendations line by line, effectively destroying the sense of fairness in the restructuring and allowing suboptimal retention of parts of the organization while gutting others whose bosses had less political power. The results were a plan in shambles and a demoralized team. In the end, the attitude of team was, "All the chief executive did was use us for cover. The end product was nothing but the work of the chief executive."

In general, teams often provide significant benefits in addition to being able to complete a greater breadth and scope of work at a finer level of detail than a group of individuals. Organizations with high-functioning teams often have lower employee-turnover rates because employees feel a greater sense of accomplishment and are often more enthusiastic about assigned tasks when working in teams. A team also helps the organization as a whole in that the strengths each individual brings are leveraged to help to support team members who are not as strong in a particular area of expertise.[3] Because teams have members from various functional areas and subunits, the team's combined problem-solving ability is greater. This enables the company as a whole to be more nimble when facing new challenges. Some firms have very flat organizational structures by design and intentionally hire generalists who operate in teams with a minimal amount of formal management oversight. This self-direction helps foster an environment of creativity and innovation.[4]

14.2. Common Misuses and Fallacies Involving Teams

As suggested in the first anecdote in the preceding section, teams are not the panacea for all organizational ills, but one might well draw the conclusion that they are if looking only at their frequent use. In today's business world teams are a vital and necessary component for business success, and leading business schools have gone to great lengths to pace students in teams to provide teamwork experience. Amidst all the emphasis on teamwork, however, businesses—and, in the interest of candor business schools as well—often provide little guidance about when and how to use and not use teams. Some common misuses of teams include the following:

1. *Hiding from problems.* It is common for management to dodge or postpone dealing with a sensitive problem by assigning it to a committee.

2. *Diffusing the blame.* Teams can provide management with political cover by allowing bosses to stipulate that the solution, albeit unpopular, was the product of a team and not the boss. It is difficult to find courageous leadership in this practice.

3. *Giving the appearance of everyone having a voice.* This tactic is frequently used in an effort to provide the feeling that all subunits have had representation in a decision. One difficulty with this misuse is loading teams with too many members and members who have little substantive contribution.

4. *Offloading undesirable work.* This occurs when mundane, undesirable tasks are assigned to teams because no one in a position of power wants to take time away from their regular duties to undertake the tasks.[5] One potential downside of this practice is that savvy team members may feel their participation as a team member is a negative signal about how their value to the organization is perceived by more senior leadership.

Although teams often have the potential to achieve a great deal more than their members individually, teams often fail to accomplish their missions for a number of reasons. One of the most common mistakes with respect to team composition is the assumption that more is better. Businesses often use the term **full-time equivalent (FTE)** to represent the amount of work that can be completed by one full-time staff person. For example, if a particular job requires 160 hours of effort it would take one FTE four weeks at 40 hours per week to complete this project. This is sometimes also referred to as a "man-month" or the amount of work a single person can do in a single month.[6] A problem occurs when leadership interprets this to mean that if one person can do the work in 160 hours, then two people can do the work in only 80 hours, and so forth. This assumption of a linear relationship frequently does not hold, however, when teams are involved because teams take time to mesh.

Consider the case of roofing a new home: expanding the roofing crew from one to two may not cut the amount of time required to do the job from 160 to 80 hours. It may even take less time because of synergies. However, at some point the addition of workers results in diminishing returns. In the software industry this concept is known as **Brooks's law**, wherein adding manpower to a late software project makes it even later.[7] In professional services firms the challenge is often more centered on managing and communicating with an ever-growing number of team members. Larger teams also have a higher probability some individual team members will not contribute to the overall success of the team. The larger the team, the easier it is to hide from work.

One potential fallacy about teams is the idea that regular turnover of team members is beneficial. Although a new team member can bring new ideas and perspectives, research indicates that the longer a team works together the better it performs. Another fallacy is that the best teams avoid conflict. When managed appropriately, conflict can be healthy for a team in forcing members to think through ideas, generate more thorough recommendations, and create a feeling of empowerment among team members by signaling their input is valued even if not always implemented. Another caution about using teams involves negotiations. Negotiations require strong leadership, and leaders often need to be both somewhat flexible and at other times firm during negotiations. Having a team of people as opposed to a team leader integrally involved in negotiations can result in mixed messages being sent that undermine the power of the negotiator arriving at agreements.[8]

One common misuse of teams is to provide political cover for decisions for senior officials after a decision has already been made. The intent is to defuse responsibility for unpopular decisions. Such was the case when the president of a small college decided to change the basis for credit hours, thereby disrupting the entire curriculum, class schedules, and degree requirements in every academic department. Failing to adequately convince the faculty that the benefit exceeded the cost of this decision, the president fell back upon appointing a team to study the issue and make a recommendation. By then, however, everyone knew of the president's intent and felt the team was simply a ruse. In the end, the political pressure became so great that the president was forced to call a faculty vote wherein his proposal was voted down. Then, against all reason, he implemented it anyway. By then, he had done more damage to his credibility and incurred more ill will than if he had simply made the decision unilaterally in the first place.

Teams also are sometimes used in an effort to convey the impression a solution to a problem is forthcoming when, in fact, no solution is intended,

in the hope the issue will die of natural causes. The oft-used statement by officials, "I've appointed a blue-ribbon committee to examine the issue and come up with a solution," is frequently nothing but a ruse for deferring a decision that will be unpopular with some constituency regardless of the result. When teams are used solely as ruses for not dealing with problems forthrightly, the results can be very demoralizing for team members. Consider the following anecdote supplied by a coauthor:

> **"The way a team plays as a whole determines its success. You may have the greatest bunch of individual stars in the world, but if they don't play together, the club won't be worth a dime."**
>
> —George Herman "Babe" Ruth

Years ago, my father-in-law was president of the state bankers association in a state struggling with revising laws capping interest rates on loans at arbitrarily low levels. There were powerful constituencies on both sides of the issue. The governor appointed a very heterogeneous "blue-ribbon committee" chaired by my father-in-law to study the problem and make recommendations. Because of its heterogeneity the governor never expected the team to be successful. To the governor's amazement and disappointment, after months of work, the committee accomplished its ostensible mission of reaching a compromise solution. When my father-in-law presented the committee's recommendations to the governor, he read the executive summary and then tossed the report in his wastebasket, saying, "It was never my intention to change interest-rate laws." The entire effort had been nothing but a ruse to avoid making a decision that would offend one political constituency or another.

Misuse of teams as illustrated in the foregoing examples not only undermines the credibility of the officials appointing teams but also makes organization members suspicious about serving on teams when significant political implications are present. Some upcoming, savvy leaders will sense when team efforts are likely to end in the political abyss and navigate deftly to avoid those teams as both a waste of time and having some career risk. For leaders, recognizing that teams are not the solution to every problem and avoiding some of the common misperceptions and misuses of teamwork can be very beneficial for the organization. In circumstances where teams are indicated, however, to be successful steps need to be taken proactively to manage team performance. A starting point is a sound knowledge of some basics of team composition and dynamics.

14.3. Some Thoughts about Team Mission, Composition, and Dynamics for Team Sponsors

Teams need a clear understanding of their **mission** and what end state constitutes its successful accomplishment. The ends/way/means model is a good starting point. Team sponsors creating teams need to clearly understand and communicate the purpose of the team to its members. As basic as this seems, such understanding does not always exist. Too often what ensues is something as follows:

Subordinate leader: "We've had a surge in customer complaints recently. I don't know the reasons, but we'd better get the problem fixed or the VP will be on our backs about it."

Leader: "Ok, go ahead and form a team to look into the problem."

What's the mission? Does "look into" it mean discover the general nature of the problem and re-

port back, or discover the specific causes of the complaint and fix them? The answer could well influence the team's charter, its size and composition, its power to exert authority, and the non-human resources required for success, such as access to information and technology. If the mission is merely to uncover the general nature of the problem, is a team the best way to accomplish that mission? If the problem results from product defects, the implications for team composition might be quite different than if the problem results from misaligned new incentives. If the team is supposed to fix the problem, what authorities and resources are necessary? The import is that, when creating teams, **team sponsors** need to specify the desired end state, create a team capable of attaining that end state, and resource it with the appropriate means to achieve its mission, to include imbuing it with the necessary authority to accomplish that mission.

Once the team mission is established, team members need to be selected based on the skills they bring to the team, with careful attention to the roles they will serve. For example, if working on a possible merger of two companies, a team may need members who are industry, financial, or legal experts that specialize in mergers and acquisitions activity. Some team members may also be specialists in important functional areas such as project management, human resources, or information technology but may not possess merger and acquisition experience. This may require time and resources necessary to educate some team members unfamiliar with the mission context.

After the team members have been selected and roles assigned, teams must be given the authority necessary to achieve the team's goals and objectives. One common method of empowering a team is to have the project sponsor notify the people and/or departments that will most likely be impacted that a team has been formed with the approval of senior leadership and that the team's efforts should be supported. Scope limitations and operating boundaries should also be defined. One of the most difficult team problems can arise when the team sponsor does not control the resources or access to information necessary for a team to accomplish its mission. Especially with projects spanning organizational boundaries that involve sensitivities, outsiders may have incentives to impede team progress or steer its actions by providing selective or notional cooperation. In such situations, sponsors may need to seek the necessary empowerment from more senior leadership having authority over those units possessing the necessary resources and information.[9]

Once assigned to a team, members need to embrace their assigned roles and perform to the best of their ability.[10] Teams perform better when members are fully committed to the project, with each person's role enabling professional growth. Commitment is more difficult to achieve when team members suspect the mission and purpose of the team have questionable organizational impact. Further, it is easy to become spread too thin by becoming involved in too many teams. The implication is that savvy leaders need to choose their teams carefully when afforded the opportunity to select into or out of particular teams, asking themselves the following questions:

> 1. Is this team's mission important to the organization?
>
> 2. Will I gain important knowledge and skills by serving?
>
> 3. Will I enjoy the transactions in which this team will engage and the other team members?
>
> 4. Is this team being formed for reasons other than the ostensible purpose?
>
> 5. Does this team have the total support of the team sponsor and senior management?

> "Coming together is a beginning. Keeping together is progress. Working together is success."
>
> —Henry Ford

6. Is this team sufficiently empowered to accomplish its mission?

In some cases, the best teams to join may not necessarily be ideal from every perspective but instead be those that enable leaders to better prepare themselves for longer-term goals. For example, an audit manager might accept a role more suited for a senior staff person because it involves a client in an industry about which the manager desires to gain knowledge.

Savvy leaders also need to understand **team dynamics**. One definition holds that, "Team dynamics are the unconscious, psychological forces that influence the direction of a team's behavior and performance. They are like undercurrents in the sea, which can carry boats in a different direction than the one they intend to sail."[11] Team dynamics influence business profitability, job satisfaction, and employee retention.[12] Team dynamics are affected by the roles and relationships among team members resulting from being assigned connected tasks. These roles and relationships are in turn affected by responsibilities for performance outcomes and productivity.[13] High-performing teams exhibit a blend of professional expertise and members' personal credibility, a strong sense of accountability to the team product, avoidance of turf wars, open communications, and a free exchange of ideas.[14]

Team dynamics are influenced by personality preferences, politics, the nature of the team's work, relationships among team members, team members' background and expertise, and organizational climate and culture. Although *teams* and *groups* are sometimes confused, they are not the same, and team dynamics can differ substantially from group dynamics. **Groups** are a social community consisting of members who may or may not share common interests. In business one hears reference to "our sales team" when this is often a misnomer because the salespeople are actually acting independently with individual performance metrics and little actual teamwork.

"The bottom line is, when people are crystal clear about the most important priorities of the organization and team, when they work with and [have] prioritized their work around those top priorities, not only are they many times more productive, they discover they have the time they need to have a whole life."

—Stephen Covey

Well-functioning teams, on the other hand, should share common goals and objectives and work interactively.[15] Technology has enabled many teams to function as a team despite the members being in different locales. This is especially important in today's multinational business environment. Despite this convenience, teams that are able to assemble together periodically often outperform those teams working remotely with little direct personal contact.[16]

Team sponsors should recognize the existence of stages in team life, the level of interaction required among team members at each stage, and the possible need to vary team composition somewhat at different stages to provide the necessary knowledge, skills, and talent. Tuckman's stages originally broke down team development

into four phases: forming, storming, norming, and performing.[17] A fifth phase, adjourning, was eventually added. An adaption of this model is shown in Figure 14.1 on the following page. In this model, teams have limited **life cycles** consisting of five somewhat overlapping stages: (1) initiation, (2) planning, (3) execution, (4) monitoring and control, and (5) closure. During the *initiation phase,* team creation mission assignment, general problem identification, and solution conceptualization occur. During the *planning phase,* possible discrete courses of action are conceptualized along with the necessary detailed framework for implementation. Discovery of additional evidence may require revisiting team mission, composition and resourcing. Once the *execution phase* begins, new issues arising may require additional planning. There is a need for *monitoring and control* throughout the process, but this need is usually greatest when planning and execution overlap the most because of the high levels of interaction among team members. The *closure phase* begins toward the end of execution when there is a need for report writing, presentations to higher-level leadership, and assessment of team members' individual performances by team leadership.

Although at times it may seem that "getting the most out of the team is often as hard as pushing water uphill with a rake: lots of activity, but only marginal results," successful teams often share similar traits that can be nurtured and used by team sponsors.[18] First and foremost is that every team needs to have a clearly defined mission that is communicated to everyone involved with the project. Not only do the team members need to understand what the goals and objectives are for the project but they also need to understand why success is important to the organization. Unfortunately, circumstances do not always afford the desired level of mission clarity, and team dynamics can become quite complicated. Consider the following example supplied by a coauthor.

Understanding the Organizational Environment

Figure 14.1. Overlapping Phases in a Team's Life

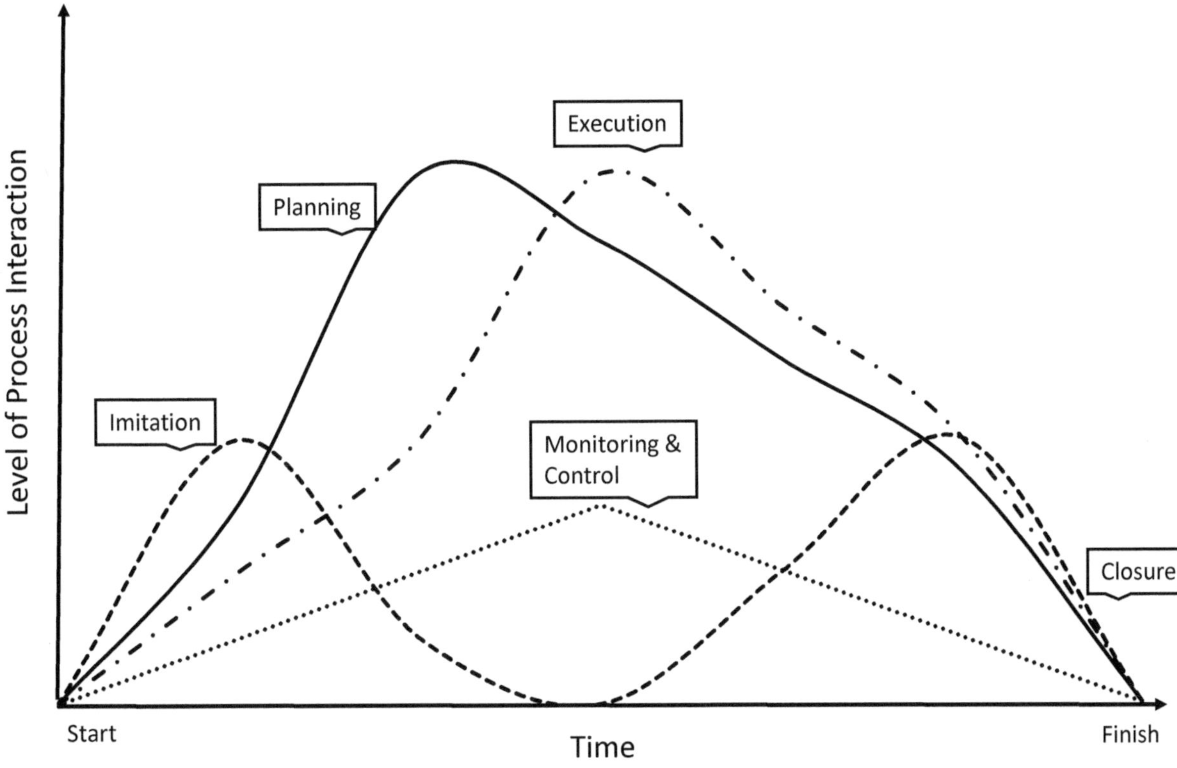

Source: Adapted from http://www.gnsegroup.com/images/logo/chart.JPG (accessed Jan 24, 2015).

A consulting firm was once asked on short notice to become a member of a team responding to a request for proposal (RFP) from potential new client—a large governmental unit within one of the United States. At that juncture, little was known about the RFP's contents except that the project was potentially lucrative and involved a service sector in which the firm did not currently operate. For the young coauthor it seemed this could become a stretch assignment providing a tremendous opportunity to develop new skills with exposure to his firm's top leadership. When the RFP was received, however, gloom fell over the team. The team would be required to take interim control of the unit because its previous head had been fired for violations of state and federal regulations. The depth and breadth of the violations were still not completely known, and news outlets were reporting that additional allegations, including some involving violent crimes, were expected. At a team meeting, the firm's CEO acknowledged the significant downside risk for anyone involved with the project, but the firm had been recommended by a good business partner who had helped the company win several major engagements. To not propose on the project could offend this business partner and make the firm look bad. Fortunately for prospective team members the firm did not get the contract.

The foregoing example illustrates the type of vagaries that can exist with team assignments as well as the political pressures that can sometimes be placed on teams when strategic issues such as entry into a new client sector and pleasing a strategic partner collide with a mission involving high political controversy. These forces impact upon team dynamics. Knowing that such a project is of strategic importance enables team members and their sponsors to engage in honest dialogue about how to best staff and plan for it. When team sponsors fail in this regard, it makes full commitment by team members significantly more difficult to achieve, and they may be more reluctant to become involved in similar projects in the future.[19]

If team sponsors are willing to expend the time and effort required to properly develop and support teams they create, they can create both short- and long-term benefits for the organization. Not only will there be a greater likelihood of team success but team members who have successful team experiences also exhibit higher job satisfaction, higher morale, and lower turnover rates than those who do not.[20]

14.4. Some Thoughts about Team Development and Functioning for Team Leaders

It is generally agreed that high-performing teams go through various stages in performing their missions. Understanding these various stages can help team sponsors and leaders identify where a specific team is in its development and provide guidance as necessary to team members to redirect the team toward mission accomplishment.[21] Allan Drexler and David Sibbett propose a model helpful in understanding how a highly performing team develops and performs during its life.[22] This **team performance model** breaks high-performing team functioning down into seven steps and provides several assessment criteria for each step.[23] Figure 14.2 depicts these steps.[24]

Step 1. Orientation: During this step teams perform initial mission analysis and begin developing

Figure 14.2. Team Performance

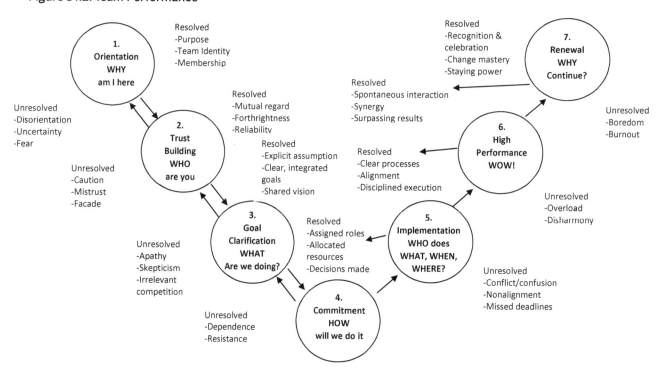

Source: Adapted from http://www.iridiumconsulting.co.uk/wp-content/uploads/2011/10/Drexler-and-Sibbet-1024x768.jpg (accessed February 10, 2015).

Understanding the Organizational Environment

a team identity essential answering the question, "Why are we here?" Although a team identity begins to form, some members may be disoriented in terms of understanding their roles and how these roles will play out in mission execution. Uncertainty and even fear of failure may be present.

Step 2. Trust Building: During this step the team answers the question, "Who are you?" Team members begin to place their teammates in roles in terms of expertise, potential contributions, reliability, and integrity. A mutual respect begins to form among members. However, some caution and mistrust may exist. Because of caution arising from mistrust, some members may use facades to present an image that does not necessarily reflect their true feelings or persona. A need may also arise to revisit step 1 to resolve newly emerging questions about team mission and member identity.

Step 3. Goal Clarification: At this step the team answers a question about its *ends:* "What are we doing?" The team completes its mission analysis to include development of clear, agreed-upon goals, identification of explicit and implicit assumptions, and development of a shared vision of what victory means for the team. Some dysfunctional behaviors may emerge to include apathy, skepticism, and competition among team members that cause a need for the team to revert back to trust building.

Step 4. Commitment: At this step the team answers the question, "How will we do it?" The team should have resolved the roles of the members at this juncture, made basic decisions about the *ways* in which the team's mission will be accomplished, and determined whether the requisite *means* exist for goal accomplishment. There may be, however, unresolved issues involving team member resistance that the team leader will need to address, requiring a return to step 3 to solidify a shared vision.

Step 5. Implementation: This step details how the *ways* will be executed, thereby making pro-

> **"A good manager doesn't try to eliminate conflict; he tries to keep it from wasting the energies of his people. If you're the boss and your people fight you openly when they think that you are wrong—that's healthy."**
>
> —Robert Townsend

cesses clear and aligning ends, ways, and means for a disciplined execution. Conflicts may possibly arise over nonalignment and how executional issues such as missed deadlines will be dealt with, requiring revisiting some of the alignment issues dealt with in step 4.

Step 6. High Performance: Upon reaching this step, high-performing teams experience spontaneous interactions among members as synergies emerge resulting from complementary abilities. Team leaders should be sensitive to indications of disharmony emerging from disparate workloads and some members—or perhaps the whole team—becoming overworked.

Step 7. Renewal: At this juncture, the team has mastered the blending of skills and abilities of the members, but, as with any extended effort, burnout can occur. Team leadership needs to sense when burnout manifests itself in the form of boredom and apathy. Leaders may need to reenergize the team by revisiting the team dynamics that make for high performance.

A caution is in order in that the foregoing model is a generalization in its nature. As Einstein observed, "In theory, theory and practice are the same. In practice, they are not."[25] There is no assurance that all teams will follow all of these steps in exactly the given order. Moreover, the steps may overlap and therefore may not always be discretely identifiable to leaders. Nonetheless, the model provides a useful guide for measuring team progress.

14.5. Conflict among Team Members

Conflict is not only possible at each step, it may persist throughout the life of a high-performing team. Nearly every successful team will experience some level of conflict, and this is not necessarily a bad thing. Although few team leaders desire excessive conflict, they should recognize that some level of conflict can be healthy in generating new ideas and finding better directions. There may be insufficient information for teams to be reasonably certain that proposed solutions will result in mission accomplishment, and circumstances

> "Great teams do not hold back with one another. They are unafraid to air their dirty laundry. They admit their mistakes, their weaknesses, and their concerns without fear of reprisal."
>
> —Patrick Lencioni

may change during team life. Disagreement over the efficacy of solutions can lead teams to develop risk-mitigation strategies and sensitivity analyses. Healthy, spirited debate over contradictory data, varying opinions, and conflicting demands can be useful in ensuring decisions are vetted with appropriate scrutiny.[26]

Consequently, teams can go too far in conflict avoidance. Some teammates may fear offending or subjecting themselves to criticism when others disagree with their ideas. This is especially prevalent in firms that have created a culture wherein challenging the status quo is unacceptable and harmony is valued over efficacy. Team leadership needs to be sensitive to this fallacy and promote candid discussion. Research indicates that a lack of candor makes it more difficult for teams to reach a decision and often results in poorer overall performance.[27]

Conflict does not always arise because of a lack of candor within the team but rather due to a lack of candor about the underlying goals of those who appoint teams. Previous sections have related examples of situations where teams are formed ostensibly for one purpose but, in reality, are put together for other reasons. These situations can present great challenges for team leaders and result in a demoralized team even if the ostensible goals are attained.

Once a coauthor was a member of a team tasked with providing advice to a midsized merchandising company that was performing poorly. Although the engagement called for the team to identify a certain amount of short-term cost savings, the assumed goal was to allow senior management time to generate additional sales to turn the company's financial performance around. The team knew that no cost-cutting measures would rectify the company's financial distress permanently absent substantial improvement in its revenues. The team approached its task with energy and creativity; but even though the consultants' recommended actions exceeded the expected annual savings goal by nearly 50 percent, management made little effort to increase sales even when pressed by the team about the lack of progress. By the conclusion of the engagement, it had become obvious that management had been less than candid about its true objectives in engaging the consultants. Despite having accomplished its mission of identifying a dollar figure of short-term cost reductions, the lack of candor between client management and the team resulted in a demoralized team.

Teams perform much better when operating with open, honest dialogue. Allowing members to set forth alternative ideas without fear of verbal reprisals leads to better decisions and higher levels of trust and commitment. However, team leaders must perform a delicate balancing act in eliciting candor without allowing it to become synonymous with disrespect. Members need to interact with civility and respect when disagreement occurs, and it is incumbent upon team leaders to enforce good behaviors. Team leaders should set the example for civility when holding teams and members accountable for results by providing criticism in a respectful and constructive manner.[28]

14.6. Preventing and Fixing Dysfunctional Teams

Teams become dysfunctional with some frequency, so team leaders need to sense when this is occurring and move rapidly and decisively to rectify the causes of the dysfunction. There is some agreement among experts that teams often experience five major dysfunctions.[29] In this regard, we define **dysfunction** as being a set of behaviors that poses a serious threat to mission accomplishment. What causes these five dysfunctions and how to fix them may vary by team, but early recognition and correction are important.

The first, and often most severe, dysfunction is the *absence of trust.*[30] An absence of trust can occur when team members do not allow themselves to be vulnerable within the group.[31] Group members are sometimes afraid of the ramifications of being wrong or accused of not being a team player. Consequently, instead of working as hard as they can to make the team a success, believing that the team will support them if they make mistakes, members lacking trust in their teammates may restrict themselves to roles well within their comfort zones, hide mistakes, or isolate themselves by refraining from interacting with other team members. One reason the absence of trust is so problematic is that it can manifest itself in many ways and is sometimes the driving force behind the other dysfunctions. As we related in part I, trust takes time to

build and is easy to destroy. Savvy leaders can help build trust among team members by being the first to demonstrate trust in others. It is vital that team leaders consistently demonstrate trust in team members as well as discussing its importance. Trust is built in such ways as keeping promises and forgiving team members when they make forgivable mistakes. Recall that in part I we defined what constitutes forgivable mistakes as mistakes not involving moral turpitude, not of a catastrophic nature, and not repeated over and over. Trust is also promoted by leaders setting an example of vulnerability by making themselves vulnerable and admitting their own mistakes.

A second dysfunction is *fear of conflict,* discussed in the previous section, which is often connected to a lack of trust.[32] When team members are afraid of conflict, they will agree with teammates despite a belief that better alternatives exist.[33] As noted previously, some level of conflict is healthy, but conflict should be factual and constructive. Team leaders should not allow attacks personal in nature or motivated by petty grievances. Similar to the steps that need to be taken to build trust, actions often speak louder than words in reducing fear of conflict. Team leaders should encourage all members of the group to debate and challenge assumptions and recommendations, including their own. Leaders may also need to elicit the ideas from more reticent team members by asking direct questions. Should the discussion become too heated, it is the team leader's responsibility to tamp emotions and ensure respectful exchange. Sometimes taking short breaks can be useful in allowing time for members' emotions to calm.

Lack of commitment is the third common dysfunction.[34] With lack of commitment decisions are sometimes made too quickly. Lack of commitment may be evinced by comments such as, "Let's get this project over with so that I can get back to my day job." Conversely, decisions may be made too slowly as evinced by behavior suggesting, "If I stay disengaged long enough, the team will eventually do it themselves or assign it to someone else." Lack of commitment is sometimes interrelated with fear of conflict and lack of trust. If decisions are routinely made without considering the opinions of some members, attitudes may arise such as, "The team leader is going to do what she wants regardless of what we say, so let's just agree with her and get this over."

"Unless commitment is made, there are only promises and hopes; but no plans."

—Peter F. Drucker

There may be times when a team selects a course of action with which some members disagree. When this happens there must be enough trust in the decision-making process for dissenting team members to give the project their full support despite having disagreed with the course of action chosen. To lay the groundwork for such situations, team leaders are well advised to agree upon the decision-making process during the commitment step in team performance. It may be desirable to explain early in team formation when and under what circumstances the team leader may need to make an executive decision to ensure the project stays on course if consensus cannot be reached among team members. There may also be times when teams become bogged down and individual members take the initiative to move projects forward. Under such circumstances team leaders should be supportive, assuming taking the initiative is undertaken with proper intent and the behaviors are consistent with good team outcomes.[35]

Avoidance of accountability is the fourth dysfunction. A common manifestation itself is the failure of individual members to support each other.[36] For example, one team member may complete tasks quickly and efficiently but then does nothing to assist less efficient team members often assuming implicitly the more efficient member will be rewarded for his or her individual performance even if the team fails to achieve its goals. Team leaders must hold each member accountable for completing his or her assignments as required but make it clear that the team as a whole is held accountable for achieving its goals and objectives. The increasing use of electronic communication contributes to this problem because team members have less visibility and more difficulty determining when a teammate needs assistance. Also, some members may infer that the greater anonymity provided by electronic communications implies less accountability. Regular interaction—face-to-face when possible—should be encouraged.[37] In our experience, when dealing with remotely located teams it is sometimes necessary on occasion to gather the team together physically despite the additional time and expense involved.

Team management tools such as RACI charts—which outline who is *responsible, accountable,* to be *consulted,* and to be *informed* for various tasks—assist in achieving greater accountability and encouraging dialogue among team members. Even if some individual members are not held accountable for specific tasks, they may be expected to provide feedback to other team members. Encouraging such interactions can be particularly useful in overcoming the problem of an individual member surfacing problems only to the team leader in a manner that leaves other members feeling as if they have been circumvented and reported upon adversely.[38] In summary, team leaders should establish both individual and team accountability by clearly communicating how each member will be measured and how the team will be rewarded for their performances.

Inattention to or disregard for team objectives[39] is a fifth common dysfunction occurring when individual members focus on achieving objectives not aligned with the team's, thereby intentionally or unintentionally interfering with the team fulfilling its mission. This can be caused by team objectives that were not clearly communicated or understood. This is especially prevalent when team members join subsequently to the early team-performance steps and are not briefed properly upon joining. Formal mission statements and regularly prepared and distributed performance reports are helpful in motivating team members to work toward the same objectives. Team leadership needs to model the way by underscoring the importance of placing team efforts over individual member concerns unrelated to the team. For example, if team leaders assign tasks to the team and then wander away for long periods of time working on matters unrelated to the team's mission, this behavior can result in team members taking their tasks less seriously. Absentee team leaders may return to find their teams off course and working at a slower-than-desired pace. Team leaders should support team activity and the individual team members, helping to cultivate high team performance by showing that the team's work product is important and team efforts have strong backing.

It is also important to know when to resist additional responsibilities being thrust upon the team once a project is underway. **Mission creep** occurs because outsiders may see a high-performing team as a vehicle for accomplishing ancillary tasks.[40] In some cases team sponsors may see additional missions as an inexpensive way of extracting additional work from an existing team rather than forming a new one. Team leaders can help avoid mission creep by clearly identifying and codifying the team's mission early during the team performance process and obtaining buy-in from team sponsors. Doing so provides team leaders the opportunity to make statements such as, "This additional mission is outside the scope of the team's responsibilities. If we are to undertake this additional mission, we will need more time and resources."

> ## "None of us, including me, ever do great things. But we can all do small things, with great love, and together we can do something wonderful."
>
> —Mother Teresa

Clearly defining team mission and obtaining buy-in from team sponsors can also avoid ultimate failure and its attendant disappointment once it is realized that the **project scope** is unattainable given the allocated manpower, time, and other resources. For example, a team of MBA-student consultants was assigned to work with a hospital chain to develop a cost/benefit analysis for installing an electronic medical records (EMR) system in one of its hospitals. At the initial meeting with key hospital staff members the team was asked to develop a return on investment (ROI) figure for the project that management would present to the company's board of directors. The team eagerly agreed with this goal before the team's faculty advisor intervened with the caution that determining an accurate ROI would likely be impossible absent an extensive market study that assessed the impact of not installing an EMR system on patient retention and growth over time. The team had neither the time nor resources to conduct such a study, so a narrower mission was agreed upon. As a result, the team was able to fulfill its more-limited responsibilities, and the company was spared potential problems associated with presenting a highly inaccurate ROI figure to its board that might have led to a suboptimal decision.

Each of the dysfunctions outlined above can derail a team and keep it from fulfilling its mission. The underlying causes can sometimes be obscure, but often the dysfunctions result from failure of team leaders to give proper attention to the seven steps involved in developing high-performance teams outlined in section 14.4. By being proactive in communicating sponsor and leader expectations and demonstrating the desired behaviors, courageous team leaders can help prevent these dysfunctions and more quickly resolve them if they occur.

14.7. Personality Preference Type in Team-Member Selection and Leadership

The Myers-Briggs Type Indicator (MBTI) introduced in chapter 5 is one tool available to help leaders better understand team members and how to motivate them. For example, when comparing how people process information, those having a preference for sensing (S) prefer facts and details. Sensing types tend to focus on "tried and true," practical ideas and base their decisions on past experiences. Conversely, those who prefer intuition (N) tend to focus more on general concepts, focusing on what is possible. They are willing to innovate, consider theoretical outcomes, value imagination, and often desire change. In terms of decision making, thinking (T) types tend to focus on the pros and cons of alternative solutions and approach the decision-making process using logic and data. They prefer decisions to be objective and fair. Feeling (F) types are more likely to approach decision making with empathy and compassion. Harmony is important for feeling types,[41] and, in contrast to thinking types, feeling types tend to focus on the values surrounding problems and often personalize decisions.

Recall from chapter 5 that tools for categorizing individuals by personality preferences such as the MBTI measure only preferences and do so nonjudgmentally in the sense that one set of preferences is in a general sense neither better nor worse than others. They are simply different. Understanding preferences, however, does enable team leaders to make some useful assessments of team members.[42] This includes how to better motivate individual members, what roles they are likely to excel in, and how to manage conflict among members. Type can also be useful in deciding upon team composition. Teams comprised of members of similar type tend to understand each other more quickly compared to teams consisting of members of different types. This itself is a nonjudgmental observation, however, because the degree of homogeneity of preferences in members can be a function of mission urgency and other considerations. There are times when teams with highly heterogeneous preferences may be preferred over teams consisting of members with homogeneous preferences and vice versa. Members usually retain their individual behavioral preferences when assigned to teams and may respond differently to team actions, events, and attempts to motivate. Learning and decision-making processes also differ.[43]

Team sponsors sometimes give insufficient attention to the personality preference dimension of team composition when creating teams despite its implications for team performance. When manpower resources permit, team performance may be enhanced by team sponsors assigning team members whose personality preferences are well aligned with the team mission. For example, if the mission necessitates a fast problem identification and solution, creating a team consisting of relatively homogeneous preferences of the right types has a greater likelihood of getting rapid results than a team consisting of members with more heterogeneous preferences because homogeneous types better understand each other and solidify faster as a team. Conversely, if the team mission calls for a high degree of creativity, heterogeneity in preferences is more likely to result in creative thinking, but more brainstorming means more time spent in the goal clarification and commitment steps of team performance.[44]

Team leaders also need to understand that, because of type differences, a one-size-fits-all approach to team leadership is unlikely to optimize team performance when teams are comprised of members with disparate preferences. Therefore, in some respects, the leadership challenge becomes greater as personality preference heterogeneity increases. Different preferences can require different motivational approaches, which, in turn, take more leadership time and effort. Recognition of this requirement when composing teams allows for team leaders to better plan for the time and interactions required to achieve high team performance.

Team size is an additional consideration because, in general, the larger the team the greater the complexity of preferences. Teams should be appropriately sized for the mission to include scope of the work and knowledge and skill sets required. As obvious as this sounds, teams are often not built to optimal size for a mission but instead sized because of various externalities such as resource availability and organizational politics. Teams may be built too small because of the nonavailability of human resources or too large because some personnel are underemployed and team sponsors view the team as a vehicle for involving idle resources in something useful.

The potentially controversial, political nature of a mission may also lead team sponsors to assign team members for reasons other than optimizing team performance. For example, a team assigned to recommend a new organization structure has a high potential of arousing concern and suspicion about its deliberations with subsequent controversy attending its recommendations. Consequently, team sponsors may decide to appoint representatives from various organizational units in an effort to portray equity and fairness in studying organizational needs. Team representation for political reasons will likely increase team-member-preference complexity and require

outstanding team leadership to motivate team members who may react quite differently to political pressure coming from various stakeholders in the organization. Some members—especially those who tend to be more sensitive to the fears of non-team-member colleagues about possible staff reductions, job reassignment, and changes in compensation—may need continuous reassurance from team leaders and reiteration of why successful completion of the team's mission will benefit the organization as a whole.

Once a team is formed, even if the team leader had little if any input into its composition, understanding the members' personality preferences can assist in maximizing team effectiveness. Team leaders should assess team members' skills, abilities, preferences, strengths, and weaknesses in relation to the team's mission, goals, and objectives. Knowing how various members are likely to react to team needs enables leaders to manage three team leadership roles appropriately.[45] In small teams, team leaders will likely perform all of these functions. In larger teams, team leaders may wish to delegate some of these functions to other members. Although it is undesirable for the team leader to be absent from the team for long periods, sometimes exigencies of the moment and prior commitments may necessitate more than a brief absence. In this event, the team leader should appoint one or more individuals to carry out these three functions.

The first key function is that of **facilitator and coordinator**. The facilitator/coordinator functions to keep the team focused on its tasks, to encourage participation from all members, to protect individuals from personal attacks by other members, to suggest alternative courses of action if the team becomes stalled, and to summarize and clarify team decisions. If this role must be temporarily assigned to another team member, the team leader should assign it to someone who has the requisite organizational skills and motivation to keep the team on track without the hubris that may accompany the team member being singled out as the backup leader. For example, if the leader will be absent from the team for several days due to other commitments and wants the team to continue to work on its current course of action, then the team leader might consider placing an ESTJ in charge. ESTJs direct activity, are pragmatic, use accepted ways of leading, have a task-centered style, and focus on task accomplishment.

A second key function associated with team leadership is that of **boundary manager.** The boundary manager serves as liaison between the team and parties external to the team, especially its stakeholders. Once again, if some of the boundary management function is to be carried out by someone other than the leader, then MBTI can help identify members best suited for this role. For example, if periodic progress presentations to top leadership are required that create significant stress, then the team leader might avoid assigning the task of boundary manager to an introverted, intuitive type because of a tendency to experience greater discomfort in making presentations and dealing with top leaders' specific concerns.

A third key team leader role is that of **project manager** who organizes work plans. An introverted sensing type may be well suited for this role because of preferences for staying focused on objectives and using well-established procedures for task accomplishment.[46]

Under ideal conditions, team leaders will know each member's personality preferences, but what if such knowledge is unavailable? Time permitting, team leaders can still make an assessment of what each member likes and dislikes in teamwork. To help in this assessment, in the *trust-building step* in team performance, team leaders can encourage members

to first write down and then openly discuss their previous experiences about working in teams by answering the following questions:

1. What did I like about the best teams with which I have worked?

2. What did I like least about the worst teams?

3. What did I like most and least about the best and worst team leaders?

4. How did I add the most value to a team?

5. When and why was I least valuable to a team?

6. How do I like to process information and make decisions?

Taking time for such discussion can help team leaders form an assessment of team members' strengths and weaknesses along with their preferences. Further, this type of exercise also allows team members to better understand their own preferences and those of their fellow team members, thereby helping to build trust through mutual understanding.[47]

14.8. Concluding Thoughts: Teaming versus Teams

Although sometimes misused, poorly directed, and even dysfunctional, the use of teams is a growing phenomenon in business, and team leadership skills are an absolutely essential tool in courageous leaders' toolkits. Twenty-five hundred years ago, Greek philosopher Heraclitus of Ephesus stated, "Everything changes and nothing remains still."[48] This applies to teamwork today. Teaming has become a way of life in business, with varying degrees of effectiveness. With increasing dynamism in business, teams are also becoming dynamic, and career professionals often engage with more than one team simultaneously. Team composition can change during the course of a single project. With increasing regularity business is moving from the concept of teams as a distinct entity to **teaming as an activity**, with teams becoming somewhat amorphous.

Amorphous teaming is perhaps easier to visualize when one considers the example of medical professionals working in a hospital handling an emergency appendectomy. When the patient is admitted to the emergency department with this potentially life-threatening condition, an initial diagnosis is immediately performed that may include a CT scan and an ultrasound test. The patient is stabilized and medicated until a surgery team with the appropriate skill set, including a general surgeon and an anesthesiologist, takes over treatment in an operating room. Following surgery and initial recovery, the patient is transferred to yet a third group of care providers that assumes control of the patient under the direction of a charge nurse with overall care continuing to be monitored by the surgeon. Even membership in this final care team changes as shifts change.[49]

There are many analogous business situations, including crisis-management teams formed on the spur of the moment to deal with rapidly evolving events such as the prospective loss of a major client, the sudden introduction of a competitive threat, or discovery of a major financial discrepancy. Harvard professor Amy Edmondson states, "We've seen fewer stable, well-designed, well-composed teams, simply because of the nature of the work, which is more uncertain and dynamic than before. As a means for getting the work done, we've got to focus on the interpersonal processes and dynamics that occur among people working together for shorter durations."[50] Team members often need to adapt

to their new teams, environments, and problem situations quickly, identify and implement solutions, and move to the next problem involving yet another team. In some cases, teams are self-formed and self-managed through various stages of team life without ever being formally designated as a team. Although the notion of self-formed and self-managed teams may make some leaders uneasy, these leaders might take some comfort in research indicating that self-directed teams have 30 percent to 40 percent higher productivity.[51]

Teaming helps organizations adapt more quickly to changes in dynamic political, social, or economic environments. Vital organizational learning takes place through the teaming process by forcing organization members out of functional silos, enabling better focus on emergent problems and engaging organization members with the appropriate skill sets irrespective of their department, formal organizational role, or functional expertise.[52] Organization members who routinely engage in teaming learn not only how to better accomplish current objectives but also how to engage with their co-workers more effectively. Building such a repository of team experience allows solution of future problems more efficiently.

Whether engaged in large or small team projects, the skills that team leaders need and the guidelines to be followed in developing high-performing teams are largely the same. To realize high team performance, team leaders must create an environment of trust, candid communication, commitment, and accountability. Although overused and misused in some instances, teamwork is an ever-more-integral part of today's business environment, and being able to employ teams properly is a crucial skill for all leaders. Savvy leaders must understand when and how to team.

CHAPTER 15

Organizational Savvy

> **"In business, courageous action is really a special kind of calculated risk taking. People who have become good leaders have a greater than average willingness to make bold moves, but they strengthen their chances of success—and avoid career suicide—through careful deliberation and preparation."**
>
> —Kathleen K. Reardon, "Courage as a Skill," *Harvard Business Review*, January 2007

The quote above makes quite clear the nexus between courageous leadership and organizational savvy. What is business organizational savvy? Is it political skill? Is it business acumen? Is it mere shrewdness? Is it just a useful tool "in navigating the minefield of office politics?"[1] Some describe it in those terms. Definitions of organizational politics and its close synonyms vary widely.[2] For the purposes of this chapter, we favor our own definition: ***Organizational savvy*** *in business is a keen acumen about what creates value in a business and the ability to apply the skills and abilities necessary to achieve both organizational and personal success in light of the organization's vision, strategy, core values, economic environment, politics, climate, culture, power structure, and resources.* This definition is intentionally broad because our belief is that organizational savvy is essential to successful leadership, and successful leaders must exercise sound judgment and business acumen about all these factors affecting the organization.

Another way to think of organizational savvy, albeit in a somewhat negative light, is *business street smarts* that allow leaders to deal with or-

ganizations the way they are rather that the way they should be.[3] Face it: we humans are a messy bunch with different personalities, likes and dislikes, attitudes, values, and expectations. The automotive genius Henry Ford was reputed to have said, "Why is it that I always get the whole person when what I really want is a pair of hands?" In other words, when businesses employ people they come with baggage, not just the desired skills and abilities.[4] It does little good to lament the necessity of having to deal with human emotions, frailties, excesses, and selfishness. These exist because people exist, and this means leaders can't just manage the business; they must also lead the people who compose it.

This chapter explores some of the several aspects of organizational savvy that one source places in the following categories: (1) personal competence to include not only technical job skills but leadership skills and self-awareness, (2) political competence to include the ability to recognize behaviors dysfunctional to the organization, (3) an understanding of the formal and informal power structures within organizations, (4) the ability to build information networks and supportive coalitions, and (5) the ability to deliver value-creating results.[5] As with virtually all our topics, this exploration is neither as exhaustive nor as deep as the topic deserves in terms of leaders' understanding. Our hope is to create awareness and whet appetites for both greater breadth and depth. Further, organizational savvy is not gained simply by reading, any more than leadership skills are in general. It must be gained through experience. Nonetheless, awareness is a good starting point for leaders who wish to accelerate their careers and avoid being ambushed because they are unwary of the dangers of naïveté.

15.1. Why Organizational Savvy?

Although we believe that organizational savvy encompasses more than just politics and political skills, a useful starting point for understanding why being savvy is important is gaining an understanding of the political nature of organizations, to include businesses. We explore the topic of business organization politics in more depth in the following section, but for the moment suffice it to say that politics is a reality in business that can create enormous stresses for leaders.[6] Moreover, politics can create enormous stress on leaders that not only interferes with their ability to accomplish their goals but may even adversely affect their health.[7] Organizational savvy in the form of political skills can reduce these stresses.[8]

Consider for a moment the political difficulties associated with being chief compliance partner for a public accounting firm charged, in part, with ensuring that audits performed by the firm comply with all regulatory requirements for financial reporting purposes. The partner-in-charge of a major audit client proposes a reporting accommodation desired by the client that the compliance partner feels is inappropriate. The intentions of both parties may be good in that the audit partner is desirous of client satisfaction and retention, whereas the compliance partner wants

> **"How is it some people seem to work effectively within an organization while others—equally competent in their respective fields—struggle to make significant progress in accomplishing broader organizational goals? Why is it some people who are so successful as individual contributors fail to achieve similar success when taking on a larger role or broader assignment within an organization? The answer often lies in a single phrase: organizational savvy."**
>
> —Harold S. Resnick, Work Systems Newsletter

to protect his or her firm. Handling such difficult and potentially tense situations without them exploding into acrimony requires a high level of political skill. This skill may be defined as "the ability to effectively understand others at work and to use this knowledge to influence others to act in ways that enhance one's personal and/or organizational objectives."[9]

Consequently, organizational political skill is often an essential component of a leader's success.[10] It is important for advancement and very necessary under conditions of ambiguity and uncertainty.[11] But the need for organizational savvy goes beyond simply being politically adept to include being *able to exercise sound judgment in assessing ethical issues and the accuracy of information.* This necessity is summed up succinctly in the following quote:

Imagine a leader who is an excellent role model of ethical behavior but who cannot

- Detect deception, either in the organization or in key external relationships.

- Filter and screen self-serving information.

- Discern who to trust and who not to trust.

- Ensure the flow of accurate and timely information.

The absence of those skills leaves a leader vulnerable, and, even with excellent personal values and intentions, she becomes an ineffective steward of the company's resources or reputation.[12]

Organizational savvy is necessary for leaders to discern many types of self-serving and opportunistic behaviors by both organizational members and outside parties, such as

> over-promising, exaggerating, lying, providing partial or misleading information, hiding bad news, giving superficial explanations, taking undeserved credit, scapegoating and blaming others, refusing to admit mistakes, unfairly tarnishing the reputation of others, sabotaging the efforts of colleagues, giving insincere flattery, telling people what they want to hear, punishing people who criticize ideas, over-controlling information.[13]

Just as with poor political skills, lacking the ability to discern such dysfunctional behaviors impedes recruiting the best people for the organization and makes leaders less effective in stewardship of organizational resources.[14] Consequently, organizational savvy is an imperative for effective leadership.

15.2. Politics: The Good, the Bad, and the Downright Ugly

Frequently regarded as a negative word, politics is both a fact of business life and a necessity in many cases. Unfortunately, the negative connotations associated with organizational politics means that it is often not legitimized by senior leadership, with the result that skills for dealing with it are rarely discussed.[15] Business politics can be good, bad, or downright ugly. Used ethically and with the organization's best interests in mind, political acumen can be a force for *good.* For example, recall the compliance partner from the previous example. If he or she uses political skill to resolve the compliance issue with the partner-in-charge and the client amenably, then the compliance partner has used his or her political skill to the firm's benefit. If instead the compliance partner is impolitic and the partner-in-charge of the audit takes the matter to the highest levels fearing the loss of the client will roll back on him, then the situation has turned *bad.* What about the *downright ugly*? Consider the following real anecdote related by one of the coauthors:

> A recently hired executive vice president employed his mistress as his administrative assistant. Word leaked out that she had held those same capacities when with his previous firm and their personal relationship had become known. It didn't help that neither the EVP nor his assistant got along well with most organization members. The relationship cast a pall over the entire group of executives and administrative assistants in the suite, with everyone tiptoeing around uneasily and lots of whispering in the background. Office politics turned really ugly, however, when the assistant began to take advantage of her relationship with the EVP, arriving late for work, taking long breaks, sitting at her desk applying nail polish, walking into her boss's office at will interrupting conversations—and even bringing her toy poodle to work. Preferential treatment also extended to a particular junior executive—the "fair-haired lad"—who was shown favoritism in assignments and giv-

en special privileges, such as access to the corporate aircraft. There was resentment about the preferential treatment the two were receiving, but no one dared raise the issue with the short-tempered EVP for fear of retribution. Morale plummeted, but the worst part was that the implicit message was sent that power, formal and informal, was what really counted, and those who had it could abuse it. Before the EVP and his assistant/mistress finally departed the firm, one high-performing young executive had bailed in disgust for another employer and the "fair-haired lad" had been fired for illegal acts.

Given circumstances such as the foregoing it is understandable why business politics carries negative connotations, but these connotations need not always hold true if leaders learn to navigate political waters deftly. If one thinks of political skill as "a critical competency for effectiveness in the ambiguous and often turbulent environments," "characterized by social perceptiveness and the ability to adjust one's behaviors to different and changing situational needs," and "the ability to understand others at work and to use such knowledge to influence others in ways that enhance one's personal or organizational objectives," business politics appears in a far more favorable light.[16] Politically skilled business leaders are seen as successful in regulating interactions with other organizational members in ways that inspire confidence, trust, and sincerity.[17]

For aspiring leaders there are *two ways of dealing with organizational politics:* **developing competence in political skills** and **acquiring power**, formal and/or informal, through *instrumental relationships.*[18] Political skills become a *buffer* between causes of stress in the workplace and the effects of this stress on leaders, leading to proficiency in coping with complexity, uncertainty, and accountability, the adverse effects of

which can be exacerbated by politics.[19] Developing instrumental relationships leads to *network centrality,* enabling leader access to important information and support from bosses, co-workers, and subordinates. Confidence, trust, and sincerity engendered through political skills assists in developing such networks and helps place leaders "in the know" when it comes to inside information about organizational matters.[20]

Some research has examined the association between employees' perception of leaders' political skills and ethical versus unethical leader behavior with somewhat intuitive results. More politically skilled leaders were perceived to be more ethical, resulting in greater commitment and lower stress levels for employees. Politically skilled leaders who engaged in unethical behaviors were perceived to be more ethical than politically unskilled leaders who engaged in these behaviors. The research also suggests that politically skilled leaders may promote more ethical behaviors among employees but with the negative caveat that political skill assists leaders in disguising unethical behaviors.[21]

Political skills and acquisition of power are critical to leadership success in business and form a component of organizational savvy. A starting point for garnering these assets is to understand what it means to have business acumen.

15.3. Business Acumen

Although in our definition of organizational savvy business acumen is but one aspect of it, it is an important aspect. "**Business acumen** is an acute understanding of how a business works and what it takes for the business to make money."[22] Consider the following quote:

> People are the most important ingredient of the organizations. This is the human capital that gives a competitive edge to an organization in the presence of abun-

dant capital and technological resources...
[and] the prime motive for joining an organization is to serve one's own interests.
People come to work situations with many
goals and objectives. These goals invoke
conflict and competition among workers to
utilize the scarce resources. This competition, in turn, affects the use of power and
politics in organizations.[23]

The starting point, then, for developing business
acumen is to understand that business is first and

> **"Managers with business
> acumen are able to break down
> organizational silos, bridge
> communication gaps, and
> engage the employees they
> manage, so the entire workforce
> can understand how the
> company operates and how each
> person can contribute to the
> company's success."**
>
> —Catherine J. Rezak, Paradigm Learning, Inc.

foremost about people. In chapter 1 we presented
the idea that leaders having their priorities right
is essential to courageous leadership. We stated
the leader's first priority is what benefits the pack.
Since for the most part people who join businesses enter thinking primarily of themselves, the
leader's task becomes one of moving attitudes
toward a mentality of thinking about what benefits the organization as well as themselves.[24] This
means several things, among them:

- Understanding which individual behaviors, decisions, and group interactions
  add value to the organization and which
  do not.

- Establishing organizational climates and
  cultures consistent with vision and strategy.

- Clearly communicating goals and objectives.

- Ensuring business performance measures and associated incentives encourage behaviors consistent with attainment
  of goals and objectives.

- Intuiting when something is wrong, why,
  and being able to intervene in a timely
  manner using political skills, influence, and
  control to correct problems without burn-
  ing down the house to get rid of a few mice.

Leaders need not only a clear understanding
of how the business works but also its success
drivers in terms of realization of it vision and strategy and the major value-creating activities that
translate into success. This is important at both
the personal and organizational levels. At the personal level, leaders must be able to demonstrate
they can contribute value to establish credibility
and earn the trust and confidence of others. At the
organizational level, leaders must direct subordinates effectively so that they, in turn, add value.
These leaders should share a common focus with
their bosses and co-workers about both their own
job responsibilities and the bigger picture of organizational success.

If anything, the need for business acumen
is increasing because the need to identify and
solve complex problems is rapidly increasing as
the speed of change in business increases due
to global competition and technological change.
Business acumen includes understanding the
competitive landscape and connecting day-to-
day decisions and activities with key business
performance metrics. In other words, savvy leaders must understand holistically how the business
makes money in order to discern which opportunities are good bets and which should be ignored.

Understanding the Organizational Environment

Some of the more important questions implied by business acumen are:

1. What are the important ways the firm makes money by creating value?

2. What does each of the firm's financial statements say about the business?

3. What is the difference between profits and cash, and why should both be carefully monitored and controlled?

4. How do initiatives such as business performance measurement, capital expenditure projects, and systems upgrades impact strategic success?

5. Are the goals of my unit aligned with those of the firm?

6. What are the key client-interface issues?

7. Are we investing for the future or the past?

Failing to ask and answer these questions correctly results in too many actions being taken that do not align with the firm's strategy, goals, and objectives. Spread across the entire organization, this means there is frequently a huge gap between leaders merely executing job tasks and leading and directing subordinates effectively. In part this is because acumen is often not taught in business or executive training programs as a core leadership competency, but business acumen can and must be learned. The leader's role is rapidly evolving from just managing for efficiency to playing a pivotal role in aligning performance with corporate strategy, making business acumen essential. Several groups of executives represent potentially good targets for business acumen training. These include high-performance-potential managers, sales, marketing, financial and technical professionals, and team leaders.

One reason developing business acumen through training programs is challenging is because its very nature requires higher-level cognitive skills in addition to a broad understanding of both business and leadership. Moreover, it is difficult to deliver effectively using passive-learning techniques. Evidence suggests that retention and utilization are lower when using only these methods. Instead, business acumen needs to be taught interactively on an experiential basis.[25] Despite the difficulties, we believe that the payoffs from developing business acumen in leaders can be great and are becoming increasingly essential for sustained organizational success.

15.4. Organizational Climate and Culture

Although the difference can at times seem rather fuzzy, researchers usually make a distinction between organizational climate and organizational culture.[26] **Climate** refers to how organization members perceive its practices and common features to include whether leadership is supportive, there is open communication, the extent to which conflict exists, and whether and how performance is rewarded. **Culture,** on the other hand, is determined by the values, norms, and behavioral practices that members share.[27] Careful examination of both definitions suggests the two are related inasmuch as perceptions can influence behaviors,

> **"To understand what goes on in an organization and why it happens the way it does, one needs several concepts. Climate and culture, if each is carefully defined, then become crucial building blocks for organization description and analysis."**
>
> —B. Schneider et al., quoting E. H. Schein, *Handbook of Organization Culture and Climate* (2000), pp. xxiv–xxv

and a focused climate could, in part, be derived from various culture-embedding mechanisms. Nonetheless, many researchers maintain the two are sufficiently distinct enough to merit being considered separate-but-related building blocks for organizational description and analysis.[28]

Organizational climate is related to factors influencing member well-being, such as job satisfaction and work-related stress. In fact, virtually any examination of the workplace related to member perceptions of their work environment involves climate. *Stressful business climates* are often characterized by conflict avoidance rather than problem surfacing and problem solving by leaders, or, alternatively, by confrontational behaviors. Other characteristics include a lack of openness, a preponderance of negative feedback rather than positive psychological rewards, lack of supportive relations between leaders and members, and limited member participation in decision making. Research has linked these stressful influences to low morale and instances of psychogenic illness.[29]

Some research has attempted to categorize organizational climate into dimensions based upon their focus. These include such foci as (1) certain behaviors, ethics, and justice, (2) involvement, participation, support, and empowerment, (3) development, innovation, and creativity, and (4) core competencies such as service.[30] So, for example, the climate in a highly technological consumer-products company such as Apple might be focused on innovation and creativity, whereas a CPA firm might be focused on core financial competencies and client service combined with strong ethics. Moreover, different climates may exist at different levels and subunits of a business, so risk factors associated with different climates may differ.[31] Inasmuch as quality of leadership can have a profound effect on aspects of organizational climate such as levels of stress, variable leadership across levels and sub-

units may explain some differences in climate. One implication is that, the greater the stress created by extraorganizational factors such as the nature of transactions with customers and clients, the more attention top leadership should pay to assigning outstanding leaders to high-stress subunits. Another implication comes from research indicating that leaders' goal orientation guides goal-oriented patterns of work groups.[32] This logically suggests that the business may benefit by inserting strong, goal-oriented leaders into work groups lacking a goal-orientation focus, a suggestion that would seem hardly surprising to experienced leaders.

Researchers have identified *five basic elements* that characterize **organizational culture.** These include (1) fundamental *assumptions* that shape views about such matters as organizational stability or hostility, (2) *values* in the form of preferences for certain outcomes, (3) *norms* about appropriate and inappropriate behavior, (4) *patterns* of activities such as how members are recognized, rewarded, or sanctioned, and (5) *statements and symbols* such as vision and mission statements used to communicate cultural messages. Like climate, cultures can differ with hierarchical levels and take fundamentally different forms that include a *dominant organizational culture, subcultures* in various subunits, and *countercultures* in subunits that are either dysfunctional or resisting the organizational culture because subunit members believe it to be dysfunctional.[33] Consider the following example of the latter related by one of the coauthors:

> During my early combat experience, the culture in our unit's parent organization was perceived by members of our unit to be flawed in that staff officers who had little or no direct experience facing the enemy were repeatedly permitted by the command to interfere with the unit's combat operations. This proved especially troublesome when

Understanding the Organizational Environment

we were in contact with the enemy and received directives via radio to take actions contraindicated by the tactical situation. As a result of this micromanagement, a practice grew in the unit whereby members began to choose when and when not to obey these directives by developing "communications difficulties." Over time, this developed beyond tactical situations into a counterculture in which selective obedience to various other directives became the norm. Efforts by the parent unit to eradicate this maverick counterculture were ineffective, in part because it often resulted in better overall outcomes—but given better leadership at the parent-unit level it should never have arisen in the first place.

The foregoing anecdote is illustrative of an important point. When top leadership is oblivious to a perverse culture growing inside the organization, this opens the door to the growth of potentially unhealthy subcultures and countercultures. Further, once embedded, cultures tend to become persistent even if organizational climate changes. The following guidelines summarize what leaders should do to embed sound cultures:

- Communicate organizational values and assumptions clearly, consistently, and recurrently to include the use of statements and symbols.

- Be continuously aware of organization members' patterns of behavior to ascertain if they are consistent with the desired culture.

- Model appropriate behaviors.

- React appropriately to crises, critical incidents, and stress situations.

- Dispense rewards, praise, and criticisms fairly and appropriately.

> **"The concepts of power and leadership have been and will continue to be interconnected. While an individual may exert power without being a leader, an individual cannot be a leader without having power."**
>
> —Vidula Bal et al., Center for Creative Leadership White Paper

- Set strong, fair, and effective standards for recruitment, selection, promotion, and termination.[34]

Culture is a potentially important tool for obtaining desired behaviors of organization members. Climate is apt to change with the organization's circumstances, but culture, especially if properly attended, can be a persistent source of reinforcement for behavioral control. However, if left unattended and unnurtured, culture can become perverse and degenerate into subcultures. Savvy leaders must therefore pay careful and continuous attention to culture.

15.5. Power: Formal and Informal

Power is defined as "the ability to act; the capacity for action and performance . . . At the heart of any relationship is the ability to influence the other person to gain support for your program."[35] Leadership and power go hand in hand. As the box on the left states, power is necessary for leaders to be effective.[36] Savvy leaders are therefore wise to have a sound understanding of power in their businesses—which members have power, its sources, how they use it, and how it can be marshaled by the leader for the betterment of the firm or the leader's unit. It is important for leaders to recognize that organizations have both formal and informal power structures. **Formal power** is usually associated with positions on organization charts and power prescribed by policies, rules, and regulations. But the reality of how decisions are made is often quite different than the power embodied in formal structure and codified in writing. The power to influence can come from a variety of sources and is often held by organization members whose titles and job descriptions belie the extent of influence they wield. This is usually referred to as **informal power**.[37] Sometimes formal power is referred to loosely as *positional power* or *legitimate power,* and informal power as *personal power.*[38] A variety of more specific sources of power have been identified as falling under these two general categories.

Leadership needs to be aware of organization members holding significant informal power because these people often have substantial influence over employee subgroups. Organizationally savvy leaders at all levels are well served by understanding who holds power, why they hold it, and the extent of their power to improve the effectiveness of their units. For example, informal power can sometimes be wielded to protect organizational units from unwarranted and dysfunctional interference from outsiders and to facilitate mission accomplishment.[39]

A useful starting point for understanding power in businesses is John French and Bertram Raven's classic schema (1959) for categorizing various sources of power that became somewhat of a cornerstone for research on power in organizations. These researchers identified five somewhat distinct powers that included *legitimate, reward, coercive, expert,* and *referent* powers. The first four are fairly self-explanatory. The fifth, referent power, emanates from other organization members having a high level of identification with and/or admiration for a member. French and Raven's seminal work was expanded upon by Paul Hersey and Ken Blanchard (1982), who added *connection power* and *information power* to the original five powers. Connection power simply refers to an organization member being connected in some way to other organizational members who hold power and is often referred to as *networking.* Information power emanates from the ability to control critical information and can be either positional or personal power.[40]

Subsequent researchers have identified many different additional forms and sources of power that fall under the two general categories or are subsets of the aforementioned seven. What follows is a reasonably inclusive list of these powers:

1. *Resource control power* comes from being given authority of resources relatively irrespective of position in the organizational hierarchy. "The classic example is the facilities manager who can override the requirements of a VP for the design of a personal office because the facilities manager has been empowered by the organization to enforce a facilities policy."[41] This specific source of control includes control of technology.[42]

2. *Coercive power* is derived from the ability to influence others using threats, punishment, or sanctions.[43]

3. *Reward power* arises from an allocation of incentives to include both intrinsic and extrinsic rewards.[44]

4. *Charisma* or *personality power* comes from charm, mode of dress, interpersonal communications skills, and other personal attributes that cause people to like the individual.[45] Great popularity can make it more difficult for leadership to sanction a

"Power is the probability that one actor within the relationship will be in a position to carry out his own will despite resistance."

—Max Weber

Understanding the Organizational Environment

subordinate and draw the ire of other subordinates because in many cases leaders should not disclose the reasons for such sanctioning.

5. *Control over decision processes* gives rise to power because approvals can be withheld to negate or force modification of proposals.[46]

Research reveals some interesting data regarding how power is used and what forms of power are most useful. For example, 28 percent of leaders surveyed in studies conducted by the Center for Creative Leadership report that power is misused by top leadership. The three most leveraged sources of informal power are expertise, information, and relationships, with the latter being used most often to promote leaders' own personal agendas. The sources of power leaders believe will be most important in the future are relationships, information, and rewards.[47] The result underscores the importance of leaders developing a strong base of informal power in order to overcome obstacles to improving organizational effectiveness.

One important concept to understand about informal power is that of **sweat equity**, a term originally used to describe the work people put into building their own houses but now more generally defined as "a party's contribution to a project in the form of effort."[48] The amount of sweat equity organization members put into a project is sometimes quite disparate, with some members having a great deal more than others. In team activities, there is a tendency to attribute more voice in decision making to those members who have put forth more effort into projects. Sweat equity is not just a quantity issue but also one of quality. If a lack of quality means some members have to spend significant time correcting other members' work, then the value of sweat equity goes down. When team members of equal formal standing

> **"I once had a project I was trying to get funded but was having trouble working my way up through the chain of command. Finally it hit me that I didn't have to be the one to sell my proposal. I arranged for a senior-level leader to brief the organization on the topic and made sure the head of my organization was invited. The briefing was a huge success, and my organization head asked what we could do to follow up. I sent in my proposal, and it was funded immediately."**
>
> —Owen Godeken, "Bridging the PM Performance Gap," *Defense AT&L* (July–August 2009)

but with far less sweat equity attempt to assert power disproportional to their equity, perceptions of unfairness can arise and result in resistance by other members. The lesson is simply this: when assigned as a team member to a project, don't expect your voice in decision making to be materially greater than your contributions. The harder and more effectively you work, the more informal power you will likely gain.

15.6. How and How Not to Use Power: Some General Remarks

As indicated by the testimony in the box on the right, power can be put to good use in achieving organizational aims. Savvy, ethical leaders understand how to use power and how not to use it. Unfortunately, survey evidence suggests that less than 30 percent of business organizations teach leaders about power and how to leverage it for the good of the organization.[49]

287

Leaders sometimes fixate on formal power, particularly position power, but there is often a gap between leaders' formal power and their responsibilities—a power mismatch.[50] For leaders to accomplish their missions this gap must be closed using informal power. For example, project managers may have authority over execution using partial funding, but further execution—and therefore project continuance—may require approval for funding the next phase. Obtaining such funding might entail going up against other fund-

"If you want to use your power effectively, learn about the other party's needs, interests, and goals."

—Allen R. Cohen

ing requests and winning. For leaders for whom failure is not an option, some of the strategies for closing this gap include networking to gain informal support from others, building reciprocal relationships with powerful organization members, and the use of expert power to convince those with approval authority. The key is understanding how power, formal and informal, is distributed in the organization and tapping into it.[51]

If one accepts that the real basis of informal power is interpersonal relationships, developing this power represents an investment in time to build and maintain relationships. Your network is not just the colleagues or those with whom you have a personal relationship. That's a support group. Your network must be broader than that.[52] Leaders often do not know when the need for informal power will arise at some future date, so they are well advised to work on retaining and expanding networks of people who might someday become valuable sources of information and expertise.[53] Years may go by before a contact becomes enormously valuable. Consider the following testimony from one of the coauthors:

Over the years I taught thousands of students and stayed in touch with a number of them. Many have gone on to become very successful in various aspects of business. After retiring from teaching I became involved with working with startup life sciences companies to commercialize intellectual property developed by university faculty. Today, I routinely call on several former students for their expertise in areas such as entrepreneurship, intellectual property protection and licensing, venture capital, and healthcare consulting. Some of these contacts have also proved valuable in getting in the doors of business prospects. I still teach occasionally and advise students to start building their network of contacts while they are in school. And, as much as I dislike social media personally, I grudgingly admit it can be a very useful tool for networking.

As the quote by Allen R. Cohen indicates, building an informal power base begins with developing an understanding of others' needs, interests, and goals. It would be unwise, however, to do this with transparent insincerity in ways that appear manipulative, and sincerity requires genuinely caring about other organizational members' welfare, showing both sympathy and empathy when appropriate. It does not mean sympathizing with co-workers when they are in the wrong merely to garner their support. It does not mean agreeing with bosses when they are wrong just to curry favor. Bosses who have an honest understanding of who they are and are humble enough to admit mistakes should appreciate polite, carefully considered advice coming from a subordinate that prevents a mistake from occurring.[54]

You may not always be fortunate in having such a boss, however, so you are well advised to assess carefully your boss's willingness to accept feedback and when asked provide it truthfully in a manner that does not appear to challenge his or her authority or wound his or her pride. In the coauthors' experience, sometimes the toughest bosses are the ones who are best able to handle—and often appreciate—honest disagreement coming from subordinates, provided their outstanding past performance has accumulated substantial balances in their organizational creditability accounts, as discussed in chapter 1. In fact, properly done, honest, accurate feedback that prevents bosses from, as one former boss of a coauthor put it, "walking off the cliff blindfolded" may actually engender additional power for the subordinate. Savvy leaders cultivate subordinates to whom they can go to for honest answers on handling difficult situations. Our advice for subordinates is to develop a reputation for being tactfully honest. When asked by a boss for your opinion, be circumspect in how you provide it—but be honest. Our experience suggests that savvy, perceptive bosses are usually able to accept critical feedback and discern honest agreement from self-serving flattery. A boss who believes that polite disagreement is being given in her best interests is far more likely to appreciate honest feedback.

One way for leaders to develop large networks of support is by mentoring, coaching, and championing others and making themselves susceptible to mentoring and coaching. Overly proud leaders who believe they are too accomplished to need mentoring and coaching not only engage in self-deception but also deny themselves an opportunity to expand their support network. Advocating for others, especially deserving subordinates and co-workers, is an excellent way to develop. By championing high-performing subordinates, leaders gain their support and loyalty while at the same time serving the organization and developing a reputation for being a leader who helps others move up faster in their careers. This can create a synergistic effect whereby promising young starts seek to be assigned as subordinates to the champion.[55]

15.7. How and How Not to Use Power: A Deeper Dive

What follows are some specific examples on how to use and not use various sources of power. As stated in chapter 12, leaders are well served to develop knowledge and expertise throughout their careers. Doing so makes them more valuable to their firms and therefore more likely to survive organizational storms and thrive in terms of advancement. It is not uncommon for subordinates to have more expertise than both their leaders and co-workers in certain matters. Withholding knowledge from co-workers, however, in an effort to continuously appear superior can easily backfire. Astute leadership eventually sees through such manipulative behaviors as the expert subordinate over time develops a reputation for not communicating important knowledge to co-workers.

As related in an earlier chapter, there are times to use authority—and use it with sufficient force to make a point—but formal, authoritarian power is easily overused and sometimes abused. If leaders find themselves having to use positional power with great frequency, this is often a sign of poor leadership. "Being the boss, however, does not guarantee that you will have followers that comply of their own free will. Using only positional power means you make decisions without consideration of personal relationships, individual needs, and personal objectives."[56] Further, an ill-disguised hunger for positional authority can easily work against a leader. Consider the following anecdote supplied by a coauthor:

> A team had begun to assemble offsite for a project, and its leader was delayed in arriving. Fearing a loss of productive time, the leader encountered a team member who was also in transit and instructed him to temporarily take control. Upon arrival, the team member immediately announced that the boss had placed him in charge and

began to issue orders in an authoritarian manner while obviously relishing his new-found power. Despite the team having already taken the initiative to organize itself cooperatively and being hard at work, the temporary boss made no attempt to ascertain what work was already under way. To make matters worse, his initial instructions were for the team to repeat tasks that it had already accomplished without supervision. When team members objected, arguments erupted with the end result that the team simply refused to accept the temporary boss's authority, the team disintegrated as a unit, and work stopped until the real boss arrived to reorganize. The one positive was that giving the temporary boss even a small amount of power exposed his lust for it—which he had previously kept concealed behind superficial congeniality—showing his frailties as a leader, and ended his hopes of progression.

Three keys to developing greater informal power are (1) investing time in others, (2) identifying specific people with whom relationships may be beneficial, and (3) repairing relationships that have fallen into disrepair through neglect. Research indicates that nearly half of executives surveyed feel they need to find the time and energy to invest more time in existing relationships to enhance their informal power. Approximately a fourth of those surveyed felt they needed to identify individuals with whom they needed to develop closer relationships including bosses, peers, and customers, and another fourth recognized the need to repair damaged relationships in order to create greater trust.[57] Leveraging the power of relationships is best used when personal relationships are strong, the leader has the trust of organization members, and the desired outcome does not conflict with the interests of those to whom the leader is attempting to relate.[58]

Despite our previous admonitions about over-use of positional power, there are times to use it, including the power to sanction subordinates. This is necessary not only to correct the subordinate's misbehavior but also to set an example for others who might be inclined to misbehave. Leaders should use coercive power if they must when:

1. There is a need to ensure rules, policies, and standards are followed.

2. Significant risks necessitate careful behaviors that do not expose the organization to loss.

3. An organization member's behavior is so bizarre, disrespectful of others, and not in keeping with the desired culture that stern corrective action, including discharge, is required.[59]

Unless necessary to prevent immediate damage to the organization and/or its members, it is best not to use coercive power at a time when leaders feel frustrated and highly emotional because emotions can interfere with sound reasoning. Before applying sanctions that might appear draconian to some organization members, it is often a good idea to consult with your boss and possibly a human resources representative for three reasons. First, the sanction should be commensurate with the infraction. Second, sanctions need to be consistent with legal and organizational rules, policies, and precedents. Third, in the event sanctions result in significant blowback in the form of adverse actions by the member being sanctioned or even legal action, you do not want your boss and the organization to be surprised. Research indicates that the **power to reward** that comes with positional power is considered by many executives to be very important as a tool to leverage in attaining organizational aims.[60] There are some general guidelines for when and when not to use reward power. It is best to use reward power when:

Understanding the Organizational Environment

1. You need something done quickly.

2. Your team needs a motivational boost.

3. You're asking your followers to go above and beyond their duty.

4. You want to create friendly competition.

It is generally best to avoid using reward power when:

1. Resources are scarce so that using rewards becomes a zero-sum game such that when someone wins someone else loses.

2. Your ability to provide an adequate reward is questionable.

3. Petty jealousies are prevalent involving team members.[61]

To summarize our discussion of organizationally savvy leaders leveraging power to achieve the organization's goals and objectives as well as their own, leaders should make relationships a priority and maximize their communications networks to gain information power but not become information hoarders. They should realize that position doesn't always equate to power and use positional power judiciously. When necessary to sanction subordinates, they should punish with purpose and never vindictively. Savvy leaders should develop expertise in activities that add significant value to the organization but avoid the hubris of becoming the proud expert. They should be careful not to overplay their personal agendas so that they appear ambitious to excess and hungry for power such that co-workers are made uneasy about the leaders' self-serving behaviors. Being reasonably generous with rewards, leaders should take care to use reward appropriately and under conditions in which they are likely to be effective. Finally, savvy leaders should invest in others, mentoring those who seek it, coaching subordinates, and extending themselves to assist co-workers with information and expertise.[62]

15.8. Assessing Environmental, Organizational, and Job Fit

Two of the most important skills organizationally savvy leaders can have at their disposal is choosing the right people to bring into the organization, be they external or internal candidates, and being able to place the right people in the right jobs and roles once they are on board. This can be summarized by asking, "Is the candidate a good **fit**?" Sometimes the need for skill in assessing fit extends to an even more general level than that of the organization—the environment. Environmental fit can be important when leaders are considering hiring someone into a particular industry, such as a pharmaceutical or professional environment like public accounting.[63]

Assessing fit is extremely important in light of the findings that 30 percent or more of people seeking employment apply for fifty or more jobs indicating they are willing to accept a wide variety of situations irrespective of whether they possess the appropriate knowledge and skills suitable for those positions.[64] Hiring decisions that don't work out are very expensive. The costs associated with terminating employees, recruiting, orienting and training replacements, and the lost productivity when positions are gapped are high. One source indicates it costs $12,000 in recruitment and training alone to replace the average nonprofessional and $35,000 to acquire a new professional. Other estimates suggest costs of as high as 75 percent of annual salaries to replace nonmanagerial employees and 150 percent of managers' annual salaries.[65] Often, one of the most significant costs is not measured in monetary terms, however, but rather in the time it takes for leaders to deal with poorly performing employees and the organizational angst associated with discharging employees.

Figure 15.1. Relationships among Different Conceptualizations of P-E Fit

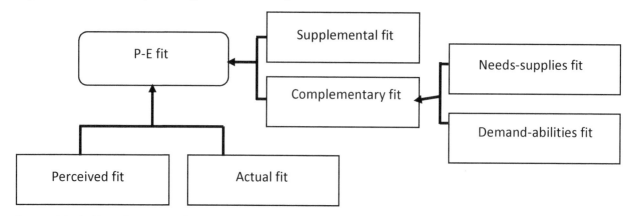

Source: Adapted from Figure 1 in T. Sekiguchi, "Person-Organization Fit and Person-Job Fit in Employee Selection: A Review of the Literature," *Osaka Keidai Ronshu,* 54 no. 6 (March 2004): 181.

Person-environment (P-E) fit is defined as the degree of congruence or match between a person and the environment, such as a particular profession or industry.[66] **Person-organization (P-O) fit** "refers to the compatibility between a person and the organization, emphasizing the extent to which a person and the organization share similar characteristics and meet each other's needs."[67] **Person-job (P-J) fit** "refers to the match between the abilities of a person and the demands of a job or the desires of a person and the attributes of a job."[68] Given these three levels of fit, assessing fit is more complex than is often believed. Take, for example, a student considering a career in public accounting in auditing. She should be asking herself at least three questions: (1) Is public accounting the right environment for me? (2) Is Ashton, Bancroft & Cressida, LLP, the right firm for me? (3) Is becoming an auditor the right job for me? Actually, two more questions are implied by these questions: (1) Do I know enough about the environment, organization, and job to adequately answer the questions? (2) If not, how do I obtain that knowledge?

P-E fit can be dimensioned into *complementary versus supplementary fit, needs-supplies versus demands-abilities fit,* and *perceived versus actual fit.* Supplementary fit refers to people perceptions that they fit in an environment because they are similar to others in the environment that is described by its inhabitants. Complementary fit occurs when the addition of a person adds to the environment defined apart from its inhabitants according to its demands and requirements. Complementary fit subsumes needs-supplies and demands-abilities fit because the latter determines the extent to which a person complements the environment. When environments meet people's needs this is described in terms of the needs-supplies dimension. On the other hand, when the environment demands particular skills, knowledge, and abilities this refers to the demands-abilities dimension. The perceived versus actual fit dimension contrasts an environment member's perceptions of his fit with the actual fit. These various dimensions impact upon one another as shown in Figure 15.1.

P-O fit is frequently measured in terms of the degree of congruence between individual and organizational values, goals, and characteristics such as personality and preferences for climate and culture. Research indicates that high levels of P-O fit are positively correlated with job satisfaction and organizational commitment, lower turnover, prosocial behaviors, teamwork, and higher performance. Consequently, employers and employees do well to pay careful attention to P-O fit. Despite these positive outcomes of P-O fit, howev-

292

er, it is often the case that employers pay the most attention to P-J fit, in that traditionally the primary concern has been finding applicants whose skills and abilities are best suited to a particular job as determined by job analysis compared to applicants' job-related attributes.[69] The implication may be that employers for which employee retention and development are priorities weighting the emphasis toward P-O fit as opposed to P-J fit may result in improved long-term outcomes.

Evidence suggests that many employees who have difficulty keeping their jobs are not lacking in the necessary technical skills. Technical ability alone does not ensure career success. Many of the transferrable skills that employees bring to a new job are related to interpersonal adeptness, so leaders are therefore well served to consider indicators beyond those of technical competence (e.g., degrees, grade-point averages, professional certifications and designations). Review each candidate's resume carefully for clues. Are there employment gaps? Are there periods in which the candidate was self-employed, and, if so, does this appear to be genuine employment or a way of hiding gaps in employment? Is there a clear record of progression over time or lots of lateral or backward movement? Draw up a list of questions in advance to include follow-on questions if you receive answers that suggest deeper digging. For example, "I notice you were self-employed as a tax accountant for 3 years. What unique challenges did self-employment present different from your prior experience with a large accounting firm?" Keep in mind that inflated or even fabricated resumes are not uncommon. Job candidates may alter job titles to make their past positions seem more important and inflate job descriptions. Be sensitive to possible evidence of resume inflating, but do not give away your suspicions.

The following is a partial list of guidelines that can easily make the difference between a successful hire and one that exits through the revolving door:

1. *Human relations skills* are essential, including good communications and harmonious interactions. A good technique is to ask the job candidate to describe situations with difficult people and how he or she handled them.

2. *Sound ethics* are essential, to include how the candidate feels about seemingly small ethical violations. Ask the candidate questions such as what he or she would do if he or she discovered an employee was taking home office supplies for the purpose of supplying his or her children for school.

3. *Extracurricular activities* can be important indicators of life balance but are easily placed on resumes and often passed by interviewers without comment. If a candidate reports being a volunteer at a children's hospital, ask such things as how that experience may have better prepared him or her to deal with adversity.

4. *Dig deeper when you sense something may be amiss.* If you sense that the hospital volunteer work may be superficial, ask more specific questions. If digging deeper makes the candidate ill at ease, this may be a signal that the resume is inflated.

5. *Don't ask leading questions.* A leading question would be, "Here at XYZ we value collegiality. Would you describe yourself as a good colleague?" This is telegraphing the desired answer to the candidate. Instead, ask the candidate to describe a situation in which he or she initially had difficulty dealing with someone but was able to resolve the difficulty and achieve good relations.

6. *Ask penetrating questions but don't be intrusive.* A penetrating question might be, "So, your last job required very long hours. How were you able to balance the time

commitment and have time for your family?" An intrusive question would be, "Didn't your family suffer because you worked so hard?"

7. *After the interview,* draw reasonable conclusions based upon what you saw and heard in the way of factual evidence and compare these to your instincts. If the two do not line up, try to understand why. For example, if a candidate appears to be well qualified but makes you uneasy, try to understand the reasons for your unease. If you cannot resolve the differences, it may be desirable to have the candidate interview with someone else to get a cross-check on your opinion.[70]

In our experience, some job candidates base their impression of a large organization upon interactions with one interviewer. Although this can be a mistake on the part of the candidate, organizations that view job interviews as a one-way interaction are missing an important point—both the interviewer and interviewee are interviewing, and many of the same principles regarding fit hold when you are assessing potential employment situations. As we discussed much earlier in the book, decades of collection experience tells us that job satisfaction is greatest when working in an environment, organization, climate, culture, and job conducive to making as many of your daily transactions as enjoyable as possible. Although it is highly unlikely there is a job situation wherein all your transactions will be enjoyable, having the majority enjoyable over the long term is a prerequisite for continuing satisfaction. Consequently, careful attention to fit when seeking employment is important to career satisfaction and success. One way to discover whether the organization you are seeking is a good fit for you is to ask penetrating questions in a nonthreatening, uncritical manner.

Many job candidates make the mistake of believing that all interview time should be dedicated to making their case for employment to the interviewer. We disagree. Much information about you can be conveyed by the quality and thoughtfulness of the questions you ask your interviewers and the ensuing dialogue in attempting to gain deeper insights into the climate and culture of the prospective employer. Consider the following story related by one of the coauthors:

The CEO, another senior officer, and I sat alone eating lunch in a private corporate dining room. This was my big job interview and, despite the excellent food and impressive surrounds, nervousness had killed my appetite. The interview began as I expected with the two top leaders asking me standard questions about my experience and qualifications, but then it took a somewhat unexpected turn. At one point the CEO remarked, "I see you have a military background. Tell me about it." So I provided a brief summation of my experiences and then asked a question myself: "How does the firm feel about the value of military experience?" This question launched the CEO on a story about having been an admiral's aide in the navy. My nervousness evaporated as the conversation became an easy dialogue with us sharing common experiences during which we both probably learned more about each other than any series of scripted questions would have unearthed. At the conclusion of lunch, the CEO pushed back from the table and said, "You'll be a fine fit for our organization. After lunch Frank will talk compensation with you. If you two agree, how soon could you start?"

Although the foregoing experience may be atypical of most employment interviews, it underscores the point that interviews should be a two-way process of discovery. Asking the right

Understanding the Organizational Environment

questions not only helps determine whether the organization is a fit for you but also communicates something about the depth of your thinking and your determination to find the best employer for your needs. Both parties should be cautious, however, to avoid any suggestion of hubris and haughtiness in their interactions. Even if the employer has ten candidates in line for each position, or even if the candidate is being heavily recruited by multiple employers, both are well advised to treat each and every employment interview with professionalism, attention, and respect. Circumstances change and employment is often not a "one-period game" in that most executives will work for several employers during their careers. In a few years you may find yourself interviewing with the very firm you turn down—or that turns you down—today, so don't "burn your bridges" behind you.

One of the coauthors notes, "When seeking admission to doctoral programs, one school wrote me back rather bluntly discouraging my applying saying that I was older than their usual doctoral students. A few years later upon graduation from a different school with my PhD, the same school contacted me asking me to consider a faculty position there." The coauthor adds wryly, "My thought at the time was, 'They think me well qualified enough to teach at their university but not qualified to learn there? That doesn't make much sense.' Because my first experience had left a bad taste, I declined the second opportunity. In retrospect, although circumstances worked out well personally, both parties were probably wrong in the manner in which they viewed the interactions."

15.9. Dealing with Uncertainty, Ambiguity, and Change

One of the most difficult challenges facing leaders is dealing with uncertainty and ambiguity on organizational, subordinate, and personal levels. The acronym VUCA (Volatility, Uncertainty, Change, and Ambiguity) quickly depicts the overall challenges. Volatility involves the cyclical, seasonal, and unexpected ups, downs, and sideways that occur. Uncertainty often involves risk and is threatening for many people. In a business world characterized by growing dynamism and the uncertainty it brings, a seemingly placid workplace can be disrupted by many sudden events, such as the announcement of a merger, an organizational restructuring, a major new initiative, the loss of a large customer, business financial distress, or the introduction of a new product by a competitor unforeseen by the firm's leadership. Major, disruptive organizational events can be very unsettling for subordinates, and leaders can find themselves caught in a web of uncertainty, followers' fears, and their own anxieties about the future. Uncertainty for leaders can also emanate from personal factors, such as getting a new boss, receiving a promotion, or being transferred to a different unit. Being able to deal with uncertainty and ambiguity is one of the most important abilities leaders can have, not only because they must keep subordinates' fears from spinning out of control but also for reasons related to their own emotional intelligence. In fact, the international CPA firm of Ernst & Young indicates that dealing with ambiguity is one of the more difficult skills to master.[71]

Space does not permit dealing with the many sources of uncertainty in business, so for illustrative purposes we focus on one of the most difficult uncertainty challenges leaders face—managing **organizational change**. Substantive change is threatening for many people, particularly those who do not feel secure in their own abilities and value to the organization. **Change resistance** is a well-known phenomenon to many experienced leaders and sometimes the subject of wry humor. Managing change is particularly difficult when organizational major restructuring is being proposed because such restructuring frequently involves downsizing the business, the elimination of some positions, and the reclassification of others. Consider the following testimony by a coauthor:

Across four and a half decades of organizational life, some of the most difficult and disconcerting tasks I have undertaken involved being an integral part of organizational restructurings. This has been true in business, academia, and the military and includes acquisitions, major program restructuring, launching new programs to replace or augment old ones, and downsizing of force structure. In most cases these restructurings were not handled as well as they might have been by leadership, probably due to a lack of understanding of the levels of fear and emotion among many organization members and how to best deal with them. These fears and emotions led to significant acrimony as jobs, power, and resources were placed in jeopardy and turf battles ensued. In all cases, my observation was that, had leaders done a better job of preparing their organizations for these changes, at least some of the uncertainties, ambiguities, and conflicts could have been eliminated or reduced.

The literature on mergers and acquisitions offers interesting insights into the effects of traumatic organizational change. Ignoring the human factor and people's resistance to change is cited as one of the key reasons for failure of 60 percent to 80 percent of organizational consolidations.[72] The acquisition of a person's employer is likely to be one of the most significant changes organization members will ever face, and how the company answers questions such as the following will have a lot to do with how committed members are to making consolidations successful: "Will I have a job? Who is my new boss going to be? Will I have to move?" Too often leaders are so concerned with getting the deal closed and moving on that they fail to consider the uncertainty and fears of those down the hierarchical ladder whose efforts will make or break the implementation.

Given the inevitably of change and its increasing frequency, leaders have but two choices in preparing themselves mentally to deal with it—dread and fear it, or learn how to embrace and manage it. A starting point is recognizing that change is a far more complicated organizational phenomenon than often realized, and, even when leadership takes measures to prepare their businesses for major changes, such preparations are often viewed in a static manner instead of a continuous process. A traditional approach for proactively dealing with change is anticipating and attempting to mitigate change resistance. Once leadership creates what it hopes is the groundwork for preparing the organization for major change, the feeling is that the problem has been resolved. Not only is this often not the case for several reasons including unforeseen emergent exigencies, but it is an inherently negative mindset that is easily transmitted by leaders to subordinates—change is a bad thing, but we're trying to ease the pain preemptively.[73]

In today's increasingly dynamic business environment, a better approach is to view change as a series of processes, with occasional crescendos of activity due to various events. Under this view of change, the role of leadership is to create a continual change readiness in organizations with change perceived as offering opportunities as opposed to threats. Needless to say, this is a daunting task that requires a deeper understanding of change than many leaders appreciate. It involves creating a change message along the dimensions organization members use to form attitudes, beliefs, and intentions. At its core, a positive message about change being an opportunity versus a threat must address several questions affirmatively in the minds of organization members to include:

1. Is the change needed and why?

2. Will the proposed change adequately address the deficiency it is intended to correct?

3. Can the change be successfully implemented with the available resources?

4. To what degree do leadership and organizational members support the change?

5. How will the proposed change affect individuals within the organization?[74]

In addition to persuasively communicating satisfactory answers to these questions for members, leaders can engage in various tactics to win members over to proposed changes that include the following:

1. Seek early volunteers that are adaptable and have good emotional intelligence to actively participate in planning for and implementing the change.

2. Take into account interpersonal dynamics such as the effects of change on existing informal coalitions inside the organization.

3. Enlist popular and respected organization members with informal power to become change agents and counter the inevitable unfounded rumors and misinformation that are propagated through the "employee grapevine."

4. Find savvy, "honest broker" constructive critics to meet periodically, critically evaluate how change is progressing, and offer solutions for correcting implementation problems.[75]

Successful leadership requires continual adjustment to a changing environment and the political skill to navigate the fearful waters change presents for many organization members including leaders. Having political skill serves to reinforce leaders' belief in their own abilities to act as causal agents in effecting change and reduces their uncertainty about outcomes.[76] This is particularly true even if leaders are successful in preparing or-

ganization members for change because change readiness and continuing commitment have been shown to be somewhat separate and distinct.

In the end, the new business environment is demanding businesses that are built for change rather than organizations that undergo change occasionally. Such organizations have a strong future focus, are flexible in redesigning themselves as required by changing environments, and are able to successfully orchestrate changes on a routine basis. In order to deal with the attendant uncertainties and associated fears, built-for-change organizations must develop among members a sense of adaptability and readiness for change, a diversity of specialization, functional differentiation among workgroups, adequate slack resources to allow rapid redeployment of human resources, and strong formal and informal communication systems capable of conveying continuous and accurate information about ongoing and prospective changes and processes that reduce the perceived risks and adverse consequences of uncertainty and ambiguity.[77] If your organization's future depends upon being built-for-change, careful consideration of how well its leaders and members are equipped to deal with uncertainty is paramount.

15.10. Concluding Thoughts on Becoming Organizationally Savvy Leaders

Becoming organizationally savvy is not the same as becoming overtly political, but the preferred behavior for leaders is not political naïveté. Successful leaders must understand who holds power, what power they hold, and how it can be used in order to navigate the political waters of business and accomplish organizational goals and objectives. Power is a necessity for leaders to be effective, so leaders need to be aware of the need for it and how to acquire and use it. Highly successful leaders exert their power in three ways: (1) They set high-but-attainable goals, objectives, and performance standards, encouraging organization members to meet these standards and insisting they do so. (2) They set forth and model outstanding values that underlie the organization's culture and direct members' actions, showing what is and is not acceptable behavior and reflecting the organization's concern for its customers and members. (3) They establish and nurture sound business and interpersonal relationships that drive the organization's value-creating activities, products, and services. Using power in these ways helps constitute the organization's personality and determines how it is viewed by its members and external constituents. It also defines to a significant extent roles, relationships, intrinsic rewards, and rites of passage among members.[78]

Using power in these ways aligns quite well with Kouzes and Posner's (1987) five keys to great leadership, which involve:

> 1. Challenging processes by finding and fixing dysfunctional systematic behaviors, rules, and procedures.

> 2. Inspiring a shared vision among organization members that creates a sense of being part of something good that is reaching for greatness.

> 3. Enabling other organization members to act by providing them with the methods and tools they need to solve problems and empowering them to accomplish greater things.

> 4. Modeling the way by "walking the walk," not just "talking the talk."

> 5. Encouraging other organization members' hearts by sharing the credit but not the disappointments.[79]

It is important to keep in mind that the source of power in business organizations is most often relationships. One of its great ironies is that those who hoard it either lose it or stifle its growth, and those who share it deftly usually see their personal power grow. Although leaders with formal authority do well to employ these five keys, one need not have a formal leadership position to use them. Informal leaders can and do emerge by subtly engaging in leader-like behaviors that inspire and enable others while removing obstacles in the way of mission accomplishment. The truth is that most organization members want to be well led, and they abhor a leadership vacuum. In the absence of formal leadership performing in the manner described above, they will often gravitate toward informal leaders who provide sound leadership without being overtly dominant. This can eventually lead to informal leaders being nominated by their bosses to become formal leaders.

So much can be said about organizational savvy that it is difficult provide anything close to holistic coverage in one chapter. We therefore leave our discussion of leadership and organizational savvy with some additional thoughts provided by the U.S. Army. Savvy leaders know their jobs, themselves, and their deficiencies and seek continuous improvement. They understand human nature and how people respond to stress, uncertainty, ambiguity, and change. They assess situations with savvy and know how to lead, follow, and communicate clearly using both formal and informal power.[80] Your career depends to a large extent upon your development of organizational savvy.

Understanding the Organizational Environment

CHAPTER 16

Customer/Client Interface:

The Bottom Line Is about the Top Line

> "Generally speaking, the more cash flow a company generates, the more valuable it is. The question then is, 'How does a company increase its cash flow and, therefore, boost the value of the business?' The best way is to address issues like leadership, strategy and management."
>
> —Kristen Hampshire, "What Drives Value?" *Smart Business*

What has client interface to do with courageous leadership? The answer is a great deal. In previous chapters we have talked about the importance of courageous savvy leaders maintaining a customer focus. As the quote above states, there is a definite connection between leadership and the value of businesses, and in the final analysis it is customers who drive this value. Leaders should never lose sight of the need for a customer focus. There is a caveat to this customer focus, however. The focus needs to be on the right customers, and herein lies one of the greatest leadership challenges.

There is an old adage that says, "The customer is always right." The underlying message in this saying is for employees to give customers what they want and never disagree. Is that best for firms? The answer is no for several reasons, including the following: (1) Customers don't always know what is best for themselves. (2) Some customers are bad for business. They demand too much, are unprofitable, and detract from the business's ability to provide high-quality service to good customers. (3) Customers who are abusive to employees destroy morale, and leaders who permit abusive behaviors in an effort to please customers lose the trust of their subordinates.[1]

On one hand customers are indispensable to business success, and establishing a sound customer/client interface is a critical leadership function. On the other hand, customers are not always easy to interface with successfully, so savvy leaders need to cultivate a keen understanding of how their organizations want this interface conducted. This chapter addresses this all-important issue of dealing with customers and clients, nouns we will hereafter use interchangeably. We begin with a discussion of why revenues are critical to the bottom line.

16.1. Why Is the Top Line So Important?

What makes a continuing business valuable? Perhaps this is best seen in mathematical terms using a simple example of how operating companies are often valued. Although there are three basic approaches to valuing companies, for ongoing

299

Figure 16.1. Comparison of Value with Sales Growth Rates for Companies in a Similar Line of Business

Company Percentile	Long-Term Growth Percentages			
	Sales	Assets	Net Income	Equity
25th Percentile	13.3%	11.1%	13.1%	8.5%
Median	17.9%	17.3%	23.0%	11.4%
75th Percentile	18.7%	28.1%	33.7%	25.4%

Source: Adapted from J. R. Hitchner, *Financial Valuation: Applications and Models,* 2nd ed. (Hoboken, N.J.: Wiley, 2006), 289.

Note: The source does not disclose the line of business nor does it stipulate the time period used for these data, but discussion elsewhere in the reference suggests a 5-year period.

enterprises a common valuation approach known as the **income approach** utilizes the company's potential to generate a future economic stream of benefits for its investors. This benefit stream is often measured as **net cash flows** (NCF) and is defined as the cash flows available to investors after all other claims on the company's cash flows have been satisfied. Under this approach, a common methodology to value common equity in a company with an expected constant growth rate in NCF is the **capitalized cash flow (CCF) method**. Using the CCF method, a company's NCF is capitalized by dividing by a **capitalization rate** calculated as a **discount rate** (k) minus the **growth rate** (g) of the NCF. This discount rate used is normally the sum of the real rate of return (i.e., risk-free rate), expected inflation, and the uncertainty associated with the realization of the expected stream of economic benefits. These relationships are expressed in the following equation:

$$FMV = NCF / (k\text{-}g)$$

Since both k and g are fractions, the lower the capitalization rate the higher the value; and, since the capitalization rate decreases as g increases, the higher the growth, the higher the value.[2] Thus, a company with an NCF of $1,000,000, a capitalization rate of 12 percent, and a growth rate of 5 percent would be valued as follows using the CCF method:

$$FMV = NCF / (k\text{-}g) = \$1,000,000 / (.12\text{-}.05)$$
$$= \$14,285,714$$

If that company is able to improve g by 1 percent without altering its capitalization rate, then the value increases as follows:

$$FMV = NCF / (k\text{-}g) = \$1,000,000 / (.12\text{-}.06)$$
$$= \$16,666,667$$

What has this got to do with revenues? The answer is that the primary driver of NCF growth is revenue growth. This can perhaps best be seen by examining financial statements on a hypothetical company under differing conditions. Consider Figure 16.1 on the following page containing data on long-term growth rates for companies in the same line of business. There is an obvious relationship between growth in revenues and growth in assets, net income, and shareholder value. Although these relationships are doubtless unsurprising to many experienced business executives and professionals, what may be informative is the magnitude. A difference of 5 percent to 6 percent in long-term sales growth is associated with approximately three times the growth rate in shareholder equity. This underscores the importance of sales to growth in value.

It is apparent from Figure 16.1 that, ceteris paribus, sales growth has a rather profound effect on the value of the companies making up the percentiles, but what about reducing costs to increase firm value? In times of economic downturn, companies often engage in cost-reduction programs in attempting to maintain their NCF growth rates.

Cost reduction programs do not, however, result in continuously decreasing costs over extended periods for the reason perhaps best analogized by picking apples. The low-hanging fruit goes first. Once that fruit is gone, it become increasing more difficult to pick the next basket of apples as one climbs higher in the tree. Ultimately, the marginal returns from additional picking do not equal the effort required. The same holds for costs. Cost reduction can sometimes maintain growth in NCF temporarily but not over longer periods. The result is that continuous growth in revenues is the real key to growing the value of businesses in perpetuity.

16.2. Six Basics of the Client Interface

Now that we have hopefully established the importance of revenue generation to business value, what are the implications? One implication is that getting the client interface right is essential to continuous long-term revenue growth. As with the association of growth in revenues and other business growth metrics, this seems obvious. Obvious though it may be, some businesses—as is equally obvious from Figure 16.1—do a much better job of this than others. So, despite being obvious, there is a need for savvy leaders to focus on the client relationship. A starting point is to reflect on some basics before plunging deeper—basics that are all too frequently lost in the complexities of transacting business day to day and the pressure to deliver on short-term goals such as monthly sales targets or billable hours.

At the most basic level, developing a good client interface involves six actions:[3]

1. *Getting to know clients*—knowing clients is far more involved than merely becoming acquainted. Knowing clients means many things. It means knowing their needs and problems, proclivities, preferences for information, how they react to new ideas, and how they see you and your firm in comparison to your competition. Over time, your depth of knowledge of clients should extend to understanding them at a personal level and learning about their professional ambitions and the challenges they face inside their organizations.

2. *Doing an exceptional job in serving clients' needs*—as with most relationships, trust is critical in the client relationship. One of the fastest ways to destroy trust is to not meet client expectations, thereby placing the clients' members with whom you interface in a bad light. One of the quickest ways to build trust is to deliver more than you promised and do it in a way that makes those with whom you interface look good in the process.

3. *Communicating regularly and effectively with clients*—there is no substitute for regular, interpersonal communication in client relations. Consider the following anecdote supplied by a coauthor:

> We were a medium-sized, well-run business that used a large CPA firm as our independent auditor. We rarely saw or heard from the partner-in-charge of our relationship in between annual audits. Communications with his subordinates were usually limited to casual, "Is everything ok?" types of inquiries with no real effort to uncover any unsatisfied needs. We strongly suspected we were being taken for granted—an easy to audit, cleanly run business with few problems. This impression deepened as we began to notice that less-experienced personnel were being used on our engagement. When asked to facilitate a connection to the auditor's consulting services (assisting in evaluating a major information technology purchase), the young manager at our site, consumed with his auditing responsibilities, forgot to make the requested connection. Concurrently, as the relationship was atrophying, our audit business was being

heavily solicited by another CPA firm. Because we weren't publicly traded, we weren't concerned about changing auditors and switched, reducing our fees in the process.

One point to glean from the above anecdote is that *regularly* and *effectively* are not synonymous. Depending upon the preferences of individuals with whom you are dealing, taking your client's time without adding any value to the relationship risks becoming annoying—superficial inquiries somewhat analogous to a waiter asking three times during a meal, "How's the food tasting?" having forgotten that he's asked twice previously.

4. *Eliciting feedback from clients and acting on that feedback*—knowing what questions to ask is critically important. Asking the client, "How is our product working out for you?" doesn't go deep enough. Drill down to discover whether or not your product or service is really meeting client needs. Ask for specifics such as, "How did well did our product solve your problem with the widget defect?" and "Is there anything our product isn't doing that you wish it would?" One critical point, however, is that uncovering problems with your offerings without a full and rapid follow-up to solve them communicates insincerity. You are probably better off not asking than asking and then failing to act in a timely manner and destroying trust. As discussed later in the section, insincerity is particularly damaging when dealing with certain types of clients who have a natural mistrust of salesmanship and especially of being hustled.

5. *Having the requisite expertise to meet client needs and applying this expertise well*—a prior chapter discussed the need to grow technical skills as well as leadership skills throughout your career. As you progress up the organizational hierarchy, it is likely that your interactions with clients will become increasingly complex. Larger and more important clients are often associated with greater complexity of operations. This means a substantial ability to exercise critical and creative thinking skills in complex-problem finding and solving. Your ability to peer incisively inside your clients' business and detect opportunities to add value has a great deal to do with your ability to grow your revenues.

6. *Cultivating the client as a partner, not a buyer*—how do you see your client, as a *buyer* or a *partner*? A buyer relationship is much easier for competition to attack than a partnership. A buyer relationship says, "I want to sell you something." A partner relationship speaks, "We're in this together. What benefits you benefits me." It's far easier to steal somebody's prom date than to break up a happy marriage.

These are just some simple basics of client relations. Before plunging deeper into interfacing with clients, we believe it is helpful to first gain a strategic perspective on the client. One way of accomplishing this is to understand that both you and your client are links in a chain of value-creating activities.

16.3. A Strategic View of Customer and Client Relations

Good client relations begin with understanding your clients. How do they make money? What do they do that creates value for *their* customers? What are their strategic opportunities and threats? What strengths and weaknesses do they have? By putting yourself in the minds of your clients you can think far more effectively about how you can provide them with products or services that will enhance their ability to generate revenues. This, in turn, generates revenues for you. With a little introspection, you may see a parallel to what was discussed in chapter 1 about getting your priorities right. If your client is your partner, then he or she is part of your pack, and your pack comes first. Your first priority is to figure out what benefits your pack. To do that you need to put yourself in the minds of your clients and think about what you would do if you were running those businesses.

It is also helpful to understand that no matter who your customer is, your product or service represents a resource to the customer. Even if you are selling electronic equipment to consumers, your service represents a *means* for them to get to some *end.* That end may be happiness and personal satisfaction that comes from interacting with family and friends. It may be the prestige that comes from owning the latest mega-G cell phone that downloads from the Internet at the speed of light. It may be a way of staying in touch with their clients. What you are selling, however, is not just a device but also a resource for reaching either a state of mind or business growth and efficiency. Most often the customer doesn't want your product or service but rather the benefits that come from it.

Steve Jobs understood this clearly when he returned to Apple to turn the company back from the economic abyss. Jobs said that most market research is focused on determining preferences among products that already exist, but it does little to get to the deeper level—what capability would the customer love to have that he or she doesn't have, perhaps a capability he or she hasn't even dreamed of having yet.[4] When you try to sell potential customers something your competition is already selling them, you have to convince them that your product performs significantly better than the existing product or that yours is sufficiently cheaper to justify switching costs. When you sell something the customer needs and wants but doesn't have, you have a unique opportunity

> **"Star performers always manage to find a way to see their work, and the product it helps to build, through the eyes of the customer. The stars work to understand what customer needs and motivations are, even though they may be far removed from the sales office."**
>
> —Robert E. Kelley, *How to Be a Star at Work*

to win a new customer and perhaps a foot in the door to sell other products and services.

Therefore, start your understanding of clients by considering three themes that basically describe how businesses function: (1) value chain, (2) value drivers, and (3) strategic positioning. "The **value chain** for any firm in any business in the linked set of value-creating activities all the way from basic raw material sources for component suppliers through to the ultimate end-use product delivered into the final consumers' hands."[5] So, for example, if you are selling consulting services to an electronics components manufacturer, from a value-chain perspective your challenge is to understand how the manufacturer's products add value to its electronics-manufacturer customers. If you can help the client upgrade its business performance measurement system so that it has better visibility over its critical value drivers such as its response to market dynamism in its clients' markets instead of focusing on labor efficiency, you may enable it to become the supplier of choice.

Value drivers are the product attributes and actions necessary to create them that make customers want to buy your clients' products or services. As discussed in chapter 13, which dealt with organization control and measurement, principal value drivers need to be aligned with clients' mis-

Figure 16.2. Porter's Five Forces

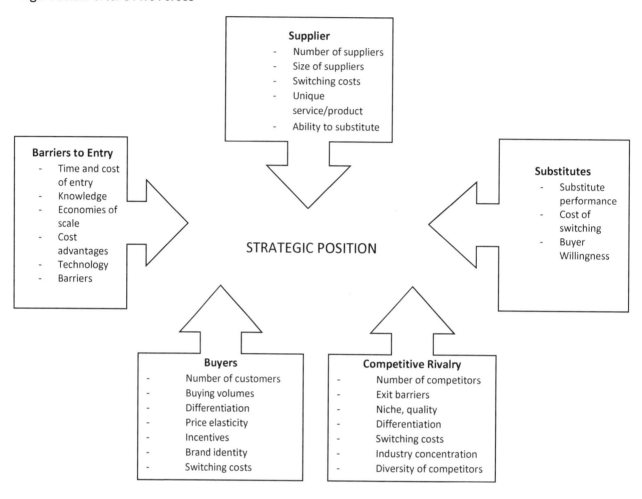

sions and strategies. Sometimes clients have no precise idea of what their value drivers may be or how to optimize them. Helping your clients identify and control value drivers can add enormously to their sales—and yours. Even though it may seem this observation is aimed only at consultants, that is not the case. Many companies report that some of the best improvement ideas come from suppliers of products or services they use. For example, through electronic data interchange a hospital supply company can assist healthcare providers by reducing order frequency and inventory hoarding, expediting shipments, and reducing suboptimal emergency purchasing decisions.[6]

Strategic positioning refers to how a client positions its products or services with respect to its competition.[7] There are various strategies customers of an electronics-component company might employ, such as being a low-cost, high-performance, or niche-need supplier. Accompanying each of these strategies is a set of value drivers for its own customers. For example, for some customers good product reliability at low cost may be a principal value driver. For those customers, being able to produce efficiently in large quantities without the need for a large investment in inventory might be a value driver. Your company's ability to help your customer meet its customer demand with a high degree of accuracy using customer-usage-data interchange might allow the client to optimize volume and minimize inventory without risk of failing to meet its customers' needs.

Another key to understanding the client's business strategically is the well-known Porter's Five Forces, as shown in Figure 16.2, which can be useful in understanding clients' strengths, weaknesses, opportunities, and threats. Many businesses have used this popular model to assist in understanding their own strategic position, but how many have used it to understand that of their clients and customers? Do you know your client's strategy? Do you understand its value drivers?

Do you know the impact of competitive rivalries, buyer power, product substitutes, and barriers to entry on their revenue streams? Keep in mind that your clients' revenue streams have a great deal to do with your firm's revenue stream. In the long run, their success is necessary for your success, but how many firms pay more than scant attention to their clients' strategic positioning? Based on his research, former Harvard professor and well-known consultant David Maister asserts the following:

> 1. There are few signs that providers are really listening to clients. Clients report that providers are only interested in selling their services, not in solving client problems, and do little to create the feeling their business is important. Providers need to focus on being useful, not "romancing" clients, and improving the quality of the work performed by their more junior personnel.

> 2. Customers want providers to earn their business, providing relationship plans, not sales plans. They want providers to identify their specific needs and provide customized suggestions for improving customer value. They want providers to have an impact on their business, spending more

time helping customers think and improve their strategies to include being involved in meetings where strategic brainstorming occurs.

> 3. Customers want providers to be more proactive, understanding where and how their businesses are moving and visualizing what they will look like in years to come. They want ideas from providers.[8]

Does this sound like firms, on average, have a clear understanding of their clients from a strategic perspective? The answer to that rhetorical question is no. The question then is, "Why not?" Maister's answer is that firms simply do not make the investment in learning about their clients, but it's time they started. As one recently retired sales executive who desires anonymity told us, "It is far more difficult to get new customers than to keep existing ones, so you need to be a lot more intensely focused on understanding, helping, and keeping the customers you've already got than my former company is."

16.4. Developing a Client-/ Customer-Centric Organization

It has been said, "The purpose of a company is to create a customer," and some firms such as Procter & Gamble have experienced tremendous revenue growth by deciding that the customer, not the CEO, is boss.[9] No, the customer isn't always right, but then again neither is the boss. So how exactly does a firm go about building a client-centric organization? A starting point is self-examination, and a starting point for self-examination is asking, "Are we even asking customers the right questions?"

In previous chapters we talked about the increasing dynamism, complexity, and globalization of business. We noted that complex problems are rarely solved using simple solutions. If they were, someone would have already solved them. One implication is that, as complexity grows and the pace of change quickens, selling the simpler solutions you sold 10 years ago probably doesn't work as well. Clients want solutions that come in multiple configurations, perform multiple tasks, and address different problems at different places in their organizations. Are you asking your customers the right questions, or the same questions you asked 10 years ago—questions that may no longer be fully responsive to their evolving needs?[10] Instead, firms should be trying to ascertain where and why their customers are experiencing pain and curing it.

Developing a client-/customer-centric focus starts with top leadership and works its way down throughout the organization. It is easy, however, for top leadership to become so caught up in strategy, finance, restructuring, spinning off a division, or working on the latest acquisition that it forgets about customers. Corporate headquarters often develop internally focused cultures. The aforementioned retired sales executive who spent a career with a Fortune 50 company that manufactures and sells highly diversified lines of consumer and industrial products tells the following story:

> I was booked on a commercial flight into our home office when our company's chief pilot called and asked if I would like to ride with a corporate vice president who was traveling there from my city on one of the company's jets. During the flight the VP asked, "Don't think we've met before. Why are you located here instead of corporate headquarters?" I replied, "Because I'm near my division's customers who generate $80 million in revenues and $32 million in profits for our company. Being near them allows me to better know their businesses and their needs." He responded, "That's a novel idea, a national sales manager locating at the source of business instead of the home office." Most division sales managers wanted to be at corporate headquarters

to be seen more frequently by top leadership—a personal strategy of putting their own welfare above that of the company, and one that was obviously effective for that selfish purpose.

For too many businesses a customer-/client-centric focus is a novelty. But even in companies where top leadership understands this, developing a client-centric organization requires more than just top-leadership emphasis. It also requires development of **internal systems** built around client needs. Too often these systems—if they exist—do not work well. For example, "Clients overwhelmingly report that many of the professional firms they deal with do *not* have internal systems in place that would allow them to manage engagements properly."[11] These firms are often unable to provide progress reports, expenditures against planned budget, and cost updates on request. Partners are often more interested in booking their own billable hours than in supervising teams they are supposed to be leading. The focus is on the individuals doing the work generating billable time, not the success of the client's project.[12]

Because of increasing dynamism in business, creating a client-/customer-centric organization is an ongoing process, not a one-time event, requiring continuous realignment of the organization around its markets. This means fluid analysis of customers' buying processes and how these processes align with the organization's selling processes. Among the key questions customer-/client-centric organizations need to keep asking are:

1. When was our last in-depth analysis of each of our important customers/clients?

2. Are our processes aligned with those of our clients? How good are the linkages?

3. What are our customers' needs, expectations, and requirements? How much value are we providing?

Figure 16.3. Example of Integrated Design to Promote Customer/Client Centricity

Typical Sales Process				
Steps:	Activities	Process Owner	Sales Activity Lead	Sales Activity Support
1. Lead Generation	• Client mapping • Research • Meeting • Pro-active selling	Sales Team	Sales Team	Executive Team & Operation
2. Solution	• Scope Q&A • Solution approach • Pricing • Program timetable • Proposal	Sales Team	Operation & Finance	Sales Team
3. Deal Closing	• Final presentations • Site visit • Inside channel feedback • Contract negotiations • Program Planning	Sales Team	Executive Team	Sales Team
4. Program Launch	• Provide contracted services	Operation	Operations & Recruitment	Finance

Source: Adapted from P. Currie, "Developing a Customer Centric and Sales Driven High Performance Organization," Ascension April 24, 2013, http://ascensionstrategy.com/blog/post/developing-customer-centric-and-sales-driven-high-performance -organization (accessed April 13, 2014).

4. Are we providing our personnel the resources necessary to help meet customer needs, expectations, and requirements?

5. Do we have a strong follow-up process designed to signal how well we are performing?

6. When advised of client needs, do we follow through and act decisively to meet those needs?

Achieving a tight fit between customers' needs, expectations, and requirements is not easy. It requires both good data and an objective analysis that those deeply involved with the customer interface may be too biased to develop. This self-examination may require the use of some internal or external group capable of unbiased assessments. One useful tool is periodic questionnaires to elicit customer satisfaction that measures customers' perceptions of the organization's professionalism, communication skills, and incisiveness in discov-

ering and curing customers' pain. Self-examination is but one piece of the system, however. A system is required. An example of one system for uncovering and curing customer pain is shown in Figure 16.3.[13]

Several insights can be gleaned from steps, activities, and human resources involved in this system for business development. First, it is not just about selling something. Rather, it is logical in sequence moving from business finding through solution finding to deal closing to program launch. Second, the activities involved include "client mapping" and research to understand the customer's business and its pain points. The system then explicitly moves to determining a solution to that pain and ensuring through such measures as site visits and feedback that the proposed solution will solve the client's problem. Third, there is a clearly stipulated "owner" of the process at each step, with other clearly designated supporting roles. Fourth, the system is integrated across organizational functions with integral involvement of the executive team. Systems may differ but ideally should at least include these same attributes.

16.5. Your Existing Customers as a Source of Additional Business: Why Cross Selling Often Fails

Cross selling of products or services has long been a sales tactic used by many businesses. **Cross selling** involves expanding customer relationships by increasing the range of products or services provided. Employees are encouraged to ask customers about additional buying, often at the point of sale. There are **three types of cross selling**: (1) Meeting an additional need discovered in the process of delivering an offering. In this type of cross selling the additional need is met by the same unit supplying the current offering. (2) Selling add-on offerings from a different part of the provider's organization. (3) Selling offerings that are bundled together to form a package.[14]

Cross selling attempts occur in many businesses ranging from fast food ("Would you like fries with that burger?") to public accounting firms attempting to sell consulting services to tax clients. In many cases these efforts fail for the simple reason that often there is *no benefit* to the client in buying the additional service from the particular vendor with which the customer is already doing business. Consider the following points made by one of the coauthors:

> I consider myself a reasonably sophisticated car buyer and a tough negotiator. After researching reports on various makes and models, dealer costs, and manufacturer's discounts and holdbacks and driving cars at whatever dealership is convenient, I negotiate to buy new automobiles cash only over the Internet when sales are slow. I don't care which dealer sells me the car if it's the car I want at the price I want. The car is exactly the same regardless of which

> dealer sells it. If a dealer doesn't have what I want in stock, it can usually get it shipped from elsewhere. I think I'm pretty good at cutting through the smoke of car-sales jargon and very savvy about cross-selling attempts. Dealers always try to sell me on additional services, but I never buy. I have no loyalty to any dealer. Even though the dealer will always try to get my service business because that is its most lucrative offering, I don't care which dealer services my car because the service is pretty much the same regardless of the dealer. Because I do my research online, I don't need to ask questions at a dealership. In short, I may be the worst-case customer for the schmoozing-one-moment, pushy-the-next car salesperson. Not only will I not tolerate cross-selling attempts, I won't even get face-to-face with him or her unless absolutely necessary.

Does this describe many business clients today in industries ranging from banking to public accounting to manufacturing? Increasingly, business customers have become very sophisticated consumers of products and services in today's highly competitive, information-rich environment. They ask, "Why should I buy a widget from you just because I'm buying your gazorkinflickin if I can get the equivalent widget cheaper from another vendor?" There is really only one good answer to this question: "The reason is that there are demonstrable benefits such as synergies and efficiencies from buying both the burger and fries from us." In other words, "Yes, you can get your burger here and your fries from the fast-food joint down the street, but you have to drive a block to get there. So buying their fries isn't really cheaper and it's also inconvenient."

A coauthor recalls that in the 1970s retail banks were focused on **service usage ratios**, the average number of services used per cus-

Understanding the Organizational Environment

tomer, as targets. Having failed to directly cross sell enough services at the point of contact, the banks attempted to **bundle** services as a means of cross selling. For a flat monthly fee customers could enjoy the benefits of a checking account with no minimum balance, a savings account (already free), a credit card with a slightly reduced but still high annual interest rate, a safe-deposit box, and—whoopee!—access to an ATM (already free). One bank even used the visual analogy of different services coming out of a box to advertise its bundled-service offering.

To illustrate how internally focused these cross-selling efforts were, safe-deposit boxes were an underutilized service at most banks, representing a sunk cost in fixed assets. Banks decided to place safe-deposit boxes in the bundle—even though customer demand for them was low—as a way of hopefully leveraging this sunk cost. This amounted to giving customers "the sleeves off our vest" in a somewhat transparent attempt to convince customers they were receiving value when the service was in fact little desired. These bundling efforts largely failed to attract customers for simple reasons. Many customers did not want all the services in the bundle, there was little or no difference in the services from one bank to another, and the services could be obtained individually, often without paying a monthly fee. In retrospect, the shallowness of this internally focused selling strategy is rather obvious, and the money spent on marketing the service bundles was largely wasted.

In more sophisticated product and service lines where it pays more to shop for lower cost and/or better results, there is evidence cross selling has never worked particularly well and is becoming harder for several reasons. First, there have often been *few incentives* for employees in one department to sell the offerings of another. If an auditor helps to sell a tax engagement, her billable hours haven't changed. Second, the cross-selling focus in most firms has mainly been

internal. In other words, it's obvious how cross selling helps our firm. Our revenues go up, but do the client's revenues go up or its costs go down? Is the client now able to produce something better and more efficiently than it did before because it purchased this additional offering from us? The answer is that often *cross selling does nothing for the customer.* Take public accounting services, for example. When a client purchases an additional offering, the services are often provided by a completely different unit with no real connection to the unit's services currently utilized. Moreover, often no integrated service plan exists.

Third, there is an implicit expectation by the provider that because the customer likes the product it is now using, it should buy more products from the provider.[15] But in the increasingly competitive, information-rich business environment, there are more products to choose from, and it is much easier to obtain information about them. The "Why us, not them?" question goes unanswered. Fourth, sometimes there is a fear within the organizational unit currently doing business with a particular customer that the unit to which business is referred will fail to provide good service and end up placing the existing relationship at risk.[16]

There are **customer-internal barriers** to cross selling in addition to the foregoing self-inflicted impediments. Some businesses have policies requiring the use of multiple vendors in order to avoid excessive reliance on one vendor—and because of fear of too-cozy relationships between employees and the provider. Also, purchasing different offerings often occurs at different points within the buyer's organization meaning that, even though one group of customer personnel may be highly satisfied, the decision to purchase an additional offering may rest with personnel who have little knowledge of or appreciation for the provider.[17]

So, should firms give up on cross selling? No, instead they should invest much more heavily in it rather than expecting it to happen with minimal investment of time and thought spent in understanding the client's business, training personnel to discover ways in which to add value for the client, and planning and executing the client engagement. The first step in effective cross selling is grasping that it takes a great deal more investment than most businesses usually give it. So shallow are many cross-selling attempts that they have the opposite effect of that desired on many customers. One of the coauthors recently called a restaurant for a takeout order. The selling spiel the person answering the phone was required to give callers was so long, detailed, and hurried that, not even able to understand what was being said, he interrupted and said, "Stop the required nonsense and just take my order." He hasn't called back for another takeout. One might be tempted to suggest, "Well, that's just a restaurant, a pretty unsophisticated business." True, but many companies selling software or financial services make the same error.

Maister says, "Firms must understand that cross-selling is like a PhD program. There are milestones that must be passed before you are eligible to even try for it."[18] The first of these milestones is ensuring that the customer is *not only satisfied but delighted.* The second is *investing in the customer relationship* to create an impression that the firm is trying hard to earn and deserve additional business over the long haul. In this regard there is no substitute for sincerity. Insincere attempts are often transparent and irritate customers. Sincerity is demonstrated by going the extra mile and sometimes giving the customer the benefit of the doubt, as seen in the following coauthor anecdote:

> We own a weekend log home in the woods that has two side-by-side chimneys. Once there was a chimney fire, and one of the chimneys was damaged. When the workmen came to place a liner to cover the damaged interior tile, they noticed that

the other chimney had been damaged in a separate fire sometime in the past. We informed our insurance company, USAA, that we didn't know whether the second fire had occurred while we owned the cabin or prior to our purchasing it and been missed by the inspector. Without being asked, USAA gave us the benefit of the doubt and paid for both chimneys. Back then we only used its insurance services. Today we use its insurance, banking, financial-management, travel, and product-purchase services. USAA earned our trust and our business. Satisfaction isn't adequate to describe our feelings about how they do business. Delight is more appropriate. Not only would we not think of using another company, we have referred many people to USAA, and referrals are an important test of customer satisfaction.[19]

Once a business has earned a high level of delight and loyalty, cross selling becomes a matter of finding customer pain to be fixed. Now it is possible to take the third step and successfully approach clients with recommendations such as, "Our knowledge of your business suggests that you can reduce inventory cost significantly and improve your customer satisfaction if we help tighten your data interchange linkages. Is this something you'd like to discuss?" Instead of clients seeing this inquiry as merely one more attempt to get into their wallets, they view it as a business partner with a genuine interest in their welfare.

16.6. Making Your Clients/ Customers Part of Your Sales Force

How do you know when you've arrived at the PhD-level of customer loyalty and delight? One way to gauge this is the extent to which you get new business referrals from existing customers. Referrals are one of the best ways to get new business because the business often comes to you with an endorsement from a delighted existing customer that the prospect trusts and respects. Popular selling literature is replete with guidance on how to ask existing customers for referrals. Consider, for example, the following statements:

1. "Ask for referrals from your clients . . . Ask for referrals from every person you know."[20]

2. "There is no cost [for referrals]."[21]

3. "Block 15 minutes at the end of each prospect or client meeting to 'brainstorm' on the subject of referrals, and communicate this ahead of time with a meeting agenda."[22]

4. "It's your job to promote referrals all the time . . . ask for the referral!!"[23]

How do these statements compare to those of Maister, whose fundamental position is that you must earn your right to ask your client for help? In his chapter appropriately titled "How Real Professionals Develop Business," you first have to ask your existing clients how to serve them better and next invest heavily in them by placing their welfare first, demonstrating both an understanding of their business and that you can add value. Don't ask from referrals until you are sure you have delighted your existing customers. Does this sound like "no cost?" Once this delight exists, even though you have earned the right to ask for referrals, sometimes you won't have to ask. If you aren't getting the referrals you need, you need to revisit whether you are delighting your existing customer base.[24]

One sales strategist states, "In all my years as a sales strategist, I've never heard of someone losing a client because they asked for an introduction. So what do you have to lose?"[25] We think a lot if done without great care. We believe there are big problems with an overbearing approach to attempting to obtain referrals. One commentator

> "Your best referrers are your customers . . . Receiving referrals from customers starts with giving great customer service."
>
> —David Frey, "How to Make It Rain Referrals"

states, "People HATE to ask for referrals. You hate it, I hate it, and the people who get asked hate it."[26] Pause and consider how something so hated will be perceived by your existing customers. This is especially true when the request comes from a vendor who presumes its own relationship with an existing customer has reached a state of delight when, in fact unknown to the vendor because he hasn't invested in existing clients, the relationship is hanging by a thread. Imagine how your existing clients feel about "blocking 15 minutes at the end of each . . . client meeting" to discuss your desire for referrals as suggested by one of the quotes above. How do your clients feel about you promoting yourself "all the time?" Just because someone likes you doesn't mean she wants to recommend you. Consider the following coauthor anecdote:

> The husband of one of my wife's good friends sold insurance. He was very friendly, but, even though he hadn't earned my trust and business, it didn't stop him from asking for referrals—calling at work and home, even asking at social engagements. Because of our spouses' affinity for one another, I was somewhat forced to listen to his requests. Knowing that if I gave him referrals he would annoy them, too—and make it sound as if I endorsed him—I asked him to desist, but he was undeterred. Eventually I asked my spouse to drop the couple from our guest list for social events.

Does the foregoing imply that referrals aren't important and you should never ask? No, referrals are a very powerful to acquire new business. For

"Marketing must be a seduction, not an assault. It must not scream 'hire me!' but must gently suggest 'Here is some concrete evidence as to why you may want to get to know me better.' Marketing is truly about attracting clients—doing something that causes them to want to take the next step."

—David H. Maister, *Managing the Professional Services Firm*

example, approximately 45 percent of most service firms are hired based upon referrals. Further, referrals from existing customers solidify their own loyalty to your business, but you have to earn them. Some actions in developing the kind of relationship that will naturally result in referrals are as follows:

1. Ask clients how to serve them better.

2. Invest heavily in existing clients by understanding their businesses and needs.

3. Design plans to demonstrate that you can add value.

4. Don't wait until you get paid to become helpful.[27]

Consider also what one sales strategist calls **"moments of truth"** that can become turning points in your relationship with an existing client and may well determine whether that client becomes a source of referrals:

1. You receive a complaint from a customer.

2. A new customer places a second order.

3. A customer thanks you.

4. A customer experiences a problem with which you are in some way involved.

5. A customer asks you for a favor.

6. You encounter your customer in a public forum.

7. Your customer brings you a referral.[28]

These "moments of truth" represent opportunities to either solidify a relationship or fix a broken one. If you go the extra mile investing in your customers by immediately solving problems, sending a thank you note, or doing the customer a favor, you earn their trust and establish a reputation for professionalism instead of begging for business.

Customer loyalty has been touted as the best metric for predicting whether customers provide referrals, but the drivers of customer loyalty are complex. Perhaps one of the greatest impediments to understanding how to get referrals is oversimplifying customer-loyalty behaviors. This oversimplification is apparent in the many simple prescriptions for getting referrals. A number of metrics have been used in attempts to measure loyalty, such as customers' satisfaction, expectations, retention, value perceptions, repurchase intentions, and spending trends among others. However, research indicates that customer loyalty behaviors are multidimensional, and no one metric predicts all these behaviors. These dimensions may vary by industry and customer characteristics. They are affected by different aspects of the customer experience. In other words, there is no substitute for a deep understanding of the customer when it comes to predicting loyalty and therefore willingness to generate referrals.[29] As Maister has stated, "The main goal of all marketing tactics should be to get away as soon as possible from 'broadcasting a general message to a wide audience' and move to a highly individualized face-to-face dialogue between prospect and partner."[30]

16.7. A Planning Frame for the Customer/Client Interface

Miscommunication and **misunderstanding** are two primary causes of failure to create delighted customers. Often this occurs because success has been inadequately defined. Maister says, "As most professionals quickly learn, the project is never about what they said during the proposal process."[31] Here again, the use of the ends/ways/means model can help avoid disappointment. This is especially important when the assigned mission does not end up addressing the real underlying problem. Consider the following example.

Your consulting firm negotiated an engagement to assist a division of a large office supply firm in installing an accounting system that accurately measures customer profitability. Your stated mission was to implement the system and determine which customers were and were not profitable with the stated goal of *rectifying a problem of declining profitability.* The company's new competitive strategy had been to offer a menu of high-intensity, specialized services, thereby turning what had been a commodity products business into a differentiated service business for those customers willing to pay for the high-intensity services. This was done in an attempt to gain a competitive advantage over other office-supply vendors. Upon implementation you discover that those customers using the new strategy are unprofitable and those not using the strategy are profitable. In other words, the real problem is the company's new strategy is costing too much to implement.[32]

By determining which customers are unprofitable you haven't really solved the underlying problem of a mismatch between strategy and profitable customers because the client is left in a quandary. If it abandons its strategy, the division is left without a way to differentiate itself from its competition. If it sticks with its strategy, the more customers who choose its strategy, the more unprofitable the division will become. This is bound to be a very disappointing result for a client expecting you to solve its profitability problem. But by more careful analysis and better communication prior to the engagement, this disappointment might have been avoided. The problem was both of you implicitly assumed that knowing which customers were unprofitable would solve the client's problem, but it didn't because there was a mission/problem mismatch. If instead you had been careful to stipulate that your task was to install an accounting system that would better enable the client to determine customer profitability—but not assume that the determination would solve the underlying problem of a strategy/customer mismatch—then the client's disappointment wouldn't extend to you. In fact, there might be an opportunity to sell additional services in assisting the client in solving the real problem without having failed to fulfill your stated mission.

Success or failure often comes down to how the customer/client interface is managed. It is always better to *underpromise and overdeliver* than the other way around. Your goal in this interface should be not a satisfied customer but a **delighted customer**! At a minimum, the principal steps in the interface should be as follows:

1. Discover what your client thinks his or her **pain** is and what he or she thinks is **causing this pain** by carefully listening and asking incisive questions. Decide if you think the real cause of the pain is that or something else. Discuss this with your client.

2. Decide if your firm **can cure all the pain, some, or none**. If some, what contribution to curing the pain is within your firm's capability? Be sure to stipulate this to the client.

3. Walk the client through **alternative courses of action** for curing the pain

and help decide on the best course of action given the client's constraints, such as time, budget, and other resources. In other words, make sure the **ends, ways, and means** of your involvement are aligned.

4. Once the contract is signed, review it with the client and confirm that it reflects what is really expected. Then memorialize this understanding in a precise **memo of understanding (MOU)** that clearly articulates the ends, ways, and means to include all significant intermediate objectives. Next ensure all the personnel involved—the client's and yours—clearly understand what constitutes victory and how together you plan to achieve it.

5. No one, least of all your clients, wants to be ambushed with unpleasant surprises. Establish a **milestone plan** with critical measures at each milestone to discuss with the client. Elicit feedback. If you are not meeting the milestones, ascertain why. If the engagement veers off track, you'll know it sooner, have a better chance of correcting problems, and your client won't be ambushed with bad news.

6. Once the engagement is reaching conclusion, review the MOU to **ensure you have accomplished your desired end state** and each significant objective.[33] Determine what possible follow-on actions beyond the scope of your MOU may be indicated and ask the client to discuss these actions.

7. Once the engagement is over, **ask the client for feedback**, pro and con. Ask, "How can we make this better if there is a next time?" Celebrate the victory with your client.

8. **Engage your cybernetic loop** and learn from the experience. Conduct your own mental review. What lessons were learned? Note what you would do differently next time. Ensure this is transmitted to team members.

A carefully planned and executed customer/client interface will go a long way toward avoiding disappointment, solidify relationships, and create delight. Once your client is delighted, your job is to perpetuate that delight by avoiding complacency and continuing to delight by keeping its welfare foremost.

16.8. The Importance of Knowing Your Clients' and Customers' Personality Preferences

Consider the following scenario. You have been working hard to get Mammoth, Inc.'s, business. Through an acquaintance inside Mammoth you have worked your way up the organization discussing this with various levels of Mammoth officials. Your meetings have entailed many presentations to operations and information-technology personnel demonstrating how your software will enable Mammoth to save a significant amount of money by providing greater visibility of key value drivers. Gradually, level by level, you have won these officials over to doing business with your firm. Now you finally have a 60-minute audience with an executive vice president who has the power to write the check. You may have but one shot, so your pitch has to be spot on.

You carefully prepare your presentation containing twenty slides, ensuring each slide contains important details about the most critical technical aspects of your software that have been persuasive to Mammoth's lower-level officials. You have included links so that you can show how the software operates in various ways. The first ten slides provide a detailed history of the problems Mammoth is experiencing with its current software. The next ten slides describe how your software will cure this pain and the various options available with attendant costs. You have carefully rehearsed your presentation three times, timing yourself so that you can finish with 20 minutes left for questions. You have prepared backup slides so that you can respond in detail to questions you've been asked previously by lower-level officials.

Five minutes and three slides into your presentation the EVP begins asking questions that focus on material you planned to cover in the last 10 minutes. Some of these questions cannot be answered without first reviewing material you had planned to cover 20 minutes into the presentation. You find yourself jumping back and forth. The presentation becomes rather confused with you attempting to respond to questions that are difficult to answer without more foundation material. When the hour is up, the EVP says, "Well, this has been somewhat informative. I need to reflect more on what we've discussed. Thank you for coming." There is no indication that an invitation for a follow-up meeting will be forthcoming. You get the feeling the EVP is unimpressed.

As you leave, you reflect on what went wrong. First, you assumed that the same points that had intrigued lower-level operations and IT officials would also hook the EVP. You didn't query those lower-level officials about the EVP's preferences for information with questions such as, "Can you tell me something about how Ms. Katzenbach prefers to receive information?" Second, you created a linearly organized presentation that relied on an inductive approach—building from data to a conclusion—that had worked well with the other officials. In retrospect, you now see that the EVP prefers a deductive approach in which she gets the big picture first and then delves selectively into details. Third, because you didn't plan for this shift in informational appetite, you weren't nimble enough to alter your presentation midstream and make the necessary adjustments.

Many sources of advice for practitioners about how to interface with customers and prospects at the interpersonal level treat the interface generically. That is, they provide rote prescriptions such as those noted previously about constantly asking for referrals. This can be a huge mistake. How you interact interpersonally can have everything to do with success or failure in getting business. In chapter 5 we introduced the idea of type when interacting with personnel inside your firm, noting sixteen different personality preference profiles. Clients and prospects are no different, so why assume implicitly that they are? A big reason is that, although it is possible to use techniques such as MBTI to type your own personnel, you cannot take clients through that assessment. Nonetheless, as the foregoing scenario illustrates, failing to take personal preferences into consideration can negate an enormous amount of time and effort expended in creating sales opportunities. So, how does one go about interfacing with clients and customers in a manner that considers personality preferences when you can't type them? The following section presents one approach for doing this, and appendix C presents a shortcut method of typing clients.

16.9. The "Platinum Rule" Approach to Understanding Personality Preferences

In *The Platinum Rule,* Tony Alessandra and Michael O'Connor present a methodology for placing personalities in business settings into four basic categories with sixteen subcategories in a somewhat analogous manner to the sixteen MBTI types. The Platinum Rule derives its name from a comparison to the Golden Rule, which says, "Do unto others as you would have them do unto you." In contrast, the Platinum Rule says, "Do unto others as they'd like done unto them," necessitating understanding others' preferences and adjusting your own behavior to conform to those preferences. Alessandra and O'Connor

Figure 16.4. Alessandra and O'Connor's Four Basic Personality Groups

Style	Description	Preferences
Director	Ambitious, firm, forceful, confident, competitive, decisive, determined, risk taking, impatient, task oriented, intensely focused, capable of multitasking, thrive on crises, become frustrated with nonperformers, take themselves seriously	Work hard, make things happen, get results, like and initiate change, delegate authority to those who produce, deal quickly with practical problems, dislike too much abstraction, like efficiency, dislike being hustled
Socializer	Outgoing, optimistic, enthusiastic, talkative, creative, self-focused, expressive, fun loving, people loving, playful, fast paced, energetic, prone to speak before thinking, spontaneous, easily bored, craves approval	Riding the crest of ideas, being where the action is, sequential projects, building networks, being admired and talked about, stimulation, new ideas but not putting them into practice
Relater	Team oriented, friendly, personable, cooperative, caring, likable, calm, low keyed, timid, slow to change, unlikely to make sudden moves, realistic, modest, unassertive, sensitive, change resistant	Stability, tranquility, being a longtime member of an ongoing team, process slowly, dislike rocking the boat, prefer actions over words, going along with others even if disagree, careful planning
Thinker	Self-controlled, serious, cautious, analytical, unemotional, starchy, contemplative, thorough, disciplined, frugal, accurate, dependable, standoffish, subject to overanalyzing, make natural engineers, computer programmers, and accountants	Clarity, order, long-range thinking, detail oriented, detailed planning, careful progress, reason, asking incisive questions, avoiding embarrassment, follow through, having a few close friendships

Source: Adapted from T. Alessandra and M. J. O'Connor, *The Platinum Rule* (New York: Business Plus, 1996), 4–6.

note psychologists have produced a number of models describing behavioral differences, but a common thread is four basic categories of preferences, as we observe with MBTI.[34] The Platinum Rule groups personalities into the following four basic styles shown in Figure 16.4: (1) directors, (2) socializers, (3) relaters, and (4) thinkers.

The authors stipulate that adjusting to people's preferences for interaction if done with integrity is not synonymous with manipulation. They also stipulate that, although many people are var-

ious blends of the four styles, most have a dominant style and signal these styles. For example, in section 16.8, Mammoth's EVP signaled a predominantly director style that was perhaps quite different from the operations- and technology-oriented officials with whom our hypothetical presenter had previously interacted. Those officials might have instead been thinkers given their apparent preference for detailed information. Different personality categories give off different verbal, vocal, and visual cues, as shown in Figure 16.5.

Figure 16.5. Alessandra and O'Connor's Four Basic Personality Groups—Cues

Style	Verbal Cues	Vocal Cues	Visual Cues
Director Example	Talk more, commanding "Let's cut to the chase."	Forceful intonation "So, by next Friday . . ."	Assertive gestures Firm handshake
Socializer Example	Talk more, friendly "Let me noodle on that."	Use variety in vocal quality "Wow! That's great!"	Animated Lots of hand movement
Relater Example	Talk less, soft response "I'm not yet sure."	Speak less forcefully "Perhaps we could . . ."	Gentle movements Intermittent eye contact
Thinker Example	Talk less, precise "Examine this logically."	Slow speak, little inflection "Let me think about that."	Little body expression Poker faced

Source: Adapted from T. Alessandra and M. J. O'Connor, *The Platinum Rule* (New York: Business Plus, 1996), 47–56.

Beyond understanding what category of individual you're dealing with, the really important question is how to best approach each personality. **Directors** want just enough information to understand the overall concept, not the details. They want facts, not to be buddies with you. They will probably be little impressed with testimonials from other customers, preferring to focus on summary metrics such as return on investment, efficiency, output, or fixing their company's pain. With directors you must be well organized, fast paced, and very time conscious. Approach them using statements such as, "If you will give me 10 minutes, I'll show you how to improve your profits significantly."

In contrast, **socializers** want to be your buddy, so be upbeat as if you are a politician running for office. Be an empathic listener, showing interest and using feeling words. Socializers like to hear about the newest product available, the latest technology, or a new idea for saving money. Use approaches such as, "Can I drop by and show you the latest office management software that will help you manage your sales force like nothing else on the market?"

Relaters should be approached with sincere interest in a nonthreatening, pleasant, friendly, and patient manner. Your credibility may be strengthened by mentioning someone who referred you or talking about mutual acquaintances. Relaters are easily threatened and feel less so when interacting with people they have confidence in and know up front what your interaction is about. Approaches such as, "May I drop by and show you how you can reduce your market risk?" may appeal to their need for security.

You have to be especially well prepared when approaching **thinkers** because they are naturally skeptical. Be prepared to offer strong evidence of the efficacy of your offering. You build credibility with thinkers slowly, so don't rush them. Don't be verbose or use too much small talk. Focus on evidence, using statements such as, "Our research conducted over the past 5 years with forty-two existing customers in your industry and of your approximate size strongly supports a 20 percent average savings in customer-support costs from using this particular software package."[35]

Before leaving this topic we would like to express one caution. As Alessandra and O'Connor point out, although most people have a dominant style, many people are blends of the four basic personality types, so be nimble in your approach. One coauthor gives an example of why this is important:

Having sat through innumerable sales pitches in a variety of settings, I abhor being hustled and know how I normally react. When approached by someone with whom I am not well acquainted making a sales pitch, I am usually in a director mode at the onset, wanting summary, factual information. The person doesn't have long to hook me. If I do become hooked, however, I often shift to being a thinker, wanting detailed proof of the claims being made. Consequently, there is double jeopardy in selling to me. You can lose by being too detailed at the onset, but lose later on by not being able to back up your claims with convincing evidence. Therefore, the best way to approach me is to come with a short presentation aimed at a high level backed up by lots of detailed support that you may or may not use.

This section has barely scratched the surface of understanding customers and clients, so readers are encouraged to obtain a copy of *The Platinum Rule* and use it to develop a deeper understanding of how to apply these principles, as well as using appendix C, which shows a shortcut way to apply MBTI.

16.10. Sorting Out the Wheat from the Chaff

Patently obvious to any experienced business leader is that not all customers and clients are equally desirable, and some even represent problems. We need to be clear that in this section we distinguish between two types of customers: (1) profitable customers your firm is at risk of losing because of its own substandard performance, and (2) situations in which the customer itself is the problem. The first type of situation represents one of those "moments of truth" we discussed previously. When you encounter that type of "moment of truth," you need to immediately re-

turn to basics and follow the procedures outlined below to bring the relationship to where it needs to be—first apologizing for the difficulties, then identifying and fixing the customer's pain, working to create a delighted business partner.

1. Be sensitive to the heartbeat of your customer relationships and move rapidly when you sense an irregular heartbeat.

2. Quickly look internally and attempt to discover why the customer is displeased.

3. Contact the client immediately, apologize, and ask for further explanation. Be sure you understand the problem. Agree on a fix for the problem.

4. Underpromise and overdeliver with the fix.

5. Elicit feedback from both your personnel and the customer to ensure the fix works and the client's pain has been fixed.

6. Conduct a lessons-learned session with the personnel involved to hopefully prevent a recurrence of customer dissatisfaction—for this customer and others with similar circumstances.[36]

The second type of customer-problem situation is another matter. Customer problems of the second type fall into several categories: (1) customers in market segments that do not provide the required rate of return; (2) customers that demand more service than the value of their business justifies; and (3) customers whose representatives are abusive, obnoxious, or overbearing. Businesses that are best at value creation avoid trying to be all things to all customers. They focus on target markets and customers so that they can become very familiar with client needs in a particular niche. They can organize around these niches in ways that allow greater efficiency and better service.

Although volume may be sometimes sacrificed, that is not necessarily the case. For example, Carlisle Companies, Inc., has grown sales dramatically despite greatly reducing its number of divisions. Having a better target focus can allow companies to increase their sales penetration into those niches and become the provider of choice.[37] Moreover, even if they reside in the same niche, all customers are not equally profitable. Some may demand a much higher level of service while paying identical prices and generating a lower volume of sales. Businesses need to identify their best customers in terms of profitability and then learn as much about them as possible.[38]

Unprofitable or limitedly profitable clients are another form of potentially undesirable customer. Often their demands far exceed their value. If you have a reasonably accurate system for determining customer profitability, list your customers from most to least profitable. You may discover that the top 20 percent create a hugely disproportionate percentage of profits and the bottom 20 percent are unprofitable or limitedly profitable because of high servicing demand relative to revenues. In *Islands of Profit in a Sea of Red Ink,* Jonathan Byrnes argues that by any way of measuring, 40 percent of customers are unprofitable. He maintains that in some companies the "20/300 Rule" applies. That is, 20 percent of the customers create 300 percent of the profits, the middle 60 percent is breakeven, and the bottom 20 percent lose 200 percent of net profits.[39] Divesting yourself of unprofitable clients can be tricky because of the adverse signals it can send other customers, but one way can be pricing your products and services so that the relationship either becomes profitable or the customers migrate to another provider. Do so carefully, however. When you decide to divest, don't simply attempt to price yourself out of the market because that may take too long and make the customer even more difficult to deal with in the interim. It is better to advise the client that, after careful study of the relationship,

> "Breaking up may be hard to do, but when a client is costing you money or making you crazy, it can be a smart move. Severing unprofitable or exhausting relationships can, after the initial fallout, boost your company's revenues."
>
> —Amy Barrett, "When, Why, and How to Fire That Customer," *Bloomberg Businessweek Magazine*

you have concluded that your services no longer meet its needs.[40] It can also be helpful to provide the customer with your reasoning and data supporting the price increase, but be prepared these conversations can sometimes get ugly. Also ensure that you convey candidly the reasoning to your own employees who may well have formed attachments to the customer. Often is possible to work with the client to adjust your servicing to make the customer profitable and salvage the relationship.[41]

Very difficult-to-deal-with clients can exhibit various behaviors, including passive aggression, never being satisfied no matter how much service your firm provides, being slow to pay while complaining that you should do more, continuously seeking uncontracted services, attempting to exert control over how your provide services, and being abusive of your personnel.[42] Assuming you have investigated and ascertained with assurance that none of these behaviors is caused by your firm's shortcomings, and assuming you have made reasonable attempts to resolve the issues and bring the relationship to a better footing, you may benefit by divesting such customers. Abusive clients sometimes cannot be transformed, and "Going into therapy with your clients is a very unlikely scenario . . . The truth is, people don't change."[43]

"Back in 2003, Trish Bear, president and CEO of I-ology, a 22-employee, $1.6 million Scottsdale (Ariz.) Internet strategy company, knew that one customer just had to go. The client, a $7 billion corporation that accounted for 24% of revenues, was constantly dissastified, requiring Bear to attend meetings two to three times a week. The client also rejected many of Bear's proposed strategies. The customer paid in 60 or 90 days, when Bear needed to be paid in 30 days. To prepare for a split, Bear told her staff to do pretty much whatever the client wanted, which allowed her to steer clear of all those meetings. She used the extra time to recruit new business. Six months later, Bear had landed a number of new accounts, and revenues were up 33%."

—Amy Barrett, "When, Why, and How to Fire That Customer," *Bloomberg Businessweek Magazine*

16.11. Concluding Thoughts

In the end, the bottom line is all about the top line because growing the latter is necessary for growing cash flow to ownership. This means upwardly bound, courageous leaders need to have a **customer perspective** focusing on what drives value creation over the long run—revenues—and act on this perspective:

- Having a strategic understanding of customers' businesses.

- Building a client-centric organization.

- Truly investing in understanding how to create synergies within your organization in serving clients so that you can sell additional services in ways that benefit them, not just your firm.

- So delighting your clients that they are happy to refer others to your business without you having to beg for referrals.

- Knowing how to interface with customers at both the organizational and individuals levels and training your personnel to do likewise.

- Being able to discern what business to keep and what to divest so that you can focus on the right clients to build profitable revenues.

Robert E. Kelley has said, "Perspective is the major work strategy ... that reflects on your standing as a brainpowered worker."[44] In our view, a good perspective is a prerequisite for good judgment. No matter what your function as a leader in the organization, understanding how businesses make money is essential for a good perspective, and a customer/client focus is essential for making money. Making a success out of stretch assignments that springboard your career frequently involves revenue growth.

Conclusion: Putting It All Together

When you reach pivotal moments in your business career—those opportunities to take stretch assignments that could become strategic inflection points in your career trajectory and set you on a faster course to top leadership—will you be ready? The answer: probably no and hopefully yes. No, you'll probably not be as ready as you would like to be. Few who have stepped into those stretch experiences have felt they were completely ready in terms of their knowledge and experience at the time. Otherwise, they would not be stretch assignments. But, yes, they were ready to accept the challenge and did so, making it—and themselves—a success. When afforded such opportunities only three choices exist. You can turn down the assignment, in which case you may never be offered such an opportunity again. You can accept it but fail with the same outcome likely. Or, you can accept the stretch assignment and succeed, in which case your career will likely move much faster than before.

The business world wants **courageous, ethical leaders who can identify and solve complex problems under conditions of uncertainty, motivate others to perform at high levels, and consistently achieve superior organizational outcomes on schedule within resource constraints.** When your pivotal moment comes to step into a stretch assignment, hopefully you will have the courage to take a career risk and make a success of it. *Courageous leadership* is not something we're endowed with but rather something leaders develop over time through focused effort. It requires the *tenacity to succeed,* the *humility to admit mistakes and learn from them,* and the *perseverance to surmount obstacles,* survive, and move on from the inevitable setbacks.

As Cathy Tang, chief legal officer at KFC Corporation, has said, "Stretch assignments aren't something posted on your company's job board. These are 'hand-selected' opportunities given to you by someone who understands your capabilities, perceives you as credible, and believes in your potential. You must put yourself in a position to be selected . . . by successfully communicating and demonstrating your knowledge, talents, and career goals."[1] Will you be selected? You have to create that opportunity through hard work. Will you be ready to succeed if you are selected? You may have little or no warning when the times comes because these opportunities usually arise when your employer is experiencing a crisis it desperately needs you to resolve.

How will you prepare yourself? First you must become a courageous leader. This starts with understanding something about leadership, but it doesn't end there. Leaders aren't made just by reading about leadership. Yes, savvy students of leadership can greatly benefit by preparing themselves intellectually for leadership roles, but leaders have to grow by experiencing leadership, especially when it makes them uncomfortable. Savvy leaders understand that leadership is a career-long journey, not a destination. Courageous leaders avoid the hubris associated with thinking themselves good leaders and instead continuously critique their own leadership performances, asking, "How could I have done that better?"

This means you need a lifelong appetite for learning—learning about others, yourself, and many other things such as ethical reasoning, critical and creative thinking, communicating with others, technical skills and technology, organizational control, performance measurement, teamwork, and how to interface with clients. It means knowing what creates value in your organization and what behaviors are valued. It means being organizationally savvy so that you can be the cook rather than just being a morsel in the firm's soup. It means you have to be able to motivate others, helping them to grow as you grow yourself. And perhaps as importantly as anything, it means keeping your priorities straight and remembering that it's about the welfare of the pack first, its members second, and then you. We firmly believe that by putting yourself last in terms of whose welfare you seek, over time you will end up being first as others are drawn to your leadership.

We hope that you have enjoyed this portion of your journey in courageous leadership and that it will be beneficial in helping make you a better leader. One of the nice things about technology is that it enables publication of this work in electronic text. This means revisions are made easier, and our intent is to continuously revise this book. We appreciate any thoughts and suggestions you may have for its improvement. Thanks for being an attentive, learning leader, and please know we part company with our best wishes for future success in your business career. The Kelley Leadership Development Team will be cheering for you!

Terry, Chris, John, Eric, Ray, and Kelly

Appendix A. Written Communication for Credible and Effective Leaders

In the professional world, you will meet many people for the first time via written communication (e-mail). In today's global economy, it is increasingly common to interact with people for months, or even years, without ever meeting them face to face.

Initially, these people will judge you based on . . . the way you type. Well, not exactly. However, these people (clients, colleagues, staff, company leadership) will form perceptions about you based on how you communicate. Your credibility will be determined by how you write and send e-mail messages, as well as how you create reports.

The importance of good written communication in the professional world cannot be overstated. The ability to write will not only improve your credibility, it will also improve your effectiveness. When you utilize good writing practices, you save time and avoid misunderstandings.

A.1. Know the Reader

Think about business negotiation. One of the first rules is to know the person with whom you are negotiating. This same negotiating principle can be used with correspondence.

The first consideration is the audience. This key concept applies to all types of written communication—from e-mail messages and handwritten notes to reports and executive summaries. You wouldn't design a product, create a marketing campaign, or open a new business without considering the customer. Use this same business principle with your professional correspondence. Who is reading what you are writing?

> Written communication is a function of conducting business—it is not simply "typing a message."

Have you ever taken a behavior profile or personality test? If so, you know that people communicate differently based on their natural tendencies. This means they like to receive communication in different ways.

For example, some behavior styles love details. Other styles dislike (and refuse to read) details. With respect to results, some personality types expect immediate answers. Others require significant time to analyze the situation.

It isn't realistic to ask every recipient of your correspondence to take a behavior profile. The point is to think about the reader. If you know the person, then you can answer a few general questions about his or her communication preferences.

Beyond personal characteristics, there are other elements to consider. Even if you don't know the reader at all, there are still questions you should ask before writing and sending communication. Here are a few examples.

EXAMPLE: QUESTIONS TO ASK ABOUT THE READER

1. What does he or she know about the information you are sending?

2. Is the message expected?

3. Will the person recognize the acronyms/abbreviations you are using?

4. Will the receiver understand any technical information?

5. How is this recipient different from your normal readers?

6. Will multiple people be reading this message?

EXERCISE: WHO IS THE AUDIENCE?

DIRECTIONS

Take a moment to think about an e-mail you need to write today. Make some notes below about the person who will be reading the message.

_____

_____

Adjusting Content

After you have identified the reader(s), you are ready to move to the next step. How will you adjust the content, as well as the tone, of your message—now that you know who will be reading it?

EXERCISE: ADJUSTING CONTENT

DIRECTIONS

Go back to the previous exercise where you made notes about who will be reading your message. How will you adjust the content of the message based on your observations?

_____

_____

SAMPLE SOLUTION

Here are a few adjustments you may have mentioned:

- Include one or two sentences to build rapport.

- Skip the "chitchat" and get straight to the point.

- Provide more details.

- Avoid details and just provide an overview.

- Offer some background information.

- Define technical terms that are specific to your industry but not theirs.

INTERNAL VERSUS EXTERNAL MESSAGES

When adjusting content for the audience/reader, there is an important distinction between internal and external messages.

For internal messages, here are points to consider:

1. *Is this a person you correspond with frequently?*

You can be more informal. The reader needs less explanation. Get to the point and get on with it.

2. *Is this someone you e-mail occasionally?*

Take a moment to build rapport. Perhaps you will need to include a little more background about the topic.

3. *Is this an important person?*

Be more formal and professional. Spend extra time writing and editing. Be as concise as possible. Think "executive summary," not in-depth report (unless that is the purpose of the message, of course).

For external messages, here are two points to consider:

1. *Is this a potential client or someone you don't know?*

Be more formal. Consider if you need to introduce yourself or explain why you are corresponding. (Remember, this is e-mail. Spend one sentence on this, not one page.)

2. *Is this someone you have built a relationship with over time?*

You can be more informal. You might inquire about family or other personal interests, if appropriate.

EXERCISE: ANOTHER ADJUSTING CONTENT

INFORMATION
You have volunteered to chair the program committee for a nonprofit professional association called BPP (Business & Professional People). You're sending an initial message to members who have agreed to serve on the committee. This message is being sent to their work e-mail addresses. The first committee meeting will be Tuesday, October 10 at 4:00 PM at your office.

DIRECTIONS
Write a message informing the committee members of the meeting.

_____

_____

Now, review the message you wrote, using the following questions:

- Did you explain that you were a volunteer with BPP—or does your signature line just have your company name? (Just because BPP is on your mind doesn't mean it's on theirs.)

- Did you explain the committee?

- Did you use any acronyms that might only make sense to seasoned members but not new ones?

- What else? There's a good chance that these questions helped you think of other issues you forgot to consider.

SAMPLE SOLUTION

Greetings! Thanks for agreeing to serve as a volunteer on the program committee for BPP (Business & Professional People).

The first meeting will be on Tuesday, October 10 at 4:00 PM at my office. The address is 123 Main Street, Suite 503. Please confirm that you can attend. I'll send an agenda next week.

Attached is a description of the committee's duties. I look forward to working with you!

Sincerely,

Spongey Robert

BPP Program Committee Chair

President, Lobster Patty Foodservice

bob@lobstersRus.com www.LobstersRus.com

A.2. Determine the Purpose

In addition to knowing the reader, another way to determine the content of a message is to consider the purpose or intent. These are the four most common purposes for business correspondence.

1. *Motivational*

The purpose is to motivate. You may want to inspire your staff, encourage a colleague, or congratulate a client.

2. *Informational*

You may be sending information, or you may be requesting that someone send **you** information. You could also be asking the reader to do something or take some basic action. If you're requesting an action that requires people to think before they agree, the message may be more persuasive.

3. *Persuasive*

The purpose could be to convince a potential client to buy your services. You could also be asking a colleague to use your market research or convincing a boss to agree with your financial analysis.

4. *Bad news*

The reason for your message may be to convey bad news. Keep in mind that what may seem informational to you may be perceived as bad news by the reader.

After identifying the purpose of the correspondence, you can determine the content. This will help you decide what information goes first, what information is excluded, and how much "extra" information is necessary.

A.3. Effective Business Correspondence—Be Organized

The most common type of business correspondence is informational. If you are sharing information, the goal is to get to the point. There is no room here for fluff and extras.

People don't read e-mail thoroughly. They skim, so make it easy for them.

Start with the main point, then provide the supporting details. Don't bury your most important points in the middle of the fourth paragraph.

Inverted pyramid

To help visualize what an informational message should look like, think about a large "V." It is wide/broad at the top. That is where you put the general information. Then, as the "V" becomes more narrow, you include more details. The message becomes more specific as you go down.

General information

V

Details

Five Ws

To assist with prioritizing, particularly in situations where you are sharing a lot of information, consider using a journalism technique called the "Five Ws":

- Who?

- What?

- When?

- Where?

- Why?

When it is appropriate, start the message by answering those five questions—briefly and in the first paragraph. These become a summary of the vital information. You can elaborate on each of these elements later in the message—after you have the reader's attention.

EXERCISE: ORGANIZE AN INFORMATIONAL MESSAGE

DIRECTIONS

Organize and rewrite this ineffective message. The audience is your staff, and the purpose is to inform.

INEFFECTIVE MESSAGE

We'll be discussing several topics at next week's staff meeting. So, we'll need to plan on starting on time. Be prepared to stay an hour. If you have anything at all to report, you'll need to let me know soon, so I can add you to the agenda. If you aren't on the agenda in advance, you won't be able to present at the meeting. No last-minute additions to the agenda will be allowed. The meeting will be on Tuesday in Conference Room B. We'll start at 9 AM and end at 10 AM.

REWRITE THE MESSAGE

_____

_____

_____

_____

As you rewrite the message, be sure to consider the personality of your staff and their specific needs/challenges. Also, is this the first time you are calling this meeting? If so, you might want to reinforce your comments about the agenda and starting promptly. (See sample solution.) If you have been following these procedures for a while, then the reminders are unnecessary and can be omitted.

SAMPLE SOLUTION

The staff meeting will be Tuesday from 9 AM to 10 AM in Conference Room B. If you have a report, let me know by noon Thursday, so I can add you to the agenda. No last-minute additions, please! We'll start promptly, since we have several topics to discuss.

A.4. Effective Business Correspondence—Be Concise

In this busy, cluttered world of information overload, there is no room for flowery discourses, ram-

> ## "I didn't have time to write a short letter, so I wrote a long one instead."
>
> —Mark Twain (also attributed to Blaise Pascal, in a different form)

bling dissertations, or verbose verbiage. If your e-mail message appears too long, the receiver may think, "I don't have time to read that" and delete it.

Messages should be short and succinct. Yes, it takes a little longer to write a concise message.

However, it is worth the effort to be brief. By keeping your correspondence short, there is a significantly better chance it will be read. You will develop a reputation . . . a good one! You will become known as someone who can communicate in a concise, professional manner. People will read your messages because they know you won't waste their time.

Unnecessary words

One way to write more concisely is to avoid unnecessary words. Take a look at your writing. Is it filled with words that provide no additional information to the reader? Here are a few examples.

EXAMPLE: UNNECESSARY WORDS

- For the most part

- Very

- Actually

- Really

- Ultimately

- Basically

Note: These aren't evil words that must be avoided at all costs. Occasional use is fine, especially verbally. The point is—when written space is limited, don't waste that valuable area with unnecessary words.

Wordy phrases

Another way to write concisely is to replace wordy phrases. Why use five words when just one will suffice?

Exercise: Replace Wordy Phrases

DIRECTIONS
Replace each long phrase with a single word.

1. A great deal	1. _____
2. As a general rule	2. _____
3. On two different occasions	3. _____
4. At this point in time	4. _____
5. Due to the fact that	5. _____
6. Despite the fact that	6. _____
7. In a careful manner	7. _____

Sample Solution

DIRECTIONS
Replace each long phrase with a single word.

1. A great deal	1. Many (a lot, much)
2. As a general rule	2. Generally
3. On two different occasions	3. Twice
4. At this point in time	4. Now
5. Due to the fact that	5. Because (due to)
6. Despite the fact that	6. Yet (however)
7. In a careful manner	7. Carefully

Another advantage

There is another advantage to writing concisely, in addition to appearing organized and professional. When you write succinctly, it helps remove wording that may sound pompous or pretentious. This concept is discussed later in the text, so keep the above techniques in mind. As a leader, you aren't impressing anyone if your wordy writing appears to be condescending.

A.5. Effective Business Correspondence—Create Proper Expectations

If you find yourself in situations where your boss or customers imply you aren't meeting their expectations, there are several possible reasons. Let's discuss one potential cause that involves communication.

Any time you are writing, there is a chance that miscommunication will occur. Recipients interpret what they read based on their own past experiences. They process the information by sending it through their own filter and looking at it from their own perspective.

When you use vague wording, you are allowing the reader to determine what you mean. Chances are that he or she will interpret the message differently from what you intended.

> The more ambiguous your wording is, the more room there is for misinterpretation and confusion.

Solution

To decrease the chances for misunderstandings and unclear expectations . . . be specific. Here are a few common areas where writers are often vague:

- Time
- Date
- Amount
- Size
- Location
- Distance

EXAMPLES

At first glance, this message looks great and responsive: "I'll respond to your request soon." In reality, it could lead to an upset boss or disappointed customer. Why? Because you were unclear. If you interpret "soon" to be next week and the customer thinks it means today, then you have a problem. Instead, be specific: "I'll respond to your request by noon on Thursday."

Here is another example: "The attachment I will send is large. Is that okay?" Well, the answer depends on how you define "large." If the person has a slow Internet connection, the response would be different than someone with a fast connection. Be specific instead: "The attachment I'll send is in PowerPoint, and it's 6 MB. Is that okay?"

Here is an exercise to help you focus on being specific.

EXERCISE: VAGUE VERSUS SPECIFIC

DIRECTIONS

Look through recent e-mails you have sent. List situations where you were too vague. Beside each one, write what you should have said instead.

A.6. E-mail and Credibility: Reply All

Just as the content of correspondence can affect your credibility, so can the mechanics. In the case of e-mail, "mechanics" refers to how messages are sent.[1] There are accepted standards for sending and responding to e-mail messages. When these standards aren't followed, you can be perceived as unprofessional, rude, or downright incompetent.

There are many mistakes that occur when sending e-mail messages. Let's look at three that

are quite common and that can also have a big impact on how others perceive you as a professional. These three mechanics are "Reply All," "cc," and "bcc."

Reply versus Reply All

There are two options for responding to e-mail messages: "Reply" and "Reply All."

- Hitting the "Reply" button sends a response to the original sender only.

- Hitting the "Reply All" button sends a response to everyone who received the original e-mail.

It is important that you understand the difference between the two buttons and that you make the correct selection.

> If your comment only applies to one person, don't send it to everyone.

This may sound simple, but it is often misused. It is annoying and unprofessional when senders abuse the "Reply All" button. Even worse, it wastes time. Recipients must read through the message only to determine that it wasn't intended for them. You can acquire a bad reputation in a hurry by using the "Reply All" function incorrectly.

EXAMPLE

A business professional named Nicole (name changed to protect the innocent) volunteered to serve on the nominating committee for one of the professional associations to which she belongs. The committee chair sent an e-mail to all members asking when they were available to meet.

All seven of the other members responded with the "Reply All" function. For two days, Nicole received messages about who was available when. This wasn't only annoying, it was a waste of her time.

Only the committee chair needed that information. The chair could compile the times, select the most appropriate one, and send one e-mail to everyone indicating the details.

The annoyances didn't stop there. The members of the committee continued to "Reply All" to *every e-mail* from the chair for the duration of the committee's project.

There were two negative consequences from this incident. First, Nicole developed a poor perception of all seven of those members. She won't be buying their products or services. Second, she didn't volunteer with that association again for 2 years. That may sound harsh, but Nicole has limited time to volunteer. She wants to maximize her efforts and spend her time doing something productive and worthwhile.

* * *

You may know the difference between "Reply" and "Reply All." But what about your colleagues? If they are abusing the function, don't sit there and whine. Be proactive. Provide your colleagues with "instructions." If you are sending an e-mail to a group of people who are known to abuse the "Reply All" function, include directions in the message for how to respond.

EXAMPLE: SAMPLE REPLY INSTRUCTIONS

The task force needs to meet next week. When are you available? Simply hit Reply and send me your dates. I'll sort through the info and find a date that works for everyone. Then, I'll send a meeting notice.

* * *

Since the directions are sent to everyone, no one will be embarrassed or feel singled out. Plus, you will avoid a lot of unnecessary e-mails. There is another highly effective technique to stop the

"Reply All" problem, and it is discussed in the section on "bcc."

A.7. E-mail and Credibility: "cc"

People waste an enormous amount of time wading through messages that don't interest them and that aren't relevant to them. What causes this massive overload of irrelevancy? One of the biggest culprits is the "cc" button. It is so easy to click on the copy ("cc") function that people abuse it. They break one of the cardinal rules of e-mail—they don't think. Instead, they just hit keys.

Who should be copied? Only those people who need the information. However, it can be difficult to know who those people are. Here are four quick tests.

1. Ask yourself this question: "If my e-mail weren't working, would I take the time to pick up the telephone and call this person, or would I walk across the hall and visit this person, just to convey this information?"

If the answer is no, then don't send the person a copy of the message. It is obviously not that relevant. If you tweak this question a little and make it apply to you and your situations, you will find it is a fairly accurate test.

2. If you exclude the person from the "cc" list, what is the worst thing that can happen? If it isn't anything serious, then removing the person from the list is worth the risk.

3. What is the proper protocol? Would you stop the president of your company or the head of your department if you saw him or her in the hallway just to discuss the contents of this e-mail message? If the answer is no, then don't use the fact that you possess his or her e-mail address as an excuse

to send irrelevant information.

Also, copying your boss on every piece of e-mail correspondence isn't an effective way to show him or her how great you are. You aren't impressing the boss; you are only annoying him or her. You are also gaining a bad reputation throughout the organization.

4. Ask! Ask the recipient if he or she wants to be included. This test works especially well for situations where you send the same documents on a regular basis (weekly reports, etc.).

"To" versus "cc"

When sending an e-mail message, how do you decide whose name to put on the "To" line and who belongs on the "cc" line? The person on the "To" line is the primary recipient of the message. This person is the only one who should respond—by answering your question or providing the information you have requested.

The people on the "cc" line may need to see the information or see that you concluded some transaction, but they aren't expected to take action. The "cc" is similar to an FYI (for your information).

A.8. E-mail and Credibility: "bcc"

Many times people confuse the "cc" (carbon copy) function with the "bcc" (blind carbon copy) function. When you type the e-mail addresses in the "bcc" field, they will appear on your screen as you type them. However, they won't show up in the recipient's window.

Back in the days when letters were typed on a typewriter and sent through the post office, the purpose of a blind carbon copy was to ensure that the original addressee didn't know another person was receiving a copy of the correspondence. How is the "bcc" function used today with e-mail?

Here are several purposes. All of these are good ways to send e-mail effectively.

1. *To avoid reading long lists of addresses*

This long list occurs because people type all the addresses into the "To" or "cc" line. If you receive a message with a few addressee names, it is no problem to skip over them. It is a different matter entirely if the list of addressees is long, and you have to scroll down through pages of "To" or "cc" names before you get to the actual message so you can read it.

There is another way this can happen. This applies to most e-mail software. For example, say you create a distribution group labeled "Task Force." In your address book, you have seventy-three names in the Task Force folder. When you type that group name into the "To" line, nothing else will appear in your box except those words. The system will now send the message to all the addresses within that group. However, when the recipients receive the message, it won't say "To: Task Force." *It will list all the addresses.*

To solve this problem, put the "Task Force" distribution group on the "bcc" line. None of the addresses will appear on the recipients' screens.

2. *To avoid printing a long list of addresses (and save a rain forest)*

Another problem arises if the recipient wants to print the message. Many newer e-mail systems won't display all the "To" names when you're previewing the message on-screen. But when you hit the "Print" button, all the names will be printed.

It is frustrating to print an e-mail and see a full page of names before you get to the message. You just wasted a bunch of ink and killed a tree for no reason.

3. *To maintain privacy for your recipients*

Let's assume you are sending a message to a lot of people. Some of these people may not want to share their contact information with others. By using the "bcc" function, the e-mail addresses will remain hidden. And, you avoid making someone really mad.

For example, a parent receives messages from his or her children's school—requesting volunteers, etc. The e-mails come from PTO leaders and other parents. These messages include the e-mail addresses for lots of other parents. Some of those people will be horrified to see their work e-mail addresses distributed.

Don't do this! You can hurt your reputation, make someone mad, or end up in a lawsuit.

4. *To avoid giving your competitors your client list*

What happens if you are sending a message, and the distribution list includes your customers as well as your competition? If you don't hide those addresses, you have just given your competitors the contact information of your clients. That is a valuable gift! It's doubtful they will send you a thank you note.

5. *To share information internally (without disclosing addresses externally)*

For example, let's say you are the primary contact or liaison with a client. You send him or her an e-mail. You want other members of your department or team to know what information you sent to the client.

However, if you include the internal names on the "cc" line, then the client will know everyone's e-mail addresses. This creates a problem, if you want the client to correspond only with you. Because the first time that client can't reach you, he will look at that e-mail and start contacting anyone and everyone on that list until he reaches someone.

To resolve the situation, include the internal addresses on the "bcc" line. Then, everyone within your company remains in the communication loop—without being visible.

6. *To stop the "Reply All" problem*

If you are sending a broadcast e-mail to a large group of people, then there is another advantage of putting the addresses in the "bcc" line. If someone mistakenly hits the dreaded "Reply All" button, the message won't go to everyone. Why? Since the addresses are listed on the "bcc" line, they are hidden, so there is no way to reply to all of them.

This makes sense, if you think about it. If you were allowed to reply to addresses in the "bcc" line, then you could access those addresses by reviewing your "Messages Sent" box. That would defeat the entire purpose of the "bcc" function being hidden.

Secrecy

There is another use for the "bcc" function, but this one isn't always recommended. The "bcc" function can be used to send a copy of a message to someone without telling the primary recipient what you are doing. Be careful when using the function in this manner. To your primary recipient, it may appear as though you are sneaking around behind his or her back.

There are a few appropriate reasons for using the function for this purpose; for example, HR or your boss requested a copy. Just make sure there is a legitimate reason before using "bcc" to hide a recipient.

A.9. Internal Correspondence— Questions

Internal correspondence is communication that occurs within the organization. This is communication with people you know and probably interact with frequently. One of the most commonly asked questions about internal e-mail is, "How can you convince people to respond to your messages?"

When you send requests, do you have difficulty obtaining answers? Most people struggle with this problem, and they deal with it by complaining about the people who aren't responding. That behavior won't solve the problem. You have no control over those people. You do, however, have control over yourself—and the messages you send—so take a look at the type of questions you

> The best way to obtain good answers is . . . ask good questions!
>
> Here are four techniques for writing questions that will get better and more rapid responses.

are asking.

1. *Understand the question*

Know what you are asking. If you aren't sure what information you want, the person on the other end certainly cannot be blamed for a poor response. The key is to recognize

when you are asking poor questions.

2. *Avoid open-ended questions*

Avoid asking open-ended questions, whenever possible. Since this requires a lot of thought on the part of the reader, he or she is less likely to respond. Plus, it is rude. It can appear that you are asking the reader to do the work for you.

Example: Effective and Ineffective Questions

Example of an ineffective open-ended question:

"How did you increase traffic to your website?"

Example of an effective specific question:

"Did you attract new clients from your banner ad campaign? If so, how many?"

* * *

The more detailed and specific your request is, the easier it is for the person to respond, and the easier it is for people to answer, the more likely they are to do so. Here are some examples of how to make your questions more effective.

Example: Rewording Questions to Obtain Fast Answers

Example of a question requiring too much thought/time:

"Let me know your views on potential members for the Annual Meeting Committee."

Example of the same question requiring minimal thought/time:

"Here are seven suggestions for members for the Annual Meeting Committee. Which four people do you recommend?"

3. Word the question for a "yes" or "no" answer

Another technique for obtaining answers to inquiries is to word the question so the reader can reply with a "yes" or "no" answer. This can often by achieved by simply rewriting the question.

4. Ask the question first

If you have a question, let the reader know immediately. Place the inquiry in the first sentence. If that isn't feasible, at least mention right away that you have a question.

If you have several questions, use a list. With questions, it is most effective to use numbers. Then, the recipient can refer to the numbers when responding. And, it serves as a checklist for you, as well as the responder, to ensure all questions were answered.

EXERCISE: ASKING EFFECTIVE QUESTIONS

DIRECTIONS

Browse some recent e-mails you have sent that contain questions. Were any of the questions vague or hard to answer? If so, list them below. Below each one, rewrite the question to be more effective.

---

* * *

A.10. Internal Correspondence—Angry Messages

When you receive an angry message, what is your first response? Anger. Next time, before you become too agitated, try these steps:

1. Breathe.

2. Reread the message. Is the person really upset/angry, or are you overreacting?

3. As you read, ignore the tone and look for the essentials. Focus on the *issues* when you type your response.

Wait!

When you think you have calmed down enough to send a rational reply, should you respond? No! Because you really aren't ready. Wait longer.

Calm wins

Don't stoop to the other person's low level by being nasty. It only makes you look bad. As you have probably experienced firsthand, it is the nasty e-mails that are most often copied to other people and shared around the office. If you respond calmly, it only makes the angry sender look more ridiculous.

Solve the problem

Start the correspondence with the solution. The person won't read the rest of the message until he or she is assured that the problem has been resolved.

Defend your position, but don't be defensive

It's okay to defend your position—just don't sound defensive.

You should tell the person what action you took and why. Leave out the emotions and stick to the facts.

EXERCISE: RESPOND TO AN ANGRY MESSAGE

In the following exercise, you have received an angry message from your boss. Also included is an initial response from you. The response is inappropriate, but it contains the facts you need to write a better answer. With your better response, be sure to tell your version of the situation by focusing on the facts. You want to defend yourself without being defensive or nasty.

DIRECTIONS
Read the message from your boss and the "original" angry response. Then, write a better response to your boss.

E-MAIL MESSAGE FROM YOUR BOSS

Jane,

Fred Flintrock, president of Flintrock Company, contacted me today. He didn't receive the shipment of boxes he was promised. He is really mad. What is the matter with you? He's one of our best customers. Take care of this immediately. I mean right now. I would've thought this was obvious, but since you seem to be brainless, let me spell it out. Do whatever it takes to make him happy. I don't care if you have to carry the boxes to him on a bicycle.

—Big Boss

YOUR ANGRY (AND INAPPROPRIATE) RESPONSE

Boss,

How am I supposed to send him something, when I don't know what the heck he wants? In the past week, he has changed his order three times. The first two times, I personally walked back to the shipping department to stop the shipment before it was put on the truck. That way, Mr. Flintrock wouldn't incur any shipping charges. The third time he called to change the stupid order, he told me to hold the order until he called back with the details. He never called me back.

Finally, I called him this morning. He started yelling at me about the order not being at his plant. He finally admitted he forgot to call me. Then, he insisted it was my fault for not calling him sooner. (By the way, last month when I called to follow up on something he told me not to call and bother him, ever again.) I finally got him to give me the necessary details.

I processed the order and walked the paperwork to the shipping department to ensure it was taken care of. Because he's such a big customer, I even agreed to express ship the order at no extra charge to him. Now, if you'd stop bugging me with this stuff, I might be able to get some work done.

—Jane

DIRECTIONS
What is a better response?

_____

_____

_____

_____

* * *

Since this situation deals with emotions and perceptions, there are many potential solutions to this exercise. Here is one sample solution.

SAMPLE SOLUTION

Boss,

The order was shipped this morning via

express shipping. Here's the background on what occurred.

Mr. Flintrock changed his order three times this week. The first two times, I walked back to the shipping department and stopped the shipment before it was put on the truck. That way, Mr. Flintrock wouldn't have to pay any shipping charges.

The third time Mr. Flintrock called, he asked me to HOLD the order until he called back. I waited 3 days. Because I understand what a valuable customer Mr. Flintrock is, I took the initiative and called him. (Note: I would've called even sooner, but last month when I called to follow up on a matter, he asked me not to call him again.)

After he provided the necessary information, I immediately walked the paperwork to the shipping department and sent the order via express shipping. I waived the extra charge—again, because Mr. Flintrock is such an important customer.

—Jane

* * *

FOLLOW-UP TO THE EXERCISE
- Spend a few minutes thinking about how your answer differed from the sample and why.

- The sample began with the resolution. Why? The boss isn't going to listen to anything until he knows the problem has been solved.

- Wouldn't it have been nice if your boss had *asked you about the situation* instead of jumping to conclusions? Of course. However, you can't control your boss.

Note: These techniques and examples refer to

internal communication. Your response would be quite different if you were corresponding directly with the customer.

You can't control other people and their unprofessional rants. However, you can control how you deal with others. Make sure you treat your employees and colleagues with respect and don't treat them the way boss treated this employee.

A.11. Business Report

The purpose of this section is to provide a big picture view of report writing in a business setting, not to teach you in-depth techniques. Let's start with perspective.

This isn't a high school English paper. The type of writing for which you received an A in English class won't be appropriate in the business world. While grammar, spelling, and punctuation are still vital, the tone and style of a report for business are quite different.

> The most common problem with reports is: the writer tries too hard to impress.

A business report must be professional and organized. In addition, it must also be concise and easy to read because it is being viewed by a busy person.

By far, the most common problem seen with new professionals is they write in a style that is stilted, verbose, pompous, and condescending. In other words, the writer is trying to impress, instead of simply being clear and concise.

Here is a list of other common errors found in the writing of business reports:

- The report rambles and is disorganized.

- The report contains tangents that aren't relevant to the main point.

- The writer fails to focus on and answer the

main question.

- The recommendations are vague, buried, or not presented with conviction.

- The writer doesn't explain the underlying assumptions that drive the results.

- There are too many details.

There are plenty of how-to books available on report writing. Find one that fits your needs. However, before you start following the detailed instructions in the book, recognize there are also some high-level concepts to be considered.

Here are several key concepts to consider when writing a report in a business setting.

1. *Know the reader*

As mentioned previously, the first step in writing any document is to know your audience. What does the reader want to know? Why did he or she request the report? What does the reader already know?

Be sure to consider the level of formality the person will expect. This will vary greatly from a law firm or audit client to an advertising agency or small business. After you have determined who is reading the report, then you can begin the writing process.

2. *Get organized*

Don't simply start writing. Brainstorm ideas, collect data, and organize the information. Use a system that works for you—outline, flowchart, mind mapping, and so forth. If you spend the majority of your time in the organization phase, everything else will fall into place.

3. *Stay focused and on topic*

If you use an organizational system, this will occur naturally. For example, assume you are outlining, and you end up with a dangling concept that doesn't fit anywhere on the outline. Guess what? That means it doesn't belong. With outlining or flowcharting, you are able to immediately identify any unnecessary information.

4. *Format for easy reading*

Remember your reader? He or she is busy. By utilizing a few formatting techniques, you can make the report faster and easier to read.

A. *Headings*

One technique is to utilize headings. Readers can see at a glance what information is being covered. There is an additional benefit of using headings: it forces you, as the writer, to stay on track and be organized.

B. *Lists*

Another formatting technique is to use lists. Don't bury important content in the middle of a paragraph. Make it stand out by creating a list. You can use numbers or bullets, depending on which is more appropriate.

In addition to helping emphasize key points, lists are easy on the eyes. Readers don't feel as overwhelmed as they do when faced with an entire page of unending typed words and no white space.

5. *Use an appendix*

While most readers only want to see key information, there are a few who will want details. You can accommodate both types of readers by keeping the body of the report clean and concise, while providing additional data in an appendix.

The concept of an appendix is to handle supplemental information, so use it. Put sources in the appendix. Even readers who want to see your sources don't want to wade through lines of citations buried within each paragraph.

6. *Addressing what the client wants versus needs*

Sometimes what a client or manager *needs* to hear from you is different from what he or she *wants* to hear. In other words, the project you have been hired by a client to complete (or the assignment you have been given by your manager) might not be the real problem.

For example, let's assume in the research phase of your project that you discover additional information. This data leads you on a path that differs from the initial request. If this occurs, you will need to deal with the situation.

Don't ignore it and hope it goes away. It might feel awkward or intimidating, but the issue must be addressed. On the positive side, this will be an opportunity for you to demonstrate your leadership skills, as well as your strategic thinking ability.

After reviewing the impact of the information on the situation, you will need to decide how to proceed. One option is to informally discuss your findings with the client or manager. This may be done verbally or via e-mail. Then you will have guidance for how to continue. In other instances, a more formal option may be necessary.

Based on the response, you may need to rewrite some of the elements or analysis of the report. If the findings of your research significantly impact the results, or force you to go in an entirely different direction, then you may need to significantly redraft the report.

7. *Be confident with your recommendations*

Resist the urge to fall back into pretentious writing to make the report seem important. Your research and expertise should stand on their own. Don't get nervous and start "padding" the report with extras. Be confident with your recommendations. Present your ideas clearly, concisely, and professionally.

A.12. Executive Summary

The most difficult part of a business report to write is the executive summary. It is also the most important part. Why is the executive summary so critical?

First, most people won't read the full report. All the vital information needs to be included in the executive summary because people may be making decisions based on those few short paragraphs.

> The viability of your recommendations will be based on your ability to write the executive summary.

Second, you need to hook readers with the executive summary in order to create interest. If you don't capture their attention with the summary, it significantly decreases the chance they will read the full report.

Third, people will judge your recommendations based on your ability to write about them.

338

Key areas

Now that you understand the importance of the executive summary, you are ready to write. Here are the key areas to include in an executive summary:

1. Statement of the problem, situation, or proposal (one or two sentences).

2. Background on the topic (key points—briefly).

3. Brief analysis.

4. Main conclusions (stated succinctly).

Final review technique

Here is one additional technique that may not be found in a typical how-to book, but it will greatly increase the chance of you writing a better executive summary: you should double-check the specifics.

After you have finished writing the summary, go back and review it. Did you include the key areas mentioned above? Take the time to identify the exact location where each of those areas is addressed. You may highlight them, circle them, or whatever works for you. The point is to specifically identify each key element. You may be surprised to discover that you didn't cover the areas as well as you originally thought. This extra review step may be a little more work, but it will strengthen your writing.

Worth the effort

Learning to write effective reports and executive summaries can be difficult. It may take time for you to perfect these skills, but it is worth the investment. When you can document your research and demonstrate your strategic thinking, your recommendations will be considered more valuable . . . and you will be perceived as more credible.

Appendix B.
A Brief Marketing Skills Tutorial

Chapter 16 discussed the bottom line being closely related to the top line and the need for businesses to have a customer- or client-centric focus. Regardless of what career track you pursue, if you climb high enough sooner or later you will have to be concerned about how the business markets its products or services. In many organizations, relative ability to generate revenues can become the distinguishing difference between progression and stalling out. Consequently, whether you are in marketing yourself, charged with overseeing some aspects of the marketing function, or required to routinely interface with marketing personnel, it behooves organizationally savvy leaders to understand the marketing skills required for success in that function. Leaders need to be able to place the right people in positions and be able to assess their needs and performance. One coauthor tells the following story:

> When I went into banking I didn't realize how much emphasis would be placed upon developing business. At first I was tasked with analyzing business others had brought in, but very quickly I learned that financial skills alone were insufficient. Sitting in the office massaging spreadsheets wasn't going to get me where I wanted to go. Somebody had to get out in the field and develop the business opportunities before I could analyze them. I also learned that those who were best capable of doing this were also the most valued. Yes, this was selling, not marketing per se, but eventually I learned that the two were interrelated. Later on, I moved into a higher-level position where marketing was one of the functions reporting to me. I felt ill prepared to oversee marketing because my limited marketing education had been acquired mostly through osmosis and one or two marketing courses in my MBA program. I felt my way along wishing I knew more. I pride myself on generally having made good hiring decisions over the years, but one of the worst I ever made was hiring a marketing director. On paper she looked great and received a good reference from her previous employer, but after a year we had to let her go because the results simply weren't there. She created professional-sounding presentations and analyses but flopped when it came to implementing plans and getting results. I suspected that the good reference by her former employer had been a well-disguised attempt to ease her out the door. Ex post, I wished I had been better able to assess whether she had the right skill set for the job.

As this anecdote suggests, knowing how to assess the performance of marketing personnel is critical given the importance of marketing to developing business. In addition to the general leadership discussed in this book, leaders within the marketing function also need to develop their technical competencies. These technical skills span two dimensions: (1) tying implementation to strategic visioning, and (2) managing product life cycles.

B.1. Tying Implementation to Strategic Vision

For example, early in a career as an associate brand manager at a men's health firm, the primary everyday focus of the job is on implementation of marketing tactics. The impact is near-term, immediately measureable, and measured in thousands to millions of dollars. Examples are Old Spice (https://www.youtube.com/watch?v=owGykVbfgUE) and Dollar Shave Club (https://www.youtube.com/watch?v=ZUG9qYTJMsI). An associate for one of these brands is likely to be working through the basics of marketing attempting to answer the following questions:

1. What is the target customer segment for my brand?

2. What is my brand's current position in the market versus what we would like for it to be?

3. What is our value proposition for the target customer?

4. How can I leverage marketing tactics to reach the target customer segment and support my brand position?

5. What is my brand message?

6. What channels (TV, print, social media, etc.) are best suited to my target customer and my brand message?

Tactics require constant monitoring and updating, so a marketing associate needs to be good at the following:

1. Executing a market research plan and translating the results into insights.

2. Influencing cross functionally and managing external agencies.

3. Evaluating the quality of creative content.

4. Converting a brand position into a marketing message.

For example, a YouTube video may be inexpensive to produce, but even when successful the impact may be very temporary.

As a marketer moves up in an organization, responsibility frequently grows from one product to several and eventually a portfolio. Through this progression, the emphasis shifts from concern with near-term impact and development of tactics to portfolio management over the long term. Senior marketing executives need to be able to answer questions such as the following:

1. Which products need to be prioritized and why?

2. From which products will future revenue growth come?

3. In which product lines should limited financial resources be invested?

4. Are their gaps in the portfolio the business could exploit?

5. How are the needs of target customers changing?

6. What external trends are shaping the industry as a whole?

7. How are distribution channels changing?

In answering these questions, marketing executives should be able to:

1. Think strategically over a 5+ year time horizon.

2. Forecast sales with good accuracy.

3. Measure results.

4. Lead cross-functional teams in discussions involving tradeoffs of one product for another.

Figure B.1. Product Life Cycles

Life Cycle: Four Basic Stages

Audience	Early Adopters	Mainstream	Late Adopters	Laggards
Market	Small	Growing	Large	Contracting
Sales	Low	High	Flattening	Moderate
Competition	Low	Moderate	High	Moderate
Business Focus	Average	Market Share	Customer Retention	Transition
Design Focus	Tuning	Scaling	Support	Transition

Source: Adapted from http://www.idea-sandbox.com/blog_images/life_cycle.png (accessed April 21, 2014).

5. Develop and/or evaluate branding plans.

6. Analyze markets, competitors, and trends.

B.2. Managing Product Life Cycles

The second dimension deals with how a marketer manages the life cycle of a product. Products usually progress through phases, starting with the *introduction phase,* moving to the *growth phase,* then to the *maturity phase,* and perhaps to a *decline phase,* as shown in Figure B.1.

Regardless of their relative positions in the organizational hierarchy, marketers need to be able to manage brands as they move through these phases. At each stage marketers must consider six aspects of a product:

1. The audience they are attempting to attract.

2. The size of the potential market.

3. The revenues likely to be generated.

4. Competitive intensity.

5. The business focus of the marketing.

6. The fundamental design of marketing plans.

Consider a new 5G cellular phone that enables high-definition TV and cloud computing. During the **introduction phase** early in the product's life cycle, the target audience may be primarily those consumers who like being on the cutting edge of technology. These customers may represent a relatively small part of the potential market, but they are important for getting the product into the public domain to create awareness and attain some revenue traction. Sales will be low relative to potential sales at this stage and competition minimal because competitors have not had time to react to the new offering. Marketers will tune their marketing campaign based upon what creates a customer response. During the introduction phase, marketers are focused on (1) building brand awareness, (2) the results of product trials, (3) establishing distribution through the channels selected, and (4) establishing the brand's position in the market.

During the **growth phase** the target market becomes larger and more mainstream, with customers focusing on the more utilitarian features of the phone. Accordingly, the organization must scale up its marketing efforts. If the product is successful, sales growth becomes exponential, with rapidly growing market share of the overall phone market. Competitors become more threatened by the new phone and start to ramp up their competitive efforts. In the **maturity phase** the marketing focus shifts to those potential customers who have yet to embrace 5G. Sales start to flatten as market growth slows and competition intensifies. Customer retention via phone replacement becomes paramount, supported by incremental product improvement. In the **decline phase**, the 5G is being replaced by 6G and sales begin to fall. The focus is now on transitioning to 6G.

During each phase the measurement of success also differs. While resources are always constrained, budget management is not always as critical in this phase of the life cycle. The product often does not generate positive return on investment in the first few months following its launch, and companies usually know that they have to invest more heavily early on to successfully launch a new product. In the introductory stage, customer awareness measures may be most important. In the growth stage, market share may be dominant over profitability, but in the maturity phase tradi-

tional financial measures such as return on investment and profit margin may replace market share in importance. Investments in product improvements may be made in attempts to hold market share. In the decline phase, the company will attempt to "harvest" its investment in the product and net cash flows used to create new products may be the paramount consideration.

Examining the product life cycle, early on marketers need to know how to:

- Build marketing campaigns.

- Establish relationships with distributors and/or retailers.

- Partner with and incentivize sales forces.

- Interpret market research results, with particular emphasis on insights that can be used to generate product trials.

As a product matures, the focus shifts away from the aforementioned, and the goals differ:

- Generate repeat use and brand loyalty.

- Defend against competitive attack.

- Establish strategic partnerships with distributors and/or retailers.

- Maintain enthusiasm with a sales force, especially as new products get added to the portfolio.

- Generate high returns on diminishing investments.

When a product truly becomes a "cash cow" (think Cheerios), marketers are counted on to maintain the brand's position in the market on extremely limited resources. Creativity is important, but less in terms of advertising and more in terms of channel management. (Often mature brands are the first to take advantage of new advertising me-

A Brief Marketing Skills Tutorial

diums like social or digital media. They are cheap and fast.) The skills necessary to be successful include:

- Creative problem solving.

- Fiscal responsibility.

- CRM system expertise, especially as it relates to "loyalty marketing."

- Sales force effectiveness.

- External relationship management, especially with retailers.

B.3. Concluding Thoughts

In summary, the foregoing provides a brief but hopefully useful overview of the marketing skills required along two major dimensions: tying implantation of marketing to the firm's strategic vision and managing products through their life cycles. Because of the criticality of revenue generation to business success, business leaders need to understand this important aspect of their businesses irrespective of the functional specialization they happen to be operating in currently. Leaders bound for top management positions need to have a customer-centric focus, and an important part of that focus is understanding how the firm markets its products or services.

Appendix C. Using MBTI SpeedReading to Assess Customer/Client Preferred Behaviors

Chapter 5 related how the Myers-Briggs Type Indicator can be used to assess subordinates' personality preferences. Chapter 16 discussed the importance of knowing customers' and clients' personality preferences in interfacing with them but noted that, since we cannot perform MBTI assessments on customers, we rarely, if ever, have the benefit of knowing their type. The same is true in intraorganizational situations in which a leader does not know type. As a result, chapter 16 presented one method for quickly assessing personality preferences; that presented by Alessandra and O'Connor in *The Platinum Rule.* This appendix presents another method for assessing personality preferences based upon MBTI SpeedReading of types.[1]

As discussed in chapter 5, recognizing, appreciating, and acting upon personality preference differences requires understanding of differences in behavior. As noted previously, MBTI considers personality preference differences as neither good nor bad, just differences in normal people behaving normally in somewhat unique ways. Chapter 5 focused on the deeper understanding of MBTI and helping ourselves and others to find their Best-Fit. SpeedReading involves determining Best-Fit more rapidly and without a formal assessment. SpeedReading requires effort at first but becomes easier, with increasing accuracy and efficiency with experience. Patience is critical because of a tendency to jump to erroneous conclusions without sufficient observation.

Reviewing a few key elements from chapter 5 helps set the stage for using this method. Now recall the discussion from chapter 5 in which we contrasted preferences across four behavioral dimensions, replicated below in Figure C.1.

Figure C.1. Preferences Across Four Behavioral Attributes

Extraversion Prefers the external world	Energy	Introversion Prefers the internal world
Sensing Prefers to scan back for data with the five senses	Perception	Intuition Prefers to scan ahead for possibilities and new ideas
Thinking Prefers to step back from the situation and make an objective and logical decision	Judgment	Feeling Prefers to place him- or herself into the situation and make a personalized subjective decision
Judging Prefers a planned approach, motivated by the deadline	Orientation	Perceiving Prefers a spontaneous approach, motivated by pulling off the task at the last minute or in the last hours

Figure C.2. Hand-Exercise Descriptors

Preferred Hand	Nonpreferred Hand
Easy	Difficult
Fluid	Awkward
Comfortable	Uncomfortable
Did not need to think	Had to think a lot
Could do this all day!	Exhausting—would not last long doing this

C.1. SpeedReading the E/I Dimension

The first step in SpeedReading is watching for preferred and nonpreferred behaviors. Recall the preferred way of handwriting example in chapter 5 replicated in Figure C.2.

One key point from the handwriting exercise was that everyone could do the nonpreferred; it was simply more effortful. The same holds true in other type behaviors; the more people use non-preferred behaviors, the more exhausted they become. Introverts can perform extraverted behaviors for a while, as noted in the anecdote about marine officers in chapter 5, but reversion to introversion restores their energy. Consequently, a good starting point in SpeedReading type is assessing introversion and extraversion through a combination of questioning and observing.

One useful technique for assessing introversion (I) versus extraversion (E) in business settings is **observing** who most often initiates contact and how individuals respond in conversation. An introvert and extravert can be best friends, but the extravert will most often initiate contact. Does a person take a moment to think before responding? Does he or she seem to want to fill a void in conversation? If so, one is likely observing an extravert. Failure to correctly assess this dimension can result in misunderstandings among different types. For example, when extraverts and introverts know very little about each other, the extravert may assume the introvert is hiding something because of a reticence to communicate, whereas the introvert may assume the extravert is loquacious. Similarly, an introvert may be exhausted by the seemingly endless list of projects started by an extravert, while the extravert is energized by the number of projects and possibilities. On the other hand, the extravert may wonder why the introvert does not engage in more activities. Either may be temporarily resentful of the other without realizing they are simply observing differences in preferences.

Observing is one key to SpeedReading the E/I dimension, but **asking** is another key if observation does not provide sufficient evidence of the E/I preference.[2] Listen for responses such as, "I enjoy doing that!" or "Oh, at work I have to be like this . . ." The "have to" phrase indicates nonpreferred behaviors. The import is enthusiastic or guarded statements can indicate one preference or the other.

C.2. SpeedReading the S/N Dimension

Imagine a sensor (S) and an intuitive (N) are examining physical objects—a tree, flower, building, car, or another person. A sensor typically will focus on facts and details, often going into more detail than an intuitive wants. The intuitive typically prefers a big-picture approach and suggests linkages to other elements. The sensor does not always understand or appreciate what he or she perceives are factual disconnects. Conversely, the intuitive does not always understand the sensor's fascination with detail. Either may be temporarily resentful of the other absent realization they are experiencing different preference behaviors.

The sensor usually thinks in linear fashion, proceeding step by step to reach conclusions. The less-linear intuitive may or may not wait for the sensor to get through the steps, sometimes completing the sensor's thoughts or interrupting and asking questions such as, "Where does this end?" The intuitive may start a story, then digress, then return to the story, and finally come to a conclusion. The sensor may interrupt, saying, "Go back to the beginning, you've lost me," or make comments such as, "That was a circuitous path."

Sensors and intuitives find organizational administration to be either a blessing or a curse, respectively. To the sensor, following facts and details in an administrative situation seems normal most all the time. To the intuitive, this seems normal only if one must do it; otherwise, facts and details are merely suggestions or for others to follow. As with the E/I dimension, observing and asking are key to SpeedReading the S/N dimension. Ask questions and listen to ascertain if the responses contain phrases similar to "Oh, this is how I have to behave at work."

C.3. SpeedReading the T/F Dimension

Thinkers (T) and feelers (F) make decisions differently.[3] Thinkers use objectivity, and feelers use subjectivity. Thinkers typically remain outside situations, even ones that affect them personally, examining facts in an objective manner and assessing costs and benefits. Thinkers seek to depersonalize outcomes, whereas feelers typically go inside situations, even if they do not affect them personally, determining how each party "feels" and attempting to personalize outcomes.

Thinkers and feelers typically do not have a mutually agreeable way of agreeing to disagree.[4] That is, thinkers will disagree vehemently about topics under discussion as if the topics are inan-imate objects. For example, in a heated debate in a faculty meeting some years ago, the voices became louder, the commentary more volatile, and the verbal daggers came out. At lunchtime, the thinker said, "Let's go to lunch," and the feeler responded, "No way." Either may be temporarily resentful of the other unless they understand the T/F dimension.

When asked questions such as, "Does this hairstyle make me look younger?" thinkers and feelers will typically respond differently. Thinkers may provide blunt or neutral assessments, while feelers may offer a compliment, hoping to avoid any criticism. In business, thinkers often criticize first and appreciate later, if at all. In contrast, feelers appreciate first and criticize later, if at all. For example, if a team has worked diligently to complete a complicated report on time and in compliance with its mandate, thinkers receiving the report will immediately give suggestions on improvements to the report, while feelers will offer appreciation immediately.

Observing and asking remain the keys to SpeedReading the T/F dimension. Listen for responses such as, "Logically this is the thing to do but I feel that..." The "logically but I feel" construction signals a nonpreferred outcome. Consider the following anecdote from a coauthor: "My feeler father, 86 years old at the time, informed me that he was scheduling a medical operation of a particular type. My thinker reaction—preferred and normal for me—'Dad, that has a negative net present value for you and for society.' Feelers will usually object to my response—even asking if the story is real. But the story is real and continues with a further dialogue months after the operation when I, the thinker son, reiterated my previous position. My father responded, 'It may represent a negative net present value in financial terms, but I am more concerned about the net personal value—and that is positive.'"

C.4. SpeedReading the J/P Dimension

Judgers (J) prefer to live their lives on a schedule, while perceivers (P) prefer to live flexibly. Judgers are not necessarily judgmental but prefer structure. Perceivers are not necessarily perceptive but prefer to keep their options open. Judgers and perceivers often miscommunicate due to differences in their underlying behavioral patterns and the concomitant assumptions they make. In a business meeting or a personal situation, judgers hear decisions being made, and perceivers hear options being discussed. Thus, the proverbial contrasting comments, "We have already decided that" versus "No way, we were just discussing options," come into play. Both judgers and perceivers may be temporarily resentful of each other unless they realize the underlying causes of their differences lie in personality preferences.

Judgers typically very quickly select their order at restaurants. If they have enjoyed a particular meal previously they tend to order the same thing. Perceivers typically prefer to hear all the options and scan the menu several times before ordering, sometimes to the consternation of the judgers, who resent the delay. Upon receiving a meal, the judgers typically are ready to eat without much ado, while the perceivers may even regret their order and wistfully wonder if they would have been better off selecting something else.

Judgers typically are capable of and satisfied with making decisions with less information than perceivers. Judgers prefer deciding now to the confusion of the perceiver, who wonders why they didn't wait for more information. Judgers and perceivers sometimes interact in such situations with fairly intense behavioral responses. If traveling together, judgers prefer to schedule activities and perceivers prefer to keep their options open. Judgers will make statements such as, "I schedule my spontaneity," while perceivers make statements such as, "Time is elastic." Once, in arriving at a dinner meeting with an important client scheduled for 8 PM, the judger (one of the coauthors) arrived at 7:45 PM, the client at 8 PM, and a third person, a perceiver, arrived at 8:20 PM. When the judger quietly asked the perceiver if he knew what time the dinner was supposed to begin, the perceiver glanced at his watch and proudly announced, "8:20, right on time!"

Just as with the other dimensions, observing remains the key to SpeedReading the J/P dimension. As with the other dimensions, if individuals do not reveal their preferences, probe gently by asking and listening carefully for phrases similar to, "I prefer to always be on time" or "I like to be more flexible than that."

C.5. An Example of Using SpeedReading in a Client Setting

You are a newly minted assurance partner in a large CPA firm. You have typed yourself an ENFP who enjoys people-to-people work, and you are generally regarded as an excellent salesperson. You are good at acting out roles and belong to a community theater group. In social settings people often regard you as charming, gentle, and sympathetic. You enjoy pursuing new and interesting things, particularly if they are out of the ordinary. Recently, you and your family took a vacation in Peru where you participated in an Amazon River adventure. You are planning a vacation next year with your spouse in Nepal and enjoy talking about these kinds of experiences.

In your new capacity at work, you have just taken over as partner-in-charge of the audit of a relatively small, publicly held furniture manufacturer, NuFurn, Inc., located in a midsized Midwestern state. The previous PIC departed the firm abruptly under less than amiable circumstances, so you have had no opportunity to discuss the client with him. Over the phone you scheduled an appointment with the company chief's financial officer, Mr. Bonn, to introduce yourself, and now you are shown into his office. The following conversation ensues.

You: "Good morning. I'm Cathy Hendrix. It is a pleasure to meet you!"

Bonn (shaking hands across the desk and sitting back in his chair): "Likewise. Have a seat."

You: "As I mentioned on the phone, I'll be heading up the audit team for NuFurn. I'm looking forward to working with you."

Bonn: Silence. Hands folded on desk, looking at you expectantly.

You (hoping to break the ice): "It's a really nice day. My family and I just got back from vacation in the tropics, so this cool air is really great."

Bonn (distractedly looking at a note on his desk): "Good. What happened to Bob Johnston?"

You: "Well, Bob left the firm. I just transferred here from San Francisco, so I didn't have an opportunity to meet him before he left, and I'm unsure why he left."

Bonn: "So your firm assigned you to the audit and didn't tell you why?"

You (starting to become uncomfortable): "I was able to review your files and discuss NuFurn with the partner-in-charge of assurance services in Chicago, but we really didn't get into why Mr. Johnston left."

Bonn: "So you don't know anything about the problems?"

You: "Uh…I confess I wasn't told anything about problems. Can you elaborate on that?"

Bonn (somewhat impatiently): "I went into all that with Johnston a month ago. You mean he didn't put anything in your files about it?"

You: "Apparently not, but I'd really appreciate knowing about any difficulties NuFurn has experienced with our services."

Bonn: "It is hard for me to understand why Johnston would not have noted that. He must have been having other difficulties and didn't want to bring ours to your firm's attention."

Based upon Bonn's behaviors so far, what can you deduce about his type? Rather obviously, he is an introvert. He waited for you to initiate conversation and sometimes only a question, not a statement, elicits a response. Also, he seems detailed oriented, wanting to delve into your predecessor's reasons for leaving the firm and why the problems weren't noted in your firm's files rather than moving on. That attention to detail suggests that he may be a sensor, not an intuitive. You decide to ask some questions to gain a better understanding of Bonn.

You: "If NuFurn has issues with our services, I am very concerned about correcting any problems as soon as possible. Perhaps if you can relate some of the details of what these difficulties are, we can decide how to go about addressing them. Will you help me better understand?"

Bonn then proceeds to go into some depth of detail about areas he believed received too little scrutiny and others than received too much during the past audit. It is clear he is focused on how the audit was structured. He talks about the audit not having really provided any "value added" and how NuFurn leadership feels it is not getting as much benefit from recent audits as it had in the past. You are impressed with his mastery of audits and audit procedures and his objective assessment of the pros and cons of the relationship.

You decide he is not asking for anything your firm could not and should not be providing. You also decide Bonn is quite intelligent and very much a deep thinker despite his plain and straightforward way of speaking.

You: "I'm impressed with your knowledge of audit procedures. Do you have a background doing assurance work in public accounting?"

Bonn: "Spent 18 years in audit with Ashton, Bancroft & Prescott before taking this job. Now, back to our discussion of the problems…"

By now you have formed your first impression of Bonn's complete MBTI. Given his apparent affinity for structure, you deem him a judger. Consequently, you decide tentatively that Bonn is an ISTJ. How does this help you resolve what is apparently a problem with a client?

Having studied MBTI types, you know that ISTJs have the following preferences:

1. Decisiveness

2. Thoroughness

3. Justice

4. Practicality

5. Smoothly working operations

6. Reliability

7. Risk aversion

Knowing these preferences, how do you now deal with the situation? First, you apologize for the difficulties, assure him that you are determined to make the relationship right, and will deal with the problem immediately and thoroughly. You want a smooth working relationship that enables him to depend upon your firm supplying NuFurn's assurance needs. You might say something to mitigate his risk aversion such as, "Despite not knowing as

much about the past as I would like to, I intend to fix that by delving into this and making NuFurn a delighted customer. I appreciate your candor and hope that you will continue to advise me of anything you feel we can do better to help NuFurn." Obviously, thorough follow-up and correction of the problems are critical to the relationship. You want to keep in touch with Bonn to ensure things go smoothly but not waste his time.

C.6. Concluding Thoughts

As we hopefully discussed convincingly in chapter 16, a customer-/client-centric focus is critical to the success of businesses. A major aspect of this focus is how you and your personnel interact interpersonally with customer/client representatives. Knowing type and the preferences associated with it can significantly improve these interactions by facilitating a greater degree of comfort on the part of those with whom you and your people interact. Once you have typed your customer or client, you can then refer back to the basic MBTI descriptions to gain a better understanding of how to temper your interactions to optimize your relationship. Figure C.3 on the following page provides a handy guide for SpeedReading type.

SpeedReading type is not science, but insights gained from it can go a long way toward recognizing, appreciating, and acting upon differences in preferences. By careful observation and questioning, you can learn how to change your own behaviors to become a better fit with those with whom you do business. As Tolstoy noted, "Everyone thinks of changing the world, but no one thinks of changing himself."[5]

Figure C.3. Handy Guide to SpeedReading MBTI

QUAD2 Consulting_____

"SpeedReading People" Using Myers-Briggs

Just as everyone has feet and toes differently shaped from everyone else, so too we have different styles behavior. The dimensions of the Myers Briggs Type Indicator (MBTI) make it relatively easy to understand one's own—and just as importantly another's—style.

Understanding and appreciating these natural differences enables one to communicate and collaborate more effectively. You can use the matrix below to get a quick, but reasonably reliable "speedread" on your own or another's MBTI Profile.

Very Clear	Clear	Moderate	Slight	Slight	Moderate	Clear	Very Clear
Extraversion (E)							Introversion (I)
• Verbal				• Independent			
• Accessible and open				• Able to work alone			
• Action oriented				• Diligent			
• Extensive interests				• Thinks before acting			
• Interacts with others				• Listens well			
• Outwardly directed				• Reflective			
• do—think—do				• think—do—think			
Sensing (S)							Intuiting (N)
• Realistic				• Imaginative			
• Memory for detail/fact				• Rapid insights			
• Careful, systematic				• Sees global picture			
• Patient with routine				• Solves novel problems			
• Practical				• Seeks possibilities			
• Enjoys the present				• Futuristic; visionary			
• Tactical				• Strategic			
Thinking (T)							Feeling (F)
• Logical, analytic				• Considers others			
• Objective				• Understands needs			
• Just				• Demonstrates feeling			
• Stands firm				• Persuades, inspires			
• Critical ability				• Compassionate			
• Organized				• Creates harmony			
Judging (J)							Perceiving (P)
• Decisive				• Spontaneous			
• Plans ahead				• Open minded			
• Exercises authority				• Understanding			
• Orders, organizes				• Curious			
• Sustains effort				• Flexible, adaptable			
• Systematic, orderly				• Tolerant			
• Acts sooner rather than later				• Holds off pending more information			
• Course-corrects if/when necessary				• Waits till we can do it right			

Source: Adapted from materials previously supplied by Quad2Consulting, www.quad2consulting.com.

Appendix D.
Activity-Based Costing

"Companies should decide what processes and competencies they must excel at and specify measures for each."

—David P. Norton and Robert S. Kaplan

On the way into the office, you swing by the local gas station to fill up and grab a cup of coffee. Without really thinking about it, you pay $2.25/gallon for the gasoline, $1.79 for the coffee, and $2.99 for the protein bar, which will become a mid-morning snack during the 9:00 AM project meeting that will most likely run until lunch.

Most of us are so comfortable buying everyday items that we don't give it a lot of thought except when costs are noticeably different. One coauthor never thinks about the amount of gas purchased for his day-to-day car, but when he fills up his 1985 Land Cruiser, which has a 50 percent larger gas tank, he sometimes has a moment of "sticker shock." Another common occurrence is to go to a discount warehouse to buy 3–4 things and still spend over $100. Yes, only one package of paper towels was purchased, but that package has twelve rolls, nine more than the three-roll package that is usually purchased at the grocery. Despite these little "surprises," most people recognize that this is simply a function of price multiplied by quantity and that if we purchase more things then we will pay a higher price.

Even as the world has moved to a more service-based economy, the price times quantity equation does not cause most consumers a great deal of grief. Consumers fully expect to pay a different price based upon the amount of service that is consumed, be it the number of nights stayed in a hotel room, the distance flown on a specific airline ticket, or the number of hours the babysitter watched the children. But what if the babysitter does more than just watch the kids? Let's say the kids are eating a pizza dinner when the babysitter shows up, and you and your spouse leave before dinner is finished. Do you expect the babysitter to clean up the leftover pizza and put the dishes in the dishwasher? If they do clean up after dinner, do you pay them more since they did more work on your behalf? When people go to the movies, they expect to pay a standard price regardless of the duration of the movie, albeit longer movies require more resources.

Activity-based costing helps managers to better quantify and understand both direct and indirect costs associated with the products and services they provide.

D.1. The ABCs of Activity-Based Costing (ABC)

As technology improved throughout the 1970s and into the 1980s, manufacturing firms found that the proportion of indirect costs associated with their products was increasing. This created significant challenges for many companies as it is more difficult to track indirect costs. Additionally, despite the fact that indirect costs were rising, the overall percentage of these costs was often significantly lower than direct costs. Let's consider the costs associated with buying a cheeseburger. One hamburger patty, one bun, and one slice of cheese are easy to track. The cost associated with the lettuce and tomato is a bit more difficult, and the ketchup and mustard harder still. Even more difficult is the cost of running the grill, the chef's labor, and the real estate taxes on the restaurant itself. While some of these indirect costs are immaterial on a per burger basis, they still represent millions of dollars per year to larger hamburger chains. Firms that can track these costs accurately and efficiently can often gain a competitive advantage over their rivals.

In the late 1980s Professors Robert S. Kaplan and William J. Bruns of the Harvard Business School helped popularize the concept of activity-based costing. Traditional costing systems usually grouped indirect costs into major categories and then allocated these costs based on arbitrary methodology such as square footage of space or headcount. ABC, on the other hand, would "first accumulate overheads for each organizational activity. They then assign[ed] the costs of these activities to products, services or customers (referred to as cost objects) causing that activity."[1]

A good application of activity-based costing is in a payroll department. If all employees are paid at the same time and use the same payroll services, then the assignment of costs is simple. However, if line staff are paid on a weekly basis and management is paid bi-weekly, the line staff uses twice as much of the payroll activity as a typical manager. Of course, staff who earn overtime or holiday pay require more payroll services than those who earn only their base pay in a given week. Other payroll-specific activities that employers may track separately include: bonus pay, stock options, employee stock purchase plans, commissions, 401k deductions, expense reimbursement, supplemental insurance coverage, etc.

Implementing ABC can be managed in four easy steps:

1. *Identify the activities associated with a given process, product, service, or customer.*

2. *Assign the costs to each activity.*

   A. Direct costs can be traced to one item; for example, one bun for each cheeseburger.

   B. Indirect costs can be traced to multiple items; for example, the cost of the stove.

   C. Administrative costs can be traced to many items and often won't change with volume; for example, the property tax on the restaurant.

3. *Identify the outputs (also known as cost objects), which may include products, services, or customers.*

4. *Assign activity costs to the outputs. The demand or volume for a specific activity is tracked using activity drivers; for example, cheeseburgers ordered or payroll checks processed.[2]*

D.2. Activity-Based Costing Example

Below is an example of how activity-based costing may be applied in a manufacturing setting.

A company sells two different types of smart phones: a 64GB and an 8GB model. These phones will be the cost objects for this example (see step 3 above). Traditionally the company allocates its $2 million manufacturing overhead budget based on 100,000 direct labor hours, or $20 per direct labor hour. Since the 64GB phone uses 5 direct labor hours per unit produced and the 8GB phone uses 3.75 hours per unit, they would be allocated $100 and $75 of manufacturing overhead respectively for each unit produced.

Figure D.1.

Activity	Activity Cost Driver	Total Activity Cost ($)	/	Activity Volume	=	Activity Rate ($)
Engineering	Engineering hours	125,000		12,500		10.00
Machine Set-up	Number of setups	300,000		300		1,000.00
Machine running	Machine-hours	1,500,000		150,000		10.00
Packaging	Packing orders	75,000		15,000		5.00

However, using an activity-based costing model, the assignment of manufacturing overhead costs would be based upon overhead-based activities performed when producing the smart phones. Step 1 is to identify the activities. The four overhead activities required to make smart phones are listed in Figure D.1. In addition to each activity, their respective cost drives, the total cost of each activity, and the number of times each activity was performed are listed. In step 2 we assign the costs to each activity. For example, the machines used to make the smart phones ran 150,000 hours during the given period. Since the total cost of running the machines was $1.5 million, it can be calculated that it costs the organization $10 for each hour the machines are run.

Once the activity rates are calculated, and since we have already identified the cost objects (step 3), we can proceed to step 4, which is to assign the costs to the smart phones. During the production of 5,000 64GB smart phones, the total activity volume required is provided in column 3 of Figure D.2. Using this volume and the activity rates calculated above, the total overhead costs and the overhead cost per unit can be assigned to the 64GB phones.

Based upon these calculations, it is easy to see that under a traditional costing methodology the amount of overhead allocated to the 64GB phone ($100/unit) was much lower than the amount of overhead activity actually required to make the phone ($155/unit). This new information will most likely lead the manufacturer to make different choices as it runs the business.

Companies have found that activity-based costing often provides not only a more accurate method of costing their products and services, but more detailed insights into what makes up these costs, such as value-added versus non-value-added activities. However, many firms also found that ABC can be very expensive to implement properly, and it can be difficult and time consuming to collect the data about activities and cost drivers on an ongoing basis.[3] Additionally, one coauthor noted, "Once ABC assumptions and results have been reasonably well accepted by all parties, there will be costs that do not attach to a product, customer, or service. These costs (fixed, usually) have not found a 'home'—making them orphan costs. Orphan costs are the costs that offer the opportunity to check your courage. Do you have the courage to eliminate orphan costs? Costs that add no value and that no one wants assigned to them via ABC? Thus, ABC offers a 'gut check' for leaders!" Finally, companies learned that although ABC could be easily implemented in small companies or departments, the process does not scale very well. As organizations grew, so did the number of activities that needed to be tracked, making the overall reporting process more cumbersome and the reporting less timely.

A third challenge that firms encountered was that when employees filled out their time cards, they reported very little, if any, idle time. Thus, the costs associated with specific activities were much too high, as all of the costs were assigned to value-added activities, when in reality some costs should have been assigned to "nonproductive" cost objects. Firms and scholars alike looked for a better way.

Figure D.2.

Activity Cost Driver	(1) Activity Rate ($)	(2) Activity Volume 64GB	(3) Total Overhead Allocated (4) = (2) × (3)	(5) = (4)/5,000 Units Overhead per Unit ($)
Engineering hours	10.00	5,000	50,000	10.00
Number of setups	1,000.00	200	200,000	40.00
Machine-hours	10.00	50,000	500,000	100.00
Packing orders	5.00	5,000	25,000	5.00
			$775,000	$155.00

D.3. Time-Driven Activity Based Costing (TDABC)

Eventually, Professor Kaplan, with the assistance of Steven R. Anderson, was among the first to simplify the process by developing time-driven activity-based costing. This is not to say that traditional ABC systems did not take time into account when identifying and costing activities; it is simply that TDABC made it more of a focal point. Instead of having each employee measure each of the activities performed directly, managers simply estimated two items: (1) the cost per time unit (minute or hour) of activity and (2) the amount of time required for each activity.

In the first instance, the manager estimates how much time is actually spent on each given activity, including idle-time or non-productive activities, for example, staff waiting for a machine to be repaired or attending a staff meeting. When that is complete, the manager estimates the amount of time required to process each activity once, for example, the time required to process a standard forty hour payroll check, over-time pay, or year-end bonuses. "The objective is to be approximately right, say within 5% to 10% of the actual number, rather than precise. If the estimate of practical capacity is grossly in error, the process of running the time-driven ABC system will reveal the error over time."[4] Finally, by multiplying the time required for each activity (e.g., 90 minute set up per machine) by the cost per time

unit ($30/hour), one would calculate the cost driver rates ($45/machine set up). This rate would then be applied to the volume of a specific cost driver (5 setups per production run) to determine the cost that should be applied to a specific cost object ($225 of setup costs per production run).

Through the use of time-driven activity-based costing, management is able to more accurately track both the costs of services and products and is also able to better measure and manage the capacity within their operations. Additionally, TDABC is easier to implement and maintain over time. If new activities are added or if processes are redesigned, then management simply needs to estimate new costs and monitor them over time.

Both traditional activity-based costing and time-driven activity-based costing can add a tremendous amount of value to a company. Management should clearly define the goals it wishes to obtain through the implementation of an activity-based costing methodology and be realistic in regards to resources that will be available to both implement and maintain the system. For a call center where a great deal of information is tracked accurately and efficiently, traditional ABC may be the best option; however in a meat processing plant, TDABC may be a better option. Either way, the organization will have a robust tool to help the leadership team be more successful.

Appendix E.
Economic Value Added (EVA)

> ## "EVA is just a way to measure profit, but one that is better than all others."
>
> —Bennett Stewart

Intuitively, we may wonder if the statement "better than all others" is possible! What we can say about Economic Value Added (EVA) is that EVA directly links the balance sheet and the income statement for performance management purposes. EVA purports to recapture the underlying economic elements into a coherent system of accounting, reporting, planning, budgeting, and financial management up to and including share price valuation. As a courageous leader, one needs to think seriously about such a claim and to assess it using critical thinking while determining its place in a leadership and team environment. What we can say quickly is that "accounting" is not perfect, nor does it capture everything in business decision making and reporting; on the other hand, accounting is the language of business and has been since ancient times, in one form or another.

Adding EVA to the performance management portfolio allows us to better equate our intuition with the economic realities. In accounting, we have the accounting equation Assets = Liabilities + Equity (Revenues - Expenses = Profit); that is, the income statement has a direct connection to the equity account in that managers make decisions on behalf of the owners with the eventual summarization "closed" to the equity account! Customers want the products or services expected at the price expected; suppliers want the payment expected at the time expected; and employees want the payroll expected at the time expected. So, why is it not consistent that owners want the dividends or share price increases expected when expected?

Given this logical consistency of expectations and the fact that "accounting" does not adequately communicate these "capital" charges vis-à-vis contemporary accounting, EVA was developed by Stern Stewart (www.sternstewart.com) and now EVA Dimensions (www.EVADimensions.com) to provide the consistency and transparency that decision makers need. EVA intends to transparently communicate to all concerned parties that there are underlying economic realities not captured in traditional accounting systems. Keep in mind that EVA is an accounting system with different assumptions designed to accomplish this goal of transparency of economic events.

EVA offers an ethically appropriate and economically-driven planning and performance management tool; yet, it is not a panacea.

E.1. The Basics of EVA

Financial reporting has made continuous improvements to get closer to the economic decision making paradigm but, as a human artifact, is still imperfect; thus, improvements are continuously being made vis-à-vis post-retirement healthcare obligations, pension assets or obligations, stock options, fair value accounting, non-

Figure E.1.

Net Sales

-	Operating Expenses
=	Operating Profit (EBIT: Earnings before Interest and Taxes)
-	Taxes
=	Net Operating Profit after Tax (NOPAT)
-	Capital Charges (Invested Capital × Cost of Capital)
=	Economic Value Added (EVA)

Source: Adapted from www.sternstewart.com, www.evadimensions.com, and www.investopedia.com/terms/e/eva.asp.

financial indicators, and integrated reporting. EVA is designed to adjust the accounting equation to represent the charge necessary to meet owners' expectations, as shown in Figure E.1.

These basics reveal some interesting characteristics. We assume net sales eventually converts to cash under most normal operation conditions.

Operating expenses include expenses that may benefit the future, yet, under current accounting standards are immediate expenses: advertising, research and development, training, and others depending on the industry parameters. Advertising has an immediate impact followed by a decaying impact process; nevertheless, there is the lingering impact as well as a cumulative impact. Thus, in EVA, advertising expense is capitalized and amortized over a number of periods, as are research and development and training expenses. These examples serve to illustrate that what is known in the accounting world as a "conservative" approach—expensing such items—is actually an "aggressive" accounting treatment of decisions taken and resources allocated to benefit more than one period.

Operating profit is the result once we have adjusted the operating expenses. We are getting closer to an "economic operating profit" as op-

posed to the accountant's operating profit! We then deduct taxes to arrive at the underlying profitability net of taxes and label this as it is— Net Operating Profit after Taxes (NOPAT)—in order to communicate the essence of the business profitability.

From NOPAT, we deduct a capital charge to account for the sources of capital used in the business. This invested capital may need some adjustments regarding restructuring, goodwill, and other accounting, but our goal for now is simply to introduce that the courageous leader will want to make sure that *all* expectations are accounted for.[1] In essence, we have now assessed a charge for the assets used in the business. Economic transparency is closer with EVA.

E.2. Implications of EVA

With an EVA system in place, we can begin the process of using the EVA metric as a planning and performance tool. We can start with either element as the process is iterative; that is, if we start with EVA results as a performance indicator, we assess the expected EVA with the actual and determine the desired EVA for the next period (or periods); if we start with the planning process EVA, we will need to assess the performance of the period to determine the next period's EVA.

Several elements require consideration in calculating EVA and using EVA for decision making. We start with the calculations:

1. *The number of adjustments to derive NOPAT is subject to a benefit-cost analysis as there are more than one hundred and fifty adjustments possible.*

2. *We select the more important adjustments to get us close to an EVA NOPAT, but we do not seek perfect accuracy.*

3. *In essence, we are adjusting accrual accounting to an economic value added accounting system (EVA).*

4. *The number of adjustments to derive invested capital is subject to a benefit-cost analysis as there are many adjustments possible:*

   A. We remove the noninterest bearing current liabilities as we are looking for assets funded by invested capital.

   B. We adjust for any goodwill to bring the full amount of the invested capital into play.

   C. We double-check our accrual adjustments to get to NOPAT—for example, advertising expense and research and development expense are capitalized; thus, we need an asset to represent this.

   D. We have several more areas such as minority interests, operating leases, etc., to consider; but in any case, we use a benefit-cost analysis.

5. *Weighted average cost of capital (WACC) requires a good estimate, not a perfect estimate.*[2]

In using EVA for decision making, we discover several key elements:

1. The change in EVA, or delta (Δ) EVA, is critical for analytical purposes as we are seeking continuous improvements.

2. Increases in EVA are the target. That is, bigger positive EVA numbers are always good—assuming we have no other issues to confound the results.

3. EVA touches both the income statement and the balance sheet. Decision makers should seek assets that generate a positive EVA and eliminate assets that generate a negative EVA.

4. With the adjustments made to the NOPAT and to the invested capital, decision makers should be focused on the long-term results, using the short-term results to inform their decision process.

5. Implementing an EVA system requires a starting point, which may be from a negative EVA situation; EVA works here as the Δ EVA is the target. This suggests that a negative EVA starting point with a positive Δ EVA is meritorious, even if the EVA has not turned positive overall![3]

Courageous leaders seek planning and performance indicators that are logically consistent, objective in their implementation, support short-term and long-term perspectives, and serve as proper motivation in both communications and commitment.[4] Using EVA in the bonus system is one way of doing this, where a bonus pool is set up to help managers realize that there are risks to the EVA results. The bonus pool holds back a portion of the EVA bonus to carry over for multiple periods. Thus, a dramatic positive or negative EVA is not rewarded or reduced immediately; this gives the decision maker incentive to make sure the next period(s) are oriented to positive Δ EVA numbers. Note that the EVA process requires a mindset shift; thus emphasizing courageous leadership.

E.3. EVA Momentum as a Ratio of Interest

EVA was adopted, refined, and improved from its inception. More recently (2007–2015), EVA Momentum has been offered as a ratio that brings the best of EVA and the best of decision making processes, where ratios are paramount, together. EVA Momentum is the change in a firm's EVA in a period divided by its sales in the previous period. The basic idea is that Δ EVA is an indicator for alarm or reinforcement for interested readers and decision makers. EVA Momentum has been developed into a "tree" diagram similar to the Du-Pont model used in financial analysis. But, where the DuPont model uses accounting data; the EVA Momentum tree uses the EVA accounting system data.[5]

E.4. EVA, EVA Momentum, and Beyond: Food for Thought

Planning and performance tools continue to be improved over time, and EVA, activity-based costing, and the balanced scorecard will no doubt see improvements in the future. However, they currently form a set of tools that can significantly inform decision makers in a logical, consistent manner to maintain objectivity in their planning and implementation, to support multiple period approaches, and to engage employees in a mindset shift. We are not so naïve as to think that these tools are a panacea; but, even though today's managers may face a volatile and changing world, their tools are gaining sophistication.

With the advent of integrated reporting, a pattern emerges of increasingly sophisticated planning and performance tools embedded in organizations of all sizes, in all industries, in all countries, and in "any other categorization." Integrated reporting is based on the premise that integrated thinking holds a key role in decision making in such complex environments. "An integrated report is a concise communication about how an organization's strategy, governance, performance and prospects, in the context of its external environment, lead to the creation of value in the short, medium and long term."[6] If we combine integrated reporting, which is a more "public-facing" reporting framework,[7] and our collection of planning and performance tools, we find a good fit. With the increased emphasis on economic, social, and governance issues, courageous leaders equipped with these tools can move to the forefront of the trend of increasingly complex reporting in both financial and nonfinancial aspects. Courageous leaders strive to get in front of trends and lead from the front.

Notes

1. It's about the Pack!

1. Angela L. Duckworth, "Research Statement," Duckworth Lab, University of Pennsylvania, https://sites.sas.upenn.edu/duckworth/pages/research-statement (accessed August 1, 2013).

2. A Philosophy of Courageous Leadership

1. Stephen R. Covey, "Three Rules of the Leader in the New Paradigm," in *The Leader of the Future,* ed. F. Hesselvein, M. Goldsmith, and R. Beckhard (New York: Drucker Foundation, 1996), 155.

2. Perry M. Smith, *Taking Charge: Making the Right Choices* (Garden City, N.Y.: Avery, 1989), 1.

3. James M. Kouzes and Barry Z. Posner, *The Leadership Challenge: How to Keep Getting Extraordinary Things Done in Organizations,* 2nd ed. (San Francisco: Jossey-Bass, 1995), 163–164.

4. August Turak, "The 11 Leadership Secrets You've Never Heard About," *Forbes,* July 17, 2012, www.forbes.com/sites/augustturak/2102/07/17/the-11-leadership-secrets-you-never-heard-about (accessed January 5, 2014).

5. Smith, *Taking Charge,* 164.

6. Peter G. Northhouse, *Leadership: Theory and Practice,* 3rd ed. (Thousand Oaks, Calif.: Sage, 2004), 88.

7. Patrick L. Townsend and Joan E. Gebhardt, *Five-Star Leadership* (Hoboken, N.J.: Wiley, 1997), 48.

8. Frances Hesselbein, Marshall Goldsmith, and Richard Beckhard, eds., *The Leader of the Future* (New York: Drucker Foundation, 1996), 103.

9. Kouzes and Posner, *The Leadership Challenge,* 288.

10. C. O'Reilly and D. F. Caldwell, "The Power of Strong Corporate Cultures in Silicon Valley Firms," presentation to the Executive Seminar in Corporate Excellence, Santa Clara University, February 13, 1985; and C. Reilly, "Corporations, Culture, and Commitment: Motivation and Social Control in Organizations," *California Management Review* 31, no. 4 (1989): 9.

11. Kouzes and Posner, *The Leadership Challenge,* 288.

12. See, for example, Jeff Hayden, "9 Things You Should Never Ask Employees to Do," *Inc.,* February 22, 2012, http://www.inc.com/jeff-haden/9-things-you-should-never-ask-employees-to-do.html (accessed January 5, 2014).

13. Hesselbein, Goldsmith, and Beckhard, *The Leader of the Future,* 225.

14. Northhouse, *Leadership,* 126.

15. David Garvin, "How Google Sold Its Engineers on Management," *Harvard Business Review,* December 2013, 76–78.

16. Walter Isaacson, "The Real Leadership Lessons of Steve Jobs," *Harvard Business Review,* April 2012, 97.

17. Isaacson, "The Real Leadership Lessons of Steve Jobs," 98.

18. Kouzes and Posner, *The Leadership Challenge,* 294–304.

19. Ron Edmondson, "7 Traits of Courageous Leadership," February 2, 2011, http://www.ronedmondson.com/2011/02/7-traits-of-courageous-leadership.html (accessed January 5, 2014).

3. Leadership Power, Theories, and Styles

1. Kendra Cherry, "What Is AutoCratic Leadership?" *About.com Psychology,* http://psychology.about.com/od/leadership/f/autocratic-leadership.htm (accessed December 31, 2013).

2. Andrew Carroll, "A Sidelined Patton Shares His Philosophy on Leadership," *Historynet.com,* May 22, 2009, http://www.historynet.com/a-sidelined-patton-shares-his-philosophy-on-leadership.htm (accessed January 2, 2014).

3. Leonard Kloeber, "Leadership Lessons from General Eisenhower," *Ezine Articles,* September 6, 2010, http://ezinearticles.com/?Leadership-Lessons-From-General-Eisenhower&id=4991281 (accessed January 2, 2014).

4. "Dwight D. Eisenhower—The Eisenhower Approach to Leadership," *Profiles of U.S. Presidents,* http://www.presidentprofiles.com/Grant-Eisenhower/Dwight-D-Eisenhower-The-eisenhower-approach-to-leadership.html (accessed December 31, 2013).

5. John R. P. French and Bertram Raven, "The Bases of Social Power," in D. Cartwright and A. Zander, *Group Dynamics* (New York: Harper & Row, 1959); and Patrick J. Montana and Bruce H. Charnov, "Leadership: Theory and Practice," in *Management,* 4th ed. (Hauppauge, N.Y.: Barron's, 2008), 253.

6. "Reward Power—The Fastest Way to Persuade," *EzineMark.com,* April 20, 2010, http://reward.ezinemark.com/reward-power-the-fastest-way-to-persuade-4cd11a8fe05.html (accessed January 2, 2014).

7. "Expert Witness Law & Legal Definition," *USLegal.com*, http://definitions.uslegal.com/e/expert -witness/ (accessed December 30, 2013).

8. Christopher Adair-Toteff, "Max Weber's Charisma," *Journal of Classical Sociology* 5, no. 2 (2005): 189–204.

9. Seth D. Kunin, *Religion: The Modern Theories* (Edinburgh: Edinburgh University Press, 2003), 40.

10. Jens Beckert and Milan Zafirovski, *International Encyclopedia of Economic Sociology* (New York: Routledge, 2006), 53.

11. Joseph C. Thomas. "Leadership Effectiveness of Referent Power as a Distinction of Personal Power," Regent University Center for Leadership Studies, LEAD605, Foundations of Effective Leadership, February 18, 2002, http://www.jctnet.us/Professional /MOL/LEAD605/ThomasJMicroBP$2.pdf (accessed January 2, 2014).

12. Quote attributed to motivational speaker Brian Tracy.

13. C. Bird, *Social Psychology* (New York: Appleton-Century, 1940); R. D. Mann, "A Review of the Relationship between Personality and Performance in Small Groups," *Psychological Bulletin* 56, no. 4 (1959): 241–270; and R. M. Stogdill, "Personal Factors Associated with Leadership: A Survey of the Literature," *Journal of Psychology* 25 (1948): 35–71.

14. See, for example, S. J. Zaccaro, "Trait-Based Perspectives of Leadership," *American Psychologist* 62 (2007): 6–16.

15. M. D. Mumford, S. J. Zaccaro, F. D. Harding, T. O. Jacobs, and E. A. Fleishman, "Leadership Skills for a Changing World: Solving Complex Social Problems," *Leadership Quarterly* 11 (2000): 11–35; and D. Magnusson, "Holistic Interactionism: A Perspective for Research on Personality Development," in L. A. Pervin and O. P. John, eds., *Handbook of Personality: Theory and Research* (New York: Guilford Press, 1995), 219–247.

16. R. Blake and J. Mouton, *The Managerial Grid: The Key to Leadership Excellence* (Houston: Gulf, 1964).

17. R. G. Miltenberger, *Behavior Modification Principles and Procedures,* 3rd ed. (Belmont, Calif.: Wadsworth/Thomson Learning, 2004).

18. See, for example, F. E. Fiedler, *A Theory of Leadership Effectiveness* (New York: McGraw-Hill, 1967); V. H. Vroom and P. W. Yetton, *Leadership and Decision-Making* (Pittsburgh: University of Pittsburgh Press, 1973); and V. H. Vroom and A. G. Jago, *The New Leadership: Managing Participation in Organization*s (Englewood Cliffs, N.J.: Prentice Hall, 1988).

19. J. R. Hackman and R. E. Walton, *Leading Groups in Organizations* (San Francisco: Jossey-Bass, 1986); J. E. McGrath, *Leadership Behavior: Some Re-quirements for Leadership Training* (Washington, D.C.: U.S. Civil Service Commission, Office of Career Development, 1962); J. Adair, *Developing Leaders: The Ten Key Principles* (Guildford, England: Talbot Adair Press, 1988); and James M. Kouzes and Barry Z. Posner, *The Leadership Challenge: How to Keep Getting Extraordinary Things Done in Organizations* (San Francisco: Jossey-Bass, 1995).

20. Eric Berne, *The Structure and Dynamics of Organizations and Groups* (New York: Ballantine, 1975).

21. John P. Howell, *Snapshots of Great Leadership* (London: Taylor and Francis, 2012), 16–17.

22. James Scouller, *The Three Levels of Leadership: How to Develop Your Leadership Presence, Knowhow and Skill* (Gloucestershire, England: Management Books 2000 Ltd., 2011).

23. D. Rock and J. Schwartz, "The Neuroscience of Leadership," *Strategy+Business* 43 (2006): 10.

24. Cherry, "What Is AutoCratic Leadership?"

25. Cherry, "What Is AutoCratic Leadership?"

26. Leadership-ToolBox, "Leadership Styles: Autocratic Leadership," http://www.leadership-toolbox.com /autocratic-leadership.html (accessed December 30, 2013).

27. G. S. Erben and A. B. Guneser, "The Relationship between Paternalistic Leadership and Organizational Commitment: Investigating the Role of Climate Regarding Ethics," *Journal of Business Ethics* 82, no. 4 (2008): 955–968.

28. Erben and Guneser, "The Relationship between Paternalistic Leadership and Organizational Commitment."

29. N. Martindale, "Leadership Styles: How to Handle the Different Personas," *Strategic Communication Management* 15, no. 8 (2011): 32–35.

30. C. E. Johnson and M. Z. Hackman, *Leadership, a Communication Perspective,* 4th ed. (Long Grove, Ill.: Waveland Press, 2003), 38.

31. J. Rowold and W. Schlotz, "Transformational and Transactional Leadership and Followers' Chronic Stress," *Leadership Review* 9 (2009): 35–48.

32. S. Wolinski, "Adaptive Leadership," (blog) July 7, 2010, http://managementhelp.org/blogs /leadership/2010/07/07/adaptive-leadership/(accessed January 2, 2014).

33. Wolinski, "Adaptive Leadership."

34. B. N. Smith, R. V. Montagno, and T. N. Kuzmenko, "Transformational and Servant Leadership: Content and Contextual Comparisons," *Journal of Leadership and Organizational Studies* 10, no. 4 (2004): 80–91.

35. A. G. Stone, R. F. Russell, and K. Patterson, "Transformational versus Servant Leadership: A Difference in Leader Focus," Servant Leadership Research

Roundtable, August 2003, http://regent.edu/acad /global/publications/sl_proceedings/2003/stone _transformation_versus.pdf (accessed December 30, 2013).

36. D. Schultz and S. E. Schultz, *Psychology and Work Today* (New York: Prentice Hall, 2010), 201–202.

37. George Pitagorsky, "The Caring Manager," *Project Times,* http://www.projecttimes.com/george -pitagorsky/the-caring-manager.html (accessed June 5, 2013).

38. B. M. Bass, *Transformational Leadership* (London: Lawrence Erlbaum, 1998), 60–61.

39. D. Goleman, "Leadership That Gets Results," *Harvard Business Review*, March 1, 2000.

40. P. Hersey and K. H. Blanchard, "Life-Cycle Theory of Leadership," *Training and Development Journal* 23 (1969): 26–34.

41. Peter G. Northhouse, *Leadership: Theory and Practice,* 3rd ed. (Thousand Oaks, Calif.: Sage, 2004), 87–96.

42. M. G. Evans, "Leadership and Motivation: A Core Concept," *Academy of Management Journal* 13 (1970): 91–102; and R. J. House, "A Path-Goal Theory of Leader Effectiveness," *Administrative Science Quarterly* 16 (1971): 81–98.

43. Northhouse, *Leadership,* 123–127.

44. Northhouse, *Leadership,* 126.

45. Northhouse, *Leadership,* 131.

4. Four Common Business Leadership Situations

1. A. Green, "5 Secrets You Should Know about HR," *U.S. News*, July 29, 2013, http://money .usnews.com/money/blogs/outside-voices -careers/2013/07/29/5-secrets-you-should-know -about-hr (accessed January 1, 2014).

2. Adapted from Problem Identification, Problem Analysis, Decision Making, and Type, TEAM International, Carouga, Switzerland.

3. S. Grier, "How to Counsel an Employee Performance Issue," *IT Managers Inbox,* http://itmanagers inbox.com/2209/how-to-counsel-an-employee -performance-issue/ (accessed December 28, 2013).

4. See, generally, Therese Haberman, "How to Give an Employee Performance Review," *Hartford Examiner*, October 25, 2010, www.examiner.com /article/how-to-give-an-employee-performance -review (accessed December 28, 2013); and "How to Give a Performance Review of an Employee," http:// www.wikihow.com/Give-a-Performance-Review -of-an-Employee (accessed December 30, 2013).

5. A. Hall, "The 7 C's: How to Find and Hire Great Employees," *Forbes*, June 19, 2012, http://www.forbes .com/sites/alanhall/2012/06/19/the-7-cs-how-to-find

-and-hire-great-employees/ (accessed January 1, 2014).

6. J. Cogen, "The Secret to Reading Resumes— Five Tips to Choosing the Right Candidates to Interview," http://ezinearticles.com/?The-Secret -to-Reading-Resumes---Five-Tips-to-Choosing -the-Right-Candidates-to-Interview&id=3618056 (accessed January 1, 2014); and C. Nepomuceno, "How to Read a Resume," http://ezinearticles. com/?How-To-Read-A-Resume&id=937720 (accessed January 1, 2014).

7. B. Libby, "How to Conduct a Job Interview," *CBS Money Watch,* March 13, 2007, http://www .cbsnews.com/news/how-to-conduct-a-job -interview/ (accessed January 1, 2014).

8. Libby, "How to Conduct a Job Interview."

9. "10 Mistakes Managers Make during Job Interviews," *CBSNews.com,* June 17, 2008, http://www .cbsnews.com/news/10-mistakes-managers-make -during-job-interviews/ (accessed January 1, 2014).

10. M. W. Berger, "Ten Critical Questions to Ask When Checking References," A Hire Authority, January 24, 2005, http://www.drgnyc.com/List_Serve /Jan24_2005.htm (accessed January 1, 2014).

11. J. Graves, "How to Fire Someone Compassionately," *U.S. News*, August 22, 2013, http://money .usnews.com/money/careers/articles/2013/08/22 /how-to-fire-someone-compassionately (accessed December 30, 2013); V. Lipman, "How to Fire Someone Effectively but (Hopefully) with Dignity," *Forbes*, April 16, 2013, http://www.forbes.com/sites/victor lipman/2013/04/16/how-to-fire-someone- effectively-but-hopefully-with-dignity/ (accessed December 30, 2013); M. Korn, "The Best Ways to Fire Someone," *Wall Street Journal*, October 26, 2012, http://online.wsj.com/news/articles/SB100008723 9639044388410457764581424927568 (accessed December 30, 2013); R. Hein, "8 Tips for How to Fire an Employee," *CIO*, January 22, 2013, http://www .cio.com/article/727127/8_Tips_for_How_to_Fire _an_Employee (accessed December 30, 2013); and C. Hamlett, "How to Fire Someone," http://www.ehow .com/how_4500247_fire-someone.html (accessed December 30, 2013).

5. Understanding Others and Yourself

1. Stephen P. Robbins and Timothy A. Judge, *Organizational Behavior,* 15th ed. (Upper Saddle River, N.J.: Prentice Hall, 2012). Several other personality models and descriptions are noted. Among these are: BIG Five personality, Core Self-Evaluation, Machiavellianism, self-monitoring, risk-taking, proactive personality, Holland's Typology, and others. We do note that

many, if not all, alternatives address the core processes of MBTI.

2. Isabel Briggs Myers, Linda K. Kirby, and Katherine D. Myers, *Introduction to Type: A Guide to Understanding Your Results on the Myers-Briggs Type Indicator* (Palo Alto, Calif.: CPP, 1998); and David J. Pittenger, "Cautionary Comments Regarding the Myers-Briggs Type Indicator," *Consulting Psychology Journal: Practice and Research* 57, no. 3 (2005): 210–221. Pittenger has numerous cautionary items but does acknowledge that "MBTI can serve as a nonthreatening vehicle to introduce the concept of individual preferences in personality and the relation between personality constructs and behavior to a general audience . . . as catalyst for exercises that lead to improved esprit de corps among employees" (p. 219).

3. Roger R. Pearman and Sarah C. Albritton, *I'm Not Crazy, I'm Just Not You: The Real Meaning of the 16 Personality Types,* 2nd ed. (Boston: Nicholas Brealey, 2010).

4. R. Bryan Kennedy and D. Ashley Kennedy, "Using the Myers-Briggs TYPE Indicator in Career Counseling," *Journal of Employment Counseling* 41, no. 1: 38–44 (2004). Business Source Premier, EBSCOhost (accessed February 1, 2014).

5. Robert M. Pirsig, "Zen and the Art of Motorcycle Maintenance: An Inquiry into Values," http://www.goodreads.com/work/quotes/175720-zen-and-the-art-of-motorcycle-maintenance-an-inquiry-into-values (accessed January 31, 2014).

6. Eleanor S. Corlett, Nancy B. Millner, and Katherine D. Myers, *Navigating Midlife: Using Typology as a Guide* (Palo Alto, Calif.: Davies-Black, 1995). Note this is not about midlife crises, but every time I have shown the book title to executives, their response is to complete the title with the word "crisis"!

7. Frank J. Landy and James L. Farr, "Performance Rating," *Psychological Bulletin* 87, no.1 (1980): 72–107. Behaviorally anchored rating scales (BARS) in one form or another have been used to assess behavioral aspects of individuals, teams, and even learning organizations.

8. Terry Campbell and *Heather Cairns*, "Developing and Measuring the Learning Organization: From Buzz Words to Behaviours," *Industrial and Commercial Training* 26, no. 7 (1994): 10–15.

9. Matthew W. Ohland, Misty L. Loughry, David J. Woehr, Lisa G. Bullard, Richard M. Felder, Cynthia J. Finelli, Richard A. Layton, Hal R. Pomeranz, and Douglas G. Schmucker, "The Comprehensive Assessment of Team Member Effectiveness: Development of a Behaviorally Anchored Rating Scale for Self- and Peer Evaluation," *Academy of Management Learning and Education* 11, no. 4 (2012): 609–630. Business Source Premier, EBSCOhost (accessed January 30, 2014).

10. Justin Kruger and David Dunning, "Unskilled and Unaware of It: How Difficulties in Recognizing One's Own Incompetence Lead to Inflated Self-Assessments," *Journal of Personality and Social Psychology* 77, no. 6 (1999): 1121–1134. Business Source Premier, EBSCOhost (accessed January 30, 2014). Kruger and Dunning demonstrated two things of concern to us: (1) in certain domains it is difficult to objectively self-assess, and (2) significant improvements are possible if directed learning is made. Thus, people improve their ability to self-assess with feedback and guidance.

11. Isabell Briggs Myers with Peter Myers, *Gifts Differing: Understanding Personality Type* (Palo Alto, Calif.: CPP, 1980).

12. www.cpp-db.com.

13. In using MBTI, many other tools have been encountered; each of these tools (e.g., 16PF, DISC, Belbin's Team, and Enneagrams) was examined for replacing and/or supplementing MBTI. In addition, Hofstede's work in national cultures as a differentiating factor was examined. See, for example, Geert Hofstede, "Cultural Constraints in Management Theories," *Academy of Management Executive* 7, no. 1 (1993): pp. 81–94. None of these provided the positive outcomes that MBTI provided and provides today.

14. Peter F. Drucker, "Managing Oneself," *Harvard Business Review* 83, no. 1 (2005): 100–109. Business Source Premier, EBSCOhost (accessed January 30, 2014). Drucker makes a strong case for knowing yourself in order to manage yourself. In fact, Drucker argued: "do not try to change yourself—you are unlikely to succeed. Work to improve the way you perform" (p. 104). This fits with our understanding of type.

15. Dorothy Leonard and Susan Straus. "Putting Your Company's Whole Brain to Work," *Harvard Business Review* 75, no. 4 (1997): 110–121. Business Source Premier, EBSCOhost (accessed January 30, 2014).

16. Katherine D. Myers and Linda K. Kirby, *Introduction to Type Dynamics and Development: Exploring the Next Level of Type* (Palo Alto, Calif.: CPP, 1994).

17. Laurie Helgoe, "Revenge of the Introvert," *Psychology Today* (September 2010), 54. Academic One-File, EBSCOhost (accessed January 30, 2014).

18. Many NPs share this "now panic" mode but not necessarily in a negative sense; rather in a positive sense that now the platform is really on fire, so time to get to it!

19. http://www.keirsey.com/4temps/overview_temperaments.asp. Keirsey has many tools available leveraging type and his sorting approach.

20. Sharon Lebovitz Richmond, *Introduction to Type and Leadership* (Palo Alto, Calif.: CPP, 2008).

21. Daniel Goleman, "What Makes a Leader?" *Harvard Business Review* 76, no. 6 (1998): 93–102. Busi-

ness Source Premier, EBSCOhost (accessed January 30, 2014). Goleman argues for five components of emotional intelligence—self-awareness, self-regulation, motivation, empathy, and social skill—as the defining variables of leadership excellence. Each of these variables is an integral part of type.

22. Oliver J. Sheldon, David Dunning, and Daniel R. Ames, "Emotionally Unskilled, Unaware, and Uninterested in Learning More: Reactions to Feedback about Deficits in Emotional Intelligence," *Journal of Applied Psychology* 99, no. 1 (2014): 125–137. Business Source Premier, EBSCOhost (accessed January 30, 2014). The argument here is once again to operationalize high-quality self-awareness so that improvements can take place. The challenge in this study versus the earlier study (Kruger and Dunning) where improvements were made is that improvements were much harder to come by. Evidently, emotional intelligence is such a "harder" topic that no one wants to admit deficiencies. Thus, they tend to allocate no or little resources to improvements.

23. J. Collins, "Level 5 Leadership," *Harvard Business Review* 79, no. 1 (2001): 66–76.

24. Will in Level 5 was not the first time to imagine will as important to achieving objectives: "as man under pressure tends to give in to physical and intellectual weakness, *only great strength of will can lead to the objective*" (emphasis added). "Carl von Clausewitz," http://www.goodreads.com/author/quotes/67848 .Carl_von_Clausewitz (accessed January 31, 2014).

25. This practice aspect is part of the argument that to become an expert one needs 10,000 hours of practice.

26. Carl von Clausewitz, *On War* (New York: Penguin Classics, 1982).

27. J. Leslie, "Leadership Skills and Emotional Intelligence" (2003), retrieved from http://www.ccl.org /leadership/pdf/assessments/skills_intelligence.pdf (accessed February 11, 2014).

28. Teams: Elizabeth Hirsh, Katherine W. Hirsh, and Sandra Krebs Hirsh, *Introduction to Type and Teams* (Palo Alto, Calif.: CPP, 2003); learning: Donna Dunning, *Introduction to Type and Learning* (Palo Alto, Calif.: CPP, 2003); organizations: Sandra K. Hirsh, *Introduction to Type and Organizations* (Palo Alto, Calif.: CPP, 1998); selling: Susan A. Brock, *Introduction to Type and Selling* (Palo Alto, Calif.: CPP, 1994); conflict resolution: Damian Killen and Danica Murphy, *Introduction to Type and Conflict* (Palo Alto, Calif.: CPP, 2003); coaching: Sandra K. Hirsh and Jane A. G. Kise, *Introduction to Type and Coaching* (Palo Alto, Calif.: CPP, 2011); careers: Allen L. Hammer, *Introduction to Type and Careers* (Palo Alto, Calif.: CPP, 2007); change: Nancy J. Barger and Linda K. Kirby, *Introduc-*

tion to Type and Change (Palo Alto, Calif.: CPP, 2004); project management: Jennifer Tucker, *Introduction to Type and Project Management* (Palo Alto, Calif.: CPP, 2008); leadership: Tucker, *Introduction to Type and Project Management,* and Richmond, *Introduction to Type and Leadership;* innovation: Damian Killen and Gareth Williams, *Introduction to Type and Innovation* (Palo Alto, Calif.: CPP, 2000); decision making: Katherine W. Hirsh and Elizabeth Hirsh, *Introduction to Type and Decision Making* (Palo Alto, Calif.: CPP, 1997); communication: Donna Dunning, *Introduction to Type and Communication* (Palo Alto, Calif.: CPP, 2003); EI: Roger Pearman, *Introduction to Type and Emotional Intelligence* (Palo Alto, Calif.: CPP, 2002); reintegration: Elizabeth Hirsh, Katherine W. Hirsh, and James Peak, *Introduction to Type and Reintegration* (Palo Alto, Calif.: CPP, 2011); and navigating midlife: Corlett, Millner, and Myers, *Navigating Midlife.*

6. Business Ethics

1. Richard Posner, *The Problems of Jurisprudence* (Cambridge, Mass.: Harvard University Press, 1990), p. 187.

2. Michael B. Metzger, Ethical Responsibilities of Managers (L533 course notes), Spring 2008, Indiana University, Bloomington.

3. http://www.brainyquote.com/quotes/quotes/w /winstonchu135210.html (accessed April 29, 2014).

4. See, e.g., Edward Broughton, "The Bhopal Disaster and Its Aftermath: A Review," National Center for Biotechnology Information, May 10, 2005, http:// www.ncbi.nlm.nih.gov/pmc/articles/PMC1142333/ (accessed January 19, 2014).

5. Alejandro Russell, "The Benefits & Importance of Ethics in the Workplace," Global Post, http://everydaylife .globalpost.com/benefits-importance-ethics -workplace-7414.html (accessed January 16, 2014).

6. Metzger, Ethical Responsibilities of Managers (L533 course notes).

7. Charles D. Kerns, "Creating and Sustaining an Ethical Workplace Culture," *Graziadio Business Review* 6, no. 3 (August 2003), http://gbr.pepperdine .edu/2010/08/creating-and-sustaining-an-ethical -workplace-culture/ (accessed January 15, 2014).

8. David Wessel, "Why the Bad Guys of the Boardroom Emerged en Masse," *Wall Street Journal,* June 20, 2002, p. A1.

9. Desmond Berghofer and Geraldine Schwartz, "Ethical Leadership: Right Relationships and the Emotional Bottom Line: The Gold Standard for Success," Institute for Ethical Leaders, http://www .ethicalleadership.com/Business /Article.htm (accessed January 15, 2014).

10. Ken Silverstein, "Enron, Ethics, and Today's Corporate Values," *Forbes.com,* May 14, 2013, http://www.forbes.com/sites/kensilverstein/2013/05/14/enron-ethics-and-todays-corporate-values/ (accessed January 15, 2014).

11. Susan M. Heathfield, "Did You Bring Your Ethics to Work Today?" *About.com,* http://humanresources.about.com/businessethics/qt/workplace-ethics.htm (accessed January 15, 2014).

12. Russell, "The Benefits & Importance of Ethics in the Workplace."

13. Russell, "The Benefits & Importance of Ethics in the Workplace."

14. Heathfield, "Did You Bring Your Ethics to Work Today?"

15. Campbell Jones, Martin Parker, and Rene Ten Bos, *For Business Ethics: A Critical Approach* (London: Routledge, 2005), p. 5.

16. "Business Ethics," http://en.wikipedia.org/wiki/Business_ethics (accessed January 15, 2014).

17. John Rawls, *A Theory of Justice* (Cambridge, Mass.: Belknap Press of Harvard University Press, 1971), p. 28.

18. Silverstein, "Corporate Values."

19. Berghofer and Schwartz, "Ethical Leadership."

20. "Ethics," http://en.wikipedia.org/wiki/Ethics (accessed January 21, 2014).

21. William S. Sahakian and Mabel L. Sahakian, *Ideas of the Great Philosophers* (New York: Barnes & Noble, 1993), p. 36.

22. Sahakian and Sahakian, *Ideas of the Great Philosophers,* pp. 38–41.

23. Sahakian and Sahakian, *Ideas of the Great Philosophers,* p. 37.

24. J. L. Mackie, *Ethics: Inventing Right and Wrong* (London: Penguin, 1990).

25. Julian Baggini and Peter S. Fosi, *The Ethics Toolkit: A Compendium of Ethical Concepts and Methods* (Malden, Mass.: Wiley-Blackwell, 2007), pp. 57–58.

26. Metzger, Ethical Responsibilities of Managers (L533 course notes).

27. "Ethics."

28. "Ethics."

29. Metzger, Ethical Responsibilities of Managers (L533 course notes), p. 4.

30. Michael J. Papa, Tom D. Daniels, and Barry K. Spiker, *Organizational Communication: Perspectives and Trends* (Los Angeles: Sage, 2007).

31. Ed Thompson, "The 4 Main Kinds of Ethics: An Introduction," http://rebirthofreason.com/Articles/Thompson/The_4_Main_Kinds_of_Ethics_An_Introduction.shtml (accessed January 21, 2014).

32. Thompson, "The 4 Main Kinds of Ethics."

33. James Rachels, "The Challenge of Cultural Relativism," citing Ruth Benedict, *Patterns of Culture* (New York: Houghton Mifflin, 1934), http://faculty.uca.edu/movy/Rachels-Cultural%20Relativism.htm (accessed April 28, 2014), p. 1.

34. Metzger, Ethical Responsibilities of Managers (L533 course notes), pp. 49, 56.

35. Metzger, Ethical Responsibilities of Managers (L533 course notes), p. 57, quoting Loyal Rue, *By the Grace of Guile* (1994).

36. As quoted in Tom Morris, *If Aristotle Ran General Motors* (New York: Henry Holt, 1997).

37. Thomas E. Ricks, "What Ever Happened to Accountability," *Harvard Business Review* 90, no. 10 (2012): 94.

38. Michael T. Robinson, "The 5 Keys to Achieving Job Satisfaction," *CareerPlanner.com,* November 24, 2012, http://www.careerplanner.com/5-Keys-To-Job-Satisfaction.cfm (accessed December 31, 2013).

39. "Ethical Dilemmas in Business," May 27, 2013, http://www.speedupcareer.com/articles/ethical-dilemmas-in-business.html (accessed January 15, 2014).

40. Chad Brooks, "7 Steps to Ethical Leadership," *FoxBusiness,* December 3, 2013, http://smallbusiness.foxbusiness.com/entrepreneurs/2013/12/03/7-steps-to-ethcial-leadership/ (accessed January 15, 2014).

41. Silverstein, "Corporate Values."

42. "Business Ethics."

43. Richard B. Schmidt, "Companies Add Ethics Training; Will It Work?" *Wall Street Journal,* November 4, 2002, p. B1.

44. Schmidt, "Companies Add Ethics Training," quoting Professor Barbara Ley Toffler of Columbia University, former partner-in-charge of Arthur Andersen's ethics practice.

45. "Business Ethics."

46. "Business Ethics."

47. Schmidt, "Companies Add Ethics Training"

48. Josephson Institute Center for Business Ethics, http://josephsoninstitute.org/business/overview/faq.html (accessed January 23, 2014).

49. A. Raghavan, K. Kranhold, and A. Barrionuevo, "How Enron Bosses Created a Culture of Pushing Limits," *Wall Street Journal,* August 26, 2002, pp. A1, A7.

50. Hope Hodge, "Corps Preparing PR Blitz for Commandant's Garrison 'Reawakening' Campaign," *Marine Corps Times,* November 27, 2013, http://www.marinecorpstimes.com/article/20131127/NEWS/311270023/Corps-preparing-PR-blitz-commandant-s-garrison-reawakening-campaign (accessed January 23, 2014).

51. Michelle Tan, "Odierno to Soldiers: Toxic Leaders Will Be Fired," *Army Times,* April 1, 2013, http://

www.armytimes.com/article/20130401
/NEWS/304010009/Odierno-soldiers-Toxic-leaders
-will-fired (accessed January 23, 2014).

52. Harvey Schachter, "The Guideposts to Follow for Ethical Leadership," *Globe and Mail,* January 12, 2014, http://www.theglobeandmail.com /report-on-business/careers/management/guide posts-for-ethical-leadership/article16277696 /?service=mobile (accessed January 23, 2014).

53. Heathfield, "Did You Bring Your Ethics to Work Today?"

54. Josephson Institute Center for Business Ethics.

55. Kirk O. Hanson, "Ethics and the Middle Manager: Creating the 'Tone in the Middle,'" Markkula Center for Applied Ethics, Santa Clara University, http://www .scu.edu/ethics/practicing/focusareas/business /middle-managers.html (accessed January 23, 2014).

56. Hanson, "Ethics and the Middle Manager."

57. Hanson, "Ethics and the Middle Manager."

7. Motivating Others and Yourself

1. Michelle Hinton and Michael Biderman, "Empirically Derived Job Characteristics Measures and the Motivating Potential Score," *Journal of Business and Psychology* 9, no. 4 (June 1995): 361.

2. "Top 5 Job Satisfaction Factors," June 16, 2010, http://www.coach4u.net/coach_4_u_blog /top-5-job-satisfaction-factors.html (accessed January 10, 2014).

3. Kendra Cherry, "Theories of Motivation," *About. com,* http://psychology.about.com/od/psychology topics/tp/theories-of-motivation.htm (accessed January 9, 2014).

4. "Work Motivation," http://en.wikipedia.org /wiki/Work_Motivation (accessed January 9, 2014).

5. "Motivating Employees," *Wall Street Journal,* April 7, 2009, extracted from http://guides.wsj.com /management/managing-your-people/how-to -motivate-employees/ (accessed January 9, 2014).

6. "Work Motivation."

7. See generally, Steve M. Jex and Thomas W. Britt, *Organizational Psychology: A Scientist Practitioner Approach* (Hoboken, N.J.: Wiley, 2008).

8. See generally, Jex and Britt, *Organizational Psychology.*

9. See generally, Jex and Britt, *Organizational Psychology;* David C. McClelland, "Toward a Theory of Motive Acquisition," *American Psychologist* 20, no. 5 (1965): 321–333.

10. T. R. Mitchell and D. Daniels, "Motivation," in *Handbook of Psychology,* vol. 12, ed. W. C. Borman, D. R. Ilgen, and R. J. Klimoski (New York: Wiley, 2003), pp. 225–254.

11. Mitchell and Daniels, "Motivation"; and Maureen L. Ambrose and Carol T. Kulik, "Old Friends, New Faces: Motivation Research in the 1990s," *Journal of Management* 25, no. 3 (1999): 231–292.

12. See generally, Jex and Britt, *Organizational Psychology;* and E. E. Lawler and G. D. Jenkins, "Strategic Reward Systems," in *Handbook of Industrial and Organizational Psychology,* 2nd ed., ed. M. D. Dunnette and J. M. Hough (Palo Alto, Calif.: CPP, 1995), pp. 1009–1055.

13. Mitchell and Daniels, "Motivation"; and D. Schultz and S. E. Schultz, *Psychology and Work Today.* (New York: Prentice Hall, 2010), pp. 38–39.

14. See generally, Jex and Britt, *Organizational Psychology;* and Schultz and Schultz, *Psychology and Work Today,* p. 227.

15. Schultz and Schultz, *Psychology and Work Today,* p. 227.

16. Paul M. Muchinsky, *Psychology Applied to Work* (Summerfield, N.C.: Hypergraph, 2012).

17. Robert H. Moorman, "The Influence of Cognitive and Affective Based Job Satisfaction Measures on the Relationship Between Satisfaction and Organizational Citizenship Behavior," *Human Relations* 46, no. 6 (1993): 759–776.

18. T. A. Judge, E. A. Locke, and C. C. Durham, "The Dispositional Causes of Job Satisfaction: A Core Evaluation Approach," *Research in Organizational Behavior* 19 (1997): 151–188.

19. Richard L. Solomon and John D. Corbit, "An Opponent-Process Theory of Motivation," *American Economic Review* 68, no. 6 (1978): 12–24.

20. Richard C. Huseman, John D. Hatfield, and Edward W. Miles, "A New Perspective on Equity Theory: The Equity Sensitivity Construct," *Academy of Management Review* 12, no. 2 (1987): 232–234; and Schultz and Schultz, *Psychology and Work Today,* p. 227.

21. Timothy J. Strauman, "Self-Discrepancies in Clinical Depression and Social Phobia: Cognitive Structures that Underlie Emotional Disorders," *Journal of Abnormal Psychology* 98, no. 1 (1989): 14–22.

22. Manfred Pfeil, "How Employee Recognition Programs Improve Retention," *CFO Insight Magazine,* January 2013, extracted from http://www.cfo-insight .com/human-capital-career/talent-management /how-employee-recognition-programmes-improve -retention/ (accessed January 13, 2014); and Freek Vermeulen, "Five Mistaken Beliefs Leaders Have about Innovation," *Forbes,* May 30, 2011, http://www .forbes.com/sites/freekvermeulen/2011/05/30 /five-mistaken-beliefs-business-leaders-have-about -innovation/ (accessed January 13, 2014).

23. Cynthia D. Fisher, "Mood and Emotions While Working: Missing Pieces of Job Satisfaction?" *Jour-

nal of Organizational Behavior 21 (2000): 185–202; Stephane Cote and Laura M. Morgan, "A Longitudinal Analysis of the Association between Emotion Regulation, Job Satisfaction, and Intentions to Quit," Journal of Organizational Behavior 23, no. 8 (2002): 947–962; Blake E. Ashforth and Ronald H. Humphrey, "Emotional Labor in Service Roles: The Influence of Identity," Academy of Management Review 18, no. 1 (1993): 88–115; A. Rafaeli and R. I. Sutton, "The Expression of Emotion in Organizational Life," Research in Organizational Behavior 11 (1989): 1–42; and Rebecca Abraham, "The Impact of Emotional Dissonance on Organizational Commitment and Intention to Turnover," Journal of Psychology 133, no. 4 (1999): 441–455.

24. Arthur P. Brief and Howard M. Weiss, "Organizational Behavior: Affect in the Workplace," Annual Review of Psychology 53 (2002): 279–307.

25. Thomas A. Wright and Russell Cropanzano, "Psychological Well-Being and Job Satisfaction as Predictors of Job Performance," Journal of Occupational Health Psychology 5, no. 1 (2000): 84–94; Nicole R. Baptiste, "Tightening the Link between Employee Wellbeing at Work and Performance: A New Dimension for HRM," Management Decision 46, no. 2 (2008): 284–309; Ivan T. Robertson, Alex J. Birch, and Cary L. Cooper, "Job and Work Attitudes, Engagement and Employee Performance: Where Does Psychological Well-Being Fit In?" Leadership & Organization Development Journal 33, no. 3 (2012): 224–232; and Thomas A. Wright, Russell Cropanzano, and Douglas G. Bonett, "The Moderating Role of Employee Positive Well Being on the Relation between Job Satisfaction and Job Performance," Journal of Occupational Health Psychology 12, no. 2 (2007): 93–104.

26. V. Lipman, "5 Easy Ways to Motivate—and Demotivate—Employees," Psychology Today, March 24, 2013, http://www.psychologytoday.com/blog /mind-the-manager/201303/5-easy-ways-motivate -and-demotivate-employees (accessed December 31, 2013).

27. James C. Petersen, Why Don't We Listen Better? Communicating and Connecting in Relationships (Portland, Ore.: Petersen, 2007), pp. 18–19.

28. See generally, Jex and Britt, Organizational Psychology.

29. See generally, Jex and Britt, Organizational Psychology.

30. Carter McNamara, "Understanding Motivation," Managementhelp.org, http: //managementhelp.org/leadingpeople/motivating -others.htm (accessed December 30, 2013).

31. See generally, Jex and Britt, Organizational Psychology.

32. Michael A. West and Neil R. Anderson, "Innovation in Top Management Teams," Journal of Applied Psychology 81, no. 6 (1996): 680–693.

33. Steve W. Kozlowski and Bradford S. Bell, "Work Groups and Teams in Organizations," in Handbook of Psychology, vol. 12, ed. W. C. Borman, D. R. Ilgen, and R. J. Klimoski (New York: Wiley, 2003), pp. 333–375.

34. Kim S. Cameron and Robert E. Quinn, Diagnosing and Changing Organizational Culture: Based on the Competing Values Framework (San Francisco: Jossey-Bass, 2006).

35. C. McNamara, "Understanding Motivation."

36. Sandra K. Hirsh and Jean M. Kummerow, Introduction to Type in Organizations: Individual Interpretive Guide, 3rd ed. (Mountain View, Calif.: CPP, 1998), p. 25.

37. Hirsh and Kummerow, Introduction to Type in Organizations, p. 25.

38. C. McNamara, "Basic Principles to Remember about Motivation," ManagementHelp.org, http: //managementhelp.org/leadingpeople/motivating -others.htm (accessed December 30, 2013).

39. Dario Nardi, Neuroscience of Personality: Brain Savvy Insights for All Types of People (Los Angeles: Radiance House, 2011).

40. M. T. Robinson, "The 5 Keys to Achieving Job Satisfaction," CareerPlanner.com, http://www .careerplanner.com/5-Keys-To-Job-Satisfaction .cfm (accessed December 31, 2013).

41. "How to Motivate Yourself—Self Motivation," pickthebrain.com, http://www.pickthebrain .com/blog/how-to-motivate-yourself/ (accessed December 30, 2013).

42. Joel Brown, "7 Unconventional Ways to Motivate Yourself," Addicted2success.com, http: //addicted2success.com/motivation /7-unconventional-ways-to-motivate-yourself / (accessed December 30, 2013).

43. "Steve Jobs' 12 Rules of Success," 1000advices.com, http://www.1000advices.com /guru/leader_corporate_12_success_rules_sj.html (accessed December 30, 2103).

8. Fostering Growth in Others and Yourself

1. "Definition of Mentoring, Benefits of Mentoring, & Other FAQs," Management-Mentors.com, http://www.management-mentors.com/resources /corporate-mentoring-programs-faqs (accessed January 2, 2014).

2. Frances Hesselbein, Marshall Goldsmith, and Richard Beckhard, eds., The Leader of the Future (New York: Drucker Foundation, 1996), p. 166.

3. Richard M. Highsmith, "Encourage Creativity and Growth among Your Employees,"

BusinessKnowHowcom, http://www .businessknowhow.com/growth/squisgcreativity .htm (accessed December 31, 2013); Jamie Walters, "How Can You Foster Growth and Get Value from Employees?" *LearningPlaceOnline.com,* http://www .learningplaceonline.com/workplace/employees /growth-value.htm (accessed December 30, 2013); and "Effective Methods for Fostering Employee Growth," *BusinessDictionary.com,* http//www .businessdictionary.com/article/419/effective -methods-for-fostering-employee-growth/ (accessed December 31, 2103).

4. Leslie Levine, "Strengthen Your Business by Developing Your Employees," *AllBusiness.com,* http://www.allbusiness.com/human-resources /employee-development/1240-1.html (accessed December 31, 2013).

5. Levine, "Strengthen Your Business by Develop- ing Your Employees."

6. Levine, "Strengthen Your Business by Develop- ing Your Employees."

7. Levine, "Strengthen Your Business by Develop- ing Your Employees."

8. Walters, "How Can You Foster Growth and Get Value from Employees?"

9. Walters, "How Can You Foster Growth and Get Value from Employees?"

10. Dick Dixon, "Fostering Employee Growth," *PerformanceBiz.com,* http://performancebiz.com /tips/fostering-employee-growth (accessed December 31, 2013).

11. Highsmith, "Encourage Creativity and Growth Among Your Employees."

12. Walters, "How Can You Foster Growth and Get Value from Employees?"

13. Dixon, "Fostering Employee Growth."

14. Highsmith, "Encourage Creativity and Growth Among Your Employees."

15. Dixon, "Fostering Employee Growth."

16. Stephen R. Covey, *Principle-Centered Leader- ship* (New York: Franklin Covey, 1992), p. 253.

17. Dixon, "Fostering Employee Growth."

18. David Keirsey and Marilyn Bates, *Please Under- stand Me: Character and Temperament Types* (Del Mar, Calif.: Prometheus Nemesis, 1984), pp. 129–130.

19. Isabel Briggs Myers, "Myers-Briggs Type Indicator," http://www.coachingwithlene.com/?page _id=369 (accessed January 2, 2014).

20. Keirsey and Bates, *Please Understand Me,* pp. 121–132.

21. Myers, "Myers-Briggs Type Indicator."

22. Susan M. Heathfield, "Use Employee Coaching to Improve Performance," *About.com,* http://humanresources.about.com/od/glossaryc /g/coaching.htm (accessed January 6, 2014).

23. Susan M. Heathfield, "Performance Improvement Strategies," *About.com,* http:// humanresources.about.com/od /manageperformance/a/manage_perform.htm (accessed January 2, 2014).

24. See generally, Heathfield, "Use Employee Coaching to Improve Performance."

25. See generally, Susan M. Heathfield, "Discipline (Progressive Discipline)," About.com, http://humanresources.about.com/od/glossaryd/a /discipline.htm (accessed January 2, 2014).

26. See, e.g., Gina Abudi, "Formal Internal Mentoring Programs," *Ezinearticles.com,* http://ezinearticles.com/?Formal-Internal-Company -Mentoring-Programs&id=3884109 (accessed January 2, 2014); and James M. Kouzes and Barry Z. Posner, *The Leadership Challenge: How to Keep Getting Extraordinary Things Done in Organizations,* 2nd ed. (San Francisco: Jossey-Bass, 1995).

27. "Definition of Mentoring, Benefits of Mentor- ing, & Other FAQs."

28. "Definition of Mentoring, Benefits of Mentoring, & Other FAQs."

29. Richard E. Boyatzis, Melvin L. Smith, and Alim J. Beveridge, "Coaching with Compassion: Inspiring Health, Well-Being, and Development in Organiza- tions," *Journal of Applied Behavioral Science* 49, no. 2 (2013): 155–156.

30. Boyatzis, Smith, and Beveridge, "Coaching with Compassion," 155.

31. "Definition of Mentoring, Benefits of Mentoring, & Other FAQs."

32. "Definition of Mentoring, Benefits of Mentoring, & Other FAQs."

33. Abudi, "Formal Internal Mentoring Programs."

34. "Definition of Mentoring, Benefits of Mentoring, & Other FAQs."

35. Tess M. S. Neal, "How to Be a Good Mentee," *Association for Psychological Science Observer* 24, no. 2 (February 2011), http://www.psychologicalscience .org/index.php/publications/observer/2011 /february-11/how-to-be-a-good-mentee.html (accessed December 31, 2013).

36. Taylor Davidson, "How to Be a Great Mentor (and a Great Mentee)," Thenextweb.com, http://thenextweb.com/entrepreneur/2012/01/25 /how-to-be-a-great-mentor-and-a-mentee/#!rA1ZI (accessed December 31, 2013).

37. "What Makes a Good Mentor and Mentee?" *Science Daily,* November 30, 2012, http://www .sciencedaily.com/releases/2012/11/121130110658 .htm (accessed December 31, 2012), citing research by Dr. Sharon Strauss, Director of Geriatric Medicine, University of Toronto.

38. "Tips for Being a Successful Mentee," *UCDavis. edu,* http://www.hr.ucdavis.edu/sdps/career -management-toolkit/explore-the-world-of-work /mentoring/tips-for-being-a-successful-mentee (accessed December 31, 2013).

39. "How to Be a Good Mentee," *CareerHQ.org,* http://www.asaecenter.org/files/FileDownloads /How_to_be_a_good_mentee.pdf (accessed December 31, 2013).

40. "How to Become Your Own Greatest Mentor in Life," http://voices.yahoo.com/how-become -own-greatest-mentor-life-3697194.html (accessed December 31, 2013).

41. Ilya Pozin, "Who Says You Need a Mentor? Be Your Own," *Parade,* October 1, 2013, http://www .parade.com/169966/ilyapozin/who-says-you-need -a-mentor-be-your-own/ (accessed December 31, 2013).

42. See, e.g., Mark Snyder, "Self-Monitoring of Expressive Behavior," *Journal of Personality and Social Psychology* 30, no. 4 (1974): 526–537; and Steven W. Gangestad and Mark Synder, "Self-Monitoring: Appraisal and Reappraisal," *Psychological Bulletin* 126, no. 4 (2000): 530–555.

43. "How to Become Your Own Greatest Mentor in Life."

9. Critical Thinking in Identifying and Solving Complex Problems

1. Chris Argyris, "Teaching Smart People How to Learn," *Harvard Business Review* 69, no. 3 (1991).

2. Joanne R. Reid and Phyllis R. Anderson, "Critical Thinking in the Business Classroom," *Journal of Education for Business* 87, no. 1 (2012): 57–58.

3. Michael B. Metzger, "Critical Thinking" (X504 course notes), Spring 2007, Kelley School of Business, Indiana University, Bloomington, 12.

4. Susan Schott Karr, "Critical Thinking: A CRITICAL Strategy for Financial Executives," *Financial Executive* 25, no. 10 (2009): 58–61.

5. Metzger, "Critical Thinking," 17.

6. Metzger, "Critical Thinking," 17.

7. Reid and Anderson, "Critical Thinking in the Business Classroom," 57–58.

8. Metzger, "Critical Thinking," 17.

9. Diane F. Halpern, "Teaching Critical Thinking for Transfer across Domains: Dispositions, Skills, Structure Training, and Metacognitive Monitoring," *American Psychologist* 53, no. 4 (1998): 450.

10. Reid and Anderson, "Critical Thinking in the Business Classroom," 52, quoting J. Reid, "Can Critical Thinking Be Learned?" paper presented at the Midwest Regional Educational Research Association, St. Louis, October 2009.

11. Reid and Anderson, "Critical Thinking in the Business Classroom," 52.

12. Reid and Anderson, "Critical Thinking in the Business Classroom," 52.

13. Metzger, "Critical Thinking," 17.

14. This section was adapted with permission from Metzger, "Critical Thinking," 12–21.

15. "The Importance of Reductionism in the Problem Solving Process," July 26, 2006, http://www .exforsys.com/career-center/problem-solving/the -importance-of-reductionism-in-the-problem-solving -process.html (accessed February 24, 2014).

16. Progressus, "Reductionism Can Reduce Everything," *ForProgressNotGrowth.com,* August 7, 2011, http://forprogressnotgrowth.com/2011/08/07 /reductionism-can-reduce-everything/(accessed February 24, 2014).

17. "Critical Thinking and Communications Skills Are the Reason We Have Universities," Foundation for Critical Thinking, 2006 slide presentation.

18. Linda Elder, "The Stages of Critical Thinking-Development,"http://www.criticalthinking.org/data /pages/14/fd4e6f74cc717ed36a9faccc870b8a2e 4fe0bd688b279.pdf (accessed February 22, 2014).

19. Alan M. Kantrow, "Why Read Peter Drucker?" *Harvard Business Review* 87, no. 11 (2009): 72, 74, 78.

10. Self-Learning

1. "Fast-Track to the Top: Developing the Next Generation of Leaders to Drive Future Growth," Deloitte, http://www.deloitte.com/assets/Dcom -Mexico/Local%20Assets/Documents/Fasttrack.pdf (accessed February 27, 2014).

2. "Leadership Development through Action Learning," Business School Netherlands, http://www .bsn.eu/bsn/news/leadership-development-through -action-learning.html (accessed February 27, 2014).

3. David L. Dotlich, James L. Noel, and Norman Walker, "Leadership Passages: The Personal and Professional Transitions That Make or Break a Leader," *CEO Refresher,* 2005, http://www.refresher .com/Archives/!dnwpassages.html (accessed February 24, 2014).

4. Dotlich, Noel, and Walker, "Leadership Passages."

5. http://4.bp.blogspot.com/-tpMvKrY54sc /UkdBTVqi59I/AAAAAAAAMdA/sK9_UeXaOl4 /s1600/OODA_Loop.png (accessed February 25, 2014).

6. Chris Argyris, "Double-Loop Learning, Teaching, and Research," *Academy of Management Learning and Education* 1, no. 2 (2002): 206.

7. Argyris, "Double-Loop Learning, Teaching, and Research," 212–215.

8. K. M. Black and R. Seaker, "Project Performance: Implications of Personality Preferences and

Double-Loop Learning," *Journal of American Academy of Business* 1, no. 1 (2004): 292–297.

9. "Self-Regulated Learning," http://en.wikipedia.org/wiki/Self-regulated_learning (accessed February 25, 2014).

10. Gerhard Fischer and Masanori Sugimoto, "Supporting Self-Directed Learners and Learning Communities with Sociotechnical Environments," *Journal of Research and Practice in Technology Enhanced Learning* 1, no. 1 (2006): 36.

11. Jeanne M. VanBriesen, "Self-Directed Learning," Carnegie Mellon University, *www.nae.edu/File.aspx?id=37803* (accessed February 25, 2014).

12. Cath Duncan, "How to Drive Your Professional Development with a Self-Directed Learning Program," Productive Flourishing, February 22, 2011, http://www.productiveflourishing.com/how-to-drive-your-professional-development-with-a-self-directed-learning-program/ (accessed February 25, 2014).

13. Phil Rosenzweig, "Making Better Decisions Over Time," *Strategy+Business,* January 6, 2014, www.strategy-business.com/article/00227?pg=all&tid=27782251 (accessed February 15, 2014).

14. R. Hiermstra, "Self-Directed Learning," in *The International Encyclopedia of Education,* 2nd ed., ed. T. Husen and T. N. Postlethwaite (Oxford: Pergamon Press, 1994), ccnmtl.columbia.edu/projects/p13p/Self-Directed%20Learning.pdf (accessed February 15, 2014).

15. Rosenzweig, "Making Better Decisions Over Time."

16. Howard Spoelstra, Peter van Rosmalen, and Peter B. Sloep, "Supporting Project Team Formation for Self-Directed Learners," Center for Learning Sciences and Technologies, July 4, 2011, http://celstec.org/content/supporting-project-team-formation-self-directed-learners (accessed February 25, 2014).

17. Barbara McIntosh, "An Employer's Guide to Older Workers: How to Win Them Back and Convince Them to Stay," www.doleta.gov/Seniors/other_docs/EmplGuide.pdf (accessed February 26, 2014).

18. "Fast-Track to the Top."

19. "Strategic Thinking: Developing Leaders' Skills Faster with Advanced Business Simulations," http://www.webex.com/webinars/Strategic-Thinking-Developing-Leaders-Skills-Faster-With-Advanced-Business-Simulations (accessed February 27, 2014).

20. "Fast-Track to the Top."

21. "Fast-Track to the Top."

22. "Why Failure Develops Leaders Faster," Riverstone Group, March 29, 2013, http://www.theriverstonegroup.com/the-secret-to-developing-leaders-faster/ (accessed February 27, 2014).

23. "Why Failure Develops Leaders Faster."

24. M. C. Higgins, "What Should C. J. Do?" *Harvard Business* 78, no. 6 (2000): 43.

25. "Never Too Old to Learn," *Economist,* May 12, 2010, http://www.economist.com/node/16036092/print (accessed February 27, 2014).

26. "Fast-Track to the Top."

27. "Workforce and Succession Management in a Changing World," *CPP Global Human Capital Report,* November 2008, https://www.cpp.com/Pdfs/Workforce_and_succession_mgmt.pdf (accessed February 27, 2014).

11. Effective Communication

1. Adapted from "Communication," *Merriam-Webster.com,* http://www.merriam-webster.com/dictionary/communication (accessed February 2, 2014).

2. *Clifford N. Lazarus.* "Simple Keys to Effective Communication: How to be a Great Communicator," *Psychology Today,* July 26, 2011. http://www.psychologytoday.com/blog/think-well/201107/simple-keys-effective-communication (accessed February 2, 2014).

3. Adapted from Lee Lefever, *The Art of Explanation: Making Your Ideas, Products and Services Easier to Understand* (Hoboken, N.J.: Wiley, 2012).

4. Calvin Sun, "10 Ways to Explain Things More Effectively," *TechRepublic,* April 1, 2008, http://www.techrepublic.com/blog/10-things/10-ways-to-explain-things-more-effectively/ (accessed February 13, 2014).

5. Sun, "10 Ways to Explain Things More Effectively."

6. Sun, "10 Ways to Explain Things More Effectively."

7. Adapted from Lefever, *The Art of Explanation.*

8. Adapted from D. Kieso, J. Weygandt, and T. Warfield, *Intermediate Accounting,* 14th ed. (Hoboken, N.J.: Wiley, 2011).

9. "Business Communication," https://en.wikipedia.org/wiki/Business_communication (accessed January 27, 2014).

10. A. Mehrabian, *Silent Messages: Implicit Communication of Emotions and Attitudes,* cited in T. Koegel, *The Exceptional Presenter* (Austin, Tex.: Greenleaf, 2007).

11. Adapted from Koegel, *The Exceptional Presenter.*

12. Ann Marie Sabath, *One Minute Manners: Quick Solutions to the Most Awkward Situations You'll Ever Face at Work,* cited in Koegel, *The Exceptional Presenter.*

13. Adapted from the work of J. Iverson, psychologist, University of Missouri, cited in Koegel, *The Exceptional Presenter.*

14. Michael Doyle and David Straus, *How to Make Meetings Work!* (New York: Berkley Books, 1976).

15. Adapted from the work of H. Reimer and cited in Doyle and Straus, *How to Make Meetings Work!*

16. R. Nichols, *Are You Listening?* (New York: Mc-Graw-Hill, 1957), cited in M. Burley-Allen, *Listening: The Forgotten Skill* (New York: Wiley, 1982).

17. Nichols, *Are You Listening?*

18. David Madden, "Semantic Noise and Interpersonal Communications," *Relating360.com,* August 27, 2007, http://www.relating360.com /index.php/semantic-noise-and-interpersonal -communications-42594/ (accessed February 15, 2014).

19. Adapted from Tom Ricci, "Public Speaking: Know Your Audience," *ASME.org.* August 2012, https://www.asme.org/career-education /articles/public-speaking/public-speaking-know -your-audience?cm_sp=Public+Speaking -_-Featured+Articles-_-Public+Speaking+Know+Your +Audience (accessed February 5, 2014)).

20. Robert E. Kelley, *How to Be a Star at Work: 9 Breakthrough Strategies You Need to Succeed* (New York: Three Rivers Press, 1999), 237.

21. Adapted from Anna Rydne, "5 Bullet-Proof Methods to Connect with Your Audience," http://communicateskills.com/2012/10/04 /communication-connect-audience/ (accessed February 5, 2014).

22. Kelley, *How to Be a Star at Work,* 239.

23. Adapted from Koegel, *The Exceptional Presenter.*

24. Adapted from Lawrence Robinson, Jeanne Segal, and Robert Segal, "Effective Communication: Improving Communication Skills in Business and Relationships," http://www.helpguide.org/mental /effective_communication_skills.htm (accessed January 27, 2014).

12. Becoming a Talent That Fits

1. Jim Murray, "Aspiring to Leadership: Technical Knowledge vs. People Skills," *CheckMark,* Summer 2008, http://www.cpaontario.ca/PD /PDarticles/1016page9923.pdf (accessed March 12, 2014).

2. "Importance of Technical Skills," http://www .indianmanpower.com/blog_Technical-Skills -Manpower-Recruitment.html (accessed March 12, 2014).

3. Murshed Chowdhury, "How Important Are Technical Skills for Managers?" *Infusive Solutions,* January 24, 2012, http://www.infusivesolutions.com /blog/bid/76847/How-Important-are-Technical -Skills-for Managers (accessed March 12, 2014).

4. Murray, "Aspiring to Leadership."

5. Kristen May, "Skills-Based Leadership Theory," *Houston Chronicle,* http://smallbusiness.chron.com /skillsbased-leadership-theory-31074.html (accessed March 13, 2014), citing R. L. Katz, "Skills of an Effective Administrator," *Harvard Business Review* 33, no. 1 (1955): 33–42.

6. Pat Sweet, "Why Technical Leadership Skills Are Critical to Your Success," http://www .engineeringandleadership.com/why-technical -leadership-skills-are-critical-to-your-success / (accessed March 10, 2014).

7. "Competent and Versatile: How Professional Accountants in Business Drive Sustainable Organizational Success," International Federation of Accountants, August 2011, 12–13, http://viewer. zmags.com/publication/b908956a#/b908956a/1 (accessed March 10, 2014).

8. "Competent and Versatile," 7.

9. "The Challenges of Doing Business Internationally," *Trekking,* http://www.trekconsulting .com/Publications/Newsletter/Issue8/Issue8.html (accessed March 13, 2014).

10. Ramona Dzinkowski, "A View from the Top," *Strategic Finance,* October 2013, 52.

11. "Competent and Versatile," 13.

12. "Competent and Versatile," 13.

13. B. Kang, "Managing the Strategic Finance Gap," *Strategic Finance,* February 2014, 44.

14. "Competent and Versatile," 10.

15. USAA Report to Members 2012, https://www .usaa.com/inet/pages/reporttomembers_main _landing?wa_ref=annual_report_2012_landing_nav _home (accessed March 15, 2014).

16. J. M. Bird, Re: Intel Update, USAA, letter to customers, March 2014.

17. "Competent and Versatile," 10–11.

18. Kurt Kuehn, "Navigating the Shoals in Fast-Moving Currents," Keynote address to the Institute of Management Accountants 90th Annual Conference and Exposition, Denver, June 6, 2009, http://pressroom.ups.com/About+UPS /UPS+Leadership/Speeches/Kurt+Kuehn /ci.Navigating+the+Shoals+in+Fast -Moving+Currents.print (accessed March 16, 2014).

19. "Easy Guide to Understanding ENRON: Scandal Summary," http://finance.laws.com/enron -scandal-summary (accessed March 17, 2014); and "WorldCom Scandal: A Look Back at One of the Biggest Corporate Scandals in U.S. History," March 8, 2007, http://voices.yahoo.com/worldcom-scandal -look-back-one-biggest-225686.html (accessed March 17, 2014).

20. "Arthur Andersen at Center of Scandal Again," *CRN.com,* June 28, 2002, http://www.crn.com/news

/channel-programs/18828554/arthur-andersen
-at-center-of-scandal-again.htm (accessed March 17,
2014).

21. "Competent and Versatile," 10–11.

22. Thomas G. Canace and Paul Jones, "CFO: From
AnalysttoCatalyst,"StrategicFinance96,no.2(2014):29.

23. Glyn Holton, "Corporate Risk Management,"
http://riskencyclopedia.com/articles/corporate_risk
_management/ (accessed February 17, 2014).

24. Kuehn, "Navigating the Shoals in Fast-Moving
Currents."

25. Douglas K. Barry, "Service Architecture,"
http://www.service-architecture.com/articles
/web-services/service-oriented_architecture_soa
_definition.html (accessed March 17, 2014).

26. "How CIOs Can Drive Growth," Business
Flexibility and Innovation, IBM Global Technology
Services, 2007, http://www.cio.com/documents
/whitepapers/IBMQ3wp072007.pdf (accessed March
17, 2014), p. 2.

27. "How CIOs Can Drive Growth."

28. "How CIOs Can Drive Growth."

29. Catherine Bolgar, "Education and Adaptability
Are Vital in Our Rapidly Evolving, Innovative World,"
Wall Street Journal Executive Digest, 2011,
http://online.wsj.com/ad/article/execdigest
-education (accessed March 17, 2014).

30. Bolgar, "Education and Adaptability Are Vital."

31. Kuehn, "Navigating the Shoals in Fast-Moving
Currents."

32. Dzinkowski, "A View from the Top," 49.

33. Dzinkowski, "A View from the Top," 52–53.

34. "Competent and Versatile," 11.

35. "Talent Management," http://en.wikipedia.org
/wiki/Talent_management (accessed March 17,
2014).

36. "Talent Management."

37. "Talent Management."

38. "Competency Dictionary," http://en.wikipedia
.org/wiki/Competency_dictionary (accessed March
17, 2014).

39. Matthew Littlefield, "An Operational Excellence
Definition Quality Executives Must Know," LNS
Research, November 20, 2012, http://blog
.lnsresearch.com/blog/bid/164666/An-Operational
-Excellence-Definition-Quality-Executives-Must-Know
(accessed March 17, 2014).

40. "Operational Excellence," http://en.wikipedia
.org/wiki/Operational_excellence (accessed March 17,
2014).

41. "Principles of Operational Excellence,"
http://www.iienet2.org/uploadedfiles/SHSNew
/Tools_and_Resources/RobertMillerOpExArticle.pdf
(accessed March 17, 2014).

42. "Principles of Operational Excellence."

43. "Competent and Versatile," 11.

44. Azriel Winnett, "Transparency in
Communication: Is It All about Truth, or about
Sincerity?" http://www.hodu.com/blog1
/transparency-in-communication/ (accessed March
18, 2014).

45. Patrick Smyth, "Transparent Communication,"
http://ezinearticles.com/?Transparent
-Communication&id=1953434 (accessed March 18,
2014).

46. Pablo Herrera, "Transparent to the Core,"
Soderquist Center, April 29, 2011, http://www.scribd
.com/doc/54173448/Transparency-in-Business
-Communication (accessed March 18, 2014).

47. Mary E. Barth and Katherine Schipper, "Financial Reporting Transparency," Journal of Accounting,
Auditing & Finance 23, no. 2 (2008): 173.

48. Ben McClure, "The Importance of Corporate
Transparency," Investopedia, January 3, 2014,
http://www.investopedia.com/articles
/fundamental/03/121703.asp (accessed March 18,
2014).

49. Smyth, "Transparent Communication."

50. Smyth, "Transparent Communication."

51. John H. Troughton, "Business Improvement
through Transparency," http://www
.themanagementpractice.com/ams/Business%20
Improvement%20by%20Transparency.pdf (accessed
March 18, 2014).

52. Lynn E. Turner, Chief Accountant, U.S.
Securities & Exchange Commission, "SEC Update:
Transparent Financial Reporting and Disclosures,"
Interagency Accounting Conference, Denver, April 3,
2001, http://www.sec.gov./news/speech/spch476
.htm (accessed March 18, 2014).

53. Kuehn, "Navigating the Shoals in Fast-Moving
Currents."

54. Dzinkowski, "A View from the Top," 51.

55. Kuehn, "Navigating the Shoals in Fast-Moving
Currents."

56. Dzinkowski, "A View from the Top," 51.

13. Organizational Control and Measurement

1. Ellen Kaufman, "What Gets Measured Gets
Done," June 3, 2013, http://www.talkativeman.com
/what-gets-measured-gets-done/ (accessed
February 15, 2014).

2. "Control (management)," http://en.wikipedia
.org/wiki/Control_(management) (accessed February
25, 2014).

3. "Culture and Control," http://facultyfp
.salisbury.edu/rchoffman/culcntl.htm (accessed
February 15, 2014).

4. "Business Performance Management,"
http://en.wikipedia.org/wiki/Business_performance
_management (accessed February 15, 2014).

5. Vince Kellen, "Business Performance Measurement: At the Crossroads of Strategy, Decision-Making, Learning and Information Visualization," School of CTI, DePaul University, February 2003, http://www.kellen.net/bpm.htm (accessed February 15, 2014).

6. "Performance Management and Measurement," U.S. Department of Health and Human Services, Health Resources and Services Administration, April 2011, http://www.hrsa.gov/quality/toolbox/508pdfs/performancemanagementandmeasurement.pdf (accessed February 25, 2014), 3.

7. Kellen, "Business Performance Measurement."

8. "What Is Performance Measurement?" Business Performance Improvement Resources, 2014, http://www.bpir.com/what-is-perfromance-measurement-bpir-com.html (accessed February 15, 2014).

9. "Business Performance Management."

10. Grigore Ana-Maria, Badea Florica, and R. Catalina, "Modern Instruments for Measuring Organizational Performance," *ResearchGate.net,* http://www.researchgate.net/publication/49615452_MODERN_INSTRUMENTS_FOR_MEASURING_ORGANIZATIONAL_PERFORMANCE (accessed March 6, 2014).

11. Ana-Maria, Florica, and Catalina, "Modern Instruments for Measuring Organizational Performance."

12. Nancy Kirkendall, "Organizational Performance Measurement in the Energy Information Administration," http://www.docstoc.com/docs/10802651/Organizational-Performance-Measurement-in-the-Energy-Information-Administration (accessed February 24, 2014).

13. "Business Performance Management."

14. Michael Donovan, "Performance Measurement: Connecting Strategy, Operations, and Actions," http://www.reliableplant.com/Articles/Print/140 (accessed February 23, 2014).

15. Ana-Maria, Florica, and Catalina, "Modern Instruments for Measuring Organizational Performance."

16. "Link Sustainability to Corporate Strategy Using the Balanced Scorecard," Balanced Scorecard Institute, http://www.balancedscorecard.org/Portals/0/PDF/LinkingSustainabilitytoCorporateStrategyUsingtheBalancedScorecard.pdf (accessed March 7, 2014).

17. Howard Rohm, "A Balancing Act," *Performance Measurement in Action* 2, no. 2 (May 2002): 3.

18. Donovan, "Performance Measurement."

19. Donovan, "Performance Measurement."

20. Kellen, "Business Performance Measurement," citing a 2000 report by Gartner, Frigo, and Krumwiede.

21. Rohm, "A Balancing Act," 4–5.

22. Rohm, "A Balancing Act," 4–5.

23. Howard Rohm and Larry Halbach, "A Balancing Act: Sustaining New Directions," *Performance Management in Action* 3, no. 2 (2005): 2–4.

24. Rohm and Halbach, "A Balancing Act," 6–7.

25. Misty Walker, "Tying Compensation to the Balanced Scorecard," http://voices.yahoo.com/tying-compensation-balanced-scorecard-1943330.html (accessed March 3, 2014).

26. Kellen, "Business Performance Measurement," citing a 2000 report by Gartner, Frigo, and Krumwiede.

27. Kellen, "Business Performance Measurement," citing a 2000 report by Gartner, Frigo, and Krumwiede.

28. Rohm and Halbach, "A Balancing Act," 7.

29. Michael J. Smith, "Gaming Nonfinancial Performance Measures," *Journal of Management Accounting Research* 14, no. 1 (2002): 120.

30. David P. Quinn, "Tying Project Measures to Performance Incentives," *Journal of Defense Software Engineering* 1 (2005): 28.

31. Kellen, "Business Performance Measurement," citing a 2000 report by Gartner, Frigo, and Krumwiede.

32. Quinn, "Tying Project Measures to Performance Incentives," 29.

33. Rohm and Halbach, "A Balancing Act," 7.

34. Pierre Gurdjian, Thomas Halbeisen, and Kevin Lane, "Why Leadership-Development Programs Fail," *McKinsey Quarterly,* January 2014, 1–6.

35. "Evidence of a Mature Scorecard: The Power of Alignment," www.balancescoreacrd.org (accessed March 6, 2014), 2.

36. Kaufman, "What Gets Measured Gets Done."

14. Teams and Teamwork

1. Federal Aviation Administration, Team Performance Module; Team Use 5–6, "When to Use Teams?" https://www.hf.faa.gov/webtraining/TeamPerfrom/Team007.htm (accessed March 13, 2014).

2. Federal Aviation Administration, "When to Use Teams?"

3. Adapted from C. T. Schlachter and T. H. Hildebrandt, "Leading Business Change of Dummies: The Importance of Teamwork to Business Change," https://www.dummies.com/how-to/content/the-importance-of-teamwork-to-business-change.html (accessed February 26, 2014).

4. Adapted from L. Magloff, "What Are the Benefits of Teamwork in Business," *Houston Chronicle,* http://smallbusiness.chron.com/benefits-teamwork-business-3250.html (accessed March 13, 2014).

5. K. J. Arnold, "Workplace Teamwork: Where NOT to USE Teams," http://www.sdoeroad.com/Team_Building/workplace-teamwork.html (accessed April 4, 2014).

6. F. Brooks, *The Mythical Man-Month: Essays on Software Engineering, Anniversary Edition* (Boston: Addison-Wesley Longman, 1995).

7. Brooks, *The Mythical Man-Month,* as referenced by E. Lau "Why and Where Is Teamwork Important?" *Forbes,* January 23, 2013, http://www.forbes.com/sites/quora/2013/01/23/why-and-where-is-teamwork-important.html (accessed February 24, 2014).

8. J. Anderson, "To Team or Not to Team, That Is the Question," http://ezinearticles.com/?To-Team-Or-Not-to-Team,-That-is-the-Question&id=3625010 (accessed April 3, 2014).

9. Adapted from S. M. Heathfield, "12 Tips for Team Building: How to Build Successful Work Teams," http://humanresources.about.com/od/involvementteams/a/twelve_tip_team.htm (accessed March 13, 2014).

10. "Building a Sense of Teamwork among Staff Members," http://www.amanet.org/training/articles/Building-a-Sense-of-Teamwork-Among-Staff-Members.aspx (accessed February 26, 2014).

11. "Team Technology," http://www.teamtechnology.co.uk/ (accessed April 3, 2014).

12. "Team Dynamics—How They Affect Performance," http://www.teamteachnology.co.uk/team/dynamics/overview/ (accessed April 4, 2014).

13. "Team Dynamics," http://www.businessdictionary.com/definition/team-dynamics.html (accessed April 3, 2014).

14. "Team Dynamics—How They Affect Performance."

15. "Team Dynamics—How They Affect Performance."

16. Adapted from J. R. Hackman, "Six Common Misperceptions about Teamwork," *Harvard Business Review,* June 2011, https://blogs.hbr.org/2011/06/six-common-mosperceptions-about-teamwork.html (accessed February 2, 2014).

17. "Tuckman's Stages of Group Development," http://en.wikipedia.org/wiki/Bruce_Tuckman (accessed March 16, 2014).

18. R. D. Duncan, "Morphing Teamwork: From Buzzword to Reality," *Forbes,* January 15, 2014, http://www.forbes.com/sites/rodgerdeanduncan/2014/01/15/morphing-teamwork-from-buzzword-to-reality/ (accessed February 26, 2014).

19. Adapted from Heathfield, "12 Tips for Team Building."

20. Adapted from Scott Span, "Promoting Teamwork? It May Be the Key to Your Organization's Success," October 8, 2013, http://www.tlnt.com/2013/10/08/is-it-possible-to-nurture-and-promote-teamwork/ (accessed February 26, 2014).

21. Adapted from Eugene E. Kim, "The Life Cycle of Groups," November 29, 2011, http://groupaya.net/the-lifecycle-of-groups/ (accessed January 26, 2014).

22. Adapted from Kim, "The Life Cycle of Groups."

23. Adapted from Kim, "The Life Cycle of Groups."

24. A. Drexler and D. Sibbet, "Team Performance Model," http://www.grove.com/site/ourwk_gm_tp.html (accessed March 15, 2014).

25. A. Einstein, http://www.goodreads.com/quotes/66864-in-theory-theory-and-practice-are-the-same-in-practice (accessed March 16, 2014).

26. Duncan, "Morphing Teamwork."

27. Adapted from Keith Ferrazzi, "Candor, Criticism, Teamwork," *Harvard Business Review,* January–February 2012, http://hbr.org/2012/01/candor-criticism-teamwork/ar/1 (accessed February 16, 2014).

28. Adapted from Christian Pielow, "5 Key Factors to Managing Successful Teams," https://www.bluesteps.com/blog/5-key-factors-to-building-and-managing-successful-teams.aspx (accessed February 16, 2014).

29. "The Five Dysfunctions of a Team," http://en.wikipedia.org/wiki/The_Five_Dysfunctions_of_a_Team (accessed March 20, 2014).

30. "The Five Dysfunctions of a Team."

31. Adapted from James Manktelow, "Lencioni's Five Dysfunctions of a Team by James Manktelow," http://www.convergingzone.com/business/lencionis-five-dysfunctions-of-a-team-by-james-manktelow/ (accessed March 20, 2014).

32. "The Five Dysfunctions of a Team."

33. Adapted from Manktelow, "Lencioni's Five Dysfunctions of a Team by James Manktelow."

34. "The Five Dysfunctions of a Team."

35. Adapted from Manktelow, "Lencioni's Five Dysfunctions of a Team by James Manktelow."

36. "The Five Dysfunctions of a Team."

37. Adapted from James M. Kouzes and Barry Z. Posner, *The Leadership Challenge: How to Keep Getting Extraordinary Things Done in Organizations,* 4th ed. (San Francisco: Jossey-Bass, 2008).

38. Adapted from Manktelow, "Lencioni's Five Dysfunctions of a Team by James Manktelow."

39. "The Five Dysfunctions of a Team."

40. Adapted from Kevin Kruse, "5 Ways to Fix Your Dysfunctional Team," *Forbes,* December 11, 2013, http://www.forbes.com/sites/kevinkruse/2013/12/11/5-ways-to-fix-your-dysfunctional-team/ (accessed February 24, 2014).

41. Adapted from Team International, "Coaching High Performance Teams: The Art of the Impossible!" Training material; and Elizabeth Hirsh, Katherine W. Hirsh, and Sandra Krebs Hirsh, *Introduction to Type and Teams* (Palo Alto, Calif.: CCP, 2003).

42. Adapted from work attributed to Mary McCaulley (1975); and Hirsh, Hirsh, and Hirsh, *Introduction to Type and Teams.*

43. Adapted from Terry Campbell, "Teams Come in All Types, Sizes, and Shapes!" Lecture material.

44. Hirsh, Hirsh, and Hirsh, *Introduction to Type and Teams,* 2.

45. Adapted from Terry Campbell, "Teams Come in All Types, Sizes, and Shapes!"

46. Steve Borgatti, "Manual for Working in Teams," 2004, http://www.analytictech.com/mb021/teamhint.htm (accessed April 2, 2014).

47. Adapted from Team International, "Coaching High Performance Teams: The Art of the Impossible!"

48. "Heraclitus," http://en.wikipedia.org/wiki/Heraclitus (accessed March 19, 2014).

49. Adapted from Amy C. Edmondson, "Teamwork on the Fly," *Harvard Business Review,* April 2012, http://hbr.org/2012/04/teamwork-on-the-fly/ar/1m (accessed February 26, 2014).

50. Adapted from Maggie Starvish, "Why Leaders Need to Rethink Teamwork," *Forbes,* December 28, 2012, http://www.forbes.com/sites/hbsworking knowledge/2012/12/28/why-leaders-need-to-rethink-teamwork/ (accessed March 28, 2014).

51. Attributed to the work of J. Osburn and adapted from C. C. Sidle, *The Leadership Wheel* (New York: Palgrave MacMillan, 2005).

52. A. Edmondson, "The Importance of Teaming," Harvard Business School, April 12, 2012, http://hbswk.hbs.edu/item/6997.html (accessed March 28, 2014).

15. Organizational Savvy

1. Lauren Yost, "Workplace Savvy," *Parks and Recreation Magazine,* March 2014, http://www.parlsandrecreation.org/2014/March/Work place-Savvy/ (accessed March 22, 2104).

2. Thomas S. Westbrook, James R. Veale, and Roger E. Karnes, "Multirater and Gender Differences in the Measurement of Political Skill in Organizations," *Journal of Leadership Studies* 7, no. 2 (2013): 6–17.

3. "Office Politics—Seven Savvy Steps," http://www.billilee.com/office_politics_tips.htm/ (accessed March 22, 2014).

4. Yost, "Workplace Savvy."

5. H. S. Resnick, "Organizational Savvy," *Worksystems Newsletter,* December 2009, http://www.worksystems.com/newsletter/dec_09.htm (accessed March 25, 2104).

6. V. Marie Vicher, "Teaching Political Savvy as a Workforce Skill," Working paper, Southern Illinois University Carbondale, http://opensiuc.lib.siu.edu/morris_opensiuc (accessed March 24, 2014), 3.

7. M. R. Leary, *Self-Preservation: Impression Management and Interpersonal Behavior* (Boulder, Colo.: Westview Press, 1996).

8. P. L. Perrewe, G. R. Ferris, D. D. Frink, and W. P. Anthony, "Political Skill: An Antidote for Workplace Stressors," *Academy of Management Executive* 14 (2000): 115–123.

9. K. K. Ahearn, G. R. Ferris, W. A. Hochwarter, C. Douglas, and A. P. Ammeter, "Leader Political Skill and Team Performance," *Journal of Management* 30, no. 3 (2004): 311.

10. Westbrook, Veale, and Karnes, "Multirater and Gender Differences in the Measurement of Political Skill in Organizations."

11. Kathleen Kelly Reardon, *The Secret Handshake: Mastering the Politics of the Business Inner Circle* (New York: Currency Doubleday, 2000); and Lee G. Bolman and Terrence E. Deal, *Reframing Organizations: Artistry, Choice, and Leadership* (San Francisco: Jossey-Bass, 2003).

12. Martin Seldman and Edward Betof, "An Illuminated Path," *T+D* 58, no. 12 (December 2004): 35.

13. Seldman and Betof, "An Illuminated Path," 36.

14. Seldman and Betof, "An Illuminated Path," 36.

15. Vicher, "Teaching Political Savvy as a Workforce Skill," 13.

16. Jeffrey Pfeffer, *Power in Organizations* (Marshfield, Mass.: Pittman, 1981); G. R. Ferris, D. C. Treadway, R. W. Kolodinsky, W. A. Hochwater, C. J. Kacmar, C. Douglas, and D. D. Frink, "Development and Validation of the Political Skill Inventory," *Journal of Management* 31, no. 1 (February 2005): 126–152; and P. L. Perrewe, K. L. Zellars, A. M. Rossi, C. J. Kacmar, and D. A. Ralston, "Neutralizing Job Stressors," *Academy of Management Journal* 47, no. 3 (2004): 141–152.

17. G. R. Ferris, W. A. Hochwater, C. Douglas, F. R. Blass, R. W. Kolodinsky, and D. C. Treadway, "Social Influence in Organizations and Human Resources Systems," in *Research in Personnel and Human Resources Management,* ed. G. R. Ferris and J. J. Martocchio (Oxford: Elsevier Science, 2002), 65–127.

18. Takuma Kimura, "The Moderating Effects of Political Skill and Leader-Member Exchange on the Relationship between Organization Politics and Affective Commitment," *Journal of Business Ethics* 116 (2013): 596.

19. Vicher, "Teaching Political Savvy as a Workforce Skill," 5.

20. I. Q. Cheema, H. A. Cheema, and K. Ashraf, "Leaders' Political Skill, Organizational Politics Savvy, and Change in Organizations—A Constellation," Servant Leadership Research Roundtable, Regent University, May 2008, http://www.regent.edu/acad/global/publications/sl_proceedings/2008/cheema-ashraf.pdf (accessed March 24, 2014), 10.

21. P. Harvey, K. J. Harris, K. M. Kacmar, A. Buck-

less, and A. T. Pescosolido, "The Impact of Political Skill on Employees' Perceptions of Ethical Leadership," *Journal of Leadership & Organizational Studies* 2, no. 1 (2014): 5.

22. C. Rezak, "Leadership White Paper: Developing Business-Savvy Leaders," Paradigm Learning, Inc., 2011, *http://www.paradigmlearning.com/Libraries/White-Papers/WP-Developing-Business-Savvy-Leaders.sflb.ashx* (accessed March 24, 2014), 2.

23. Cheema, Cheema, and Ashraf, "Leaders' Political Skill, Organizational Politics Savvy, and Change in Organizations," 10.

24. P. A. Wilson, "The Effects of Politics and Power on the Organizational Commitment of Federal Executives," *Journal of Management* 21, no. 1 (Spring 1995): 101–118.

25. Rezak, "Leadership White Paper," 4–5.

26. J. Martin, *Cultures in Organizations: Three Perspectives* (New York: Oxford University Press, 1992), 112.

27. D. M. Rousseau, "Organizational Climate and Culture," in *Macro-Organizational Factors,* ed. J. J, Hurrell, Jr., L. Levi, L. R. Murphy, and S. L. Sauter, Encyclopedia of Occupational Health & Safety, 2011, http://www.ilo.org/oshenc/part-v/psychosocial-and-organizational-factors/macro-organizational-factors/item/29-organizational-climate-and-culture (accessed March 24, 2014).

28. B. Schneider, M. G. Ehrhart, and W. H. Macey, "Perspectives on Organization Climate and Culture, Building and Developing the Organization," in *APA Handbook of Industrial and Organizational Psychology,* ed. S. Zedeck (Washington, D.C.: American Psychological Association, 2011), 373.

29. Rousseau, "Organizational Climate and Culture."

30. Schneider, Ehrhart, and Macey, "Perspectives on Organization Climate and Culture," 383.

31. Rousseau, "Organizational Climate and Culture."

32. Schneider, Ehrhart, and Macey, "Perspectives on Organization Climate and Culture," 388.

33. Rousseau, "Organizational Climate and Culture."

34. Schneider, Ehrhart, and Macey, "Perspectives on Organization Climate and Culture," 389–390.

35. O. Godeken, "Bridging the PM Performance Gap," *Defense AT&L* (July–August 2009): 37.

36. Vidula Bal, M. Campbell, J. Steed, and K. Meddings, "The Role of Power in Effective Leadership: A CCL Research White Paper," Center for Creative Leadership, 2008, http://www.ccl.org/leadership/pdf/research/roleOfPower.pdf (accessed March 27, 2014), 5.

37. Resnick, "Organizational Savvy."

38. T. Stimson, "Sources of Power," *CLI,* 2011, http://www.consultcli.com/Sourcespower.htm (accessed March 25, 2014).

39. Seldman and Betof, "An Illuminated Path," 39.

40. Stimson, "Sources of Power," citing John R. P. French and Bertram Raven, "The Bases of Social Power," in D. Cartwright and A. Zander, *Group Dynamics* (New York: Harper & Row, 1959); and P. Hersey and K. Blanchard, *Management of Organizational Behavior* (Upper Saddle River, N.J.: Prentice Hall, 1982).

41. R. Woldring, "Power in Organizations: A Way of Thinking about What You've Got, and How to Use It," Workplace Competence International Limited, 2001, http://www.wciltd.com/pdfquark/powerorgv2.pdf (accessed March 29, 2014).

42. "Various Sources of Power in an Organization," blog, December, 23, 2013, http://bankofinfo.com/sources-of-power-in-an-organization/ (accessed March 25, 2014).

43. P. Merchant, "5 Sources of Power in Organizations," *Small Business Chronicle,* http://smallbusiness.chron.com/5-sources-power-organizations-14467.html (accessed March 25, 2014).

44. S. Stapleton, "The Five Sources of a Leader's Power, and How (and How Not) to Use Them," *SimonStapleton.com,* December 17, 2007, http://www.simonstapleton.com/wordpress/2007/12/17/the-five-sources-of-a-leader%E2%80%99s-power-and-how-and-how-not-to-use-them/ (accessed March 25, 2014).

45. Woldring, "Power in Organizations."

46. "Various Sources of Power in an Organization."

47. Bal et al., "The Role of Power in Effective Leadership," 4.

48. "Sweat Equity," http://en.wikipedia.org/wiki/Sweat_equity (accessed March 31, 2014).

49. Bal et al., "The Role of Power in Effective Leadership," 15.

50. Woldring, "Power in Organizations."

51. Godeken, "Bridging the PM Performance Gap," 35, 37–38.

52. "Office Politics—Seven Savvy Steps."

53. Godeken, "Bridging the PM Performance Gap," 36–37.

54. Donald Clark, "Concepts of Leadership," http://www.nmlink.com/~donclark/leader/leadcon.html (accessed March 25, 2014).

55. Bal et al., "The Role of Power in Effective Leadership," 12–13.

56. Stapleton, "The Five Sources of a Leader's Power."

57. Bal et al., "The Role of Power in Effective Leadership," 13–14.

58. Stapleton, "The Five Sources of a Leader's Power."

59. Stapleton, "The Five Sources of a Leader's Power."

60. Bal et al., "The Role of Power in Effective Leadership," 4.

61. Stapleton, "The Five Sources of a Leader's Power."

62. Bal et al., "The Role of Power in Effective Leadership," 17–19.

63. T. Sekiguchi, "Person-Organization Fit and Person-Job Fit in Employee Selection: A Review of the Literature," *Osaka Keidai Ronshu* 54, no. 6 (March 2004): 179.

64. "Increase Hiring Effectiveness," Business Success Tools, LLC, http://business successtools.biz /assessmenets/candidate-assessment-toolsov.shtml (accessed March 31, 2014).

65. J. K. Ustin, "Assessing Job Candidates for Fit," http://http://www.joankustin.com/N5content/PDF /Assessing_Job_Candidates_for_Fit.pdf (accessed March 31, 2014).

66. Sekiguchi, "Person-Organization Fit and Person-Job Fit in Employee Selection," 179.

67. A. L. Kristof, "Person-Organization Fit: An Integrative Review of Its Conceptualizations, Measurement and Implications," *Personnel Psychology* 49, no. 1 (1996): 1–49.

68. J. R. Edwards, "Person-Job Fit: A Conceptual Integration, Literature Review, and Methodological Critique," in *International Review of Industrial & Organizational* Psychology, ed. C. L. Cooper and I. T. Robertson (New York: Wiley, 1991), 283–357.

69. Sekiguchi, "Person-Organization Fit and Person-Job Fit in Employee Selection," 181–183.

70. "Insights: Assessing Job Candidates beyond the Technical Skills," 2013, http://www.printlink.com /resources_insight051.php (accessed April 1, 2014).

71. "Learning Agility and Emotional Intelligence Competencies," Ernst & Young slide presentation.

72. E. Coghlan, "Why Do Mergers and Acquisitions Fail?" *American News Report,* June 19, 2013, http:// americannewsreport.com/why-do-mergers-and -acquisitions-fail-8819047 (accessed April 2, 2014).

73. G. W. Stevens, "Toward a Process-Based Approach of Conceptualizing Change Readiness," *Journal of Applied Behavioral Science* 49, no. 3 (2013): 339–341.

74. Stevens, "Toward a Process-Based Approach of Conceptualizing Change Readiness," 335, 347.

75. Q. N. Huy, "In Praise of Middle Managers," *Harvard Business Review* September 2001, 75.

76. Cheema, Cheema, and Ashraf, "Leaders' Political Skill, Organizational Politics Savvy, and Change in Organizations," 10.

77. Stevens, "Toward a Process-Based Approach of Conceptualizing Change Readiness," 341–342.

78. Clark, "Concepts of Leadership."

79. James M. Kouzes and Barry Z. Posner, *The Leadership Challenge* (San Francisco: Jossey-Bass, 1987).

80. U.S. Army, *Military Leadership,* Field Manual 22-100 (Washington, D.C.: U.S. Government Printing Office, 1983).

16. Customer/Client Interface

1. A. Kjerulf, "Top 5 Reasons Why 'The Customer Is Always Right' Is Wrong," July 12, 2006, http://positivesharing.com/2006/07/why-the -customer-is-always-right-results-in-bad-customer -service/ (accessed April 9, 2014).

2. J. R. Hitchner, *Financial Valuation: Applications and Models,* 2nd ed. (Hoboken, N.J.: Wiley, 2006), 98–103.

3. Alyssa Gregory, "How to Strengthen Relationships with Your Client," http://sbinformation .about.com/od/businessmanagemen1/a/strengthen -client-relationships.htm (accessed March 31, 2014).

4. Peter N. Murray, "How Steve Jobs Knew What You Wanted," *Psychology Today,* October 31, 2011, http://www.psychologytoday.com/blog/inside-the -consumer-mind/201110/how-steve-jobs-knew-what -you-wanted (accessed April 11, 2014).

5. John Shank and Vijay Govindarajan, *Strategic Cost Management* (New York: Free Press, 1993), 13.

6. "Reducing Cost-to-Serve in the Supply Chain," Buffalo Hospital Supply, June 18, 2013, http://www.buffalohospital.com/news/article:06-18 -2013-reducing-cost-to-serve-in-the-supply-chain/ (accessed April 12, 2014.

7. Shank and Govindarajan, *Strategic Cost Management,* 17.

8. David Maister, "Key Account Management," 1997, http://davidmaister.com/articles/key-account -management/ (accessed April, 12, 2014).

9. Alan M. Kantrow, "Why Read Peter Drucker?" *Harvard Business Review* 87, no. 11 (November 2009): 72–82.

10. Sarah Earnell, "The Value of Training Customer-Facing Staff in Sales," PROFORCE, http:// www.proforce.net.au/media/4954/customer%20 facing%20people%20as%20salespeople.pdf (accessed April 12, 2014).

11. David Maister, *True Professionalism: The Courage to Care about Your People, Your Clients, and Your Career* (New York: Simon & Schuster, 1997), 133.

12. Maister, *True Professionalism,* 133–134.

13. Pamela Currie, "Developing a Customer Centric and Sales Driven High Performance Organization," *Ascension,* April 24, 2013, http://ascensionstrategy.com/blog/post /developing-customer-centric-and-sales-driven-high -performance-organization (accessed April 13, 2014).

14. "Cross-selling," http://en.wikipedia.org/wiki /Cross-selling (accessed April 14, 2014).

15. Maister, *True Professionalism,* 178–181.

16. "Cross-selling."

17. "Cross-selling."

18. Maister, *True Professionalism,* 185.

19. Timothy L. Keiningham, Bruce Cooil, Lerzan Aksoy, Tor W. Andreassen, and Jay Weiner, "The Value of Different Customer Satisfaction and Loyalty Metrics in Predicting Customer Retention, Recommendation, and Share-of-Wallet," *Managing Service Quality* 17, no. 4 (2007): 377.

20. Dorie Clark, "Five Ways to Get Clients Now," February 23, 2012, http://www.huffingtonpost.com /dorie-clark/five-ways-to-get-clients-_b_1296558 .html (accessed April 15, 2014).

21. Mark Wayshak, "Every Business Needs a Referral System," August 16, 2013, http://www .huffingtonpost.com/marc-wayshak/why-every -business-needs-_b_3767485.html (accessed April 15, 2014).

22. Daryl Logullo, "Five Outstanding Client Referral Tactics (and Action Steps)," September 25, 2007, http://www.marketingprofs.com/7 /five-outstanding-client-referral-tactics-logullo.asp (accessed April 15, 2014).

23. Wayshak, "Every Business Needs a Referral System."

24. Maister, *True Professionalism,* 168–169.

25. Wayshak, "Every Business Needs a Referral System."

26. David Frey, "Stop Begging for Referrals," http://www.evancarmichael.com/Marketing/77 /Stop-Begging-for-Referrals.html (accessed April 15, 2014).

27. Maister, *True Professionalism,* 168–170.

28. David Frey, "How to Make It Rain Referrals," http://www-rohan.sdsu.edu/~renglish/377/notes /chapt07/raining_referra.htm (accessed April 15, 2014).

29. Keiningham et al., "The Value of Different Customer Satisfaction and Loyalty Metrics," 363–365, 378.

30. David Maister, *Managing the Professional Services Firm* (New York: Simon & Schuster, 1997), 121–122.

31. Maister, *True Professionalism,* 175.

32. Adapted from John Shank, "Allied Stationery," in *Cases in Cost Management,* 3rd ed. (New York: Cengage Learning, 2005).

33. Adapted from Maister, *Managing the Professional Services Firm,* 171–177.

34. T. Alessandra and M. J. O'Connor, *The Platinum Rule* (New York: Business Plus, 1996), 3–4.

35. Adapted from Alessandra and O'Connor, *The Platinum Rule,* 229–231.

36. Ross Beard, "How Do the Best Companies Deal with At-Risk Clients?" http://blog.clientheartbest .com/dealing-with-at-risk-clients/ (accessed March 31, 2014).

37. Kristen Hampshire, "What Drives Value?" *Smart Business,* December 31, 2006, http://www .sbnonline.com/component/k2/16-philadelphia -editions/12154 (accessed April 9, 2014).

38. L. G. Godard, "Understanding the Needs of Your Clients," March 2009, http://www .thegodardgroup.com/wp-content/up- loads/2011/03/Understanding-the-Needs-of-Your -Clients.pdf (accessed April 15, 2014).

39. Leland Putterman, "Cumulative Customer Profitability—the 20/300 Rule," May 5, 2011, http://www.acornsys.com/The-Acorn-Blog /bid/56484/Cumulative-Customer-Profitability-The -20-300-Rule, (accessed April 17, 2014), citing J. S. Byrnes, *Islands of Profit in a Sea of Red Ink: Why 40 Percent of Your Business Is Unprofitable and How to Fix It* (New York: Penguin, 2010).

40. Amy Barrett, "When, Why, and How to Fire That Customer," *Bloomberg Businessweek Magazine,* October 28, 2007, http://www.businessweek.com /stories/2007-10-28/when-why-and-how-to-fire -that-customer (accessed April 17).

41. Barrett, "When, Why, and How to Fire That Customer."

42. Robert Bowen, "How to Identify and Deal with Different Types of Clients," *Smashing Magazine,* October 15, 2009, http://www.smashingmagazine .com/2009/10/15/identifying-and-dealing-with -different-types-of-clients/ (accessed April 17, 2014).

43. Barrett, "When, Why, and How to Fire That Customer," quoting Professor G. Richard Shell of the Wharton School, University of Pennsylvania.

44. R. E. Kelley, *How to Be a Star at Work: 9 Breakthrough Strategies You Need to Succeed* (New York: Three Rivers Press, 1999), 148.

Conclusion

1. C. Tang, speech at event titled "Celebration of Women," Greater Louisville International Professionals, March 20, 2014.

Appendix A

1. Kelly Watkins, *Email Etiquette Made Easy* (Petite Press, 2009), 108.

Appendix C

1. We provide a link to a document with some questions and/or behaviors shown in just one page to SpeedRead! https://www.hbanet.org/sites/hba /files/docs/Corporate/Leadership_ Conference/2010_Leadership_Conference/2010

_Art_of_theAsk_Speed_Reading_People.pdf. This page is also inserted in this document with thanks to the Quad2 Consulting Group.

2. A quote that is useful in E/I discovery: "If you do not know what an introvert is thinking, you have not asked; if you do not know what an extravert is thinking, you have not been listening."

3. Caution is urged in assessing the T/F preferences, as the peer pressure to be objective may be very high to be a T in decision making.

4. Emotional intelligence and a willingness to explore the other types for recognizing, appreciating, and acting upon differences mitigates this and other issues discussed here.

5. http://www.brainyquote.com/quotes /quotes/l/leotolstoy105644.html (accessed April 22, 2014).

Appendix D

1. Stephanie Edwards and Technical Information Service, "Activity Based Costing: Topic Gateway Series No. 1," Revised November 2008, http://www .cimaglobal.com/Documents/ImportedDocuments /cid_tg_activity_based_costing_nov08.pdf.pdf (accessed December 27, 2014).

2. Adapted from Edwards, "Activity Based Costing."

3. Adapted from Edwards, "Activity Based Costing."

4. Robert S. Kaplan and Steven R. Anderson, "Time-Driven Activity-Based Costing," *Harvard Business Review,* November 2004, https://hbr .org/2004/11/time-driven-activity-based-costing (accessed December 27, 2014).

Appendix E

1. For more information, see the Amazon case study provided by EVA Dimensions, which demonstrates these concepts: http://evadimensions.com/sites /default/files/fileupload/Amazon.pdf.

2. Adapted from EVA Dimensions LLC. "How EVA Works." 2010, http://evadimensions.com/sites /default/files/fileupload/EVAReference/EVA_White _Papers/How%20EVA%20Works.pdf (accessed January 6, 2015).

3. Adapted from "Five EVA Metrics That Every CFO Should Know" *EVADimensions.com.* http://evadimensions.com/5EVAMetricsCFO (accessed January 6, 2015).

4. John A. Hayes. "2013 Letter to Our Shareholders," in "2013 Ball Annual Report," by Ball Corporation, 1, http://www.ball.com/2013annualreport /pdf/2013BallAnnualReport.pdf (accessed January 6, 2015).

5. For the interested reader, please note that www.EVADimensions.com contains information in far more depth than we can explicate here.

6. *Integrated Reporting <IR>,* http://www.theiirc.org/ (accessed January 6, 2015).

7. The Sustainability Accounting Standards Board (www.sasb.org) is now in operation with the intentions of informing FASB, IASB, and other accounting standard setters on sustainability accounting.

Bibliography

Abraham, Rebecca. "The Impact of Emotional Dissonance on Organizational Commitment and Intention to Turnover." *Journal of Psychology* 133, no. 4 (1999): 441–455.

Abudi, Gina. "Formal Internal Company Mentoring Programs." Ezinearticles.com. http://ezinearticles.com/?Formal-Internal-Company-Mentoring-Programs&id=3884109 (accessed January 2, 2014).

Adair, J. *Developing Leaders: The Ten Key Principles* (Guildford, England: Talbot Adair Press, 1988).

Adair-Toteff, Christopher. "Max Weber's Charisma." *Journal of Classical Sociology* 5, no. 2 (2005): 189–204.

Ahearn, K. K., G. R. Ferris, W. A. Hochwarter, C. Douglas, and A. P. Ammeter. "Leader Political Skill and Team Performance." *Journal of Management* 30, no. 3 (2004): 309–327.

Alessandra, T., and M. J. O'Connor. *The Platinum Rule* (New York: Business Plus, 1996).

Ambrose, Maureen L., and Carol T. Kulik. "Old Friends, New Faces: Motivation Research in the 1990s." *Journal of Management* 25, no. 3 (1999): 231–292.

Ana-Maria, Grigore, Badea Florica, and Catalina Radu. "Modern Instruments for Measuring Organizational Performance." Researchgate.net. http://www.researchgate.net/publication/49615452_MODERN_INSTRUMENTS_FOR_MEASURING_ORGANIZATIONAL_PERFORMANCE (accessed March 6, 2014).

Anderson, J. "To Team or Not to Team, That Is the Question." http://ezinearticles.com/?To-Team-Or-Not-to-Team,-That-is-the-Question&id=3625010 (accessed April 3, 2014).

Argyris, Chris. "Double-Loop Learning, Teaching, and Research." *Academy of Management Learning and Education* 1, no. 2 (2002): 206–218.

———. "Teaching Smart People How to Learn." *Harvard Business Review* 69, no. 3 (1991).

Arnold, K. J. "Workplace Teamwork: Where NOT to USE Teams." http://www.sdoeroad.com/Team_Building/workplace-teamwork.html (accessed April 4, 2014).

"Arthur Andersen at Center of Scandal Again." CRN.com, June 28, 2002. http://www.crn.com/news/channel-programs/18828554/arthur-andersen-at-center-of-scandal-again.htm (accessed March 17, 2014).

Ashforth, Blake E., and Ronald H. Humphrey. "Emotional Labor in Service Roles: The Influence of Identity." *Academic Management Review* 18, no. 1 (1993): 88–115.

Baggini, Julian, and Peter S. Fosi. *The Ethics Toolkit: A Compendium of Ethical Concepts and Methods.* (Malden, Mass.: Wiley-Blackwell, 2007).

Bal, Vidula, M. Campbell, J. Steed, and K. Meddings. "The Role of Power in Effective Leadership: A CCL Research White Paper." Center for Creative Leadership, 2008. http://www.ccl.org/leadership/pdf/research/roleOfPower.pdf (accessed March 27, 2014).

Baptiste, Nicole R. "Tightening the Link between Employee Wellbeing at Work and Performance: A New Dimension for HRM." *Management Decision* 46, no. 2 (2008): 284–309.

Barger, Nancy J., and Linda K. Kirby. *Introduction to Type and Change* (Palo Alto, Calif.: CPP, 2004).

Barrett, Amy. "When, Why, and How to Fire That Customer." *Bloomberg Businessweek Magazine,* October 28, 2007. http://www.businessweek.com/stories/2007-10-28/when-why-and-how-to-fire-that-customer (accessed April 17, 2014).

Barry, Douglas K. "Service Architecture." http://www.service-architecture.com/articles/web-services/service-oriented_architecture_soa_definition.html (accessed March 17, 2014).

Barth, Mary E., and Katherine Schipper. "Financial Reporting Transparency." *Journal of Accounting, Auditing & Finance* 23, no. 2 (2008): 173–190.

Bass, B. M. *Transformational Leadership* (London: Lawrence Erlbaum, 1998).

Beard, Ross. "How Do the Best Companies Deal with At-Risk Clients?" http://blog.clientheartbest.com/dealing-with-at-risk-clients/ (accessed March 31, 2014).

Beckert, Jens, and Milan Zafirovski. *International Encyclopedia of Economic Sociology* (New York: Routledge, 2005).

Berger, M. W. "Ten Critical Questions to Ask When Checking References." A Hire Authority, January 24, 2005. http://www.drgnyc.com /List_Serve/Jan24_2005.htm (accessed January 1, 2014).

Berghofer, Desmond, and Geraldine Schwartz. "Ethical Leadership: Right Relationships and the Emotional Bottom Line: The Gold Standard for Success." Ethicalleadership. com. http://www.ethicalleadership.com /BusinessArticle.htm (accessed January 15, 2014).

Berne, Eric. *The Structure and Dynamics of Organizations and Groups* (New York: Ballantine, 1975).

Bird, C. *Social Psychology* (New York: Appleton-Century, 1940).

Bird, J. M. "Re: Intel Update." USAA letter to customers, March 2014.

Black, K. M., and R. Seaker. "Project Performance: Implications of Personality Preferences and Double-Loop Learning." *Journal of American Academy of Business* 1, no. 1 (2004): 292–297.

Blake, R., and J. Mouton. *The Managerial Grid: The Key to Leadership Excellence* (Houston: Gulf, 1964).

Bolgar, Catherine. "Education and Adaptability Are Vital in Our Rapidly Evolving, Innovative World." *Wall Street Journal Executive Digest,* 2011. http://online.wsj.com/ad/article /execdigest-education (accessed March 17, 2014).

Bolman Lee G., and Terrence E. Deal. *Reframing Organizations: Artistry, Choice, and Leadership* (San Francisco: Jossey-Bass, 2003).

Borgatti, Steve. "Manual for Working in Teams." 2004. http://www.analytictech.com/mb021 /teamhint.htm (accessed April 2, 2014).

Bowen, Robert. "How to Identify and Deal with Different Types of Clients." *Smashing Magazine,* October 15, 2009. http://www .smashingmagazine.com/2009/10/15 /identifying-and-dealing-with-different -types-of-clients/ (accessed April 17, 2014).

Boyatzis, Richard E., Melvin L. Smith, and Alim J. Beveridge. "Coaching with Compassion: Inspiring Health, Well-Being, and Development in Organizations." *Journal of Applied Behavioral Science* 49, no. 2 (2013): 153–178.

Brief, Arthur P., and Howard M. Weiss. "Organizational Behavior: Affect in the Workplace." *Annual Review of Psychology* 53 (2002): 279–307.

Brock, Susan A. *Introduction to Type and Selling* (Palo Alto, Calif.: CPP, 1994).

Brooks, Chad. "7 Steps to Ethical Leadership." *FoxBusiness.com.* http://smallbusiness.foxbusiness.com /entrepreneurs/2013/12/03/7-steps-to -ethical-leadership/ (accessed January 15, 2014).

Brooks, F. *The Mythical Man-Month: Essays on Software Engineering, Anniversary Edition* (Boston: Addison-Wesley Longman, 1995).

Broughton, Edward. "The Bhopal Disaster and Its Aftermath: A Review." *Ncbi.nlm.nih.gov.* http://www.ncbi.nlm.nih.gov/pmc/articles /PMC1142333/ (accessed January 19, 2014).

Brown, Joel. "7 Unconventional Ways to Motivate Yourself." *Addicted2success.com.* http:// addicted2success.com/motivation/7 -unconventional-ways-to-motivate-yourself/ (accessed December 30, 2013).

"Building a Sense of Teamwork among Staff Members." http://www.amanet.org/training /articles/Building-a-Sense-of-Teamwork -Among-Staff-Members.aspx (accessed February 26, 2014).

Burley-Allen, M. *Listening: The Forgotten Skill* (New York: Wiley, 1982).

"Business Communication." https://en.wikipedia.org /wiki/Business_communication (accessed January 27, 2014).

"Business Ethics." http://en.wikipedia.org/wiki /Business_ethics (accessed January 15, 2014).

"Business Performance Management." http:// en.wikipedia.org/wiki/Business _performance_management (accessed February 15, 2014).

Cameron, Kim S., and Robert E. Quinn. *Diagnosing and Changing Organizational Culture: Based on the Competing Values Framework* (San Francisco: Jossey-Bass, 2006).

Campbell, Terry. "Teams Come in All Types, Sizes, and Shapes!" Lecture material.

Campbell, Terry, and Heather Cairns. "Developing and Measuring the Learning Organization: From Buzz Words to Behaviors." *Industrial and Commercial Training* 26, no. 7 (1994): 10–15.

Canace, Thomas G., and Paul Juras. "CFO: From Analyst to Catalyst." *Strategic Finance* 96, no. 2 (2014): 27–33.

"Career: Claims Vice President." *MyMajors.com.* http://www.mymajors.com/skills-and -knowledge/Claims-Vice-President (accessed March 15, 2014).

Carroll, Andrew. "A Sidelined Patton Shares His Philosophy on Leadership." *Historynet.com,* May 22, 2009. http://www.historynet.com/a -sidelined-patton-shares-his-philosophy-on -leadership.htm (accessed January 2, 2014).

"The Challenges of Doing Business Internationally." *Trekking.* http://www.trekconsulting.com /Publications/Newsletter/Issue8/Issue8. html (accessed March 13, 2014).

Cheema, I. Q., H. A. Cheema, and K. Ashraf. "Leaders' Political Skill, Organizational Politics Savvy, and Change in Organizations—A Constellation." Servant Leadership Research Roundtable, Regent University, May 2008 http://www.regent.edu/acad/global /publications/sl_proceedings/2008 /cheema-ashraf.pdf, (accessed March 24, 2014).

Cherry, Kendra. "Theories of Motivation." *About.com.* http://psychology.about.com /od/psychologytopics/tp/theories-of -motivation.htm (accessed January 9, 2014).

———. "What Is AutoCratic Leadership?" *About.com.* http://psychology.about.com/od /leadership/f/autocratic-leadership.htm (accessed December 31, 2013).

Chowdhury, Murshed. "How Important Are Technical Skills for Managers?" *Infusive Solutions,* January 24, 2012. http://www .infusivesolutions.com/blog/bid/76847 /How-Important-are-Technical-Skills-for Managers (accessed March 12, 2014).

"Claims Examiners Property Casualty Insurance Job Description." http://www.insurancejobs .com/claims-examiners-property-casualty -insurance-job-description.htm (accessed March 15, 2014).

Clark, Donald. "Concepts of Leadership." http://www .nmlink.com/~donclark/leader/leadcon .html (accessed March 25, 2014).

Clark, Dorie. "Five Ways to Get Clients Now." February 23, 2012. http://www.huffingtonpost.com /dorie-clark/five-ways-to-get-clients -_b_1296558.html (accessed April 15, 2014).

Cogen, J. "The Secret to Reading Resumes—Five Tips to Choosing the Right Candidates to Interview." http://ezinearticles.com/?The -Secret-to-Reading-Resumes—-Five-Tips -to-Choosing-the-Right-Candidates-to -Interview&id=3618056 (accessed January 1, 2014).

Coghlan, E. "Why Do Mergers and Acquisitions Fail?" *American News Report,* June 19, 2013. http://americannewsreport.com/why-do -mergers-and-acquisitions-fail-8819047 (accessed April 2, 2014).

Collins, J. "Level 5 Leadership." *Harvard Business Review* 79, no. 1 (2001): 66–76.

"Communication." *Merriam-Webster.com.* http://www.merriam-webster.com /dictionary/communication (accessed February 2, 2014).

"Competency Dictionary." http://en.wikipedia.org /wiki/Competency_dictionary (accessed March 17, 2014).

"Competent and Versatile: How Professional Accountants in Business Drive Sustainable Organizational Success." International Federation of Accountants, August 2011. http://viewer.zmags.com/publication /b908956a#/b908956a/1 (accessed March 10, 2014).

"Control (Management)." http://en.wikipedia.org /wiki/Control_(management) (accessed February 25, 2014).

Corlett, Eleanor S., Nancy B. Millner, and Katharine D. Myers. *Navigating Midlife: Using Typology as a Guide* (Palo Alto, Calif.: Davies-Black, 1995).

Cote, Stephane, and Laura M. Morgan. "A Longitudinal Analysis of the Association between Emotion Regulation, Job Satisfaction, and Intentions to Quit." *Journal of Organizational Behavior* 23, no. 8 (2002): 947–962.

Covey, Stephen R. *Principle-Centered Leadership* (New York: Franklin Covey, 1992).

"Critical Thinking and Communication Skills Are the Reason We Have Universities." Slide presentation, Foundation for Critical Thinking, 2006.

"Cross-Selling." http://en.wikipedia.org/wiki/Cross -selling (accessed April 14, 2014).

"Culture and Control." http://facultyfp.salisbury.edu /rchoffman/culcntl.htm (accessed February 15, 2014).

Currie, Pamela. "Developing a Customer Centric and Sales Driven High Performance Organization." *Ascension,* April 24, 2013. http://ascensionstrategy.com/blog/post /developing-customer-centric-and-sales -driven-high-performance-organization (accessed April 13, 2014).

Davidson, Taylor. "How to Be a Great Mentor (and a Great Mentee)." *TheNextWeb.com.* http://thenextweb.com/entrepreneur /2012/01/25/how-to-be-a

-great-mentor-and-a-mentee/
#!rA1ZI (accessed December 31, 2013).

"Definition of Mentoring, Benefits of Mentoring, & Other FAQs." *Management-Mentors.com.* http://www.management-mentors.com /resources/corporate-mentoring-programs -faqs (accessed January 2, 2014).

Dixon, Dick. "Fostering Employee Growth." *PerformanceBiz.com.* http://performancebiz .com/tips/fostering-employee-growth (accessed December 31, 2013).

Donovan, Michael. "Performance Measurement: Connecting Strategy, Operations and Actions." http://www.reliableplant.com /Articles/Print/140 (accessed February 23, 2014).

Dotlich, David L., James L. Noel, and Norman Walker. "Leadership Passages: The Personal and Professional Transitions That Make or Break a Leader." *CEO Refresher,* 2005. http://www .refresher.com/Archives/!dnwpassages.html (accessed February 24, 2014).

Doyle, Michael, and David Straus. *How to Make Meetings Work!* (New York: Berkley Books, 1976).

Drexler, A., and D. Sibbet. "Team Performance Model." http://www.grove.com/site/ourwk_gm _tp.html (accessed March 15, 2014).

Drucker, Peter F. "Managing Oneself." *Harvard Business Review* 83, no. 1 (2005): 100–109.

Duckworth, Angela L. "Research Statement." Duckworth Lab, University of Pennsylvania. https://sites.sas.upenn.edu/duckworth /pages/research-statement (accessed August 1, 2013).

Duncan, Cath. "How to Drive Your Professional Development with a Self-Directed Learning Program." *Productive Flourishing,* February 22, 2011. http://www.productiveflourishing .com/how-to-drive-your-professional -development-with-a-self-directed-learning -program/ (accessed February 25, 2014).

Duncan, R. D. "Morphing Teamwork: From Buzzword to Reality." *Forbes,* January 15, 2014. http://www.forbes.com/sites /rodgerdeanduncan/2014/01/15/morphing -teamwork-from-buzzword-to-reality/ (accessed February 26, 2014).

Dunning, Donna. *Introduction to Type and Communication* (Palo Alto, Calif.: CPP, 2003).

———. *Introduction to Type and Learning* (Palo Alto, Calif.: CPP, 2003).

"Dwight D. Eisenhower—The Eisenhower Approach to Leadership." *Profiles of U.S. Presidents.*

http://www.presidentprofiles.com/Grant -Eisenhower/Dwight-D-Eisenhower-The -eisenhower-approach-to-leadership.html (accessed December 31, 2013).

Dzinkowski, Ramona. "A View from the Top." *Strategic Finance,* October 2013.

Earnell, Sarah. "The Value of Training Customer -Facing Staff in Sales." *PROFORCE.* http://www.proforce.net.au/media/4954 /customer%20facing%20people%20 as%20salespeople.pdf (accessed April 12, 2014).

"Easy Guide to Understanding ENRON: Scandal Summary." http://finance.laws.com/enron -scandal-summary (accessed March 17, 2014).

Edmondson Amy C. "The Importance of Teaming." Harvard Business School, April 12, 2012. http://hbswk.hbs.edu/item/6997.html (accessed March 28, 2014).

———. "Teamwork on the Fly." *Harvard Business Review,* April 2012. http://hbr.org/2012/04 /teamwork-on-the-fly/ar/1m (accessed February 26, 2014).

Edmondson, Ron. "7 Traits of Courageous Leadership." February 2, 2011. http://ronedmondson.com/2011/02 /7-traits-of-courageous-leadership.html.

Edwards, J. R. "Person-Job Fit: A Conceptual Integration, Literature Review, and Methodological Critique." In *International Review of Industrial & Organizational Psychology,* ed. C. L. Cooper and I. T. Robertson (New York: Wiley, 1991), 283–357.

Edwards, Stephanie, and Technical Information Service, "Activity Based Costing: Topic Gateway Series No. 1," Revised November 2008. http://www.cimaglobal.com /Documents/ImportedDocuments/cid _tg_activity_based_costing_nov08.pdf.pdf (accessed December 27, 2014).

"Effective Methods for Fostering Employee Growth." *Businessdictionary.com.* http://www .businessdictionary.com/article/419 /effective-methods-for-fostering-employee -growth/ (accessed December 31, 2013).

Einstein, A. http://www.goodreads.com/ quotes/66864-in-theory-theory-and- practice-are-the-same-in-practice (accessed March 16, 2014).

Elder, Linda. "The Stages of Critical Thinking Development." http://www.criticalthinking. org/data/pages/14

/fd4e6f74cc717ed36a9faccc870b8a2
e4fe0bd688b279.pdf
(accessed February 22, 2014).

Erben, G. S., and A. B. Guneser. "The Relationship
between Paternalistic Leadership and
Organizational Commitment: Investigating
the Role of Climate Regarding Ethics."
Journal of Business Ethics 82, no. 4 (2008):
955–968.

"Ethical Dilemmas in Business." *SpeedUpCareer.com.*
http://www.speedupcareer.com
/articles/ethical-dilemmas-in-business.html
(accessed January 15, 2014).

"Ethics." http://en.wikipedia.org/wiki/Ethics
(accessed January 21, 2014).

EVA Dimensions LLC. "How EVA Works." 2010.
http://evadimensions.com/sites/default
/files/fileupload/EVAReference/EVA
_White_Papers/How%20EVA%20Works.pdf
(accessed January 6, 2015).

Evans, M. G. "Leadership and Motivation: A Core
Concept." *Academy of Management Journal*
13 (1970): 91–102.

"Evidence of a Mature Scorecard: The Power
of Alignment." *BalancedScorecard.org*
(accessed March 6, 2014).

"Expert Witness Law & Legal Definition." *USLegal.
com.* http://definitions.uslegal.com/e
/expert-witness/ (accessed December 30,
2013).

"Fast-Track to the Top: Developing the Next
Generation of Leaders to Drive Future
Growth." Deloitte. http://www.deloitte.com
/assets/Dcom-Mexico/Local%20Assets
/Documents/Fasttrack.pdf (accessed
February 27, 2014).

Federal Aviation Administration. Team Performance
Module. Team Use 5–6. "When to Use
Teams?" https://www.hf.faa.gov
/webtraining/TeamPerfrom/Team007.htm
(accessed March 13, 2014).

Ferrazzi, Keith. "Candor, Criticism, Teamwork."
Harvard Business Review, January–February
2012. http://hbr.org/2012/01/candor
-criticism-teamwork/ar/1 (accessed
February 16, 2014).

Ferris, G. R., W. A. Hochwater, C. Douglas, F. R. Blass,
R. W. Kolodinsky, and D. C. Treadway. "Social
Influence in Organizations and Human
Resources Systems." In *Research in Personnel
and Human Resources Management,* ed. G. R.
Ferris and J. J. Martocchio (Oxford: Elsevier
Science, 2002), 65–127.

Ferris, G. R., D. C. Treadway, R. W. Kolodinsky,
W. A. Hochwarter, C. J. Kacmar, C. Douglas,
and D. W. Frink. "Development and Validation
of the Political Skill Inventory." *Journal of
Management* 31, no. 1 (February 2005):
126–152.

Fiedler, F. E. *A Theory of Leadership Effectiveness*
(New York: McGraw-Hill, 1967).

Fischer, Gerhard, and Masanori Sugimoto.
"Supporting Self-Directed Learners and
Learning Communities with Sociotechnical
Environments." *Journal of Research and
Practice in Technology Enhanced Learning*
1, no. 1 (2006): 36.

Fisher, Cynthia D. "Mood and Emotions While
Working: Missing Pieces of Job Satisfaction."
Journal of Organizational Behavior 21 (2000):
185–202.

"Five EVA Metrics That Every CFO Should Know."
EVADimensions.com. http://evadimensions
.com/5EVAMetricsCFO (accessed January
6, 2015).

"The Five Dysfunctions of a Team."
http://en.wikipedia.org/wiki/The_Five
_Dysfunctions_of_a_Team (accessed March
20, 2014).

French, John R. P., and Bertram Raven. "The Bases of
Social Power." In D. Cartwright and A. Zander,
Group Dynamics (New York: Harper & Row,
1959).

Frey, David. "How to Make It Rain Referrals."
http://www-rohan.sdsu.edu/~renglish/377
/notes/chapt07/raining_referra.htm
(accessed April 15, 2014).

———. "Stop Begging for Referrals." http://www
.evancarmichael.com/Marketing/77/Stop
-Begging-for-Referrals.html (accessed April
15, 2014).

Gangestad, Steven W., and Mark Snyder. "Self-
Monitoring: Appraisal and Reappraisal."
Psychological Bulletin 126, no. 4 (2000):
530–555.

Garvin, David. "How Google Sold Its Engineers on
Management." *Harvard Business Review,*
December 2013, 76–78.

Godard L. G. "Understanding the Needs of Your
Clients." March 2009. http://www
.thegodardgroup.com/wp-content
/uploads/2011/03/Understanding-the
-Needs-of-Your-Clients.pdf(accessed April
15, 2014).

Godeken, O. "Bridging the PM Performance Gap."
Defense AT&L, July–August 2009, 34–38.

Goleman, D. "Leadership That Gets Results." *Harvard Business Review,* March 1, 2000.

Goleman, Daniel. "What Makes a Leader?" *Harvard Business Review* 76, no. 6 (1998): 93–102.

Graves, J. "How to Fire Someone Compassionately." *U.S. News,* August 22, 2013. http://money.usnews.com/money/careers /articles/2013/08/22/how-to-fire -someone-compassionately (accessed December 30, 2013).

Green, A. "5 Secrets You Should Know about HR." *U.S. News,* July 29, 2013. http://money.usnews .com/money/blogs/outside-voices -careers/2013/07/29/5-secrets-you -should-know-about-hr (accessed January 1, 2014).

Gregory, Alyssa. "How to Strengthen Relationships with Your Client." http://sbinformation.about .com/od/businessmanagemen1/a /strengthen-client-relationships.htm (accessed March 31, 2014).

Grier, S. "How to Counsel an Employee Performance Issue." *IT Managers Inbox.* http://itmanagersinbox.com/2209/how -to-counsel-an-employee-performance -issue/ (accessed December 28, 2013).

Gurdjian, Pierre, Thomas Halbeisen, and Kevin Lane. "Why Leadership-Development Programs Fail." *McKinsey Quarterly,* January 2014, 1–6.

Haberman, Therese. "How to Give an Employee Performance Review." *Hartford Examiner,* October 25, 2010. www.examiner.com /article/how-to-give-an-employee -performance-review (accessed December 28, 2013).

Hackman J. R. "Six Common Misperceptions about Teamwork." *Harvard Business Review,* June 2011. https://blogs.hbr.org/2011/06/six -common-mosperceptions-about-teamwork. html (accessed February 2, 2014).

Hackman, J. R., and R. E. Walton, *Leading Groups in Organizations* (San Francisco: Jossey-Bass, 1986).

Hall, H. "The 7 C's: How to Find and Hire Great Employees." *Forbes,* June 19, 2012. http://www.forbes.com/sites /alanhall/2012/06/19/the-7-cs-how-to -find-and-hire-great-employees/ (accessed January 1, 2014).

Halpern, Diane F. "Teaching Critical Thinking for Transfer across Domains: Disposition, Skills, Structure Training, and Metacognitive Monitoring." *American Psychologist* 53, no. 4 (1998): 449–455.

Hamlett, C. "How to Fire Someone." http://www.ehow .com/how_4500247_fire-someone.html (accessed December 30, 2013).

Hammer, Allen L. *Introduction to Type and Careers* (Palo Alto, Calif.: CPP, 2007).

Hampshire, Kristen. "What Drives Value?" *Smart Business,* December 31, 2006. http://www.sbnonline.com/component /k2/16-philadelphia-editions/12154 (accessed April 9, 2014).

Hanson, Kirk O. "Ethics and the Middle Manager: Creating the 'Tone in the Middle.'" Markkula Center for Applied Ethics, Santa Clara University. http://www.scu.edu/ethics /practicing/focusareas/business/middle -managers.html (accessed January 23, 2014).

Harvey P., K. J. Harris, K. M. Kacmar, A. Buckless, and A. T. Pescosolido. "The Impact of Political Skill on Employees' Perceptions of Ethical Leadership." *Journal of Leadership & Organizational Studies.* 2, no. 1 (2014): 5–16.

Hayden, Jeff. "9 Things You Should Never Ask Employees to Do." *Inc.com.* http://www .inc.com/jeff-haden/9-things-you-should -never-ask-employees-to-do.html (accessed January 5, 2014).

Hayes, John A. "2013 Letter to Our Shareholders." In "2013 Ball Annual Report," by Ball Corporation, 1, http://www .ball.com/2013annualreport /pdf/2013BallAnnualReport.pdf (accessed January 6, 2015).

Heathfield, Susan M. "Did You Bring Your Ethics to Work Today?" *About.com.* http://humanresources.about.com /businessethics/qt/workplace-ethics.htm (accessed January 15, 2014).

——. "Discipline (Progressive Discipline)." *About. com.* http://humanresources.about.com /od/glossaryd/a/discipline.htm (accessed January 2, 2014).

——. "Performance Improvement Strategies." *About.com.* http://humanresources.about .com/od/manageperformance/a/manage _perform.htm (accessed January 2, 2014).

——. "12 Tips for Team Building: How to Build Successful Work Teams." *About.com.* http://humanresources.about.com/od /involvementteams/a/twelve_tip_team.htm (accessed March 13, 2014).

——. "Use Employee Coaching to Improve Performance." *About.com.* http://humanresources.about.com/od

/glossaryc/g/coaching.htm (accessed January 6, 2014).

Hein, R. "8 Tips for How to Fire an Employee." *CIO,* January 22, 2013. http://www.cio.com /article/727127/8_Tips_for_How_to_Fire _an_Employee (accessed December 30, 2013).

Helgoe, Laurie. "Revenge of the Introvert." *Psychology Today,* September 2010, 54.

"Heraclitus." http://en.wikipedia.org/wiki/Heraclitus (accessed March 19, 2014).

Herrera, Pablo. "Transparent to the Core." Soderquist Center, April 29, 2011. http://www.scribd .com/doc/54173448/Transparency-in -Business-Communication (accessed March 18, 2014).

Hersey, P., and K. Blanchard. "Life-Cycle Theory of Leadership." *Training and Development Journal* 23 (1969): 26–34.

———. *Management of Organizational Behavior* (Upper Saddle River, N.J.: Prentice Hall, 1982).

Hesselbein, Frances, Marshall Goldsmith, and Richard Beckhard, eds. *The Leader of the Future* (New York: Drucker Foundation, 1996).

Hiermstra, R. "Self-Directed Learning." In *The International Encyclopedia of Education,* 2nd ed., ed. T. Husen and T. N. Postlethwaite (Oxford: Pergamon Press, 1994). ccnmtl .columbia.edu/projects/p13p/Self -Directed%20Learning.pdf (accessed February 15, 2014).

Higgins, M. C. "What Should C.J. Do?" *Harvard Business Review* 78, no. 6 (2000): 43–52.

Highsmith, Richard M. "Encourage Creativity and Growth among Your Employees." Businessknowhow.com. http://www .businessknowhow.com/growth /squishcreativity.htm (accessed December 31, 2013).

Hinton, Michelle, and Michael Biderman. "Empirically Derived Job Characteristics Measures and the Motivating Potential Score." *Journal of Business and Psychology* 9, no.4 (1995): 355–364.

Hirsh, Elizabeth, Katherine W. Hirsh, and Sandra Krebs Hirsh. *Introduction to Type and Teams* (Palo Alto, Calif.: CPP, 2003).

Hirsh, Elizabeth, Katherine W. Hirsh, and James Peak. *Introduction to Type and Reintegration* (Palo Alto, Calif.: CPP, 2011).

Hirsh, Katherine W., and Elizabeth Hirsh. *Introduction to Type and Decision Making* (Palo Alto, Calif.: CPP, 1997).

Hirsh, Sandra K. *Introduction to Type and Organizations* (Palo Alto, Calif.: CPP, 1998).

Hirsh, Sandra K., and Jane A. G. Kise. *Introduction to Type and Coaching* (Palo Alto, Calif.: CPP, 2011).

Hirsh, Sandra K., and Jean M. Kummerow. *Introduction to Type in Organizations: Individual Interpretive Guide,* 3rd ed. (Mountain View, Calif.: CPP, 1998).

Hitchner, James R. *Financial Valuation: Applications and Models,* 2nd ed. (Hoboken, N.J.: Wiley, 2006).

Hodge, Hope. "Corps Preparing PR Blitz for Commandant's Garrison 'Reawakening' Campaign." *Marine Corps Times,* November 27, 2013. http://www.marinecorpstimes .com/article/20131127/NEWS/311270023 /Corps-preparing-PR-blitz-commandant-s -garrison-reawakening-campaign (accessed January 23, 2014).

Hofstede, Geert. "Cultural Constraints in Management Theories." *Academy of Management Executive* 7, no. 1 (1993): 81–94.

Holton, Glyn A. "Corporate Risk Management." http://riskencyclopedia.com/articles /corporate_risk_management/ (accessed February 17, 2014).

House, R. J. "A Path-Goal Theory of Leader Effectiveness." *Administrative Science Quarterly* 16 (1971): 81–98.

"How CIOs Can Drive Growth." Business Flexibility and Innovation, IBM Global Technology Services, 2007. http://www.cio.com /documents/whitepapers/IBMQ3wp072007 .pdf (accessed March 17, 2014).

Howell, John P. *Snapshots of Great Leadership* (London: Taylor and Francis, 2012).

"How to Be a Good Mentee." CareerHQ.com. http://www.asaecenter.org/files /FileDownloads/How_to_be_a_good_ mentee.pdf (accessed December 31, 2013).

"How to Become Your Own Greatest Mentor in Life." http://voices.yahoo.com/how-become -own-greatest-mentor-life-3697194.html (accessed December 31, 2013).

"How to Give a Performance Review of an Employee." http://www.wikihow.com/Give -a-Performance-Review-of-an-Employee (accessed December 30, 2013).

"How to Motivate Yourself—Self Motivation." *PicktheBrain.com.* http://www.pickthebrain .com/blog/how-to-motivate-yourself/ (accessed December 30, 2013).

Huseman, Richard C., John D. Hatfield, and Edward W. Miles. "A New Perspective on Equity Theory: The Equity Sensitivity Construct." *Academy of Management Review* 12, no. 2 (1987): 222–234.

Husen, T., and T. N. Postlethwaite, eds. *The International Encyclopedia of Education,* 2nd ed. (Oxford: Pergamon Press, 1994).

Huy, Q. N. "In Praise of Middle Managers." *Harvard Business Review,* September 2001, 72–79.

"The Importance of Reductionism in the Problem Solving Process." Exforsys Inc., July 20, 2006. http://www.exforsys.com/career -center/problem-solving/the-importance -of-reductionism-in-the-problem-solving -process.html (accessed February 24, 2014).

"Importance of Technical Skills." http://www .indianmanpower.com/blog_Technical-Skills -Manpower-Recruitment.html (accessed March 12, 2014).

"Increase Hiring Effectiveness." Business Success Tools, LLC. http://business successtools.biz /assessmenets/candidate-assessment -toolsov.shtml (accessed March 31, 2014).

"Insights: Assessing Job Candidates beyond the Technical Skills." 2013. http://www.printlink .com/resources_insight051.php (accessed April 1, 2014).

Integrated Reporting <IR>. http://www.theiirc.org /the-iirc/ (accessed January 6, 2015).

Isaacson, Walter. "The Real Leadership Lessons of Steve Jobs." *Harvard Business Review,* April 2012, 97, 98.

Jex, Steve M., and Thomas W. Britt. *Organizational Psychology: A Scientist Practitioner Approach.* (Hoboken, N.J.: Wiley, 2008).

Johnson, C. E., and M. Z. Hackman. *Leadership, a Communication Perspective,* 4th ed. (Long Grove, Ill.: Waveland Press, 2003).

Jones, Campbell, Martin Parker, and Rene Ten Bos. *For Business Ethics: A Critical Approach* (London: Routledge, 2005).

Josephson Institute Center for Business Ethics. "Frequently Asked Questions." *JosephsonInstitute.org.* http://josephsoninstitute.org/business /overview/faq.html (accessed January 23, 2014).

Judge, T. A., E. A. Locke, and C. C. Durham. "The Dispositional Causes of Job Satisfaction: A Core Evaluation Approach." *Research in Organizational Behavior* 19 (1997): 151–188.

Kang, B. "Managing the Strategic Finance Gap." *Strategic Finance,* February 2014.

Kantrow, Alan M. "Why Read Peter Drucker?" *Harvard Business Review* 87, no. 11 (2009): 72–82.

Kaplan, Robert S., and Steven R. Anderson, "Time-Driven Activity-Based Costing," *Harvard Business Review,* November 2004. https://hbr.org/2004/11/time-driven -activity-based-costing (accessed December 27, 2014).

Kaufman, Ellen. "What Gets Measured Gets Done." June 3, 2013. http://www.talkativeman.com /what-gets-measured-gets-done/ (accessed February 15, 2014).

Keiningham, Timothy L., Bruce Cooil, Lerzan Aksoy, Tor W. Andreassen, and Jay Weiner. "The Value of Different Customer Satisfaction and Loyalty Metrics in Predicting Customer Retention, Recommendation, and Share-of -Wallet." *Managing Service Quality* 17, no. 4 (2007): 361–384.

Keirsey, David, and Marilyn Bates. *Please Understand Me: Character and Temperament Types* (Del Mar, Calif.: Prometheus Nemesis, 1984).

Kellen, Vince. "Business Performance Measurement: At the Crossroads of Strategy, Decision -Making, Learning and Information Visualization." School of CTI, DePaul University, February 2003. http://www .kellen.net/bpm.htm (accessed February 15, 2014).

Kelley, Robert E. *How to Be a Star at Work: 9 Breakthrough Strategies You Need to Succeed* (New York: Three Rivers Press, 1999).

Kennedy, R. Bryan, and D. Ashley Kennedy. "Using the Myers-Briggs Type Indicator in Career Counseling." *Journal of Employment Counseling* 41, no. 1 (2004): 38–44.

Kerns, Charles D. "Creating and Sustaining an Ethical Workplace Culture." *Graziadio Business Review* 6, no. 3 (2003).

Kieso, D., J Weygandt, and Terry D. Warfield. *Intermediate Accounting,* 14th ed. (Hoboken, N.J.: Wiley, 2011).

Killen, Damian, and Danica Murphy. *Introduction to Type and Conflict* (Palo Alto, Calif.: CPP, 2003).

Killen, Damian, and Gareth Williams. *Introduction to Type and Innovation* (Palo Alto, Calif.: CPP, 2000).

Kim, Eugene E. "The Life Cycle of Groups." November 29, 2011. http://groupaya.net/the-lifecycle -of-groups/ (accessed January 26, 2014).

Kimura, Takuma. "The Moderating Effects of Political Skill and Leader-Member Exchange on the Relationship between Organization Politics and Affective Commitment." *Journal of Business Ethics* 116 (2013): 587–599.

Kirkendall, Nancy. "Organizational Performance Measurement in the Energy Information Administration." http://www.docstoc.com/docs/10802651/Organizational-Performance-Measurement-in-the-Energy-Information—Administration (accessed February 24, 2014).

Kjerulf, A. "Top 5 Reasons Why 'The Customer Is Always Right' Is Wrong." July 12, 2006. http://positivesharing.com/2006/07/why-the-customer-is-always-right-results-in-bad-customer-service/ (accessed April 9, 2014).

Kloeber, Leonard. "Leadership Lessons from General Eisenhower." *Ezinearticles.com,* September 6, 2010. http://ezinearticles.com/?Leadership-Lessons-From-General-Eisenhower&id=4991281 (accessed January 2, 2014).

Koegel, T. *The Exceptional Presenter* (Austin, Tex.: Greenleaf, 2007).

Korn, M. "The Best Ways to Fire Someone." *Wall Street Journal,* October 26, 2012. http://online.wsj.com/news/articles/SB10000872396390443884104577645814249927568 (accessed December 30, 2013).

Kouzes, James M., and Barry Z. Posner. *The Leadership Challenge* (San Francisco: Jossey-Bass, 1987).

———. *The Leadership Challenge: How to Keep Getting Extraordinary Things Done in Organizations,* 2nd ed. (San Francisco: Jossey-Bass, 1995).

———. *The Leadership Challenge: How to Keep Getting Extraordinary Things Done in Organizations,* 4th ed. (San Francisco: Jossey-Bass, 2008).

Kozlowski, Steve W., and Bradford S. Bell. "Work Groups and Teams in Organizations." In *Handbook of Psychology,* vol. 12, ed. W. C. Borman, D. R. Ilgen, and R. J. Klimoski (New York: Wiley, 2003), 333–375.

Kristof A. L. "Person-Organization Fit: An Integrative Review of Its Conceptualizations, Measurement and Implications." *Personnel Psychology* 49, no. 1 (1996): 1–49.

Kruger, Justin, and David Dunning. "Unskilled and Unaware of It: How Difficulties in Recognizing One's Own Incompetence Lead to Inflated Self-Assessments." *Journal of Personality and Social Psychology* 77, no. 6 (1999): 1121–1134.

Kruse, Kevin. "5 Ways to Fix Your Dysfunctional Team." *Forbes,* December 11, 2013. http://www.forbes.com/sites/kevinkruse/2013/12/11/5-ways-to-fix-your-dysfunctional-team/ (accessed February 24, 2014).

Kuehn, Kurt. "Navigating the Shoals in Fast-Moving Currents." Keynote Address to the Institute of Management Accountants 90th Annual Conference and Exposition, Denver, June 6, 2009. http://pressroom.ups.com/About+UPS/UPS+Leadership/Speeches/Kurt+Kuehn/ci.Navigating+the+Shoals+in+Fast-Moving+Currents.print (accessed March 16, 2014).

Kunin, Seth D. *Religion: The Modern Theories* (Edinburgh: Edinburgh University Press, 2003).

Landy, Frank J., and James L. Farr. "Performance Rating." *Psychological Bulletin* 87, no. 1 (1980): 72–107.

Lau, E. "Why and Where Is Teamwork Important?" *Forbes,* January 23, 2013. http://www.forbes.com/sites/quora/2013/01/23/why-and-where-is-teamwork-important.html (accessed February 24, 2014).

Lawler, E. E., and G. D. Jenkins, "Strategic Reward Systems." In *Handbook of Industrial and Organizational Psychology,* 2nd ed., ed. M. D. Dunnette and L. M. Hough (Palo Alto, Calif.: CPP, 1995), 1009–1055.

Lazarus, Clifford N. "Simple Keys to Effective Communication: How to Be a Great Communicator." *Psychology Today,* July 26, 2011. http://www.psychologytoday.com/blog/think-well/201107/simple-keys-effective-communication (accessed February 2, 2014).

"Leadership Development through Action Learning." Business School Netherlands. http://www.bsn.eu/bsn/news/leadership-development-through-action-learning.html (accessed February 27, 2014).

Leadership-Toolbox. "Leadership Styles: Autocratic Leadership." http://www.leadership-toolbox.com/autocratic-leadership.html (accessed December 30, 2013).

"Learning Agility and Emotional Intelligence Competencies." Ernst & Young slide presentation.

Leary, M. R. *Self-Preservation: Impression Management and Interpersonal Behavior* (Boulder, Colo.: Westview Press, 1996).

LeFever, Lee. *The Art of Explanation: Making Your Ideas, Products, and Services Easier to Understand* (Hoboken, N.J.: Wiley, 2012).

Leonard, Dorothy, and Susan Straus. "Putting Your Company's Whole Brain to Work." *Harvard*

Business Review 75, no. 4 (1997): 110–121.

Leslie, J. "Leadership Skills and Emotional Intelligence." Center for Creative Leadership. http://www.ccl.org/leadership/pdf /assessments/skills_intelligence.pdf (accessed February 11, 2014).

Levine, Leslie. "Strengthen Your Business by Developing Your Employees." *Allbusiness. com.* http://www.allbusiness.com/human -resources/employee-development/1240-1. html (accessed December 31, 2013).

Libby, B. "How to Conduct a Job Interview." *CBS Money Watch,* March 13, 2007. http://www .cbsnews.com/news/how-to-conduct-a-job -interview/ (accessed January 1, 2014).

"Link Sustainability to Corporate Strategy Using the Balanced Scorecard." Balanced Scorecard Institute. http://www.balancedscorecard .org/Portals/0/PDF /LinkingSustainabilitytoCorporateStrategy UsingtheBalancedScorecard.pdf (accessed March 7, 2014).

Lipman, V. "5 Easy Ways to Motivate—and Demotivate—Employees." *Psychology Today,* March 24, 2013. http://www .psychologytoday.com/blog/mind-the -manager/201303/5-easy-ways-motivate -and-demotivate-employees (accessed December 31, 2013).

——. "How to Fire Someone Effectively but (Hopefully) with Dignity." *Forbes,* April 16, 2013. http://www.forbes.com/sites /victorlipman/2013/04/16/how-to-fire -someone-effectively-but-hopefully-with -dignity/ (accessed December 30, 2013).

Littlefield, Matthew. "An Operational Excellence Definition Quality Executives Must Know." LNS Research, November 20, 2012. http://blog.lnsresearch.com/blog /bid/164666/An-Operational-Excellence -Definition-Quality-Executives-Must-Know (accessed March 17, 2014).

Logullo, Daryl. "Five Outstanding Client Referral Tactics (and Action Steps)." September 25, 2007. http://www.marketingprofs.com/7 /five-outstanding-client-referral-tactics -logullo.asp (accessed April 15, 2014).

Mackie, J. L. *Ethics: Inventing Right and Wrong* (London: Penguin, 1990).

Madden, David. "Semantic Noise and Interpersonal Communications." *Relating360.com,* August 27, 2007. http://www.relating360.com/index .php/semantic-noise-and-interpersonal -communications-42594/ (accessed February 15, 2014).

Magloff, L. "What Are the Benefits of Teamwork in Business?" *Houston Chronicle.* http://smallbusiness.chron.com/benefits -teamwork-business-3250.html (accessed March 13, 2014).

Magnusson, D. "Holistic Interactionism: A Perspective for Research on Personality Development." In L. A. Pervin and O. P. John, eds., *Handbook of Personality: Theory and Research* (New York: Guilford Press, 1995), 219–247.

Maister, David. "Key Account Management." 1997. http://davidmaister.com/articles/key -account-management/ (accessed April, 12, 2014).

——. *Managing the Professional Services Firm* (New York: Simon & Schuster, 1997).

——. *True Professionalism: The Courage to Care about Your People, Your Clients, and Your Career* (New York: Simon & Schuster, 1997).

Manktelow, James. "Lencioni's Five Dysfunctions of a Team by James Manktelow." http://www .convergingzone.com/business/lencionis -five-dysfunctions-of-a-team-by-james -manktelow/ (accessed March 20, 2014).

Mann, R. D. "A Review of the Relationships between Personality and Performance in Small Groups." *Psychological Bulletin* 56, no. 4 (1959): 241–270.

Martin, J. *Cultures in Organizations: Three Perspectives* (New York: Oxford University Press, 1992).

Martindale, N. "Leadership Styles: How to Handle the Different Personas." *Strategic Communication Management* 15, no. 8 (2011): 32–35.

May, Kristen. "Skills-Based Leadership Theory." *Houston Chronicle.* http://smallbusiness .chron.com/skillsbased-leadership -theory-31074.html (accessed March 13, 2014).

McClelland, David C. "Toward a Theory of Motive Acquisition." *American Psychologist* 20, no. 5 (1965): 321–333.

McClure, Ben. "The Importance of Corporate Transparency." *Investopedia,* January 3, 2014. http://www.investopedia.com/articles /fundamental/03/121703.asp (accessed March 18, 2014).

McGrath, J. E. *Leadership Behavior: Some Requirements for Leadership Training* (Washington, D.C.: U.S. Civil Service Commission, Office of Career Development, 1962).

McIntosh, Barbara. "An Employer's Guide to Older Workers: How to Win Them Back and Convince Them to Stay." http://www.doleta

.gov/Seniors/other_docs/EmplGuide.pdf (accessed February 26, 2014).

McNamara, Carter. "Basic Principles to Remember about Motivation." *ManagementHelp.org.* http://managementhelp.org/leadingpeople /motivating-others.htm (accessed December 30, 2013).

———. "Understanding Motivation." *ManagementHelp .org.* http://managementhelp.org /leadingpeople/motivating-others.htm (accessed December 30, 2013).

Merchant, P. "5 Sources of Power in Organizations." *Small Business Chronicle.* http://smallbusiness.chron.com/5-sources -power-organizations-14467.html (accessed March 25, 2014).

Metzger, Michael B. "Critical Thinking." X504 Course Notes. Spring 2007. Indiana University, Bloomington.

———. "Ethical Responsibilities of Managers." L533 Course Notes. Spring 2008. Indiana University, Bloomington.

Miltenberger, R. G. *Behavior Modification Principles and Procedures,* 3rd ed. (Belmont, Calif.: Wadsworth/Thomson Learning, 2004).

Mitchell, T. R., and D. Daniels. "Motivation." In *Handbook of Psychology,* vol. 12, ed. W. C. Borman, D. R. Ilgen, and R. J. Klimoski (New York: Wiley, 2003), 225–254.

Montana, Patrick J., and Bruce H. Charnov, "Leadership: Theory and Practice." In *Management,* 4th ed. (Hauppage, N.Y.: Barron's, 2008).

Moorman, Robert H. "The Influence of Cognitive and Affective Based Job Satisfaction Measures on the Relationship between Satisfaction and Organizational Citizenship Behavior." *Human Relations* 46, no. 6 (1993): 759–776.

Morris, Tom. *If Aristotle Ran General Motors* (New York: Henry Holt, 1997).

"Motivating Employees." *Wall Street Journal,* April 7, 2009. http://guides.wsj.com/management /managing-your-people/how-to-motivate -employees/ (accessed January 9, 2014).

Muchinsky, Paul M. *Psychology Applied to Work* (Summerfield, N.C.: Hypergraph, 2012).

Mumford, M. D., S. J. Zaccaro, F. D. Harding, T. O. Jacobs, and E. A. Fleishman. "Leadership Skills for a Changing World: Solving Complex Social Problems." *Leadership Quarterly* 11 (2000): 11–35.

Murray, Jim. "Aspiring to Leadership: Technical Knowledge vs. People Skills." *Checkmark,* Summer 2008. http://www.cpaontario.ca

/PD/PDarticles/1016page9923.pdf (accessed March 12, 2014).

Murray, Peter N. "How Steve Jobs Knew What You Wanted." *Psychology Today,* October 31, 2011. http://www.psychologytoday.com /blog/inside-the-consumer-mind/201110 /how-steve-jobs-knew-what-you-wanted (accessed April 11, 2014).

Myers, Isabel Briggs. "Myers-Briggs Type Indicator." http://www.coachingwithlebe.com/?page _id=369 (accessed January 2, 2014).

Myers, Isabel Briggs, and Peter B. Meyers. *Gifts Differing: Understanding Personality Type* (Palo Alto, Calif.: CPP, 1980).

Myers, Isabel Briggs, Linda K. Kirby, and Katherine D. Myers. *Introduction to Type: A Guide to Understanding your Results on the Myers-Briggs Type Indicator* (Palo Alto, Calif.: CPP, 1998).

Myers, Katharine D., and Linda K. Kirby. *Introduction to Type Dynamics and Development: Exploring the Next Level of Type* (Palo Alto, Calif.: CPP, 1994).

Nardi, Dario. *Neuroscience of Personality: Brain Savvy Insights for All Types of People* (Los Angeles: Radiance House, 2011).

Neal, Tess M. S. "How to Be a Good Mentee." *Association for Psychological Science Observer* 24, no. 2 (February 2011). http://www.psychologicalscience.org /index.php/publications/observer/2011 /february-11/how-to-be-a-good-mentee .html (accessed December 31, 2013).

Nepomuceno, C. "How to Read a Resume." http://ezinearticles.com/?How-To-Read-A -Resume&id=937720 (accessed January 1, 2014).

"Never Too Old to Learn." *Economist,* May 12, 2010. http://www.economist.com /node/16036092/print (accessed February 27, 2014).

Northhouse, Peter G. *Leadership: Theory and Practice,* 3rd ed. (Thousand Oaks, Calif.: Sage, 2004).

"Office Politics—Seven Savvy Steps." http://www .billilee.com/office_politics_tips.htm/ (accessed March 22, 2014).

Ohland, Matthew W., Misty L. Loughry, David J. Woehr, Lisa G. Bullard, Richard M. Felder, Cynthia J. Finelli, Richard A. Layton, Hal R. Pomeranz, and Douglas G. Schmucker. "The Comprehensive Assessment of Team Member Effectiveness: Development of a Behaviorally Anchored Rating Scale for Self- and Peer Evaluation." *Academy of*

Management Learning and Education 11, no. 4 (2012): 609–630.

"Operational Excellence." http://en.wikipedia.org /wiki/Operational_excellence (accessed March 17, 2014).

O'Reilly, C. "Corporations, Culture, and Commitment: Motivation and Social Control in Organizations." *California Management Review* 31, no. 4 (1989): 9–17.

O'Reilly, C., and D. F. Caldwell. "The Power of Strong Corporate Cultures in Silicon Valley Firms." Presentation to the Executive Seminar in Corporate Excellence, Santa Clara University, February 13, 1985.

"Overview of the Four Temperaments." *Keirsey.com.* http://www.keirsey.com/4temps/overview _temperaments.asp.

Papa, Michael J., Tom D. Daniels, and Barry K. Spiker. *Organizational Communication: Perspectives and Trends* (Los Angeles: Sage, 2007).

Pearman, Roger. *Introduction to Type and Emotional Intelligence* (Palo Alto, Calif.: CPP, 2002).

Pearman, Roger, and Sarah C. Albritton. *I'm Not Crazy, I'm Just Not You: The Real Meaning of the 16 Personality Types,* 2nd ed. (Boston: Nicholas Brealey, 2010).

"Performance Management & Measurement." U.S. Department of Health and Human Services, Health Resources and Services Administration, April 2011. http://www .hrsa.gov/quality/toolbox/508pdfs/per formancemanagementandmeasurement.pdf (accessed February 25, 2014).

Perrewe, P. L., G. R. Ferris, D. D. Frink, and W. P. Anthony. "Political Skill: An Antidote for Workplace Stressors." *Academy of Management Executive* 14 (2000): 115–123.

Perrewe, P. L., K. L. Zellars, G. R. Ferris, A. M. Rossi, C. J. Kacmar, and D. A. Ralston. "Neutralizing Job Stressors." *Academy of Management Journal* 47, no. 3 (2004): 141–152.

Petersen, James C. *Why Don't We Listen Better? Communicating and Connecting in Relationships* (Portland, Ore.: Petersen, 2007).

Pfeffer, Jeffrey. *Power in Organizations* (Marshfield, Mass.: Pittman, 1981).

Pfeil, Manfred. "How Employee Recognition Programs Improve Retention." *CFO Insight Magazine,* January 2013. http://www.cfo-insight.com /human-capital-career/talent -management/how-employee-recognition -programmes-improve-retention/ (accessed January 13, 2014).

Pielow, Christian. "5 Key Factors to Managing Successful Teams." https://www.bluesteps .com/blog/5-key-factors-to-building-and -managing-successful-teams.aspx (accessed February 16, 2014).

Pirsig, Robert M. "Zen and the Art of Motorcycle Maintenance: An Inquiry into Values." *Goodreads.com.* http://www.goodreads .com/work/quotes/175720-zen-and-the-art -of-motorcycle-maintenance-an-inquiry-into -values (accessed January 31, 2014).

Pitagorsky, George. "The Caring Manager." *ProjectTimes.com.* http://www.projecttimes .com/george-pitagorsky/the-caring -manager.html (accessed June 5, 2013).

Pittenger, David J. "Cautionary Comments Regarding the Myers-Briggs Type Indicator." *Consulting Psychology Journal: Practice and Research* 57, no. 3 (2005): 210–221.

Posner, Richard. *The Problems of Jurisprudence* (Cambridge, Mass.: Harvard University Press, 1990).

Pozin, Ilya. "Who Says You Need A Mentor? Be Your Own." *Parade,* October 1, 2013. http://www .parade.com/169966/ilyapozin/who-says -you-need-a-mentor-be-your-own/ (accessed December 31, 2013).

"Principles of Operational Excellence." http://www .iienet2.org/uploadedfiles/SHSNew/Tools _and_Resources/RobertMillerOpExArticle .pdf (accessed March 17, 2014).

Progressus. "Reductionism Can Reduce Everything." *ForProgressNotGrowth.com,* August 7, 2011. http://forprogressnotgrowth.com /2011/08/07/reductionism-can -reduce-everything/ (accessed February 24, 2014).

Putterman, Leland. "Cumulative Customer Profitability—the 20/300 Rule." May 5, 2011. http://www.acornsys.com/The-Acorn -Blog/bid/56484/Cumulative-Customer -Profitability-The-20-300-Rule, (accessed April 17, 2014), citing Byrnes, J. S., *Islands of Profit in a Sea of Red Ink: Why 40 Percent of Your Business Is Unprofitable and How to Fix It* (New York: Penguin, 2010).

Quinn, David P. "Tying Project Measures to Performance Incentives." *Journal of Defense Software Engineering* 1 (2005): 28–30.

Rafaeli, A., and R. I. Sutton. "The Expression of Emotion in Organizational Life." *Research in Organizational Behavior* 11 (1989): 1–42.

Raghavan, A., K. Kranhold, and A. Barrionuevo. "How Enron Bosses Created a Culture of Pushing Limits." *Wall Street Journal,* August 26, 2002.

Rawls, John. *A Theory of Justice* (Cambridge, Mass.: Belknap Press of Harvard University Press, 1971).

Reardon, Kathleen Kelly. *The Secret Handshake: Mastering the Politics of the Business Inner Circle* (New York: Currency Doubleday, 2000).

"Reducing Cost-to-Serve in the Supply Chain." *Buffalo Hospital Supply,* June 18, 2013. http://www.buffalohospital.com/news/article:06-18-2013-reducing-cost-to-serve-in-the-supply-chain/ (accessed April 12, 2014).

Reid, Joanne R., and Phyllis R. Anderson. "Critical Thinking in the Business Classroom." *Journal of Education for Business* 87, no. 1 (2012): 52–59.

Resnick, H. S. "Organizational Savvy." *Worksystems Newsletter,* December 2009. http://www.worksystems.com/newszletter/dec_09.html (accessed March 25, 2014).

"Reward Power—The Fastest Way to Persuade." *EzineMark.com,* April 20, 2010. http://reward.ezinemark.com/reward-power-the-fastest-way-to-persuade-4cd11a8fe05.html (accessed January 2, 2014).

Rezak, C. "Leadership White Paper: Developing Business-Savvy Leaders." Paradigm Learning, Inc., 2011. http://www.paradigmlearning.com/Libraries/White-Papers/WP-Developing-Business-Savvy-Leaders.sflb.ashx (accessed March 24, 2014).

Ricci, Tom. "Public Speaking: Know Your Audience." *ASME.org,* August 2012. https://www.asme.org/career-education/articles/public-speaking/public-speaking-know-your-audience?cm_sp=Public+Speaking-_-Featured+Articles-_-Public+Speaking+Know+Your+Audience (accessed February 5, 2014).

Richmond, Sharon Lebovitz. *Introduction to Type and Leadership* (Palo Alto, Calif.: CPP, 2008).

Ricks, Thomas E. "What Ever Happened to Accountability." *Harvard Business Review* 90, no. 10 (2012): 93–100.

Robbins, Stephen P., and Timothy A. Judge. *Organizational Behavior,* 15th ed. (Upper Saddle River, N.J.: Prentice Hall, 2012).

Robertson, Ivan T., Alex J. Birch, and Cary L. Cooper. "Job and Work Attitudes, Engagement and Employee Performance: Where Does Psychological Well-Being Fit In?" *Leadership & Organization Development Journal* 33, no. 3 (2012): 224–232.

Robinson, Lawrence, Jeanne Segal, and Robert Segal. "Effective Communication: Improving Communication Skills in Business and Relationships." http://www.helpguide.org/mental/effective_communication_skills.htm (accessed January 27, 2014).

Robinson, Michael T. "The 5 Keys to Achieving Job Satisfaction." *CareerPlanner.com.* http://www.careerplanner.com/5-Keys-To-Job-Satisfaction.cfm (accessed December 31, 2013).

Rock, D., and J. Schwartz. "The Neuroscience of Leadership." *Strategy+Business* 43 (2006): 10.

Rohm, Howard. "A Balancing Act." *Performance Measurement in Action* 2, no. 2 (2002): 1–8.

Rohm, Howard, and Larry Halbach. "A Balancing Act: Sustaining New Directions." *Performance Management in Action* 3, no. 2 (2005): 1–8.

Rosenzweig, Phil. "Making Better Decisions Over Time." *Strategy + Business,* January 6, 2014. www.strategy-business.com/article/00227?pg=all&tid=27782251 (accessed February 15, 2014).

Rousseau, D. M. "Organizational Climate and Culture." In *Macro-Organizational Factors,* ed. J. J. Hurrell, Jr., J. Levi, I. R. Murphy, and S. L. Sauter. Encyclopedia of Occupational Health & Safety, 2011. http://www.ilo.org/oshenc/part-v/psychosocial-and-organizational-factors/macro-organizational-factors/item/29-organizational-climate-and-culture (accessed March 24, 2014).

Rowold, J., and W. Schlotz. "Transformational and Transactional Leadership and Followers' Chronic Stress." *Leadership Review* 9 (2009): 35–48.

Russell, Alejandro. "The Benefits & Importance of Ethics in the Workplace." *GlobalPost.com.* http://everydaylife.globalpost.com/benefits-importance-ethics-workplace-7414.html (accessed January 16, 2014).

Rydne, Anna. "5 Bullet-Proof Methods to Connect with Your Audience." http://communicateskills.com/2012/10/04/communication-connect-audience/ (accessed February 5, 2014).

Sahakian William S., and Mabel L. Sahakian. *Ideas of the Great Philosophers* (New York: Barnes & Noble, 1993).

Schachter, Harvey. "The Guideposts to Follow for Ethical Leadership." *Globe and Mail,* January 12, 2014. http://www.theglobeandmail.com/report-on-business/careers/management/guideposts-for-ethical-leadership

/article16277696/?service=mobile (accessed January 23, 2014).

Schlachter, C. T., and T. H. Hilderbrandt. "Leading Business Change of Dummies: The Importance of Teamwork to Business Change." *For Dummies.* https://www .dummies.com/how-to/content/the -importance-of-teamwork-to-business -change.html (accessed February 26, 2014).

Schmidt, Richard B. "Companies Add Ethics Training: Will It Work?" *Wall Street Journal,* November 4, 2002.

Schneider, B., M. G. Ehrhart, and W. H. Macey. "Perspectives on Organization Climate and Culture, Building and Developing the Organization." In *APA Handbook of Industrial and Organizational Psychology,* ed. S. Zedeck (Washington, D.C.: American Psychological Association, 2011), 373–414.

Schott Karr, Susan. "Critical Thinking: A CRITICAL Strategy for Financial Executives." *Financial Executive* 25, no. 10 (2009): 58–61.

Schultz, D., and S. E. Schultz. *Psychology and Work Today* (New York: Prentice Hall, 2010).

Scouller, James. *The Three Levels of Leadership: How to Develop Your Leadership Presence, Knowhow and Skill* (Cirencester, England: Management Books 2000 Ltd., 2011).

Sekiguchi, T. "Person-Organization Fit and Person-Job Fit in Employee Selection: A Review of the Literature." *Osaka Keidai Ronshu* 54, no. 6 (March 2004): 179–196.

Seldman, Martin, and Edward Betof. "An Illuminated Path." *T+D* 58, no. 12 (December 2004): 35–39.

"Self-Regulated Learning." http://en.wikipedia.org /wiki/Self-regulated_learning (accessed February 25, 2014).

Shank, John. "Allied Stationery." In *Cases in Cost Management,* 3rd ed. (New York: Cengage Learning, 2005).

Shank, John, and Vijay Govindarajan. *Strategic Cost Management* (New York: Free Press, 1993).

Sheldon, Oliver J., David Dunning, and Daniel R. Ames. "Emotionally Unskilled, Unaware, and Uninterested in Learning More: Reactions to Feedback about Deficits in Emotional Intelligence." *Journal of Applied Psychology* 99, no. 1 (2014): 125–137.

Sidle, C. Clinton. *The Leadership Wheel* (New York: Palgrave MacMillan, 2005).

Silverstein, Ken. "Enron, Ethics and Today's Corporate Values." *Forbes,* May 14, 2013. http://www .forbes.com/sites/kensilverstein /2013/05/14/enron-ethics-and-todays -corporate-values/ (accessed January 15, 2014).

"Skills, Knowledge, Abilities and Tasks." *Career Guide for Insurance Manager.* http://jobs.virginia .gov/careerguides/InsuranceMgr.htm (accessed March 15, 2014).

Smith, B. N., R. V. Montagno, and T. N. Kuzmenko. "Transformational and Servant Leadership: Content and Contextual Comparisons," *Journal of Leadership and Organizational Studies* 10, no. 4 (2004): 80–91.

Smith, Michael J. "Gaming Nonfinancial Performance Measures." *Journal of Management Accounting Research* 14, no. 1 (2002): 119–133.

Smith, Perry M. *Taking Charge: Making the Right Choices* (Garden City, N.Y.: Avery, 1989).

Smyth, Patrick. "Transparent Communication." http://ezinearticles.com/?Transparent -Communication&id=1953434 (accessed March 18, 2014).

Snyder, Mark. "Self-Monitoring of Expressive Behavior." *Journal of Personality and Social Psychology* 30, no. 4 (1974): 526–537.

Solomon, Richard L., and John D. Corbit. "An Opponent-Process Theory of Motivation." *American Economic Review* 68, no. 6 (1978): 12–24.

Span, Scott. "Promoting Teamwork? It May Be the Key to Your Organization's Success." October 8, 2013. http://www.tlnt.com/2013/10/08 /is-it-possible-to-nurture-and-promote -teamwork/ (accessed February 26, 2014).

Spoelstra, Howard, Peter Van Rosmalen, and Peter B. Sloep. "Supporting Project Team Formation for Self-Directed Learners." Center for Learning Sciences and Technologies, July 4, 2011. http://celstec.org/content/supporting -project-team-formation-self-directed -learners (accessed February 25, 2014).

Stapleton, S. "The Five Sources of a Leader's Power, and How (and How Not) to Use Them." SimonStapleton.com, December 17, 2007. http://www.simonstapleton.com /wordpress/2007/12/17/the-five-sources -of-a-leader%E2%80%99s-power-and-how -and-how-not-to-use-them/ (accessed March 25, 2014).

Starvish, Maggie. "Why Leaders Need to Rethink Teamwork." *Forbes,* December 28, 2012. http://www.forbes.com/sites /hbsworkingknowledge/2012/12/28 /why-leaders-need-to-rethink-teamwork/ (accessed March 28, 2014).

"Steve Jobs' 12 Rules of Success." *1000Advices .com.* http://www.1000advices.com/guru /leader_corporate_12_success_rules_sj.html (accessed December 30, 2013).

Stevens, G. W. "Toward a Process-Based Approach of Conceptualizing Change Readiness." *Journal of Applied Behavioral Science* 49, no. 3 (2013): 333–349.

Stimson, T. "Sources of Power." *CLI,* 2011. http://www.consultcli.com/Sourcespower .htm (accessed March 25, 2014).

Stogdill, R. M. "Personal Factors Associated with Leadership: A Survey of the Literature." *Journal of Psychology* 25 (1948): 35–71.

Stone, A. G., R. F. Russell, and K. Patterson. "Transformational versus Servant Leadership: A Difference in Leader Focus." Servant Leadership Research Roundtable, August 2003. http://regent.edu/acad /global/publications/sl_proceedings/2003 /stone_transformation_versus.pdf (accessed December 30, 2013).

"Strategic Thinking: Developing Leaders' Skills Faster with Advanced Business Simulations." http://www.webex.com/webinars/Strategic -Thinking-Developing-Leaders-Skills-Faster -With-Advanced-Business-Simulations (accessed February 27, 2014).

Strauman, Timothy J. "Self-Discrepancies in Clinical Depression and Social Phobia: Cognitive Structures That Underlie Emotional Disorders." *Journal of Abnormal Psychology* 98, no. 1 (1989): 14–22.

Sun, Calvin. "10 Ways to Explain Things More Effectively." *TechRepublic,* April 1, 2008. http://http://www.techrepublic.com /blog/10-things/10-ways-to-explain-things -more-effectively/ (accessed February 13, 2014).

"Sweat Equity." http://en.wikipedia.org/wiki/Sweat _equity (accessed March 31, 2014).

Sweet, Pat. "Why Technical Leadership Skills Are Critical to Your Success." http://www .engineeringandleadership.com/why -technical-leadership-skills-are-critical-to -your-success/ (accessed March 10, 2014).

"Talent Management." http://en.wikipedia.org/wiki /Talent_management (accessed March 17, 2014).

Tan, Michelle. "Odierno to Soldiers: Toxic Leaders Will Be Fired." *Army Times,* April 1, 2013. http://www.armytimes.com /article/20130401/NEWS/304010009 /Odierno-soldiers-Toxic-leaders-will-fired (accessed January 23, 2014).

Tang, C. Speech at event titled "Celebration of Women," Greater Louisville International Professionals, March 20, 2014.

"Team Dynamics." http://www.businessdictionary .com/definition/team-dynamics.html (accessed April 3, 2014).

"Team Dynamics—How They Affect Performance." http://www.teamteachnology.co.uk/team /dynamics/overview/ (accessed April 4, 2014).

Team International. "Coaching High Performance Teams: The Art of the Impossible!" Training Material.

"Team Technology." http://www.teamtechnology .co.uk/ (accessed April 3, 2014).

"10 Mistakes Managers Make during Job Interviews." *CBSNews.com,* June 17, 2008. http://www .cbsnews.com/news/10-mistakes -managers-make-during-job-interviews / (accessed January 1, 2014).

Thomas, Joseph C. "Leadership Effectiveness of Referent Power as a Distinction of Personal Power." Regent University Center for Leadership Studies. LEAD605, Foundations of Effective Leadership, February 18, 2002. http://www.jctnet.us/Professional /MOL/LEAD605/ThomasJMicroBP$2.pdf (accessed January 2, 2014).

Thompson, Ed. "The 4 Main Kinds of Ethics: An Introduction." *RebirthofReason.com.* http://rebirthofreason.com/Articles /Thompson/The_4_Main_Kinds_of_Ethics _An_Introduction.shtml (accessed January 21, 2014).

"Tips for Being a Successful Mentee." *UCDavis.edu.* http://www.hr.ucdavis.edu/sdps /career-management-toolkit/explore-the -world-of-work/mentoring/tips-for-being-a -successful-mentee (accessed December 31, 2013).

"Top 5 Job Satisfaction Factors." *Coach4U.net,* June 4, 2010. http://www.coach4u.net/coach_4_u _blog/top-5-job-satisfaction-factors.html (accessed January 10, 2014).

Townsend, Patrick L., and Joan E. Gebhardt. *Five-Star Leadership* (Hoboken, N.J.: Wiley, 1997).

Tracy, Brian. "100 Best Quotes on Leadership." *Forbes,* October 16, 2012. http://www.forbes.com /sites/kevinkruse/2012/10/16/quotes-on -leadership/.

Troughton, John H. "Business Improvement through Transparency." http://www .themanagementpractice.com/ams /Business%20Improvement%20by%20 Transparency.pdf (accessed March 18, 2014).

Tucker, Jennifer. *Introduction to Type and Project Management* (Palo Alto, Calif.: CPP, 2008).

"Tuckman's Stages of Group Development." http://en.wikipedia.org/wiki/Bruce _Tuckman (accessed March 16, 2014).

Turak, August. "The 11 Leadership Secrets You've Never Heard About." *Forbes,* July 17, 2012. http://www.forbes.com/sites/augustturak /2012/07/17/the-11-leadership-secrets-you -never-heard-about (accessed January 5, 2014).

Turner, Lynn E., Chief Accountant, U.S. Securities & Exchange Commission. "SEC Update: Transparent Financial Reporting and Disclosures." Interagency Accounting Conference, Denver, April 3, 2001. http://www.sec.gov./news/speech/spch476 .htm (accessed March 18, 2014).

USAA Report to Members 2012. https://www.usaa .com/inet/pages/reporttomembers_main _landing?wa_ref=annual_report_2012 _landing_nav_home&akredirect=true (accessed March 15, 2014).

U.S. Army. *Military Leadership,* Field Manual 22–100 (Washington, D.C.: U.S. Government Printing Office, 1983).

Useem, Michael. "Four Lessons in Adaptive Leadership." *Harvard Business Review,* November 2010.

Ustin, J. K. "Assessing Job Candidates for Fit." http://http://www.joankustin.com /N5content/PDF/Assessing_Job _Candidates_for_Fit.pdf (accessed March 31, 2014).

VanBriesen, Jeanne M. "Self-Directed Learning." Carnegie Mellon University. www.nae.edu /File.aspx?id=37803 (accessed February 25, 2014).

"Various Sources of Power in an Organization" (blog). December 23, 2013. http://bankofinfo .com/sources-of-power-in-an-organization/ (accessed March 25, 2014).

Vermeulen, Freek. "Five Mistaken Beliefs Business Leaders Have about Innovation." *Forbes,* May 30, 2011. http://www.forbes.com/sites /freekvermeulen/2011/05/30/five -mistaken-beliefs-business-leaders-have -about-innovation/ (accessed January 13, 2014).

Vicher, V. Marie. "Teaching Political Savvy as a Workforce Skill." Working paper. Southern Illinois University Carbondale. http:// opensiuc.lib.siu.edu/morris_opensiuc (accessed March 24, 2014).

Von Clausewitz, Carl. "Carl Von Clausewitz: Quotes." *Goodreads.com.* http://www.goodreads. com/author/quotes/67848.Carl_von _Clausewitz (accessed January 31, 2014).

———. *On War* (New York: Penguin Classics, 1982).

Vroom, V. H., and A. J. Jago. *The New Leadership: Managing Participation in Organizations.* (Englewood Cliffs, N.J.: Prentice Hall, 1988).

Vroom, V. H., and P. W. Yetton. *Leadership and Decision-Making* (Pittsburgh: University of Pittsburgh Press, 1973).

Walker, Misty. "Tying Compensation to the Balanced Scorecard." http://voices.yahoo.com/tying -compensation-balanced-scorecard -1943330.html (accessed March 3, 2014).

Walters, Jamie. "How Can You Foster Growth and Get Value from Employees?" *LearningPlaceOnline.com.* http://www .learningplaceonline.com/workplace /employees/growth-value.htm (accessed December 30, 2013).

Watkins, Kelly. *Email Etiquette Made Easy* (Petite Press, 2009).

Wayshak, Mark. "Every Business Needs a Referral System." August 16, 2013. http://www .huffingtonpost.com/marc-wayshak/why -every-business-needs-_b_3767485.html (accessed April 15, 2014).

Wessell, David. "Why the Boardroom Bad Guys Have Now Emerged en Masse." *Wall Street Journal,* June 20, 2002. http://latrobefinancialmanagement .com/Research/Governance/Why%20 Boardroom%20Bad%20Guys%20Have%20 Now%20Emerged%20en%20Masse.pdf (accessed January 15, 2014).

West, Michael A., and Neil R. Anderson. "Innovation in Top Management Teams." *Journal of Applied Psychology* 81, no. 6 (1996): 680–693.

Westbrook, Thomas S., James R. Veale, and Roger E. Karnes. "Multirater and Gender Differences in the Measurement of Political Skill in Organizations." *Journal of Leadership Studies* 7, no. 2 (2013): 6–17.

"What Is Performance Measurement?" *Business Performance Improvement Resources,* 2014. http://www.bpir.com/what-is-perfromance -measurement-bpir.com.html (accessed February 15, 2014).

"What Makes a Good Mentor and Mentee?" *Science Daily,* November 30, 2012. http://www .sciencedaily.com/releases /2012/11/121130110658.htm (accessed December 31, 2013).

"Why Failure Develops Leaders Faster." Riverstone Group, March 29, 2013. http://www.theriverstonegroup.com/the-secret-to-developing-leaders-faster/ (accessed February 27, 2014).

Wilson, P. A. "The Effects of Politics and Power on the Organizational Commitment of Federal Executives." *Journal of Management* 21, no. 1 (Spring 1995): 101–118.

Winnett, Azriel. "Transparency in Communication: Is It All about Truth, or about Sincerity?" http://www.hodu.com/blog1/transparency-in-communication/ (accessed March 18, 2014).

Woldring, R. "Power in Organizations: A Way of Thinking about What You've Got, and How to Use It." Workplace Competence International Limited, 2001. http://www.wciltd.com/pdfquark/powerorgv2.pdf (accessed March 29, 2014).

Wolinski, S. "Adaptive Leadership" (blog). July 7, 2010. http://managementhelp.org/blogs/leadership/2010/07/07/adaptive-leadership/ (accessed January 2, 2014).

"Workforce and Succession Management in a Changing World." CPP Global Human Capital Report, November 2008. https://www.cpp.com/Pdfs/Workforce_and_succession_mgmt.pdf (accessed February 27, 2014).

"Work Motivation." http://en.wikipedia.org/wiki/Work_Motivation (accessed January 9, 2014).

"WorldCom Scandal: A Look Back at One of the Biggest Corporate Scandals in U.S. History." March 8, 2007. http://voices.yahoo.com/worldcom-scandal-look-back-one-biggest-225686.html (accessed March 17, 2014).

Wright, Thomas A., and Russell Cropanzano. "Psychological Well-Being and Job Satisfaction as Predictors of Job Performance." *Journal of Occupational Health Psychology* 5, no. 1 (2000): 84–94.

Wright, Thomas A., Russell Cropanzano, and Douglas G. Bonett. "The Moderating Role of Employee Positive Well Being on the Relation between Job Satisfaction and Job Performance." *Journal of Occupational Health Psychology* 12, no. 2 (2007): 93–104.

Yost, Lauren. "Workplace Savvy." *Parks and Recreation Magazine,* March 2014. http://www.parlsandrecreation.org/2014/March/Workplace-Savvy/ (accessed March 22, 2014).

Zaccaro, Stephen J. "Trait-Based Perspectives of Leadership." *American Psychologist* 62 (2007): 6–16.

Lightning Source UK Ltd.
Milton Keynes UK
UKHW050741090421
381703UK00005B/12